SCHAUM'S OUTLINE OF

THEORY AND PROBLEMS

of

BEGINNING
LINEAR ALGEBRA

•

SEYMOUR LIPSCHUTZ, Ph.D.

Professor of Mathematics
Temple University

•

SCHAUM'S OUTLINE SERIES
McGRAW-HILL
New York   Chicago   San Francisco   Lisbon   London
Madrid   Mexico City   Milan   New Delhi   San Juan
Seoul   Singapore   Sydney   Toronto

SEYMOUR LIPSCHUTZ, who is presently on the mathematics faculty of Temple University, formerly taught at the Polytechnic Institute of Brooklyn and was visiting professor in the Computer Science Department of Brooklyn College. He received his Ph.D. in 1960 at the Courant Institute of Mathematical Sciences of New York University. Some of his other books in the Schaum's Outline Series are *Discrete Mathematics*, *Probability*, and *Linear Algebra*, 2nd ed.

Schaum's Outline of Theory and Problems of
BEGINNING LINEAR ALGEBRA

8 9 10 11 12 13 14 15 16 17 18 19 20   CUS CUS   10 09 08

ISBN 0-07-038037-6

Sponsoring Editor: Arthur Biderman
Production Supervisor: Suzanne Rapcavage
Editing Supervisor: Maureen Walker

Library of Congress Cataloging-in-Publication Data
Lipschutz, Seymour.
    Schaum's outline of theory and problems of beginning linear
algebra / Seymour Lipschutz.
        p. cm. — (Schaum's outline series)
    Includes index.
    ISBN 0-07-038037-6
    1. Algebras, Linear—Problems, exercises, etc. 2. Algebras,
Linear—Outlines, syllabi, etc. I. Title.
QA184.5.L57 1997
512'.5'076—dc20   96-9004
                                                                   CIP

McGraw-Hill
A Division of The McGraw-Hill Companies

Preface

Linear algebra has recently become an essential part of the undergraduate mathematical training of students from many different fields besides mathematics and physics, such as, biology, chemistry, economics, statistics, and all fields of engineering. This requirement reflects the fact that linear algebra has many important and widespread applications.

The purpose of this text is to present a modern elementary introduction to linear algebra which will be found useful to all individuals regardless of their fields of specialization. It should be easily accessible to readers who have had a year of mathematics beyond high school algebra, such as, calculus, discrete mathematics, or probability and statistics. It is designed for use as a textbook for a formal course in linear algebra or as a supplement to all current standard texts.

Each chapter begins with clear statements of pertinent definitions, theorems and principles together with illustrative and other descriptive material. This is followed by graded sets of solved and supplementary problems. The solved problems illustrate and amplify the theory, and provide the repetition of basic principles so vital to effective teaching. Many proofs of theorems are included among the solved problems. The large number of supplementary problems, with answers, serve as a complete review of the material of each chapter.

Every effort has been made to ease the reader's entry into linear algebra. This is especially true with respect to the graded solved and supplementary problems. Furthermore, the text mainly uses the real number system **R** as the underlying field of scalars. However, formal abstract definitions and proofs are given. We do not lose sight of the fact that one main purpose of linear algebra is to help students develop the capability of handling abstract concepts.

The first part of the book deals with vectors and matrices, and systems of linear equations. This leads naturally to the topics of vector spaces and subspaces, and to the formal definition of linear dependence and independence, and dimension. Next comes a chapter on inner product spaces. This is followed by a chapter on linear mappings, and a chapter on the relationship between linear transformations and matrices. The chapter on eigenvalues and eigenvectors and the diagonalization of linear operators is preceded by a chapter on determinants. The final chapter deals with quadratic forms.

The text includes more material than can be covered in most first courses. This has been done to make the text more flexible, to provide a useful book of reference, and to stimulate further interest in the subject.

I wish to thank the staff of the McGraw-Hill Schaum Outline Series for invaluable suggestions and for their helpful cooperation. I also wish to thank Michel Falus for careful review of the manuscript. Lastly, I want to express my gratitude to Wilhelm Magnus, my teacher, advisor, and friend, who introduced me to the beauty of mathematics.

Temple University   SEYMOUR LIPSCHUTZ

Contents

Chapter 1

Vectors and Matrix Algebra

1.1 INTRODUCTION

Suppose the weights (in pounds) of eight students are listed as follows:

$$134, \quad 156, \quad 127, \quad 145, \quad 203, \quad 186, \quad 145, \quad 138$$

One can denote all the values in the list using only one symbol, say w, but with different subscripts, that is,

$$w_1, \quad w_2, \quad w_3, \quad w_4, \quad w_5, \quad w_6, \quad w_7, \quad w_8$$

Observe that each subscript denotes the position of the value in the list. For example, $w_1 = 134$, the first number; $w_2 = 156$, the second number; .... Such a list of values is called a *linear array* or *vector*.

Using such subscript notation, one can write the sum S and the average A of the weights as follows:

$$S = \sum_{k=1}^{8} w_k = w_1 + w_2 + \cdots + w_8 \quad \text{and} \quad A = \frac{S}{8} = \frac{\left(\sum_{k=1}^{8} w_k \right)}{8}$$

(See Section 1.5.) Subscript notation is indispensable in developing concise expressions for arithmetic manipulations of such lists of values.

Analogously, a chain of 28 stores, each store having 4 departments, could list its weekly sales (say, to the nearest dollar) as in Table 1-1. Again, we need only one symbol, say s, to denote all the values in the table, but now we need two subscripts, that is,

$$s_{1,1}, \quad s_{1,2}, \quad s_{1,3}, \quad s_{1,4}, \quad s_{2,1}, \quad s_{2,2}, \quad \ldots, \quad s_{28,4}$$

where $s_{i,j}$ denotes the sales in store i, department j. (We shall simplify the notation to s_{ij} instead of $s_{i,j}$ when there is no possibility of a misunderstanding.) Thus

$$s_{11} = 2872, \quad s_{12} = 805, \quad s_{13} = 3211, \quad \ldots$$

Such a rectangular array of numbers is called a *two-dimensional array* or *matrix*.

Table 1-1

Store \ Dept.	1	2	3	4
1	2872	805	3211	1560
2	2196	1223	2525	1744
3	3257	1017	3686	1951
⋮	⋮	⋮	⋮	⋮
28	2618	931	2333	982

This chapter will investigate such vectors and matrices, as well as certain algebraic operations involving them. Unless otherwise stated or implied, all entries will be real numbers, that is, elements of the real number system, denoted by

$$\mathbf{R}$$

In the context of vectors and matrices, the numbers themselves are called *scalars*.

1.2 VECTORS IN $\mathbf{R}^n$

By a *vector u* we simply mean a list of numbers, say, $a_1, a_2, \ldots a_n$. Such a vector is denoted by

$$u = (a_1, a_2, \ldots, a_n)$$

The numbers a_i are called the *components* or *entries* of u. If all the $a_i = 0$, then u is called the *zero vector*. Two such vectors, u and v, are *equal*, written $u = v$, if they have the same number of components and if the corresponding components are equal. The set of all vectors with n real components is denoted by $\mathbf{R}^n$.

EXAMPLE 1.1

(a) The following are vectors:

$$(3, -5), \qquad (7, 9), \qquad (0, 0, 0), \qquad (3, 4, 5)$$

The first two vectors belong to $\mathbf{R}^2$, whereas the last two vectors belong to $\mathbf{R}^3$. The third vector is the zero vector in $\mathbf{R}^3$.

(b) Although vectors $(1, 2, 3)$ and $(2, 3, 1)$ contain the same numbers, they are not equal since corresponding elements are not equal.

Vector Addition and Scalar Multiplication

Consider two arbitrary vectors u and v in $\mathbf{R}^n$, say,

$$u = (a_1, a_2, \ldots, a_n) \qquad \text{and} \qquad v = (b_1, b_2, \ldots, b_n)$$

Their *sum*, written $u + v$, is the vector obtained by adding corresponding components from u and v. That is,

$$u + v = (a_1 + b_1, a_2 + b_2, \ldots, a_n + b_n)$$

The *scalar product* or, simply, *product* of a scalar k and the vector u, written ku, is the vector obtained by multiplying each component of u by k. That is,

$$ku = k(a_1, a_2, \ldots, a_n) = (ka_1, ka_2, \ldots, ka_n)$$

We also define

$$-u = (-1)u \qquad \text{and} \qquad u - v = u + (-v)$$

The vector $-u$ is called the *negative* of u. We also use 0 for the zero vector.

EXAMPLE 1.2   Let $u = (2, 4, -5)$ and $v = (1, -6, 9)$.   Then

$$u + v = (2 + 1, \ 4 + (-6), \ -5 + 9) = (3, -2, 4)$$
$$6u = (6(2), 6(4), 6(-5)) = (12, 24, -30)$$
$$-v = (-1)(1, -6, 9) = (-1, 6, -9)$$
$$2u - 3v = (4, 8, -10) + (-3, 18, -27) = (1, 26, -37)$$

The vector $2u - 3v$ is called a *linear combination* of u and v.

Inner Product, Orthogonality, and Length

Again let u and v be the above arbitrary vectors in $\mathbf{R}^n$.   The *inner product* or *dot product* of u and v, denoted by $u \cdot v$, is the scalar obtained by multiplying corresponding components and adding the resulting products.   That is,

$$u \cdot v = a_1 b_1 + a_2 b_2 + \cdots + a_n b_n$$

The vectors u and v are said to be *orthogonal* (or *perpendicular*) if their dot product is zero, that is, if $u \cdot v = 0$.

The *norm* (or *length*) of the vector u is denoted and defined by

$$\|u\| = \sqrt{u \cdot u} = \sqrt{a_1^2 + a_2^2 + \cdots + a_n^2}$$

Observe that if $u \neq 0$, then $\|u\| > 0$; if $u = 0$, we have $\|u\| = \|0\| = 0$.   Also, we say that u is a *unit* vector when $\|u\| = 1$.

EXAMPLE 1.3

(a)   Let $u = (1, -2, 3)$, $v = (4, 5, -1)$, and $w = (2, 7, 4)$.   Then

$$u \cdot v = 1(4) - 2(5) + 3(-1) = 4 - 10 - 3 = -9$$
$$u \cdot w = 1(2) - 2(7) + 3(4) = 2 - 14 + 12 = 0$$

Thus u and w are orthogonal.

(b)   Let $u = (1, -3, 4)$ and $v = (\tfrac{2}{3}, \tfrac{1}{3}, -\tfrac{2}{3})$.   Then

$$\|u\| = \sqrt{1^2 + (-3)^2 + 4^2} = \sqrt{1 + 9 + 16} = \sqrt{26}$$
$$\|v\| = \sqrt{\tfrac{4}{9} + \tfrac{1}{9} + \tfrac{4}{9}} = \sqrt{1} = 1$$

Thus v is a unit vector.

Column Vectors

Frequently we will write a list of numbers vertically rather than horizontally.   Such a list is called a *column vector*.   In contrast, using similar notation, the above horizontally written vectors are called *row vectors*.   Furthermore, the above operations for row vectors are defined analogously for column vectors.

EXAMPLE 1.4

(a) The following are column vectors:

$$\begin{bmatrix} 0 \\ 1 \end{bmatrix}, \qquad \begin{bmatrix} 1 \\ -2 \end{bmatrix}, \qquad \begin{bmatrix} 1 \\ 5 \\ -6 \end{bmatrix}, \qquad \begin{bmatrix} 1.4 \\ \frac{3}{4} \\ -17 \end{bmatrix}$$

The first two vectors have two components, whereas the last two have three components.

(b) Let $\quad u = \begin{bmatrix} 2 \\ 3 \\ -4 \end{bmatrix}$ and $\quad v = \begin{bmatrix} 3 \\ -1 \\ -2 \end{bmatrix}.$ Then $\quad 2u - 3v = \begin{bmatrix} 4 \\ 6 \\ -8 \end{bmatrix} + \begin{bmatrix} -9 \\ 3 \\ 6 \end{bmatrix} = \begin{bmatrix} -5 \\ 9 \\ -2 \end{bmatrix},$

$u \cdot v = 6 - 3 + 8 = 11$, and $\|u\| = \sqrt{4 + 9 + 16} = \sqrt{29}.$

1.3 MATRICES

A *matrix A* is a rectangular array of numbers usually presented in the form

$$A = \begin{bmatrix} a_{11} & a_{12} & \cdots & a_{1n} \\ a_{21} & a_{22} & \cdots & a_{2n} \\ \cdots & \cdots & \cdots & \cdots \\ a_{m1} & a_{m2} & \cdots & a_{mn} \end{bmatrix}$$

The m horizontal lists of numbers are called the *rows* of A, and the n vertical lists of numbers are its *columns*. Thus the element a_{ij}, called the ij entry, appears in row i and column j. We frequently denote such a matrix simply by writing $A = [a_{ij}]$.

A matrix with m rows and n columns is called an *m by n* matrix, written $m \times n$. The pair of numbers m and n is called the *size* of the matrix. Two matrices A and B are equal, written $A = B$, if they have the same size and if corresponding elements are equal. Thus the equality of two $m \times n$ matrices is equivalent to a system of mn equalities, one for each corresponding pair of elements.

A matrix with only one row is called a *row matrix* or *row vector*, and a matrix with only one column is called a *column matrix* or *column vector*. A matrix whose entries are all zero is called a *zero matrix* and will usually be denoted by 0.

Matrices whose entries are all real numbers are called *real matrices* or are said to be *matrices over* **R**. This book will be mainly concerned with such real matrices.

EXAMPLE 1.5

(a) The rectangular array $A = \begin{bmatrix} 1 & -4 & 5 \\ 0 & 3 & -2 \end{bmatrix}$ is a 2×3 matrix. Its rows are $[1, -4, 5]$ and

$[0, 3, -2]$, and its columns are $\begin{bmatrix} 1 \\ 0 \end{bmatrix}, \begin{bmatrix} -4 \\ 3 \end{bmatrix},$ and $\begin{bmatrix} 5 \\ -2 \end{bmatrix}.$

(b) The 2×4 zero matrix is the matrix $0 = \begin{bmatrix} 0 & 0 & 0 & 0 \\ 0 & 0 & 0 & 0 \end{bmatrix}.$

(c) Suppose

$$\begin{bmatrix} x + y & 2z + t \\ x - y & z - t \end{bmatrix} = \begin{bmatrix} 3 & 7 \\ 1 & 5 \end{bmatrix}$$

Then the four corresponding entries must be equal. That is,

$$x + y = 3, \qquad x - y = 1, \qquad 2z + t = 7, \qquad z - t = 5$$

The solution of the system of equations is

$$x = 2, \qquad y = 1, \qquad z = 4, \qquad t = -1.$$

1.4 MATRIX ADDITION AND SCALAR MULTIPLICATION

Let $A = [a_{ij}]$ and $B = [b_{ij}]$ be two matrices of the same size, say, $m \times n$ matrices. The *sum* of A and B, written $A + B$, is the matrix obtained by adding corresponding elements from A and B. That is,

$$A + B = \begin{bmatrix} a_{11} + b_{11} & a_{12} + b_{12} & \cdots & a_{1n} + b_{1n} \\ a_{21} + b_{21} & a_{22} + b_{22} & \cdots & a_{2n} + b_{2n} \\ \cdots\cdots\cdots\cdots\cdots\cdots\cdots\cdots\cdots\cdots \\ a_{m1} + b_{m1} & a_{m2} + b_{m2} & \cdots & a_{mn} + b_{mn} \end{bmatrix}$$

The *product* of matrix A by a scalar k, written $k \cdot A$ or simply kA, is the matrix obtained by multiplying each element of A by k. That is,

$$kA = \begin{bmatrix} ka_{11} & ka_{12} & \cdots & ka_{1n} \\ ka_{21} & ka_{22} & \cdots & ka_{2n} \\ \cdots\cdots\cdots\cdots\cdots\cdots\cdots \\ ka_{m1} & ka_{m2} & \cdots & ka_{mn} \end{bmatrix}$$

Observe that $A + B$ and kA are also $m \times n$ matrices. We also define

$$-A = (-1)A \qquad \text{and} \qquad A - B = A + (-B)$$

Matrix $-A$ is called the *negative* of matrix A. The sum of matrices having different sizes is not defined.

EXAMPLE 1.6　Let $A = \begin{bmatrix} 1 & -2 & 3 \\ 0 & 4 & 5 \end{bmatrix}$ and $B = \begin{bmatrix} 4 & 6 & 8 \\ 1 & -3 & -7 \end{bmatrix}$. Then

$$A + B = \begin{bmatrix} 1+4 & -2+6 & 3+8 \\ 0+1 & 4+(-3) & 5+(-7) \end{bmatrix} = \begin{bmatrix} 5 & 4 & 11 \\ 1 & 1 & -2 \end{bmatrix}$$

$$3A = \begin{bmatrix} 3(1) & 3(-2) & 3(3) \\ 3(0) & 3(4) & 3(5) \end{bmatrix} = \begin{bmatrix} 3 & -6 & 9 \\ 0 & 12 & 15 \end{bmatrix}$$

$$2A - 3B = \begin{bmatrix} 2 & -4 & 6 \\ 0 & 8 & 10 \end{bmatrix} + \begin{bmatrix} -12 & -18 & -24 \\ -3 & 9 & 21 \end{bmatrix} = \begin{bmatrix} -10 & -22 & -18 \\ -3 & 17 & 31 \end{bmatrix}$$

Basic properties of matrices under the operations of matrix addition and scalar multiplication follow.

Theorem 1.1:　Consider any matrices A, B, C (having the same size) and any scalars k and k'. Then

(i)	$(A + B) + C = A + (B + C)$	(v)　$k(A + B) = kA + kB$
(ii)	$A + 0 = 0 + A = A$	(vi)　$(k + k')A = kA + k'A$
(iii)	$A + (-A) = (-A) + A = 0$	(vii)　$(kk')A = k(k'A)$
(iv)	$A + B = B + A$	(viii)　$1 \cdot A = A$

Note first that the 0 in (ii) and (iii) refers to the zero matrix.   Also, by (i) and (iv), any sum of matrices

$$A_1 + A_2 + \cdots + A_n$$

requires no parentheses, and the sum does not depend on the order of the matrices.   Furthermore, using (vi) and (viii), we also have $A + A = 2A$, $A + A + A = 3A$, ... Lastly, since vectors in $\mathbf{R}^n$ may be viewed as row (or column) matrices, Theorem 1.1 also holds for vectors in $\mathbf{R}^n$.

The proof of Theorem 1.1 reduces to showing that the ij entries on both sides of each matrix equation are equal.   (See Problem 1.46.)

1.5 SUMMATION SYMBOL

Before we define matrix multiplication, it will be convenient to introduce first the *summation symbol* Σ (the Greek capital letter sigma).

Suppose $f(k)$ is an algebraic expression involving the variable k.   Then the expression

$$\sum_{k=1}^{n} f(k) \qquad \text{or equivalently} \qquad \sum_{k=1}^{n} f(k)$$

has the following meaning.   First we let $k = 1$ in $f(k)$, obtaining

$$f(1)$$

Then we let $k = 2$ in $f(k)$, obtaining $f(2)$, and add this to $f(1)$, obtaining

$$f(1) + f(2)$$

Next we let $k = 3$ in $f(k)$, obtaining $f(3)$, and add this to the previous sum, obtaining

$$f(1) + f(2) + f(3)$$

We continue this process until we obtain the sum

$$f(1) + f(2) + f(3) + \cdots + f(n-1) + f(n)$$

Observe that at each step we increase the value of k by 1 until k is equal to n.   Naturally we may use a variable other than k.

We also generalize our definition by allowing the sum to range from any integer n_1 to any integer n_2, where $n_1 \leq n_2$.   That is, we define

$$\sum_{k=n_1}^{n_2} f(k) = f(n_1) + f(n_1 + 1) + f(n_1 + 2) + \cdots + f(n_2)$$

EXAMPLE 1.7

(a) $\displaystyle\sum_{k=1}^{5} x_k = x_1 + x_2 + x_3 + x_4 + x_5$

(b) $\displaystyle\sum_{i=1}^{n} a_i b_i = a_1 b_1 + a_2 b_2 + \cdots + a_n b_n$

(c) $\displaystyle\sum_{j=2}^{5} j^2 = 2^2 + 3^2 + 4^2 + 5^2 = 4 + 9 + 16 + 25 = 54$

(d) $\displaystyle\sum_{i=0}^{n} a_i x^i = a_0 + a_1 x + a_2 x^2 + \cdots + a_n x^n$

(e) $\displaystyle\sum_{k=1}^{p} a_{ik} b_{kj} = a_{i1} b_{1j} + a_{i2} b_{2j} + a_{i3} b_{3j} + \cdots + a_{ip} b_{pj}$

1.6 MATRIX MULTIPLICATION

The product of matrices A and B, written AB, is somewhat complicated. For this reason, we first begin with a special case.

The product AB of a row matrix $A = [a_i]$ and a column matrix $B = [b_i]$ with the same number of elements is defined to be the scalar (or 1×1 matrix) obtained by multiplying corresponding entries and adding. That is,

$$AB = [a_1, a_2, \ldots, a_n] \begin{bmatrix} b_1 \\ b_2 \\ \vdots \\ b_n \end{bmatrix} = a_1 b_1 + a_2 b_2 + \cdots + a_n b_n = \sum_{k=1}^{n} a_k b_k$$

We emphasize that AB is a scalar (or 1×1 matrix). The product AB is not defined when A and B have different numbers of elements.

EXAMPLE 1.8

(a) $[7, \; -4, \; 5] \begin{bmatrix} 3 \\ 2 \\ -1 \end{bmatrix} = 7(3) + (-4)(2) + 5(-1) = 21 - 8 - 5 = 8$

(b) $[6, \; -1, \; 8, \; 3] \begin{bmatrix} 4 \\ -9 \\ -2 \\ 5 \end{bmatrix} = 24 + 9 - 16 + 15 = 32$

We are now ready to define matrix multiplication in general.

Definition: Suppose $A = [a_{ik}]$ and $B = [b_{kj}]$ are matrices such that the number of columns of A is equal to the number of rows of B, say, A is an $m \times p$ matrix and B is a $p \times n$ matrix. Then the product AB is the $m \times n$ matrix whose ij entry is obtained by multiplying the ith row A_i of A by the jth column B^j of B,

$$AB = \begin{bmatrix} A_1B^1 & A_1B^2 & \cdots & A_1B^n \\ A_2B^1 & A_2B^2 & \cdots & A_2B^n \\ \cdots\cdots\cdots\cdots\cdots\cdots\cdots\cdots\cdots \\ A_mB^1 & A_mB^2 & \cdots & A_mB^n \end{bmatrix}$$

That is,

$$\begin{bmatrix} a_{11} & \cdots & a_{1p} \\ & \cdots & \\ a_{i1} & \cdots & a_{ip} \\ & \cdots & \\ a_{m1} & \cdots & a_{mp} \end{bmatrix} \begin{bmatrix} b_{11} & \cdots & b_{ij} & \cdots & b_{1n} \\ \cdot & \cdots & \cdot & \cdots & \cdot \\ \cdot & \cdots & \cdot & \cdots & \cdot \\ \cdot & \cdots & \cdot & \cdots & \cdot \\ b_{p1} & \cdots & b_{pj} & \cdots & b_{pn} \end{bmatrix} = \begin{bmatrix} c_{11} & \cdots & c_{1n} \\ \cdot & \cdots & \cdot \\ \cdot & c_{ij} & \cdot \\ \cdot & \cdots & \cdot \\ c_{m1} & \cdots & c_{mn} \end{bmatrix}$$

where $c_{ij} = a_{i1}b_{1j} + a_{i2}b_{2j} + \cdots + a_{ip}b_{pj} = \sum_{k=1}^{p} a_{ik}b_{kj}$.

We emphasize that the product AB is not defined if A is an $m \times p$ matrix and B is a $q \times n$ matrix, where $p \neq q$.

EXAMPLE 1.9 Find AB, where $A = \begin{bmatrix} 1 & 3 \\ 2 & -1 \end{bmatrix}$ and $B = \begin{bmatrix} 2 & 0 & -4 \\ 5 & -2 & 6 \end{bmatrix}$.

Since A is 2×2 and B is 2×3, the product AB is defined and AB is a 2×3 matrix. To obtain the first row of the product matrix AB, multiply the first row $[1, 3]$ of A times each column of B,

$$\begin{bmatrix} 2 \\ 5 \end{bmatrix}, \quad \begin{bmatrix} 0 \\ -2 \end{bmatrix}, \quad \begin{bmatrix} -4 \\ 6 \end{bmatrix}$$

That is,

$$AB = \begin{bmatrix} 2+15 & 0-6 & -4+18 \end{bmatrix} = \begin{bmatrix} 17 & -6 & 14 \end{bmatrix}$$

To obtain the second row of the product AB, multiply the second row $[2, -1]$ of A times each column of B. Thus

$$AB = \begin{bmatrix} 17 & -6 & 14 \\ 4-5 & 0+2 & -8-6 \end{bmatrix} = \begin{bmatrix} 17 & -6 & 14 \\ -1 & 2 & -14 \end{bmatrix}$$

EXAMPLE 1.10 Suppose $A = \begin{bmatrix} 1 & 2 \\ 3 & 4 \end{bmatrix}$ and $B = \begin{bmatrix} 5 & 6 \\ 0 & -2 \end{bmatrix}$. Then

$$AB = \begin{bmatrix} 1(5)+2(0) & 1(6)+2(-2) \\ 3(5)+4(0) & 3(6)+4(-2) \end{bmatrix} = \begin{bmatrix} 5 & 2 \\ 15 & 10 \end{bmatrix}$$

$$BA = \begin{bmatrix} 5(1)+6(3) & 5(2)+6(4) \\ 0(1)+(-2)(3) & 0(2)+(-2)(4) \end{bmatrix} = \begin{bmatrix} 23 & 34 \\ -6 & -8 \end{bmatrix}$$

The above example shows that matrix multiplication is not commutative, i.e., the products AB and BA of matrices need not be equal.

Matrix multiplication does, however, satisfy the following properties.

Theorem 1.2: Let A, B, and C be matrices. Then, whenever the products and sums are defined,

(i) $(AB)C = A(BC)$ (associative law)

(ii) $A(B + C) = AB + AC$ (left distributive law)
(iii) $(B + C)A = BA + CA$ (right distributive law)
(iv) $k(AB) = (kA)B = A(kB)$, where k is a scalar

We note that $0A = 0$ and $B0 = 0$, where 0 is the zero matrix.

1.7   TRANSPOSE OF A MATRIX

The *transpose* of a matrix A, written A^T, is the matrix obtained by writing the columns of A, in order, as rows.   For example,

$$\begin{bmatrix} 1 & 2 & 3 \\ 4 & 5 & 6 \end{bmatrix}^T = \begin{bmatrix} 1 & 4 \\ 2 & 5 \\ 3 & 6 \end{bmatrix} \quad \text{and} \quad [1, -3, -5]^T = \begin{bmatrix} 1 \\ -3 \\ -5 \end{bmatrix}$$

In other words, if $A = [a_{ij}]$ is an $m \times n$ matrix, then $A^T = [b_{ij}]$ is the $n \times m$ matrix, where $b_{ij} = a_{ji}$.

Observe that the transpose of a row vector is a column vector.   Similarly, the transpose of a column vector is a row vector.

The next theorem lists basic properties of the transpose operation.

Theorem 1.3:   Let A and B be matrices and k a scalar.   Then, whenever the sum and product are defined,

(i) $(A + B)^T = A^T + B^T$ (iii) $(kA)^T = kA^T$
(ii) $(A^T)^T = A$ (iv) $(AB)^T = B^T A^T$

We emphasize that, by (iv), the transpose of a product is the product of the transposes, but in the reverse order.

1.8   BLOCK MATRICES

Using a system of horizontal and vertical (dashed) lines, we can partition a matrix A into submatrices called *blocks* (or *cells*) of A.   Clearly a given matrix may be divided into blocks in different ways.   For example,

$$\begin{bmatrix} 1 & -2 & 0 & 1 & 3 \\ 2 & 3 & 5 & 7 & -2 \\ 3 & 1 & 4 & 5 & 9 \end{bmatrix} = \left[\begin{array}{cc:ccc} 1 & -2 & 0 & 1 & 3 \\ 2 & 3 & 5 & 7 & -2 \\ \hdashline 3 & 1 & 4 & 5 & 9 \end{array}\right] = \left[\begin{array}{c:cc:cc} 1 & -2 & 0 & 1 & 3 \\ \hdashline 2 & 3 & 5 & 7 & -2 \\ 3 & 1 & 4 & 5 & 9 \end{array}\right]$$

The convenience of the partition of matrices, say A and B, into blocks is that the result of operations on A and B can be obtained by carrying out the computation with the blocks, just as if they were the actual elements of the matrices.   This is illustrated next.

Suppose A and B are partitioned into the same number of row and column blocks and suppose corresponding blocks have the same size.   Say,

$$A = \begin{bmatrix} A_{11} & A_{12} & \cdots & A_{1n} \\ A_{21} & A_{22} & \cdots & A_{2n} \\ \cdots\cdots\cdots\cdots\cdots\cdots \\ A_{m1} & A_{m2} & \cdots & A_{mn} \end{bmatrix} \quad \text{and} \quad B = \begin{bmatrix} B_{11} & B_{12} & \cdots & B_{1n} \\ B_{21} & B_{22} & \cdots & B_{2n} \\ \cdots\cdots\cdots\cdots\cdots\cdots \\ B_{m1} & B_{m2} & \cdots & B_{mn} \end{bmatrix}$$

Adding the corresponding blocks of A and B also adds the corresponding elements of A and B. Also, multiplying each block of A by a scalar k multiplies each element of A by k. Thus

$$A + B = \begin{bmatrix} A_{11} + B_{11} & A_{12} + B_{12} & \cdots & A_{1n} + B_{1n} \\ A_{21} + B_{21} & A_{22} + B_{22} & \cdots & A_{2n} + B_{2n} \\ \cdots\cdots\cdots\cdots\cdots\cdots\cdots\cdots\cdots\cdots\cdots\cdots \\ A_{m1} + B_{m1} & A_{m2} + B_{m2} & \cdots & A_{mn} + B_{mn} \end{bmatrix}$$

and

$$kA = \begin{bmatrix} kA_{11} & kA_{12} & \cdots & kA_{1n} \\ kA_{21} & kA_{22} & \cdots & kA_{2n} \\ \cdots\cdots\cdots\cdots\cdots\cdots\cdots \\ kA_{m1} & kA_{m2} & \cdots & kA_{mn} \end{bmatrix}$$

The case of matrix multiplication is less obvious, but still true. Suppose matrices U and V are partitioned into blocks as follows:

$$U = \begin{bmatrix} U_{11} & U_{12} & \cdots & U_{1p} \\ U_{21} & U_{22} & \cdots & U_{2p} \\ \cdots\cdots\cdots\cdots\cdots\cdots \\ U_{m1} & U_{m2} & \cdots & U_{mp} \end{bmatrix} \quad \text{and} \quad V = \begin{bmatrix} V_{11} & V_{12} & \cdots & V_{1n} \\ V_{21} & V_{22} & \cdots & V_{2n} \\ \cdots\cdots\cdots\cdots\cdots\cdots \\ V_{p1} & V_{p2} & \cdots & V_{pn} \end{bmatrix}$$

Also assume that the number of columns of each block U_{ik} is equal to the number of rows of each block V_{kj}. (Thus each product $U_{ik}V_{kj}$ is defined.) Then

$$UV = \begin{bmatrix} W_{11} & W_{12} & \cdots & W_{1n} \\ W_{21} & W_{22} & \cdots & W_{2n} \\ \cdots\cdots\cdots\cdots\cdots\cdots \\ W_{m1} & W_{m2} & \cdots & W_{mn} \end{bmatrix}$$

where

$$W_{ij} = U_{i1}V_{1j} + U_{i2}V_{2j} + \cdots + U_{ip}V_{pj}$$

The proof of the formula for UV is straightforward, but detailed and lengthy. It is left as an exercise. (See Problem 1.96.)

1.9 VECTORS IN $\mathbf{R}^2$ AND $\mathbf{R}^3$, SPATIAL VECTORS

Vectors in the plane $\mathbf{R}^2$ and vectors in the space $\mathbf{R}^3$ (called *spatial vectors*) can be pictured geometrically as directed line segments (arrows), and the vector space operations on them have a geometrical interpretation. For this reason, many of our examples in this text will be in $\mathbf{R}^2$ or $\mathbf{R}^3$. We discuss these ideas in this section. In order to avoid repetition, we will mainly restrict our discussion to $\mathbf{R}^3$. It will also be convenient to distinguish here between a triple $P(a, b, c)$ of real numbers representing a point in space $\mathbf{R}^3$ and a triple $u = [a, b, c]$ representing a vector in $\mathbf{R}^3$.

Coordinate System and Arrow Vectors

First we review the representation of points in space by ordered triples of real numbers, as indicated in Fig. 1-1. Specifically, we first choose a point in space, called the *origin* and denoted by O. Next we choose three mutually perpendicular real number lines containing the point O, called the x, y, and z *axes*, where the zero on each number line is chosen to be the common origin point O and the unit lengths of the three axes are (usually) chosen to be equal. Also, as pictured in Fig. 1-1, the positive direction of each axis is indicated by an arrow head at the end of the axis, and the directions are chosen so that the axes form a right-handed coordinate system. Given any such coordinate system, any point P in space is represented by an ordered triple (a, b, c) of real numbers, called the *coordinates* of P, as indicated in Fig. 1-1, and any ordered triple of real numbers corresponds to a point in space. [We will frequently write $P(a, b, c)$ to denote the point P with coordinates a, b, c.] This representation of points in space is called 3-space and is denoted by $\mathbf{R}^3$.

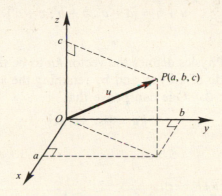

Fig. 1-1 $\mathbf{R}^3$ space.

A *vector* u in $\mathbf{R}^3$ is a 1×3 (or 3×1) matrix or, simply, a triple of real numbers. We identify the vector $u = [a, b, c]$ with the arrow (directed line segment) from the origin $O(0, 0, 0)$, called the *initial point* (or *tail*) of the arrow u, to the point $P(a, b, c)$, called the *terminal point* (or *head*) of u, as indicated in Fig. 1-1. The length of the arrow u is given by

$$\|u\| = \sqrt{a^2 + b^2 + c^2}$$

This formula can be derived using the Pythagorean theorem.

Any pair of points in $\mathbf{R}^3$, say $A(a_1, a_2, a_3)$ and $B(b_1, b_2, b_3)$, defines the *located vector* or *directed line segment from A to B*, written $\overrightarrow{AB}$. Since vectors (arrows) with the same magnitude and direction are usually identified, we identify $\overrightarrow{AB}$ with the vector

$$u = B - A = [b_1 - a_1, b_2 - a_2, b_3 - a_3]$$

since $\overrightarrow{AB}$ and u have the same magnitude and direction, as pictured in Fig. 1-2.

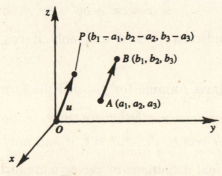

Fig. 1-2 $u = B - A$.

Vector Operations

Consider vectors (arrows) $u = [a, b, c]$ and $v = [a', b', c']$ in $\mathbf{R}^3$. Next we discuss the geometrical interpretation of our vector operations.

(a) **Addition:** Physics defines the sum $u + v$ of the vectors u and v by the so-called *parallelogram law*, i.e., $u + v$ is the diagonal of the parallelogram formed by u and v. One can prove that

$$u + v = [a + a', b + b', c + c']$$

[See Fig. 1-3(a).]

(b) **Scalar Multiplication:** Physics defines the vector ku to be the vector obtained from u by multiplying the magnitude of u by k, and by retaining the same direction if $k > 0$ or the opposite direction if $k < 0$. One can prove that

$$ku = [ka, kb, kc]$$

[See Fig. 1-3(b).]

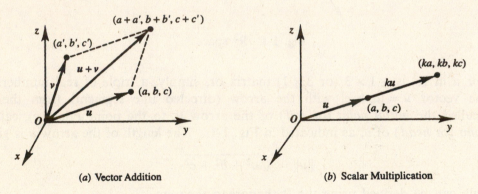

(a) Vector Addition   (b) Scalar Multiplication

Fig. 1-3

(c) **Inner (Dot) Product:** Physics defines the dot (inner) product of u and v to be the scalar:

$$u \cdot v = \|u\|\|v\| \cos \alpha$$

where α is the angle between the arrows u and v. (See Fig. 1-4.) One can show that

$$u \cdot v = aa' + bb' + cc'$$

Accordingly, u is perpendicular to v if and only if $\cos \alpha = 0$, i.e., if and only if $\alpha = \pi/2 = 90°$.

(d) **Norm (Length):** The above formula for $\|u\|$ and the formula for $u \cdot v$ indicate that

$$\|u\| = \sqrt{u \cdot u}$$

Hence a vector u is a *unit* vector, i.e., $\|u\| = 1$, if and only if $u \cdot u = 1$.

Thus we see that our original definitions of vector addition, scalar multiplication, inner product, and length agree with the physical definitions of these operations.

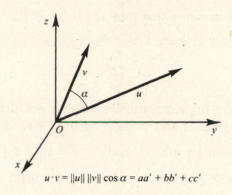

$$u \cdot v = \|u\| \, \|v\| \cos \alpha = aa' + bb' + cc'$$

Fig. 1-4

ijk Notation

Vectors in $\mathbf{R}^3$ are sometimes expressed using a special **ijk** notation. Specifically,

$\mathbf{i} = [1, 0, 0]$ denotes the unit vector in the x direction.
$\mathbf{j} = [0, 1, 0]$ denotes the unit vector in the y direction.
$\mathbf{k} = [0, 0, 1]$ denotes the unit vector in the z direction.

Then any vector $u = [a, b, c]$ can be expressed uniquely in the form

$$u = [a, b, c] = a\mathbf{i} + b\mathbf{j} + c\mathbf{k}$$

Since $\mathbf{i}, \mathbf{j}, \mathbf{k}$ are unit vectors and mutually orthogonal, we have

$$\mathbf{i} \cdot \mathbf{i} = 1, \qquad \mathbf{j} \cdot \mathbf{j} = 1, \qquad \mathbf{k} \cdot \mathbf{k} = 1 \quad \text{and} \quad \mathbf{i} \cdot \mathbf{j} = 0, \qquad \mathbf{i} \cdot \mathbf{k} = 0, \qquad \mathbf{j} \cdot \mathbf{k} = 0$$

Furthermore, the vector operations discussed above may be expressed in the **ijk** notation as follows. Suppose

$$u = a_1\mathbf{i} + a_2\mathbf{j} + a_3\mathbf{k} \qquad \text{and} \qquad v = b_1\mathbf{i} + b_2\mathbf{j} + b_3\mathbf{k}$$

Then $$u + v = (a_1 + b_1)\mathbf{i} + (a_2 + b_2)\mathbf{j} + (a_3 + b_3)\mathbf{k}$$

and $$cu = ca_1\mathbf{i} + ca_2\mathbf{j} + ca_3\mathbf{k}$$

where c is a scalar. Also,

$$u \cdot v = a_1 b_1 + a_2 b_2 + a_3 b_3 \qquad \text{and} \qquad \|u\| = \sqrt{u \cdot u} = \sqrt{a_1^2 + a_2^2 + a_3^2}$$

EXAMPLE 1.11 Suppose $u = 3\mathbf{i} + 5\mathbf{j} - 2\mathbf{k}$ and $v = 4\mathbf{i} - 3\mathbf{j} + 7\mathbf{k}$.

(a) To find $u + v$, add the corresponding components, yielding

$$u + v = 7\mathbf{i} + 2\mathbf{j} + 5\mathbf{k}$$

(b) To find $3u - 2v$, first multiply the vectors by the scalars and then add,

$$3u - 2v = (9\mathbf{i} + 15\mathbf{j} - 6\mathbf{k}) + (-8\mathbf{i} + 6\mathbf{j} - 14\mathbf{k}) = \mathbf{i} + 21\mathbf{j} - 20\mathbf{k}$$

(c) To find $u \cdot v$, multiply the corresponding components and then add,

$$u \cdot v = 12 - 15 - 14 = -17$$

(d) To find $\|u\|$, square each component and then add to get $\|u\|^2$,

$$\|u\|^2 = 9 + 25 + 4 = 38 \qquad \text{and hence} \qquad \|u\| = \sqrt{38}$$

Cross Product (Optional)

There is a special operation for vectors in $\mathbf{R}^3$ which is not defined in $\mathbf{R}^n$ for $n \neq 3$. This operation is called the *cross product* and is denoted by $u \times v$. Specifically, suppose

$$u = a_1\mathbf{i} + a_2\mathbf{j} + a_3\mathbf{k} \qquad \text{and} \qquad v = b_1\mathbf{i} + b_2\mathbf{j} + b_3\mathbf{k}$$

Then $\qquad\qquad u \times v = (a_2b_3 - a_3b_2)\mathbf{i} + (a_3b_1 - a_1b_3)\mathbf{j} + (a_1b_2 - a_2b_1)\mathbf{k}$

Note that $u \times v$ is a vector; hence $u \times v$ is sometimes called the *vector product* or *outer product* of u and v. The formula for the cross product is usually easily remembered using the expression

$$u \times v = \begin{vmatrix} a_2 & a_3 \\ b_2 & b_3 \end{vmatrix}\mathbf{i} - \begin{vmatrix} a_1 & a_3 \\ b_1 & b_3 \end{vmatrix}\mathbf{j} + \begin{vmatrix} a_1 & a_2 \\ b_1 & b_2 \end{vmatrix}\mathbf{k}$$

This expression uses the determinant notation $\begin{vmatrix} a & b \\ c & d \end{vmatrix} = ad - bc$, which is discussed in detail in Chapter 10.

EXAMPLE 1.12

(a) Suppose $u = 4\mathbf{i} + 3\mathbf{j} + 6\mathbf{k}$ and $v = 2\mathbf{i} + 5\mathbf{j} - 3\mathbf{k}$. Then

$$u \times v = \begin{vmatrix} 3 & 6 \\ 5 & -3 \end{vmatrix}\mathbf{i} - \begin{vmatrix} 4 & 6 \\ 2 & -3 \end{vmatrix}\mathbf{j} + \begin{vmatrix} 4 & 3 \\ 2 & 5 \end{vmatrix}\mathbf{k} = -39\mathbf{i} + 24\mathbf{j} + 14\mathbf{k}$$

(b) Suppose $u = [2, -1, 5]$ and $v = [3, 7, 6]$. Then

$$u \times v = \left[\begin{vmatrix} -1 & 5 \\ 7 & 6 \end{vmatrix}, \ -\begin{vmatrix} 2 & 5 \\ 3 & 6 \end{vmatrix}, \begin{vmatrix} 2 & -1 \\ 3 & 7 \end{vmatrix} \right] = [-41, 3, 17]$$

Here we find the cross product without using the **ijk** notation.

(c) The cross products of the vectors **i, j, k** are as follows:

$$\mathbf{i} \times \mathbf{j} = \mathbf{k}, \qquad \mathbf{j} \times \mathbf{k} = \mathbf{i}, \qquad \mathbf{k} \times \mathbf{i} = \mathbf{j}, \qquad \text{and} \qquad \mathbf{j} \times \mathbf{i} = -\mathbf{k}, \qquad \mathbf{k} \times \mathbf{j} = -\mathbf{i}, \qquad \mathbf{i} \times \mathbf{k} = -\mathbf{j}$$

In other words, if we view the triple (**i, j, k**) as a cyclic permutation, say, as arranged clockwise around a circle, then the product of two of them in the given direction is the third one, but the product of two of them in the opposite direction is the negative of the third one.

Two important properties of the cross product are contained in the following theorem.

Theorem 1.4: Let u, v, and w be vectors in $\mathbf{R}^3$.

(i) The vector $u \times v$ is orthogonal to both u and v.

(ii) The absolute value of the "triple product"

$$u \cdot v \times w$$

represents the volume of the parallelepiped formed by the vectors u, v, and w. (See Fig. 1-5.)

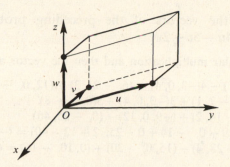

Fig. 1-5

We note that the vectors $u, v,$ and $u \times v$ form a right-handed system, and the following formula gives the magnitude of $u \times v$:

$$\|u \times v\| = \|u\|\|v\| \sin \alpha$$

where α is the angle between u and v.

Solved Problems

VECTORS

1.1. Determine which of the following vectors, if any, are equal:

$$u_1 = (1, 2, 3), \qquad u_2 = (2, 3, 1), \qquad u_3 = (1, 3, 2), \qquad u_4 = (2, 3, 1)$$

Vectors are equal only when the corresponding entries are equal; hence only u_2 and u_4 are equal.

1.2. Let $u = (2, -7, 1)$, $v = (-3, 0, 4)$, and $w = (0, 5, -8)$. Find: *(a)* $u + v$; *(b)* $v + w$; *(c)* $-3u$; *(d)* $-w$.

(a) Add corresponding components:

$$u + v = (2, -7, 1) + (-3, 0, 4) = (2 - 3, \ -7 + 0, \ 1 + 4) = (-1, -7, 5)$$

(b) Add corresponding components:

$$v + w = (-3, 0, 4) + (0, 5, -8) = (-3 + 0, 0 + 5, 4 - 8) = (-3, 5, -4)$$

(c) Multiply each component of u by the scalar -3:

$$-3u = -3(2, -7, 1) = (-6, 21, -3)$$

(d) Multiply each component of w by -1, i.e., change the sign of each component:

$$-w = -(0, 5, -8) = (0, -5, 8)$$

1.3. Let u, v, and w be the vectors of the preceding problem. Find: (a) $3u - 4v$; (b) $2u + 3v - 5w$;   (c) $4u - 5v + 2w$.

First perform the scalar multiplication and then the vector addition.

(a) $3u - 4v = 3(2, -7, 1) - 4(-3, 0, 4) = (6, -21, 3) + (12, 0, -16) = (18, -21, -13)$
(b) $2u + 3v - 5w = 2(2, -7, 1) + 3(-3, 0, 4) - 5(0, 5, -8)$
$$= (4, -14, 2) + (-9, 0, 12) + (0, -25, 40)$$
$$= (4 - 9 + 0, \ -14 + 0 - 25, \ 2 + 12 + 40) = (-5, -39, 54)$$
(c) $4u - 5v + 2w = (8, -28, 4) + (15, 0, -20) + (0, 10, -16) = (23, -18, -32)$

1.4. Given: $u = (1, -2, 3, -4, 5)$, $v = (2, 3, 4, 5, 6)$, and $w = (3, 0, -4, 1, -2)$. Find: (a) $5u - 2v$;   (b) $3u + 2v - 4w$.

First perform the scalar multiplication and then the vector addition.

(a) $5u - 2v = (5, -10, 15, -20, 25) + (-4, -6, -8, -10, -12)$
$$= (1, -16, 7, -30, 13)$$
(b) $3u + 2v - 4w = (3, -6, 9, -12, 15) + (4, 6, 8, 10, 12) + (-12, 0, 16, -4, 8)$
$$= (-5, 0, 33, -6, 35)$$

1.5. Find x and y if $x(1, 1) + y(2, -1) = (1, 4)$.

First multiply by the scalars x and y and then add:

$$x(1, 1) + y(2, -1) = (x, x) + (2y, -y) = (x + 2y, x - y) = (1, 4)$$

Two vectors are equal only when their corresponding components are equal. Hence set corresponding components equal to each other to obtain

$$x + 2y = 1 \quad \text{and} \quad x - y = 4$$

Solve the system of equations to obtain $x = 3$ and $y = -1$.

1.6. Suppose $u = \begin{bmatrix} 5 \\ 3 \\ -4 \end{bmatrix}$, $v = \begin{bmatrix} -1 \\ 5 \\ 2 \end{bmatrix}$, and $w = \begin{bmatrix} 3 \\ -1 \\ -2 \end{bmatrix}$. Find: (a) $5u - 2v$; (b) $-2u + 4v - 3w$.

(a) $5u - 2v = 5\begin{bmatrix} 5 \\ 3 \\ -4 \end{bmatrix} - 2\begin{bmatrix} -1 \\ 5 \\ 2 \end{bmatrix} = \begin{bmatrix} 25 \\ 15 \\ -20 \end{bmatrix} + \begin{bmatrix} 2 \\ -10 \\ -4 \end{bmatrix} = \begin{bmatrix} 27 \\ 5 \\ -24 \end{bmatrix}$

(b) $-2u + 4v - 3w = \begin{bmatrix} -10 \\ -6 \\ 8 \end{bmatrix} + \begin{bmatrix} -4 \\ 20 \\ 8 \end{bmatrix} + \begin{bmatrix} -9 \\ 3 \\ 6 \end{bmatrix} = \begin{bmatrix} -23 \\ 17 \\ 22 \end{bmatrix}$

INNER (DOT) PRODUCT, ORTHOGONALITY, LENGTH (NORM) IN $\mathbf{R}^n$

1.7. Compute $u \cdot v$, where: (a) $u = (2, -5, 6)$ and $v = (8, 2, -3)$; (b) $u = (3, -5, 2, 1)$ and $v = (4, 1, -2, 7)$; (c) $u = (4, 2, -3, 5, -1)$ and $v = (2, 6, -1, -4, 8)$.

Multiply corresponding components and add.

(a) $u \cdot v = 2(8) - 5(2) + 6(-3) = 16 - 10 - 18 = -12$

(b) $u \cdot v = 12 - 5 - 4 + 7 = 10$
(c) $u \cdot v = 8 + 12 + 3 - 20 - 8 = -5$

1.8.   Suppose $u = (3, 2, 1)$, $v = (5, -3, 4)$, and $w = (1, 6, -7)$. Find: (a) $(u + v) \cdot w$;
(b) $u \cdot w + v \cdot w$.

(a)   First calculate $u + v$ by adding corresponding components:

$$u + v = (3 + 5, 2 - 3, 1 + 4) = (8, -1, 5)$$

Then compute the inner product:

$$(u + v) \cdot w = (8, -1, 5) \cdot (1, 6, -7) = 8 - 6 - 35 = -33$$

(b)   First find

$$u \cdot w = 3 + 12 - 7 = 8 \qquad \text{and} \qquad v \cdot w = 5 - 18 - 28 = -41$$

Then $u \cdot w + v \cdot w = 8 - 41 = -33$.

(Note that both values are equal.)

1.9.   Let $u = (5, 4, 1)$, $v = (3, -4, 1)$, and $w = (1, -2, 3)$.   Which pair of vectors, if any, are perpendicular (orthogonal)?

Find the dot product of each pair of vectors:

$$u \cdot v = 15 - 16 + 1 = 0 \qquad v \cdot w = 3 + 8 + 3 = 14 \qquad u \cdot w = 5 - 8 + 3 = 0$$

Thus vectors u and v and vectors u and w are orthogonal, but vectors v and w are not.

1.10.   Determine k so that the vectors u and v are orthogonal, where: (a) $u = (1, k, -3)$ and $v = (2, -5, 4)$; (b) $u = (2, 3k, -4, 1, 5)$ and $v = (6, -1, 3, 7, 2k)$.

Compute $u \cdot v$, set it equal to 0, and then solve for k.

(a) $u \cdot v = 1(2) + k(-5) - 3(4) = 2 - 5k - 12 = -5k - 10$.   Then

$$-5k - 10 = 0 \qquad \text{or} \qquad k = -2$$

(b) $u \cdot v = 12 - 3k - 12 + 7 + 10k = 7k + 7$.   Then

$$7k + 7 = 0 \qquad \text{or} \qquad k = -1$$

1.11.   Find $\|u\|$, where: (a) $u = (3, -12, -4)$; (b) $u = (2, -3, 8, -7)$.

First find $\|u\|^2 = u \cdot u$ by squaring the components and adding.   Then $\|u\| = \sqrt{\|u\|^2}$.

(a) $\|u\|^2 = (3)^2 + (-12)^2 + (-4)^2 = 9 + 144 + 16 = 169$.   Hence $\|u\| = \sqrt{169} = 13$.
(b) $\|u\|^2 = 4 + 9 + 64 + 49 = 126$.   Hence $\|u\| = \sqrt{126}$.

1.12. Determine k such that $\|u\| = \sqrt{39}$, where $u = (1, k, -2, 5)$.

First find $\|u\|^2 = 1 + k^2 + 4 + 25 = k^2 + 30$. Then solve $k^2 + 30 = 39$ and obtain $k = 3, -3$.

1.13. For any nonzero vector v, the following vector is a unit vector (i.e., length 1) in the same direction of v:

$$\hat{v} = \frac{1}{\|v\|} v$$

The process of finding $\hat{v}$ is called *normalizing* v. Normalize: (*a*) $u = (3, -4)$; (*b*) $w = (4, -2, -3, 8)$; (*c*) $v = (\frac{1}{2}, \frac{2}{3}, -\frac{1}{4})$.

(*a*) First find $\|u\|^2 = 9 + 16 = 25$. Hence $\|u\| = 5$. Divide each component of u by 5 to get

$$\hat{u} = (\tfrac{3}{5}, -\tfrac{4}{5})$$

(*b*) First find $\|w\|^2 = 16 + 4 + 9 + 64 = 93$. Divide each component of w by $\|w\| = \sqrt{93}$ to obtain

$$\hat{w} = \frac{w}{\|w\|} = \left(\frac{4}{\sqrt{93}}, \frac{-2}{\sqrt{93}}, \frac{-3}{\sqrt{93}}, \frac{8}{\sqrt{93}} \right)$$

(*c*) Note that v and any positive multiple of v will have the same normalized form. Hence first multiply v by 12 to "clear fractions", that is, first find $12v = (6, 8, -3)$. Then

$$\|12v\|^2 = 36 + 64 + 9 = 109 \quad \text{and} \quad \hat{v} = \widehat{12v} = \frac{12v}{\|12v\|} = \left(\frac{6}{\sqrt{109}}, \frac{8}{\sqrt{109}}, \frac{-3}{\sqrt{109}} \right)$$

MATRIX ADDITION AND SCALAR MULTIPLICATION

1.14. Given: $A = \begin{bmatrix} 1 & 2 & -3 \\ 4 & -5 & 6 \end{bmatrix}$ and $B = \begin{bmatrix} 1 & -1 & 2 \\ 0 & 3 & -5 \end{bmatrix}$. Find: (*a*) $A + B$; (*b*) $3A$ and $-4B$.

(*a*) Add corresponding elements:

$$A + B = \begin{bmatrix} 1+1 & 2+(-1) & -3+2 \\ 4+0 & -5+3 & 6+(-5) \end{bmatrix} = \begin{bmatrix} 2 & 1 & -1 \\ 4 & -2 & 1 \end{bmatrix}$$

(*b*) Multiply each entry by the given scalar:

$$3A = \begin{bmatrix} 3(1) & 3(2) & 3(-3) \\ 3(4) & 3(-5) & 3(6) \end{bmatrix} = \begin{bmatrix} 3 & 6 & -9 \\ 12 & -15 & 18 \end{bmatrix}$$

$$-4B = \begin{bmatrix} -4(1) & -4(-1) & -4(2) \\ -4(0) & -4(3) & -4(-5) \end{bmatrix} = \begin{bmatrix} -4 & 4 & -8 \\ 0 & -12 & 20 \end{bmatrix}$$

1.15. Find $2A - 3B$, where $A = \begin{bmatrix} 1 & -2 & 3 \\ 4 & 5 & -6 \end{bmatrix}$ and $B = \begin{bmatrix} 3 & 0 & 2 \\ -7 & 1 & 8 \end{bmatrix}$.

First perform the scalar multiplications and then a matrix addition:

$$2A - 3B = \begin{bmatrix} 2 & -4 & 6 \\ 8 & 10 & -12 \end{bmatrix} + \begin{bmatrix} -9 & 0 & -6 \\ 21 & -3 & -24 \end{bmatrix} = \begin{bmatrix} -7 & -4 & 0 \\ 29 & 7 & -36 \end{bmatrix}$$

(Note that we multiply B by -3 and then add, rather than multiplying B by 3 and subtracting. This usually prevents errors.)

1.16. Find $3A + 4B - 2C$, where $A = \begin{bmatrix} 2 & -5 & 1 \\ 3 & 0 & -4 \end{bmatrix}$, $B = \begin{bmatrix} 1 & -2 & -3 \\ 0 & -1 & 5 \end{bmatrix}$, and $C = \begin{bmatrix} 0 & 1 & -2 \\ 1 & -1 & -1 \end{bmatrix}$.

First perform the scalar multiplication and then the matrix addition:

$$3A + 4B - 2C = \begin{bmatrix} 6 & -15 & 3 \\ 9 & 0 & -12 \end{bmatrix} + \begin{bmatrix} 4 & -8 & -12 \\ 0 & -4 & 20 \end{bmatrix} + \begin{bmatrix} 0 & -2 & 4 \\ -2 & 2 & 2 \end{bmatrix} = \begin{bmatrix} 10 & -25 & -5 \\ 7 & -2 & 10 \end{bmatrix}$$

1.17. Find x, y, z and t if $3\begin{bmatrix} x & y \\ z & t \end{bmatrix} = \begin{bmatrix} x & 6 \\ -1 & 2t \end{bmatrix} + \begin{bmatrix} 4 & x+y \\ z+t & 3 \end{bmatrix}$.

First write each side as a single matrix:

$$\begin{bmatrix} 3x & 3y \\ 3z & 3t \end{bmatrix} = \begin{bmatrix} x+4 & x+y+6 \\ z+t-1 & 2t+3 \end{bmatrix}$$

Set corresponding entries equal to each other to obtain the system of four equations:

$$\begin{array}{cc} 3x = x+4 & 2x = 4 \\ 3y = x+y+6 & 2y = 6+x \\ 3z = z+t-1 \quad \text{or} \quad & 2z = t-1 \\ 3t = 2t+3 & t = 3 \end{array}$$

The solution is $x = 2$, $y = 4$, $z = 1$, and $t = 3$.

MATRIX MULTIPLICATION

1.18. Calculate: (a) $[8, -4, 5]\begin{bmatrix} 3 \\ 2 \\ -1 \end{bmatrix}$; (b) $[6, -1, 7, 5]\begin{bmatrix} 4 \\ -9 \\ -3 \\ 2 \end{bmatrix}$; (c) $[3, 8, -2, 4]\begin{bmatrix} 5 \\ -1 \\ 6 \end{bmatrix}$

(a) Multiply corresponding entries and add:

$$[8, -4, 5]\begin{bmatrix} 3 \\ 2 \\ -1 \end{bmatrix} = 8(3) + (-4)(2) + 5(-1) = 24 - 8 - 5 = 11$$

(b) Multiply corresponding entries and add:

$$[6, -1, 7, 5] \begin{bmatrix} 4 \\ -9 \\ -3 \\ 2 \end{bmatrix} = 24 + 9 - 21 + 10 = 22$$

(c) The product is not defined when the row matrix and the column matrix have different numbers of elements.

1.19. Let $(r \times s)$ denote an $r \times s$ matrix. Find the sizes of those matrix products that are defined:

(a) $(2 \times 3)(3 \times 4)$ (c) $(1 \times 2)(3 \times 1)$ (e) $(4 \times 4)(3 \times 3)$
(b) $(4 \times 1)(1 \times 2)$ (d) $(5 \times 2)(2 \times 3)$ (f) $(2 \times 2)(2 \times 4)$

    In each case the product is defined if the inner numbers are equal, and then the product will have the size of the outer numbers in the given order.

(a) 2×4 (c) not defined   (e) not defined
(b) 4×2 (d) 5×3 (f) 2×4

1.20. Let $A = \begin{bmatrix} 1 & 3 \\ 2 & -1 \end{bmatrix}$ and $B = \begin{bmatrix} 2 & 0 & -4 \\ 3 & -2 & 6 \end{bmatrix}$. Find: (a) AB; (b) BA.

(a) Since A is 2×2 and B is 2×3, the product AB is defined and is a 2×3 matrix. To obtain the entries in the first row of AB, multiply the first row $[1, 3]$ of A by the columns

$\begin{bmatrix} 2 \\ 3 \end{bmatrix}$, $\begin{bmatrix} 0 \\ -2 \end{bmatrix}$, and $\begin{bmatrix} -4 \\ 6 \end{bmatrix}$ of B, respectively:

$$\begin{bmatrix} \boxed{1 \quad 3} \\ 2 \quad -1 \end{bmatrix} \begin{bmatrix} \boxed{2} & \boxed{0} & \boxed{-4} \\ \boxed{3} & \boxed{-2} & \boxed{6} \end{bmatrix} = [1(2) + 3(3) \quad 1(0) + 3(-2) \quad 1(-4) + 3(6)]$$

$$= [2 + 9 \quad 0 - 6 \quad -4 + 18] = [11 \quad -6 \quad 14]$$

To obtain the entries in the second row of AB, multiply the second row $[2, -1]$ of A by the columns of B:

$$\begin{bmatrix} 1 \quad 3 \\ \boxed{2 \quad -1} \end{bmatrix} \begin{bmatrix} \boxed{2} & \boxed{0} & \boxed{-4} \\ \boxed{3} & \boxed{-2} & \boxed{6} \end{bmatrix} = \begin{bmatrix} 11 & -6 & 14 \\ 4 - 3 & 0 + 2 & -8 - 6 \end{bmatrix}$$

Thus
$$AB = \begin{bmatrix} 11 & -6 & 14 \\ 1 & 2 & -14 \end{bmatrix}$$

(b) Note that B is 2×3 and A is 2×2. Since the inner numbers 3 and 2 are not equal, the product BA is not defined.

1.21. Given: $A = \begin{bmatrix} 2 & -1 \\ 1 & 0 \\ -3 & 4 \end{bmatrix}$ and $B = \begin{bmatrix} 1 & -2 & -5 \\ 3 & 4 & 0 \end{bmatrix}$. Find: (a) AB; (b) BA.

(a) Since A is 3×2 and B is 2×3, the product AB is defined and is a 3×3 matrix. To obtain the first row of AB, multiply the first row of A by each column of B:

$$\begin{bmatrix} 2 & -1 \\ 1 & 0 \\ -3 & 4 \end{bmatrix} \begin{bmatrix} 1 \\ 3 \end{bmatrix} \begin{bmatrix} -2 \\ 4 \end{bmatrix} \begin{bmatrix} -5 \\ 0 \end{bmatrix} = \begin{bmatrix} 2-3 & -4-4 & -10+0 \end{bmatrix} = \begin{bmatrix} -1 & -8 & -10 \end{bmatrix}$$

To obtain the second row of AB, multiply the second row of A by each column of B:

$$\begin{bmatrix} 2 & -1 \\ 1 & 0 \\ -3 & 4 \end{bmatrix} \begin{bmatrix} 1 \\ 3 \end{bmatrix} \begin{bmatrix} -2 \\ 4 \end{bmatrix} \begin{bmatrix} -5 \\ 0 \end{bmatrix} = \begin{bmatrix} -1 & -8 & -10 \\ 1+0 & -2+0 & -5+0 \end{bmatrix} = \begin{bmatrix} -1 & -8 & -10 \\ 1 & -2 & -5 \end{bmatrix}$$

To obtain the third row of AB, multiply the third row of A by each column of B:

$$\begin{bmatrix} 2 & -1 \\ 1 & 0 \\ -3 & 4 \end{bmatrix} \begin{bmatrix} 1 \\ 3 \end{bmatrix} \begin{bmatrix} -2 \\ 4 \end{bmatrix} \begin{bmatrix} -5 \\ 0 \end{bmatrix} = \begin{bmatrix} -1 & -8 & -10 \\ 1 & -2 & -5 \\ -3+12 & 6+16 & 15+0 \end{bmatrix} = \begin{bmatrix} -1 & -8 & -10 \\ 1 & -2 & -5 \\ 9 & 22 & 15 \end{bmatrix}$$

Thus
$$AB = \begin{bmatrix} -1 & -8 & -10 \\ 1 & -2 & -5 \\ 9 & 22 & 15 \end{bmatrix}$$

(b) Since B is 2×3 and A is 3×2, the product BA is defined and is a 2×2 matrix. To obtain the first row of BA, multiply the first row of B by each column of A:

$$\begin{bmatrix} 1 & -2 & -5 \\ 3 & 4 & 0 \end{bmatrix} \begin{bmatrix} 2 \\ 1 \\ -3 \end{bmatrix} \begin{bmatrix} -1 \\ 0 \\ 4 \end{bmatrix} = \begin{bmatrix} 2-2+15 & -1+0-20 \end{bmatrix} = \begin{bmatrix} 15 & -21 \end{bmatrix}$$

To obtain the second row of BA, multiply the second row of B by each column of A:

$$\begin{bmatrix} 1 & -2 & -5 \\ 3 & 4 & 0 \end{bmatrix} \begin{bmatrix} 2 \\ 1 \\ -3 \end{bmatrix} \begin{bmatrix} -1 \\ 0 \\ 4 \end{bmatrix} = \begin{bmatrix} 15 & -21 \\ 6+4+0 & -3+0+0 \end{bmatrix} = \begin{bmatrix} 15 & -21 \\ 10 & -3 \end{bmatrix}$$

Thus
$$BA = \begin{bmatrix} 15 & -21 \\ 10 & -3 \end{bmatrix}$$

Remark: Observe that in this problem both AB and BA are defined, but they are not equal; in fact, they do not even have the same shape.

1.22. Find: (a) $\begin{bmatrix} 1 & 6 \\ -3 & 5 \end{bmatrix} \begin{bmatrix} 2 \\ -7 \end{bmatrix}$; (b) $\begin{bmatrix} 2 \\ -7 \end{bmatrix} \begin{bmatrix} 1 & 6 \\ -3 & 5 \end{bmatrix}$; (c) $[2, -7] \begin{bmatrix} 1 & 6 \\ -3 & 5 \end{bmatrix}$; (d) $\begin{bmatrix} 1 & 6 \\ -3 & 5 \end{bmatrix} [2, -7]$.

(a) The first factor is 2×2 and the second is 2×1, so the product is defined as a 2×1 matrix:

$$\begin{bmatrix} 1 & 6 \\ -3 & 5 \end{bmatrix} \begin{bmatrix} 2 \\ -7 \end{bmatrix} = \begin{bmatrix} 2-42 \\ -6-35 \end{bmatrix} = \begin{bmatrix} -40 \\ -41 \end{bmatrix}$$

(b) The product is not defined since the first factor is 2×1 and the second factor is 2×2.

(c) The first factor is 1×2 and the second factor is 2×2, so the product is defined as a 1×2 (row) matrix:

$$[2, -7]\begin{bmatrix} 1 & 6 \\ -3 & 5 \end{bmatrix} = [2 + 21, 12 - 35] = [23, -23]$$

(d) The product is not defined since the first factor is 2×2 and the second factor is 1×2.

1.23. Let $A = \begin{bmatrix} 2 \\ 3 \\ -1 \end{bmatrix}$ and $B = [6, -4, 5]$, a column vector and a row vector, respectively.
Find: (a) AB; (b) BA.

(a) The first factor is 3×1 and the second factor is 1×3, so the product AB is defined as a 3×3 matrix:

$$AB = \begin{bmatrix} 2 \\ 3 \\ -1 \end{bmatrix}[6, -4, 5] = \begin{bmatrix} 2(6) & 2(-4) & 2(5) \\ 3(6) & 3(-4) & 3(5) \\ -1(6) & -1(-4) & -1(5) \end{bmatrix} = \begin{bmatrix} 12 & -8 & 10 \\ 18 & -12 & 15 \\ -6 & 4 & -5 \end{bmatrix}$$

(b) The first factor is 1×3 and the second factor is 3×1, so the product BA is defined as a 1×1 matrix, which we write as a scalar:

$$BA = [6, -4, 5]\begin{bmatrix} 2 \\ 3 \\ -1 \end{bmatrix} = 12 - 12 - 5 = -5$$

1.24. Clearly $0A = 0$ and $A0 = 0$, where the 0s are *zero matrices* (all entries 0) with possibly different sizes. Construct a suitable example to show that we can have $AB = 0$, with $A \neq 0$ and $B \neq 0$.

Let $A = \begin{bmatrix} 1 & 2 \\ 2 & 4 \end{bmatrix}$ and $B = \begin{bmatrix} 6 & 2 \\ -3 & -1 \end{bmatrix}$. Then

$$AB = \begin{bmatrix} 1 & 2 \\ 2 & 4 \end{bmatrix}\begin{bmatrix} 6 & 2 \\ -3 & -1 \end{bmatrix} = \begin{bmatrix} 6-6 & 2-2 \\ 12-12 & 4-4 \end{bmatrix} = \begin{bmatrix} 0 & 0 \\ 0 & 0 \end{bmatrix}$$

TRANSPOSE

1.25. Find the transpose of each matrix:

$$A = \begin{bmatrix} 1 & -2 & 3 \\ 7 & 8 & -9 \end{bmatrix}, \qquad B = \begin{bmatrix} 1 & 2 & 3 \\ 2 & 4 & 5 \\ 3 & 5 & 6 \end{bmatrix}, \qquad C = [1, -3, 5, -7], \qquad D = \begin{bmatrix} 2 \\ -4 \\ 6 \end{bmatrix}$$

Rewrite the rows of each matrix as columns to obtain the transpose of the matrix:

$$A^T = \begin{bmatrix} 1 & 7 \\ -2 & 8 \\ 3 & -9 \end{bmatrix}, \qquad B^T = \begin{bmatrix} 1 & 2 & 3 \\ 2 & 4 & 5 \\ 3 & 5 & 6 \end{bmatrix}, \qquad C^T = \begin{bmatrix} 1 \\ -3 \\ 5 \\ -7 \end{bmatrix}, \qquad D^T = [2, -4, 6]$$

(Note that $B^T = B$; such a matrix is said to be *symmetric*. Note also that the transpose of the row vector C is a column vector, and the transpose of the column vector D is a row vector.)

1.26. Find AA^T and A^TA, where $A = \begin{bmatrix} 1 & 2 & 0 \\ 3 & -1 & 4 \end{bmatrix}$.

Obtain A^T by rewriting the rows of A as columns:

$$A^T = \begin{bmatrix} 1 & 3 \\ 2 & -1 \\ 0 & 4 \end{bmatrix} \quad \text{and hence} \quad AA^T = \begin{bmatrix} 1 & 2 & 0 \\ 3 & -1 & 4 \end{bmatrix}\begin{bmatrix} 1 & 3 \\ 2 & -1 \\ 0 & 4 \end{bmatrix} = \begin{bmatrix} 5 & 1 \\ 1 & 26 \end{bmatrix}$$

$$A^TA = \begin{bmatrix} 1 & 3 \\ 2 & -1 \\ 0 & 4 \end{bmatrix}\begin{bmatrix} 1 & 2 & 0 \\ 3 & -1 & 4 \end{bmatrix} = \begin{bmatrix} 1+9 & 2-3 & 0+12 \\ 2-3 & 4+1 & 0-4 \\ 0+12 & 0-4 & 0+16 \end{bmatrix} = \begin{bmatrix} 10 & -1 & 12 \\ -1 & 5 & -4 \\ 12 & -4 & 16 \end{bmatrix}$$

BLOCK MATRICES

1.27. Consider the following block matrices (which are partitions of the same matrix):

$$(a) \begin{bmatrix} 1 & -2 & 0 & 1 & 3 \\ 2 & 3 & 5 & 7 & -2 \\ 3 & 1 & 4 & 5 & 9 \end{bmatrix} \qquad (b) \begin{bmatrix} 1 & -2 & 0 & 1 & 3 \\ 2 & 3 & 5 & 7 & -2 \\ 3 & 1 & 4 & 5 & 9 \end{bmatrix}$$

Find the size of each block matrix and also the size of each block.

(a) The block matrix has two rows of matrices and three columns of matrices; hence its size is 2×3. The block sizes are 2×2, 2×2, and 2×1 for the first row; and 1×2, 1×2, and 1×1 for the second row.

(b) The size of the block matrix is 3×2; and the block sizes are 1×3 and 1×2 for each of the three rows.

1.28. Compute AB using block multiplication, where

$$A = \begin{bmatrix} 1 & 2 & 1 \\ 3 & 4 & 0 \\ 0 & 0 & 2 \end{bmatrix} \quad \text{and} \quad B = \begin{bmatrix} 1 & 2 & 3 & 1 \\ 4 & 5 & 6 & 1 \\ 0 & 0 & 0 & 1 \end{bmatrix}$$

Here $A = \begin{bmatrix} E & F \\ 0_{1\times 2} & G \end{bmatrix}$ and $B = \begin{bmatrix} R & S \\ 0_{1\times 3} & T \end{bmatrix}$, where E, F, G, R, S, and T are the given blocks. Hence

$$AB = \begin{bmatrix} ER & ES+FT \\ 0_{1\times 3} & GT \end{bmatrix} = \begin{bmatrix} \begin{bmatrix} 9 & 12 & 15 \\ 19 & 26 & 33 \end{bmatrix} & \begin{bmatrix} 3 \\ 7 \end{bmatrix}+\begin{bmatrix} 1 \\ 0 \end{bmatrix} \\ [0 \quad 0 \quad 0] & 2 \end{bmatrix} = \begin{bmatrix} 9 & 12 & 15 & 4 \\ 19 & 26 & 33 & 7 \\ 0 & 0 & 0 & 2 \end{bmatrix}$$

1.29. Compute CD by block multiplication, where

$$C = \begin{bmatrix} 1 & 2 & 0 & 0 & 0 \\ 3 & 4 & 0 & 0 & 0 \\ 0 & 0 & 5 & 1 & 2 \\ 0 & 0 & 3 & 4 & 1 \end{bmatrix} \quad \text{and} \quad D = \begin{bmatrix} 3 & -2 & 0 & 0 \\ 2 & 4 & 0 & 0 \\ 0 & 0 & 1 & 2 \\ 0 & 0 & 2 & -1 \\ 0 & 0 & -4 & 1 \end{bmatrix}$$

We obtain:

$$CD = \begin{bmatrix} \begin{bmatrix} 1 & 2 \\ 3 & 4 \end{bmatrix}\begin{bmatrix} 3 & -2 \\ 2 & 4 \end{bmatrix} & 0_{2\times2} \\ 0_{2\times2} & \begin{bmatrix} 5 & 1 & 2 \\ 3 & 4 & 1 \end{bmatrix}\begin{bmatrix} 1 & 2 \\ 2 & -3 \\ -4 & 1 \end{bmatrix} \end{bmatrix}$$

$$= \begin{bmatrix} \begin{bmatrix} 3+4 & -2+8 \\ 9+8 & -6+16 \end{bmatrix} & 0_{2\times2} \\ 0_{2\times2} & \begin{bmatrix} 5+2-8 & 10-3+2 \\ 3+8-4 & 6-12+1 \end{bmatrix} \end{bmatrix} = \begin{bmatrix} 7 & 6 & 0 & 0 \\ 17 & 10 & 0 & 0 \\ 0 & 0 & -1 & 9 \\ 0 & 0 & 7 & -5 \end{bmatrix}$$

POINTS, LINES, AND HYPERPLANES IN $\mathbf{R}^n$

Here we distinguish between a list $P(a_1, a_2, \ldots, a_n) \equiv P(a_i)$ viewed as a point in $\mathbf{R}^n$ and a list $v = [c_1, c_2, \ldots, c_n]$ viewed as a vector (arrow) from the origin O to the point $C(c_1, c_2, \ldots, c_n)$. We also use the following additional definitions.

A *hyperplane* H in $\mathbf{R}^n$ is the solution set of a linear equation,

$$a_1x_1 + a_2x_2 + \cdots + a_nx_n = b \tag{1}$$

where $u = [a_1, a_2, a_3, \ldots, a_n] \neq 0$. (Note that a hyperplane H in $\mathbf{R}^2$ is a line and a hyperplane H in $\mathbf{R}^3$ is a plane.) The vector u is said to be *normal* to the hyperplane H since it is orthogonal to any directed line segment $\overrightarrow{PQ}$, where P and Q are points in H. (This fact in $\mathbf{R}^3$ is pictured in Fig. 1-6, and it is proved in Problem 1.51.)

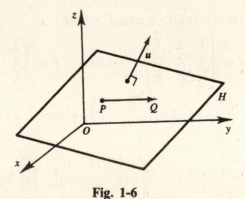

Fig. 1-6

The *line* L in $\mathbf{R}^n$ passing through the point $P(b_i)$ and in the direction of the nonzero vector $u = [a_i]$ consists of the points $X = (x_i)$ which satisfy the equation

$$X = P + tu \quad \text{or} \quad x_i = a_it + b_i \quad \text{or} \quad L(t) = (a_it + b_i) \tag{2}$$

where $i = 1, 2, \ldots, n$ and where the parameter t takes on all real values. (See Fig. 1-7.)

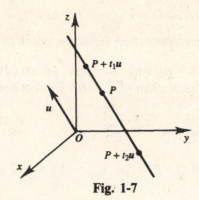

Fig. 1-7

1.30. Find the vector v identified with the directed line segment $\overrightarrow{PQ}$ for the points: (a) $P(5, 2)$ and $Q(3, -1)$ in $\mathbf{R}^2$; (b) $P(1, -5, 8)$ and $Q(4, 0, 2)$ in $\mathbf{R}^3$.

(a) $v = \overrightarrow{PQ} = Q - P = [3 - 5, -1 - 2] = [-2, -3]$

(b) $v = \overrightarrow{PQ} = Q - P = [4 - 1, 0 + 5, 2 - 8] = [3, 5, -6]$

1.31. Find an equation of the hyperplane H in $\mathbf{R}^4$ which passes through $P(3, -4, 1, -2)$ and is normal to $u = [2, 5, -6, -3]$.

The coefficients of the unknowns of an equation of H are the components of the normal vector u as indicated by Eq. (1). Thus an equation of H is of the form $2x_1 + 5x_2 - 6x_3 - 3x_4 = c$. Substitute P into the equation to obtain

$$2(3) + 5(-4) - 6(1) - 3(-2) = c \quad \text{or} \quad 6 - 20 - 6 + 6 = c \quad \text{or} \quad c = -14$$

Thus an equation of H is $2x_1 + 5x_2 - 6x_3 - 3x_4 = -14$.

1.32. Find an equation of the plane H in $\mathbf{R}^3$ which contains $P(1, -3, -4)$ and is parallel to the plane H' determined by $3x - 6y + 5z = 2$.

The planes H and H' are parallel if and only if their normals are parallel or antiparallel (opposite direction). Hence an equation of H is of the form $3x - 6y + 5z = c$. Substitute P into this equation to obtain

$$3(1) - 6(-3) + 5(-4) = c \quad \text{or} \quad 3 + 18 - 20 = c \quad \text{or} \quad c = 1$$

Thus an equation of H is $3x - 6y + 5z = 1$.

1.33. Find a parametric representation of the line L in $\mathbf{R}^4$ passing through $P(3, 1, -7, 9)$ and in the direction of the vector $u = [4, 5, 6, -2]$. Also, find the point Q on L when $t = 1$.

Substitution in Eq. (2) yields the following parametric representation of L:

$$x_1 = 4t + 3, \qquad x_2 = 5t + 1, \qquad x_3 = 6t - 7, \qquad x_4 = -2t + 9$$

or, equivalently,

$$L(t) = (4t + 3, \quad 5t + 1, \quad 6t - 7, \quad -2t + 9)$$

Substitution of $t = 1$ in this representation yields the point $Q(7, 6, -1, 7)$.

1.34. Consider the line L in $\mathbf{R}^3$ passing through points $P(5, 4, -3)$ and $Q(1, -3, 2)$. (a) Find a parametric representation of L. (b) Find a nonparametric representation of L.

(a)   First compute the vector

$$u = \overrightarrow{PQ} = Q - P = [1 - 5, \quad -3 - 4, \quad 2 + 3] = [-4, -7, 5]$$

Then use Eq. (2) to obtain

$$x = -4t + 5, \qquad y = -7t + 4, \qquad z = 5t - 3$$

(b)   Solve each coordinate equation for t and equate the results to obtain

$$\frac{x - 5}{-4} = \frac{y - 4}{-7} = \frac{z + 3}{5}$$

or the pair of linear equations $7x - 4y = 19$ and $5x + 4z = 13$.

1.35. Consider the following curve C in $\mathbf{R}^4$, where $0 \le t \le 4$:

$$F(t) = (t^2, \quad 3t - 2, \quad t^3, \quad t^2 + 5)$$

(a)   Find the point P on C corresponding to $t = 2$.
(b)   Find the initial point Q and terminal point Q' of C.
(c)   Find the unit tangent vector $\mathbf{T}$ to the curve C when $t = 2$.

(a)   Substitute $t = 2$ into $F(t)$ to get $P = F(2) = (4, 4, 8, 9)$.
(b)   The parameter t ranges from $t = 0$ to $t = 4$. Thus

$$Q = F(0) = (0, -2, 0, 5) \qquad \text{and} \qquad Q' = F(4) = (16, 10, 64, 21)$$

(c)   Take the derivative of $F(t)$, i.e., each component of $F(t)$, to obtain a vector V which is tangent to the curve:

$$V(t) = \frac{dF(t)}{dt} = [2t, 3, 3t^2, 2t]$$

Now find V when $t = 2$; that is, substitute $t = 2$ in the equation for $V(t)$ to obtain $V = V(2) = [4, 3, 12, 4]$. Now normalize V to obtain the unit tangent vector $\mathbf{T}$. Then

$$\|V\|^2 = 16 + 9 + 144 + 16 = 185 \qquad \text{or} \qquad \|V\| = \sqrt{185}$$

Thus
$$\mathbf{T} = \left[\frac{4}{\sqrt{185}}, \frac{3}{\sqrt{185}}, \frac{12}{\sqrt{185}}, \frac{4}{\sqrt{185}} \right]$$

SPATIAL VECTORS (VECTORS IN $\mathbf{R}^3$), ijk NOTATION

1.36. Consider the vectors $u = 2\mathbf{i} - 3\mathbf{j} + 4\mathbf{k}$, $v = 3\mathbf{i} + \mathbf{j} - 2\mathbf{k}$, and $w = \mathbf{i} + 5\mathbf{j} + 3\mathbf{k}$. Find:
(a) $u + v$;   (b) $3u$;   (c) $2u - 3v + 4w$.

Treat the coefficients of $\mathbf{i}$, $\mathbf{j}$, and $\mathbf{k}$ just like the components of a vector.

(a) Add corresponding coefficients:

$$u + v = (2 + 3)\mathbf{i} + (-3 + 1)\mathbf{j} + (4 - 2)\mathbf{k} = 5\mathbf{i} - 2\mathbf{j} + 2\mathbf{k}$$

(b) Multiply each coefficient by the scalar:

$$3u = 3(2)\mathbf{i} + 3(-3)\mathbf{j} + 3(4)\mathbf{k} = 6\mathbf{i} - 9\mathbf{j} + 12\mathbf{k}$$

(c) First perform the scalar multiplication and then the vector addition:

$$2u - 3v + 4w = (4\mathbf{i} - 6\mathbf{j} + 8\mathbf{k}) + (-9\mathbf{i} - 3\mathbf{j} + 6\mathbf{k}) + (4\mathbf{i} + 20\mathbf{j} + 12\mathbf{k})$$
$$= -\mathbf{i} + 11\mathbf{j} + 26\mathbf{k}$$

1.37. Let u, v, and w be the vectors in the preceding problem. Find: (a) $u \cdot v$ and $u \cdot w$;
(b) $\|u\|$, $\|v\|$, and $\|w\|$.

(a) Multiply corresponding coefficients and add:

$$u \cdot v = 6 - 3 - 8 = -5 \quad \text{and} \quad u \cdot w = 2 - 15 + 12 = -1$$

(b) To obtain $\|u\|$, first find $\|u\|^2$ by finding the sum of the squares of the coefficients.   Then

$$\|u\|^2 = 4 + 9 + 16 = 29 \quad \text{and} \quad \|u\| = \sqrt{29}$$
$$\|v\|^2 = 9 + 1 + 4 = 14 \quad \text{and} \quad \|v\| = \sqrt{14}$$
$$\|w\|^2 = 1 + 25 + 9 = 35 \quad \text{and} \quad \|w\| = \sqrt{35}$$

1.38. Find the equation of the plane H in $\mathbf{R}^3$ such that:

(a) H has normal direction $\mathbf{N} = 5\mathbf{i} - 6\mathbf{j} + 7\mathbf{k}$ and contains $P(3, 4, -2)$.
(b) H is parallel to $4x + 7y - 12z$ and contains $P(2, 3, -1)$.

(a) By Eq. (1), the equation has the form $5x - 6y + 7z = c$. Substitution of P in the equation
yields

$$5(3) - 6(4) + 7(-2) = c \quad \text{or} \quad 15 - 24 - 14 = c \quad \text{or} \quad c = -23$$

Thus $5x - 6y + 7z = -23$ is an equation of H.
(b) H and the given plane have the same normal direction. Hence the equation has the
form $4x + 7y - 12z = c$. Substitution of P in the equation yields $c = 41$. Thus
$4x + 7y - 12z = 41$ is an equation of H.

1.39. Find the (parametric) equation of the line L through:

    (a)   Point $P(3, 4, -2)$ and in the direction of $u = 5\mathbf{i} - \mathbf{j} + 3\mathbf{k}$

    (b)   Points $P(1, 3, 2)$ and $Q(2, 5, -6)$

    (a)   Use Eq. (2) to obtain

$$L(t) = (5t + 3, \; -t + 4, \; 3t - 2) = (5t + 3)\mathbf{i} + (-t + 4)\mathbf{j} + (3t - 2)\mathbf{k}$$

    (b)   First find $v = \overrightarrow{PQ} = Q - P = [1, 2, -8] = \mathbf{i} + 2\mathbf{j} - 8\mathbf{k}$. Then, use Eq. (2) with one of the points, say P, to get

$$L(t) = (t + 1, \; 2t + 3, \; -8t + 2) = (t + 1)\mathbf{i} + (2t + 3)\mathbf{j} + (-8t + 2)\mathbf{k}$$

1.40. Let H be the plane $3x + 5y + 7z = 15$. Find the equation of the line L perpendicular to H and containing the point $P(1, -2, 4)$.

    Since L is perpendicular to H, the line L is in the same direction as the normal vector $\mathbf{N} = 3\mathbf{i} + 5\mathbf{j} + 7\mathbf{k}$ to H. Use Eq. (2) with the point P and vector $\mathbf{N}$ to get

$$L(t) = (3t + 1, \; 5t - 2, \; 7t + 4) = (3t + 1)\mathbf{i} + (5t - 2)\mathbf{j} + (7t + 4)\mathbf{k}$$

1.41. Let S be the surface $xy^2 + 2yz = 16$ in $\mathbf{R}^3$.

    (a)   Find the normal vector $\mathbf{N}(x, y, z)$ to the surface S.

    (b)   Find the tangent plane H to S at the point $P(1, 2, 3)$.

    (a)   The formula for the normal vector to a surface $F(x, y, z) = 0$ is

$$\mathbf{N}(x, y, z) = F_x\mathbf{i} + F_y\mathbf{j} + F_z\mathbf{k}$$

where F_x, F_y, and F_z are the partial derivatives. Using $F(x, y, z) = xy^2 + 2yz - 16$, we obtain

$$F_x = y^2, \qquad F_y = 2xy + 2z, \qquad F_z = 2y$$

Thus $\mathbf{N}(x, y, z) = y^2\mathbf{i} + (2xy + 2z)\mathbf{j} + 2y\mathbf{k}$.

    (b)   The normal to the surface S at the point P is

$$\mathbf{N}(P) = \mathbf{N}(1, 2, 3) = 4\mathbf{i} + 10\mathbf{j} + 4\mathbf{k}$$

Hence $\mathbf{N} = 2\mathbf{i} + 5\mathbf{j} + 2\mathbf{k}$ is also normal to S at P. Thus an equation of H has the form $2x + 5y + 2z = c$. Substitute P in this equation to obtain $c = 18$. Thus the tangent plane H to S at P is $2x + 5y + 2z = 18$.

CROSS PRODUCT

    The cross product is defined only for vectors in $\mathbf{R}^3$.

1.42. Evaluate the following determinants and negatives of determinants of order 2:

(a) (i) $\begin{vmatrix} 3 & 4 \\ 5 & 9 \end{vmatrix}$; (ii) $\begin{vmatrix} 2 & -1 \\ 4 & 3 \end{vmatrix}$; (iii) $\begin{vmatrix} 4 & 5 \\ 3 & -2 \end{vmatrix}$

(b) (i) $-\begin{vmatrix} 3 & 6 \\ 4 & 2 \end{vmatrix}$; (ii) $-\begin{vmatrix} 7 & -5 \\ 3 & 2 \end{vmatrix}$; (iii) $-\begin{vmatrix} 4 & -1 \\ 8 & -3 \end{vmatrix}$

(a) Use $\begin{vmatrix} a & b \\ c & d \end{vmatrix} = ad - bc$, the product ad of the diagonal elements minus the product bc of the nondiagonal elements.   (i) $3(9) - 4(5) = 7$;   (ii) $6 + 4 = 10$;   (iii) $-8 - 15 = -23$

(b) Use $-\begin{vmatrix} a & b \\ c & d \end{vmatrix} = -(ad - bc) = bc - ad$, the product bc of the nondiagonal elements minus the product ad of the diagonal elements, called taking the determinant "*backward*".
   (i) $6(4) - 3(2) = 18$;   (ii) $-15 - 14 = -29$;   (iii) $-8 + 12 = 4$

1.43. Find $u \times v$, where: (a) $u = (1, 2, 3)$ and $v = (4, 5, 6)$;   (b) $u = (7, 3, 1)$ and $v = (1, 1, 1)$; (c) $u = (-4, 12, 2)$ and $v = (6, -18, 3)$.

The cross product of vectors $u = [a_1, a_2, a_3]$ and $v = [b_1, b_2, b_3]$ may be obtained as follows. Put the second vector v under the first vector u to obtain the array

$$\begin{bmatrix} a_1 & a_2 & a_3 \\ b_1 & b_2 & b_3 \end{bmatrix}$$

Then

$$u \times v = \left[\begin{vmatrix} a_1 & a_2 & a_3 \\ b_1 & b_2 & b_3 \end{vmatrix}, -\begin{vmatrix} a_1 & a_2 & a_3 \\ b_1 & b_2 & b_3 \end{vmatrix}, \begin{vmatrix} a_1 & a_2 & a_3 \\ b_1 & b_2 & b_3 \end{vmatrix} \right]$$
$$= [a_2 b_3 - a_3 b_2, \; a_3 b_1 - a_1 b_3, \; a_1 b_2 - a_2 b_1]$$
$$= (a_2 b_3 - a_3 b_2)\mathbf{i} + (a_3 b_1 - a_1 b_3)\mathbf{j} + (a_1 b_2 - a_2 b_1)\mathbf{k}$$

That is, the three components of $u \times v$ are obtained from the array as follows:

(1) Cover the first column and take the determinant to obtain the first component.
(2) Cover the second column and take the determinant "backward" to obtain the second component.
(3) Cover the third column and take the determinant to obtain the third component.

(a) Use $\begin{bmatrix} 1 & 2 & 3 \\ 4 & 5 & 6 \end{bmatrix}$ to get $u \times v = [12 - 15, \, 12 - 6, \, 5 - 8] = [-3, 6, -3]$

(b) Use $\begin{bmatrix} 7 & 3 & 1 \\ 1 & 1 & 1 \end{bmatrix}$ to get $u \times v = [3 - 1, \, 1 - 7, \, 7 - 3] = [2, -6, 4]$

(c) Use $\begin{bmatrix} -4 & 12 & 2 \\ 6 & -18 & 3 \end{bmatrix}$ to get $u \times v = [36 + 36, \, 12 + 12, \, 72 - 72] = [72, 24, 0]$

1.44. Consider the vectors $u = 2\mathbf{i} - 3\mathbf{j} + 4\mathbf{k}$, $v = 3\mathbf{i} + \mathbf{j} - 2\mathbf{k}$, and $w = \mathbf{i} + 5\mathbf{j} + 3\mathbf{k}$. Find:
(a) $u \times v$;   (b) $u \times w$;   (c) $v \times w$.

Use the array $\begin{bmatrix} a_1 & a_2 & a_3 \\ b_1 & b_2 & b_3 \end{bmatrix}$ as in the preceding problem to find $u \times v$, where $u = a_1\mathbf{i} + a_2\mathbf{j} + a_3\mathbf{k}$ and $v = b_1\mathbf{i} + b_2\mathbf{j} + b_3\mathbf{k}$.

(a)   Use $\begin{bmatrix} 2 & -3 & 4 \\ 3 & 1 & -2 \end{bmatrix}$ to get $u \times v = (6 - 4)\mathbf{i} + (12 + 4)\mathbf{j} + (2 + 9)\mathbf{k} = 2\mathbf{i} + 16\mathbf{j} + 11\mathbf{k}$

(b)   Use $\begin{bmatrix} 2 & -3 & 4 \\ 1 & 5 & 3 \end{bmatrix}$ to get $u \times w = (-9 - 20)\mathbf{i} + (4 - 6)\mathbf{j} + (10 + 3)\mathbf{k} = -29\mathbf{i} - 2\mathbf{j} + 13\mathbf{k}$

(c)   Use $\begin{bmatrix} 3 & 1 & -2 \\ 1 & 5 & 3 \end{bmatrix}$ to get $v \times w = (3 + 10)\mathbf{i} + (-2 - 9)\mathbf{j} + (15 - 1)\mathbf{k} = 13\mathbf{i} - 11\mathbf{j} + 14\mathbf{k}$

1.45.   Find a unit vector u orthogonal to $v = [1, 3, 4]$ and $w = [2, -6, -5]$.

First find $v \times w$, which is orthogonal to v and w. The array $\begin{bmatrix} 1 & 3 & 4 \\ 2 & -6 & -5 \end{bmatrix}$ gives

$v \times w = [-15 + 24, \quad 8 + 5, \quad -6 - 6] = [9, 13, -12]$.   Now normalize $v \times w$ to get

$$u = \left[\frac{9}{\sqrt{394}}, \frac{13}{\sqrt{394}}, \frac{-12}{\sqrt{394}} \right]$$

PROOFS

1.46.   Prove Theorem 1.1(v): $k(A + B) = kA + kB$.

Let $A = [a_{ij}]$ and $B = [b_{ij}]$.   Then the ij entry of $A + B$ is $a_{ij} + b_{ij}$.   Hence $k(a_{ij} + b_{ij})$ is the ij entry of $k(A + B)$.   On the other hand, the ij entries of kA and kB are ka_{ij} and kb_{ij}, respectively.   Thus $ka_{ij} + kb_{ij}$ is the ij entry.   However, for scalars, $k(a_{ij} + b_{ij}) = ka_{ij} + kb_{ij}$. Thus $k(A + B)$ and $kA + kB$ have the same ij entries.   Therefore $k(A + B) = kA + kB$.

1.47.   Prove Theorem 1.2(i): $(AB)C = A(BC)$.

Let $A = [a_{ij}]$, $B = [b_{jk}]$, and $C = [c_{kl}]$.   Furthermore, let $AB = S = [s_{ik}]$ and $BC = T = [t_{jl}]$. Then

$$s_{ik} = a_{i1}b_{1k} + a_{i2}b_{2k} + \cdots + a_{im}b_{mk} = \sum_{j=1}^{m} a_{ij}b_{jk}$$

$$t_{jl} = b_{j1}c_{1l} + b_{j2}c_{2l} + \cdots + b_{jn}c_{nl} = \sum_{k=1}^{n} b_{jk}c_{kl}$$

Now multiplying S by C, i.e., (AB) by C, the element in the ith row and lth column of the matrix $(AB)C$ is

$$s_{i1}c_{1l} + s_{i2}c_{2l} + \cdots + s_{in}c_{nl} = \sum_{k=1}^{n} s_{ik}c_{kl} = \sum_{k=1}^{n} \sum_{j=1}^{m} (a_{ij}b_{jk})c_{kl}$$

On the other hand, multiplying A by T, i.e., A by BC, the element in the ith row and lth column of the matrix $A(BC)$ is

$$a_{i1}t_{1l} + a_{i2}t_{2l} + \cdots + a_{im}t_{ml} = \sum_{j=1}^{m} a_{ij}t_{jl} = \sum_{j=1}^{m}\sum_{k=1}^{n} a_{ij}(b_{jk}c_{kl})$$

Since the above sums are equal, the theorem is proven.

1.48. Prove Theorem 1.2(ii): $A(B+C) = AB + AC$.

Let $A = [a_{ij}]$, $B = [b_{jk}]$, and $C = [c_{jk}]$.   Furthermore, let $D = B + C = [d_{jk}]$, $E = AB = [e_{ik}]$, and $F = AC = [f_{ik}]$.   Then

$$d_{jk} = b_{jk} + c_{jk}$$

$$e_{ik} = a_{i1}b_{1k} + a_{i2}b_{2k} + \cdots + a_{im}b_{mk} = \sum_{j=1}^{m} a_{ij}b_{jk}$$

$$f_{ik} = a_{i1}c_{1k} + a_{i2}c_{2k} + \cdots + a_{im}c_{mk} = \sum_{j=1}^{m} a_{ij}c_{jk}$$

Hence the element in the ith row and kth column of the matrix $AB + AC$ is

$$e_{ik} + f_{ik} = \sum_{j=1}^{m} a_{ij}b_{jk} + \sum_{j=1}^{m} a_{ij}c_{jk} = \sum_{j=1}^{m} a_{ij}(b_{jk} + c_{jk})$$

On the other hand, the element in the ith row and kth column of the matrix $AD = A(B+C)$ is

$$a_{i1}d_{1k} + a_{i2}d_{2k} + \cdots + a_{im}d_{mk} = \sum_{j=1}^{m} a_{ij}d_{jk} = \sum_{j=1}^{m} a_{ij}(b_{jk} + c_{jk})$$

Thus $A(B+C) = AB + AC$ since the corresponding elements are equal.

1.49. Prove Theorem 1.3(iv): $(AB)^T = B^T A^T$.

If $A = [a_{ij}]$ and $B = [b_{kj}]$, the ij entry of AB is

$$a_{i1}b_{1j} + a_{i2}b_{2j} + \cdots + a_{im}b_{mj} \tag{1}$$

Thus expression (1) is the ji entry (reverse order) of $(AB)^T$.

On the other hand, column j of B becomes row j of B^T, and row i of A becomes column i of A^T.   Consequently, the ji entry of $B^T A^T$ is

$$[b_{1j}, b_{2j}, \ldots, b_{mj}] \begin{bmatrix} a_{i1} \\ a_{i2} \\ \cdots \\ a_{im} \end{bmatrix} = b_{1j}a_{i1} + b_{2j}a_{i2} + \cdots + b_{mj}a_{im}$$

Thus $(AB)^T = B^T A^T$, since corresponding entries are equal.

1.50. Prove Theorem 1.4(i):   The vector $u \times v$ is orthogonal to both u and v.

Suppose $u = [a_1, a_2, a_3]$ and $v = [b_1, b_2, b_3]$.   Then

$$u \cdot (u \times v) = a_1(a_2 b_3 - a_3 b_2) + a_2(a_3 b_1 - a_1 b_3) + a_3(a_1 b_2 - a_2 b_1)$$
$$= a_1 a_2 b_3 - a_1 a_3 b_2 + a_2 a_3 b_1 - a_1 a_2 b_3 + a_1 a_3 b_2 - a_2 a_3 b_1 = 0$$

Thus $u \times v$ is orthogonal to u. Similarly, $u \times v$ is orthogonal to v.

1.51. Consider a hyperplane H in $\mathbf{R}^n$ which is the solution of the linear equation

$$a_1 x_1 + a_2 x_2 + \cdots + a_n x_n = b \qquad\qquad (1)$$

where $u = [a_1, a_2, \ldots, a_n] \neq 0$. Show that the directed line segment $\overrightarrow{PQ}$ of any pair of points $P(p_i)$ and $Q(q_i)$ in H is orthogonal to u.

Since $P(p_i)$ and $Q(q_i)$ belong to H they satisfy Eq. (1), that is,

$$a_1 p_1 + a_2 p_2 + \cdots + a_n p_n = b \qquad \text{and} \qquad a_1 q_1 + a_2 q_2 + \cdots + a_n q_n = b$$

Let
$$v = \overrightarrow{PQ} = Q - P = [q_1 - p_1, q_2 - p_2, \ldots, q_n - p_n]$$

Then

$$u \cdot v = a_1(q_1 - p_1) + a_2(q_2 - p_2) + \cdots + a_n(q_n - p_n)$$
$$= (a_1 q_1 + a_2 q_2 + \ldots + a_n q_n) - (a_1 p_1 + a_2 p_2 + \ldots + a_n p_n)$$
$$= b - b = 0$$

Thus $v = \overrightarrow{PQ}$ is orthogonal to u.

1.52. Let A and B be matrices for which AB is defined. Prove:

(a) If A has a zero row, then AB has a zero row.
(b) If B has a zero column, then AB has a zero column.

(a) Let R_i be the zero row of A, and let $B^1, B^2, \ldots, B^n$ be the columns of B. Then the ith row of AB is

$$(R_i \cdot B^1, R_i \cdot B^2, \ldots, R_i \cdot B^n) = (0, 0, \ldots, 0)$$

(b) If B has a zero column, then B^T has a zero row. Hence, by (a), $B^T A^T = (AB)^T$ has a zero row. Accordingly, AB has a zero column.

1.53. Suppose u and v are distinct vectors. Show that, for distinct values of k, the vectors $u + k(u - v)$ are distinct.

We need to show that if

$$u + k_1(u - v) = u + k_2(u - v)$$

then $k_1 = k_2$. Suppose the above equation is true. Then

$$k_1(u - v) = k_2(u - v) \qquad \text{or} \qquad (k_1 - k_2)(u - v) = 0$$

Since u and v are distinct, $u - v \neq 0$. Hence $k_1 - k_2 = 0$. Thus $k_1 = k_2$.

Supplementary Problems

VECTORS IN R^n

1.54. Let $v_1 = (2, 5, 6)$, $v_2 = (5, 6, 2)$, $v_3 = (2, 5, 6)$, and $v_4 = (6, 5, 2)$.   Which of the vectors, if any, are equal?

1.55. Let $u = (1, -2, 4)$, $v = (3, 5, 1)$, and $w = (2, 1, -3)$.   Find: (a) $3u - 2v$;   (b) $4u - v - 3w$;   (c) $5u + 7v - 2w$.

1.56. For the vectors in Problem 1.55, find: (a) $u \cdot v$, $u \cdot w$, $v \cdot w$;   (b) $\|u\|$, $\|v\|$, $\|w\|$.

1.57. Let $u = (2, -5, 4, 6, -3)$ and $v = (5, -2, 1, -7, -4)$.   Find: (a) $4u - 3v$;   (b) $5u + 2v$; (c) $u \cdot v$; (d) $\|u\|$ and $\|v\|$.

1.58. Let $u = (2, -1, 0, -3)$, $v = (1, -1, -1, 3)$, and $w = (1, 3, -2, 2)$.   Find: (a) $2u - 3v$; (b) $5u - 3v - 4w$;   (c) $-u + 2v - 2w$;   (d) $u \cdot v$, $u \cdot w$, $v \cdot w$;   (e) $\|u\|$, $\|v\|$, $\|w\|$.

1.59. Let $u = \begin{bmatrix} 1 \\ 3 \\ -4 \end{bmatrix}$, $v = \begin{bmatrix} 2 \\ 1 \\ 5 \end{bmatrix}$, and $w = \begin{bmatrix} 3 \\ -2 \\ 6 \end{bmatrix}$.   Find: (a) $5u - 3v$;   (b) $2u + 4v - 6w$;   (c) $u \cdot v$, $u \cdot w$, $v \cdot w$;   (d) $\|u\|$, $\|v\|$, $\|w\|$.

1.60. Determine k so that u and v are orthogonal: (a) $u = (3, k, -2)$, $v = (6, -4, -3)$; (b) $u = (5, k, -4, 2)$, $v = (1, -3, 2, 2k)$;   (c) $u = (1, 7, k + 2, -2)$, $v = (3, k, -3, k)$.

1.61. Find x and y, where: (a) $(x, x + y) = (y - 2, 6)$;   (b) $x(1, 2) = -4(y, 3)$.

1.62. Find x and y, where: (a) $x(3, 2) = 2(y, -1)$;   (b) $x(2, y) = y(1, -2)$.

1.63. Find x and y, where: (a) $x(2, 5) + y(4, -3) = (0, 13)$;   (b) $x(1, 4) + y(2, -5) = (7, 2)$.

1.64. Find x, y, z, where $x \begin{bmatrix} 1 \\ 2 \\ 3 \end{bmatrix} + y \begin{bmatrix} 2 \\ 5 \\ -1 \end{bmatrix} + z \begin{bmatrix} 4 \\ -2 \\ 3 \end{bmatrix} = \begin{bmatrix} 9 \\ -3 \\ 16 \end{bmatrix}$.

1.65. Normalize each vector: (a) $u = (5, -7)$;   (b) $v = (1, 2, -2, 4)$;   (c) $w = (\frac{1}{2}, -\frac{1}{3}, \frac{3}{4})$.

1.66. Let $u = (1, 2, -2)$, $v = (3, -12, 4)$, and $k = -3$.   (a) Find $\|u\|$, $\|v\|$, $\|u + v\|$, and $\|ku\|$. (b) Verify that $\|ku\| = |k|\|u\|$ and $\|u + v\| \leq \|u\| + \|v\|$.

MATRIX OPERATIONS

Problems 1.67 to 1.71 refer to the following matrices:

$$A = \begin{bmatrix} 1 & 2 \\ 3 & -4 \end{bmatrix}, \qquad B = \begin{bmatrix} 5 & 0 \\ -6 & 7 \end{bmatrix}, \qquad C = \begin{bmatrix} 1 & -3 & 4 \\ 2 & 6 & -5 \end{bmatrix}, \qquad D = \begin{bmatrix} 3 & 7 & -1 \\ 4 & -8 & 9 \end{bmatrix}$$

1.67. Find: (a) $5A - 2B$;   (b) $C + D$;   (c) $2C - 3D$.

1.68. Find: (a) AB; (b) BA.

1.69. Find: (a) AC; (b) AD; (c) BC; (d) BD.

1.70. Find: (a) A^T; (b) C^T; (c) C^TC; (d) CC^T.

1.71. Find: (a) $A^2 = AA$; (b) $B^2 = BB$; (c) $C^2 = CC$.

Problems 1.72 to 1.75 refer to the following matrices:

$$A = \begin{bmatrix} 1 & -1 & 2 \\ 0 & 3 & 4 \end{bmatrix}, \qquad B = \begin{bmatrix} 4 & 0 & -3 \\ -1 & -2 & 3 \end{bmatrix}, \qquad C = \begin{bmatrix} 2 & -3 & 0 & 1 \\ 5 & -1 & -4 & 2 \\ -1 & 0 & 0 & 3 \end{bmatrix}, \qquad D = \begin{bmatrix} 2 \\ -1 \\ 3 \end{bmatrix}$$

1.72. Find: (a) $A + B$; (b) $A + C$; (c) $3A - 4B$.

1.73. Find: (a) AB; (b) AC; (c) AD.

1.74. Find: (a) BC; (b) BD; (c) CD.

1.75. Find: (a) A^T; (b) A^TB; (c) A^TC.

1.76. Let $A = \begin{bmatrix} 1 & 2 \\ 3 & 6 \end{bmatrix}$. Find a 2×3 matrix B with distinct entries such that $AB = 0$.

1.77. Answer True or False, where A and B are matrices.
 (a) If $A + B$ is defined, then $B + A$ is always defined.
 (b) If AB is defined, then BA is always defined.
 (c) $A + A^T$ is always defined.
 (d) AA^T is always defined.
 (e) If AB^T is defined, then BA^T is always defined.

1.78. Suppose $e_1 = [1, 0, 0]$, $e_2 = [0, 1, 0]$, $e_3 = [0, 0, 1]$, and suppose $A = \begin{bmatrix} a_1 & a_2 & a_3 & a_4 \\ b_1 & b_2 & b_3 & b_4 \\ c_1 & c_2 & c_3 & c_4 \end{bmatrix}$. Find e_1A, e_2A, and e_3A.

1.79. Let $e_i = (0, \ldots, 0, 1, 0, \ldots, 0)$, where 1 is the ith component. Show the following:
 (a) $e_iA = A_i$, the ith row of a matrix A.
 (b) $Be_j^T = B^j$, the jth column of B.
 (c) If $e_iA = e_iB$ for each i, then $A = B$.
 (d) If $Ae_j^T = Be_j^T$ for each j, then $A = B$.

POINTS, LINES, AND HYPERPLANES IN $\mathbf{R}^n$

1.80. Find the vector v identified with the directed line segment $\overrightarrow{PQ}$ for the points: (a) $P(2, 3, -7)$ and $Q(1, -6, -5)$ in $\mathbf{R}^3$; (b) $P(1, -8, -4, 6)$ and $Q(3, -5, 2, -4)$ in $\mathbf{R}^4$.

1.81. Find and equation of the hyperplane H in $\mathbf{R}^4$ which:
 (a) Contains $P(1, 2, -3, 2)$ and is normal to $u = [2, 3, -5, 6]$.
 (b) Contains $P(3, -1, 2, 5)$ and is parallel to $2x_1 - 3x_2 + 5x_3 - 7x_4 = 4$.

1.82. Find a parametric representation of the line L in $\mathbf{R}^4$ which:

    (a) Passes through $P(1, 2, 3, 4)$ in the direction of $u = [5, 6, 7, 8]$.

    (b) Passes through points $P(1, 2, 1, 2)$ and $Q(3, -5, 7, -9)$.

    (c) Passes through $P(1, 1, 3, 3)$ and is perpendicular to the hyperplane

        $2x_1 + 4x_2 + 6x_3 - 8x_4 = 5$.

SPATIAL VECTORS (VECTORS IN $\mathbf{R}^3$), ijk NOTATION

1.83. Given: $u = 3\mathbf{i} - 4\mathbf{j} + 2\mathbf{k}$, $v = 2\mathbf{i} + 5\mathbf{j} - 3\mathbf{k}$, and $w = 4\mathbf{i} + 7\mathbf{j} + 2\mathbf{k}$. Find: (a) $2u - 3v$; (b) $3u + 4v - 2w$; (c) $u \cdot v$, $u \cdot w$, $v \cdot w$; (d) $\|u\|$, $\|v\|$, $\|w\|$.

1.84. Find the equation of plane H:

    (a) With normal $\mathbf{N} = 3\mathbf{i} - 4\mathbf{j} + 5\mathbf{k}$ and containing the point $P(1, 2, -3)$.

    (b) Parallel to $4x + 3y - 2z = 11$ and containing the point $Q(2, -1, 3)$.

1.85. Find the (parametric) equation of line L:

    (a) Through the point $P(2, 5, -3)$ and in the direction of $v = 4\mathbf{i} - 5\mathbf{j} + 7\mathbf{k}$.

    (b) Through the points $P(1, 2, -4)$ and $Q(3, -7, 2)$.

    (c) Perpendicular to the plane $2x - 3y + 7z = 4$ and containing $P(1, -5, 7)$.

1.86. Consider the following curve C in $\mathbf{R}^3$, where $0 \le t \le 5$:

$$F(t) = t^3\mathbf{i} - t^2\mathbf{j} + (2t - 3)\mathbf{k}$$

    (a) Find the point P on C corresponding to $t = 2$.

    (b) Find the initial point Q and the terminal point Q'.

    (c) Find the unit tangent vector $\mathbf{T}$ to the curve C when $t = 2$.

1.87. Find a normal vector $\mathbf{N}$ and the tangent plane H to the surface at the given point:

    (a) Surface $x^2y + 3yz = 20$ and point $P(1, 3, 2)$.

    (b) Surface $x^2 + 3y^2 - 5z^2 = 16$ and point $P(3, -2, 1)$.

1.88. Given the surface $z = f(x, y) = x^2 + 2xy$, find a normal vector $\mathbf{N}$ and tangent plane H when $x = 3$ and $y = 1$.

1.89. We have chosen a right-handed coordinate system for $\mathbf{R}^3$, that is, if the fingers of the right hand are curled around the z axis in the same direction as the positive x axis rotates toward the

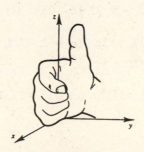

Fig.1-8

positive y axis, then the thumb points in the direction of the positive z axis. (See Fig. 1-8.) Draw a picture of a left-handed coordinate system.

CROSS PRODUCT

The cross product is defined only for vectors in $\mathbf{R}^3$.

1.90. Given: $u = 3\mathbf{i} - 4\mathbf{j} + 2\mathbf{k}$, $v = 2\mathbf{i} + 5\mathbf{j} - 3\mathbf{k}$, $w = 4\mathbf{i} + 7\mathbf{j} + 2\mathbf{k}$. Find: (a) $u \times v$; (b) $u \times w$; (c) $v \times w$; (d) $v \times u$.

1.91. Given: $u = [2, 1, 3]$, $v = [4, -1, 2]$, $w = [1, 1, 5]$. Find: (a) $u \times v$; (b) $u \times w$; (c) $v \times w$; (d) $v \times u$.

1.92. Find the volume V of the parallelepiped formed by the vectors u, v, w in: (a) Problem 1.90; (b) Problem 1.91.

1.93. Find a unit vector w orthogonal to: (a) $u = [1, 2, 3]$ and $v = [1, -1, 2]$; (b) $u = 3\mathbf{i} - \mathbf{j} + 2\mathbf{k}$ and $v = 4\mathbf{i} - 2\mathbf{j} - \mathbf{k}$.

PROOFS

1.94. Prove Theorem 1.2: (iii) $(B + C)A = BA + CA$; (iv) $k(AB) = (kA)B = A(kB)$.

1.95. Prove Theorem 1.3: (i) $(A + B)^T = A^T + B^T$; (ii) $(A^T)^T = A$; (iii) $(kA)^T = kA^T$.

1.96. Suppose $U = [U_{ik}]$ and $V = [V_{kj}]$ are block matrices for which UV is defined and the number of columns of each block U_{ik} is equal to the number of rows of each block V_{kj}. Show that $UV = [W_{ij}]$, where $W_{ij} = \sum_k U_{ik} V_{kj}$.

Answers to Supplementary Problems

1.54. Only v_1 and v_3 are equal.

1.55. (a) $(-3, -16, 10)$; (b) $(-5, -16, 24)$; (c) $(22, 23, 33)$

1.56. (a) $-3, -12, 8$; (b) $\sqrt{21}, \sqrt{35}, \sqrt{14}$

1.57. (a) $(-7, -14, 13, 45, 0)$; (b) $(20, -29, 22, 16, -23)$; (c) -6; (d) $\sqrt{90} = 3\sqrt{10}$ and $\sqrt{95}$

1.58. (a) $(1, 1, 3, -15)$; (b) $(3, -14, 11, -32)$; (c) $(-2, -7, 2, 5)$; (d) $-6, -7, 6$; (e) $\sqrt{14}, \sqrt{12} = 2\sqrt{3}, \sqrt{18} = 3\sqrt{2}$

1.59. (a) $(-1, 12, -35)^T$; (b) $(-8, 22, -24)^T$; (c) $-15, -27, 34$; (d) $\sqrt{26}, \sqrt{30}, 7$

1.60. (a) 6; (b) 3; (c) $\frac{3}{2}$

1.61. (a) $x = 2, y = 4$; (b) $x = -6, y = \frac{3}{2}$

1.62. (a) $x = -1, y = -\frac{3}{2}$; (b) $x = 0, y = 0$, or $x = -2, y = -4$

1.63. (a) $x = 2, y = -1$; (b) $x = 3, y = 2$

1.64. $x = 3, y = -1, z = 2$

1.65. (a) $\hat{u} = \left(\dfrac{5}{\sqrt{74}}, \dfrac{-7}{\sqrt{74}} \right)$; (b) $\hat{v} = (\frac{1}{5}, \frac{2}{5}, -\frac{2}{5}, \frac{4}{5})$; (c) $\hat{w} = \left(\dfrac{6}{\sqrt{133}}, \dfrac{-4}{\sqrt{133}}, \dfrac{9}{\sqrt{133}} \right)$

1.66. (a) $\|u\| = 3, \|v\| = 13, \|u+v\| = \sqrt{120} = 2\sqrt{30}, \|ku\| = 9$

1.67. (a) $\begin{bmatrix} -5 & 10 \\ 27 & -34 \end{bmatrix}$; (b) $\begin{bmatrix} 4 & 4 & 3 \\ 6 & -2 & 4 \end{bmatrix}$; (c) $\begin{bmatrix} -7 & -27 & 11 \\ -8 & 36 & -37 \end{bmatrix}$

1.68. (a) $AB = \begin{bmatrix} -7 & 14 \\ 39 & -28 \end{bmatrix}$; (b) $BA = \begin{bmatrix} 5 & 10 \\ 15 & -40 \end{bmatrix}$

1.69. (a) $AC = \begin{bmatrix} 5 & 9 & -6 \\ -5 & -33 & 32 \end{bmatrix}$; (b) $AD = \begin{bmatrix} 11 & -9 & 17 \\ -7 & 53 & -39 \end{bmatrix}$; (c) $BC = \begin{bmatrix} 5 & -15 & 20 \\ 8 & 60 & -59 \end{bmatrix}$;

(d) $BD = \begin{bmatrix} 15 & 35 & -5 \\ 10 & -98 & 69 \end{bmatrix}$

1.70. (a) $A^T = \begin{bmatrix} 1 & 3 \\ 2 & -4 \end{bmatrix}$; (b) $C^T = \begin{bmatrix} 1 & 2 \\ -3 & 6 \\ 4 & -5 \end{bmatrix}$; (c) $C^T C = \begin{bmatrix} 5 & 9 & -6 \\ 9 & 45 & -42 \\ -6 & -42 & 41 \end{bmatrix}$;

(d) $CC^T = \begin{bmatrix} 26 & -36 \\ -36 & 65 \end{bmatrix}$

1.71. (a) $A^2 = \begin{bmatrix} 7 & -6 \\ -9 & 22 \end{bmatrix}$; (b) $B^2 = \begin{bmatrix} 25 & 0 \\ -72 & 49 \end{bmatrix}$; (c) C^2 not defined

1.72. (a) $A + B = \begin{bmatrix} 5 & -1 & -1 \\ -1 & 1 & 7 \end{bmatrix}$; (b) $A + C$ not defined; (c) $3A - 4B = \begin{bmatrix} -13 & -3 & 18 \\ 4 & 17 & 0 \end{bmatrix}$

1.73. (a) AB not defined; (b) $AC = \begin{bmatrix} -5 & -2 & 4 & 5 \\ 11 & -3 & -12 & 18 \end{bmatrix}$; (c) $AD = \begin{bmatrix} 9 \\ 9 \end{bmatrix}$

1.74. (a) $BC = \begin{bmatrix} 11 & -12 & 0 & -5 \\ -15 & 5 & 8 & 4 \end{bmatrix}$; (b) $BD = \begin{bmatrix} -1 \\ 9 \end{bmatrix}$; (c) CD not defined

1.75. (a) $A^T = \begin{bmatrix} 1 & 0 \\ -1 & 3 \\ 2 & 4 \end{bmatrix}$; (b) $A^T B = \begin{bmatrix} 4 & 0 & -3 \\ -7 & -6 & 12 \\ 4 & -8 & 6 \end{bmatrix}$; (c) $A^T C$ not defined

1.76. $B = \begin{bmatrix} 2 & 8 & 10 \\ -1 & -4 & -5 \end{bmatrix}$ (not unique).

1.77. (a) T; (b) F; (c) F; (d) T; (e) T

1.78. $e_1 A = (a_1, a_2, a_3, a_4)$, $e_2 A = (b_1, b_2, b_3, b_4)$, $e_3 A = (c_1, c_2, c_3, c_4)$, that is, the rows of A

1.80. (a) $v = [-1, -9, 2]$; (b) $v = [2, 3, 6, -10]$

1.81. (a) $2x_1 + 3x_2 - 5x_3 + 6x_4 = 35$; (b) $2x_1 - 3x_2 + 5x_3 - 7x_4 = -16$

1.82. (a) $x_1 = 5t + 1, x_2 = 6t + 2, x_3 = 7t + 3, x_4 = 8t + 4$
(b) $x_1 = 2t + 1, x_2 = -7t + 2, x_3 = 6t + 1, x_4 = -11t + 2$
(c) $x_1 = 2t + 1, x_2 = 4t + 1, x_3 = 6t + 3, x_4 = -8t + 3$

1.83. (a) $-23\mathbf{j} + 13\mathbf{k}$; ($b$) $9\mathbf{i} - 6\mathbf{j} - 10\mathbf{k}$; ($c$) $u \cdot v = -20, u \cdot w = -12, v \cdot w = 37$;
(d) $\|u\| = \sqrt{29}, \|v\| = \sqrt{38}, \|w\| = \sqrt{69}$

1.84. (a) $3x - 4y + 5z = -20$; (b) $4x + 3y - 2z = -1$

1.85. (a) $x = 4t + 2, y = -5t + 5, z = 7t - 3$; ($b$) $x = 2t + 1, y = -9t + 2, z = 6t - 4$;
(c) $x = 2t + 1, y = -3t - 5, z = 7t + 7$

1.86. (a) $P = F(2) = 8\mathbf{i} - 4\mathbf{j} + \mathbf{k}$; ($b$) $Q = F(0) = -3\mathbf{k}, Q' = F(5) = 125\mathbf{i} - 25\mathbf{j} + 7\mathbf{k}$;
(c) $\mathbf{T} = (6\mathbf{i} - 2\mathbf{j} + \mathbf{k})/\sqrt{41}$

1.87. (a) $\mathbf{N} = 6\mathbf{i} + 7\mathbf{j} + 9\mathbf{k}, 6x + 7y + 9z = 45$; ($b$) $\mathbf{N} = 6\mathbf{i} - 12\mathbf{j} - 10\mathbf{k}, 3x - 6y - 5z = 16$

1.88. $\mathbf{N} = 8\mathbf{i} + 6\mathbf{j} - \mathbf{k}, 8x + 6y - z = 15$

1.89. Interchange the x and y axes, or the y and z axes, or the x and z axes.

1.90. (a) $2\mathbf{i} + 13\mathbf{j} + 23\mathbf{k}$; ($b$) $-22\mathbf{i} + 2\mathbf{j} + 37\mathbf{k}$; ($c$) $31\mathbf{i} - 16\mathbf{j} - 6\mathbf{k}$; ($d$) $-2\mathbf{i} - 13\mathbf{j} - 23\mathbf{k}$

1.91. (a) $[5, 8, -6]$; (b) $[2, -7, 1]$; (c) $[-7, -18, 5]$; (d) $[-5, -8, 6]$

1.92. Use Theorem 1.4(b). (a) $V = |u \cdot v \times w| = |145| = 145$; ($b$) $V = |u \cdot v \times w| = |-17| = 17$

1.93. (a) $(7, 1, -3)/\sqrt{59}$; (b) $(5\mathbf{i} + 11\mathbf{j} - 2\mathbf{k})/\sqrt{150}$

Chapter 2

Systems of Linear Equations

2.1 INTRODUCTION

The theory of systems of linear equations plays an important and motivating role in the subject of linear algebra. In fact, the solution of many problems in linear algebra reduces to solving a system of linear equations. Thus the techniques introduced in this chapter will frequently be used in studying and understanding abstract concepts of linear algebra appearing in later chapters. On the other hand, some of the results of the abstract theory will give us new insights into the structure of "concrete" systems of linear equations.

This chapter investigates systems of linear equations and describes in detail the Gaussian elimination algorithm, which is used to find the solution of such systems. One can also solve a system of linear equations using a matrix format. This is done in the latter part of the chapter. Accordingly, we also describe the Gaussian elimination algorithm as applied to a given matrix. This algorithm yields the row canonical form of the matrix, which will also be used for the solution of certain problems in linear algebra.

A system of m linear equations in n unknowns will be called an $m \times n$ (read: m by n) *system*. A system with the same number of equations as unknowns, that is, an $n \times n$ system, is called a *square* system, and such systems play an important role in the theory. In fact, a whole section will treat 2×2 systems (two equations in two unknowns) in detail since the solution of such a system can be described geometrically, and it is representative of the solution of larger systems.

All our equations will involve specific numbers, called *constants* or *scalars*. For simplicity, we will assume that all our scalars are real numbers, that is, that they belong to the real field **R**. The solution of our systems of linear equations will involve lists $(k_1, k_2, \ldots, k_n)$ of real numbers, and hence the solution of those systems are vectors in $\mathbf{R}^n$.

2.2 LINEAR EQUATIONS, SOLUTIONS

This section gives basic definitions which are connected with the solution of systems of linear equations. The actual algorithm for finding such solutions will be treated later.

Linear Equation

By a *linear equation* in n unknowns $x_1, x_2, \ldots, x_n$ we mean an equation that can be put in the *standard form*

$$a_1 x_1 + a_2 x_2 + \cdots + a_n x_n = b \tag{2.1}$$

where $a_1, a_2, \ldots, a_n$, and b are constants. (We assume, unless otherwise stated or implied, that all constants are real numbers.) The number a_k is called the *coefficient* of x_k, and b is called the *constant* of the equation.

A *solution* of the linear equation (2.1) is a list of values for the unknowns or, equivalently,

39

a vector in $\mathbf{R}^n$, say,

$$x_1 = k_1, \ x_2 = k_2, \ldots, x_n = k_n \qquad \text{or} \qquad u = (k_1, k_2, \ldots, k_n)$$

such that the following statement (obtained by substituting each k_i for x_i in the equation) is true:

$$a_1 k_1 + a_2 k_2 + \cdots + a_n k_n = b$$

In this case we say that u *satisfies* the equation.

Remark: Equation (2.1) implicitly assumes that there is an ordering of the unknowns. In order to avoid subscripts, we will usually use variables, x, y, as ordered, to denote two unknowns, x, y, z, as ordered, to denote three unknowns, and x, y, z, t, as ordered, to denote four unknowns.

EXAMPLE 2.1 Let L be the following linear equation in unknowns x, y, and z:

$$2x - 3y + 4z = 5$$

Consider the following vectors in $\mathbf{R}^3$:

$$u = (5, 3, 1), \qquad v = (8, 1, -2), \qquad w = (1, 2, 3)$$

Then u is a solution of L since substituting $x = 5$, $y = 3$, and $z = 1$ in the equation yields

$$2(5) - 3(3) + 4(1) = 5 \qquad \text{or} \qquad 10 - 9 + 4 = 5 \qquad \text{or} \qquad 5 = 5$$

which is a true statement. Also v is a solution of L since substituting v in the equation yields

$$2(8) - 3(1) + 4(-2) = 5 \qquad \text{or} \qquad 16 - 3 - 8 = 5 \qquad \text{or} \qquad 5 = 5$$

which is a true statement. On the other hand, w is not a solution of L since substituting w in L yields

$$2(1) - 3(2) + 4(3) = 5 \qquad \text{or} \qquad 2 - 6 + 12 = 5 \qquad \text{or} \qquad 8 = 5$$

which is not a true statement.

Systems of Linear Equations

A *system of linear equations* is a list of linear equations with the same unknowns. For example,

$$2x - 3y + 4z = 5$$
$$5x - 7y + 9z = 13$$

is a system of two linear equations in the three unknowns x, y, and z. (Thus, using the notation introduced above, it is a 2×3 system.)

A *solution* of a system of linear equations is a vector that is a solution of all the equations. The set of all solutions of a system is called the *solution set* or *general solution* or, simply, the *solution* of the system. By a *particular solution* of a system we mean one of the elements of the general solution. By *solving* a system of linear equations we mean a process of determining the solution set of the system.

EXAMPLE 2.2 Consider the above 2×3 system of linear equations and the vectors u, v, and w in Example 2.1. As shown in Example 2.1, u and v are solutions of the first equation of the system. The vector $u = (5, 3, 1)$ is also a solution of the second equation since

$$5(5) - 7(3) + 9(1) = 13 \qquad \text{or} \qquad 25 - 21 + 9 = 13 \qquad \text{or} \qquad 13 = 13$$

is a true statement. Hence u is a solution of the system. The vector $v = (8, 1, -2)$ is not a solution of the second equation since

$$5(8) - 7(1) + 9(-2) = 13 \qquad \text{or} \qquad 40 - 7 - 18 = 13 \qquad \text{or} \qquad 15 = 13$$

is not a true statement. Hence v is not a solution of the system. The vector $w = (1, 2, 3)$ is not a solution of the first equation, hence automatically it cannot be a solution of the system.

One main result about systems of linear equations follows.

Theorem 2.1:   Any system of linear equations has either: (i) a unique solution, (ii) no solution, or (iii) an infinite number of solutions.

A system of linear equations is said to be *consistent* if it has one or more solutions [case (i) or (iii) in Theorem 2.1], and it is said to be *inconsistent* if it has no solution [case (ii) in Theorem 2.1]. Figure 2-1 illustrates this situation.

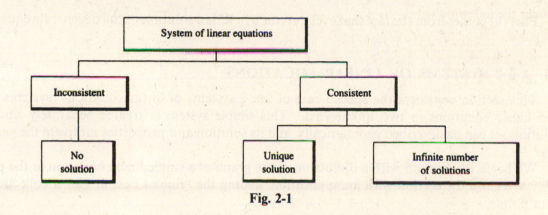

Fig. 2-1

Degenerate Equations

A linear equation is said to be *degenerate* if all the coefficients are zero, that is, if it has the form

$$0x_1 + 0x_2 + \cdots + 0x_n = b \qquad\qquad (2.2)$$

The solution of such an equation only depends on the value of the constant b. Specifically,

(i)   If $b \neq 0$, then the equation has no solution.

(ii)   If $b = 0$, then every vector $u = (k_1, k_2, \ldots, k_n)$ in $\mathbf{R}^n$ is a solution.

Thus such an equation cannot have a unique solution.

EXAMPLE 2.3

(a)   Describe the solution of $4y - x - 3y + 3 = 2 + x - 2x + y + 1$.
    Rewrite in standard form by collecting terms and transposing:

$$y - x + 3 = y - x + 3 \qquad \text{or} \qquad 0x + 0y = 0$$

The equation is degenerate with constant $b = 0$. Thus every vector $u = (a, b)$ in $\mathbf{R}^2$ is a solution.

(b) Describe the solution of $3x - 4y - x + 2 = 4 - 7y + 2x + 3y + 1$.

Rewrite in standard form:

$$2x - 4y + 2 = 2x - 4y + 5 \qquad \text{or} \qquad 0x + 0y = 3$$

The equation is degenerate with nonzero constant $b = 3$. Hence no vector in $\mathbf{R}^2$ is a solution.

The following theorem tells us how a degenerate equation affects a system of linear equations.

Theorem 2.2: Suppose a system of linear equations contains a degenerate equation with the constant b.

   (i) If $b \neq 0$, then the degenerate equation and, hence, the system have no solution.

   (ii) If $b = 0$, then the degenerate equation may be deleted from the system without changing the solution set of the system.

Part (ii) comes from the fact that every vector u in $\mathbf{R}^n$ is a solution of the degenerate equation.

2.3   2 × 2 SYSTEMS OF LINEAR EQUATIONS

This section considers the special case of 2×2 systems of linear equations (systems with two linear equations in two unknowns). This simple system is treated separately since its solution set can be described geometrically, and its solution and properties motivate the general case.

We begin this section with a discussion of the graph of a single linear equation in the plane $\mathbf{R}^2$. We close the section with an application, finding the "line of best fit" for a collection of data points.

Linear Equation in Two Unknowns

Consider a single linear equation in two unknowns x and y, that is, an equation that can be put in the standard form

$$Ax + By = C$$

where A, B, and C are real numbers. We assume that the equation is nondegenerate, i.e., that A and B are not both zero.

Each solution of the above equation is a pair (k_1, k_2) of real numbers, which can be found by assigning an arbitrary value to x and solving for y, or vice versa. Such a solution corresponds to a point in the cartesian plane $\mathbf{R}^2$. Since A and B are not both zero, all such solutions correspond precisely to the points on a straight line (whence the term "linear equation"). This line is called the *graph* of the equation.

EXAMPLE 2.4 Plot the graph of the linear equation $2x + y = 4$.

First find, say, three solutions of the equation as follows. Choose any value for either unknown, say, $x = -2$. Substitute $x = -2$ into the equation to obtain

$$2(-2) + y = 4 \qquad \text{or} \qquad -4 + y = 4 \qquad \text{or} \qquad y = 8$$

Thus $x = -2$, $y = 8$ or, equivalently, the point $(-2, 8)$ in $\mathbf{R}^2$ is a solution of the equation. Now find a second solution point, say, the y intercept. That is, substitute $x = 0$ into the equation to get $y = 4$. Hence the point $(0, 4)$ on the y axis is a solution. Next find a third solution point, say, the x intercept. That is, substitute $y = 0$ into the equation to get $x = 2$. Hence the point $(2, 0)$ on the x axis is a solution.

To plot the graph of the equation, first plot the three solutions $(-2, 8)$, $(0, 4)$, and $(2, 0)$ in the plane $\mathbf{R}^2$, as pictured in Fig. 2-2. Then draw the line L determined by two of the solution points and note that the line L also passes through the third solution point. (Indeed, L is the set of all solutions of the equation.) The line L is the graph of the equation.

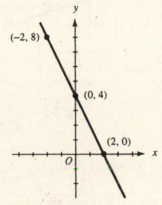

Fig. 2-2 Graph of $2x + y = 4$.

Remark: Suppose a line $Ax + By = C$ is not vertical, that is, suppose $B \neq 0$. Then one can rewrite the equation in the form

$$y = mx + b$$

This is called the *slope-intercept* form of the equation since m is the *slope* of the line and b is the *y intercept*.

Systems of Two Linear Equations in Two Unknowns (2 × 2 Systems)

Consider a system of two linear equations in two unknowns x and y, which can be put in the standard form

$$\begin{aligned} A_1 x + B_1 y &= C_1 \\ A_2 x + B_2 y &= C_2 \end{aligned} \qquad (2.3)$$

We assume that both equations are nondegenerate, that is, that A_1 and B_1 are not both zero and that A_2 and B_2 are not both zero. Thus the graph of each equation is a line in the plane $\mathbf{R}^2$.

A solution of system (2.3) is a pair (x_1, y_1) of real numbers which satisfies both equations. Thus such a solution is a point of intersection of the two lines corresponding to the equations.

The general solution of system (2.3) belongs to one of three types, and these three types may be described geometrically as pictured in Fig. 2-3.

(1) **The system has exactly one solution:** Here the two lines intersect in one point [Fig. 2-3(a)]. This occurs when the coefficients of x and y are not proportional, that is, when

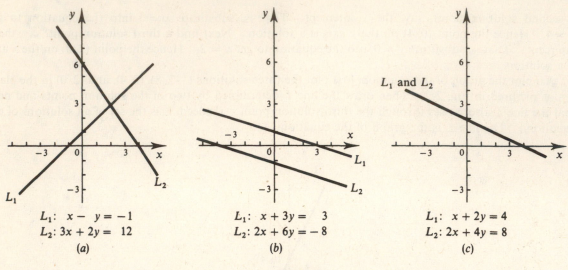

$$L_1: x - y = -1$$
$$L_2: 3x + 2y = 12$$
$$(a)$$

$$L_1: x + 3y = 3$$
$$L_2: 2x + 6y = -8$$
$$(b)$$

$$L_1: x + 2y = 4$$
$$L_2: 2x + 4y = 8$$
$$(c)$$

Fig. 2-3

$$\frac{A_1}{A_2} \neq \frac{B_1}{B_2} \qquad \text{or equivalently} \qquad A_1 B_2 - A_2 B_1 \neq 0$$

For example, for the lines in Fig. 2-3(a), we have $\frac{1}{3} \neq -\frac{1}{2}$.

(2) **The system has no solution:** Here the lines are parallel [Fig. 2-3(b)]. This occurs when the coefficients are proportional with each other, but not with the constants; that is, when

$$\frac{A_1}{A_2} = \frac{B_1}{B_2} \neq \frac{C_1}{C_2}$$

For example, for the lines in Fig. 2-3(b) we have $\frac{1}{2} = \frac{3}{6} \neq -\frac{3}{8}$.

(3) **The system has an infinite number of solutions:** Here the lines coincide [Fig. 2-3(c)]. This occurs when the coefficients and the constants are proportional, that is, when

$$\frac{A_1}{A_2} = \frac{B_1}{B_2} = \frac{C_1}{C_2}$$

For example, for the lines in Fig. 2-3(c) we have $\frac{1}{2} = \frac{2}{4} = \frac{4}{8}$.

Remark: The following expression and its value is called a *determinant of order* 2:

$$\begin{vmatrix} A_1 & B_1 \\ A_2 & B_2 \end{vmatrix} = A_1 B_2 - A_2 B_1$$

Determinants will be studied in Chapter 10. Thus the system (2.3) has a unique solution if and only if the determinant of its coefficients is not zero.

Elimination Algorithm

The solution to system (2.3) can be obtained by the process known as (Gaussian) elimination. This algorithm, which follows, has two parts.

Algorithm 2.3   (Gaussian Elimination):   The input consists of two linear equations L_1 and L_2 in two unknowns.

Part A (Forward Elimination):

(1)   Multiply each equation by a constant so that the resulting coefficients of one unknown are negatives of each other.

(2)   Add the two equations obtained in (1). This yields a new equation L, which has only one unknown.

Part B (Back-Substitution):

(1)   Solve for the unknown in the new equation L (which contains only one unknown).

(2)   Substitute the value of the unknown obtained in (1) (Part B) into one of the original equations, and then solve to obtain the value of the other unknown.

EXAMPLE 2.5   Solve the system

$$L_1:\quad 2x - 3y = -8$$

$$L_2:\quad 3x + 4y = \quad 5$$

We eliminate x from the equations by forming the new equation $L = -3L_1 + 2L_2$, that is, we multiply L_1 by -3 and L_2 by 2 and add the resulting equations:

$$
\begin{array}{rl}
-3L_1: & -6x + 9y = 24 \\
2L_2: & 6x + 8y = 10 \\
\hline
\text{Addition:} & 17y = 34
\end{array}
$$

Solving the new equation for y yields $y = 2$. Substituting $y = 2$ into one of the original equations, say L_1, yields

$$2x - 3(2) = -8 \quad\text{or}\quad 2x - 6 = -8 \quad\text{or}\quad 2x = -2 \quad\text{or}\quad x = -1$$

Thus $x = -1$, $y = 2$ or the pair $(-1, 2)$ is the unique solution of the system. Geometrically, the lines intersect at the point $(-1, 2)$, as shown in Fig. 2-4. (This is expected since $\frac{2}{3} \neq -\frac{3}{4}$.)

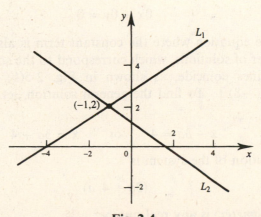

Fig. 2-4

EXAMPLE 2.6   (Nonunique Cases)

(a) Solve the system

$$L_1: \qquad x - 3y = 4$$
$$L_2: \quad -2x + 6y = 5$$

Eliminate x from the equations by multiplying L_1 by 2 and adding it to L_2, that is, by forming the new equation $L = 2L_1 + L_2$.   This yields the equation

$$0x + 0y = 13$$

which is degenerate with a nonzero constant $b = 13$.   Thus this equation and the system have no solution.   Geometrically, the lines are parallel, as shown in Fig. 2-5(a).   [This is expected since $1/(-2) = -3/6 \neq 4/5$.]

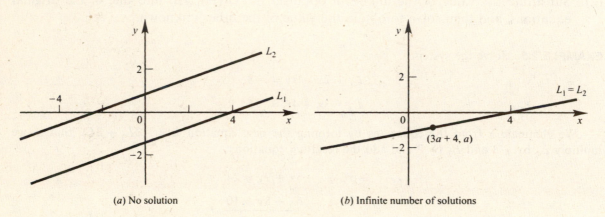

(a) No solution   (b) Infinite number of solutions

Fig. 2-5

(b) Solve the system

$$L_1: \qquad x - 3y = \quad 4$$
$$L_2: \quad -2x + 6y = -8$$

Eliminate x by multiplying L_1 by 2 and adding it to L_2, that is, by forming the new equation $L = 2L_1 + L_2$.   This yields the equation

$$0x + 0y = 0$$

which is a degenerate equation where the constant term is also zero.   Thus the system has an infinite number of solutions, which correspond to the solutions of either equation. Geometrically, the lines coincide, as shown in Fig. 2-5(b).   [This is expected since $1/(-2) = -3/6 = 4/(-8)$.]   To find the general solution, let $y = a$ and substitute into L_1 to obtain

$$x - 3a = 4 \qquad \text{or} \qquad x = 3a + 4$$

Thus the general solution of the system is

$$(3a + 4, a)$$

where a (called a *parameter*) is any real number.

Application: Line of Best Fit (Least Squares)

Consider N points in the plane, say,

$$A_1(x_1, y_1), A_2(x_2, y_2), \ldots, A_N(x_N, y_N)$$

Assuming the points lie approximately on a line, we seek the line L which "best" describes the points, called the *line of best fit*. Specifically, as illustrated in Fig. 2-6, we seek the line L such that the sum of the squares of the vertical distances of the points to the line is a minimum (hence the name "least squares").

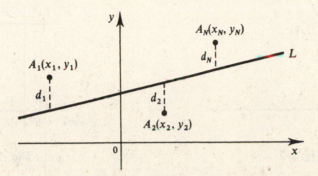

Fig. 2-6   Line L of best fit where sum $d_1^2 + d_2^2 + \cdots + d_N^2$ is a minimum

Now it can be shown that the slope m and the y intercept b of the line L of best fit (pictured in Fig. 2-6) are obtained from the following two equations in the two unknowns m and b:

$$\begin{aligned} Nb + (\Sigma x)m &= \Sigma y \\ (\Sigma x)b + (\Sigma x^2)m &= \Sigma xy \end{aligned} \qquad (2.4)$$

where

$$N = \text{number of points}$$
$$\Sigma x = x_1 + x_2 + \cdots + x_N \qquad (\text{sum of } x \text{ values})$$
$$\Sigma y = y_1 + y_2 + \cdots + y_N \qquad (\text{sum of } y \text{ values})$$
$$\Sigma x^2 = x_1^2 + x_2^2 + \cdots + x_N^2$$
$$\Sigma xy = x_1 y_1 + x_2 y_2 + \cdots + x_N y_N$$

The symbol Σ is the Greek capital letter *sigma*, and it is frequently used to denote summations, as above.

EXAMPLE 2.7   Find the line L of best fit for the following four points, which are plotted in Fig. 2-7:

$$A(1, 2), \qquad B(2, 3), \qquad C(4, 6), \qquad D(5, 9)$$

Form the table in Fig. 2-8. Specifically, first list the x values and their sum Σx and the y values and their sum Σy. Next list the x^2 values and their sum Σx^2 to the left of the x values, and then list the xy values and their sum Σxy to the right of the y values. Using this table we obtain

$$N = 4, \qquad \Sigma x = 12, \qquad \Sigma y = 20, \qquad \Sigma xy = 77, \qquad \Sigma x^2 = 46$$

Substitution into formula (2.4) yields the system

$$\begin{aligned} 4b + 12m &= 20 \\ 12b + 46m &= 77 \end{aligned} \qquad \text{or} \qquad \begin{aligned} b + 3m &= 5 \\ 12b + 46m &= 77 \end{aligned}$$

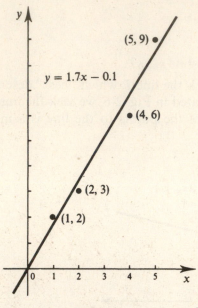

Fig. 2-7

x^2	x	y	xy
1	1	2	2
4	2	3	6
16	4	6	24
25	5	9	45
Sums: 46	12	20	77

Fig. 2-8

(We multiplied the first equation by $\frac{1}{4}$ to obtain a simpler first equation.)   Eliminate b by forming the new equation $L = -12L_1 + L_2$:

$$-12L_1: \quad -12b - 36m = -60$$
$$L_2: \quad \underline{\quad 12b + 46m = \quad 77}$$
$$\text{Addition:} \quad 10m = \quad 17$$

Solve the new equation for m to obtain $m = 1.7$.   Substitute $m = 1.7$ in the first equation $b + 3m = 5$ to obtain $b = -0.1$.   Thus the line L of best fit is

$$y = 1.7x - 0.1$$

This line is also plotted in Fig. 2-7.

2.4 3 × 3 SYSTEMS OF LINEAR EQUATIONS, ELEMENTARY OPERATIONS

Consider now a system of three linear equations in three unknowns x, y, and z, which can be put in the *standard form*

$$a_{11}x + a_{12}y + a_{13}z = b_1$$
$$a_{21}x + a_{22}y + a_{23}z = b_2 \tag{2.5}$$
$$a_{31}x + a_{32}y + a_{33}z = b_3$$

We assume no equation is degenerate, that is, no equation is of the form

$$0x + 0y + 0z = c$$

where all three coefficients are zero.

A *solution* of system (2.5) is a triple (x_1, y_1, z_1) of real numbers that satisfy all three equations.   Geometrically speaking, each equation represents a plane H in space (three dimensions), and so any solution of the system, if it exists, is a point of intersection of the three planes.

The *general solution* or *solution set* of system (2.5) is the collection of all solutions of the system, and it belongs to one of three types. These three types may be described geometrically as pictured in Fig. 2-9, where H_1, H_2, and H_3 are the planes corresponding to the given linear equations. Specifically:

(1) *The system has a unique solution.* Here [Fig. 2-9(a)] the three planes intersect in one point.

(2) *The system has no solution.* Here [Fig. 2-9(b)] the planes may intersect pairwise, but with no common point of intersection, as in (i), or two of the planes may be parallel, as in (ii) to (iv).

(3) *The system has an infinite number of solutions.* Here [Fig. 2-9(c)] the three planes may intersect in a line, as in (i) and (ii), or the three planes may coincide, as in (iii).

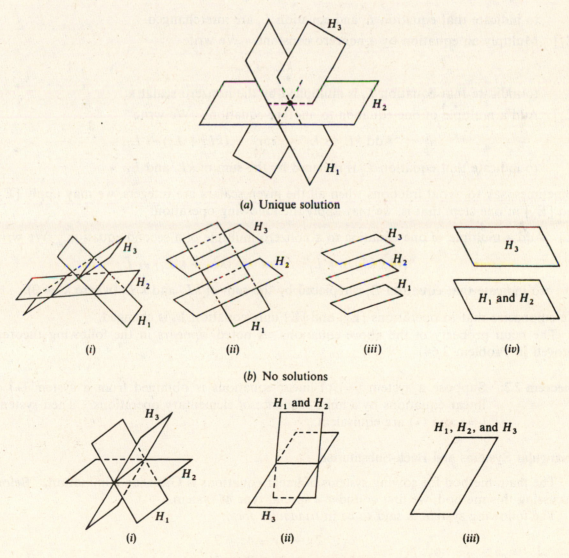

(a) Unique solution

(i) (ii) (iii) (iv)

(b) No solutions

(i) (ii) (iii)

(c) Infinite number of solutions

Fig. 2-9

This section discusses the solution of 3×3 systems of linear equations with unique solutions. The solution of systems with nonunique solutions will be discussed in later sections.

First, however, we need to introduce the notion of equivalent systems and certain elementary operations which will also apply to general systems of linear equations.

Equivalent Systems, Elementary Operations

Systems of linear equations in the same unknowns are said to be *equivalent* if the systems have the same solution set. One way of producing a system ($\#$) that is equivalent to a given system ($\star$) is by applying a sequence of the following operations, called *elementary operations* (where $L_1, L_2, \ldots$ denote linear equations):

[E_1] Interchange two of the equations. We write

$$L_i \leftrightarrow L_j$$

to indicate that equation L_i and equation L_j are interchanged.

[E_2] Multiply an equation by a nonzero constant. We write

$$kL_i \to L_i$$

to indicate that equation L_i is multiplied by the nonzero scalar k.

[E_3] Add a multiple of one equation to another equation. We write

$$\text{``Add } kL_i \text{ to } L_j\text{''} \qquad \text{or} \qquad (kL_i + L_j) \to L_j$$

to indicate that equation L_j is replaced by the sum of kL_i and L_j.

Sometimes, say to avoid fractions when all the given scalars are integers, we may apply [E_2] and [E_3] in one step, that is, we may apply the following operation:

[E] Add a multiple of one equation to a nonzero multiple of a second equation. We write

$$\text{``Add } kL_i \text{ to } k'L_j\text{''} \qquad \text{or} \qquad (kL_i + k'L_j) \to L_j$$

to indicate that equation L_j is replaced by the sum of kL_i and $k'L_j$ (where $k' \neq 0$).

We emphasize that in operations [E_3] and [E] only equation L_j is changed.

The main property of the above equations, as noted, appears in the following theorem (proved in Problem 2.64).

Theorem 2.3: Suppose a system ($\#$) of linear equations is obtained from a system ($\star$) of linear equations by a finite sequence of elementary operations. Then systems ($\#$) and ($\star$) are equivalent.

Triangular Systems and Back-Substitution

The main method for solving systems of linear equations is Gaussian elimination. Before discussing this method, we first consider a special type of system.

The following system is said to be in *triangular form*:

$$
\begin{aligned}
L_1: &\quad 2x + y - 4z = 3 \\
L_2: &\quad \quad\quad 3y - 8z = 1 \\
L_3: &\quad \quad\quad\quad\quad 2z = 5
\end{aligned}
$$

That is, the first unknown appearing in each equation is, respectively, x, y, and z. The unique solution to such a triangular system can be found easily by the process known as *back-substitution*, that is,

(i)   Solve the last equation L_3 for the last unknown z, obtaining $z = \frac{5}{2}$.

(ii)   Substitute the value of z in the second equation L_2 and solve for y. This yields

$$3y - 8(\tfrac{5}{2}) = 1 \quad \text{or} \quad 3y - 20 = 1 \quad \text{or} \quad 3y = 21 \quad \text{or} \quad y = 7$$

(iii)   Substitute the values $z = \frac{5}{2}$, $y = 7$ into the first equation L_1 and then solve for x:

$$2x + 7 - 4(\tfrac{5}{2}) = 3 \quad \text{or} \quad 2x + 7 - 10 = 3 \quad \text{or} \quad 2x = 6 \quad \text{or} \quad x = 3$$

Thus the solution of the triangular system is $x = 3$, $y = 7$, $z = \frac{5}{2}$ or, equivalently, the vector $u = (3, 7, \frac{5}{2})$.

Gaussian Elimination for 3 × 3 Systems

The method of *Gaussian elimination*, one of the oldest and most frequently used methods for finding the solution of systems of linear equations, is made up of two parts:

Part A: Step-by-step reduction of the system to a simpler (triangular or, more generally, echelon) form

Part B: Solving the simpler system by back-substitution

The details of this method for general systems will be treated later. Here we illustrate the basic ideas of this method using a 3×3 system with a unique system. In this case, Part A will lead to a triangular system.

Gaussian Elimination Example

Consider the following system of three equations in three unknowns:

$$\begin{aligned}
L_1: & \quad x - 3y - 2z = 6 \\
L_2: & \quad 2x - 4y - 3z = 8 \\
L_3: & \quad -3x + 6y + 8z = -5
\end{aligned}$$

We solve the system by Gaussian elimination.

Part A: First we want to eliminate x from the second equation L_2 and the third equation L_3. This is accomplished by the operations "Add $-2L_1$ to L_2" and "Add $3L_1$ to L_3", that is, by multiplying L_1 by -2 and adding it to L_2, and then multiplying L_1 by 3 and adding it to L_3. This yields

$$\begin{array}{ll}
(-2)L_1: & -2x + 6y + 4z = -12 \\
L_2: & \underline{2x - 4y - 3z = 8} \\
\text{New } L_2: & 2y + z = -4
\end{array} \qquad
\begin{array}{ll}
3L_1: & 3x - 9y - 6z = 18 \\
L_3: & \underline{-3x + 6y + 8z = -5} \\
\text{New } L_3: & -3y + 2z = 13
\end{array}$$

Thus the original system is changed to

$$\begin{aligned}
L_1: & \quad x - 3y - 2z = 6 \\
L_2: & \quad 2y + z = -4 \\
L_3: & \quad -3y + 2z = 13
\end{aligned}$$

(Note that equations L_2 and L_3 form a subsystem with one less unknown than the original system.)

Next we want to eliminate y from the (new) third equation L_3 using only (new) equation L_2 and L_3. This is accomplished by the operation "Add $(\frac{3}{2})L_2$ to L_3" or, alternately, by "Add $3L_2$ to $2L_3$". In other words, we apply the operation $(\frac{3}{2}L_2 + L_3) \to L_3$ or $(3L_2 + 2L_3) \to L_3$. This yields

$$
\begin{array}{rrl}
\frac{3}{2}L_2: & 3y + \frac{3}{2}z = & -6 \\
L_3: & -3y + 2z = & 13 \\
\hline
\text{New } L_3: & \frac{7}{2}z = & 7
\end{array}
\qquad \text{or} \qquad
\begin{array}{rrl}
3L_2: & 6y + 3z = & -12 \\
2L_3: & -6y + 4z = & 26 \\
\hline
\text{New } L_3: & 7z = & 14
\end{array}
$$

Thus our system is changed to

$$
\begin{array}{ll}
L_1: & x - 3y - 2z = 6 \\
L_2: & 2y + z = -4 \\
L_3: & 7z = 14 \qquad (\text{or} \quad \frac{7}{2}z = 7)
\end{array}
$$

The system is now in triangular form.

Part B: The values for the unknowns are obtained in reverse order by back-substitution. Specifically, we obtain $z = 2$ from L_3, then $y = -3$ from L_2, and finally $x = 1$ from L_1. Thus the solution of the triangular system and hence the original system is $x = 1$, $y = -3$, $z = 2$ or, in other words, the vector $u = (1, -3, 2)$.

Remark: In the first stage of Gaussian elimination the coefficient of x in the first equation L_1 is called the *pivot*. Similarly, in the second stage the coefficient of y in the second equation L_2 is the pivot. Clearly, one must have a nonzero pivot in order for the process to work. Thus one may need to interchange equations first in order to obtain a nonzero pivot. (See Problem 2.28.)

Condensed Format

The Gaussian elimination algorithm involves rewriting systems of linear equations. Sometimes we can avoid excessive recopying of some of the linear system. This format for the solution of the above system follows.

Number	Equation	Operation
(1)	$x - 3y - 2z = 6$	
(2)	$2x - 4y - 3z = 8$	
(3)	$-3x + 6y + 8z = -5$	
(2')	$2y + z = -4$	Add $-2L_1$ to L_2.
(3')	$-3y + 2z = 13$	Add $3L_1$ to L_3.
(3'')	$7z = 14$	Add $3L_2$ to $2L_3$.

That is, first we write down the number of each of the original equations. As we apply the Gaussian elimination algorithm to the system, we only write down the new equations, and we label each new equation using the same number as the original corresponding equation, but with an added prime. (After each new equation we will indicate the elementary operation that yields the new equation.)

The system in triangular form consists of Eqs. (1), $(2')$, and $(3'')$, the numbers with the largest number of primes. Applying back-substitution to these equations yields $x = 1$, $y = -3$, $z = 2$.

Remark: If two of the equations need to be interchanged, say to obtain a nonzero pivot, then this is easily accomplished in the format by simply renumbering the two equations rather than changing their positions.

EXAMPLE 2.8 Solve the system

$$2x + y - 3z = 1$$
$$5x + 2y - 6z = 5$$
$$3x - y - 4z = 7$$

Using the condensed format, we reduce the system to triangular form as follows:

Number	Equation	Operation
(1)	$2x + y - 3z = 1$	
(2)	$5x + 2y - 6z = 5$	
(3)	$3x - y - 4z = 7$	
$(2')$	$-y + 3z = 5$	Add $-5L_1$ to $2L_2$.
$(3')$	$-5y + z = 11$	Add $-3L_1$ to $2L_3$.
$(3'')$	$-14z = -14$	Add $-5L_2$ to L_3.

Equations (1), $(2')$, and $(3'')$ form the triangular system.

Using back-substitution with the triangular system yields $z = 1$ from $(3'')$, $y = -2$ from $(2')$, and $x = 3$ from (1). Thus $x = 3$, $y = -2$, $z = 1$ or, equivalently, the vector $u = (3, -2, 1)$ is the unique solution of the system.

2.5 SYSTEMS OF LINEAR EQUATIONS

Consider a system of m linear equations $L_1, L_2, \ldots, L_m$ in n unknowns $x_1, x_2, \ldots, x_n$. Such a system can be put in the *standard form*

$$a_{11}x_1 + a_{12}x_2 + \cdots + a_{1n}x_n = b_1$$
$$a_{21}x_1 + a_{22}x_2 + \cdots + a_{2n}x_n = b_2$$
$$\cdots\cdots\cdots\cdots\cdots\cdots\cdots\cdots\cdots$$
$$a_{m1}x_1 + a_{m2}x_2 + \cdots + a_{mn}x_n = b_m$$

$$(2.6)$$

where the a_{ij} and b_i are constants. The number a_{ij} is the *coefficient* of the unknown x_j in equation L_i, and the number b_i is the *constant* of the equation L_i.

A *solution* (or a *particular solution*) of system (2.6) is a list of values for the unknowns or, equivalently, a vector in $\mathbf{R}^n$, say,

$$x_1 = k_1, x_2 = k_2, \ldots, x_n = k_n \qquad \text{or} \qquad u = (k_1, k_2, \ldots, k_n)$$

which is a solution of each equation of the system, i.e., substituting k_i for x_i in every equation in (2.6) yields a true statement. The set of all solutions is called the *solution set* or the *general solution* of the system.

EXAMPLE 2.9   Consider the system

$$x + 2y - 4z = 1$$
$$2x + 5y - 7z = 4$$

Determine whether or not $u = (1, 2, 1)$ or $v = (3, 1, 1)$ is a solution of the system.

Substitute the values of u into each equation to obtain

(*1*) $1 + 2(2) - 4(1) = 1$ or $1 + 4 - 4 = 1$ or $1 = 1$
(*2*) $2(1) + 5(2) - 7(1) = 4$ or $2 + 10 - 7 = 4$ or $5 = 4$

No, u is not a solution of the system since it is not a solution of the second equation.

Substitute the values of v into each equation to obtain

(*1*) $3 + 2(1) - 4(1) = 1$ or $3 + 2 - 4 = 1$ or $1 = 1$
(*2*) $2(3) + 5(1) - 7(1) = 4$ or $6 + 5 - 7 = 4$ or $4 = 4$

Yes, v is a solution of the system since it is a solution of both equations.

Augmented and Coefficient Matrices

Every system of linear equations has associated with it an *augmented matrix M* and the *coefficient matrix A*. For example, the augmented matrix M and the coefficient matrix A of the system in Example 2.9 follow:

$$M = \begin{bmatrix} 1 & 2 & -4 & 1 \\ 2 & 5 & -7 & 4 \end{bmatrix} \quad \text{and} \quad A = \begin{bmatrix} 1 & 2 & -4 \\ 2 & 5 & -7 \end{bmatrix}$$

Observe that each row of M corresponds to an equation of the system, and each column of M corresponds to the coefficients of an unknown, except for the last column, which corresponds to the constants of the system. The coefficient matrix A is simply the matrix of coefficients, that is, the augmented matrix M without the last column of constants. Some texts write $M = [A, b]$ to emphasize the two parts of M, where b denotes the column vector of constants.

Clearly, a system is completely determined by its augmented matrix M and vice versa. One way of solving a system of linear equations is by working with its augmented matrix M instead of the system itself. This relationship is discussed in Section 2.9.

Matrix Equation and Vector Equation of a System of Linear Equations

Every system of linear equations is equivalent to a matrix equation of the form $Ax = b$, where A is the coefficient matrix, x is the column vector of unknowns, and b is the column vector of constants of the system. For example, the system in Example 2.9 is equivalent to the matrix equation

$$\begin{bmatrix} 1 & 2 & -4 \\ 2 & 5 & -7 \end{bmatrix} \begin{bmatrix} x \\ y \\ z \end{bmatrix} = \begin{bmatrix} 1 \\ 4 \end{bmatrix}$$

The statement that the system of linear equations and the matrix equation are equivalent means that any vector solution of the system is a solution of the matrix equation, and vice versa.

Every system of linear equations is also equivalent to a vector equation. For example, the system of linear equations in Example 2.9 is also equivalent to the vector equation

$$x\begin{bmatrix}1\\2\end{bmatrix} + y\begin{bmatrix}2\\5\end{bmatrix} + z\begin{bmatrix}-4\\-7\end{bmatrix} = \begin{bmatrix}1\\4\end{bmatrix}$$

That is, any solution of the system is a solution of the vector equation, and vice versa.

Remark: The matrix form $Ax = b$ of a system of linear equations is notationally very convenient when discussing and proving properties of systems of linear equations.

2.6 SYSTEMS IN TRIANGULAR AND ECHELON FORM

The main method for solving systems of linear equations, Gaussian elimination, is treated in Section 2.7. Here we consider two simple types of systems of linear equations: systems in triangular form and the more general systems in echelon form.

Triangular Form

The following system of linear equations is in *triangular form*:

$$\begin{aligned}2x - 3y + 5z - 2t &= 9\\5y - z + 3t &= 1\\7z - t &= 3\\2t &= 8\end{aligned}$$

That is, the first unknown x is the *leading unknown* (i.e., the first unknown with a nonzero coefficient) in the first equation, the second unknown y is the leading unknown in the second equation, and so on. Thus in particular, the system is square and each leading unknown is *directly* to the right of the leading unknown in the preceding equation.

Such a triangular system always has a unique solution, which may be obtained by back-substitution. That is,

(i) First solve the last equation for the last unknown to get $t = 4$.

(ii) Then substitute this value $t = 4$ into the next-to-last equation and solve for the next-to-last unknown z as follows:

$$7z - 4 = 3 \quad\text{or}\quad 7z = 7 \quad\text{or}\quad z = 1$$

(iii) Now substitute $z = 1$ and $t = 4$ into the second equation and solve for the second unknown y as follows:

$$5y - 1 + 12 = 1 \quad\text{or}\quad 5y + 11 = 1 \quad\text{or}\quad 5y = -10 \quad\text{or}\quad y = -2$$

(iv) Finally, substitute $y = -2$, $z = 1$, and $t = 4$ into the first equation and solve for the first unknown x as follows:

$$2x + 6 + 5 - 8 = 9 \quad\text{or}\quad 2x + 3 = 9 \quad\text{or}\quad 2x = 6 \quad\text{or}\quad x = 3$$

Thus $x = 3$, $y = -2$, $z = 1$, $t = 4$ or, equivalently, the vector $u = (3, -2, 1, 4)$ is the unique solution of the system.

Remark: There is an alternate form for back-substitution (which will be used when solving a system using the matrix format). Specifically, after first finding the value of the last unknown, we substitute this value for the last unknown in all the preceding equations before solving for the next-to-last unknown. This yields a triangular system with one less equation and one less unknown. For example, in the above triangular system, we substitute $t = 4$ in all the preceding equations to obtain the triangular system

$$
\begin{aligned}
2x - 3y + 5z &= 17 \\
5y - z &= -11 \\
7z &= 7
\end{aligned}
$$

We then repeat the process using the new last equation, and so on.

Echelon Form, Basic and Free Variables

The following system of linear equations is in *echelon form*:

$$
\begin{aligned}
2x + 6y - z + 4s - 2t &= 15 \\
z + 2s + 2t &= 5 \\
3s - 9t &= 6
\end{aligned}
\tag{2.7}
$$

That is, no equation is degenerate, and the leading unknown in each equation other than the first is to the right of the leading unknown in the preceding equation.

The leading unknowns in an echelon system of linear equations are called *basic* (or *dependent* or *nonfree*) *variables*, and all the other unknowns are called *free* (or *independent*) *variables*. Thus in the above system, x, z, and s are the basic variables, and y and t are the free variables.

The solution set of any echelon system is described in the following theorem (proved in Problem 2.66).

Theorem 2.4: Consider a system of linear equations in echelon form, say with r equations in n unknowns. There are two cases.

    (i) $r = n$. That is, there are as many equations as unknowns (triangular form). Then the system has a unique solution.

    (ii) $r < n$. That is, there are more unknowns than equations. Then we can arbitrarily assign values to the $n - r$ free variables and solve uniquely for the r basic variables, obtaining a solution of the system.

Suppose an echelon system does contain more unknowns than equations. Then the system has an infinite number of solutions since each of the $n - r$ free variables may be assigned any real number. The general solution of the system may be obtained in either of two equivalent ways, which we illustrate using the echelon system (2.7), where there are $r = 3$ equations and $n = 5$ unknowns.

(a) **(Parametric Form):** Assign arbitrary values, called *parameters*, to the free variables y and t, say $y = a$ and $t = b$, and then use back-substitution to obtain values for the basic variables x, z, and s in terms of the parameters a and b. Specifically,

    (1)   Substitute $t = b$ into the last equation and solve for s:

$$
3s - 9b = 6 \qquad \text{or} \qquad 3s = 6 + 9b \qquad \text{or} \qquad s = 2 + 3b
$$

(2)   Substitute $s = 2 + 3b$ and $t = b$ into the second equation and solve for z:

$$z + 2(2 + 3b) + 2b = 5 \qquad \text{or} \qquad z + 4 + 8b = 5 \qquad \text{or} \qquad z = 1 - 8b$$

(3)   Substitute $y = a$, $z = 1 - 8b$, $s = 2 + 3b$, and $t = b$ into the first equation and solve for x:

$$2x + 6a - (1 - 8b) + 4(2 + 3b) - 2b = 15 \qquad \text{or} \qquad x = 4 - 3a - 9b$$

Accordingly,

$$x = 4 - 3a - 9b, \qquad y = a, \qquad z = 1 - 8b, \qquad s = 2 + 3b, \qquad t = b$$

or, equivalently,

$$u = (4 - 3a - 9b, a, 1 - 8b, 2 + 3b, b)$$

where a and b are arbitrary numbers, is the general solution in *parametric form*.

(b)   **(Free-Variable Form):**   Use back-substitution to solve for the basic variables x, z, and s directly in terms of the free variables y and t. That is, the last equation gives $s = 2 + 3t$. Substitution in the second equation yields $z = 1 - 8t$, and then substitution in the first equation yields $x = 4 - 3y - 9t$. Accordingly,

$$x = 4 - 3y - 9t$$
$$y = \text{free variable}$$
$$z = 1 - 8t$$
$$s = 2 + 3t$$
$$t = \text{free variable}$$

is the *free-variable form* for the general solution of the system.

We emphasize that there is no difference between the above two forms of the general solution, and the use of one or the other to represent the general solution is simply a matter of taste.

Remark: A particular solution of system (2.7) can be found by assigning any values to the free variables and then solving for the basic variables by back-substitution.   For example, setting $y = 1$ and $t = 1$, we obtain

$$s = 2 + 3 = 5, \qquad z = 1 - 8 = -7, \qquad x = 4 - 3 - 9 = -8$$

Thus $u = (-8, 1, -7, 5, 1)$ is the particular solution corresponding to $y = 1$ and $t = 1$.

2.7   GAUSSIAN ELIMINATION

The main method for solving system (2.6) of linear equations is called *Gaussian elimination*. It essentially consists of two parts:

Part A   (*Forward Elimination*):   Step-by-step reduction of the system yielding either a degenerate equation with no solution (which indicates the system has no solution) or an equivalent simpler system in triangular or echelon form.

Part B   (*Backward Elimination*):   Step-by-step back-substitution to find the solution of the simpler system.

Part B was already investigated in Section 2.6. Accordingly, we need only give the algorithm for Part A, which follows.

Algorithm 2.7   (Forward Elimination):   The input is an $m \times n$ system of linear equations.

Step 1.   Find the first unknown in the system with a nonzero coefficient (which now must be x_1).

(a)   Arranged so that $a_{11} \neq 0$. That is, if necessary, interchange equations so that the first unknown x_1 appears with a nonzero coefficient in the first equation.

(b)   Use a_{11} as a *pivot* to eliminate x_1 from all equations except the first equation. That is, for $i > 1$,

(1)   Set $m = -a_{i1}/a_{11}$.

(2)   Add mL_1 to L_i.

In other words, apply the elementary operation

$$-(a_{i1}/a_{11})L_1 + L_i \to L_i$$

which replaces equation L_i by $-(a_{i1}/a_{11})L_1 + L_i$.

(c)   Examine each new equation L.

(1)   If L has the form $0x_1 + 0x_2 + \cdots + 0x_n = 0$ or if L is a multiple of another equation, then delete L from the system.

(2)   If L has the form $0x_1 + 0x_2 + \cdots + 0x_n = b$ with $b \neq 0$, then *stop*. The system has no solution.

Step 2.   Repeat Step 1 with the subsystem formed by all the equations, excluding the first equation. Here we let x_{j_2} denote the first unknown in the subsystem with a nonzero coefficient. Hence at the end of Step 2, we have $a_{2j_2} \neq 0$.

Step 3 to m.   Continue the above process until the system is reduced to triangular or echelon form, or until a degenerate equation with no solution is obtained.

Remark 1:   The justification of Step 1(c) is Theorem 2.2 and the fact that if $L = kL'$ for some other equation L', then the operation $(-kL' + L) \to L$ replaces L by $0x_1 + 0x_2 + \cdots + 0x_n = 0$ (which again may be deleted by Theorem 2.2).

Remark 2:   The number in Step 1(b),

$$m = -\frac{a_{i1}}{a_{11}} = -\frac{\text{coefficient to be deleted}}{\text{pivot}}$$

is called the *multiplier*.

Remark 3:   One could replace the operation in Step 1(b) by

$$(-a_{i1}L_1 + a_{11}L_i) \to L_i$$

This would avoid fractions if all the scalars were originally integers.

EXAMPLE 2.10 Solve the system

$$x + 2y - 3z = 1$$
$$2x + 5y - 8z = 4$$
$$3x + 8y - 13z = 7$$

We use Gaussian elimination.

Part A (*Forward Elimination*): First we eliminate x from the second and third equations by the operations "Add $-2L_1$ to L_2" and "Add $-3L_1$ to L_3", that is, by applying the operations $(-2L_1 + L_2) \rightarrow L_2$ and $(-3L_1 + L_3) \rightarrow L_3$. This yields

$$
\begin{aligned}
x + 2y - 3z &= 1 \\
y - 2z &= 2 \\
2y - 4z &= 4
\end{aligned}
\qquad \text{or} \qquad
\begin{aligned}
x + 2y - 3z &= 1 \\
y - 2z &= 2
\end{aligned}
$$

(The third equation is deleted since it is a multiple of the second equation.) The system is now in echelon form with basic variables x and y and free variable z.

Part B (*Backward Elimination*): To obtain the general solution, let $z = a$ and solve for x and y by back-substitution. Substitute $z = a$ into the second equation to obtain $y = 2 + 2a$. Then substitute $z = a$ and $y = 2 + 2a$ into the first equation to obtain

$$x + 2(2 + 2a) - 3a = 1 \qquad \text{or} \qquad x + 4 + 4a - 3a = 1 \qquad \text{or} \qquad x = -3 - a$$

Thus the general solution is

$$x = -3 - a, \qquad y = 2 + 2a, \qquad z = a \qquad \text{or} \qquad (-3 - a, 2 + 2a, a)$$

where a is a parameter.

EXAMPLE 2.11 Solve the 3×4 system

$$x + 3y - 2z + 5t = 4$$
$$2x + 8y - z + 9t = 9$$
$$3x + 5y - 12z + 17t = 7$$

We use Gaussian elimination.

Part A (*Forward Elimination*): First we eliminate x from the second and third equations by applying the operations "Add $-2L_1$ to L_2" and "Add $-3L_1$ to L_3", that is, by applying the operations $(-2L_1 + L_2) \rightarrow L_2$ and $(-3L_1 + L_3) \rightarrow L_3$. This yields

$$
\begin{aligned}
x + 3y - 2z + 5t &= 4 \\
2y + 3z - t &= 1 \\
-4y - 6z + 2t &= -5
\end{aligned}
$$

We eliminate y from the third equation by applying the operation "Add $2L_2$ to L_3", that is, $(2L_2 + L_3) \rightarrow L_3$. This yields the degenerate equation

$$0x + 0y + 0z = -3$$

Thus this equation and, hence, the original system have no solution. (*Do not continue.*)

Remark: As in the above example, Part A of Gaussian elimination always tells us whether or not the system has a solution, i.e., is consistent. Accordingly, Part B need never be applied when a system has no solution.

EXAMPLE 2.12 Solve the system

$$x - 2y + 2z = 6$$
$$2x - 5y + 7z = 20$$
$$5x - 8y + 4z = 14$$
$$x + y - 5z = -12$$

First we reduce the system to echelon form. To eliminate x from the second, third, and fourth equations, we first "Add $-2L_1$ to L_2", then "Add $-5L_1$ to L_3", and lastly "Add $-L_1$ to L_4". This yields

$$x - 2y + 2z = 6$$
$$-y + 3z = 8$$
$$2y - 6z = -16$$
$$3y - 7z = -18$$

or

$$x - 2y + 2z = 6$$
$$-y + 3z = 8$$
$$3y - 7z = -18$$

(The third equation is deleted since it is a multiple of the second equation.) To eliminate y from the (new) third equation, we "Add $3L_2$ to L_3". This yields

$$x - 2y + 2z = 6$$
$$-y + 3z = 8$$
$$2z = 6$$

The system is now in echelon form. In fact, the system is in triangular form, and hence there are no free variables. Back-substitution yields the unique solution $x = 2$, $y = 1$, $z = 3$ or the vector $u = (2, 1, 3)$.

Remark 1: The condensed format described in Section 2.4 for solving square 3×3 systems of linear equations can also be used for solving general systems.

Remark 2: If there are more than four equations, then it may be more convenient to use the matrix format for solving systems. That is discussed in Sections 2.9.

2.8 MATRICES: ROW EQUIVALENCE AND ELEMENTARY ROW OPERATIONS

Section 2.9 rediscusses the Gaussian elimination algorithm for the solution of a system of linear equations using the matrix representation (format) of the system. The present section discusses the matrix terminology and concepts which are required for such a discussion.

Remark: By the *leading nonzero* element of a row R of a matrix A we mean the first nonzero number in R. Of course if R is a *zero row*, that is, all elements of R are zero, then R has no leading nonzero element.

Echelon Matrices

A matrix A is called an *echelon matrix*, or is said to be in *echelon form*, if the following two conditions hold:

(1) All zero rows, if any, are at the bottom of the matrix.

(2)   Each leading nonzero entry in a row is to the right of the leading nonzero entry in the preceding row.

That is, $A = [a_{ij}]$ is an echelon matrix if there exist nonzero entries

$$a_{1j_1}, a_{2j_2}, \ldots, a_{rj_r}, \qquad \text{where} \qquad j_1 < j_2 < \cdots < j_r$$

with the property that

$$a_{ij} = 0 \qquad \text{for} \qquad \text{(i) } i \le r, j < j_i \qquad \text{and} \qquad \text{(ii) } i > r$$

In this case $a_{1j_1}, a_{2j_2}, \ldots, a_{rj_r}$ are the leading nonzero entries of A. These leading nonzero entries will be called the *pivots*.

EXAMPLE 2.13   The following are echelon matrices whose pivots (leading nonzero entries) have been circled:

$$\begin{bmatrix} ② & 3 & 2 & 0 & 4 & 5 & -6 \\ 0 & 0 & ① & 1 & -3 & 2 & 0 \\ 0 & 0 & 0 & 0 & 0 & ⑥ & 2 \\ 0 & 0 & 0 & 0 & 0 & 0 & 0 \end{bmatrix} \qquad \begin{bmatrix} ① & 2 & 3 \\ 0 & 0 & ① \\ 0 & 0 & 0 \end{bmatrix} \qquad \begin{bmatrix} 0 & ① & 3 & 0 & 0 & 4 \\ 0 & 0 & 0 & ① & 0 & -3 \\ 0 & 0 & 0 & 0 & ① & 2 \end{bmatrix}$$

Row Canonical Form

A matrix A is said to be in *row canonical form* (or *row reduced echelon form*) if A is an echelon matrix, that is, A satisfies properties (1) and (2) above, and if A satisfies the following additional two properties:

(3)   Each pivot (leading nonzero entry) is equal to 1.

(4)   Each pivot is the only nonzero entry in its column.

The major difference between an echelon matrix and a matrix in row canonical form is that in an echelon matrix there must be zeros below the pivots [properties (1) and (2)], but in a matrix in row canonical form there must be zeros both below and above the pivots [property (4)].

   The third matrix above is an example of a matrix in row canonical form. The second matrix is not in row canonical form since it does not satisfy property (4), that is, there is a nonzero entry above the pivot in the second row. The first matrix is not in row canonical form since it satisfies neither property (3) nor property (4), that is, some pivots are not equal to 1 and there are nonzero entries above the pivots.

   The zero matrix 0, for any number of rows or columns, is also an example of a matrix in row canonical form.

Elementary Row Operations, Row Equivalence

Suppose A is a matrix with rows $R_1, R_2, \ldots, R_m$. The following operations on A are called *elementary row operations*:

[E_1]   *(Row Interchange):*   Interchange two of the rows. We write

$$R_i \leftrightarrow R_j$$

to indicate that rows R_i and R_j are interchanged.

[E₂] *(Row Scaling):* Multiply a row by a nonzero constant.   We write

$$kR_i \to R_i$$

to indicate that row R_i is multiplied by the nonzero scalar k.

[E₃] *(Row Addition):* Add a multiple of one row to another row.   We write

$$\text{"Add } kR_i \text{ to } R_j\text{"} \qquad \text{or} \qquad (kR_i + R_j) \to R_j$$

to indicate that row R_j is replaced by the sum of kR_i and R_j.

Sometimes, say, to avoid fractions when all the given scalars are integers, we may apply [E₂] and [E₃] in one step, that is, we may apply the following operation:

[E] Add a multiple of one row to a nonzero multiple of a second row.   We write

$$\text{"Add } kR_i \text{ to } k'R_j\text{"} \qquad \text{or} \qquad (kR_i + k'R_j) \to R_j$$

to indicate that row R_j is replaced by the sum of kR_i and $k'R_j$ (where $k' \neq 0$).

We emphasize that in operations [E₃] and [E] only row R_j is changed.

The reader no doubt recognizes the similarity of the above operations and those used for solving systems of linear equations.

A matrix A is said to be *row equivalent* to a matrix B, written

$$A \sim B$$

if B can be obtained from A by a sequence of elementary row operations.   We note that row equivalence is an equivalence relation, that is,

(1) $A \sim A$ for any matrix A.

(2)   If $A \sim B$, then $B \sim A$.

(3)   If $A \sim B$ and $B \sim C$, then $A \sim C$.

Property (2) comes from the fact that the elementary row operations are invertible.   (This is discussed in Section 3.7.)

2.9 GAUSSIAN ELIMINATION—MATRIX FORMULATION

Any matrix A can be transformed into an echelon form by Algorithm 2.9A.   The echelon matrix can then be transformed into row canonical form by Algorithm 2.9B.   These algorithms, which use the elementary row operations, are simply restatements of Gaussian elimination as applied to matrices rather than linear equations.   (The term "row reduce" or simply "reduce" shall mean to transform a matrix by the row operations.)

Algorithm 2.9A   (Forward Elimination):   The input is an arbitrary matrix $A = [a_{ij}]$.

Step 1.   Find the first column with a nonzero entry.   Let j_1 denote this column.

(a)   Arrange so that $a_{1j_1} \neq 0$.   That is, if necessary, interchange rows so that a nonzero entry appears in the first row in column j_1.

(b)   Use a_{1j_1} as a *pivot* to obtain 0s below a_{1j_1}.   That is, for $i > 1$,

    (1)   Set $m = -a_{ij_1}/a_{1j_1}$.

    (2)   Add mR_1 to R_i.

In other words, apply the elementary row operation

$$-(a_{ij_1}/a_{1j_1})R_1 + R_i \to R_i$$

[This replaces row R_i by $-(a_{ij_1}/a_{1j_1})R_1 + R_i$.]

Step 2. Repeat Step 1 with the submatrix formed by all the rows excluding the first row.   Here we let j_2 denote the first column in the submatrix with a nonzero entry.   Hence at the end of Step 2 we have $a_{2j_2} \neq 0$.

Steps 3 to r + 1. Continue the above process until the submatrix has no nonzero entry.

We emphasize that at the end of the algorithm, the pivot (leading nonzero) entries will be

$$a_{1j_1}, a_{2j_2}, \ldots, a_{rj_r}$$

where r denotes the number of nonzero rows in the matrix in echelon form.

Remark 1: The number in Step 1(b),

$$m = -\frac{a_{ij_1}}{a_{ij_1}} = -\frac{\text{coefficient to be deleted}}{\text{pivot}}$$

is called the *multiplier.*

Remark 2: One could replace the operation in Step 1(b) by

$$(-a_{ij_1}R_1 + a_{1j_1}R_i) \to R_i$$

This would avoid fractions if all the scalars were originally integers.

Algorithm 2.9B (Backward Elimination): The input is a matrix $A = [a_{ij}]$ in echelon form with pivot entries $a_{1j_1}, a_{2j_2}, \ldots, a_{rj_r}$.

Step 1. (a) Multiply the last nonzero row R_r by $1/a_{rj_r}$ so that the pivot entry is equal to 1.

    (b) Use $a_{rj_r} = 1$ to obtain 0s above the pivot.   That is, for $i = r-1, r-2, \ldots, 1$,

        (1)   Set $m = -a_{ij_i}$.

        (2)   Add mR_r to R_i.

In other words, apply the elementary row operations

$$-a_{ij_i}R_r + R_i \to R_i$$

(This replaces row R_i by $-a_{ij_i}R_r + R_i$.)

Steps 2 to r − 1. Repeat Step 1 for rows $R_{r-1}, R_{r-2}, \ldots, R_2$.

Step r. Multiply R_1 by $1/a_{1j_1}$.

There is an alternate form for Algorithm 2.9B where one first puts 0s above all the pivot entries before one sets the pivot entries equal to 1.

Algorithm 2.9B (Alternate Form):

Steps $r - k + 1$ (for $k = r, r - 1, \ldots, 2$): For $i > k$,

(1) Set $m = -a_{ik_i}/a_{1k_1}$.

(2) Add mR_k to R_i.

Step r. For $i = 1$ to r, multiply R_i by $1/a_{ij_i}$.

Remark: We emphasize that Gaussian elimination is a two-part process: Part A (Algorithm 2.9A) puts 0s below the pivot entries working from the top row R_1 down; and Part B (Algorithm 2.9B) puts 0s above the pivot entries working from the bottom row R_r up. There is another algorithm, called Gauss–Jordan, which also row reduces a matrix to row canonical form. The difference is that Gauss–Jordan puts 0s both below and above each pivot as it works its way from the top row R_1 down. Although Gauss–Jordan may be easier to state, it is less efficient than Gaussian elimination.

EXAMPLE 2.14 The matrix $A = \begin{bmatrix} 1 & 2 & -3 & 1 & 2 \\ 2 & 4 & -4 & 6 & 10 \\ 3 & 6 & -6 & 9 & 13 \end{bmatrix}$ is reduced (a) to echelon form by Algorithm 2.9A and then (b) to row canonical form by Algorithm 2.9B as follows:

(a) Use $a_{11} = 1$ as a pivot to obtain 0s below a_{11}, that is, add $-2R_1$ to R_2 and then add $-3R_1$ to R_3 to obtain the matrix

$$\begin{bmatrix} 1 & 2 & -3 & 1 & 2 \\ 0 & 0 & 2 & 4 & 6 \\ 0 & 0 & 3 & 6 & 7 \end{bmatrix}$$

Next use $a_{23} = 2$ as a pivot to obtain 0 below a_{23}, that is, add $(-\frac{3}{2})R_2$ to R_3 to obtain the matrix

$$\begin{bmatrix} 1 & 2 & -3 & 1 & 2 \\ 0 & 0 & 2 & 4 & 6 \\ 0 & 0 & 0 & 0 & -2 \end{bmatrix}$$

The matrix is now in echelon form.

(b) Multiply R_3 by $-\frac{1}{2}$ so that the pivot entry $a_{35} = 1$, and then use $a_{35} = 1$ as a pivot to obtain 0s above it by the operations "Add $-6R_3$ to R_2" and then "Add $-2R_3$ to R_1". This yields

$$A \sim \begin{bmatrix} 1 & 2 & -3 & 1 & 2 \\ 0 & 0 & 2 & 4 & 6 \\ 0 & 0 & 0 & 0 & 1 \end{bmatrix} \sim \begin{bmatrix} 1 & 2 & -3 & 1 & 0 \\ 0 & 0 & 2 & 4 & 0 \\ 0 & 0 & 0 & 0 & 1 \end{bmatrix}$$

Multiply R_2 by $\frac{1}{2}$ so that the pivot entry $a_{23} = 1$, and then use $a_{23} = 1$ as a pivot to obtain 0s above it by the operation "Add $3R_2$ to R_1". This yields

$$A \sim \begin{bmatrix} 1 & 2 & -3 & 1 & 0 \\ 0 & 0 & 1 & 2 & 0 \\ 0 & 0 & 0 & 0 & 1 \end{bmatrix} \sim \begin{bmatrix} 1 & 2 & 0 & 7 & 0 \\ 0 & 0 & 1 & 2 & 0 \\ 0 & 0 & 0 & 0 & 1 \end{bmatrix}$$

The last matrix is the row canonical form of A.

Algorithms 2.9A and 2.9B show that any matrix A is row equivalent to at least one matrix in row canonical form. We prove in Chapter 4 that such a matrix is unique. That is,

Theorem 2.5:   Any matrix A is row equivalent to a unique matrix in row canonical form, called the *row canonical form* of A.

Application to Systems of Linear Equations

One way to solve a system of linear equations is by working with its augmented matrix M rather than the equations themselves.   Specifically, we reduce M to echelon form (which tells whether the system has a solution) and then further reduce M to its row canonical form (which essentially gives the solution of the original system of linear equations).   The justification of this process comes from the following facts.

(1)   Any elementary row operation on the augmented matrix M of the system is equivalent to applying the corresponding operation on the system itself.

(2)   The system has a solution if and only if the echelon form of the augmented matrix M does not have a row of the form $(0, 0, \ldots, 0, b)$ with $b \neq 0$.

(3)   In the row canonical form of the augmented matrix M (excluding zero rows) the coefficient of each basic variable is a pivot entry equal to 1, and it is the only nonzero entry in its respective column.   Hence the free-variable form of the solution of the system of linear equations is obtained by simply transferring the free variables to the other side.

This process is illustrated below.

EXAMPLE 2.15   Solve the system

$$x + y - 2z + 4t = 5$$
$$2x + 2y - 3z + t = 3$$
$$3x + 3y - 4z - 2t = 1$$

Reduce its augmented matrix M to echelon form and then to row canonical form as follows:

$$M = \begin{bmatrix} 1 & 1 & -2 & 4 & 5 \\ 2 & 2 & -3 & 1 & 3 \\ 3 & 3 & -4 & -2 & 1 \end{bmatrix} \sim \begin{bmatrix} 1 & 1 & -2 & 4 & 5 \\ 0 & 0 & 1 & -7 & -7 \\ 0 & 0 & 2 & -14 & -14 \end{bmatrix} \sim \begin{bmatrix} 1 & 1 & 0 & -10 & -9 \\ 0 & 0 & 1 & -7 & -7 \\ 0 & 0 & 0 & 0 & 0 \end{bmatrix}$$

Thus the free-variable form of the general solution is

$$\begin{aligned} x + y \quad\;\; - 10t &= -9 \\ z - \;\; 7t &= -7 \end{aligned} \qquad \text{or} \qquad \begin{aligned} x &= -9 - y + 10t \\ y &= -7 + 7t \end{aligned}$$

(The zero row is omitted in the solution.)   Observe that x and z are the basic variables, and y and t are the free variables.

EXAMPLE 2.16   Solve the system

$$x_1 + x_2 - 2x_3 + 3x_4 = 4$$
$$2x_1 + 3x_2 + 3x_3 - x_4 = 3$$
$$5x_1 + 7x_2 + 4x_3 + x_4 = 5$$

First reduce its augmented matrix M to echelon form as follows:

$$M = \begin{bmatrix} 1 & 1 & -2 & 3 & 4 \\ 2 & 3 & 3 & -1 & 3 \\ 5 & 7 & 4 & 1 & 5 \end{bmatrix} \sim \begin{bmatrix} 1 & 1 & -2 & 3 & 4 \\ 0 & 1 & 7 & -7 & -5 \\ 0 & 2 & 14 & -14 & -15 \end{bmatrix} \sim \begin{bmatrix} 1 & 1 & -2 & 3 & 4 \\ 0 & 1 & 7 & -7 & -5 \\ 0 & 0 & 0 & 0 & -5 \end{bmatrix}$$

There is no need to continue to find the row canonical form of M since the echelon matrix already tells us that the system has no solution. Specifically, the third row of the echelon matrix corresponds to the degenerate equation

$$0x_1 + 0x_2 + 0x_3 + 0x_4 = -5$$

which has no solution.

EXAMPLE 2.17   Solve the system

$$x + 2y + z = 3$$
$$2x + 5y - z = -4$$
$$3x - 2y - z = 5$$

Reduce its augmented matrix M to echelon form and then to row canonical form as follows:

$$M = \begin{bmatrix} 1 & 2 & 1 & 3 \\ 2 & 5 & -1 & -4 \\ 3 & -2 & -1 & 5 \end{bmatrix} \sim \begin{bmatrix} 1 & 2 & 1 & 3 \\ 0 & 1 & -3 & -10 \\ 0 & -8 & -4 & -4 \end{bmatrix} \sim \begin{bmatrix} 1 & 2 & 1 & 3 \\ 0 & 1 & -3 & -10 \\ 0 & 0 & -28 & -84 \end{bmatrix}$$

$$\sim \begin{bmatrix} 1 & 2 & 1 & 3 \\ 0 & 1 & -3 & -10 \\ 0 & 0 & 1 & 3 \end{bmatrix} \sim \begin{bmatrix} 1 & 2 & 0 & 0 \\ 0 & 1 & 0 & -1 \\ 0 & 0 & 1 & 3 \end{bmatrix} \sim \begin{bmatrix} 1 & 0 & 0 & 2 \\ 0 & 1 & 0 & -1 \\ 0 & 0 & 1 & 3 \end{bmatrix}$$

Thus the system has the unique solution $x = 2$, $y = -1$, $z = 3$, or, equivalently, the vector $u = (2, -1, 3)$. We note that the echelon form of M already indicated that the solution was unique since it corresponded to a triangular system.

2.10   HOMOGENEOUS SYSTEMS OF LINEAR EQUATIONS

A system of linear equations is said to be *homogeneous* if all the constant terms are zero. Thus a homogeneous system has the form $Ax = 0$. Clearly, such a system always has a solution, namely, the zero vector $0 = (0, 0, \ldots, 0)$, called the *zero* or *trivial* solution. Frequently we are interested in whether or not a nonzero solution exists.

Since a homogeneous system $Ax = 0$ does have at least the zero solution, it can always be reduced to an equivalent homogeneous system in echelon form, say,

$$a_{11}x_1 + a_{12}x_2 + a_{13}x_3 + a_{14}x_4 + \cdots\cdots\cdots + a_{1n}x_n = 0$$
$$a_{2j_2}x_{j_2} \quad + a_{2, j_2+1}x_{j_2+1} + \cdots + a_{2n}x_n = 0$$
$$\cdots\cdots\cdots\cdots\cdots\cdots\cdots\cdots\cdots\cdots$$
$$a_{rj_r}x_{j_r} + \cdots + a_{rn}x_n = 0$$

where r denotes the number of equations in echelon form and n denotes the number of unknowns. There are two possibilities:

(i) $r = n$.   The system has only the zero solution.

(ii) $r < n$.   The system has a nonzero solution.

Accordingly, if we begin with fewer equations than unknowns then, in echelon form, $r < n$, and therefore the system has a nonzero solution. This proves the following important theorem.

Theorem 2.6:   A homogeneous system with more unknowns than equations has a nonzero solution.

EXAMPLE 2.18

(a) Consider the homogeneous system

$$x + 2y - 3z + \ t = 0$$
$$2x - 3y + \ z - 2t = 0$$
$$7x + 4y - 5z + 6t = 0$$

It has a nonzero solution since there are four unknowns but only three equations.

(b) The following system is reduced to echelon form:

$$
\begin{array}{ccc}
x + \ y - \ z = 0 & \quad x + \ y - \ z = 0 & \quad x + \ y - \ z = 0 \\
2x - 3y + \ z = 0 & \quad -5y + 3z = 0 & \quad -5y + 3z = 0 \\
x - 4y + 2z = 0 & \quad -5y + 3z = 0 &
\end{array}
$$

The system has a nonzero solution since there are only two equations in three unknowns in echelon form. Here z is a free variable. Let, say, $z = 5$; then $y = 3$ and $x = 2$. In other words, the vector $u = (2, 3, 5)$ is a particular nonzero solution.

(c) The following system is reduced to echelon form:

$$
\begin{array}{ccc}
x + \ y - \ z = 0 & \quad x + \ y - \ z = 0 & \quad x + \ y - \ z = 0 \\
2x + 4y - \ z = 0 & \quad 2y + \ z = 0 & \quad 2y + \ z = 0 \\
3x + 2y + 2z = 0 & \quad -y + 5z = 0 & \quad 11z = 0
\end{array}
$$

In echelon form there are three equations in three unknowns. Thus the given system has only the zero solution.

Basis for the General Solution of a Homogeneous System

Let W denote the general solution of a homogeneous system $Ax = 0$. A list of nonzero solution vectors $u_1, u_2, \ldots, u_s$ of the system is said to be a *basis* of W if every solution vector w in W can be expressed uniquely as a *linear combination* of $u_1, u_2, \ldots, u_s$. That is, there exist unique scalars $a_1, a_2, \ldots, a_s$ such that

$$w = a_1 u_1 + a_2 u_2 + \cdots + a_s u_s$$

The number s of such basis vectors is called the *dimension* of W, written $\dim W = s$. In the case where $W = \{0\}$, that is, the system has only the zero solution, we define $\dim W = 0$.

The following theorem, proved in Chapter 5, tells us how to find such a basis.

Theorem 2.7: Let W be the general solution of a homogeneous system $Ax = 0$, and suppose that the echelon form of the homogeneous system has s free variables. Let $u_1, u_2, \ldots, u_s$ be the solutions obtained by setting one of the free variables equal to 1 (or any nonzero constant) and the remaining free variables equal to 0. Then $\dim W = s$ and the vectors $u_1, u_2, \ldots, u_s$ form a basis of W.

EXAMPLE 2.19 Find the dimension and a basis for the general solution W of the homogeneous system

$$x + \ 2y - \ 3z + 2s - \ 4t = 0$$
$$2x + \ 4y - \ 5z + \ s - \ 6t = 0$$
$$5x + 10y - 13z + 4s - 16t = 0$$

First reduce the system to echelon form.   Apply the following operations: "Add $-2L_1$ to L_2" and "Add $-5L_1$ to L_3", and then "Add $-2L_2$ to L_3".   This yields

$$
\begin{aligned}
x + 2y - 3z + 2s - 4t &= 0 \\
z - 3s + 2t &= 0 \\
2z - 6s + 4t &= 0
\end{aligned}
\qquad \text{and} \qquad
\begin{aligned}
x + 2y - 3z + 2s - 4t &= 0 \\
z - 3s + 2t &= 0
\end{aligned}
$$

In echelon form the system has three free variables, y, s, and t; hence dim $W = 3$.   Three solution vectors which form a basis for W are obtained as follows:

(1)   Set $y = 1$, $s = 0$, $t = 0$.   Back-substitution yields the solution $u_1 = (-2, 1, 0, 0, 0)$.
(2)   Set $y = 0$, $s = 1$, $t = 0$.   Back-substitution yields the solution $u_2 = (7, 0, 3, 1, 0)$.
(3)   Set $y = 0$, $s = 0$, $t = 1$.   Back-substitution yields the solution $u_3 = (-2, 0, -2, 0, 1)$.

The list u_1, u_2, u_3 is a basis for W.
Now any solution of the system can be written in the form

$$au_1 + bu_2 + cu_3 = a(-2, 1, 0, 0, 0) + b(7, 0, 3, 1, 0) + c(-2, 0, -2, 0, 1)$$

$$= (-2a + 7b - 2c, a, 3b - 2c, b, c)$$

where a, b, and c are arbitrary constants.   Observe that this representation is nothing more than the parametric form of the general solution under the choice of parameters $y = a$, $s = b$, and $t = c$.

Nonhomogeneous and Associated Homogeneous Systems

Let $Ax = b$ be an arbitrary nonhomogeneous system of linear equations.   Then $Ax = 0$ is called the *homogeneous system associated with the system* $Ax = b$.   For example,

$$
\begin{aligned}
x + 2y - 4z &= 1 \\
2x + 5y - 7z &= 4
\end{aligned}
\qquad \text{and} \qquad
\begin{aligned}
x + 2y - 4z &= 0 \\
2x + 5y - 7z &= 0
\end{aligned}
$$

shows a nonhomogeneous system and its associated homogeneous system.
The relationship between the solution U of a nonhomogeneous system $Ax = b$ and the solution W of a homogeneous system $Ax = 0$ is contained in the following theorem.

Theorem 2.8:   Let v_0 be a particular solution of $Ax = b$, and let W be the general solution of $Ax = 0$.   Then

$$U = v_0 + W = \{v_0 + w : \quad w \in W\}$$

is the general solution of $Ax = b$.

That is, $U = v_0 + W$ may be obtained by adding v_0 to each element of W.   We note that this theorem has a geometrical interpretation in $\mathbf{R}^3$.   Specifically, suppose W is a line through the origin O.   Then, as pictured in Fig. 2-10, $U = v_0 + W$ is the line parallel to W which can be obtained by adding v_0 to each element of W.   Similarly, whenever W is a plane through the origin O, then $U = v_0 + W$ is a plane parallel to W.

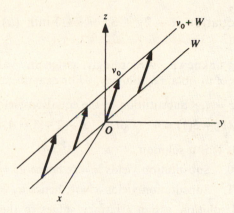

Fig. 2-10

Solved Problems

LINEAR EQUATIONS, SOLUTIONS

2.1. Determine whether each equation is linear.

(a) $5x + 7y - 8yz = 16$;   (b) $x + \pi y + ez = \log 5$;   (c) $3x + ky - 8z = 16$.

(a) No, since the product yz of two unknowns is of second degree.
(b) Yes, since π, e, and $\log 5$ are constants.
(c) As it stands, there are four unknowns: x, y, z, and k. Because of the term ky it is not a linear equation. However, assuming k is a constant, the equation is linear in the unknowns x, y, and z.

2.2. Consider the linear equation $x + 2y - 3z = 4$. Determine whether $u = (8, 1, 2)$ is a solution.

Since x, y, z is the ordering of the unknowns, $u = (8, 1, 2)$ is short for $x = 8$, $y = 1$, $z = 2$. Substitute into the equation to obtain

$$8 + 2(1) - 3(2) = 4 \quad \text{or} \quad 8 + 2 - 6 = 4 \quad \text{or} \quad 4 = 4$$

Yes, it is a solution.

2.3. Determine whether (a) $u = (3, 2, 1, 0)$ and (b) $v = (1, 2, 4, 5)$ are solutions of the equation $x_1 + 2x_2 - 4x_3 + x_4 = 3$.

(a) Substitute to obtain $3 + 2(2) - 4(1) + 0 = 3$, or $3 = 3$; yes, it is a solution.
(b) Substitute to obtain $1 + 2(2) - 4(4) + 5 = 3$, or $-6 = 3$; no, it is not a solution.

2.4. Is $u = (6, 4, -2)$ a solution of the equation $3x_2 + x_3 - x_1 = 4$?

By convention, the components of u are ordered according to the subscripts on the unknowns. That is, $u = (6, 4, -2)$ is short for $x_1 = 6$, $x_2 = 4$, $x_3 = -2$. Substitute into the equation to obtain $3(4) - 2 - 6 = 4$, or $4 = 4$. Yes, it is a solution.

2.5. Consider the linear equation $x - 2y + 3z = 4$. Find: (a) three particular solutions; (b) the general solution.

(a) Here x is the leading unknown. Accordingly, assign any values to the free variables y and z, and then solve for x to obtain a solution. For example:

    (1) Set $y = 1$ and $z = 1$. Substitution in the equation yields

$$x - 2(1) + 3(1) = 4 \quad \text{or} \quad x - 2 + 3 = 4 \quad \text{or} \quad x = 3$$

    Thus $u_1 = (3, 1, 1)$ is a solution.

    (2) Set $y = 1$, $z = 0$. Substitution yields $x = 6$; hence $u_2 = (6, 1, 0)$ is a solution.

    (3) Set $y = 0$, $z = 1$. Substitution yields $x = 1$; hence $u_3 = (1, 0, 1)$ is a solution.

(b) To find the general solution, assign arbitrary values to the free variables, say $y = a$ and $z = b$. (We call a and b parameters of the solution.) Then substitute into the equation to obtain

$$x - 2a + 3b = 4 \quad \text{or} \quad x = 4 + 2a - 3b$$

Thus $u = (4 + 2a - 3b, a, b)$ is the general solution.

2.6. Describe the solutions of each equation:

(a) $2x + y + x - 5 = 2y + 3x - y + 4$.
(b) $2y + 3x - y + 4 = x + 3 + y + 1 + 2x$.

(a) Rewrite in standard form by collecting terms and transposing:

$$3x + y - 5 = y + 3x + 4 \quad \text{or} \quad 0x + 0y = 9$$

The equation is degenerate with a nonzero constant; thus it has no solution.

(b) Rewrite in standard form by collecting terms and transposing:

$$y + 3x + 4 = 3x + 4 + y \quad \text{or} \quad 0x + 0y = 0$$

The equation is degenerate with a zero constant; thus every vector $u = (a, b)$ in $\mathbf{R}^2$ is a solution.

2×2 SYSTEMS

2.7. Solve the system

$$2x - 5y = 11$$
$$3x + 4y = 5$$

Eliminate x from the equations by forming the new equation $L = -3L_1 + 2L_2$. That is, multiply the first equation L_1 by -3 and the second equation L_2 by 2 so that the coefficients of x are negative of each other, and then add the resulting equations:

$$
\begin{array}{rl}
-3L_1: & -6x + 15y = -33 \\
2L_2: & \underline{6x + 8y = 10} \\
\text{Addition:} & 23y = -23
\end{array}
$$

Solve the new equation for y to obtain $y = -1$. Substitute $y = -1$ into one of the original equations, say L_1, to get

$$2x - 5(-1) = 11 \quad \text{or} \quad 2x + 5 = 11 \quad \text{or} \quad 2x = 6 \quad \text{or} \quad x = 3$$

Thus $x = 3$, $y = -1$ or the pair $u = (3, -1)$ is the unique solution of the system.

2.8.   Solve the system

$$3x + 4y = 10$$
$$5x - 4y = 6$$

Here the coefficients of y are already negatives of each other.   Thus first eliminate y by simply adding the equations, that is, by forming the new equation $L = L_1 + L_2$:

$$
\begin{aligned}
L_1: \quad & 3x + 4y = 10 \\
L_2: \quad & 5x - 4y = 6 \\
\hline
\text{Addition:} \quad & 8x \qquad = 16
\end{aligned}
$$

Solve the new equation for x to get $x = 2$.   Substitute $x = 2$ into L_1 to obtain

$$3(2) + 4y = 10 \quad \text{or} \quad 6 + 4y = 10 \quad \text{or} \quad 4y = 4 \quad \text{or} \quad y = 1$$

Thus $x = 2$, $y = 1$ or the pair $u = (2, 1)$ is the unique solution of the system.

2.9.   Solve the system

$$2x - 3y = 8$$
$$-6x + 9y = 6$$

Eliminate x from the equations by forming the new equation $L = 3L_1 + L_2$, that is, by multiplying the first equation L_1 by 3 and adding it to the second equation L_2:

$$
\begin{aligned}
3L_1: \quad & 6x - 9y = 24 \\
L_2: \quad & -6x + 9y = 6 \\
\hline
\text{Addition:} \quad & 0x + 0y = 30
\end{aligned}
$$

This new equation $0x + 0y = 30$ is a degenerate equation with a nonzero constant 30; therefore the equation and the system have no solution.   (Geometrically, the lines corresponding to the equations are parallel.)

2.10.   Solve the system

$$2x - 3y = 8$$
$$-4x + 6y = -16$$

Eliminate x from the equations by forming the new equation $L = 2L_1 + L_2$, that is, by multiplying the first equation L_1 by 2 and adding it to the second equation L_2:

$$
\begin{aligned}
2L_1: \quad & 4x - 6y = 16 \\
L_2: \quad & -4x + 6y = -16 \\
\hline
\text{Addition:} \quad & 0x + 0y = 0
\end{aligned}
$$

This new equation $0x + 0y = 0$ is a degenerate equation where the constant term is also zero.   Thus the system has an infinite number of solutions, which correspond to the solutions of either equation.   (Geometrically, the lines corresponding to the equations coincide.)

To find the general solution of the system, set $y = a$ and substitute in L_1 to obtain

$$2x - 3a = 8 \quad \text{or} \quad 2x = 3a + 8 \quad \text{or} \quad x = \tfrac{3}{2}a + 4$$

Thus the general solution of the system is

$$x = \tfrac{3}{2}a + 4, \ y = a \quad \text{or} \quad u = (\tfrac{3}{2}a + 4, a)$$

where a is any real number.

2.11. Solve the system

$$2x - 3y = 4$$
$$7x + 4y = 5$$

Eliminate x from the equations by forming the new equation $L = -7L_1 + 2L_2$:

$$
\begin{array}{rl}
-7L_1: & -14x + 21y = -28 \\
2L_2: & \underline{14x + 8y = 10} \\
\text{Addition:} & 29y = -18
\end{array}
$$

Solve for y to obtain $y = -18/29$. Now eliminate y from the original equations by forming the new equation $L' = 4L_1 + 3L_2$:

$$
\begin{array}{rl}
4L_1: & 8x - 12y = 16 \\
3L_2: & \underline{21x + 12y = 15} \\
\text{Addition:} & 29x = 31
\end{array}
$$

Solve for x to obtain $x = 31/29$. Thus $x = 31/29$, $y = -18/29$ or the pair $u = (31/29, -18/29)$ is the unique solution of the system.

   Remark: A fraction was obtained for the value of y. Hence it is usually easier (by hand) to solve for x independently, as above, instead of using the fractional value of y to find x.

2.12. Without solving, determine whether the solution of each 2×2 system is unique, empty (no solution), or infinite.

(a) $2x + y = 5$ (b) $-x + 3y = 5$ (c) $3x - 6y = -15$
   $x + 2y = 5$ $2x - 6y = 10$ $-x + 2y = 5$

(d) $3x - 2y = 7$ (e) $3x + 5y = 15$ (f) $7y = 2$
   $5x = 4$ $5x + 3y = 9$ $3x + 5y = 4$

   If the lines are neither horizontal nor vertical, the solution of the system

$$A_1 x + B_1 y = C_1$$
$$A_2 x + B_2 y = C_2$$

is unique, empty, or infinite according to

$$\frac{A_1}{A_2} \neq \frac{B_1}{B_2}, \qquad \frac{A_1}{A_2} = \frac{B_1}{B_2} \neq \frac{C_1}{C_2} \qquad \text{or} \qquad \frac{A_1}{A_2} = \frac{B_1}{B_2} = \frac{C_1}{C_2}$$

(a)   Since $2/1 \neq 1/2$, the solution is unique (intersecting lines).

(b)   Since $-1/2 = 3/-6 \neq 5/10$, the solution is empty (parallel lines).

(c)   Since $3/-1 = -6/2 = -15/5$, the solution is infinite (coincident lines).

(d)   The vertical line $5x = 4$ intersects the nonvertical line in a single solution point.

(e)   Since $3/5 \neq 5/3$, the solution is unique.

(f)   The horizontal line $7y = 2$ intersects the nonhorizontal line in a single solution point.

2.13. For which value(s) of k is the solution of each system (1) unique, (2) empty, (3) infinite?

(a) $2x + ky = 5$ (b) $kx + y = 3$
     $kx + 8y = 10$ $x + ky = 3$

(a) The solution is unique when

$$2/k \neq k/8 \quad \text{or} \quad k^2 \neq 16 \quad \text{or} \quad k \neq \pm 4$$

If $k = 4$, then $2/4 = 4/8 = 5/10$, and hence the solution is infinite. On the other hand, if $k = -4$, then $2/-4 = -4/8 \neq 5/10$, and the solution is empty.

(b) The solution is unique when

$$k/1 \neq 1/k \quad \text{or} \quad k^2 \neq 1 \quad \text{or} \quad k \neq \pm 1$$

If $k = 1$, then $1/1 = 1/1 = 3/3$, and hence the solution is infinite. On the other hand, if $k = -1$, then $-1/1 = 1/-1 \neq 3/3$, and the solution is empty.

LINE OF BEST FIT (LEAST SQUARES)

2.14. Find the line L of best fit for each set of points:

(a) $(1,1)$, $(2,6)$, $(3,9)$, $(4,13)$, $(5,15)$

(b) $(1,3)$, $(3,4)$, $(4,6)$, $(7,8)$, $(10,9)$

Use formula (2.4) to find the slope m and the y intercept b of line L, where N is the number of points.

(a) Here $N = 5$. First form the table in Fig. 2-11(a). Specifically, list (in columns with their sums) the x values and the y values. Then list the x^2 values to the left of the x values and the xy values to the right of the y values. Substitution in formula (2.4) yields the system

$$5b + 15m = 44$$
$$15b + 55m = 167$$

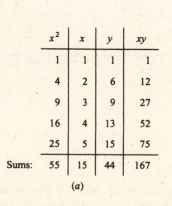

x^2	x	y	xy
1	1	1	1
4	2	6	12
9	3	9	27
16	4	13	52
25	5	15	75
Sums: 55	15	44	167

(a)

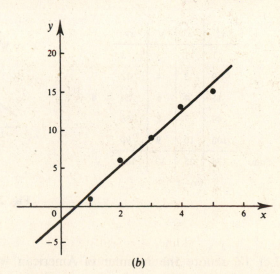

(b)

Fig. 2-11

Eliminate b by forming the new equation $L = -3L_1 + L_2$:

$$
\begin{array}{rl}
-3L_1: & -15b - 45m = -132 \\
L_2: & \underline{15b + 55m = 167} \\
\text{Addition:} & 10m = 35
\end{array}
$$

Thus $m = 3.5$. Substitute $m = 3.5$ into the first equation to obtain

$$5b + 15(3.5) = 44 \quad \text{or} \quad 5b + 52.5 = 44 \quad \text{or} \quad 5b = -8.5 \quad \text{or} \quad b = -1.7$$

Thus $y = 3.5x - 1.7$ is the equation of line L. The original points and line L are plotted in Fig. 2-11(b).

(b)   Here $N = 5$. Form, as above, the table in Fig. 2-12(a). Substitution in formula (2.4) yields the system

$$
\begin{array}{rlcrl}
5b + & 25m = & 30 & \quad \text{or} \quad & b + & 5m = & 6 \\
25b + & 175m = & 185 & & 5b + & 35m = & 37
\end{array}
$$

Eliminate b by forming the new equation $L = -5L_1 + L_2$:

$$
\begin{array}{rl}
-5L_1: & -5b - 25m = -30 \\
L_2: & \underline{5b + 35m = 37} \\
\text{Addition:} & 10m = 7
\end{array}
$$

Thus $m = 0.7$. Substitute $m = 0.7$ into the first equation to obtain

$$b + 5(0.7) = 6 \quad \text{or} \quad b + 3.5 = 6 \quad \text{or} \quad b = 2.5$$

Thus $y = 0.7x + 2.5$ is the equation of line L. The original points and line L are plotted in Fig. 2-12(b).

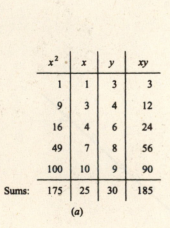

x^2	x	y	xy
1	1	3	3
9	3	4	12
16	4	6	24
49	7	8	56
100	10	9	90
Sums: 175	25	30	185

(a)

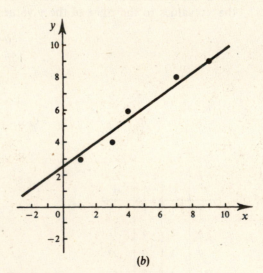

(b)

Fig. 2-12

2.15. Let W denote the number of American women graduating with a doctoral degree in mathematics in a given year. Suppose, for certain years, W has the following values:

Year	1975	1980	1985	1990
W	28	36	40	45

Assuming the increase, year by year, is approximately linear and that it will increase linearly in the near future, estimate W for the years 1995, 1998, and 2000.

Find the line L of best fit for the data.   There are $N = 4$ points.   Form, as above, the table in Fig. 2-13(a).   Substitution in formula (2.4) yields the system

$$4b + \quad 330m = \quad 149 \quad \text{or} \quad 4b + \quad 330m = \quad 149$$
$$330b + 27{,}350m = 12{,}430 \qquad 33b + 2735m = 1243$$

Eliminate b by forming the new equation $L = -33L_1 + 4L_2$.   This gives $50m = 55$, and hence $m = 1.1$.   Substitute $m = 1.1$ into the first equation to obtain $b = -53.5$.   Thus

$$y = 1.1x - 53.5 \tag{1}$$

is the equation of line L.   The original points and line L are plotted in Fig. 2-13(b).

Substitute 95, 98, and 100 in Eq. (1) to obtain 51, 54.3, and 56.5, respectively.   Thus one would expect that, approximately, $W = 51$, $W = 54$, and $W = 57$ women will receive doctoral degrees in mathematics in the years 1995, 1998, and 2000, respectively.

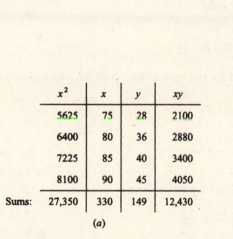

x^2	x	y	xy
5625	75	28	2100
6400	80	36	2880
7225	85	40	3400
8100	90	45	4050
Sums: 27,350	330	149	12,430

(a)

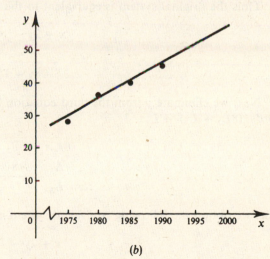

(b)

Fig. 2-13

3 × 3 SYSTEMS

2.16. Solve the system

$$5x - 3y + 2z = 1$$
$$2y - 5z = 2$$
$$4z = 8$$

The system is in triangular form; hence solve by back-substitution. The last equation yields $z = 2$. Substitute $z = 2$ in the second equation to obtain

$$2y - 5(2) = 2 \quad \text{or} \quad 2y - 10 = 2 \quad \text{or} \quad 2y = 12 \quad \text{or} \quad y = 6$$

Substitute $z = 2$ and $y = 6$ in the first equation to obtain

$$5x - 3(6) + 2(2) = 1 \quad \text{or} \quad 5x - 14 = 1 \quad \text{or} \quad 5x = 15 \quad \text{or} \quad x = 3$$

Thus $x = 3$, $y = 6$, $z = 2$ or the triple $u = (3, 6, 2)$ is the unique solution of the system.

2.17. Solve the system

$$\begin{aligned}
x + 2y - 4z &= -4 \\
5x + 11y - 21z &= -22 \\
3x - 2y + 3z &= 11
\end{aligned}$$

Reduce the system to triangular form. First eliminate x from the second and third equations by applying the operations "Add $-5L_1$ to L_2" and "Add $-3L_1$ to L_3", or, in other words, by applying $(-5L_1 + L_2) \to L_2$ and $(-3L_1 + L_3) \to L_3$:

$$
\begin{array}{rl}
-5L_1\text{:} & -5x - 10y + 20z = 20 \\
L_2\text{:} & \underline{5x + 11y - 21z = -22} \\
\text{New } L_2\text{:} & y - z = -2
\end{array}
\qquad
\begin{array}{rl}
-3L_1\text{:} & -3x - 6y + 12z = 12 \\
L_3\text{:} & \underline{3x - 2y + 3z = 11} \\
\text{New } L_3\text{:} & -8y + 15z = 23
\end{array}
$$

Thus the original system is equivalent to the system

$$\begin{aligned}
x + 2y - 4z &= -4 \\
y - z &= -2 \\
-8y + 15z &= 23
\end{aligned}$$

Next we eliminate y from the third equation by the operation "Add $8L_2$ to L_3" or, in other words, $(8L_2 + L_3) \to L_3$:

$$
\begin{array}{rl}
8L_2\text{:} & 8y - 8z = -16 \\
L_3\text{:} & \underline{-8y + 15z = 23} \\
\text{New } L_3\text{:} & 7z = 7
\end{array}
$$

Thus we obtain the following equivalent system in triangular form:

$$\begin{aligned}
x + 2y - 4z &= -4 \\
y - z &= -2 \\
7z &= 7
\end{aligned}$$

Now solve the simpler triangular system by back-substitution. The last equation yields $z = 1$. Substitute $z = 1$ into the second equation to obtain $y = -1$. Now substitute $z = 1$ and $y = -1$ into the first equation to obtain

$$x + 2(-1) - 4(1) = -4 \quad \text{or} \quad x - 2 - 4 = -4 \quad \text{or} \quad x - 6 = -4 \quad \text{or} \quad x = 2$$

Thus $x = 2$, $y = -1$, $z = 1$ or, in other words, the triple $u = (2, -1, 1)$ is the unique solution of the system.

2.18. Solve the system

$$2x + y - 2z = 10$$
$$3x + 2y + 2z = 1$$
$$5x + 4y + 3z = 4$$

Reduce the system to triangular form. First eliminate x from the second and third equations by applying the operations "Add $-3L_1$ to $2L_2$" and "Add $-5L_1$ to $2L_3$" or, in other words, by applying $(-3L_1 + 2L_2) \to L_2$ and $(-5L_1 + 2L_3) \to L_3$:

$-3L_1$:	$-6x - 3y + 6z = -30$	$-5L_1$:	$-10x - 5y + 10z = -50$
$2L_2$:	$6x + 4y + 4z = 2$	$2L_3$:	$10x + 8y + 6z = 8$
New L_2:	$y + 10z = -28$	New L_3:	$3y + 16z = -42$

Thus the original system is equivalent to the system

$$2x + y - 2z = 10$$
$$y + 10z = -28$$
$$3y + 16z = -42$$

Next we eliminate y from the third equation by the operation "Add $-3L_2$ to L_3" or, in other words, $(-3L_2 + L_3) \to L_3$:

$-3L_2$:	$-3y - 30z = 84$
L_3:	$3y + 16z = -42$
New L_3:	$-14z = 42$

Thus we obtain the following equivalent system in triangular form:

$$2x + y - 2z = 10$$
$$y + 10z = -28$$
$$-14z = 42$$

The triangular system could have been obtained by using the condensed format as follows:

Number	Equation	Operation
(1)	$2x + y - 2z = 10$	
(2)	$3x + 2y + 2z = 1$	
(3)	$5x + 4y + 3z = 4$	
(2′)	$y + 10z = -28$	Add $-3L_1$ to $2L_2$.
(3′)	$3y + 16z = -42$	Add $-5L_1$ to $2L_3$.
(3″)	$-14z = 42$	Add $-3L_2$ to L_3.

Here Eqs. (1), (2′), and (3″) form the triangular system.

Now use back-substitution to obtain the unique solution from the triangular system. The last equation yields $z = -3$. Substitute $z = -3$ in the second equation to obtain $y = 2$. Then substitute $y = 2$ and $z = -3$ in the first equation to get $x = 1$. Thus $x = 1$, $y = 2$, $z = -3$ or, equivalently, $u = (1, 2, -3)$ is the unique solution of the system.

2.19. Solve the system

$$x + 2y - 3z = -1$$
$$-3x + y - 2z = -7$$
$$5x + 3y - 4z = 2$$

Eliminate x from the second and third equations by the operations "Add $3L_1$ to L_2" and "Add $-5L_1$ to L_3". This gives the equivalent system

$$x + 2y - 3z = -1$$
$$7y - 11z = -10$$
$$-7y + 11z = 7$$

Next eliminate y from the third equation by adding the second equation to the third equation, that is, by applying the operation "Add L_2 to L_3". This yields the equation

$$0x + 0y + 0z = -3$$

This is a degenerate equation with a nonzero constant -3. Thus this equation and, hence, the system have no solution.

2.20. Solve the system

$$x + 2y - 3z = 1$$
$$2x + 5y - 8z = 4$$
$$3x + 8y - 13z = 7$$

Eliminate x from the second and third equations by applying the operations "Add $-2L_1$ to L_2" and "Add $-3L_1$ to L_3". This yields the new system

$$
\begin{array}{ccc}
x + 2y - 3z = 1 & & x + 2y - 3z = 1 \\
y - 2z = 2 & \text{or} & y - 2z = 2 \\
2y - 4z = 4 & &
\end{array}
$$

(The third equation is deleted since it is a multiple of the second equation.) Observe that any value for z gives a triangular system involving x and y or, in other words, z is a free variable. Hence the system has an infinite number of solutions, one for each value of z.

To obtain the general solution, set $z = a$ and solve for x and y by back-substitution. Substitute $z = a$ in the second equation to obtain $y = 2 + 2a$. Then substitute $z = a$ and $y = 2 + 2a$ into the first equation to obtain

$$x + 2(2 + 2a) - 3a = 1 \qquad \text{or} \qquad x + 4 + 4a - 3a = 1 \qquad \text{or} \qquad x = -3 - a$$

Thus the general solution is

$$x = -3 - a, \ y = 2 + 2a, \ z = a \qquad \text{or} \qquad u = (-3 - a, 2 + 2a, a)$$

where a (called a parameter) is any real number.

2.21. Solve the system

$$2y + 3z = 3$$
$$x + y + z = 4$$
$$4x + 8y - 3z = 35$$

Since the coefficient of x (the pivot) is zero in the first equation, begin by interchanging L_1 and L_2 to obtain the following (equivalent) system with a nonzero pivot:

$$\begin{aligned} x + y + z &= 4 \\ 2y + 3z &= 3 \\ 4x + 8y - 3z &= 35 \end{aligned}$$

Now eliminate x from the third equation L_3 by applying "Add $-4L_1$ to L_3" and then eliminate y from the (new) third equation L_3 by applying "Add $-2L_2$ to L_3". This yields

$$\begin{aligned} x + y + z &= 4 \\ 2y + 3z &= 3 \\ 4y - 7z &= 19 \end{aligned} \quad \text{and then} \quad \begin{aligned} x + y + z &= 4 \\ 2y + 3z &= 3 \\ -13z &= 13 \end{aligned}$$

where the last system is in triangular form.

The triangular system could have been obtained by using the condensed format as follows:

Number		Equation	Operation
(2)	(1)	$2y + 3z = 3$	$L_1 \leftrightarrow L_2$
(1)	(2)	$x + y + z = 4$	$L_1 \leftrightarrow L_2$
	(3)	$4x + 8y - 3z = 35$	
	(3')	$4y - 7z = 19$	Add $-4L_1$ to L_3.
	(3")	$-13z = 13$	Add $-2L_2$ to L_3.

Here Eqs. (1), (2), and (3") form the triangular system. (We emphasize that the interchange $L_1 \leftrightarrow L_2$ is accomplished by simply renumbering L_1 and L_2 as above.)

Using back-substitution with the triangular system yields $z = -1$ from L_3, $y = 3$ from L_2, and $x = 2$ from L_1. Thus $x = 2$, $y = 3$, $z = -1$ or the triple $u = (2, 3, -1)$ is the unique solution of the system.

$m \times n$ SYSTEMS, ECHELON FORM

2.22. Determine the basic and free variables in each system:

(a) $\begin{aligned} 3x + 2y - 5z - 6s + 2t &= 4 \\ z + 8s - 3t &= 6 \\ s - 5t &= 5 \end{aligned}$ (b) $\begin{aligned} 5x - 3y + 7z &= 1 \\ 4y + 5z &= 6 \\ 4z &= 9 \end{aligned}$ (c) $\begin{aligned} x + 2y - 3z &= 2 \\ 2x - 3y + z &= 1 \\ 5x - 4y - z &= 4 \end{aligned}$

(a) In echelon form, the leading variables are the basic variables, and the others are the free variables. Here x, z, and s are the basic variables and y and t are the free variables.
(b) The leading unknowns are x, y, and z, so they are the basic variables; there are no free variables (as in any triangular system).
(c) The notion of basic and free variables applies only to a system in echelon form.

2.23. Find the general solution of the echelon system

$$\begin{aligned} x - 2y - 3z + 5s - 2t &= 4 \\ 2z - 6s + 3t &= 2 \\ 5t &= 10 \end{aligned}$$

The equations begin with the unknowns x, z, and t, so these are the basic variables. The other unknowns y and s are the free variables. To find the general solution, assign parameters to the free variables, say $y = a$ and $s = b$, and use back-substitution to solve for the basic variables x, z, and t.

(i)   The last equation yields $t = 2$.

(ii) Substitute $t = 2$, $s = b$ in the second equation to obtain

$$2z - 6b + 3(2) = 2 \quad \text{or} \quad 2z - 6b + 6 = 2 \quad \text{or} \quad 2z = 6b - 4 \quad \text{or} \quad z = 3b - 2$$

(iii) Substitute $t = 2$, $s = b$, $z = 3b - 2$, and $y = a$ in the first equation to obtain

$$x - 2a - 3(3b - 2) + 5b - 2(2) = 4 \quad \text{or} \quad x - 2a - 9b + 6 + 5b - 4 = 4 \quad \text{or} \quad x = 2a + 4b + 2$$

Thus

$$x = 2a + 4b + 2, \qquad y = a, \qquad z = 3b - 2, \qquad s = b, \qquad t = 2$$

or, equivalently,

$$u = (2a + 4b + 2, a, 3b - 2, b, 2)$$

is the parametric form of the general solution.

Alternatively, solving for x, z, and t in terms of the free variables y and s yields the following free-variable form of the general solution:

$$x = 2y + 4s + 2, \qquad z = 3s - 2, \qquad t = 2$$

2.24. Solve the system

$$\begin{aligned} x - 3y + 2z - s + 2t &= 2 \\ 3x - 9y + 7z - s + 3t &= 7 \\ 2x - 6y + 7z + 4s - 5t &= 7 \end{aligned}$$

Reduce the system to echelon form. Apply the operations "Add $-3L_1$ to L_2" and "Add $-2L_1$ to L_3". This yields

$$\begin{aligned} x - 3y + 2z - s + 2t &= 2 \\ z + 2s - 3t &= 1 \\ 3z + 6s - 9t &= 3 \end{aligned} \qquad \text{or} \qquad \begin{aligned} x - 3y + 2z - s + 2t &= 2 \\ z + 2s - 3t &= 1 \end{aligned}$$

(We delete L_3 because it is a multiple of L_2.) The system is now in echelon form with free variables y, s, and t. To obtain the parametric form of the general solution, set $y = a$, $s = b$, and $t = c$, where a, b, and c are parameters. Back-substitution yields $z = 1 - 2b + 3c$ and then $x = 3a + 5b - 8c$. Thus the general solution is $x = 3a + 5b - 8c$, $y = a$, $z = 1 - 2b + 3c$, $s = b$, $t = c$ or, equivalently $u = (3a + 5b - 8c, a, 1 - 2b + 3c, b, c)$.

2.25. Solve the system

$$x + 2y - 3z + 4t = 2$$
$$2x + 5y - 2z + t = 1$$
$$5x + 12y - 7z + 6t = 7$$

Reduce the system to echelon form. Eliminate x from the second and third equations by the operations "Add $-2L_1$ to L_2" and "Add $-5L_1$ to L_3". This yields the system

$$x + 2y - 3z + 4t = 2$$
$$y + 4z - 7t = -3$$
$$2y + 8z - 14t = -3$$

The operation "Add $-2L_2$ to L_3" yields the degenerate equation $0 = 3$. Thus the system has no solution (even though the system has more unknowns than equations).

2.26. Solve the system

$$x + 2y - 3z + 5t = 1$$
$$x + y - 2z + 7t = 4$$
$$2x + 7y - 7z + 7t = 2$$
$$4x + 9y - 10z + 14t = 6$$

Reduce the system to echelon form using the condensed format, as follows:

Number	Equation	Operation
(1)	$x + 2y - 3z + 5t = 1$	
(2')	$-y + z + 2t = 3$	Add $-L_1$ to L_2.
(3')	$3y - z - 3t = 0$	Add $-2L_1$ to L_3.
(4')	$y + 2z - 6t = 2$	Add $-4L_1$ to L_4.
(3")	$2z + 3t = 9$	Add $3L_2$ to L_3.
(4")	$3z - 4t = 5$	Add $L_2 + L_4$.
(4''')	$-17t = -17$	Add $-3L_3$ to $2L_4$.

The Eqs. (1), (2'), (3"), and (4''') form a system in echelon form. In fact, it is in triangular form. Back-substitution yields $t = 1$ from Eq. (4'''), $z = 3$ from Eq. (3"), $y = 2$ from Eq. (2'), and $x = 1$ from Eq. (1). Thus the unique solution is $x = 1$, $y = 2$, $z = 3$, $t = 1$ or, equivalently, $u = (1, 2, 3, 1)$.

2.27. Solve the system

$$2x - 5y + 3z - 4s + 2t = 4$$
$$3x - 7y + 2z - 5s + 4t = 9$$
$$5x - 10y - 5z - 4s + 7t = 22$$

Reduce the system to echelon form using the condensed format, as follows:

Number	Equation	Operation
(1)	$2x - 5y + 3z - 4s + 2t = 4$	
(2')	$y - 5z + 2s + 2t = 6$	Add $-3L_1$ to $2L_2$.
(3')	$5y - 25z - 12s + 4t = 24$	Add $-5L_1$ to $2L_3$.
(3'')	$2s - 6t = -6$	Add $-5L_2$ to L_3.

The Eqs. (1), (2'), and (3'') form a system in echelon form with basic variables x, y, and s and free variables z and t. Use back-substitution to solve for the basic variables in terms of the free variables to obtain the following free-variable form of the general solution:

$$x = 26 + 11z - 15t, \qquad y = 12 + 5z - 8t, \qquad s = -3 + 3t$$

From this follows at once the parametric form of the general solution (where $z = a$, $t = b$):

$$x = 26 + 11a - 15b, \qquad y = 12 + 5a - 8b, \qquad z = a, \qquad s = -3 + 3b, \qquad t = b$$

2.28. Solve the system

$$\begin{aligned} 2y - 3z + t &= 1 \\ x + y - z - 2t &= -2 \\ -2x + 2y - 5z + 7t &= 9 \\ -x + 5y - 9z + 6t &= 8 \end{aligned}$$

First interchange the first and second equations to obtain a nonzero pivot for x. Then, using the condensed format, reduce the system to echelon form as follows:

Number	Equation	Operation
(1)	$x + y - z - 2t = -2$	$L_1 \longleftrightarrow L_2$
(2)	$2y - 3z + t = 1$	
(3)	$-2x + 2y - 5z + 7t = 9$	
(4)	$-x + 5y - 9z + 6t = 8$	
(3')	$4y - 7z + 3t = 5$	Add $2L_1$ to L_3.
(4')	$6y - 10z + 4t = 6$	Add L_1 to L_4.
(3'')	$-z + t = 3$	Add $-2L_2$ to L_3.
(4'')	$-z + t = 3$	Add $-3L_2$ to L_4.

Equation (4'') is deleted since it is a multiple of Eq. (3''). [In fact, Eq. (4'') is identical to Eq. (3'').] The Eqs. (1), (2), and (3'') form a system in echelon form with basic variables x, y, and z and free variable t. Set $t = a$, a parameter, and solve by back-substitution to obtain the general solution $x = -1 + 2a$, $y = -4 + a$, $z = -3 + a$, $t = a$ or, equivalently,

$$u = (-1 + 2a, -4 + a, -3 + a, a)$$

2.29. Solve the system

$$\begin{aligned}
x + y + 2z - s + t &= 3 \\
2x + y + 7z - 4s + t &= 7 \\
x + 3y - 2z + 6s + 5t &= 4 \\
3x + 4y + 5z + 5s + 7t &= 13 \\
-x - 4y + 11z + 5s + 3t &= 7
\end{aligned}$$

Reduce the system to echelon form using the condensed format as follows:

Number	Equation	Operation
(1)	$x + y + 2z - s + t = 3$	
$(2')$	$-y + 3z - 2s - t = 1$	Add $-2L_1$ to L_2.
$(3')$	$2y - 4z + 7s + 4t = 1$	Add $-L_1$ to L_3.
$(4')$	$y - z + 8s + 4t = 4$	Add $-3L_1$ to L_4.
$(5')$	$-3y + 13z + 4s + 4t = 10$	Add L_1 to L_5.
$(3'')$	$2z + 3s + 2t = 3$	Add $2L_2$ to L_3.
$(4'')$	$2z + 6s + 3t = 5$	Add L_2 to L_4.
$(5'')$	$4z + 10s + 7t = 7$	Add $-3L_2$ to L_5.
$(4''')$	$3s + t = 2$	Add $-L_3$ to L_4.
$(5''')$	$4s + 3t = 1$	Add $-2L_3$ to L_5.
$(5'''')$	$5t = -5$	Add $-4L_4$ to $3L_5$.

The Eqs. (1), $(2')$, $(3'')$, $(4''')$, and $(5'''')$ form a system in echelon form. In fact, it is in triangular form. Back-substitution yields the unique solution $x = 2$, $y = 1$, $z = 1$, $s = 1$, $t = -1$ or, equivalently, $u = (2, 1, 1, 1, -1)$.

2.30. Determine the values of k so that the following system in unknowns x, y, z has (i) a unique solution, (ii) no solution, (iii) an infinite number of solutions:

$$\begin{aligned}
x + y - z &= 1 \\
2x + 3y + kz &= 3 \\
x + ky + 3z &= 2
\end{aligned}$$

Reduce the system to echelon form. Eliminate x from the second and third equations by the operations "Add $-2L_1$ to L_2" and "Add $-L_1$ to L_3". This yields

$$\begin{aligned}
x + y - z &= 1 \\
y + (k + 2)z &= 1 \\
(k - 1)y + 4z &= 1
\end{aligned}$$

To eliminate y from the third equation, apply the operation "Add $-(k - 1)L_2$ to L_3". This yields

$$\begin{aligned}
x + y - z &= 1 \\
y + (k + 2)z &= 1 \\
(3 + k)(2 - k)z &= 2 - k
\end{aligned}$$

The system has a unique solution if the coefficient of z in the third equation is not zero, that is, if $k \neq 2$ and $k \neq -3$. In case $k = 2$, the third equation reduces to $0 = 0$ and the system has an infinite number of solutions (one for each value of z). In case $k = -3$, the third equation reduces to $0 = 5$ and the system has no solution. Summarizing: (*i*) $k \neq 2$ and $k \neq -3$, (*ii*) $k = -3$, (*iii*) $k = 2$.

2.31. What condition must be placed on a, b, and c so that the following system in unknowns x, y, and z has a solution:

$$\begin{aligned} x + 2y - 3z &= a \\ 2x + 6y - 11z &= b \\ x - 2y + 7z &= c \end{aligned}$$

Reduce the system to echelon form. Eliminate x from the second and third equations by the operations "Add $-2L_1$ to L_2" and "Add $-L_1$ to L_3". This yields the equivalent system

$$\begin{aligned} x + 2y - 3z &= a \\ 2y - 5z &= b - 2a \\ -4y + 10z &= c - a \end{aligned}$$

To eliminate y from the third equation, apply the operation "Add $2L_2$ to L_3". This yields the equivalent system

$$\begin{aligned} x + 2y - 3z &= a \\ 2y - 5z &= b - 2a \\ 0 &= c + 2b - 5a \end{aligned}$$

The system will have no solution if $c + 2b - 5a \neq 0$. Thus the system will have at least one solution if $c + 2b - 5a = 0$ or $5a = 2b + c$. Note that in this case the system will have infinitely many solutions. In other words, the system cannot have a unique solution.

ECHELON MATRICES, ROW REDUCTION

2.32. Interchange the rows in each of the following matrices to obtain an echelon matrix:

(*a*) $\begin{bmatrix} 0 & 1 & -3 & 4 & 6 \\ 4 & 0 & 2 & 5 & -3 \\ 0 & 0 & 7 & -2 & 8 \end{bmatrix}$ (*b*) $\begin{bmatrix} 0 & 0 & 0 & 0 & 0 \\ 1 & 2 & 3 & 4 & 5 \\ 0 & 0 & 5 & -4 & 7 \end{bmatrix}$ (*c*) $\begin{bmatrix} 0 & 2 & 2 & 2 & 2 \\ 0 & 3 & 1 & 0 & 0 \\ 0 & 0 & 0 & 0 & 0 \end{bmatrix}$

(*a*) Interchange the first and second rows, i.e., apply the elementary row operation $R_1 \leftrightarrow R_2$.

(*b*) Bring the zero row to the bottom of the matrix, i.e., apply $R_1 \leftrightarrow R_2$ and then $R_2 \leftrightarrow R_3$.

(*c*) No amount of row interchanges can produce an echelon matrix.

2.33. Row reduce the following matrix to echelon form:

$$A = \begin{bmatrix} 1 & 2 & -3 & 0 \\ 2 & 4 & -2 & 2 \\ 3 & 6 & -4 & 3 \end{bmatrix}$$

Use a_{11} as a pivot to obtain 0s below a_{11}, that is, apply the row operations "Add $-2R_1$ to R_2" and "Add $-3R_1$ to R_3". This yields the matrix

$$\begin{bmatrix} 1 & 2 & -3 & 0 \\ 0 & 0 & 4 & 2 \\ 0 & 0 & 5 & 3 \end{bmatrix}$$

Now use $a_{23} = 4$ as a pivot to obtain a 0 below a_{23}, that is, apply the row operation "Add $-5R_2$ to $4R_3$" to obtain the matrix

$$\begin{bmatrix} 1 & 2 & -3 & 0 \\ 0 & 0 & 4 & 2 \\ 0 & 0 & 0 & 2 \end{bmatrix}$$

which is in echelon form.

2.34. Row reduce the following matrix to echelon form:

$$B = \begin{bmatrix} -4 & 1 & -6 \\ 1 & 2 & -5 \\ 6 & 3 & -4 \end{bmatrix}$$

Hand calculations are usually simpler if the pivot element equals 1. Therefore, first interchange R_1 and R_2; then apply the operations "Add $4R_1$ to R_2" and "Add $-6R_1$ to R_3"; and then apply the operation "Add R_2 to R_3". These operations yield

$$B \sim \begin{bmatrix} 1 & 2 & -5 \\ -4 & 1 & -6 \\ 6 & 3 & -4 \end{bmatrix} \sim \begin{bmatrix} 1 & 2 & -5 \\ 0 & 9 & -26 \\ 0 & -9 & 26 \end{bmatrix} \sim \begin{bmatrix} 1 & 2 & -5 \\ 0 & 9 & -26 \\ 0 & 0 & 0 \end{bmatrix}$$

The matrix is now in echelon form.

2.35. Describe the *pivoting* row-reduction algorithm. Also describe the advantages, if any, of using this pivoting algorithm.

The row-reduction algorithm becomes a pivoting algorithm if the entry in column j of greatest absolute value is chosen as the pivot a_{1j_1} and if one uses the row operation

$$(-a_{ij_1}/a_{1j_1})R_1 + R_i \to R_i$$

The main advantage of the pivoting algorithm is that the above row operation involves division by the (current) pivot a_{1j_1}, and on the computer, roundoff errors may be substantially reduced when one divides by a number as large in absolute value as possible.

2.36. Use the pivoting algorithm to reduce the following matrix to echelon form:

$$A = \begin{bmatrix} 2 & -2 & 2 & 1 \\ -3 & 6 & 0 & -1 \\ 1 & -7 & 10 & 2 \end{bmatrix}$$

First interchange R_1 and R_2 so that -3 can be used as the pivot, and then apply the operations "Add $\frac{2}{3}R_1$ to R_2" and "Add $\frac{1}{3}R_1$ to R_3". These operations yield

$$A \sim \begin{bmatrix} -3 & 6 & 0 & -1 \\ 2 & -2 & 2 & 1 \\ 1 & -7 & 10 & 2 \end{bmatrix} \sim \begin{bmatrix} -3 & 6 & 0 & -1 \\ 0 & 2 & 2 & \frac{1}{3} \\ 0 & -5 & 10 & \frac{5}{3} \end{bmatrix}$$

Now interchange R_2 and R_3 so that -5 may be used as the pivot, and then apply the operation "Add $\frac{2}{5}R_2$ to R_3". We obtain

$$A \sim \begin{bmatrix} -3 & 6 & 0 & -1 \\ 0 & -5 & 10 & \frac{5}{3} \\ 0 & 2 & 2 & \frac{1}{3} \end{bmatrix} \sim \begin{bmatrix} -3 & 6 & 0 & -1 \\ 0 & -5 & 10 & \frac{5}{3} \\ 0 & 0 & 6 & 1 \end{bmatrix}$$

The matrix has been brought to echelon form using partial pivoting.

ROW CANONICAL FORM

2.37. Which of the following echelon matrices are in row canonical form?

$$\begin{bmatrix} 1 & 2 & -3 & 0 & 1 \\ 0 & 0 & 5 & 2 & -4 \\ 0 & 0 & 0 & 7 & 3 \end{bmatrix} \quad \begin{bmatrix} 0 & 1 & 7 & -5 & 0 \\ 0 & 0 & 0 & 0 & 1 \\ 0 & 0 & 0 & 0 & 0 \end{bmatrix} \quad \begin{bmatrix} 1 & 0 & 5 & 0 & 2 \\ 0 & 1 & 2 & 0 & 4 \\ 0 & 0 & 0 & 1 & 7 \end{bmatrix}$$

The first matrix is not in row canonical form since, for example, two leading nonzero entries are 5 and 7, not 1. Also, there are nonzero entries above the leading nonzero entries 5 and 7. The second and third matrices are in row canonical form.

2.38. Reduce the following matrix to row canonical form:

$$A = \begin{bmatrix} 1 & -2 & 3 & 1 & 2 \\ 1 & 1 & 4 & -1 & 3 \\ 2 & 5 & 9 & -2 & 8 \end{bmatrix}$$

First reduce A to echelon form by applying the operations "Add $-R_1$ to R_2" and "Add $-2R_1$ to R_3", and then apply the operation "Add $-3R_2$ to R_3". These operations yield

$$A \sim \begin{bmatrix} 1 & -2 & 3 & 1 & 2 \\ 0 & 3 & 1 & -2 & 1 \\ 0 & 9 & 3 & -4 & 4 \end{bmatrix} \sim \begin{bmatrix} 1 & -2 & 3 & 1 & 2 \\ 0 & 3 & 1 & -2 & 1 \\ 0 & 0 & 0 & 2 & 1 \end{bmatrix}$$

Now use back-substitution on the echelon matrix to obtain the row canonical form of A. Specifically, first multiply R_3 by $\frac{1}{2}$ to obtain the pivot $a_{34} = 1$, and then apply the operations "Add $2R_3$ to R_2" and "Add $-R_3$ to R_1". These operations yield

$$A \sim \begin{bmatrix} 1 & -2 & 3 & 1 & 2 \\ 0 & 3 & 1 & -2 & 1 \\ 0 & 0 & 0 & 1 & \frac{1}{2} \end{bmatrix} \sim \begin{bmatrix} 1 & -2 & 3 & 0 & \frac{3}{2} \\ 0 & 3 & 1 & 0 & 2 \\ 0 & 0 & 0 & 1 & \frac{1}{2} \end{bmatrix}$$

Now multiply R_2 by $\frac{1}{3}$, making the pivot $a_{22} = 1$, and then apply the operation "Add $2R_2$ to R_1".

We obtain

$$A \sim \begin{bmatrix} 1 & -2 & 3 & 0 & \frac{3}{2} \\ 0 & 1 & \frac{1}{3} & 0 & \frac{2}{3} \\ 0 & 0 & 0 & 1 & \frac{1}{2} \end{bmatrix} \sim \begin{bmatrix} 1 & 0 & \frac{11}{3} & 0 & \frac{17}{6} \\ 0 & 1 & \frac{1}{3} & 0 & \frac{2}{3} \\ 0 & 0 & 0 & 1 & \frac{1}{2} \end{bmatrix}$$

Since $a_{11} = 1$, the last matrix is the desired row canonical form of A.

2.39. Reduce the following matrix to row canonical form:

$$B = \begin{bmatrix} 2 & 2 & -1 & 6 & 4 \\ 4 & 4 & 1 & 10 & 13 \\ 6 & 6 & 0 & 20 & 19 \end{bmatrix}$$

First reduce B to echelon form by applying the operations "Add $-2R_1$ to R_2" and "Add $-3R_1$ to R_3", and then apply the operation "Add $-R_2$ to R_3". These operations yield

$$B \sim \begin{bmatrix} 2 & 2 & -1 & 6 & 4 \\ 0 & 0 & 3 & -2 & 5 \\ 0 & 0 & 3 & 2 & 7 \end{bmatrix} \sim \begin{bmatrix} 2 & 2 & -1 & 6 & 4 \\ 0 & 0 & 3 & -2 & 5 \\ 0 & 0 & 0 & 4 & 2 \end{bmatrix}$$

Now use back-substitution on the echelon matrix to obtain the row canonical form of B. Specifically, first multiply R_3 by $\frac{1}{4}$ to obtain the pivot $b_{34} = 1$, and then apply the operations "Add $2R_3$ to R_2" and "Add $-6R_3$ to R_1". These operations yield

$$B \sim \begin{bmatrix} 2 & 2 & -1 & 6 & 4 \\ 0 & 0 & 3 & -2 & 5 \\ 0 & 0 & 0 & 1 & \frac{1}{2} \end{bmatrix} \sim \begin{bmatrix} 2 & 2 & -1 & 0 & 1 \\ 0 & 0 & 3 & 0 & 6 \\ 0 & 0 & 0 & 1 & \frac{1}{2} \end{bmatrix}$$

Now multiply R_2 by $\frac{1}{3}$, making the pivot $b_{23} = 1$, and then apply the operation "Add R_2 to R_1". We obtain

$$B \sim \begin{bmatrix} 2 & 2 & -1 & 0 & 1 \\ 0 & 0 & 1 & 0 & 2 \\ 0 & 0 & 0 & 1 & \frac{1}{2} \end{bmatrix} \sim \begin{bmatrix} 2 & 2 & 0 & 0 & 3 \\ 0 & 0 & 1 & 0 & 2 \\ 0 & 0 & 0 & 1 & \frac{1}{2} \end{bmatrix}$$

Finally, multiply R_1 by $\frac{1}{2}$, making $b_{11} = 1$. Thus we obtain the following matrix, which is the row canonical form of B:

$$B \sim \begin{bmatrix} 1 & 1 & 0 & 0 & \frac{3}{2} \\ 0 & 0 & 1 & 0 & 2 \\ 0 & 0 & 0 & 1 & \frac{1}{2} \end{bmatrix}$$

2.40. Reduce the following echelon matrix to row canonical form:

$$C = \begin{bmatrix} 5 & -9 & 6 \\ 0 & 2 & 3 \\ 0 & 0 & 7 \end{bmatrix}$$

(In fact, the matrix C is a triangular matrix with nonzero diagonal entries.)

Since C is in echelon form, use back-substitution to obtain

$$C \sim \begin{bmatrix} 5 & -9 & 6 \\ 0 & 2 & 3 \\ 0 & 0 & 1 \end{bmatrix} \sim \begin{bmatrix} 5 & -9 & 0 \\ 0 & 2 & 0 \\ 0 & 0 & 1 \end{bmatrix} \sim \begin{bmatrix} 5 & -9 & 0 \\ 0 & 1 & 0 \\ 0 & 0 & 1 \end{bmatrix} \sim \begin{bmatrix} 5 & 0 & 0 \\ 0 & 1 & 0 \\ 0 & 0 & 1 \end{bmatrix} \sim \begin{bmatrix} 1 & 0 & 0 \\ 0 & 1 & 0 \\ 0 & 0 & 1 \end{bmatrix}$$

The last matrix, which is the row canonical form of C, is the 3×3 identity matrix I.   (See Problem 2.90.)

2.41. Describe the Gauss–Jordan elimination algorithm which also reduces an arbitrary matrix A to its row canonical form.

The Gauss–Jordan algorithm is similar in some ways to the Gaussian elimination algorithm, except that here each pivot is used to place 0s both below and above the pivot, not just below the pivot, before working with the next pivot.   Also, one variation of the algorithm first normalizes each row to obtain a unit pivot before it is used to produce 0s in the other rows, rather than normalizing the rows at the end of the algorithm.

2.42. Use Gauss–Jordan elimination to obtain the row canonical form of the matrix A in Problem 2.38.

Use the leading nonzero entry $a_{11} = 1$ as a pivot to put 0s below it by applying the operations "Add $-R_1$ to R_2" and "Add $-2R_1$ to R_3".   This yields

$$A \sim \begin{bmatrix} 1 & -2 & 3 & 1 & 2 \\ 0 & 3 & 1 & -2 & 1 \\ 0 & 9 & 3 & -4 & 4 \end{bmatrix}$$

Multiply R_2 by $\frac{1}{3}$ to make the pivot $a_{22} = 1$, and then produce 0s below and above a_{22} by applying the operations "Add $-9R_2$ to R_3" and "Add $2R_2$ to R_1".   These operations yield

$$A \sim \begin{bmatrix} 1 & -2 & 3 & 1 & 2 \\ 0 & 1 & \frac{1}{3} & -\frac{2}{3} & \frac{1}{3} \\ 0 & 9 & 3 & -4 & 4 \end{bmatrix} \sim \begin{bmatrix} 1 & 0 & \frac{11}{3} & -\frac{1}{3} & \frac{8}{3} \\ 0 & 1 & \frac{1}{3} & -\frac{2}{3} & \frac{1}{3} \\ 0 & 0 & 0 & 2 & 1 \end{bmatrix}$$

Last, multiply R_3 by $\frac{1}{2}$ to make the pivot $a_{34} = 1$, and then produce 0s above a_{34} by applying the operations "Add $\frac{2}{3}R_3$ to R_2" and "Add $\frac{1}{3}R_3$ to R_1".   We obtain

$$A \sim \begin{bmatrix} 1 & 0 & \frac{11}{3} & -\frac{1}{3} & \frac{8}{3} \\ 0 & 1 & \frac{1}{3} & -\frac{2}{3} & \frac{1}{3} \\ 0 & 0 & 0 & 1 & \frac{1}{2} \end{bmatrix} \sim \begin{bmatrix} 1 & 0 & \frac{11}{3} & 0 & \frac{17}{6} \\ 0 & 1 & \frac{1}{3} & 0 & \frac{2}{3} \\ 0 & 0 & 0 & 1 & \frac{1}{2} \end{bmatrix}$$

which is the row canonical form of A.   (The same matrix was obtained in Problem 2.38.)

2.43. One speaks of "an" echelon form of a matrix A, but "the" row canonical form of A. Why?

An arbitrary matrix A may be row equivalent to many echelon matrices.   On the other hand, regardless of the algorithm used, a matrix A is row equivalent to a unique matrix in row canonical form.   (This fact is the content of Theorem 2.5.)   We note that the term "canonical" usually connotes some type of uniqueness.

MATRIX NOTATION AND 3 × 3 SYSTEMS

2.44. Find the augmented matrix M and the coefficient matrix A of the following system:

$$x + 2y - 3z = 4$$
$$3y - 4z + 7x = 5$$
$$6z + 8x - 9y = 1$$

First align the unknowns in the system to obtain

$$x + 2y - 3z = 4$$
$$7x + 3y - 4z = 5$$
$$8x - 9y + 6z = 1$$

Each row of the augmented matrix M consists of the coefficients and the constant of the corresponding equation, and the coefficient matrix A is simply the matrix of coefficients or, in other words, the augmented matrix M without the last column of constants. Accordingly,

$$M = \begin{bmatrix} 1 & 2 & -3 & 4 \\ 7 & 3 & -4 & 5 \\ 8 & -9 & 6 & 1 \end{bmatrix} \quad \text{and} \quad A = \begin{bmatrix} 1 & 2 & -3 \\ 7 & 3 & -4 \\ 8 & -9 & 6 \end{bmatrix}$$

2.45. Solve the following system using its augmented matrix M:

$$2x + 3y - 4z = 4$$
$$3x + 4y - 3z = 8$$
$$7x + 12y - 12z = 19$$

Write down the coefficients and constants to obtain

$$M = \begin{bmatrix} 2 & 3 & -4 & 4 \\ 3 & 4 & -3 & 8 \\ 7 & 12 & -12 & 19 \end{bmatrix}$$

First reduce M to echelon form. This is accomplished by applying the operations "Add $-3R_1$ to $2R_2$" and "Add $-7R_1$ to $2R_3$", and then the operation "Add $3R_2$ to R_3". These operations yield

$$M \sim \begin{bmatrix} 2 & 3 & -4 & 4 \\ 0 & -1 & 6 & 4 \\ 0 & 3 & 4 & 10 \end{bmatrix} \sim \begin{bmatrix} 2 & 3 & -4 & 4 \\ 0 & -1 & 6 & 4 \\ 0 & 0 & 22 & 22 \end{bmatrix}$$

We can now proceed in two ways.

(1) Write down the corresponding triangular system

$$2x + 3y - 4z = 4$$
$$-y + 6z = 4$$
$$22z = 22$$

Solve by back-substitution to obtain $x = 1$, $y = 2$, $z = 1$.

(2)   Reduce the echelon form of M to row canonical form as follows.   Multiply R_3 by $\frac{1}{22}$ so that the third diagonal entry is 1.   (This essentially solves for z.)   Then put 0s above this diagonal entry by applying the operations "Add $-6R_3$ to R_2" and "Add $4R_3$ to R_1".   (This essentially eliminates z from the second and first equations.)   These operations yield

$$M \sim \begin{bmatrix} 2 & 3 & -4 & 4 \\ 0 & -1 & 6 & 4 \\ 0 & 0 & 1 & 1 \end{bmatrix} \sim \begin{bmatrix} 2 & 3 & 0 & 8 \\ 0 & -1 & 0 & -2 \\ 0 & 0 & 1 & 1 \end{bmatrix}$$

Now multiply R_2 by -1 so that the second diagonal entry is 1.   (This essentially solves for y.)   Then put 0 above this diagonal entry by applying "Add $-3R_2$ to R_1".   (This essentially eliminates y from the first equation.)   These operations yield

$$M \sim \begin{bmatrix} 2 & 3 & 0 & 8 \\ 0 & 1 & 0 & 2 \\ 0 & 0 & 1 & 1 \end{bmatrix} \sim \begin{bmatrix} 2 & 0 & 0 & 2 \\ 0 & 1 & 0 & 2 \\ 0 & 0 & 1 & 1 \end{bmatrix}$$

Lastly, multiply R_1 by $\frac{1}{2}$ so that the first diagonal entry is 1.   (This essentially solves for x.) This operation yields the canonical form

$$\begin{bmatrix} 1 & 0 & 0 & 1 \\ 0 & 1 & 0 & 2 \\ 0 & 0 & 1 & 1 \end{bmatrix}$$

which corresponds to the unique solution $x = 1$, $y = 2$, $z = 1$.

2.46. Solve the following system using its augmented matrix M:

$$2x + 6y - 5z = 2$$
$$2y - 4z + x = -3$$
$$3x - 4z + 11y = 12$$

To obtain the augmented matrix M of the system, first put the system in standard form (with the same unknowns under each other).   This yields

$$\begin{aligned} 2x + 6y - 5z &= 2 \\ x + 2y - 4z &= -3 \\ 3x + 11y - 4z &= 12 \end{aligned} \quad \text{and so} \quad M = \begin{bmatrix} 2 & 6 & -5 & 2 \\ 1 & 2 & -4 & -3 \\ 3 & 11 & -4 & 12 \end{bmatrix}$$

Reduce the augmented matrix M to echelon form.   Since (by hand) it is easier to work with a pivot that is unity, first interchange rows R_1 and R_2.   We get

$$M \sim \begin{bmatrix} 1 & 2 & -4 & -3 \\ 2 & 6 & -5 & 2 \\ 3 & 11 & -4 & 12 \end{bmatrix} \sim \begin{bmatrix} 1 & 2 & -4 & -3 \\ 0 & 2 & 3 & 8 \\ 0 & 5 & 8 & 21 \end{bmatrix} \sim \begin{bmatrix} 1 & 2 & -4 & -3 \\ 0 & 2 & 3 & 8 \\ 0 & 0 & 1 & 2 \end{bmatrix}$$

where the last two matrices were obtained by applying the operations "Add $-2R_1$ to R_2" and "Add $-3R_1$ to R_3" and then applying "Add $-5R_2$ to $2R_3$".   We can now proceed in two ways.

Write down the corresponding triangular system

$$\begin{aligned} x + 2y - 4z &= -3 \\ 2y + 3z &= 8 \\ z &= 2 \end{aligned}$$

Solve by back-substitution to obtain the unique solution $x = 3$, $y = 1$, $z = 2$ or $u = (3, 1, 2)$. Alternately, reduce the echelon form of M to row canonical form, obtaining

$$M \sim \begin{bmatrix} 1 & 2 & 0 & 5 \\ 0 & 2 & 0 & 2 \\ 0 & 0 & 1 & 2 \end{bmatrix} \sim \begin{bmatrix} 1 & 2 & 0 & 5 \\ 0 & 1 & 0 & 1 \\ 0 & 0 & 1 & 2 \end{bmatrix} \sim \begin{bmatrix} 1 & 0 & 0 & 3 \\ 0 & 1 & 0 & 1 \\ 0 & 0 & 1 & 2 \end{bmatrix}$$

Again we obtain the solution $x = 3$, $y = 1$, $z = 2$.

2.47. Solve the following system using the augmented matrix M:

$$\begin{aligned} x + 2y - 4z &= 3 \\ 2x + 6y - 5z &= 10 \\ 3x + 10y - 6z &= 14 \end{aligned}$$

Write down the coefficients and constants to obtain

$$M = \begin{bmatrix} 1 & 2 & -4 & 3 \\ 2 & 6 & -5 & 10 \\ 3 & 10 & -6 & 14 \end{bmatrix}$$

Reduce M to echelon form by first applying the operations "Add $-2R_1$ to R_2" and "Add $-3R_1$ to R_3" and then applying "Add $-2R_2$ to R_3". This yields

$$M \sim \begin{bmatrix} 1 & 2 & -4 & 3 \\ 0 & 2 & 3 & 4 \\ 0 & 4 & 6 & 5 \end{bmatrix} \sim \begin{bmatrix} 1 & 2 & -4 & 3 \\ 0 & 2 & 3 & 4 \\ 0 & 0 & 0 & -3 \end{bmatrix}$$

The last row corresponds to the degenerate equation $0x + 0y + 0z = -3$, which has no solution. Thus *do not continue*. The original system also has no solution.

2.48. Solve the following system using its augmented matrix M:

$$\begin{aligned} x + 2y - z &= 3 \\ x + 3y + z &= 5 \\ 3x + 8y + 4z &= 17 \end{aligned}$$

Reduce the augmented matrix M to echelon form:

$$M = \begin{bmatrix} 1 & 2 & -1 & 3 \\ 1 & 3 & 1 & 5 \\ 3 & 8 & 4 & 17 \end{bmatrix} \sim \begin{bmatrix} 1 & 2 & -1 & 3 \\ 0 & 1 & 2 & 2 \\ 0 & 2 & 7 & 8 \end{bmatrix} \sim \begin{bmatrix} 1 & 2 & -1 & 3 \\ 0 & 1 & 2 & 2 \\ 0 & 0 & 3 & 4 \end{bmatrix}$$

Now write down the corresponding triangular system

$$\begin{aligned} x + 2y - z &= 3 \\ y + 2z &= 2 \\ 3z &= 4 \end{aligned}$$

and solve by back-substitution to obtain the unique solution

$$x = \frac{17}{3}, \quad y = -\frac{2}{3}, \quad z = \frac{4}{3} \qquad \text{or} \qquad u = \left(\frac{17}{3}, -\frac{2}{3}, \frac{4}{3} \right)$$

Alternately, reduce the echelon form of M to row canonical form, obtaining

$$M \sim \begin{bmatrix} 1 & 2 & -1 & 3 \\ 0 & 1 & 2 & 2 \\ 0 & 0 & 1 & \frac{4}{3} \end{bmatrix} \sim \begin{bmatrix} 1 & 2 & 0 & \frac{13}{3} \\ 0 & 1 & 0 & -\frac{2}{3} \\ 0 & 0 & 1 & \frac{4}{3} \end{bmatrix} \sim \begin{bmatrix} 1 & 0 & 0 & \frac{17}{3} \\ 0 & 1 & 0 & -\frac{2}{3} \\ 0 & 0 & 1 & \frac{4}{3} \end{bmatrix}$$

This also corresponds to the above solution.

2.49. Solve the system in Problem 2.45 using the Gauss–Jordan algorithm.

The Gauss–Jordan algorithm reduces the augmented matrix M of the system to row canonical form pivot by pivot as follows. First multiply R_1 by $\frac{1}{2}$ so that the pivot equals 1, and then put 0s below the pivot using the operations "Add $-3R_1$ to R_2" and "Add $-7R_1$ to R_3". This yields

$$M \sim \begin{bmatrix} 1 & \frac{3}{2} & -2 & 2 \\ 3 & 4 & -3 & 8 \\ 7 & 12 & -12 & 19 \end{bmatrix} \sim \begin{bmatrix} 1 & \frac{3}{2} & -2 & 2 \\ 0 & -\frac{1}{2} & 3 & 2 \\ 0 & \frac{3}{2} & 2 & 5 \end{bmatrix}$$

Next multiply R_2 by -2 so that the pivot equals 1, and then use the operations "Add $-\frac{3}{2}R_2$ to R_1" and "Add $-\frac{3}{2}R_2$ to R_3" to put 0s above and below the pivot. This yields

$$M \sim \begin{bmatrix} 1 & \frac{3}{2} & -2 & 2 \\ 0 & 1 & -6 & -4 \\ 0 & \frac{3}{2} & 2 & 5 \end{bmatrix} \sim \begin{bmatrix} 1 & 0 & 7 & 8 \\ 0 & 1 & -6 & -4 \\ 0 & 0 & 11 & 11 \end{bmatrix}$$

Lastly, multiply R_3 by $\frac{1}{11}$ so that the pivot equals 1, and then use the operations "Add $6R_3$ to R_2" and "Add $-7R_3$ to R_1" to put 0s above the pivot. This yields

$$M \sim \begin{bmatrix} 1 & 0 & 7 & 8 \\ 0 & 1 & -6 & -4 \\ 0 & 0 & 1 & 1 \end{bmatrix} \sim \begin{bmatrix} 1 & 0 & 0 & 1 \\ 0 & 1 & 0 & 2 \\ 0 & 0 & 1 & 1 \end{bmatrix}$$

The last matrix corresponds to the solution $x = 1$, $y = 2$, $z = 1$.

2.50. Discuss advantages of Gaussian elimination over the Gauss–Jordan algorithm.

First of all one can show that Gaussian elimination uses fewer arithmetic operations than the Gauss–Jordan algorithm. Second, if the system is inconsistent, i.e. has no solution, then this will be known during the first part (triangularization) of the Gaussian elimination algorithm, whereas it may not be known until the end of the Gauss–Jordan algorithm.

MATRIX NOTATION AND $m \times n$ SYSTEMS

2.51. Solve the following system using the augmented matrix M:

$$\begin{aligned} x + 3y - 2z + t &= 3 \\ 2x + 6y - 3z - 3t &= 7 \end{aligned}$$

Reduce the augmented matrix M to echelon form and then to row canonical form:

$$M = \begin{bmatrix} 1 & 3 & -2 & 1 & 3 \\ 2 & 6 & -3 & -3 & 7 \end{bmatrix} \sim \begin{bmatrix} 1 & 3 & -2 & 1 & 3 \\ 0 & 0 & 1 & -5 & 1 \end{bmatrix} \sim \begin{bmatrix} 1 & 3 & 0 & -9 & 5 \\ 0 & 0 & 1 & -5 & 1 \end{bmatrix}$$

Write down the system corresponding to the row canonical form of M and then transfer the free variables to the other side to obtain the free-variable form of the solution:

$$x + 3y \quad - 9t = 5 \qquad \text{and then} \qquad x = 5 - 3y + 9t$$
$$z - 5t = 1 \qquad\qquad\qquad\qquad z = 1 + 5t$$

Here x and z are the basic variables, and y and t are the free variables. Recall that the parametric form of the solution can be obtained from the free-variable form of the solution by simply setting the free variables equal to parameters, say $y = a$, $t = b$. This process yields

$$x = 5 - 3a + 9b, \; y = a, \; z = 1 + 5b, \; t = b \qquad \text{or} \qquad u = (5 - 3a + 9b, \; a, \; 1 + 5b, \; b)$$

(which is another form of the solution).

2.52. Solve the following system using the augmented matrix M:

$$x + y - 2z + 4t = 5$$
$$2x + 2y - 3z + t = 4$$
$$3x + 3y - 4z - 2t = 3$$

Reduce the augmented matrix M to echelon form and then to row canonical form:

$$M = \begin{bmatrix} 1 & 1 & -2 & 4 & 5 \\ 2 & 2 & -3 & 1 & 4 \\ 3 & 3 & -4 & -2 & 3 \end{bmatrix} \sim \begin{bmatrix} 1 & 1 & -2 & 4 & 5 \\ 0 & 0 & 1 & -7 & -6 \\ 0 & 0 & 2 & -14 & -12 \end{bmatrix} \sim \begin{bmatrix} 1 & 1 & 0 & -10 & -7 \\ 0 & 0 & 1 & -7 & -6 \end{bmatrix}$$

(The third row of the second matrix is deleted since it is a multiple of the second row and will result in a zero row.) Write down the system corresponding to the row canonical form of M and then transfer the free variables to the other side to obtain the free-variable form of the solution:

$$x + y \quad - 10t = -7 \qquad \text{and then} \qquad x = -7 - y + 10t$$
$$z - 7t = -6 \qquad\qquad\qquad\qquad z = -6 + 7t$$

Here x and z are the basic variables and y and t the free variables.

2.53. Solve the following system using the augmented matrix M:

$$x - 2y + 4z = 2$$
$$2x - 3y + 5z = 3$$
$$3x - 4y + 6z = 7$$

First row reduce the augmented matrix M to echelon form:

$$M = \begin{bmatrix} 1 & -2 & 4 & 2 \\ 2 & -3 & 5 & 3 \\ 3 & -4 & 6 & 7 \end{bmatrix} \sim \begin{bmatrix} 1 & -2 & 4 & 2 \\ 0 & 1 & -3 & -1 \\ 0 & 2 & -6 & 1 \end{bmatrix} \sim \begin{bmatrix} 1 & -2 & 4 & 2 \\ 0 & 1 & -3 & -1 \\ 0 & 0 & 0 & 3 \end{bmatrix}$$

In echelon form, the third row corresponds to the degenerate equation

$$0x + 0y + 0z = 3$$

Thus the system has no solution. (Note that the echelon form indicates whether or not the system has a solution.)

2.54. Solve the following system using the augmented matrix M:

$$
\begin{aligned}
x_1 + 2x_2 - 3x_3 - 2x_4 + 4x_5 &= 1 \\
2x_1 + 5x_2 - 8x_3 - x_4 + 6x_5 &= 4 \\
x_1 + 4x_2 - 7x_3 + 5x_4 + 2x_5 &= 8
\end{aligned}
$$

Reduce the augmented matrix M to echelon form and then to row canonical form:

$$
M = \begin{bmatrix} 1 & 2 & -3 & -2 & 4 & 1 \\ 2 & 5 & -8 & -1 & 6 & 4 \\ 1 & 4 & -7 & 5 & 2 & 8 \end{bmatrix} \sim \begin{bmatrix} 1 & 2 & -3 & -2 & 4 & 1 \\ 0 & 1 & -2 & 3 & -2 & 2 \\ 0 & 2 & -4 & 7 & -2 & 7 \end{bmatrix} \sim \begin{bmatrix} 1 & 2 & -3 & -2 & 4 & 1 \\ 0 & 1 & -2 & 3 & -2 & 2 \\ 0 & 0 & 0 & 1 & 2 & 3 \end{bmatrix}
$$

$$
\sim \begin{bmatrix} 1 & 2 & -3 & 0 & 8 & 7 \\ 0 & 1 & -2 & 0 & -8 & -7 \\ 0 & 0 & 0 & 1 & 2 & 3 \end{bmatrix} \sim \begin{bmatrix} 1 & 0 & 1 & 0 & 24 & 21 \\ 0 & 1 & -2 & 0 & -8 & -7 \\ 0 & 0 & 0 & 1 & 2 & 3 \end{bmatrix}
$$

Write down the system corresponding to the row canonical form of M and then transfer the free variables to the other side to obtain the free-variable form of the solution:

$$
\begin{aligned}
x_1 + \quad\quad x_3 + \quad\quad 24x_5 &= 21 \\
x_2 - 2x_3 - \quad\quad 8x_5 &= -7 \quad\quad \text{and} \\
x_4 + \quad 2x_5 &= 3
\end{aligned}
\quad\quad
\begin{aligned}
x_1 &= 21 - x_3 - 24x_5 \\
x_2 &= -7 + 2x_3 + 8x_5 \\
x_4 &= 3 - 2x_5
\end{aligned}
$$

2.55. Solve the following system using the augmented matrix M:

$$
\begin{aligned}
x + y + 3z &= 1 \\
2x + 3y - z &= 3 \\
5x + 7y + z &= 7
\end{aligned}
$$

Reduce the augmented matrix M to echelon form and then to row canonical form:

$$
M = \begin{bmatrix} 1 & 1 & 3 & 1 \\ 2 & 3 & -1 & 3 \\ 5 & 7 & 1 & 7 \end{bmatrix} \sim \begin{bmatrix} 1 & 1 & 3 & 1 \\ 0 & 1 & -7 & 1 \\ \cancel{0 \quad 2 \quad -14 \quad 2} \end{bmatrix} \sim \begin{bmatrix} 1 & 0 & 10 & 0 \\ 0 & 1 & -7 & 1 \end{bmatrix}
$$

(The third row of the second matrix is deleted since it is a multiple of the second row and will result in a zero row.) Write down the system corresponding to the row canonical form of M and then transfer the free variables to the other side to obtain the free-variable form of the solution:

$$
\begin{aligned}
x \quad\quad 10z &= 0 \\
y - 7z &= 1
\end{aligned}
\quad\quad \text{and} \quad\quad
\begin{aligned}
x &= -10z \\
y &= 1 + 7z
\end{aligned}
$$

Here z is the only free variable. The parametric solution, using $z = a$, is as follows:

$$
x = -10a, \ y = 1 + 7a, \ z = a \quad\quad \text{or} \quad\quad u = (-10a, \ 1 + 7a, \ a)
$$

2.56. Solve the following system using the augmented matrix M:

$$
\begin{aligned}
x + 2y + 3z &= 7 \\
x + 3y + z &= 6 \\
2x + 6y + 5z &= 15 \\
3x + 10y + 7z &= 23
\end{aligned}
$$

Reduce the augmented matrix M to echelon form and then to row canonical form:

$$M = \begin{bmatrix} 1 & 2 & 3 & 7 \\ 1 & 3 & 1 & 6 \\ 2 & 6 & 5 & 15 \\ 3 & 10 & 7 & 23 \end{bmatrix} \sim \begin{bmatrix} 1 & 2 & 3 & 7 \\ 0 & 1 & -2 & -1 \\ 0 & 2 & -1 & 1 \\ 0 & 4 & -2 & 2 \end{bmatrix} \sim \begin{bmatrix} 1 & 2 & 3 & 7 \\ 0 & 1 & -2 & -1 \\ 0 & 0 & 3 & 3 \end{bmatrix}$$

$$\sim \begin{bmatrix} 1 & 2 & 3 & 7 \\ 0 & 1 & -2 & -1 \\ 0 & 0 & 1 & 1 \end{bmatrix} \sim \begin{bmatrix} 1 & 2 & 0 & 4 \\ 0 & 1 & 0 & 1 \\ 0 & 0 & 1 & 1 \end{bmatrix} \sim \begin{bmatrix} 1 & 0 & 0 & 2 \\ 0 & 1 & 0 & 1 \\ 0 & 0 & 1 & 1 \end{bmatrix}$$

(The fourth row of the second matrix is deleted since it is a multiple of the third row and will result in a zero row.) The system has the unique solution $x = 2$, $y = 1$, $z = 1$.

HOMOGENEOUS SYSTEMS

2.57. Determine whether or not each system has a nonzero solution:

(a)
$$x - 2y + 3z - 2t = 0$$
$$3x - 7y - 2z + 4t = 0$$
$$4x + 3y + 5z + 2t = 0$$

(b)
$$x + 2y - 3z = 0$$
$$2x + 5y + 2z = 0$$
$$3x - y - 4z = 0$$

(c)
$$x + 2y - z = 0$$
$$2x + 5y + 2z = 0$$
$$x + 4y + 7z = 0$$
$$x + 3y + 3z = 0$$

(a) The system must have a nonzero solution since there are more unknowns than equations.

(b) Reduce to echelon form:

$$\begin{aligned} x + 2y - 3z &= 0 \\ 2x + 5y + 2z &= 0 \\ 3x - y - 4z &= 0 \end{aligned} \quad\text{to}\quad \begin{aligned} x + 2y - 3z &= 0 \\ y + 8z &= 0 \\ -7y + 5z &= 0 \end{aligned} \quad\text{to}\quad \begin{aligned} x + 2y - 3z &= 0 \\ y + 8z &= 0 \\ 61z &= 0 \end{aligned}$$

In echelon form there are exactly three equations in the three unknowns; hence the system has a unique solution, the zero solution.

(c) Reduce to echelon form:

$$\begin{aligned} x + 2y - z &= 0 \\ 2x + 5y + 2z &= 0 \\ x + 4y + 7z &= 0 \\ x + 3y + 3z &= 0 \end{aligned} \quad\text{to}\quad \begin{aligned} x + 2y - z &= 0 \\ y + 4z &= 0 \\ 2y + 8z &= 0 \\ y + 4z &= 0 \end{aligned} \quad\text{to}\quad \begin{aligned} x + 2y - z &= 0 \\ y + 4z &= 0 \end{aligned}$$

In echelon form there are only two equations in the three unknowns; hence the system has a nonzero solution.

2.58. Find the dimension and a basis for the general solution W of the homogeneous system

$$x + 3y - 2z + 5s - 3t = 0$$
$$2x + 7y - 3z + 7s - 5t = 0$$
$$3x + 11y - 4z + 10s - 9t = 0$$

Show how the basis gives the parametric form of the general solution of the system.

Reduce the system to echelon form. Apply the operations "Add $-2L_1$ to L_2" and "Add $-3L_1$ to L_3" and then the operation "Add $-2L_2$ to L_3". This yields

$$x + 3y - 2z + 5s - 3t = 0 \qquad\qquad x + 3y - 2z + 5s - 3t = 0$$
$$y + z - 3s + t = 0 \quad \text{and} \qquad y + z - 3s + t = 0$$
$$2y + 2z - 5s = 0 \qquad\qquad\qquad\qquad s - 2t = 0$$

In echelon form, the system has two free variables, z and t; hence dim $W = 2$. A basis $\{\cdots\}$ for W may be obtained as follows:

(1) Set $z = 1$, $t = 0$. Back-substitution yields $s = 0$, then $y = -1$, and then $x = 5$. Therefore $u_1 = (5, -1, 1, 0, 0)$.

(2) Set $z = 0$, $t = 1$. Back-substitution yields $s = 2$, then $y = 5$, and then $x = -22$. Therefore $u_2 = (-22, 5, 0, 2, 1)$.

Multiplying the basis vectors by the parameters a and b, respectively, yields

$$au_1 + bu_2 = a(5, -1, 1, 0, 0) + b(-22, 5, 0, 2, 1) = (5a - 22b, -a + 5b, a, 2b, b)$$

This is the parametric form of the general solution.

2.59. Find the dimension and a basis for the general solution W of the homogeneous system

$$2x + 4y - 5z + 3t = 0$$
$$3x + 6y - 7z + 4t = 0$$
$$5x + 10y - 11z + 6t = 0$$

Reduce the system to echelon form. Apply the operations "Add $-3L_1$ to $2L_2$" and "Add $-5L_1$ to $2L_3$" and then the operation "Add $-3L_2$ to L_3". This yields

$$2x + 4y - 5z + 3t = 0 \qquad\qquad 2x + 4y - 5z + 3t = 0$$
$$z - t = 0 \quad \text{and} \qquad\qquad z - t = 0$$
$$3z - 3t = 0$$

In echelon form, the system has two free variables, y and t; hence dim $W = 2$. A basis $\{u_1, u_2\}$ for W may be obtained as follows:

(1) Set $y = 1$, $t = 0$. Back-substitution yields the solution $u_1 = (-2, 1, 0, 0)$.

(2) Set $y = 0$, $t = 1$. Back-substitution yields the solution $u_2 = (1, 0, 1, 1)$.

2.60. Find the dimension and a basis for the general solution W of the homogeneous system

$$x - 2y - 5z = 0$$
$$2x + y - z = 0$$
$$3x - 4y - 8z = 0$$

Reduce the system to echelon form. Apply the operations "Add $-2L_1$ to L_2" and "Add $-3L_1$ to L_3" and then the operation "Add $-2L_2$ to $5L_3$". This yields

$$x - 2y - 5z = 0 \qquad\qquad x - 2y - 5z = 0$$
$$5y + 9z = 0 \quad \text{and} \qquad 5y + 9z = 0$$
$$2y + 7z = 0 \qquad\qquad\qquad 17z = 0$$

There are no free variables (the system is in triangular form). Hence dim $W = 0$ and W has no basis. Specifically, W consists only of the zero solution, that is, $W = \{0\}$.

2.61. Find the dimension and a basis for the general solution W of the homogeneous system using matrix notation:

$$x + 2y + 3z - 2s + 4t = 0$$
$$2x + 4y + 8z + s + 9t = 0$$
$$3x + 6y + 13z + 4s + 14t = 0$$

When a system is homogeneous, we represent the system by its coefficient matrix A rather than by its augmented matrix M, since the last column of the augmented matrix M is a zero column, and it will remain a zero column during any row-reduction process. Reduce the coefficient matrix A to echelon form:

$$A = \begin{bmatrix} 1 & 2 & 3 & -2 & 4 \\ 2 & 4 & 8 & 1 & 9 \\ 3 & 6 & 13 & 4 & 14 \end{bmatrix} \sim \begin{bmatrix} 1 & 2 & 3 & -2 & 4 \\ 0 & 0 & 2 & 5 & 1 \\ 0 & 0 & 4 & 10 & 2 \end{bmatrix} \sim \begin{bmatrix} 1 & 2 & 3 & -2 & 4 \\ 0 & 0 & 2 & 5 & 1 \end{bmatrix}$$

(The third row of the second matrix is deleted since it is a multiple of the second row and will result in a zero row.) We can now proceed in two ways.

(a) Write down the corresponding homogeneous system in echelon form

$$x + 2y + 3z - 2s + 4t = 0$$
$$2z + 5s + t = 0$$

In echelon form, the system has three free variables, y, s, and t; hence dim $W = 3$. A basis $\{\cdots\}$ for W may be obtained as follows:

(1) Set $y = 1$, $s = 0$, $t = 0$. Back-substitution yields $z = 0$ and then $x = -2$. Thus let $u_1 = [-2, 1, 0, 0, 0]$.

(2) Set $y = 0$, $s = 2$, $t = 0$. Back-substitution yields $z = -5$ and then $x = 19$. Thus let $u_2 = [19, 0, -5, 2, 0]$.

(3) Set $y = 0$, $s = 0$, $t = 2$. Back-substitution yields $z = -1$ and then $x = -5$. Thus let $u_3 = [-5, 0, -1, 0, 2]$.

[In order to avoid fractions, we chose $s = 2$ in (2) and $t = 2$ in (3).]

(b) Reduce the echelon form of A to row canonical form:

$$A \sim \begin{bmatrix} 1 & 2 & 3 & -2 & 4 \\ 0 & 0 & 1 & \frac{5}{2} & \frac{1}{2} \end{bmatrix} \sim \begin{bmatrix} 1 & 2 & 0 & -\frac{19}{2} & \frac{5}{2} \\ 0 & 0 & 1 & \frac{5}{2} & \frac{1}{2} \end{bmatrix}$$

Write down the corresponding free-variable solution:

$$x = -2y + \tfrac{19}{2}s - \tfrac{5}{2}t$$
$$z = -\tfrac{5}{2}s - \tfrac{1}{2}t$$

Using these equations for the basic variables x and z, repeat the above process to obtain the three vector solutions u_1, u_2, u_3, which form a basis for W. That is, set $y = 1$, $s = 0$, $t = 0$ to get u_1, set $y = 0$, $s = 2$, $t = 0$ to get u_2, and set $y = 0$, $s = 0$, $t = 2$ to get u_3.

PROOFS

2.62. Show that each of the elementary operations $[E_1]$, $[E_2]$, and $[E_3]$ has an inverse operation of the same type.

(a) Interchanging the same two equations L_i and L_j twice yields the same system. That is, $L_i \leftrightarrow L_j$ is its own inverse.

(b) Multiplying equation L_i by k and then by k^{-1}, or by k^{-1} and then by k, yields the same system. That is, the operations $kL_i \rightarrow L_i$ and $k^{-1}L_i \rightarrow L_i$ are inverses.

(c) Applying the operation "Add kL_i to L_j" and then the operation "Add $-kL_i$ to L_j", or vice versa, yields the same system. Thus the operations are inverses of each other.

2.63. Consider a system $L_1, L_2, \ldots, L_m$ of linear equations in unknowns $x_1, x_2, \ldots, x_n$, say,

$$L_i: \quad a_{i1}x_1 + a_{i2}x_2 + \cdots + a_{in}x_n = b_i \quad (i = 1, 2, \ldots, m)$$

Suppose L is the equation obtained by multiplying each equation L_i by a constant c_i and then adding the resulting equations, that is, suppose L is the equation

$$(c_1 a_{11} + \cdots + c_m a_{m1})x_1 + \cdots + (c_1 a_{1n} + \cdots + c_m a_{mn})x_n = c_1 b_1 + \cdots + c_m b_m$$

Such an equation L is called a *linear combination* of the equations L_i. Show that any solution of the system is also a solution of L.

Suppose $u = (k_1, k_2, \ldots, k_n)$ is a solution of the system. Then,

$$a_{i1}k_1 + a_{i2}k_2 + \cdots + a_{in}k_n = b_i \quad (i = 1, 2, \ldots, m) \qquad (\star)$$

To show that u is a solution of L, we must verify the equation

$$(c_1 a_{11} + \cdots + c_m a_{m1})k_1 + \cdots + (c_1 a_{1n} + \cdots + c_m a_{mn})k_n = c_1 b_1 + \cdots + c_m b_m$$

But this can be rearranged into

$$c_1(a_{11}k_1 + \cdots + a_{1n}k_n) + \cdots + c_m(a_{m1} + \cdots + a_{mn}k_n) = c_1 b_1 + \cdots + c_m b_m$$

or, by $(\star)$,

$$c_1 b_1 + \cdots + c_m b_m = c_1 b_1 + \cdots + c_m b_m$$

which is clearly a true statement.

2.64. Prove Theorem 2.3: Suppose a system ($\#$) of linear equations is obtained from a system ($\star$) of linear equations by a finite sequence of elementary operations. Then ($\#$) and ($\star$) are equivalent.

We need only show that the theorem holds if ($\#$) is obtained from ($\star$) by one elementary operation. In such a case, each equation in ($\#$) is a linear combination of equations in ($\star$). Therefore, by Problem 2.63, each solution of ($\star$) is a solution of each equation of ($\#$). However, by Problems 2.62, any elementary operations can be reversed by an elementary operation. Thus each solution of ($\#$) is a solution of ($\star$). Accordingly, systems ($\#$) and ($\star$) have the same solutions or, in other words, the systems are equivalent.

2.65. Prove the following two lemmas:

Lemma 1: Suppose $ax = b$ and $a \neq 0$. Then $x = b/a$ is the unique solution of the equation $ax = b$.

Lemma 2: Suppose $a_1 x_1 + a_2 x_2 + \cdots + a_n x_n = b$ is a nondegenerate equation with, say, leading unknown x_p. Then

    (i) Any set of values for the unknowns x_j with $j \neq p$ will yield a unique solution of the equation.

    (ii) Every solution of the equation is obtained in (i).

Proof of Lemma 1: Since $a \neq 0$, the scalar b/a exists. Substituting b/a in $ax = b$ yields $a(b/a) = b$ or $b = b$; hence b/a is a solution. On the other hand, suppose x_0 is a solution to $ax = b$, so $ax_0 = b$. Multiplying both sides by $1/a$ yields $x_0 = b/a$. Hence b/a is the unique solution of $ax = b$.

Proof of Lemma 2: First we prove (i). Set $x_j = k_j$ for $j \neq p$. Since $a_j = 0$ for $j < p$, substitution in the equation yields

$$a_p x_p + a_{p+1} k_{p+1} + \cdots + a_n k_n = b \quad \text{or} \quad a_p x_p = b - a_{p+1} k_{p+1} - \cdots - a_n k_n$$

with $a_p \neq 0$. Thus, by Lemma 1, x_p is uniquely determined as

$$x_p = \frac{1}{a_p}(b - a_{p+1} k_{p+1} - \cdots - a_n k_n)$$

Hence (i) is proved.

Next we prove (ii). Suppose $u = (k_1, k_2, \ldots, k_n)$ is a solution. Then

$$a_p k_p + a_{p+1} k_{p+1} + \cdots + a_n k_n = b \quad \text{or} \quad k_p = \frac{1}{a_p}(b - a_{p+1} k_{p+1} - \cdots - a_n k_n)$$

This, however, is precisely the solution

$$u = \left(k_1, \ldots, k_{p-1}, \frac{b - a_{p+1} k_{p+1} - \cdots - a_n k_n}{a_p}, k_{p+1}, \ldots, k_n \right)$$

obtained in (i). Hence (ii) is proved.

2.66. **Prove Theorem 2.4:** Consider a system in echelon form, say with r equations in n unknowns. There are two cases:

(i) $r = n$. The system has a unique solution.

(ii) $r < n$. We can assign any values to the $n - r$ free variables and solve uniquely for the r basic variables, obtaining a solution of the system.

The proof is by induction on the number r of equations in the system. If $r = 1$, then Lemma 1 (Problem 2.65) applies when $n = 1 = r$, and Lemma 2 (Problem 2.65) applies when $n > 1 = r$. Thus the theorem holds for $r = 1$.

Suppose $r > 1$ and suppose the following is the system in echelon form:

$$a_{11} x_1 + a_{12} x_2 + a_{13} x_3 + \cdots\cdots\cdots\cdots\cdots\cdots + a_{1n} x_n = b_1$$
$$a_{2j_2} x_{j_2} + a_{2j_2+1} x_{j_2+1} + \cdots + a_{2n} x_n = b_2$$
$$\cdots\cdots\cdots\cdots\cdots\cdots\cdots\cdots$$
$$a_{rj_r} x_{j_r} + \cdots + a_{rn} x_n = b_n$$

We view the last $r - 1$ equations as a system with the unknowns $x_{j_2}, x_{j_2+1}, \ldots, x_n$. The subsystem is in echelon form and hence, by the inductive hypothesis, the theorem holds for the subsystem. Thus we can arbitrarily assign values to the $(n - j_2 + 1) - (r - 1)$ free variables in the reduced system to obtain a solution (say $x_{j_2} = k_{j_2}, \ldots, x_n = k_n$). As in the case $r = 1$, these values together with arbitrary values for the additional $j_2 - 2$ free variables (say $x_2 = k_2, \ldots, x_{j_2-1} = k_{j_2-1}$) yield a solution of the first equation with

$$x_1 = \frac{1}{a_{11}}(b_1 - a_{12} k_2 - \cdots - a_{1n} k_n)$$

[Note that there are $(n - j_2 + 1) - (r - 1) + (j_2 - 2) = n - r$ free variables.] Furthermore, these values for $x_1, \ldots, x_n$ also satisfy the other equations since, in these equations, the coefficients of $x_1, \ldots, x_{j_2 - 1}$ are zero.

Now if $r = n$, then $j_2 = 2$. Thus by induction we obtain a unique solution of the subsystem and then a unique solution of the entire system. Accordingly, the theorem is proven.

2.67. Prove Theorem 2.1: Any system of linear equations has either: (i) a unique solution, (ii) no solution, or (iii) an infinite number of solutions.

The theorem follows directly from the fact that applying the Gaussian elimination algorithm to the system either yields a degenerate equation with no solution [case (ii)] or a system in echelon form for which Theorem 2.4 applies [cases (i) and (iii)].

2.68. Prove Theorem 2.8: Let v_0 be a particular solution of $Ax = b$, and let W be the general solution of $Ax = 0$. Then $U = v_0 + W = \{v_0 + w: \ w \in W\}$ is the general solution of $Ax = b$.

Let w be any solution of $Ax = 0$. Then

$$A(v_0 + w) = Av_0 + Aw = b + 0 = b$$

Thus the sum $v_0 + w$ is a solution of $Ax = b$. On the other hand, suppose v is a solution of $Ax = b$. Then

$$A(v - v_0) = Av - Av_0 = b - b = 0$$

and hence $v - v_0$ belongs to W. Since $v = v_0 + (v - v_0)$, we get that any solution v of $Ax = b$ can be obtained by adding a solution of $Ax = 0$ to a solution of $Ax = b$. Thus the theorem is proved.

2.69. Prove that the following three statements about a system of linear equations are equivalent:

(i)   The system is consistent (has a solution).

(ii) No linear combination of the equations yields a degenerate equation L with a nonzero constant.

(iii) The system is reducible to echelon form.

Suppose the system is reducible to echelon form. The echelon form has a solution, and hence the original system has a solution. Thus (iii) implies (i).

Suppose the system has a solution. Then, by Problem 2.63, any linear combination of the equations also has a solution. But L has no solution; hence L is not a linear combination of the equations. Thus (i) implies (ii).

Finally, suppose the system is not reducible to echelon form. Then, in the Gaussian elimination algorithm, it must yield an equation of the form L. Hence L is a linear combination of the equations. Thus not-(iii) implies not-(ii) or, equivalently, (ii) implies (iii).

The three results, (iii) implies (i), (i) implies (ii), and (ii) implies (iii), prove that (i), (ii), and (iii) are equivalent.

Supplementary Problems

2×2 SYSTEMS

2.70. Solve each system:

$$
\begin{array}{lll}
(a) \quad 2x - 5y = 1 & (b) \quad 2x + 3y = 1 & (c) \quad 3x - 2y = 7 \\
 3x + 2y = 11 & 5x + 7y = 3 & x + 3y = -16
\end{array}
$$

2.71. Solve each system:

$$
\begin{array}{lll}
(a) \quad 2x + 4y = 10 & (b) \quad 4x - 2y = 5 & (c) \quad 2x - 4 = 3y \\
 3x + 6y = 15 & -6x + 3y = 1 & 5y - x = 5
\end{array}
$$

2.72. Find the values of k so that each of the following systems in unknowns x and y has: (i) a unique solution, (ii) no solution, (iii) an infinite number of solutions.

$$
\begin{array}{lll}
(a) \quad x - ky = 1 & (b) \quad x + ky = 2 & (c) \quad kx + 3y = 2 \\
 kx - 4y = 2 & 2x + 5y = k & 12x + ky = -4
\end{array}
$$

LINE OF BEST FIT (LEAST SQUARES)

2.73. Find the line L of best fit for each set of points:

    (a) $(1, 4)$, $(2, 6)$, $(3, 10)$, $(4, 15)$, $(5, 20)$

    (b) $(1, 3)$, $(3, 5)$, $(4, 10)$, $(7, 12)$, $(10, 20)$

2.74. Let E denote the average life span of people in Europe during the following years:

Year	1975	1980	1985	1990
E	68	72	74	78

Assuming the increase, year by year, is approximately linear, and that the life span will continue to increase linearly in the near future, estimate E for the years of 1995, 1998, and 2000.

3×3 SYSTEMS

2.75. Solve each system:

$$
\begin{array}{ll}
(a) \quad x + y - 3z = 5 & (b) \quad r - 2s + t = 2 \\
 2y + z = 8 & 3s - 4t = 9 \\
 3z = 6 & 2t = 6
\end{array}
$$

2.76. Solve each system:

$$
\begin{array}{lll}
(a) \quad x - y + z = 6 & (b) \quad x + 2y - z = 3 & (c) \quad 2x + y - 2z = 1 \\
 2x + y + z = 3 & 2x + 5y - 4z = 5 & 3x + 2y - 4z = 1 \\
\phantom{(a) \quad } x + y + z = 2 & 3x + 4y + 2z = 12 & 5x + 4y - z = 8
\end{array}
$$

2.77. Solve each system:

$$(a)\quad \begin{aligned} 2x - y - 3z &= 11 \\ 3x - 2y + 2z &= 5 \\ 4x + y - z &= 3 \end{aligned} \qquad (b)\quad \begin{aligned} x - 2y + 3z &= 2 \\ 2x - 3y + 8z &= 7 \\ 3x - 4y + 13z &= 8 \end{aligned} \qquad (c)\quad \begin{aligned} x + 2y + 3z &= 3 \\ 2x + 3y + 8z &= 4 \\ 5x + 8y + 19z &= 11 \end{aligned}$$

2.78. Solve each system:

$$(a)\quad \begin{aligned} x + y + 2z &= 3 \\ 2x + 3y + 5z &= 7 \\ 3x + 5y + 7z &= 12 \end{aligned} \qquad (b)\quad \begin{aligned} x - 2y - 3z &= 2 \\ x - 4y - 13z &= 14 \\ -3x + 5y + 4z &= 2 \end{aligned} \qquad (c)\quad \begin{aligned} x - 2y - 3z &= 2 \\ x - 4y - 13z &= 14 \\ -3x + 5y + 4z &= 0 \end{aligned}$$

GENERAL $m \times n$ SYSTEMS

2.79. Solve each system:

$$(a)\quad \begin{aligned} x + 3y - z - 2t &= 13 \\ 2y + 4z - t &= 10 \\ 5z - 2t &= 7 \\ 3t &= 12 \end{aligned} \qquad (b)\quad \begin{aligned} 2x + 4y - 3z + 2t &= 6 \\ 3y - 5z + 3t &= 2 \\ 4z - t &= 5 \\ 5t &= 15 \end{aligned}$$

2.80. Solve each system:

$$(a)\quad \begin{aligned} 2x + 3y &= 3 \\ x - 2y &= 5 \\ 3x + 2y &= 7 \end{aligned} \qquad (b)\quad \begin{aligned} x + 2y - 3z + 2t &= 2 \\ 2x + 5y - 8z + 6t &= 5 \\ 3x + 4y - 5z + 2t &= 4 \end{aligned} \qquad (c)\quad \begin{aligned} x + 2y - z + 3t &= 3 \\ 2x + 4y + 4z + 3t &= 9 \\ 3x + 6y - z + 8t &= 10 \end{aligned}$$

2.81. Solve each system:

$$(a)\quad \begin{aligned} x + 2y + 2z &= 2 \\ 3x - 2y - z &= 5 \\ 2x - 5y + 3z &= -4 \\ x + 4y + 6z &= 0 \end{aligned} \qquad (b)\quad \begin{aligned} x + 5y + 4z - 13t &= 3 \\ 3x - y + 2z + 5t &= 2 \\ 2x + 2y + 3z - 4t &= 1 \end{aligned}$$

2.82. Find the values of k so that each of the following systems in unknowns x, y, and z has (i) a unique solution, (ii) no solution, (iii) an infinite number of solutions.

$$(a)\quad \begin{aligned} x - 2y &= 1 \\ x - y + kz &= -2 \\ ky + 4z &= 6 \end{aligned} \qquad (b)\quad \begin{aligned} x + y + kz &= 1 \\ x + ky + z &= 1 \\ kx + y + z &= 1 \end{aligned} \qquad (c)\quad \begin{aligned} x + 2y + 2z &= 5 \\ x + ky + 3z &= 7 \\ x + 11y + kz &= 11 \end{aligned}$$

HOMOGENEOUS SYSTEMS

2.83. Determine whether or not each system has a nonzero solution.

$$(a)\quad \begin{aligned} x + 3y - 2z &= 0 \\ x - 8y + 8z &= 0 \\ 3x - 2y + 4z &= 0 \end{aligned} \qquad (b)\quad \begin{aligned} x + 3y - 2z &= 0 \\ 2x - 3y + z &= 0 \\ 3x - 2y + 2z &= 0 \end{aligned} \qquad (c)\quad \begin{aligned} x + 2y - 5z + 4t &= 0 \\ 2x - 3y + 2z + 3t &= 0 \\ 4x - 7y + z - 6t &= 0 \end{aligned}$$

2.84. Find the dimension and a basis of the general solution W of each homogeneous system.

(a) $\quad x - y + 2z = 0$ (b) $\quad x + 2y - 3z = 0$ (c) $\quad x + 2y + 3z + t = 0$
$\qquad 2x + y + z = 0$ $2x + 5y + 2z = 0$ $2x + 4y + 7z + t = 0$
$\qquad 5x + y + 4z = 0$ $3x - y - 4z = 0$ $3x + 6y + 10z + 2t = 0$

2.85. Find the dimension and a basis of the general solution W of each homogeneous system.

(a) $\quad x + 3y + 2z - s - t = 0$ (b) $\quad 2x - 4y + 3z - s + 2t = 0$
$\qquad 2x + 6y + 5z + s - t = 0$ $3x - 6y + 5z - 2s + 4t = 0$
$\qquad 5x + 15y + 12z + s - 3t = 0$ $5x - 10y + 7z - 3s + t = 0$

ECHELON MATRICES AND ELEMENTARY ROW OPERATIONS

2.86. Reduce A to echelon form and then to row canonical form.

(a) $\quad A = \begin{bmatrix} 1 & 2 & -1 & 2 & 1 \\ 2 & 4 & 1 & -2 & 3 \\ 3 & 6 & 2 & -6 & 5 \end{bmatrix}$ (b) $\quad A = \begin{bmatrix} 2 & 3 & -2 & 5 & 1 \\ 3 & -1 & 2 & 0 & 4 \\ 4 & -5 & 6 & -5 & 7 \end{bmatrix}$

2.87. Reduce A to echelon form and then to row canonical form.

(a) $\quad A = \begin{bmatrix} 1 & 3 & -1 & 2 \\ 0 & 11 & -5 & 3 \\ 2 & -5 & 3 & 1 \\ 4 & 1 & 1 & 5 \end{bmatrix}$ (b) $\quad A = \begin{bmatrix} 0 & 1 & 3 & -2 \\ 0 & 4 & -1 & 3 \\ 0 & 0 & 1 & 1 \\ 0 & 5 & -3 & 4 \end{bmatrix}$

2.88. Using only 0s and 1s, list all possible 2×2 matrices in row canonical form.

2.89. Using only 0s and 1s, list all possible 3×3 matrices in row canonical form.

2.90. Suppose $A = [a_{ij}]$ is an $n \times n$ triangular matrix with nonzero diagonal entries, that is, $a_{ij} = 0$ for $i < j$ and $a_{ij} \neq 0$ for $i = j$. Show that the row canonical form of A is the identity matrix I. [$I = [c_{ij}]$ is the identity matrix if $c_{ij} = 0$ for $i \neq j$ but $c_{ij} = 1$ for $i = j$.]

MISCELLANEOUS PROBLEMS

2.91. Let $Ax = b$ be an $n \times n$ system of linear equations.

(a) Suppose $Ax = 0$ has only the zero solution. Show that $Ax = b$ has a unique solution for any choice of vector b.

(b) Suppose $Ax = 0$ has a nonzero solution. Show that the system $Ax = b$ cannot have a unique solution, and that there are vectors b for which $Ax = b$ has no solution.

2.92. Consider the following system in unknowns x and y:

$$ax + by = 1$$
$$cx + dy = 0$$

Show that if $ad - bc \neq 0$, then the system has the unique solution

$$x = \frac{d}{ad - bc}, \qquad y = -\frac{c}{ad - bc}$$

Also show that if $ad - bc = 0$ and if $c \neq 0$ or $d \neq 0$, then the system has no solution.

Answers to Supplementary Problems

2.70. (a) $x = 3$, $y = 1$; (b) $x = 2$, $y = -1$; (c) $x = -1$, $y = -5$

2.71. (a) $x = -2a + 5$, $y = a$; (b) no solution; (c) $x = 5$, $y = 2$

2.72. (a) (i) $k \neq \pm 2$; (ii) $k = -2$; (iii) $k = 2$
(b) (i) $k \neq \frac{5}{2}$; (ii) $k = \frac{5}{2}$; (iii) never has an infinite number of solutions
(c) (i) $k \neq \pm 6$; (ii) $k = 6$; (iii) $k = -6$

2.73. (a) $y = 4.1x - 1.3$; (b) $y = 1.84x + 0.8$

2.74. Use 1970 as base zero to get $y = 0.64x + 65$, so $E = 0.64(N - 1970) + 65$, where N is the year. $E(1995) = 81$, $E(1998) = 82.92$, $E(2000) = 84.2$

2.75. (a) $x = 8$, $y = 3$, $z = 2$; (b) $r = 13$, $s = 7$, $t = 3$

2.76. (a) $x = 1$, $y = -2$, $z = 3$; (b) $x = 2$, $y = 1$, $z = 1$; (c) $x = 1$, $y = 1$, $z = 1$

2.77. (a) $x = 1$, $y = -3$, $z = -2$; (b) no solution;
(c) $(-7a - 1, 2a + 2, a)$ or $x = -7z - 1$, $y = 2z + 2$

2.78. (a) $x = 3$, $y = 2$, $z = -1$; (b) no solution;
(c) $(-7a - 10, -5a - 6, a)$ or $x = -7z - 10$, $y = -5z - 6$

2.79. (a) $x = 21$, $y = 1$, $z = 3$, $t = 4$; (b) $x = 1$, $y = 1$, $z = 2$, $t = 3$

2.80. (a) $x = 3$, $y = -1$; (b) $(-a + 2b, 1 + 2a - 2b, a, b)$ or $x = -z + 2t$, $y = 1 + 2z - 2t$;
(c) $\left(\frac{7}{2} - \frac{5b}{2} - 2a, a, \frac{1}{2} + \frac{b}{2}, b \right)$ or $x = \frac{7}{2} - \frac{5t}{2} - 2y$, $z = \frac{1}{2} + \frac{t}{2}$

2.81. (a) $x = 2$, $y = 1$, $z = -1$; (b) no solution

2.82. (a) (i) $k \neq \pm 2$; (ii) $k = 2$; (iii) $k = -2$
(b) (i) $k \neq -2$ and $k \neq 1$; (ii) $k = -2$; (iii) $k = 1$
(c) (i) $k \neq 5$ and $k \neq -1$; (ii) $k = -1$; (iii) $k = 5$

2.83. (a) yes; (b) no; (c) yes, by Theorem 2.6

2.84. (a) dim $W = 1$; $u = (-1, 1, 1)$; (b) dim $W = 0$; no basis;
(c) dim $W = 2$; $u_1 = (-2, 1, 0, 0)$, $u_2 = (-4, 0, 1, 1)$

2.85. (a) dim $W = 3$; $u_1 = (-3, 1, 0, 0, 0)$, $u_2 = (7, 0, -3, 1, 0)$, $u_3 = (3, 0, -1, 0, 1)$;

(b) dim $W = 2$; $u_1 = (2, 1, 0, 0, 0)$, $u_2 = (5, 0, -5, -3, 1)$

2.86. (a) $\begin{bmatrix} 1 & 2 & -1 & 2 & 1 \\ 0 & 0 & 3 & -6 & 1 \\ 0 & 0 & 0 & -6 & 1 \end{bmatrix}$ and $\begin{bmatrix} 1 & 2 & 0 & 0 & \frac{4}{3} \\ 0 & 0 & 1 & 0 & 0 \\ 0 & 0 & 0 & 1 & -\frac{1}{6} \end{bmatrix}$;

(b) $\begin{bmatrix} 2 & 3 & -2 & 5 & 1 \\ 0 & -11 & 10 & -15 & 5 \\ 0 & 0 & 0 & 0 & 0 \end{bmatrix}$ and $\begin{bmatrix} 1 & 0 & \frac{4}{11} & \frac{5}{11} & \frac{13}{11} \\ 0 & 1 & -\frac{10}{11} & \frac{15}{11} & -\frac{5}{11} \\ 0 & 0 & 0 & 0 & 0 \end{bmatrix}$

2.87. (a) $\begin{bmatrix} 1 & 3 & -1 & 2 \\ 0 & 11 & -5 & 3 \\ 0 & 0 & 0 & 0 \\ 0 & 0 & 0 & 0 \end{bmatrix}$ and $\begin{bmatrix} 1 & 0 & \frac{4}{11} & \frac{13}{11} \\ 0 & 1 & -\frac{5}{11} & \frac{3}{11} \\ 0 & 0 & 0 & 0 \\ 0 & 0 & 0 & 0 \end{bmatrix}$;

(b) $\begin{bmatrix} 0 & 1 & 3 & -2 \\ 0 & 0 & -13 & 11 \\ 0 & 0 & 0 & 24 \\ 0 & 0 & 0 & 0 \end{bmatrix}$ and $\begin{bmatrix} 0 & 1 & 0 & 0 \\ 0 & 0 & 1 & 0 \\ 0 & 0 & 0 & 1 \\ 0 & 0 & 0 & 0 \end{bmatrix}$

2.88. There are five: $\begin{bmatrix} 1 & 0 \\ 0 & 1 \end{bmatrix}$, $\begin{bmatrix} 1 & 1 \\ 0 & 0 \end{bmatrix}$, $\begin{bmatrix} 1 & 0 \\ 0 & 0 \end{bmatrix}$, $\begin{bmatrix} 0 & 1 \\ 0 & 0 \end{bmatrix}$, $\begin{bmatrix} 0 & 0 \\ 0 & 0 \end{bmatrix}$

2.89. There are sixteen.

Chapter 3

Square Matrices; Elementary Matrices

3.1 INTRODUCTION

Matrices with the same number of rows and columns are called *square matrices*. These matrices play a major role in linear algebra and will be used throughout the text. This chapter introduces us to these matrices and certain of their elementary properties.

This chapter also introduces us to elementary matrices that are closely related to the elementary row operations discussed in Chapter 2. The scalars in this chapter are real numbers unless otherwise stated or implied.

3.2 SQUARE MATRICES

A *square matrix* is a matrix with the same number of rows as columns. An $n \times n$ square matrix is said to be of *order n* and is sometimes called an *n-square matrix*.

Recall that not every two matrices can be added or multiplied. However, if we only consider square matrices of some given order n, then this inconvenience disappears. Specifically, the operations of addition, multiplication, scalar multiplication, and transpose can be performed on any *n*-square matrices, and the result is again an *n*-square matrix.

EXAMPLE 3.1 The following are square matrices of order 3:

$$A = \begin{bmatrix} 1 & 2 & 3 \\ -4 & -4 & -4 \\ 5 & 6 & 7 \end{bmatrix} \quad \text{and} \quad B = \begin{bmatrix} 2 & -5 & 1 \\ 0 & 3 & -2 \\ 1 & 2 & -4 \end{bmatrix}$$

The following are also matrices of order 3:

$$A + B = \begin{bmatrix} 3 & -3 & 4 \\ -4 & -1 & -6 \\ 6 & 8 & 3 \end{bmatrix}, \quad 2A = \begin{bmatrix} 2 & 4 & 6 \\ -8 & -8 & -8 \\ 10 & 12 & 14 \end{bmatrix}, \quad A^T = \begin{bmatrix} 1 & -4 & 5 \\ 2 & -4 & 6 \\ 3 & -4 & 7 \end{bmatrix}$$

$$AB = \begin{bmatrix} 2+0+3 & -5+6+6 & 1-4-12 \\ -8+0-4 & 20-12-8 & -4+8+16 \\ 10+0+7 & -25+18+14 & 5-12-28 \end{bmatrix} = \begin{bmatrix} 5 & 7 & -15 \\ -12 & 0 & 20 \\ 17 & 7 & -35 \end{bmatrix}$$

Diagonal and Trace

Consider an *n*-square matrix $A = [a_{ij}]$. The *diagonal* or *main diagonal* of A consists of the numbers

$$a_{11}, a_{22}, \ldots, a_{nn}$$

that is, the elements from the upper left-hand corner of A to the lower right-hand corner of A.

The *trace* of A, written $\operatorname{tr}(A)$, is the sum of the diagonal elements.   That is,

$$\operatorname{tr}(A) = a_{11} + a_{22} + \cdots + a_{nn} = \sum_{i=1}^{n} a_{ii}$$

The following theorem applies.

Theorem 3.1:   Suppose $A = [a_{ij}]$ and $B = [b_{ij}]$ are n-square matrices and k is any scalar. Then:

  (i) $\operatorname{tr}(A + B) = \operatorname{tr}(A) + \operatorname{tr}(B)$

 (ii) $\operatorname{tr}(kA) = k(\operatorname{tr}(A))$

(iii) $\operatorname{tr}(A) = \operatorname{tr}(A^T)$

(iv) $\operatorname{tr}(AB) = \operatorname{tr}(BA)$

EXAMPLE 3.2   Consider matrices A and B in Example 3.1.   Then the diagonal of A consists of the numbers 1, -4, and 7, and the diagonal of B consists of the numbers 2, 3, and -4.   Accordingly,

$$\operatorname{tr}(A) = 1 - 4 + 7 = 4 \qquad \text{and} \qquad \operatorname{tr}(B) = 2 + 3 - 4 = 1$$

Also, as expected from Theorem 3.1,

$$\operatorname{tr}(A + B) = 3 - 1 + 3 = 5 = \operatorname{tr}(A) + \operatorname{tr}(B)$$

$$\operatorname{tr}(2A) = 2 - 8 + 14 = 8 = 2\operatorname{tr}(A)$$

$$\operatorname{tr}(A^T) = 1 - 4 + 7 = 4 = \operatorname{tr}(A)$$

Identity Matrix

The n-square *identity* or *unit* matrix, denoted by I_n, or simply I, is the matrix with 1s on the diagonal and 0s elsewhere.   The matrix I is similar to the scalar 1 in that, for any n-square matrix A,

$$AI = IA = A$$

More generally, if B is an $m \times n$ matrix, then $BI_n = I_m B = B$.

For any scalar k, the matrix kI which contains k's on the diagonal and 0s elsewhere is called the *scalar matrix*, corresponding to the scalar k.

EXAMPLE 3.3

(a)   The identity matrices of orders 2, 3, and 4 are as follows:

$$\begin{bmatrix} 1 & 0 \\ 0 & 1 \end{bmatrix}, \qquad \begin{bmatrix} 1 & 0 & 0 \\ 0 & 1 & 0 \\ 0 & 0 & 1 \end{bmatrix}, \qquad \begin{bmatrix} 1 & & & \\ & 1 & & \\ & & 1 & \\ & & & 1 \end{bmatrix}$$

It is common practice to omit blocks or patterns of 0s when there is no ambiguity, as in the third matrix.

(b) The scalar matrices of order 2, 3, and 4 corresponding to scalar $k = 5$ are as follows:

$$\begin{bmatrix} 5 & 0 \\ 0 & 5 \end{bmatrix}, \qquad \begin{bmatrix} 5 & 0 & 0 \\ 0 & 5 & 0 \\ 0 & 0 & 5 \end{bmatrix}, \qquad \begin{bmatrix} 5 & & & \\ & 5 & & \\ & & 5 & \\ & & & 5 \end{bmatrix}$$

(c) The *Kronecker delta function* δ_{ij} is defined by

$$\delta_{ij} = \begin{cases} 0 & \text{if } i \neq j \\ 1 & \text{if } i = j \end{cases}$$

Thus the identity matrix may be defined by $I = [\delta_{ij}]$.

3.3 POWERS OF MATRICES, POLYNOMIALS IN MATRICES

Consider any n-square matrix A. *Powers of* A are defined as follows:

$$A^2 = AA, \quad A^3 = A^2A, \quad \ldots, \quad A^{n+1} = A^nA, \quad \ldots, \quad A^0 = I$$

Polynomials in the matrix A are also defined. Specifically, for any polynomial

$$f(x) = a_0 + a_1x + a_2x^2 + \cdots + a_nx^n$$

where the a_i are scalars, we define $f(A)$ to be the matrix

$$f(A) = a_0I + a_1A + a_2A^2 + \cdots + a_nA^n$$

Note that $f(A)$ is obtained from $f(x)$ by substituting the matrix A for the variable x and the scalar matrix a_0I for the scalar term a_0. In the case that $f(A)$ is the zero matrix, the matrix A is then called a *zero* or *root* of the polynomial $f(x)$.

EXAMPLE 3.4 Suppose $A = \begin{bmatrix} 1 & 2 \\ 3 & -4 \end{bmatrix}$. Then

$$A^2 = \begin{bmatrix} 1 & 2 \\ 3 & -4 \end{bmatrix}\begin{bmatrix} 1 & 2 \\ 3 & -4 \end{bmatrix} = \begin{bmatrix} 7 & -6 \\ -9 & 22 \end{bmatrix}$$

$$A^3 = A^2A = \begin{bmatrix} 7 & -6 \\ -9 & 22 \end{bmatrix}\begin{bmatrix} 1 & 2 \\ 3 & -4 \end{bmatrix} = \begin{bmatrix} -11 & 38 \\ 57 & -106 \end{bmatrix}$$

Suppose $f(x) = 2x^2 - 3x + 5$. Then

$$f(A) = 2\begin{bmatrix} 7 & -6 \\ -9 & 22 \end{bmatrix} - 3\begin{bmatrix} 1 & 2 \\ 3 & -4 \end{bmatrix} + 5\begin{bmatrix} 1 & 0 \\ 0 & 1 \end{bmatrix} = \begin{bmatrix} 16 & -18 \\ -27 & 61 \end{bmatrix}$$

Suppose $g(x) = x^2 + 3x - 10$. Then

$$g(A) = \begin{bmatrix} 7 & -6 \\ -9 & 22 \end{bmatrix} + 3\begin{bmatrix} 1 & 2 \\ 3 & -4 \end{bmatrix} - 10\begin{bmatrix} 1 & 0 \\ 0 & 1 \end{bmatrix} = \begin{bmatrix} 0 & 0 \\ 0 & 0 \end{bmatrix}$$

Thus A is a zero of the polynomial $g(x)$.

3.4 INVERTIBLE (NONSINGULAR) MATRICES, INVERSES

A square matrix A is said to be *invertible* or *nonsingular* if there exists a matrix B with the property that

$$AB = BA = I, \qquad \text{the identity matrix}$$

Such a matrix B is unique. See Problem 3.50. It is called the *inverse* of A and is denoted by A^{-1}. Observe that B is the inverse of A if and only if A is the inverse of B. For example, suppose

$$A = \begin{bmatrix} 2 & 5 \\ 1 & 3 \end{bmatrix} \qquad \text{and} \qquad B = \begin{bmatrix} 3 & -5 \\ -1 & 2 \end{bmatrix}$$

Then

$$AB = \begin{bmatrix} 6-5 & -10+10 \\ 3-3 & -5+6 \end{bmatrix} = \begin{bmatrix} 1 & 0 \\ 0 & 1 \end{bmatrix} \qquad \text{and} \qquad BA = \begin{bmatrix} 6-5 & 15-15 \\ -2+2 & -5+6 \end{bmatrix} = \begin{bmatrix} 1 & 0 \\ 0 & 1 \end{bmatrix}$$

Thus A and B are inverses.

It is known that $AB = I$ if and only if $BA = I$ (Theorem 3.8). Hence it is necessary to test only one product to determine whether two given matrices are inverses. (See Problem 3.7).

Inverse of a 2 × 2 Matrix

Let A be an arbitrary 2×2 matrix, say,

$$A = \begin{bmatrix} a & b \\ c & d \end{bmatrix}$$

We want to derive a formula for A^{-1}, the inverse of A. Specifically, we seek $2^2 = 4$ scalars, say x_1, y_1, x_2, y_2, such that

$$\begin{bmatrix} a & b \\ c & d \end{bmatrix}\begin{bmatrix} x_1 & x_2 \\ y_1 & y_2 \end{bmatrix} = \begin{bmatrix} 1 & 0 \\ 0 & 1 \end{bmatrix} \qquad \text{or} \qquad \begin{bmatrix} ax_1 + by_1 & ax_2 + by_2 \\ cx_1 + dy_1 & cx_2 + dy_2 \end{bmatrix} = \begin{bmatrix} 1 & 0 \\ 0 & 1 \end{bmatrix}$$

Setting the four entries equal to the corresponding entries in the identity matrix yields four equations, which can be partitioned into two 2×2 systems as follows:

$$\begin{array}{ll} ax_1 + by_1 = 1 & ax_2 + by_2 = 0 \\ cx_1 + dy_1 = 0 & cx_2 + dy_2 = 1 \end{array}$$

Observe that the augmented matrices of the two systems are

$$\begin{bmatrix} a & b & 1 \\ c & d & 0 \end{bmatrix} \qquad \text{and} \qquad \begin{bmatrix} a & b & 0 \\ c & d & 1 \end{bmatrix}$$

where the original matrix A is the coefficient matrix of both systems.

Suppose we let

$$|A| = ad - bc$$

(called the *determinant* of A). Assuming $|A| \neq 0$, we can solve uniquely for the above unknowns x_1, y_1, x_2, y_2, obtaining

$$x_1 = \frac{d}{ad - bc} = \frac{d}{|A|}, \qquad y_1 = \frac{-c}{ad - bc} = \frac{-c}{|A|}, \qquad x_2 = \frac{-b}{ad - bc} = \frac{-b}{|A|}, \qquad y_2 = \frac{a}{ad - bc} = \frac{a}{|A|}$$

Accordingly,

$$A^{-1} = \begin{bmatrix} a & b \\ c & d \end{bmatrix}^{-1} = \begin{bmatrix} d/|A| & -b/|A| \\ -c/|A| & a/|A| \end{bmatrix} = \frac{1}{|A|} \begin{bmatrix} d & -b \\ -c & a \end{bmatrix}$$

In other words, when $|A| \neq 0$, the inverse of a 2×2 matrix A may be obtained from A as follows:

(1)   Interchange the two elements on the diagonal.

(2)   Take the negatives of the other two elements.

(3)   Multiply the resultant matrix by $1/|A|$ or, equivalently, divide each element by $|A|$.

In case $|A| = 0$, A is not invertible.

Remark 1:   The above property that A is invertible if and only if A has a nonzero determinant is true for square matrices of any order.   (See Chapter 8.)

Remark 2:   If A and B are invertible, then AB is invertible and $(AB)^{-1} = B^{-1}A^{-1}$.   More generally, if $A_1, A_2, \ldots, A_k$ are invertible, then their product is invertible and

$$(A_1 A_2 \cdots A_k)^{-1} = A_k^{-1} \cdots A_2^{-1} A_1^{-1}$$

the product of the inverses in the reverse order.

EXAMPLE 3.5   Find the inverse of $A = \begin{bmatrix} 2 & 3 \\ 4 & 5 \end{bmatrix}$ and $B = \begin{bmatrix} 1 & 3 \\ 2 & 6 \end{bmatrix}$.

Evaluate

$$|A| = 2(5) - 3(4) = 10 - 12 = -2$$

Thus the matrix A has an inverse and

$$A^{-1} = \frac{1}{-2} \begin{bmatrix} 5 & -3 \\ -4 & 2 \end{bmatrix} = \begin{bmatrix} -\frac{5}{2} & \frac{3}{2} \\ 2 & -1 \end{bmatrix}$$

Now evaluate

$$|B| = 1(6) - 3(2) = 6 - 6 = 0$$

Thus matrix B has no inverse.

Inverse of an $n \times n$ Matrix

Consider an arbitrary 3×3 matrix $A = [a_{ij}]$.   Finding its inverse $A^{-1} = [x_{ij}]$ reduces, as above, to find the solution of three 3×3 systems of linear equations whose augmented matrices follow:

$$\begin{bmatrix} a_{11} & a_{12} & a_{13} & 1 \\ a_{21} & a_{22} & a_{23} & 0 \\ a_{31} & a_{32} & a_{33} & 0 \end{bmatrix}, \quad \begin{bmatrix} a_{11} & a_{12} & a_{13} & 0 \\ a_{21} & a_{22} & a_{23} & 1 \\ a_{31} & a_{32} & a_{33} & 0 \end{bmatrix}, \quad \begin{bmatrix} a_{11} & a_{12} & a_{13} & 0 \\ a_{21} & a_{22} & a_{23} & 0 \\ a_{31} & a_{32} & a_{33} & 1 \end{bmatrix},$$

Note that the original matrix A is the coefficient matrix of all three systems.   Also, note that the three columns of constants form the identity matrix I.   These three systems of linear equations can be solved simultaneously by the following algorithm, which holds for any $n \times n$ matrix.

Algorithm 3.4:   Find the inverse of a given $n \times n$ matrix A.

Step 1.   Form the $n \times 2n$ (block) matrix $M = [A, I]$, that is, A is in the left half of M and the identity matrix I is in the right half of M.

Step 2.   Row reduce M to an echelon form.   If the process generates a zero row in the A half of M, then *stop* (A has no inverse).   Otherwise the A half of M is in triangular form.

Step 3.   Further row reduce M to its row canonical form,

$$M \sim [I, B]$$

where the identity matrix I has replaced A in the left half of the matrix.

Step 4.   Set $A^{-1} = B$, the matrix that is now in the right half of M.

EXAMPLE 3.6   Suppose we want to find the inverse of

$$A = \begin{bmatrix} 1 & 0 & 2 \\ 2 & -1 & 3 \\ 4 & 1 & 8 \end{bmatrix}$$

First we form the (block) matrix $M = [A, I]$ and reduce M to echelon form:

$$M = \begin{bmatrix} 1 & 0 & 2 & | & 1 & 0 & 0 \\ 2 & -1 & 3 & | & 0 & 1 & 0 \\ 4 & 1 & 8 & | & 0 & 0 & 1 \end{bmatrix} \sim \begin{bmatrix} 1 & 0 & 2 & | & 1 & 0 & 0 \\ 0 & -1 & -1 & | & -2 & 1 & 0 \\ 0 & 1 & 0 & | & -4 & 0 & 1 \end{bmatrix} \sim \begin{bmatrix} 1 & 0 & 2 & | & 1 & 0 & 0 \\ 0 & -1 & -1 & | & -2 & 1 & 0 \\ 0 & 0 & -1 & | & -6 & 1 & 1 \end{bmatrix}$$

In echelon form, the left half of M is in triangular form; hence A has an inverse.   Next we further row reduce M to its row canonical form:

$$M \sim \begin{bmatrix} 1 & 0 & 0 & | & -11 & 2 & 2 \\ 0 & -1 & 0 & | & 4 & 0 & -1 \\ 0 & 0 & 1 & | & 6 & -1 & -1 \end{bmatrix} \sim \begin{bmatrix} 1 & 0 & 0 & | & -11 & 2 & 2 \\ 0 & 1 & 0 & | & -4 & 0 & 1 \\ 0 & 0 & 1 & | & 6 & -1 & -1 \end{bmatrix}$$

The identity matrix is now in the left half of the final matrix; hence the right half is A^{-1}.   In other words,

$$A^{-1} = \begin{bmatrix} -11 & 2 & 2 \\ -4 & 0 & 1 \\ 6 & -1 & -1 \end{bmatrix}$$

3.5   SPECIAL TYPES OF SQUARE MATRICES

This section describes a number of special kinds of square matrices which play an important role in linear algebra.

Diagonal and Triangular Matrices

A square matrix $D = [d_{ij}]$ is *diagonal* if its nondiagonal entries are all zero.   Such a matrix is sometimes denoted by

$$D = \text{diag}(d_{11}, d_{22}, \ldots, d_{nn})$$

where some or all of the d_{ii} may be zero. For example,

$$\begin{bmatrix} 3 & 0 & 0 \\ 0 & -7 & 0 \\ 0 & 0 & 2 \end{bmatrix}, \quad \begin{bmatrix} 4 & 0 \\ 0 & -5 \end{bmatrix}, \quad \begin{bmatrix} 6 & & & \\ & 0 & & \\ & & -9 & \\ & & & 1 \end{bmatrix}$$

are diagonal matrices which may be represented, respectively, by

$$\operatorname{diag}(3, -7, 2), \quad \operatorname{diag}(4, -5), \quad \operatorname{diag}(6, 0, -9, 1)$$

(Observe that patterns of 0s in the third matrix have been omitted.)

A square matrix $A = [a_{ij}]$ is an *upper triangular matrix* or simply a *triangular matrix* if all entries below the (main) diagonal are equal to 0, that is, if $a_{ij} = 0$ for $i > j$. Generic upper triangular matrices of orders 2, 3, and 4 are as follows:

$$\begin{bmatrix} a_{11} & a_{12} \\ 0 & a_{22} \end{bmatrix}, \quad \begin{bmatrix} b_{11} & b_{12} & b_{13} \\ & b_{22} & b_{23} \\ & & b_{33} \end{bmatrix}, \quad \begin{bmatrix} c_{11} & c_{12} & c_{13} & c_{14} \\ & c_{22} & c_{23} & c_{24} \\ & & c_{33} & c_{34} \\ & & & c_{44} \end{bmatrix}$$

(As in diagonal matrices, it is common practice to omit patterns of 0s.)

Analogously, a *lower triangular matrix* is a square matrix whose entries above the diagonal are all zero.

Remark: One can easily show that the sum, scalar product, and product of diagonal matrices are, again, diagonal. Also, a diagonal matrix D has an inverse if and only if no diagonal entry is zero and D^{-1}, if it exists, is also diagonal. These properties also are true for upper and lower triangular matrices.

Symmetric Matrices

A matrix A is *symmetric* if $A^T = A$. Equivalently, $A = [a_{ij}]$ is symmetric if the *symmetric elements* a_{ij} and a_{ji} (mirror images in the diagonal) are equal, that is, if each $a_{ij} = a_{ji}$. (Note that A must be square in order for $A^T = A$.)

A matrix A is *skew-symmetric* if $A^T = -A$. Equivalently, $A = [a_{ij}]$ is skew-symmetric if $a_{ij} = -a_{ji}$. Note that the diagonal elements of a skew-symmetric matrix must be zero since $a_{ii} = -a_{ii}$ implies $a_{ii} = 0$.

EXAMPLE 3.7 Consider the following matrices:

$$A = \begin{bmatrix} 2 & -3 & 5 \\ -3 & 6 & 7 \\ 5 & 7 & -8 \end{bmatrix}, \quad B = \begin{bmatrix} 0 & 3 & -4 \\ -3 & 0 & 5 \\ 4 & -5 & 0 \end{bmatrix}, \quad C = \begin{bmatrix} 1 & 0 & 0 \\ 0 & 0 & 1 \end{bmatrix}$$

(a) By inspection, the symmetric elements in A are equal or $A^T = A$. Thus A is symmetric.

(b) By inspection, the diagonal elements of B are 0 and the symmetric elements are negatives of each other. Thus B is skew-symmetric.

(c) Since C is not square, C is neither symmetric nor skew-symmetric.

Suppose A and B are symmetric matrices.   One can easily show that $A + B$ and kA are symmetric.   However, the product AB need not be symmetric.   For example, $A = \begin{bmatrix} 1 & 2 \\ 2 & 3 \end{bmatrix}$ and $B = \begin{bmatrix} 4 & 5 \\ 5 & 6 \end{bmatrix}$ are symmetric, but $AB = \begin{bmatrix} 14 & 17 \\ 23 & 28 \end{bmatrix}$ is not symmetric.

The following theorem applies.

Theorem 3.2:   Let A be any square matrix.   Then

(i) $A + A^T$ is symmetric.

(ii) $A - A^T$ is skew-symmetric.

(iii) $A = B + C$, where $B = \frac{1}{2}(A + A^T)$ is symmetric and $C = \frac{1}{2}(A - A^T)$ is skew-symmetric.

Orthogonal Matrices

A real matrix A is *orthogonal* if $AA^T = A^TA = I$.   Alternatively, A is orthogonal if A is square and invertible and $A^T = A^{-1}$.

EXAMPLE 3.8   Suppose

$$A = \begin{bmatrix} \frac{1}{9} & \frac{8}{9} & -\frac{4}{9} \\ \frac{4}{9} & -\frac{4}{9} & -\frac{7}{9} \\ \frac{8}{9} & \frac{1}{9} & \frac{4}{9} \end{bmatrix}$$

Then

$$AA^T = \begin{bmatrix} \frac{1}{9} & \frac{8}{9} & -\frac{4}{9} \\ \frac{4}{9} & -\frac{4}{9} & -\frac{7}{9} \\ \frac{8}{9} & \frac{1}{9} & \frac{4}{9} \end{bmatrix} \begin{bmatrix} \frac{1}{9} & \frac{4}{9} & \frac{8}{9} \\ \frac{8}{9} & -\frac{4}{9} & \frac{1}{9} \\ -\frac{4}{9} & -\frac{7}{9} & \frac{4}{9} \end{bmatrix} = \frac{1}{81} \begin{bmatrix} 1 + 64 + 16 & 4 - 32 + 28 & 8 + 8 - 16 \\ 4 - 32 + 28 & 16 + 16 + 49 & 32 - 4 - 28 \\ 8 + 8 - 16 & 32 - 4 - 28 & 64 + 1 + 16 \end{bmatrix}$$

$$= \frac{1}{81} \begin{bmatrix} 81 & 0 & 0 \\ 0 & 81 & 0 \\ 0 & 0 & 81 \end{bmatrix} = \begin{bmatrix} 1 & 0 & 0 \\ 0 & 1 & 0 \\ 0 & 0 & 1 \end{bmatrix} = I$$

This means that $A^T = A^{-1}$, and so $A^TA = I$ as well.   Thus A is orthogonal.

Consider an arbitrary 3×3 matrix

$$A = \begin{bmatrix} a_1 & a_2 & a_3 \\ b_1 & b_2 & b_3 \\ c_1 & c_2 & c_3 \end{bmatrix}$$

Suppose A is orthogonal.   Then

$$AA^T = \begin{bmatrix} a_1 & a_2 & a_3 \\ b_1 & b_2 & b_3 \\ c_1 & c_2 & c_3 \end{bmatrix} \begin{bmatrix} a_1 & b_1 & c_1 \\ a_2 & b_2 & c_2 \\ a_3 & b_3 & c_3 \end{bmatrix} = \begin{bmatrix} 1 & 0 & 0 \\ 0 & 1 & 0 \\ 0 & 0 & 1 \end{bmatrix} = I$$

This yields

$$a_1^2 + a_2^2 + a_3^2 = 1 \qquad a_1b_1 + a_2b_2 + a_3b_3 = 0 \qquad a_1c_1 + a_2c_2 + a_3c_3 = 0$$
$$b_1a_1 + b_2a_2 + b_3a_3 = 0 \qquad b_1^2 + b_2^2 + b_3^2 = 1 \qquad b_1c_1 + b_2c_2 + b_3c_3 = 0$$
$$c_1a_1 + c_2a_2 + c_3a_3 = 0 \qquad c_1b_1 + c_2b_2 + c_3b_3 = 0 \qquad c_1^2 + c_2^2 + c_3^2 = 1$$

or, in other words,

$$u_1 \cdot u_1 = 1 \qquad u_1 \cdot u_2 = 0 \qquad u_1 \cdot u_3 = 0$$
$$u_2 \cdot u_1 = 0 \qquad u_2 \cdot u_2 = 1 \qquad u_2 \cdot u_3 = 0$$
$$u_3 \cdot u_1 = 0 \qquad u_3 \cdot u_2 = 0 \qquad u_3 \cdot u_3 = 1$$

where $u_1 = (a_1, a_2, a_3)$, $u_2 = (b_1, b_2, b_3)$, $u_3 = (c_1, c_2, c_3)$ are the rows of A. Thus the rows u_1, u_2, u_3 of A are orthogonal to each other and have unit lengths, or, in other words, u_1, u_2, u_3 form an *orthonormal set of vectors*. The condition $A^T A = I$ similarly shows that the columns of A form an orthonormal set of vectors. Furthermore, since each step is reversible, the converse is true.

The above result for 3×3 matrices is true in general.

Theorem 3.3: Let A be a real matrix. Then the following are equivalent:

    (a) A is orthogonal.

    (b)   The rows of A form an orthonormal set.

    (c)   The columns of A form an orthonormal set.

For $n = 2$, we have the following result.

Theorem 3.4: Every 2×2 orthogonal matrix has the form

$$\begin{bmatrix} \cos\theta & \sin\theta \\ -\sin\theta & \cos\theta \end{bmatrix} \qquad \text{or} \qquad \begin{bmatrix} \cos\theta & \sin\theta \\ \sin\theta & -\cos\theta \end{bmatrix}$$

for some real number θ.

Remark: The condition that vectors $u_1, u_2, \ldots, u_m$ form an orthonormal set may be described simply by $u_i \cdot u_j = \delta_{ij}$, where δ_{ij} is the Kronecker delta function [Example 3.3(c)].

3.6 SQUARE BLOCK MATRICES

A block matrix A is called a *square block matrix* if (i) A is a square matrix, (ii) the blocks form a square matrix, and (iii) the diagonal blocks are also square matrices. The latter two conditions will occur if and only if there are the same number of horizontal and vertical lines and they are placed symmetrically.

Consider the following two block matrices:

$$A = \begin{bmatrix} 1 & 2 & 3 & 4 & 5 \\ 1 & 1 & 1 & 1 & 1 \\ 9 & 8 & 7 & 6 & 5 \\ 4 & 4 & 4 & 4 & 4 \\ 3 & 5 & 3 & 5 & 3 \end{bmatrix}, \qquad B = \begin{bmatrix} 1 & 2 & 3 & 4 & 5 \\ 1 & 1 & 1 & 1 & 1 \\ 9 & 8 & 7 & 6 & 5 \\ 4 & 4 & 4 & 4 & 4 \\ 3 & 5 & 3 & 5 & 3 \end{bmatrix}$$

Block matrix A is not a square block matrix since the second and third diagonal blocks are not square matrices. On the other hand, block matrix B is a square block matrix.

A *block diagonal matrix* M is a square block matrix where the nondiagonal blocks are all zero matrices. The importance of block diagonal matrices is that the algebra of the block matrix is frequently reduced to the algebra of the individual blocks. Specifically, suppose M

is a block diagonal matrix and $f(x)$ is any polynomial.   Then M and $f(M)$ have the following form:

$$
M = \begin{bmatrix} A_{11} & & & \\ & A_{22} & & \\ & & \cdots & \\ & & & A_{rr} \end{bmatrix}, \qquad
f(M) = \begin{bmatrix} f(A_{11}) & & & \\ & f(A_{22}) & & \\ & & \cdots & \\ & & & f(A_{rr}) \end{bmatrix}
$$

(As usual, we use blank spaces for patterns of zeros or zero blocks.)

Analogously, a square block matrix is called a *block upper triangular matrix* if the blocks below the diagonal are zero matrices, and a *block lower triangular matrix* if the blocks above the diagonal are zero matrices.

3.7   ELEMENTARY MATRICES AND APPLICATIONS

Consider a matrix A with rows $R_1, R_2, \ldots, R_m$. Recall (Section 2.8) the following operations on A, called *elementary row operations*:

[E_1]   *(Row Interchange)*:   Interchange row R_i and row R_j, denoted by

$$R_i \leftrightarrow R_j$$

[E_2]   *(Row Scaling)*:   Multiply row R_i by a nonzero scalar k, written

$$kR_i \rightarrow R_i \quad (k \neq 0)$$

[E_3]   *(Row Addition)*:   Add k times row R_i to row R_j, written

$$\text{"Add } kR_i \text{ to } R_j \text{"} \quad \text{or} \quad (kR_i + R_j) \rightarrow R_j$$

We note that each of the above operations has an inverse operation of the same type. Specifically:

(1)   "Interchange R_i and R_j" is its own inverse.

(2)   "Multiply R_i by nonzero k" and "Multiply R_i by $1/k$" are inverses.

(3)   "Add kR_i to R_j" and "Add $-kR_i$ to R_j" are inverses.

Also recall (Section 2.8) that a matrix A is said to be *row equivalent* to a matrix B, written $A \sim B$, if B can be obtained from A by a sequence of elementary row operations.

Since the elementary row operations are reversible, the relation of row equivalence is an equivalence relation, that is,

(1) $A \sim A$ for any matrix A.

(2)   If $A \sim B$, then $B \sim A$.

(3)   If $A \sim B$ and $B \sim C$, then $A \sim C$.

We also state the following basic result on row equivalence.

Theorem 3.5:   Every matrix A is row equivalent to a unique matrix in row canonical form.

Elementary Matrices

Let e denote an elementary row operation and let $e(A)$ denote the result of applying the operation e to a matrix A. The matrix E obtained by applying e to the identity matrix,

$$E = e(I)$$

is called the *elementary matrix* corresponding to the elementary row operation e. Note that E is always a square matrix.

EXAMPLE 3.9 Consider the following three elementary row operations:

(1) Interchange R_2 and R_3.
(2) Multiply R_2 by $k = -6$.
(3) Add $-4R_1$ to R_3.

The 3-square elementary matrices corresponding to the above elementary row operations are as follows:

$$E_1 = \begin{bmatrix} 1 & 0 & 0 \\ 0 & 0 & 1 \\ 0 & 1 & 0 \end{bmatrix}, \qquad E_2 = \begin{bmatrix} 1 & 0 & 0 \\ 0 & -6 & 0 \\ 0 & 0 & 1 \end{bmatrix}, \qquad E_3 = \begin{bmatrix} 1 & 0 & 0 \\ 0 & 1 & 0 \\ -4 & 0 & 1 \end{bmatrix}$$

The following theorem, proved in Problem 3.62, shows the fundamental relationship between the elementary row operations and their corresponding matrices.

Theorem 3.6: Let e be an elementary row operation and let E be the corresponding m-square elementary matrix. Then

$$e(A) = EA$$

where A is any $m \times n$ matrix.

In other words, the result of applying an elementary row operation e to a matrix A can be obtained by premultiplying A by the corresponding elementary matrix E.

Applications

Using Theorem 3.6, we are able to prove the following important properties of matrices.

Theorem 3.7: Let A be a square matrix. Then the following are equivalent:

    (a) A is invertible (nonsingular).
    (b) A is row equivalent to the identity matrix I.
    (c) A is a product of elementary matrices.

Recall that square matrices A and B are inverses if

$$AB = BA = I$$

The next theorem shows that we need only show that one of the products is true, say $AB = I$, to prove that matrices are inverses.

Theorem 3.8:   If $AB = I$, then $BA = I$, and hence $B = A^{-1}$.

Row equivalent can also be defined in terms of matrix multiplication.

Theorem 3.9: B is row equivalent to A if and only if there exists a nonsingular matrix P such that $B = PA$.

3.8   ELEMENTARY COLUMN OPERATION, MATRIX EQUIVALENCE

This section repeats some of the discussion of the previous section using the columns of a matrix instead of the rows.   The choice of first using rows comes from the fact that the row operations are closely related to operations with systems of linear equations.

Consider a matrix A with columns $C_1, C_2, \ldots, C_n$.   The following operations on A, called *elementary column operations*, are analogous to the above elementary row operations:

[F$_1$]   *(Column Interchange)*:   Interchange column C_i and column C_j, denoted by

$$C_i \leftrightarrow C_j$$

[F$_2$]   *(Column Scaling)*:   Multiply column C_i by a nonzero scalar k, written

$$kC_i \rightarrow C_i \quad (k \neq 0)$$

[F$_3$]   *(Column Addition)*:   Add k times column C_i to column C_j, written

$$\text{``Add } kC_i \text{ to } C_j\text{''} \quad \text{or} \quad (kC_i + C_j) \rightarrow C_j$$

Each of the above operations has an inverse operation of the same type, just like the corresponding row operations.

Elementary Matrices and Column Operations

Let f denote an elementary column operation and let $f(A)$ denote the result of applying the operation f to a matrix A.   The matrix F obtained by applying f to the identity matrix,

$$F = f(I)$$

is called the *elementary matrix*, corresponding to the elementary column operation f.   Note that F is always a square matrix.

EXAMPLE 3.10   Consider the following elementary column operations:

(1)   Interchange C_1 and C_3.
(2)   Multiply C_3 by $k = -2$.
(3)   Add $-3C_2$ to C_3.

The 3-square elementary matrices corresponding to the above elementary column operations are as follows:

$$F_1 = \begin{bmatrix} 0 & 0 & 1 \\ 0 & 1 & 0 \\ 1 & 0 & 0 \end{bmatrix}, \qquad F_2 = \begin{bmatrix} 1 & 0 & 0 \\ 0 & 1 & 0 \\ 0 & 0 & -2 \end{bmatrix}, \qquad F_3 = \begin{bmatrix} 1 & 0 & 0 \\ 0 & 1 & -3 \\ 0 & 0 & 1 \end{bmatrix}$$

Relationship between Elementary Row and Column Operations

Suppose e and f denote corresponding elementary row and column operations,

$$e: \text{``Add } -3R_1 \text{ to } R_2\text{''} \qquad f: \text{``Add } -3C_1 \text{ to } C_2\text{''}$$

Since the columns of A are the rows of A^T, and vice versa, applying f to a matrix A can be accomplished by the following three steps:

(1) Write down A^T, the transpose of A.

(2) Find $e(A^T)$, that is, apply e to A^T.

(3) Write down $[e(A^T)]^T$, the transpose of $e(A^T)$.

This is illustrated below:

$$\begin{bmatrix} 1 & 3 \\ 2 & 4 \\ 3 & 5 \end{bmatrix} \rightarrow \begin{bmatrix} 1 & 2 & 3 \\ 3 & 4 & 5 \end{bmatrix} \rightarrow \begin{bmatrix} 1 & 2 & 3 \\ 0 & -2 & -4 \end{bmatrix} \rightarrow \begin{bmatrix} 1 & 0 \\ 2 & -2 \\ 3 & -4 \end{bmatrix}$$

$$A \qquad\qquad A^T \qquad\qquad e(A^T) \qquad f(A) = [e(A^T)]^T$$

We state this result formally.

Lemma 3.10: Suppose A is any matrix. Then $f(A) = [e(A^T)]^T$.

Suppose now E and F are the elementary matrices corresponding, respectively, to the elementary row and column operations e and f. Using Lemma 3.10, we obtain:

Corollary 3.11: F is the transpose of E.

Thus by the above lemma,

$$f(A) = [e(A^T)]^T = [EA^T]^T = (A^T)^T E^T = AF$$

This proves the following theorem (which is analogous to Theorem 3.6 for the elementary row operations).

Theorem 3.12: For any matrix A, $f(A) = AF$.

That is, the result of applying an elementary column operation f on a matrix A can be obtained by postmultiplying A by the corresponding elementary matrix F.

A matrix A is *column equivalent* to a matrix B if B can be obtained from A by a sequence of elementary column operations. Column equivalence, like row equivalence, is an equivalence relation and can be defined in terms of matrix multiplication. Specifically:

Theorem 3.13: B is column equivalent to A if and only if there exists a nonsingular matrix Q such that $B = AQ$.

Matrix Equivalence

A matrix B is *equivalent* to a matrix A if B can be obtained from A by a sequence of elementary row and column operations. Alternatively, B is equivalent to A if there exist nonsingular matrices P and Q such that $B = PAQ$. Just like row and column equivalence, equivalence of matrices is an equivalence relation.

The main result of this subsection follows.

Theorem 3.14: Every $m \times n$ matrix A is equivalent to a unique block matrix of the form

$$\begin{bmatrix} I_r & 0 \\ 0 & 0 \end{bmatrix}$$

where I_r is the $r \times r$ identity matrix.

Remark: The nonnegative integer r in Theorem 3.14 is called the *rank* of A. There will be many other equivalent definitions of rank throughout the text.

3.9 *LU* FACTORIZATION

Suppose A is a nonsingular matrix which can be brought into (upper) triangular form U using only row-addition operations, that is, suppose A can be triangularized by the following algorithm, which we write using computer algorithmic notation.

Algorithm 3.9: Transform a matrix $A = [a_{ij}]$ into a triangular form U.

Step 1. Repeat for $j = 1, 2, \ldots, n-1$;

Step 2.   Repeat for $i = j + 1, \ldots, n$

   (a) Set $m_{ij} := -a_{ij}/a_{jj}$

   (b) Set $R_i := m_{ij}R_j + R_i$

   [End of Step 2 inner loop.]
   [End of Step 1 outer loop.]

Step 3. Exit.

The numbers m_{ij} are called *multipliers*. Sometimes we keep track of these multipliers by means of the following lower triangular matrix L:

$$L = \begin{bmatrix} 1 & 0 & 0 & \ldots & 0 & 0 \\ -m_{21} & 1 & 0 & \ldots & 0 & 0 \\ -m_{31} & -m_{32} & 1 & \ldots & 0 & 0 \\ \hdotsfor{6} \\ -m_{n1} & -m_{n2} & -m_{n3} & \ldots & -m_{n,n-1} & 1 \end{bmatrix}$$

That is, L has 1s on the diagonal, 0s above the diagonal, and the negative of m_{ij} as its ij entry below the diagonal.

The above matrix L and the triangular matrix U obtained in Algorithm 3.9 give us the classical LU factorization of such a matrix A. That is,

Theorem 3.15: Let A be a nonsingular matrix which can be brought into triangular form U using only row-addition operations.   Then $A = LU$, where L is the above lower triangular matrix with 1s on the diagonal, and U is an upper triangular matrix with no 0s on the diagonal.

EXAMPLE 3.11 Suppose $A = \begin{bmatrix} 1 & 2 & -3 \\ -3 & -4 & 13 \\ 2 & 1 & -5 \end{bmatrix}$.   Observe that A may be reduced to triangular form by the operations "Add $3R_1$ to R_2", "Add $-2R_1$ to R_3", and then "Add $\frac{3}{2}R_2$ to R_3".   That is,

$$A \sim \begin{bmatrix} 1 & 2 & -3 \\ 0 & 2 & 4 \\ 0 & -3 & 1 \end{bmatrix} \sim \begin{bmatrix} 1 & 2 & -3 \\ 0 & 2 & 4 \\ 0 & 0 & 7 \end{bmatrix}$$

This gives us the factorization $A = LU$, where

$$L = \begin{bmatrix} 1 & 0 & 0 \\ -3 & 1 & 0 \\ 2 & -\frac{3}{2} & 1 \end{bmatrix}, \qquad U = \begin{bmatrix} 1 & 2 & -3 \\ 0 & 2 & 4 \\ 0 & 0 & 7 \end{bmatrix}$$

We emphasize that the entries -3, 2, and $-\frac{3}{2}$ in L come from the above elementary row operations, i.e., they are the negatives of the multipliers, and that U is the triangular form of A.

Applications to Linear Equations

Consider a computer algorithm M.   Let $C(n)$ denote the running time of the algorithm as a function of the size n of the input data.   [The function $C(n)$ is sometimes called the *time complexity* or simply the *complexity* of the algorithm M.]   Frequently $C(n)$ simply counts the number of multiplications and divisions executed by M, but does not count the number of additions and subtractions since they take much less time to execute.

Now consider a square system of linear equations

$$AX = B$$

where $A = [a_{ij}]$ has an LU factorization and

$$X = (x_1, \ldots, x_n)^T \qquad \text{and} \qquad B = (b_1, \ldots, b_n)^T$$

Then the system may be brought into triangular form (in order to apply back-substitution) by applying the above algorithm to the augmented matrix $M = (A, B)$ of the system.   The time complexity of the above algorithm and that of the back-substitution are, respectively,

$$C(n) \approx n^3/3 \qquad \text{and} \qquad C(n) \approx n^2/2$$

where n is the number of equations.

On the other hand, suppose we already have the factorization $A = LU$.   Then to triangularize the system, we need only apply the row operations in the algorithm (retained by the matrix L) to the column vector B.   In this case, the time complexity is

$$C(n) \approx n^2/2$$

Of course, to obtain the factorization $A = LU$ requires the original algorithm, where $C(n) \approx n^3/3$. Thus nothing may be gained by first finding the LU factorization when a single system is involved.   However, there are situations, illustrated below, where the LU factorization is useful.

Suppose that for a given matrix A we need to solve the system

$$AX = B$$

repeatedly for a sequence of different constant vectors, say $B_1, B_2, \ldots, B_k$. Also, suppose some of the B_i depend on the solution of the system obtained while using preceding vectors B_j. In such a case it is more efficient to find first the LU factorization of A, and then to use this factorization to solve the system for each new B.

EXAMPLE 3.12   Consider the system

$$
\begin{aligned}
x - y - z &= k_1 \\
3x - 4y - 2z &= k_2 \qquad \text{or} \qquad AX = B \\
2x - 3y - 2z &= k_3
\end{aligned}
$$

where

$$
A = \begin{bmatrix} 1 & -1 & -1 \\ 3 & -4 & -2 \\ 2 & -3 & -2 \end{bmatrix} \quad \text{and} \quad B = \begin{bmatrix} k_1 \\ k_2 \\ k_3 \end{bmatrix}
$$

Suppose we want to solve the system for B_1, B_2, B_3, B_4, where $B_0 = [1, 2, 3]^T$ and

$$B_{j+1} = B_j + X_j \qquad (\text{for } j > 1)$$

where X_j is the solution of the system $AX = B_j$. Here it is more efficient to obtain first the LU factorization for A and then use the LU factorization to solve the system for each of the B's. (See Problems 3.49 and 3.107.)

Solved Problems

ALGEBRA OF MATRICES

3.1.   Find the diagonal and trace of each matrix:

$$
(a) \quad A = \begin{bmatrix} 1 & 3 & 6 \\ 2 & -5 & 8 \\ 4 & -2 & 9 \end{bmatrix}; \qquad (b) \quad B = \begin{bmatrix} 2 & 4 & 8 \\ 3 & -7 & 9 \\ -5 & 0 & 2 \end{bmatrix}; \qquad (c) \quad C = \begin{bmatrix} 1 & 2 & -3 \\ 4 & -5 & 6 \end{bmatrix}
$$

(a)   The diagonal of A consists of the elements from the upper left corner of A to the lower right corner of A or, in other words, the elements a_{11}, a_{22}, a_{33}. Thus the diagonal of A consists of the numbers 1, -5, and 9. The trace of A is the sum of the diagonal elements. Thus

$$\text{tr}(A) = 1 - 5 + 9 = 5$$

(b)   The diagonal of B consists of the numbers 2, -7, and 2. Hence

$$\text{tr}(B) = 2 - 7 + 2 = -3$$

(c)   The diagonal and trace are only defined for square matrices.

3.2. Exhibit: (a) the identity matrix I_n of order $n = 3$ and 5; (b) the scalar matrix kI_n for $k = 7$ and order $n = 3$ and 5.

(a) Write 1s on the diagonal and 0s elsewhere:

$$I_3 = \begin{bmatrix} 1 & 0 & 0 \\ 0 & 1 & 0 \\ 0 & 0 & 1 \end{bmatrix} \quad \text{and} \quad I_5 = \begin{bmatrix} 1 & & & & \\ & 1 & & & \\ & & 1 & & \\ & & & 1 & \\ & & & & 1 \end{bmatrix}$$

We frequently omit patterns of zeros, as illustrated for I_5.

(b) Write 7s on the diagonal and 0s elsewhere:

$$I_3 = \begin{bmatrix} 7 & 0 & 0 \\ 0 & 7 & 0 \\ 0 & 0 & 7 \end{bmatrix} \quad \text{and} \quad I_5 = \begin{bmatrix} 7 & & & & \\ & 7 & & & \\ & & 7 & & \\ & & & 7 & \\ & & & & 7 \end{bmatrix}$$

3.3. Let $A = \begin{bmatrix} 1 & 2 \\ 4 & -3 \end{bmatrix}$. Find: (a) A^2; (b) A^3.

(a) $A^2 = AA = \begin{bmatrix} 1 & 2 \\ 4 & -3 \end{bmatrix}\begin{bmatrix} 1 & 2 \\ 4 & -3 \end{bmatrix} = \begin{bmatrix} 1+8 & 2-6 \\ 4-12 & 8+9 \end{bmatrix} = \begin{bmatrix} 9 & -4 \\ -8 & 17 \end{bmatrix}$

(b) $A^3 = AA^2 = \begin{bmatrix} 1 & 2 \\ 4 & -3 \end{bmatrix}\begin{bmatrix} 9 & -4 \\ -8 & 17 \end{bmatrix} = \begin{bmatrix} 9-16 & -4+34 \\ 36+24 & -16-51 \end{bmatrix} = \begin{bmatrix} -7 & 30 \\ 60 & -67 \end{bmatrix}$

3.4. For the matrix A in Problem 3.3, find:

(a) $f(A)$ for the polynomial $f(x) = 2x^3 - 4x + 5$.

(b) $g(A)$ for the polynomial $g(x) = x^2 + 2x - 11$.

(a) First substitute A for x and $5I$ for the constant in $f(x) = 2x^3 - 4x + 5$, obtaining

$$f(A) = 2A^3 - 4A + 5I = 2\begin{bmatrix} -7 & 30 \\ 60 & -67 \end{bmatrix} - 4\begin{bmatrix} 1 & 2 \\ 4 & -3 \end{bmatrix} + 5\begin{bmatrix} 1 & 0 \\ 0 & 1 \end{bmatrix}$$

Then multiply each matrix by its respective scalar:

$$f(A) = \begin{bmatrix} -14 & 60 \\ 120 & -134 \end{bmatrix} + \begin{bmatrix} -4 & -8 \\ -16 & 12 \end{bmatrix} + \begin{bmatrix} 5 & 0 \\ 0 & 5 \end{bmatrix}$$

Lastly, add the corresponding elements in the matrices:

$$f(A) = \begin{bmatrix} -14-4+5 & 60-8+0 \\ 120-16+0 & -134+12+5 \end{bmatrix} = \begin{bmatrix} -13 & 52 \\ 104 & -117 \end{bmatrix}$$

(b) Substitute A for x and $11I$ for the constant 11 in $g(x) = x^2 + 2x - 11$, and then calculate as follows:

$$g(A) = A^2 + 2A - 11I = \begin{bmatrix} 9 & -4 \\ -8 & 17 \end{bmatrix} + 2\begin{bmatrix} 1 & 2 \\ 4 & -3 \end{bmatrix} - 11\begin{bmatrix} 1 & 0 \\ 0 & 1 \end{bmatrix}$$

$$= \begin{bmatrix} 9 & -4 \\ -8 & 17 \end{bmatrix} + \begin{bmatrix} 2 & 4 \\ 8 & -6 \end{bmatrix} + \begin{bmatrix} -11 & 0 \\ 0 & -11 \end{bmatrix}$$

$$= \begin{bmatrix} 9+2-11 & -4+4+0 \\ -8+8+0 & 17-6-11 \end{bmatrix} = \begin{bmatrix} 0 & 0 \\ 0 & 0 \end{bmatrix}$$

Since $g(A)$ is the zero matrix, A is a root of the polynomial $g(x)$.

3.5.   Let $B = \begin{bmatrix} 1 & 3 \\ 5 & 3 \end{bmatrix}$.   Find:

(a) $f(B)$ for the polynomial $f(x) = 2x^2 - 4x + 3$.

(b) $g(B)$ for the polynomial $g(x) = x^2 - 4x - 12$.

(a)   First calculate B^2:

$$B^2 = BB = \begin{bmatrix} 1 & 3 \\ 5 & 3 \end{bmatrix}\begin{bmatrix} 1 & 3 \\ 5 & 3 \end{bmatrix} = \begin{bmatrix} 1+15 & 3+9 \\ 5+15 & 15+9 \end{bmatrix} = \begin{bmatrix} 16 & 12 \\ 20 & 24 \end{bmatrix}$$

Then

$$f(B) = 2B^2 - 4B + 3I = 2\begin{bmatrix} 16 & 12 \\ 20 & 24 \end{bmatrix} - 4\begin{bmatrix} 1 & 3 \\ 5 & 3 \end{bmatrix} + 3\begin{bmatrix} 1 & 0 \\ 0 & 1 \end{bmatrix}$$

$$= \begin{bmatrix} 32 & 24 \\ 40 & 48 \end{bmatrix} + \begin{bmatrix} -4 & -12 \\ -20 & -12 \end{bmatrix} + \begin{bmatrix} 3 & 0 \\ 0 & 3 \end{bmatrix} = \begin{bmatrix} 31 & 12 \\ 20 & 39 \end{bmatrix}$$

(b)   We already know B^2.   Thus

$$g(B) = B^2 - 4B - 12I = \begin{bmatrix} 16 & 12 \\ 20 & 24 \end{bmatrix} - 4\begin{bmatrix} 1 & 3 \\ 5 & 3 \end{bmatrix} - 12\begin{bmatrix} 1 & 0 \\ 0 & 1 \end{bmatrix}$$

$$= \begin{bmatrix} 16 & 12 \\ 20 & 24 \end{bmatrix} + \begin{bmatrix} -4 & -12 \\ -20 & -12 \end{bmatrix} + \begin{bmatrix} -12 & 0 \\ 0 & -12 \end{bmatrix} = \begin{bmatrix} 0 & 0 \\ 0 & 0 \end{bmatrix}$$

Note that B is a zero of the polynomial $g(x)$.

3.6.   Let $A = \begin{bmatrix} 1 & 3 \\ 4 & -3 \end{bmatrix}$.

(a)   Find a nonzero column vector $u = \begin{bmatrix} x \\ y \end{bmatrix}$ such that $Au = 3u$.

(b)   Describe all such vectors.

(a)   First set up the matrix equation $Au = 3u$:

$$\begin{bmatrix} 1 & 3 \\ 4 & -3 \end{bmatrix}\begin{bmatrix} x \\ y \end{bmatrix} = 3\begin{bmatrix} x \\ y \end{bmatrix}$$

Write each side as a single matrix (column vector):

$$\begin{bmatrix} x+3y \\ 4x-3y \end{bmatrix} = \begin{bmatrix} 3x \\ 3y \end{bmatrix}$$

Set corresponding elements equal to each other to obtain the system of equations, and reduce it to echelon form:

$$\left.\begin{array}{r} x + 3y = 3x \\ 4x - 3y = 3y \end{array}\right\} \rightarrow \left.\begin{array}{r} 2x - 3y = 0 \\ 4x - 6y = 0 \end{array}\right\} \rightarrow \left.\begin{array}{r} 2x - 3y = 0 \\ 0 = 0 \end{array}\right\} \rightarrow 2x - 3y = 0$$

The system reduces to one nondegenerate linear equation in two unknowns, and so has an infinite number of solutions. To obtain a nonzero solution let, say, $y = 2$; then $x = 3$. Thus $u = (3, 2)^T$ is a desired nonzero vector.

(b) To find the general solution, set $y = a$, where a is a parameter. Substitute $y = a$ into $2x - 3y = 0$ to obtain $x = 3a/2$. Thus $u = (3a/2, a)^T$ represents all such solutions.

INVERTIBLE MATRICES, INVERSES

3.7. Show that $A = \begin{bmatrix} 1 & 0 & 2 \\ 2 & -1 & 3 \\ 4 & 1 & 8 \end{bmatrix}$ and $B = \begin{bmatrix} -11 & 2 & 2 \\ -4 & 0 & 1 \\ 6 & -1 & -1 \end{bmatrix}$ are inverses.

Compute the product AB, obtaining

$$AB = \begin{bmatrix} -11 + 0 + 12 & 2 + 0 - 2 & 2 + 0 - 2 \\ -22 + 4 + 18 & 4 + 0 - 3 & 4 - 1 - 3 \\ -44 - 4 + 48 & 8 + 0 - 8 & 8 + 1 - 8 \end{bmatrix} = \begin{bmatrix} 1 & 0 & 0 \\ 0 & 1 & 0 \\ 0 & 0 & 1 \end{bmatrix} = I$$

Since $AB = I$, we can conclude (Theorem 3.8) that $BA = I$. Accordingly, A and B are inverses.

3.8. Find the inverse, if possible, of each matrix:

(a) $A = \begin{bmatrix} 5 & 3 \\ 4 & 2 \end{bmatrix};$ (b) $B = \begin{bmatrix} 2 & -3 \\ 1 & 3 \end{bmatrix};$ (c) $\begin{bmatrix} -2 & 6 \\ 3 & -9 \end{bmatrix}.$

Use the formula for the inverse of a 2×2 matrix appearing in Section 3.4.

(a) First find $|A| = 5(2) - 3(4) = 10 - 12 = -2$. Next interchange the diagonal elements, take the negatives of the nondiagonal elements, and multiply by $1/|A|$:

$$A^{-1} = -\frac{1}{2}\begin{bmatrix} 2 & -3 \\ -4 & 5 \end{bmatrix} = \begin{bmatrix} -1 & \frac{3}{2} \\ 2 & -\frac{5}{2} \end{bmatrix}$$

(b) First find $|B| = 2(3) - (-3)(1) = 6 + 3 = 9$. Next interchange the diagonal elements, take the negatives of the nondiagonal elements, and multiply by $1/|B|$:

$$B^{-1} = \frac{1}{9}\begin{bmatrix} 3 & 3 \\ -1 & 2 \end{bmatrix} = \begin{bmatrix} \frac{1}{3} & \frac{1}{3} \\ -\frac{1}{9} & \frac{2}{9} \end{bmatrix}$$

(c) First find $|C| = -2(-9) - 6(3) = 18 - 18 = 0$. Since $|C| = 0$, C has no inverse.

3.9. Find the inverse of $A = \begin{bmatrix} 1 & -2 & 2 \\ 2 & -3 & 6 \\ 1 & 1 & 7 \end{bmatrix}$.

Form the matrix $M = [A, I]$ and row reduce M to echelon form:

$$M = \begin{bmatrix} 1 & -2 & 2 & | & 1 & 0 & 0 \\ 2 & -3 & 6 & | & 0 & 1 & 0 \\ 1 & 1 & 7 & | & 0 & 0 & 1 \end{bmatrix} \sim \begin{bmatrix} 1 & -2 & 2 & | & 1 & 0 & 0 \\ 0 & 1 & 2 & | & -2 & 1 & 0 \\ 0 & 3 & 5 & | & -1 & 0 & 1 \end{bmatrix} \sim \begin{bmatrix} 1 & -2 & 2 & | & 1 & 0 & 0 \\ 0 & 1 & 2 & | & -2 & 1 & 0 \\ 0 & 0 & -1 & | & 5 & -3 & 1 \end{bmatrix}$$

In echelon form, the left half of M is in triangular form; hence A has an inverse.   Further reduce M to row canonical form:

$$M \sim \begin{bmatrix} 1 & -2 & 0 & | & 11 & -6 & 2 \\ 0 & 1 & 0 & | & 8 & -5 & 2 \\ 0 & 0 & 1 & | & -5 & 3 & -1 \end{bmatrix} \sim \begin{bmatrix} 1 & 0 & 0 & | & 27 & -16 & 6 \\ 0 & 1 & 0 & | & 8 & -5 & 2 \\ 0 & 0 & 1 & | & -5 & 3 & -1 \end{bmatrix}$$

The final matrix has the form $[I, A^{-1}]$, that is, A^{-1} is the right half of the last matrix.   Thus

$$A^{-1} = \begin{bmatrix} 27 & -16 & 6 \\ 8 & -5 & 2 \\ -5 & 3 & -1 \end{bmatrix}$$

3.10. Find the inverse of $B = \begin{bmatrix} 1 & 2 & -4 \\ -1 & -1 & 5 \\ 2 & 7 & -3 \end{bmatrix}$.

Form the matrix $M = [B, I]$ and row reduce M to echelon form:

$$M = \begin{bmatrix} 1 & 2 & -4 & | & 1 & 0 & 0 \\ -1 & -1 & 5 & | & 0 & 1 & 0 \\ 2 & 7 & -3 & | & 0 & 0 & 1 \end{bmatrix} \sim \begin{bmatrix} 1 & 2 & -4 & | & 1 & 0 & 0 \\ 0 & 1 & 1 & | & 1 & 1 & 0 \\ 0 & 3 & 5 & | & -2 & 0 & 1 \end{bmatrix} \sim \begin{bmatrix} 1 & 2 & -4 & | & 1 & 0 & 0 \\ 0 & 1 & 1 & | & 1 & 1 & 0 \\ 0 & 0 & 2 & | & -5 & -3 & 1 \end{bmatrix}$$

In echelon form, the left half of M is in triangular form; hence B has an inverse.   Further reduce M to row canonical form:

$$M \sim \begin{bmatrix} 1 & 2 & 0 & | & -9 & -6 & 2 \\ 0 & 1 & 0 & | & \frac{7}{2} & \frac{5}{2} & -\frac{1}{2} \\ 0 & 0 & 1 & | & -\frac{5}{2} & -\frac{3}{2} & \frac{1}{2} \end{bmatrix} \sim \begin{bmatrix} 1 & 0 & 0 & | & -16 & -11 & 3 \\ 0 & 1 & 0 & | & \frac{7}{2} & \frac{5}{2} & -\frac{1}{2} \\ 0 & 0 & 1 & | & -\frac{5}{2} & -\frac{3}{2} & \frac{1}{2} \end{bmatrix}$$

The final matrix has the form $[I, B^{-1}]$, that is, B^{-1} is the right half of the last matrix.   Thus

$$B^{-1} = \begin{bmatrix} -16 & -11 & 3 \\ \frac{7}{2} & \frac{5}{2} & -\frac{1}{2} \\ -\frac{5}{2} & -\frac{3}{2} & \frac{1}{2} \end{bmatrix}$$

3.11. Find the inverse of $C = \begin{bmatrix} 1 & 3 & -4 \\ 1 & 5 & -1 \\ 3 & 13 & -6 \end{bmatrix}$.

Form the matrix $M = [C, I]$ and row reduce M to echelon form:

$$M = \begin{bmatrix} 1 & 3 & -4 & | & 1 & 0 & 0 \\ 1 & 5 & -1 & | & 0 & 1 & 0 \\ 3 & 13 & -6 & | & 0 & 0 & 1 \end{bmatrix} \sim \begin{bmatrix} 1 & 3 & -4 & | & 1 & 0 & 0 \\ 0 & 2 & 3 & | & -1 & 1 & 0 \\ 0 & 4 & 6 & | & -3 & 0 & 1 \end{bmatrix} \sim \begin{bmatrix} 1 & 3 & -4 & | & 1 & 0 & 0 \\ 0 & 2 & 3 & | & -1 & 1 & 0 \\ 0 & 0 & 0 & | & -1 & -2 & 1 \end{bmatrix}$$

In echelon form, M has a zero row in its left half, that is, C is not row reducible to triangular form. Accordingly, C has no inverse.

ELEMENTARY MATRICES

3.12. Let e_1, e_2, e_3 denote, respectively, the elementary row operations "Interchange rows R_1 and R_2", "Multiply R_3 by $k = 7$", and "Add $-3R_1$ to R_2". Find the corresponding 3-square elementary matrices E_1, E_2, and E_3.

Apply each operation to the 3×3 identity matrix I_3 to obtain

$$E_1 = \begin{bmatrix} 0 & 1 & 0 \\ 1 & 0 & 0 \\ 0 & 0 & 1 \end{bmatrix}, \qquad E_2 = \begin{bmatrix} 1 & 0 & 0 \\ 0 & 1 & 0 \\ 0 & 0 & 7 \end{bmatrix}, \qquad E_3 = \begin{bmatrix} 1 & 0 & 0 \\ -3 & 1 & 0 \\ 0 & 0 & 1 \end{bmatrix}$$

3.13. Consider the elementary row operations in Problem 3.12.

(a) Describe the inverse operations e_1^{-1}, e_2^{-1}, and e_3^{-1}.

(b) Find the corresponding 3-square elementary matrices E_1', E_2', and E_3'.

(c) What is the relationship between the matrices E_1', E_2', and E_3' and the matrices E_1, E_2, and E_3?

(a) The inverse of e_1 is itself, that is, the operation "Interchange rows R_1 and R_2" is its own inverse. The inverse of e_2 is "Multiply R_3 by $k^{-1} = \frac{1}{7}$". The inverse of e_3 is "Add $3R_1$ to R_2". (See Problem 3.55.)

(b) Apply each inverse operation to the 3×3 identity matrix I_3 to obtain

$$E_1' = \begin{bmatrix} 0 & 1 & 0 \\ 1 & 0 & 0 \\ 0 & 0 & 1 \end{bmatrix}, \qquad E_2' = \begin{bmatrix} 1 & 0 & 0 \\ 0 & 1 & 0 \\ 0 & 0 & \frac{1}{7} \end{bmatrix}, \qquad E_3' = \begin{bmatrix} 1 & 0 & 0 \\ 3 & 1 & 0 \\ 0 & 0 & 1 \end{bmatrix}$$

(c) The matrices E_1', E_2', and E_3' are the inverses of the matrices E_1, E_2, and E_3, respectively.

3.14. Consider the elementary row operations in Problem 3.12.

(a) Describe the corresponding elementary column operations f_1, f_2, and f_3.

(b) Find the corresponding 3-square elementary matrices F_1, F_2, and F_3.

(c) What is the relationship between the matrices F_1, F_2, and F_3 and the matrices E_1, E_2, and E_3?

(a) Simply replace row by column to obtain the corresponding column operations "Interchange columns C_1 and C_2", "Multiply C_3 by $k = 7$", and "Add $-3C_1$ to C_2".

(b) Apply each column operation to the 3×3 identity matrix I_3 to obtain

$$F_1 = \begin{bmatrix} 0 & 1 & 0 \\ 1 & 0 & 0 \\ 0 & 0 & 1 \end{bmatrix}, \qquad F_2 = \begin{bmatrix} 1 & 0 & 0 \\ 0 & 1 & 0 \\ 0 & 0 & 7 \end{bmatrix}, \qquad F_3 = \begin{bmatrix} 1 & -3 & 0 \\ 0 & 1 & 0 \\ 0 & 0 & 1 \end{bmatrix}$$

(c) The matrices F_1, F_2, and F_3 are the transpose of the matrices E_1, E_2, and E_3, respectively.

3.15. Write $A = \begin{bmatrix} 1 & -3 \\ -2 & 4 \end{bmatrix}$ as a product of elementary matrices.

There are three steps:

Step 1. Row reduce A to the identity matrix I, keeping track of the elementary row operations. (If A is not row equivalent to the identity matrix I, then A cannot be written as a product of elementary matrices.) We have

$$A = \begin{bmatrix} 1 & -3 \\ -2 & 4 \end{bmatrix} \sim \begin{bmatrix} 1 & -3 \\ 0 & -2 \end{bmatrix} \sim \begin{bmatrix} 1 & -3 \\ 0 & 1 \end{bmatrix} \sim \begin{bmatrix} 1 & 0 \\ 0 & 1 \end{bmatrix} = I$$

where the row operations are, respectively, "Add $2R_1$ to R_2", "Multiply R_2 by $k = -\frac{1}{2}$", and "Add $3R_2$ to R_1".

Step 2. Write down the inverse row operations. These are "Add $-2R_1$ to R_2", "Multiply R_2 by $k^{-1} = -2$", and "Add $-3R_2$ to R_1".

Step 3. Write A as the product of the elementary matrices corresponding to the inverse operations. Thus

$$A = \begin{bmatrix} 1 & 0 \\ -2 & 1 \end{bmatrix} \begin{bmatrix} 1 & 0 \\ 0 & -2 \end{bmatrix} \begin{bmatrix} 1 & -3 \\ 0 & 1 \end{bmatrix}$$

which gives us our desired product.

3.16. Write $B = \begin{bmatrix} 1 & 2 & 3 \\ 0 & 1 & 4 \\ 0 & 0 & 1 \end{bmatrix}$ as a product of elementary matrices.

There are three steps:

Step 1. Row reduce B to the identity matrix I, keeping track of the elementary row operations. We have

$$B = \begin{bmatrix} 1 & 2 & 3 \\ 0 & 1 & 4 \\ 0 & 0 & 1 \end{bmatrix} \sim \begin{bmatrix} 1 & 2 & 0 \\ 0 & 1 & 0 \\ 0 & 0 & 1 \end{bmatrix} \sim \begin{bmatrix} 1 & 0 & 0 \\ 0 & 1 & 0 \\ 0 & 0 & 1 \end{bmatrix} = I$$

where the row operations are, respectively, "Add $-4R_3$ to R_2", "Add $-3R_3$ to R_1", and "Add $-2R_2$ to R_1".

Step 2. Write down the inverse row operations. These are "Add $4R_3$ to R_2", "Add $3R_3$ to R_1", and "Add $2R_2$ to R_1".

Step 3. Write B as the product of the elementary matrices corresponding to the inverse operations. Thus

$$B = \begin{bmatrix} 1 & 0 & 0 \\ 0 & 1 & 4 \\ 0 & 0 & 1 \end{bmatrix} \begin{bmatrix} 1 & 0 & 3 \\ 0 & 1 & 0 \\ 0 & 0 & 1 \end{bmatrix} \begin{bmatrix} 1 & 2 & 0 \\ 0 & 1 & 0 \\ 0 & 0 & 1 \end{bmatrix}$$

which gives us our desired product.

3.17. Write $C = \begin{bmatrix} 1 & 1 & 2 \\ 2 & 3 & 8 \\ -3 & -1 & 2 \end{bmatrix}$ as a product of elementary matrices.

There are three steps:

Step 1. Row reduce C to the identity matrix I, keeping track of the elementary row operations. This is done by first reducing C to echelon form. We have

$$C = \begin{bmatrix} 1 & 1 & 2 \\ 2 & 3 & 8 \\ -3 & -1 & 2 \end{bmatrix} \sim \begin{bmatrix} 1 & 1 & 2 \\ 0 & 1 & 4 \\ 0 & 2 & 8 \end{bmatrix} \sim \begin{bmatrix} 1 & 1 & 2 \\ 0 & 1 & 4 \\ 0 & 0 & 0 \end{bmatrix}$$

In echelon form, C has a zero row. *Stop.* The matrix C cannot be row reduced to the identity matrix I, and so C cannot be written as a product of elementary matrices. (We note, in particular, that C has no inverse.)

DIAGONAL AND TRIANGULAR MATRICES

3.18. Write out the diagonal matrices

$$A = \mathrm{diag}(4, -3, 7), \; B = \mathrm{diag}(2, -6), \text{ and } C = \mathrm{diag}(3, -8, 0, 5)$$

Put the given scalars on the diagonal and 0s elsewhere:

$$A = \begin{bmatrix} 4 & 0 & 0 \\ 0 & -3 & 0 \\ 0 & 0 & 7 \end{bmatrix}, \quad B = \begin{bmatrix} 2 & 0 \\ 0 & -6 \end{bmatrix}, \quad C = \begin{bmatrix} 3 & & & \\ & -8 & & \\ & & 0 & \\ & & & 5 \end{bmatrix}$$

3.19. Let $A = \mathrm{diag}(2, 3, 5)$ and $B = \mathrm{diag}(7, 1, -4)$. Find: (a) AB, A^2, B^2; (b) $f(A)$ where $f(x) = x^2 + 3x - 2$; (c) A^{-1} and B^{-1}.

(a) The product matrix AB is a diagonal matrix obtained by multiplying corresponding diagonal entries.   Hence

$$AB = \mathrm{diag}(2(7), 3(1), +5(-4)) = \mathrm{diag}(14, 3, -20)$$

The squares A^2 and B^2 are diagonal matrices obtained by squaring each diagonal entry. Thus

$$A^2 = \mathrm{diag}(2^2, 3^2, 5^2) = \mathrm{diag}(4, 9, 25) \quad \text{and} \quad B^2 = \mathrm{diag}(49, 1, 16)$$

(b) $f(A)$ is a diagonal matrix obtained by evaluating $f(x)$ at each diagonal entry.   We have

$$f(2) = 4 + 6 - 2 = 8, \quad f(3) = 9 + 9 - 2 = 16, \quad f(5) = 25 + 15 - 2 = 38$$

Thus $f(A) = \mathrm{diag}(8, 16, 38)$.

(c) The inverse of a diagonal matrix is a diagonal matrix obtained by taking the inverse (reciprocal) of each diagonal entry.   Thus

$$A^{-1} = \mathrm{diag}(\tfrac{1}{2}, \tfrac{1}{3}, \tfrac{1}{5}) \quad \text{and} \quad B^{-1} = \mathrm{diag}(\tfrac{1}{7}, 1, -\tfrac{1}{4})$$

3.20. Find the inverse of $A = \text{diag}(4, \frac{2}{3}, -5, 7)$ and $B = \text{diag}(\frac{3}{4}, -8, 0, 1)$.

Take the inverse of each diagonal entry to obtain

$$A^{-1} = \text{diag}(\tfrac{1}{4}, \tfrac{3}{2}, -\tfrac{1}{5}, \tfrac{1}{7})$$

The matrix B has no inverse since one of its diagonal entries is zero.

3.21. Using only the scalars 0 and 1, find: (*a*) all 2×2 diagonal matrices; (*b*) all 2×2 upper triangular matrices.

(*a*) Diagonal matrices must have 0s off the diagonal. Hence we get

$$\begin{bmatrix} 1 & 0 \\ 0 & 1 \end{bmatrix}, \quad \begin{bmatrix} 1 & 0 \\ 0 & 0 \end{bmatrix}, \quad \begin{bmatrix} 0 & 0 \\ 0 & 1 \end{bmatrix}, \quad \begin{bmatrix} 0 & 0 \\ 0 & 0 \end{bmatrix}$$

(*b*) Upper triangular matrices must have 0s below the diagonal. This gives the four matrices of part (*a*) plus the matrices

$$\begin{bmatrix} 1 & 1 \\ 0 & 1 \end{bmatrix}, \quad \begin{bmatrix} 1 & 1 \\ 0 & 0 \end{bmatrix}, \quad \begin{bmatrix} 0 & 1 \\ 0 & 1 \end{bmatrix}, \quad \begin{bmatrix} 0 & 1 \\ 0 & 0 \end{bmatrix}$$

3.22. Find an upper triangular matrix A such that $A^3 = \begin{bmatrix} 8 & -57 \\ 0 & 27 \end{bmatrix}$.

Set $A = \begin{bmatrix} x & y \\ 0 & z \end{bmatrix}$. Then $x^3 = 8$, so $x = 2$; and $z^3 = 27$, so $z = 3$. Next calculate A^3 using $x = 2$ and $z = 3$:

$$A^2 = \begin{bmatrix} 2 & y \\ 0 & 3 \end{bmatrix}\begin{bmatrix} 2 & y \\ 0 & 3 \end{bmatrix} = \begin{bmatrix} 4 & 5y \\ 0 & 9 \end{bmatrix} \quad \text{and} \quad A^3 = \begin{bmatrix} 2 & y \\ 0 & 3 \end{bmatrix}\begin{bmatrix} 4 & 5y \\ 0 & 9 \end{bmatrix} = \begin{bmatrix} 8 & 19y \\ 0 & 27 \end{bmatrix}$$

Thus $19y = -57$, or $y = -3$. Accordingly, $A = \begin{bmatrix} 2 & -3 \\ 0 & 3 \end{bmatrix}$.

3.23. Answer true or false.   If false, give a counterexample.

(*a*) All square echelon matrices are upper triangular matrices.

(*b*) All upper triangular matrices are in echelon form.

(*c*) If A is an upper triangular matrix, then A^2 is upper triangular.

(*d*) If A^2 is an upper triangular matrix, then A is upper triangular.

(*a*) True.

(*b*) False. $A = \begin{bmatrix} 0 & 1 \\ 0 & 1 \end{bmatrix}$ is upper triangular but not in echelon form.

(*c*) True.   In fact, A^n and $f(A)$ are upper triangular matrices for any n and for any polynomial $f(x)$.

(*d*) False. $A = \begin{bmatrix} 1 & 2 \\ 3 & -1 \end{bmatrix}$ is not upper triangular, but $A^2 = \begin{bmatrix} 7 & 0 \\ 0 & 7 \end{bmatrix}$ is upper triangular.

3.24. What kinds of matrices are both upper triangular and lower triangular?

If A is both upper triangular and lower triangular, then every entry off the main diagonal must be zero. Hence A is diagonal.

3.25. Display the generic tridiagonal matrices of orders 4 and 5.

A square matrix is *tridiagonal* if the nonzero entries occur only on the diagonal, directly above the diagonal (on the *superdiagonal*), or directly below the diagonal (on the *subdiagonal*). Thus in each case, put 0s outside the diagonal, superdiagonal, and subdiagonal. This gives

$$\begin{bmatrix} a_{11} & a_{12} & & \\ a_{21} & a_{22} & a_{23} & \\ & a_{32} & a_{33} & a_{34} \\ & & a_{43} & a_{44} \end{bmatrix}, \qquad \begin{bmatrix} b_{11} & b_{12} & & & \\ b_{21} & b_{22} & b_{23} & & \\ & b_{32} & b_{33} & b_{34} & \\ & & b_{43} & b_{44} & b_{45} \\ & & & b_{54} & b_{55} \end{bmatrix}$$

3.26. Show that the product of tridiagonal matrices need not be tridiagonal.

We have

$$\begin{bmatrix} 1 & 1 & 0 \\ 1 & 1 & 1 \\ 0 & 1 & 1 \end{bmatrix} \begin{bmatrix} 1 & 1 & 0 \\ 1 & 1 & 1 \\ 0 & 1 & 1 \end{bmatrix} = \begin{bmatrix} 2 & 2 & 1 \\ 2 & 3 & 2 \\ 1 & 2 & 2 \end{bmatrix}$$

which is not tridiagonal.

SYMMETRIC AND SKEW-SYMMETRIC MATRICES

3.27. Determine whether or not each matrix is symmetric or skew-symmetric:

(a) $\quad A = \begin{bmatrix} 5 & -7 & 1 \\ -7 & 8 & 2 \\ 1 & 2 & -4 \end{bmatrix}$;   (b) $\quad B = \begin{bmatrix} 0 & 4 & -3 \\ -4 & 0 & 5 \\ 3 & -5 & 0 \end{bmatrix}$;   (c) $\quad C = \begin{bmatrix} 0 & 0 & 0 \\ 0 & 0 & 0 \end{bmatrix}$.

(a) By inspection, the symmetric elements (mirror images in the diagonal) are -7 and -7, 1 and 1, and 2 and 2. Thus A is symmetric since symmetric elements are equal.

(b) By inspection, the diagonal elements are all 0 and the symmetric elements 4 and -4, -3 and 3, and 5 and -5 are negatives of each other. Hence B is skew-symmetric.

(c) Since C is not square, C is neither symmetric nor skew-symmetric.

3.28. Determine whether or not each matrix is symmetric or skew-symmetric: (a) $D = \begin{bmatrix} 1 & 1 \\ 1 & 0 \end{bmatrix}$;

(b) $E = \begin{bmatrix} 1 & -1 \\ 1 & 0 \end{bmatrix}$; (c) $F = \begin{bmatrix} 0 & -1 \\ 1 & 0 \end{bmatrix}$; (d) $G = \begin{bmatrix} 0 & 0 \\ 0 & 0 \end{bmatrix}$.

(a) By inspection, $D^T = D$. Hence D is symmetric.

(b) We see that $E^T \neq \pm E$. Thus E is neither symmetric nor skew-symmetric.

(c) By inspection, $F^T = -F$. Hence F is skew-symmetric.

(d) Both, since $0^T = 0 = -0$ when 0 is square. [Compare with Problem 3.27(c).]

3.29. Find x, y, z, t if $A = \begin{bmatrix} 5 & 2 & x \\ y & z & -3 \\ 4 & t & -7 \end{bmatrix}$ is symmetric.

Equate symmetric elements (mirror images in the diagonal) to obtain $x = 4$, $y = 2$, and $t = -3$. The unknown z on the diagonal is indeterminate, i.e., it can be any scalar.

3.30. Find x and B if $B = \begin{bmatrix} 4 & x+2 \\ 2x-3 & x+1 \end{bmatrix}$ is symmetric.

Set the symmetric elements $x + 2$ and $2x - 3$ equal to each other, obtaining $2x - 3 = x + 2$ or $x = 5$.   Hence $B = \begin{bmatrix} 4 & 7 \\ 7 & 6 \end{bmatrix}$.

3.31. Write $A = \begin{bmatrix} 2 & 3 \\ 7 & 8 \end{bmatrix}$ as the sum of a symmetric matrix B and a skew-symmetric matrix C.

Use Theorem 3.2.   Calculate

$$A^T = \begin{bmatrix} 2 & 7 \\ 3 & 8 \end{bmatrix}, \qquad A + A^T = \begin{bmatrix} 4 & 10 \\ 10 & 16 \end{bmatrix}, \qquad A - A^T = \begin{bmatrix} 0 & -4 \\ 4 & 0 \end{bmatrix}$$

Then $A = B + C$, where

$$B = \tfrac{1}{2}(A + A^T) = \begin{bmatrix} 2 & 5 \\ 5 & 8 \end{bmatrix}, \qquad C = \tfrac{1}{2}(A - A^T) = \begin{bmatrix} 0 & -2 \\ 2 & 0 \end{bmatrix}$$

ORTHOGONAL MATRICES

All problems use Theorem 3.3, stating that a matrix A is orthogonal if and only if the rows (columns) form an orthonormal set of vectors, that is, the rows (columns) are unit vectors and are orthogonal to each other.   (Here we assume that all scalars are real numbers.)

3.32. Suppose $A = \begin{bmatrix} \frac{4}{5} & \frac{3}{5} \\ x & y \end{bmatrix}$ is orthogonal.   Find x and y.

Since the rows are orthogonal, we get $\frac{4}{5}x + \frac{3}{5}y = 0$ or $4x + 3y = 0$.   Since the first column is a unit vector, we get $x^2 + \frac{16}{25} = 1$ or $x^2 = \frac{9}{25}$ or $x = \pm\frac{3}{5}$.

Case (i): $x = \frac{3}{5}$.   Then $4x + 3y = 0$ yields $y = -\frac{4}{5}$.
Case (ii): $x = -\frac{3}{5}$.   Then $4x + 3y = 0$ yields $y = \frac{4}{5}$.

In other words, there are two possibilities:

$$A = \begin{bmatrix} \frac{4}{5} & \frac{3}{5} \\ \frac{3}{5} & -\frac{4}{5} \end{bmatrix} \qquad \text{or} \qquad A = \begin{bmatrix} \frac{4}{5} & \frac{3}{5} \\ -\frac{3}{5} & \frac{4}{5} \end{bmatrix}$$

3.33. Find x, y, z, s, and t if $A = \begin{bmatrix} x & \frac{2}{3} & \frac{2}{3} \\ \frac{2}{3} & \frac{1}{3} & y \\ z & s & t \end{bmatrix}$ is orthogonal.

Let R_1, R_2, R_3 denote the rows of A. Since R_1 and R_2 are unit vectors, we get

$$x^2 + \frac{4}{9} + \frac{4}{9} = 1 \quad \text{or} \quad x = \pm\frac{1}{3} \quad \text{and} \quad \frac{4}{9} + \frac{1}{9} + y^2 = 1 \quad \text{or} \quad y = \pm\frac{2}{3}$$

Since R_1 and R_2 are orthogonal, we get $2x/3 + \frac{2}{9} + 2y/3 = 0$ or $3x + 3y = -1$. The only possibility is that $x = \frac{1}{3}$ and $y = -\frac{2}{3}$. Thus

$$A = \begin{bmatrix} \frac{1}{3} & \frac{2}{3} & \frac{2}{3} \\ \frac{2}{3} & \frac{1}{3} & -\frac{2}{3} \\ z & s & t \end{bmatrix}$$

Let C_1, C_2, C_3 denote the columns of A. Since the columns are unit vectors,

$$\frac{1}{9} + \frac{4}{9} + z^2 = 1, \qquad \frac{4}{9} + \frac{1}{9} + s^2 = 1, \qquad \frac{4}{9} + \frac{4}{9} + t^2 = 1$$

Thus $z = \pm\frac{2}{3}$, $s = \pm\frac{2}{3}$, and $t = \pm\frac{1}{3}$.

Case (i): $z = \frac{2}{3}$. Since C_1 and C_2 are orthogonal, $s = -\frac{2}{3}$; since C_1 and C_3 are orthogonal, $t = \frac{1}{3}$.
Case (ii): $z = -\frac{2}{3}$. Since C_1 and C_2 are orthogonal, $s = \frac{2}{3}$; since C_1 and C_3 are orthogonal, $t = -\frac{1}{3}$.

Hence there are exactly two possible solutions:

$$A = \begin{bmatrix} \frac{1}{3} & \frac{2}{3} & \frac{2}{3} \\ \frac{2}{3} & \frac{1}{3} & -\frac{2}{3} \\ \frac{2}{3} & -\frac{2}{3} & \frac{1}{3} \end{bmatrix} \quad \text{and} \quad A = \begin{bmatrix} \frac{1}{3} & \frac{2}{3} & \frac{2}{3} \\ \frac{2}{3} & \frac{1}{3} & -\frac{2}{3} \\ -\frac{2}{3} & \frac{2}{3} & -\frac{1}{3} \end{bmatrix}$$

3.34. Find a 3×3 orthogonal matrix P whose first two rows are multiples of $u_1 = [1, 1, 1]$ and $u_2 = [0, -1, 1]$, respectively.

Let $u_3 = (x, y, z)$ be a nonzero vector orthogonal to u_1 and u_2. Then

$$x + y + z = 0 \quad \text{and} \quad -y + z = 0$$

Here z is a free variable. Set $z = -1$ to obtain $y = -1$ and $x = 2$. So $u_3 = (2, -1, -1)$. Let A be the matrix whose rows are u_1, u_2, u_3; and let P be the matrix obtained from A by normalizing the rows of A. Thus

$$A = \begin{bmatrix} 1 & 1 & 1 \\ 0 & -1 & 1 \\ 2 & -1 & -1 \end{bmatrix} \quad \text{and} \quad P = \begin{bmatrix} \dfrac{1}{\sqrt{3}} & \dfrac{1}{\sqrt{3}} & \dfrac{1}{\sqrt{3}} \\ 0 & \dfrac{-1}{\sqrt{2}} & \dfrac{1}{\sqrt{2}} \\ \dfrac{2}{\sqrt{6}} & \dfrac{-1}{\sqrt{6}} & \dfrac{-1}{\sqrt{6}} \end{bmatrix}$$

3.35. Let A be an arbitrary 2×2 orthogonal matrix, say, with first row $[a, b]$. Show that $a^2 + b^2 = 1$ and $A = \begin{bmatrix} a & b \\ b & -a \end{bmatrix}$ or $A = \begin{bmatrix} a & b \\ -b & a \end{bmatrix}$.

Suppose $A = \begin{bmatrix} a & b \\ c & d \end{bmatrix}$, where a, b, c, and d are real numbers. Since the rows of A form an orthonormal set, we get

$$a^2 + b^2 = 1, \qquad c^2 + d^2 = 1, \qquad ac + bd = 0$$

Similarly, the columns form an orthonormal set, so

$$a^2 + c^2 = 1, \qquad b^2 + d^2 = 1, \qquad ab + cd = 0$$

Therefore $c^2 = 1 - a^2 = b^2$, and hence $c = \pm b$.

Case (i): $c = +b$. Then $b(a + d) = 0$, so $d = -a$. The corresponding matrix is $\begin{bmatrix} a & b \\ b & -a \end{bmatrix}$.

Case (ii): $c = -b$. Then $b(d - a) = 0$, so $d = a$. The corresponding matrix is $\begin{bmatrix} a & b \\ -b & a \end{bmatrix}$.

SQUARE BLOCK MATRICES

3.36. Determine which matrix is a square block matrix.

$$A = \left[\begin{array}{cc|c|cc} 1 & 2 & 3 & 4 & 5 \\ 1 & 1 & 1 & 1 & 1 \\ \hline 9 & 8 & 7 & 6 & 5 \\ 3 & 3 & 3 & 3 & 3 \\ \hline 1 & 3 & 5 & 7 & 9 \end{array}\right], \qquad B = \left[\begin{array}{cc|c|cc} 1 & 2 & 3 & 4 & 5 \\ 1 & 1 & 1 & 1 & 1 \\ 9 & 8 & 7 & 6 & 5 \\ \hline 3 & 3 & 3 & 3 & 3 \\ \hline 1 & 3 & 5 & 7 & 9 \end{array}\right]$$

Although A is a 5×5 square matrix and a 3×3 block matrix, the second and third diagonal blocks are not square matrices. Thus A is not a square block matrix.

B is a square block matrix.

3.37. Complete the partitioning of

$$C = \left[\begin{array}{ccccc} 1 & 2 & 3 & 4 & 5 \\ 1 & 1 & 1 & 1 & 1 \\ \hline 9 & 8 & 7 & 6 & 5 \\ 3 & 3 & 3 & 3 & 3 \\ \hline 1 & 3 & 5 & 7 & 9 \end{array}\right]$$

into a square block matrix.

One horizontal line is between the second and third rows; hence add a vertical line between the second and third columns. The other horizontal line is between the fourth and fifth rows; hence add a vertical line between the fourth and fifth columns. (The horizontal lines and the vertical lines must be placed symmetrically to obtain a square block matrix.) This yields the square block matrix

$$C = \begin{bmatrix} 1 & 2 & 3 & 4 & 5 \\ 1 & 1 & 1 & 1 & 1 \\ 9 & 8 & 7 & 6 & 5 \\ 3 & 3 & 3 & 3 & 3 \\ 1 & 3 & 5 & 7 & 9 \end{bmatrix}$$

3.38. Determine which of the following square block matrices are lower triangular, upper triangular, or diagonal

$$A = \begin{bmatrix} 1 & 2 & 0 \\ 3 & 4 & 5 \\ 0 & 0 & 6 \end{bmatrix}, \qquad B = \begin{bmatrix} 1 & 0 & 0 & 0 \\ 2 & 3 & 4 & 0 \\ 5 & 0 & 6 & 0 \\ 0 & 7 & 8 & 9 \end{bmatrix}, \qquad C = \begin{bmatrix} 1 & 0 & 0 \\ 0 & 2 & 3 \\ 0 & 4 & 5 \end{bmatrix}, \qquad D = \begin{bmatrix} 1 & 2 & 0 \\ 3 & 4 & 5 \\ 0 & 6 & 7 \end{bmatrix}$$

A is upper triangular since the block below the diagonal is a zero block.

B is lower triangular since all blocks above the diagonal are zero blocks.

C is diagonal since the blocks above and below the diagonal are zero blocks.

D is neither upper triangular nor lower triangular. Furthermore, no other partitioning of D will make it into either a block upper triangular matrix or a block lower triangular matrix.

3.39. Suppose M and N are block diagonal matrices and the corresponding diagonal blocks have the same size. Say, $M = \operatorname{diag}(A_1, A_2, \ldots, A_r)$ and $N = \operatorname{diag}(B_1, B_2, \ldots, B_r)$. Find (a) $M + N$; (b) kM; (c) MN; (d) $f(M)$ for a given polynomial $f(x)$.

(a) Simply add the diagonal blocks: $M + N = \operatorname{diag}(A_1 + B_1, A_2 + B_2, \ldots, A_r + B_r)$.

(b) Simply multiply the diagonal blocks by k: $kM = \operatorname{diag}(kA_1, kA_2, \ldots, kA_r)$.

(c) Simply multiply corresponding diagonal blocks: $MN = \operatorname{diag}(A_1 B_1, A_2 B_2, \ldots, A_r B_r)$.

(d) Find $f(A_i)$ for each diagonal block A_i. Then $f(M) = \operatorname{diag}(f(A_1), f(A_2), \ldots, f(A_r))$.

3.40. Find M^2, where $M = \begin{bmatrix} 1 & 2 & & & \\ 3 & 4 & & & \\ & & 5 & & \\ & & & 1 & 3 \\ & & & 5 & 7 \end{bmatrix}$.

Since M is block diagonal, square each block:

$$\begin{bmatrix} 1 & 2 \\ 3 & 4 \end{bmatrix}\begin{bmatrix} 1 & 2 \\ 3 & 4 \end{bmatrix} = \begin{bmatrix} 7 & 10 \\ 15 & 22 \end{bmatrix}, \qquad [5][5] = [25], \qquad \begin{bmatrix} 1 & 3 \\ 5 & 7 \end{bmatrix}\begin{bmatrix} 1 & 3 \\ 5 & 7 \end{bmatrix} = \begin{bmatrix} 16 & 24 \\ 40 & 64 \end{bmatrix}$$

Then $M^2 = \begin{bmatrix} 7 & 10 & & & \\ 15 & 22 & & & \\ & & 25 & & \\ & & & 16 & 24 \\ & & & 40 & 64 \end{bmatrix}$

LU FACTORIZATION

3.41. Find the LU decomposition of $A = \begin{bmatrix} 1 & 3 & 2 \\ 2 & 5 & 6 \\ -3 & -2 & 7 \end{bmatrix}$.

Reduce A to triangular form by applying the operations "Add $-2R_1$ to R_2" and "Add $3R_1$ to R_3", and then "Add $7R_2$ to R_3". These operations yield

$$A \sim \begin{bmatrix} 1 & 3 & 2 \\ 0 & -1 & 2 \\ 0 & 7 & 13 \end{bmatrix} \sim \begin{bmatrix} 1 & 3 & 2 \\ 0 & -1 & 2 \\ 0 & 0 & 27 \end{bmatrix}$$

Use the negatives of the multipliers $-2, 3$, and 7 in the above row operations to form the matrix L, and use the triangular form of A to obtain the matrix U. That is

$$L = \begin{bmatrix} 1 & 0 & 0 \\ 2 & 1 & 0 \\ -3 & -7 & 1 \end{bmatrix} \quad \text{and} \quad U = \begin{bmatrix} 1 & 3 & 2 \\ 0 & -1 & 2 \\ 0 & 0 & 27 \end{bmatrix}$$

(As a check, multiply L and U to verify $A = LU$.)

3.42. Find the LDU factorization of the matrix A in Problem 3.41.

The $A = LDU$ factorization refers to the situation where L is a lower triangular matrix with 1s on the diagonal (as in the LU factorization of A), D is a diagonal matrix, and U is an upper triangular matrix with 1s on the diagonal. Thus simply factor out the diagonal entries in the matrix U in the above LU factorization of A to obtain the matrices D and U. Hence

$$L = \begin{bmatrix} 1 & 0 & 0 \\ 2 & 1 & 0 \\ -3 & -7 & 1 \end{bmatrix}, \quad D = \begin{bmatrix} 1 & 0 & 0 \\ 0 & -1 & 0 \\ 0 & 0 & 27 \end{bmatrix}, \quad U = \begin{bmatrix} 1 & 3 & 2 \\ 0 & 1 & -2 \\ 0 & 0 & 1 \end{bmatrix}$$

3.43. Find the LU decomposition of $B = \begin{bmatrix} 1 & -3 & 5 \\ 2 & -4 & 7 \\ -1 & -2 & 1 \end{bmatrix}$.

Reduce B to triangular form by applying the operations "Add $-2R_1$ to R_2" and "Add R_1 to R_3", and then "Add $\frac{5}{2}R_2$ to R_3". These operations yield

$$B \sim \begin{bmatrix} 1 & -3 & 5 \\ 0 & 2 & -3 \\ 0 & -5 & 6 \end{bmatrix} \sim \begin{bmatrix} 1 & -3 & 5 \\ 0 & 2 & -3 \\ 0 & 0 & -\frac{3}{2} \end{bmatrix}$$

Use the negatives of the multipliers $-2, 1$, and $\frac{5}{2}$ in the above row operations to form the matrix L, and use the triangular form of B to obtain the matrix U. That is

$$L = \begin{bmatrix} 1 & 0 & 0 \\ 2 & 1 & 0 \\ -1 & -\frac{5}{2} & 1 \end{bmatrix} \quad \text{and} \quad U = \begin{bmatrix} 1 & -3 & 5 \\ 0 & 2 & -3 \\ 0 & 0 & -\frac{3}{2} \end{bmatrix}$$

(As a check, multiply L and U to verify $B = LU$.)

3.44. Find the LU factorization of $C = \begin{bmatrix} 1 & 4 & -3 \\ 2 & 8 & 1 \\ -5 & -9 & 7 \end{bmatrix}$.

Reduce C to triangular form by first applying the operations "Add $-2R_1$ to R_2" and "Add $5R_1$ to R_3". These operations yield

$$C \sim \begin{bmatrix} 1 & 4 & -3 \\ 0 & 0 & 7 \\ 0 & 11 & -8 \end{bmatrix}$$

Observe that the second diagonal entry is 0. Thus C cannot be brought into triangular form without row interchange operations. Accordingly, C is not LU-factorable.

3.45. Find the LU factorization of $A = \begin{bmatrix} 1 & 2 & -3 & 4 \\ 2 & 3 & -8 & 5 \\ 1 & 3 & 1 & 3 \\ 3 & 8 & -1 & 13 \end{bmatrix}$ by a direct method.

First form the following matrices L and U:

$$L = \begin{bmatrix} 1 & 0 & 0 & 0 \\ l_{21} & 1 & 0 & 0 \\ l_{31} & l_{32} & 1 & 0 \\ l_{41} & l_{42} & l_{43} & 1 \end{bmatrix} \quad \text{and} \quad U = \begin{bmatrix} u_{11} & u_{12} & u_{13} & u_{14} \\ 0 & u_{22} & u_{23} & u_{24} \\ 0 & 0 & u_{33} & u_{34} \\ 0 & 0 & 0 & u_{44} \end{bmatrix}$$

The part of the product LU that determines the first row of A yields the four equations

$$u_{11} = 1, \quad u_{12} = 2, \quad u_{13} = -3, \quad u_{14} = 4$$

and the part of the product LU that determines the first column of A yields the equations

$$l_{21}u_{11} = 2, \quad l_{31}u_{11} = 1, \quad l_{41}u_{11} = 3 \quad \text{or} \quad l_{21} = 2, \quad l_{31} = 1, \quad l_{41} = 3$$

Thus at this point, the matrices L and U have the form

$$L = \begin{bmatrix} 1 & 0 & 0 & 0 \\ 2 & 1 & 0 & 0 \\ 1 & l_{32} & 1 & 0 \\ 3 & l_{42} & l_{43} & 1 \end{bmatrix} \quad \text{and} \quad U = \begin{bmatrix} 1 & 2 & -3 & 4 \\ 0 & u_{22} & u_{23} & u_{24} \\ 0 & 0 & u_{33} & u_{34} \\ 0 & 0 & 0 & u_{44} \end{bmatrix}$$

The part of the product LU that determines the remaining entries in the second row of A yields the equations

$$4 + u_{22} = 3, \quad -6 + u_{23} = -8, \quad 8 + u_{24} = 5$$

and so

$$u_{22} = -1, \quad u_{23} = -2, \quad u_{24} = -3$$

Lastly the part of the product LU that determines the remaining entries in the second column of A yields the equations

$$2 + l_{32}u_{22} = 3, \quad 6 + l_{42}u_{22} = 8$$

and so

$$l_{32} = -1, \quad l_{42} = -2$$

Thus L and U now have the form

$$L = \begin{bmatrix} 1 & 0 & 0 & 0 \\ 2 & 1 & 0 & 0 \\ 1 & -1 & 1 & 0 \\ 3 & -2 & l_{43} & 1 \end{bmatrix} \quad \text{and} \quad U = \begin{bmatrix} 1 & 2 & -3 & 4 \\ 0 & -1 & -2 & -3 \\ 0 & 0 & u_{33} & u_{34} \\ 0 & 0 & 0 & u_{44} \end{bmatrix}$$

Continuing, using the third row, third column, and the fourth row of A, we get

$$u_{33} = 2, \quad u_{34} = -4, \quad \text{then} \quad l_{43} = 2, \quad \text{and lastly} \quad u_{44} = 3$$

Thus $\quad L = \begin{bmatrix} 1 & 0 & 0 & 0 \\ 2 & 1 & 0 & 0 \\ 1 & -1 & 1 & 0 \\ 3 & -2 & 2 & 1 \end{bmatrix} \quad \text{and} \quad U = \begin{bmatrix} 1 & 2 & -3 & 4 \\ 0 & -1 & -2 & -3 \\ 0 & 0 & 2 & -4 \\ 0 & 0 & 0 & 3 \end{bmatrix}$

3.46. Find the *LDU* factorization of the matrix A in Problem 3.45.

Here U should have 1s on the diagonal and D is a diagonal matrix. Thus using the LU factorization of A in Problem 3.45, factor out the diagonal entries in that U to obtain

$$D = \begin{bmatrix} 1 & & & \\ & -1 & & \\ & & 2 & \\ & & & 3 \end{bmatrix} \quad \text{and} \quad U = \begin{bmatrix} 1 & 2 & -3 & 4 \\ & 1 & 2 & 3 \\ & & 1 & -2 \\ & & & 1 \end{bmatrix}$$

The matrix L is the same as in Problem 3.45.

3.47. Given: the factorization $A = LU$, where $L = [l_{ij}]$ and $U = [u_{ij}]$. Consider the system $AX = B$. Determine: (a) the algorithm to find $L^{-1}B$; (b) the algorithm that solves $UX = B$ by back-substitution.

   (a) The entry l_{ij} in matrix L corresponds to the elementary row operation "Add $-l_{ij}R_j$ to R_i". Thus the algorithm which transforms B to B' is as follows:

Algorithm P3.47A   (Evaluation of $L^{-1}B$):

Step 1. Repeat for $j = 1$ to $n - 1$:

Step 2.   Repeat for $i = j + 1$ to n:
      $b_i := -l_{ij}b_j + b_i$
      [End of Step 2 inner loop.]
      [End of Step 1 outer loop.]

Step 3. Exit.

      [The complexity of this algorithm is $C(n) \approx n^2/2$.]

   (b) The back-substitution algorithm follows.

Algorithm P3.47B   (Back-Substitution for System $UX = B$):

Step 1. $x_n = b_n/U_{nn}$

Step 2. Repeat for $i = n - 1, n - 2, \ldots, 1$
$$x_i = (b_i - u_{i, i+1} x_{i+1} - \cdots - u_{in} x_n)/u_{ii}$$

Step 3. Exit.

[The complexity here is also $C(n) \approx n^2/2$.]

3.48. Find the *LU* factorization of the matrix $A = \begin{bmatrix} 1 & 2 & 1 \\ 2 & 3 & 3 \\ -3 & -10 & 2 \end{bmatrix}$.

Reduce A to triangular form by the operations (1) "Add $-2R_1$ to R_2", (2) "Add $3R_1$ to R_3", then (3) "Add $-4R_2$ to R_3". This yields

$$A \sim \begin{bmatrix} 1 & 2 & 1 \\ 0 & -1 & 1 \\ 0 & -4 & 5 \end{bmatrix} \sim \begin{bmatrix} 1 & 2 & 1 \\ 0 & -1 & 1 \\ 0 & 0 & 1 \end{bmatrix}$$

Thus
$$L = \begin{bmatrix} 1 & 0 & 0 \\ 2 & 1 & 0 \\ -3 & 4 & 1 \end{bmatrix} \quad \text{and} \quad U = \begin{bmatrix} 1 & 2 & 1 \\ 0 & -1 & 1 \\ 0 & 0 & 1 \end{bmatrix}$$

The entries 2, -3, and 4 in L are the negatives of the multipliers in the above row operations.

3.49. Solve the system $AX = B$, where A is the matrix in Problem 3.48 and where: (*a*) $B = B_1 = (1, 1, 1)$; (*b*) $B = B_2 = B_1 + X_1$ where X_1 is the solution of $AX = B_1$; (*c*) $B = B_3 = B_2 + X_2$ where X_2 is the solution of $AX = B_2$.

(*a*) Find $L^{-1}B_1$ or, equivalently, apply the row operations (1), (2), and (3) in Problem 3.48 to B_1 to yield

$$B_1 = \begin{bmatrix} 1 \\ 1 \\ 1 \end{bmatrix} \xrightarrow{\text{(1) and (2)}} \begin{bmatrix} 1 \\ -1 \\ 4 \end{bmatrix} \xrightarrow{\text{(3)}} \begin{bmatrix} 1 \\ -1 \\ 8 \end{bmatrix}$$

Solve $UX = B$ for $B = (1, -1, 8)$ by back-substitution to obtain $X_1 = (-25, 9, 8)$.

(*b*) Find $B_2 = B_1 + X_1 = (1, 1, 1) + (-25, 9, 8) = (-24, 10, 9)$. Apply operations (1), (2), and (3) to B_2 to obtain $(-24, 58, -63)$, and then $B = (-24, 58, -295)$. Solve $UX = B$ by back-substitution to obtain $X_2 = (977 - 353, -295)$.

(*c*) Find $B_3 = B_2 + X_2 = (-24, 10, 9) + (977, -353, -295) = (953, -343, -286)$. Apply operations (1), (2), and (3) to B_3 to obtain $(953, -2249, 2573)$, and then $B = (953, -2249, 11569)$. Solve $UX = B$ by back-substitution to obtain $X_3 = (-38252, 13818, 11569)$.

ELEMENTARY PROOFS

3.50. Suppose A is an $n \times n$ matrix and $AB = BA = I$. Show that such a matrix B is unique, that is, show that inverses are unique.

Suppose $AB_1 = B_1A = I$ and $AB_2 = B_2A = I$. Then $B_1 = B_1I = B_1(AB_2) = (B_1A)B_2 = IB_2 = B_2$. Thus inverses are unique.

3.51. Prove the following:

(a)   If A and B are invertible, then AB is invertible and $(AB)^{-1} = B^{-1}A^{-1}$.

(b)   If $A_1, A_2, \ldots, A_n$ are invertible, then $(A_1 A_2 \cdots A_n)^{-1} = A_n^{-1} \cdots A_2^{-1} A_1^{-1}$.

(c) A is invertible if and only if A^T is invertible.

(d)   The operations of inversion and transposing commute: $(A^T)^{-1} = (A^{-1})^T$.

(a)   We have

$$(AB)(B^{-1}A^{-1}) = A(BB^{-1})A^{-1} = AIA^{-1} = AA^{-1} = I$$

$$(B^{-1}A^{-1})(AB) = B^{-1}(A^{-1}A)B = B^{-1}IB = B^{-1} = I$$

Thus $B^{-1}A^{-1}$ is the inverse of AB.

(b)   By induction on n and using part (a), we have

$$(A_1 \cdots A_{n-1} A_n)^{-1} = [(A_1 \cdots A_{n-1})A_n]^{-1} = A_n^{-1}(A_1 \cdots A_{n-1})^{-1} = A_n^{-1} \cdots A_2^{-1} A_1^{-1}$$

(c)   If A is invertible, then there exists a matrix B such that $AB = BA = I$. Then

$$(AB)^T = (BA)^T = I^T \quad \text{and so} \quad B^T A^T = A^T B^T = I$$

Hence A^T is invertible, with inverse B^T. The converse follows from the fact that $(A^T)^T = A$.

(d)   By part (c), B^T is the inverse of A^T, that is, $B^T = (A^T)^{-1}$. But $B = A^{-1}$; hence $(A^{-1})^T = (A^T)^{-1}$.

3.52. Let $D_k = kI$, the scalar matrix belonging to the scalar k. Show that: (a) $D_k A = kA$; (b) $BD_k = kB$; (c) $D_k + D_{k'} = D_{k+k'}$; (d) $D_k D_{k'} = D_{kk'}$.

(a) $D_k A = (kI)A = k(IA) = kA$

(b) $BD_k = B(kI) = k(BI) = kB$

(c) $D_k + D_{k'} = kI + k'I = (k + k')I = D_{k+k'}$

(d) $D_k D_{k'} = (kI)(k'I) = kk'(II) = kk'I = D_{kk'}$

3.53. For $i = 1, \ldots, n$, let $e_i = (0, \ldots, 1, \ldots, 0)^T$ be the (column) vector in $\mathbf{R}^n$ with 1 in the ith position and 0 elsewhere. Let A and B be any $m \times n$ matrices.

(a)   Show that Ae_i is the ith column of A.

(b)   Suppose $Ae_i = Be_i$ for each i. Show that $A = B$.

(c)   Suppose $Au = Bu$ for every vector u in $\mathbf{R}^n$. Show that $A = B$.

(a)   Let $A = [a_{ij}]$ and let $Ae_i = (b_1, \ldots, b_n)^T$. Then

$$b_k = R_k e_i = (a_{k1}, \ldots, a_{kn})(0, \ldots, 1, \ldots, 0)^T = a_{ki}$$

where R_k is the kth row of A. Thus $Ae_i = (a_{1i}, a_{2i}, \ldots, a_{ni})^T$, the ith column of A.

(b) $Ae_i = Be_i$ means A and B have the same ith column for each i. Thus $A = B$.

(c)   If $Au = Bu$ for every vector u in $\mathbf{R}^n$, then $Ae_i = Be_i$ for each i. Thus $A = B$.

3.54. Suppose a matrix A has a zero row (column).   Show that A is not invertible.

Let R_i be the zero row of A.   Suppose A is invertible and $AB = I$.   Then the ith row of AB is

$$(R_i B^1, R_i B^2, \ldots, R_i B^n) = (0, 0, \ldots, 0)$$

where B^j is the jth column of B.   This contradicts the fact that I has no zero row.   Thus A is not invertible.

On the other hand, suppose A has a zero column.   Then A^T has a zero row; and so A^T would not be invertible.   Thus, again, A is not invertible.

3.55. Show that each of the following elementary row operations has an inverse operation of the same type.   (Compare with Problem 2.62.)

[E_1]   Interchange rows R_i and R_j.

[E_2]   Multiply row R_i by a nonzero scalar k.

[E_3]   Add kR_i to R_j.

Each operation is treated separately.

(1)   Interchanging the same two rows twice yields the same matrix.   Thus this operation is its own inverse.

(2)   Multiplying R_i by k and then by k^{-1}, or by k^{-1} and then by k, yields the same matrix.   Thus the operations "Multiply R_i by k" and "Multiply R_i by k^{-1}" are inverses.

(3)   Applying the operation "Add kR_i to R_j" and then the operation "Add $-kR_i$ to R_j", or vice versa, yields the same matrix.   Thus the operations are inverses of each other.

3.56. Show that every elementary matrix E is invertible and its inverse is an elementary matrix.

Let E be the elementary matrix corresponding to the elementary operation e, that is, $e(I) = E$.   Let e' be the inverse operation of e and let E' be the corresponding elementary matrix, that is, $e'(I) = E'$.   (By Problem 3.55, the operation e' exists.)   Then

$$I = e'(e(I)) = e'(E) = E'E \qquad \text{and} \qquad I = e(e'(I)) = e(E') = EE'$$

Therefore E' is the inverse of E.

3.57. Let A be any n-square symmetric matrix and let P be any $m \times n$ matrix.   Show that $P^T A P$ is also symmetric.

Taking the transpose of $P^T A P$, we get

$$(P^T A P)^T = P^T A (P^T)^T = P^T A P$$

Thus $P^T A P$ is its own transpose, that is, $P^T A P$ is symmetric.

PROOFS

3.58. Prove Theorem 3.1(iv): $\text{tr}(AB) = \text{tr}(BA)$.

Suppose $A = [a_{ij}]$ and $B = [b_{ij}]$. Let $AB = [c_{ij}]$ and $BA = [d_{ij}]$. Then $c_{ij} = \sum_{k=1}^{n} a_{ik}b_{kj}$ and $d_{ij} = \sum_{k=1}^{n} b_{ik}a_{kj}$, and hence

$$\text{tr}(AB) = \sum_{i=1}^{n} c_{ii} = \sum_{i=1}^{n} \sum_{k=1}^{n} a_{ik}b_{ki} = \sum_{k=1}^{n} \sum_{i=1}^{n} b_{ki}a_{ik} = \sum_{k=1}^{n} d_{kk} = \text{tr}(BA)$$

3.59. Prove: Let $f(x)$ and $g(x)$ be polynomials and let A be any square matrix. Then

(i) $(f + g)(A) = f(A) + g(A)$

(ii) $(fg)(A) = f(A)g(A)$

(iii) $f(A)g(A) = g(A)f(A)$

Suppose $f(x) = \sum_{i=1}^{r} a_i x^i$ and $g(x) = \sum_{j=1}^{s} b_j x^j$.

(i)   We can assume $r = s = n$ by adding powers of x with 0 as their coefficients. Then

$$f(x) + g(x) = \sum_{i=1}^{n} (a_i + b_i)x^i$$

Hence $(f + g)(A) = \sum_{i=1}^{n} (a_i + b_i)A^i = \sum_{i=1}^{n} a_i A^i + \sum_{i=1}^{n} b_i A^i = f(A) + g(A)$

(ii) We have $f(x)g(x) = \sum_{i,j} a_i b_j x^{i+j}$. Then

$$f(A)g(A) = \left(\sum_{i} a_i A^i\right)\left(\sum_{j} b_j A^j\right) = \sum_{i,j} a_i b_j A^{i+j} = (fg)(A)$$

(iii) Using $f(x)g(x) = g(x)f(x)$, we have

$$f(A)g(A) = (fg)(A) = (gf)(A) = g(A)f(A)$$

3.60. Prove Theorem 3.2: Let A be a square matrix. Then:

(i) $A + A^T$ is symmetric.

(ii) $A - A^T$ is skew-symmetric.

(iii) $A = B + C$, where $B = \frac{1}{2}(A + A^T)$ is symmetric and $C = \frac{1}{2}(A - A^T)$ is skew-symmetric.

(i) $(A + A^T)^T = A^T + (A^T)^T = A^T + A = A + A^T$.

(ii) $(A - A^T)^T = A^T - (A^T)^T = A^T - A = -(A - A^T)$.

(iii) Choose $B \equiv \frac{1}{2}(A + A^T)$ and $C \equiv \frac{1}{2}(A - A^T)$ and appeal to (i) and (ii). (We note that no other choice is possible.)

3.61. Prove Theorem 3.4:   Every 2×2 orthogonal matrix has the form

$$\begin{bmatrix} \cos\theta & \sin\theta \\ -\sin\theta & \cos\theta \end{bmatrix} \quad \text{or} \quad \begin{bmatrix} \cos\theta & \sin\theta \\ \sin\theta & -\cos\theta \end{bmatrix}$$

for some real number θ.

   Let a and b be real numbers such that $a^2 + b^2 = 1$.   Then there exists a real number θ such that $a = \cos\theta$ and $b = \sin\theta$.   The result now follows from Problem 3.35.

3.62. Prove Theorem 3.6:   Let e be an elementary row operation and let E be the corresponding m-square elementary matrix, that is, $E = e(I)$.   Then $e(A) = EA$, where A is any $m \times n$ matrix.

   Let R_i be the ith row of A; we denote this by writing $A = (R_1, \ldots, R_m)$.   If B is a matrix for which AB is defined, then it follows directly from the definition of matrix multiplication that $AB = (R_1 B, \ldots, R_m B)$.   We also let

$$e_i = (0, \ldots, 0, \widehat{1}, 0, \ldots, 0), \qquad \widehat{} = i$$

Here $\widehat{} = i$ means that 1 is the ith component.   By Problem 3.35, $e_i A = R_i$.   We also remark that $I = (e_1, \ldots, e_m)$ is the identity matrix.

   (i)   Let e be the elementary row operation "Interchange rows R_i and R_j".   Then, for $\widehat{} = i$ and $\widehat{\widehat{}} = j$,

$$E = e(I) = (e_1, \ldots, \widehat{e_j}, \ldots, \widehat{\widehat{e_i}}, \ldots, e_m)$$

and
$$e(A) = (R_1, \ldots, \widehat{R_j}, \ldots, \widehat{\widehat{R_i}}, \ldots, R_m)$$

Thus $EA = (e_1 A, \ldots, \widehat{e_j}A, \ldots, \widehat{\widehat{e_i}}A, \ldots, e_m A) = (R_1, \ldots, \widehat{R_j}, \ldots, \widehat{\widehat{R_i}}, \ldots, R_m) = e(A)$

   (ii)   Let e be the elementary row operation "Multiply R_i by a nonzero scalar k".   Then, for $\widehat{} = i$,

$$E = e(I) = (e_1, \ldots, \widehat{ke_i}, \ldots, e_m) \quad \text{and} \quad e(A) = (R_1, \ldots, \widehat{kR_i}, \ldots, R_m)$$

Thus $EA = (e_1 A, \ldots, \widehat{ke_i}A, \ldots, e_m A) = (R_1, \ldots, \widehat{kR_i}, \ldots, R_m) = e(A)$

   (iii)   Let e be the elementary row operation "Add kR_j to R_i".   Then, for $\widehat{} = i$.

$$E = e(I) = (e_1, \ldots, \widehat{ke_j + e_i}, \ldots, e_m) \quad \text{and} \quad e(A) = (R_1, \ldots, \widehat{kR_j + R_i}, \ldots, R_m)$$

Using $(ke_j + e_i)A = k(e_j A) + e_i A = kR_j + R_i$, we have

$$EA = (e_1 A, \ldots, \widehat{(ke_j + e_i)A}, \ldots, e_m A) = (R_1, \ldots, \widehat{kR_j + R_i}, \ldots, R_m) = e(A)$$

Thus we have proved the theorem.

3.63. Prove Theorem 3.7:   Let A be a square matrix.   Then the following are equivalent:

(a) A is invertible (nonsingular).

(b) A is row equivalent to the identity matrix I.

(c) A is a product of elementary matrices.

   Suppose A is invertible and suppose A is row equivalent to a matrix B in row canonical form.   Then there exist elementary matrices $E_1, E_2, \ldots, E_s$ such that $E_s \cdots E_2 E_1 A = B$.   Since

A is invertible and each elementary matrix E_i is invertible, B is invertible. But if $B \neq I$, then B has a zero row; hence B is not invertible. Thus $B = I$, and (a) implies (b).

If (b) holds, then there exist elementary matrices $E_1, E_2, \ldots, E_s$ such that $E_s \cdots E_2 E_1 A = I$, and so $A = (E_s \cdots E_2 E_1)^{-1} = E_1^{-1} E_2^{-1} \cdots E_s^{-1}$. But the E_i^{-1} are also elementary matrices. Thus (b) implies (c).

If (c) holds, then $A = E_1 E_2 \cdots E_s$. The E_i are invertible matrices; hence their product A is also invertible. Thus (c) implies (a). Accordingly, the theorem is proved.

3.64. Prove Theorem 3.8:   If $AB = I$, then $BA = I$, and hence $B = A^{-1}$.

Suppose A is not invertible. Then A is not row equivalent to the identity matrix I, and so A is row equivalent to a matrix with a zero row. In other words, there exist elementary matrices $E_1, \ldots, E_s$ such that $E_s \cdots E_2 E_1 A$ has a zero row. Hence $E_s \cdots E_2 E_1 AB = E_s \cdots E_2 E_1$, an invertible matrix, also has a zero row. But invertible matrices cannot have zero rows; hence A is invertible, with inverse A^{-1}. Then also,

$$B = IB = (A^{-1}A)B = A^{-1}(AB) = A^{-1}I = A^{-1}$$

3.65. Prove Theorem 3.9 B is row equivalent to A if and only if there exists a nonsingular matrix P such that $B = PA$.

If $B \sim A$, then $B = e_s(\cdots(e_2(e_1(A)))\cdots) = E_s \cdots E_2 E_1 A = PA$, where $P = E_s \cdots E_2 E_1$ is nonsingular. Conversely, suppose $B = PA$ where P is nonsingular. By Theorem 3.7, P is a product of elementary matrices and hence B can be obtained from A by a sequence of elementary row operations, i.e., $B \sim A$. Thus the theorem is proved.

3.66. Prove Theorem 3.14:   Every $m \times n$ matrix A is equivalent to a unique block matrix of the form $\begin{bmatrix} I_r & 0 \\ 0 & 0 \end{bmatrix}$, where I_r is the $r \times r$ identity matrix.

The proof is constructive, in the form of an algorithm.

Step 1.   Row reduce A to row canonical form, with leading nonzero entries $a_{1j_1}, a_{2j_2}, \ldots, a_{rj_r}$.

Step 2.   Interchange C_1 and C_{1j_1}, interchange C_2 and C_{2j_2}, ..., and interchange C_r and C_{j_r}. This gives a matrix in the form $\begin{bmatrix} I_r & B \\ \hline 0 & 0 \end{bmatrix}$, with leading nonzero entries $a_{11}, a_{22}, \ldots, a_{rr}$.

Step 3.   Use column operations, with the a_{ii} as pivots, to replace each entry in B with a zero, i.e., for $i = 1, 2, \ldots, r$ and $j = r+1, r+2, \ldots, n$, apply the operation $-b_{ij}C_i + C_j \to C_j$.

The final matrix has the desired form $\begin{bmatrix} I_r & 0 \\ \hline 0 & 0 \end{bmatrix}$.

3.67. Suppose $A = [a_{ij}]$ and $B = [b_{ij}]$ are $n \times n$ upper triangular matrices. Prove that the product AB is upper triangular with diagonal elements $a_{11}b_{11}, a_{22}b_{22}, \ldots, a_{nn}b_{nn}$.

Suppose $AB = [c_{ij}]$. Then

$$c_{ij} = \sum_{k=1}^{n} a_{ik}b_{kj} \quad \text{and} \quad c_{ii} = \sum_{k=1}^{n} a_{ik}b_{ki}$$

Suppose $i > j$. Then, for any k, either $i > k$ or $k > j$, so that either $a_{ik} = 0$ or $b_{kj} = 0$. Thus $c_{ik} = 0$ and AB is upper triangular. Suppose $i = j$. Then $k < i$, $a_{ik} = 0$; and for $k > i$, $b_{ki} = 0$. Hence $c_{ii} = a_{ii}b_{ii}$, as claimed.

Supplementary Problems

ALGEBRA OF MATRICES

3.68. Find the diagonal and the trace of each matrix:

(a) $A = \begin{bmatrix} 2 & -5 & 8 \\ 3 & -6 & -7 \\ 4 & 0 & -1 \end{bmatrix}$; (b) $B = \begin{bmatrix} 1 & 3 & -4 \\ 6 & 1 & 7 \\ 2 & -5 & -1 \end{bmatrix}$; (c) $C = \begin{bmatrix} 4 & 3 & -6 \\ 2 & -5 & 0 \end{bmatrix}$

3.69. Let $A = \begin{bmatrix} 2 & -5 \\ 3 & 1 \end{bmatrix}$. Find: (a) A^2 and A^3; (b) $f(A)$ where $f(x) = x^3 - 2x^2 - 5$; (c) $g(A)$ where $g(x) = x^2 - 3x + 17$.

3.70. Let $B = \begin{bmatrix} 4 & -2 \\ 1 & -6 \end{bmatrix}$. Find: (a) B^2 and B^3; (b) $f(B)$ where $f(x) = x^2 + 2x - 22$; (c) $g(B)$ where $g(x) = x^2 - 3x - 6$.

3.71. Let $A = \begin{bmatrix} 6 & -4 \\ 3 & -2 \end{bmatrix}$. Find a nonzero vector $u = \begin{bmatrix} x \\ y \end{bmatrix}$ such that $Au = 4u$.

3.72. Let $A = \begin{bmatrix} 1 & 2 \\ 0 & 1 \end{bmatrix}$. Find A^n.

3.73. Let $A = \begin{bmatrix} 5 & 2 \\ 0 & k \end{bmatrix}$. Find all numbers k for which A is a root of the polynomial:

(a) $f(x) = x^2 - 7x + 10$; (b) $g(x) = x^2 - 25$; (c) $h(x) = x^2 - 4$.

3.74. Let $B = \begin{bmatrix} 1 & 0 \\ 26 & 27 \end{bmatrix}$. Find a matrix A such that $A^3 = B$.

3.75. Let $A = \begin{bmatrix} 0 & 1 & 0 & 0 \\ 0 & 0 & 1 & 0 \\ 0 & 0 & 0 & 1 \\ 0 & 0 & 0 & 0 \end{bmatrix}$ and $B = \begin{bmatrix} 1 & 1 & 0 \\ 0 & 1 & 1 \\ 0 & 0 & 1 \end{bmatrix}$. Find: (a) A^n and (b) B^n for all positive integers n.

3.76. Find conditions on matrices A and B so that $A^2 - B^2 = (A + B)(A - B)$.

INVERTIBLE MATRICES, INVERSES, ELEMENTARY MATRICES

3.77. Find the inverse of each matrix (if it exists):

$$A = \begin{bmatrix} 7 & 4 \\ 5 & 3 \end{bmatrix}, \qquad B = \begin{bmatrix} 2 & 3 \\ 4 & 5 \end{bmatrix}, \qquad C = \begin{bmatrix} 4 & -6 \\ -2 & 3 \end{bmatrix}, \qquad D = \begin{bmatrix} 5 & -2 \\ 6 & -3 \end{bmatrix}$$

3.78. Find the inverse of each matrix (if it exists):

$$A = \begin{bmatrix} 1 & 2 & -4 \\ -1 & -1 & 5 \\ 2 & 7 & -4 \end{bmatrix}, \qquad B = \begin{bmatrix} 1 & -1 & 1 \\ 0 & 2 & -2 \\ 1 & 3 & -1 \end{bmatrix}, \qquad C = \begin{bmatrix} 1 & 2 & 3 \\ 2 & 5 & -1 \\ 5 & 12 & 1 \end{bmatrix}$$

3.79. Find the inverse of each matrix (if it exists):

$$A = \begin{bmatrix} 1 & 3 & -2 \\ 2 & 8 & -3 \\ 1 & 7 & 1 \end{bmatrix}, \qquad B = \begin{bmatrix} 2 & 1 & -1 \\ 5 & 2 & -3 \\ 0 & 2 & 1 \end{bmatrix}, \qquad C = \begin{bmatrix} 1 & -2 & 0 \\ 2 & -3 & 1 \\ 1 & 1 & 5 \end{bmatrix}$$

3.80. Find the inverse of each matrix (where patterns of zeros have been omitted):

$$A = \begin{bmatrix} 1 & 2 & & & \\ & 1 & 2 & & \\ & & 1 & 2 & \\ & & & 1 & 2 \\ & & & & 1 \end{bmatrix}, \qquad B = \begin{bmatrix} 1 & 1 & 1 & 1 & 1 \\ & 1 & 1 & 1 & 1 \\ & & 1 & 1 & 1 \\ & & & 1 & 1 \\ & & & & 1 \end{bmatrix}$$

3.81. Express each matrix as a product of elementary matrices:

(a) $A = \begin{bmatrix} 1 & 2 \\ 3 & 4 \end{bmatrix}$;   (b) $B = \begin{bmatrix} 3 & -6 \\ -2 & 4 \end{bmatrix}$;   (c) $C = \begin{bmatrix} 2 & 6 \\ -3 & -7 \end{bmatrix}$.

3.82. Express $A = \begin{bmatrix} 1 & 2 & 0 \\ 0 & 1 & 3 \\ 3 & 8 & 7 \end{bmatrix}$ as a product of elementary matrices.

3.83. (a) Give an example of a nonzero matrix A such that $AB = AC$ but $B \neq C$. (b) Suppose A is invertible. Show that if $AB = AC$, then $B = C$.

3.84. Find 2×2 invertible matrices A and B such that $A + B \neq 0$ and $A + B$ is not invertible.

DIAGONAL AND TRIANGULAR MATRICES

3.85. Write out the matrices $A = \text{diag}(2, 4, -9)$, $B = \text{diag}(3, -5)$, and $C = \text{diag}(1, 2, 3)$.

3.86. Let $A = \text{diag}(1, 2, 3)$ and $B = \text{diag}(2, -5, 0)$. Find: (a) AB, A^2, B^2; (b) $f(A)$ where $f(x) = x^2 + 4x - 3$; (c) A^{-1} and B^{-1}.

3.87. Using only the elements 0 and 1, find all 3×3 nonsingular upper triangular matrices.

3.88. Using only the elements 0 and 1, find the number of: (a) 3×3 diagonal matrices; (b) 3×3 upper triangular matrices. Generalize to $n \times n$ matrices.

3.89. Find all real triangular matrices A such that $A^2 = B$, where:

(a) $B = \begin{bmatrix} 4 & 21 \\ 0 & 25 \end{bmatrix}$; (b) $B = \begin{bmatrix} 1 & 4 \\ 0 & -9 \end{bmatrix}$.

3.90. Let $B = \begin{bmatrix} 1 & 8 & 5 \\ 0 & 9 & 5 \\ 0 & 0 & 4 \end{bmatrix}$. Find a triangular matrix A with positive diagonal entries such that $A^2 = B$.

3.91. Find 2×2 nonzero matrices A, B, and C, where A and C are upper triangular and $AB = C$, but B is not upper triangular.

3.92. Suppose $AB = C$. Show that if A and C are upper triangular and A is invertible, then B is also upper triangular. (Compare with Problem 3.91.)

SYMMETRIC AND SKEW-SYMMETRIC MATRICES

3.93. Find x, y, and z so that each matrix is symmetric:

(a) $A = \begin{bmatrix} 2 & x & 3 \\ 4 & 5 & y \\ z & 1 & 7 \end{bmatrix}$; (b) $B = \begin{bmatrix} 7 & -6 & 2x \\ y & z & -2 \\ x & -2 & 5 \end{bmatrix}$.

3.94. Find x and C if $C = \begin{bmatrix} 7 & x+1 \\ 3x-7 & x-2 \end{bmatrix}$ is symmetric.

3.95. Write A as the sum of a symmetric matrix B and a skew-symmetric matrix C, where:

(a) $A = \begin{bmatrix} 4 & 5 \\ 1 & 3 \end{bmatrix}$; (b) $A = \begin{bmatrix} 4 & 1 & 2 \\ 3 & 8 & 7 \\ 6 & 5 & 9 \end{bmatrix}$.

3.96. Suppose A and B are $n \times n$ symmetric matrices. Show that each of the following is symmetric: (a) $A + B$; (b) kA for any scalar k; (c) A^2; (d) A^n for $n > 0$; (e) $f(A)$ for any polynomial $f(x)$.

ORTHOGONAL MATRICES

3.97. Find a 2×2 orthogonal matrix P whose first row is: (a) $(\frac{5}{13}, \frac{12}{13})$; (b) $(2/\sqrt{29}, 5/\sqrt{29})$.

3.98. Find a 2×2 orthogonal matrix P whose first row is a multiple of: (a) $(3, -4)$; (b) $(1, 2)$.

3.99. Find a 3×3 orthogonal matrix P whose first two rows are multiples of: (a) $(1, 2, 3)$ and $(0, -3, 2)$, respectively; (b) $(1, 3, 1)$ and $(1, 0, -1)$, respectively.

3.100. Suppose A and B are orthogonal matrices. Show that A^T, A^{-1}, and AB are also orthogonal.

SQUARE BLOCK MATRICES

3.101. Using vertical lines, complete the partitioning of each matrix so that it is a square block matrix:

$$A = \begin{bmatrix} 1 & 2 & 3 & 4 & 5 \\ \hline 1 & 1 & 1 & 1 & 1 \\ 9 & 8 & 7 & 6 & 5 \\ \hline 2 & 2 & 2 & 2 & 2 \\ \hline 3 & 3 & 3 & 3 & 3 \end{bmatrix}, \qquad B = \begin{bmatrix} 1 & 2 & 3 & 4 & 5 \\ 1 & 1 & 1 & 1 & 1 \\ \hline 9 & 8 & 7 & 6 & 5 \\ \hline 2 & 2 & 2 & 2 & 2 \\ 3 & 3 & 3 & 3 & 3 \end{bmatrix}$$

3.102. Partition each of the following matrices so that it becomes a diagonal block matrix with as many diagonal blocks as possible:

$$A = \begin{bmatrix} 1 & 0 & 0 \\ 0 & 0 & 2 \\ 0 & 0 & 3 \end{bmatrix}, \qquad B = \begin{bmatrix} 1 & 2 & 0 & 0 & 0 \\ 3 & 0 & 0 & 0 & 0 \\ 0 & 0 & 4 & 0 & 0 \\ 0 & 0 & 5 & 0 & 0 \\ 0 & 0 & 0 & 0 & 6 \end{bmatrix}, \qquad C = \begin{bmatrix} 0 & 1 & 0 \\ 0 & 0 & 0 \\ 2 & 0 & 0 \end{bmatrix}$$

3.103. Find M^2 and M^3 for each matrix M:

$$(a) \quad M = \begin{bmatrix} 2 & 0 & 0 & 0 \\ \hline 0 & 1 & 4 & 0 \\ 0 & 2 & 1 & 0 \\ \hline 0 & 0 & 0 & 3 \end{bmatrix}, \qquad (b) \quad M = \begin{bmatrix} 1 & 1 & 0 & 0 \\ 2 & 3 & 0 & 0 \\ \hline 0 & 0 & 1 & 2 \\ 0 & 0 & 4 & 5 \end{bmatrix}.$$

3.104. For each of the matrices M in Problem 3.103, find $f(M)$, where $f(x) = x^2 + 4x - 5$.

LU FACTORIZATION

3.105. Find the LU and LDU factorization of each matrix:

$$(a) \quad \begin{bmatrix} 1 & 4 \\ 2 & 7 \end{bmatrix}; \qquad (b) \quad B = \begin{bmatrix} 2 & 6 \\ -3 & 1 \end{bmatrix}.$$

3.106. Find the LU and LDU factorization of each matrix:

$$(a) \quad A = \begin{bmatrix} 1 & 3 & -1 \\ 2 & 5 & 1 \\ 3 & 4 & 2 \end{bmatrix}; \qquad (b) \quad B = \begin{bmatrix} 2 & 3 & 6 \\ 4 & 7 & 9 \\ 3 & 5 & 4 \end{bmatrix}.$$

3.107. Let $A = \begin{bmatrix} 1 & -1 & -1 \\ 3 & -4 & -2 \\ 2 & -3 & -2 \end{bmatrix}$.

  (a) Find the LU factorization of A.

  (b) Let X_k denote the solution of $AX = B_k$. Find X_1, X_2, X_3, X_4 and B_2, B_3, B_4 where $B_1 = (1, 1, 1)^T$ and $B_{k+1} = B_k + X_k$ for $k = 1, 2, 3$.

Answers to Supplementary Problems

3.68. (a) 2, −6, −1, tr(A) = −5; (b) 1, 1, −1, tr(B) = 1; (c) not defined

3.69. (a) $A^2 = \begin{bmatrix} -11 & -15 \\ 9 & -14 \end{bmatrix}$, $A^3 = \begin{bmatrix} -67 & 40 \\ -24 & -59 \end{bmatrix}$;   (b) $f(A) = \begin{bmatrix} -50 & 70 \\ -42 & -36 \end{bmatrix}$;   (c) $g(A) = 0$

3.70. (a) $B^2 = \begin{bmatrix} 14 & 4 \\ -2 & 34 \end{bmatrix}$, $B^3 = \begin{bmatrix} 60 & -52 \\ 26 & -200 \end{bmatrix}$;   (b) $f(B) = 0$;   (c) $g(B) = \begin{bmatrix} -4 & 10 \\ -5 & 46 \end{bmatrix}$

3.71. $u = (2a, a)^T$ for any nonzero a

3.72. $A^n = \begin{bmatrix} 1 & 2n \\ 0 & 1 \end{bmatrix}$

3.73. (a) $k = 2$; (b) $k = -5$; (c) none

3.74. $A = \begin{bmatrix} 1 & 0 \\ 2 & 3 \end{bmatrix}$

3.75. (a) $A^2 = \begin{bmatrix} 0 & 0 & 1 & 0 \\ 0 & 0 & 0 & 1 \\ 0 & 0 & 0 & 0 \\ 0 & 0 & 0 & 0 \end{bmatrix}$, $A^3 = \begin{bmatrix} 0 & 0 & 0 & 1 \\ 0 & 0 & 0 & 0 \\ 0 & 0 & 0 & 0 \\ 0 & 0 & 0 & 0 \end{bmatrix}$, $A^n = 0$ for $n > 3$;   (b) $B^n = \begin{bmatrix} 1 & n & n(n-1)/2 \\ 0 & 1 & n \\ 0 & 0 & 1 \end{bmatrix}$

3.76. $AB = BA$

3.77. $A^{-1} = \begin{bmatrix} 3 & -4 \\ -5 & 7 \end{bmatrix}$, $B^{-1} = \begin{bmatrix} -\frac{5}{2} & \frac{3}{2} \\ 2 & -1 \end{bmatrix}$, C^{-1} not defined, $D^{-1} = \begin{bmatrix} 1 & -\frac{2}{3} \\ 2 & -\frac{5}{3} \end{bmatrix}$

3.78. $A^{-1} = \begin{bmatrix} -31 & -20 & 6 \\ 6 & 4 & -1 \\ -5 & -3 & 1 \end{bmatrix}$, $B^{-1} = \begin{bmatrix} 1 & \frac{1}{2} & 0 \\ -\frac{1}{2} & -\frac{1}{2} & \frac{1}{2} \\ -\frac{1}{2} & -1 & \frac{1}{2} \end{bmatrix}$, C^{-1} not defined

3.79. $A^{-1} = \begin{bmatrix} \frac{29}{2} & -\frac{17}{2} & \frac{7}{2} \\ -\frac{5}{2} & \frac{3}{2} & -\frac{1}{2} \\ 3 & -2 & 1 \end{bmatrix}$, $B^{-1} = \begin{bmatrix} 8 & -3 & -1 \\ -5 & 2 & 1 \\ 10 & -4 & -1 \end{bmatrix}$, $C^{-1} = \begin{bmatrix} -8 & 5 & -1 \\ -\frac{9}{2} & \frac{5}{2} & -\frac{1}{2} \\ \frac{5}{2} & -\frac{3}{2} & \frac{1}{2} \end{bmatrix}$

3.80. $A^{-1} = \begin{bmatrix} 1 & -2 & 4 & -8 & 16 \\ & 1 & -2 & 4 & -8 \\ & & 1 & -2 & 4 \\ & & & 1 & -2 \\ & & & & 1 \end{bmatrix}$, $B^{-1} = \begin{bmatrix} 1 & -1 & & & \\ & 1 & -1 & & \\ & & 1 & -1 & \\ & & & 1 & -1 \\ & & & & 1 \end{bmatrix}$

3.81. (a) $A = \begin{bmatrix} 1 & 0 \\ 3 & 1 \end{bmatrix}\begin{bmatrix} 1 & -1 \\ 0 & 1 \end{bmatrix}\begin{bmatrix} 1 & 0 \\ 0 & -2 \end{bmatrix}$ or $\begin{bmatrix} 1 & 0 \\ 3 & 1 \end{bmatrix}\begin{bmatrix} 1 & 0 \\ 0 & -2 \end{bmatrix}\begin{bmatrix} 1 & 2 \\ 0 & 1 \end{bmatrix}$; (b) no product: B has no

inverse; (c) $C = \begin{bmatrix} 1 & 0 \\ -\frac{3}{2} & 1 \end{bmatrix}\begin{bmatrix} 1 & 0 \\ 0 & 2 \end{bmatrix}\begin{bmatrix} 1 & 6 \\ 0 & 1 \end{bmatrix}\begin{bmatrix} 2 & 0 \\ 0 & 1 \end{bmatrix}$

3.82. $A = \begin{bmatrix} 1 & 0 & 0 \\ 0 & 1 & 0 \\ 3 & 0 & 1 \end{bmatrix}\begin{bmatrix} 1 & 0 & 0 \\ 0 & 1 & 0 \\ 0 & 2 & 1 \end{bmatrix}\begin{bmatrix} 1 & 0 & 0 \\ 0 & 1 & 3 \\ 0 & 0 & 1 \end{bmatrix}\begin{bmatrix} 1 & 2 & 0 \\ 0 & 1 & 0 \\ 0 & 0 & 1 \end{bmatrix}$

3.83. (a) $A = \begin{bmatrix} 1 & 2 \\ 1 & 2 \end{bmatrix}$, $B = \begin{bmatrix} 0 & 0 \\ 1 & 1 \end{bmatrix}$, $C = \begin{bmatrix} 2 & 2 \\ 0 & 0 \end{bmatrix}$

3.84. $A = \begin{bmatrix} 1 & 2 \\ 0 & 3 \end{bmatrix}$, $B = \begin{bmatrix} 4 & 3 \\ 3 & 0 \end{bmatrix}$

3.85. $A = \begin{bmatrix} 2 & 0 & 0 \\ 0 & 4 & 0 \\ 0 & 0 & -9 \end{bmatrix}$, $B = \begin{bmatrix} 3 & 0 \\ 0 & -5 \end{bmatrix}$, $C = \begin{bmatrix} 1 & 0 & 0 \\ 0 & 2 & 0 \\ 0 & 0 & 3 \end{bmatrix}$

3.86. (a) $AB = \text{diag}(2, -10, 0)$, $A^2 = \text{diag}(1, 4, 9)$, $B^2 = \text{diag}(4, 25, 0)$; (b) $f(A) = \text{diag}(2, 9, 18)$; (c) $A^{-1} = \text{diag}(1, \frac{1}{2}, \frac{1}{3})$, B^{-1} does not exist.

3.87. All entries below the diagonal must be 0 to be upper triangular, and all diagonal entries must be 1 to be nonsingular. There are eight possible choices for entries above the diagonal as follows:

$$\begin{bmatrix} 0 & 0 \\ * & 0 \end{bmatrix}, \begin{bmatrix} 0 & 0 \\ * & 1 \end{bmatrix}, \begin{bmatrix} 0 & 1 \\ * & 0 \end{bmatrix}, \begin{bmatrix} 0 & 1 \\ * & 1 \end{bmatrix}, \begin{bmatrix} 1 & 0 \\ * & 0 \end{bmatrix}, \begin{bmatrix} 1 & 0 \\ * & 1 \end{bmatrix}, \begin{bmatrix} 1 & 1 \\ * & 0 \end{bmatrix}, \begin{bmatrix} 1 & 1 \\ * & 1 \end{bmatrix}$$

3.88. (a) 8 $[2^n]$; (b) 2^6 $[2^{n(n+1)/2}]$

3.89. (a) $\begin{bmatrix} 2 & 3 \\ 0 & 5 \end{bmatrix}, \begin{bmatrix} 2 & -7 \\ 0 & -5 \end{bmatrix}, \begin{bmatrix} -2 & 7 \\ 0 & 5 \end{bmatrix}, \begin{bmatrix} -2 & -3 \\ 0 & -5 \end{bmatrix}$; (b) none

3.90. $A = \begin{bmatrix} 1 & 2 & 1 \\ & 3 & 1 \\ & & 2 \end{bmatrix}$

3.91. $A = \begin{bmatrix} 1 & 1 \\ 0 & 0 \end{bmatrix}$, $B = \begin{bmatrix} 1 & 2 \\ 3 & 4 \end{bmatrix}$, $C = \begin{bmatrix} 4 & 6 \\ 0 & 0 \end{bmatrix}$

3.93. (a) $x = 4$, $y = 1$, $z = 3$; (b) $x = 0$, $y = -6$, z any real number

3.94. $x = 4$, $C = \begin{bmatrix} 7 & 5 \\ 5 & 2 \end{bmatrix}$

3.95. (a) $B = \begin{bmatrix} 4 & 3 \\ 3 & 3 \end{bmatrix}$, $C = \begin{bmatrix} 0 & 2 \\ -2 & 0 \end{bmatrix}$; (b) $B = \begin{bmatrix} 4 & 2 & 4 \\ 2 & 8 & 6 \\ 4 & 6 & 9 \end{bmatrix}$, $C = \begin{bmatrix} 0 & -1 & -2 \\ 1 & 0 & 1 \\ 2 & -1 & 0 \end{bmatrix}$

3.97. (a) $P = \begin{bmatrix} \frac{5}{13} & \frac{12}{13} \\ -\frac{12}{13} & \frac{5}{13} \end{bmatrix}$; (b) $P = \begin{bmatrix} 2/\sqrt{29} & 5/\sqrt{29} \\ 5/\sqrt{29} & -2/\sqrt{29} \end{bmatrix}$ (or the negative of the second row in each case)

3.98. (a) $P = \begin{bmatrix} \frac{3}{5} & -\frac{4}{5} \\ \frac{4}{5} & \frac{3}{5} \end{bmatrix}$; (b) $P = \begin{bmatrix} 1/\sqrt{5} & 2/\sqrt{5} \\ 2/\sqrt{5} & -1/\sqrt{5} \end{bmatrix}$

3.99. (a) $P = \begin{bmatrix} 1/\sqrt{14} & 2/\sqrt{14} & 3/\sqrt{14} \\ 0 & -3/\sqrt{13} & 2/\sqrt{13} \\ 13/\sqrt{182} & -2/\sqrt{182} & -3/\sqrt{182} \end{bmatrix}$; (b) $P = \begin{bmatrix} 1/\sqrt{11} & 3/\sqrt{11} & 1/\sqrt{11} \\ 1/\sqrt{2} & 0 & -1/\sqrt{2} \\ 3/\sqrt{22} & -2/\sqrt{22} & 3/\sqrt{22} \end{bmatrix}$

3.101. $A = \left[\begin{array}{c|cc|cc} 1 & 2 & 3 & 4 & 5 \\ \hline 1 & 1 & 1 & 1 & 1 \\ 9 & 8 & 7 & 6 & 5 \\ \hline 2 & 2 & 2 & 2 & 2 \\ 3 & 3 & 3 & 3 & 3 \end{array}\right]$, $\quad B = \left[\begin{array}{cc|c|cc} 1 & 2 & 3 & 4 & 5 \\ 1 & 1 & 1 & 1 & 1 \\ \hline 9 & 8 & 7 & 6 & 5 \\ 2 & 2 & 2 & 2 & 2 \\ 3 & 3 & 3 & 3 & 3 \end{array}\right]$

3.102. $A = \left[\begin{array}{c|cc} 1 & 0 & 0 \\ \hline 0 & 0 & 2 \\ 0 & 0 & 3 \end{array}\right]$, $\quad B = \left[\begin{array}{cc|cc|c} 1 & 2 & 0 & 0 & 0 \\ 3 & 0 & 0 & 0 & 0 \\ \hline 0 & 0 & 4 & 0 & 0 \\ 0 & 0 & 5 & 0 & 0 \\ \hline 0 & 0 & 0 & 0 & 6 \end{array}\right]$, $\quad C = \begin{bmatrix} 0 & 1 & 0 \\ 0 & 0 & 0 \\ 2 & 0 & 0 \end{bmatrix}$

(C itself is a block diagonal matrix; no further partitioning of C is possible.)

3.103. (a) $M^2 = \begin{bmatrix} 4 & & & \\ & 9 & 8 & \\ & 4 & 9 & \\ & & & 9 \end{bmatrix}$, $M^3 = \begin{bmatrix} 8 & & & \\ & 25 & 44 & \\ & 22 & 25 & \\ & & & 27 \end{bmatrix}$

(b) $M^2 = \begin{bmatrix} 3 & 4 & & \\ 8 & 11 & & \\ & & 9 & 12 \\ & & 24 & 33 \end{bmatrix}$, $M^3 = \begin{bmatrix} 11 & 15 & & \\ 30 & 41 & & \\ & & 57 & 78 \\ & & 156 & 213 \end{bmatrix}$

3.104. (a) $f(M) = \begin{bmatrix} 7 & & & \\ & 8 & 24 & \\ & 12 & 8 & \\ & & & 16 \end{bmatrix}$; (b) $f(M) = \begin{bmatrix} 2 & 8 & & \\ 16 & 18 & & \\ & & 8 & 20 \\ & & 40 & 48 \end{bmatrix}$

3.105. (a) $A = \begin{bmatrix} 1 & 0 \\ 2 & 1 \end{bmatrix}\begin{bmatrix} 1 & 0 \\ 0 & -1 \end{bmatrix}\begin{bmatrix} 1 & 4 \\ 0 & 1 \end{bmatrix}$; (b) $B = \begin{bmatrix} 1 & 0 \\ -\frac{3}{2} & 1 \end{bmatrix}\begin{bmatrix} 2 & 0 \\ 0 & 10 \end{bmatrix}\begin{bmatrix} 1 & 3 \\ 0 & 1 \end{bmatrix}$

3.106. (a) $A = \begin{bmatrix} 1 & & \\ 2 & 1 & \\ 3 & 5 & 1 \end{bmatrix}\begin{bmatrix} 1 & & \\ & -1 & \\ & & -10 \end{bmatrix}\begin{bmatrix} 1 & 3 & -1 \\ & 1 & -3 \\ & & 1 \end{bmatrix}$

(b) $B = \begin{bmatrix} 1 & & \\ 2 & 1 & \\ \frac{3}{2} & \frac{1}{2} & 1 \end{bmatrix}\begin{bmatrix} 2 & & \\ & 1 & \\ & & -\frac{7}{2} \end{bmatrix}\begin{bmatrix} 1 & \frac{3}{2} & 3 \\ & 1 & -3 \\ & & 1 \end{bmatrix}$

3.107. (a) $A = \begin{bmatrix} 1 & 0 & 0 \\ 3 & 1 & 0 \\ 2 & 1 & 1 \end{bmatrix}\begin{bmatrix} 1 & -1 & -1 \\ 0 & -1 & 1 \\ 0 & 0 & -1 \end{bmatrix}$; (b) $X_1 = \begin{bmatrix} 1 \\ 1 \\ -1 \end{bmatrix}$, $B_2 = \begin{bmatrix} 2 \\ 2 \\ 0 \end{bmatrix}$, $X_2 = \begin{bmatrix} 6 \\ 4 \\ 0 \end{bmatrix}$, $B_3 = \begin{bmatrix} 8 \\ 6 \\ 0 \end{bmatrix}$,

$X_3 = \begin{bmatrix} 22 \\ 16 \\ -2 \end{bmatrix}$, $B_4 = \begin{bmatrix} 30 \\ 22 \\ -2 \end{bmatrix}$, $X_4 = \begin{bmatrix} 86 \\ 62 \\ -6 \end{bmatrix}$

Chapter 4

Vector Spaces and Subspaces

4.1 INTRODUCTION

This chapter and the next define the underlying structure of linear algebra, that is, finite-dimensional vector space. The definition of a vector space V, whose elements are called *vectors*, involves an arbitrary field K, whose elements are called *scalars*. Almost nothing essential is lost if the reader assumes that K is the real field **R**.

The following notation will be used (unless otherwise stated or implied):

$$
\begin{array}{ll}
V & \text{given vector space} \\
u, v, w & \text{vectors in } V \\
K & \text{given number field} \\
a, b, c, \text{ or } k & \text{scalars in } K
\end{array}
$$

Length and orthogonality are not covered in these chapters since they are not considered part of the underlying structure of a vector space V. These concepts will be included as an additional structure on V, which will be introduced in Chapter 7.

4.2 VECTOR SPACES

The following defines the notion of a vector space V, where K is the field of scalars.

Definition: Let V be a nonempty set with two operations:
    (1) Rule of *vector addition*, which assigns to any $u, v \in V$ a *sum* $u + v$ in V.
    (2) Rule of *scalar multiplication*, which assigns to any $u \in V$, $k \in K$ a *product* $ku \in V$.

Then V is called a *vector space* (over the field K) if the following axioms hold:

[A_1]   For any vectors $u, v, w \in V$, $(u + v) + w = u + (v + w)$.

[A_2]   There is a vector in V, denoted by 0 and called the *zero vector*, for which $u + 0 = 0 + u = u$ for any vector $u \in V$.

[A_3]   For each vector $u \in V$ there is a vector in V, denoted by $-u$, for which $u + (-u) = (-u) + u = 0$.

[A_4]   For any vectors $u, v \in V$, $u + v = v + u$.

[M_1]   For any scalar $k \in K$ and any vectors $u, v \in V$, $k(u + v) = ku + kv$.

[M_2]   For any scalars $a, b \in K$ and any vector $u \in V$, $(a + b)u = au + bu$.

[M_3]   For any scalars $a, b \in K$ and any vector $u \in V$, $(ab)u = a(bu)$.

[M_4]   For the unit scalar $1 \in K$, $1u = u$ for any vector $u \in V$.

The above axioms naturally split into two sets. The first four are only concerned with the additive structure of V and can be summarized by saying that V is a *commutative group* under addition.   It follows that any sum of vectors of the form

$$v_1 + v_2 + \cdots + v_m$$

requires no parentheses and does not depend on the order of the summands, the zero vector 0 is unique, the *negative* $-u$ of u is unique, and the *cancellation law* holds, that is, for any vectors $u, v, w \in V$, we have

$$u + w = v + w \qquad \text{implies} \qquad u = v$$

Also, *subtraction* is defined by

$$u - v \equiv u + (-v)$$

where $-v$ is the unique negative of the vector v.

On the other hand, the remaining four axioms are concerned with the "action" of the field K of scalars on the vector space V.   Observe that the labeling of the axioms reflects this splitting.   Using these additional axioms we prove (Problem 4.7) the following simple properties of a vector space.

Theorem 4.1:   Let V be a vector space over a field K.

   (i)   For any scalar $k \in K$ and $0 \in V$, $k0 = 0$.

   (ii)   For $0 \in K$ and any vector $u \in V$, $0u = 0$.

   (iii)   If $ku = 0$, where $k \in K$ and $u \in V$, then $k = 0$ or $u = 0$.

   (iv)   For any $k \in K$ and any $u \in V$, $(-k)u = k(-u) = -ku$.

4.3   EXAMPLES OF VECTOR SPACES

This section lists important examples of vector spaces which will be used throughout the text.

Space $\mathbf{R}^n$

Recall that $\mathbf{R}^n$ denotes the set of all n-tuples of real numbers.   Here $\mathbf{R}^n$ is viewed as a vector space over $\mathbf{R}$, where vector addition and scalar multiplication are defined by

$$(a_1, a_2, \ldots, a_n) + (b_1, b_2, \ldots, b_n) = (a_1 + b_1, a_2 + b_2, \ldots, a_n + b_n)$$

and

$$k(a_1, a_2, \ldots, a_n) = (ka_1, ka_2, \ldots, ka_n)$$

The zero vector in $\mathbf{R}^n$ is the n-tuple of zeros,

$$0 = (0, 0, \ldots, 0)$$

and the negative of a vector is defined by

$$-(a_1, a_2, \ldots, a_n) = (-a_1, -a_2, \ldots, -a_n)$$

Observe that these are the same as the operations defined in Chapter 1.

Polynomial Space $\mathbf{P}(t)$

Let $\mathbf{P}(t)$ denote the set of all real polynomials

$$p(t) = a_0 + a_1 t + a_2 t^2 + \cdots + a_s t^s$$

where the coefficients a_i belong to the real field $\mathbf{R}$.   Then $\mathbf{P}(t)$ is a vector space over $\mathbf{R}$

using the operations:

(1) Vector addition $p(t) + q(t)$ in $\mathbf{P}(t)$ is the usual operation of addition of polynomials.
(2) Scalar multiplication $kp(t)$ in $\mathbf{P}(t)$ is the usual operation of the product of a scalar k and a polynomial $p(t)$.

The zero polynomial 0 is the zero vector in $\mathbf{P}(t)$.

Polynomial Space $\mathbf{P}_n(t)$

Let $\mathbf{P}_n(t)$ denote the set of all real polynomials

$$p(t) = a_0 + a_1 t + a_2 t^2 + \cdots + a_s t^s$$

where the degree of $p(t)$ is less than or equal to n, that is, $s \leq n$. Then $\mathbf{P}_n(t)$ is a vector space over $\mathbf{R}$ with respect to the usual operations of addition of polynomials and of multiplication of a polynomial by a constant [just like the vector space $\mathbf{P}(t)$ above]. We include the zero polynomial 0 as an element of $\mathbf{P}_n(t)$ even though its degree is undefined.

Matrix Space $\mathbf{M}_{m,n}$

The notation $\mathbf{M}_{m,n}$ or simply $\mathbf{M}$, will be used to denote the set of all $m \times n$ matrices whose entries are real numbers. Then $\mathbf{M}_{m,n}$ is a vector space over $\mathbf{R}$ with respect to the usual operations of matrix addition and scalar multiplication of matrices.

Function Space $\mathbf{F}(X)$

Let X be a nonempty set. Let $\mathbf{F}(X)$ denote the set of all functions of X into the real field $\mathbf{R}$. [Note that $\mathbf{F}(X)$ is nonempty since X is nonempty.] The sum of two functions f and g in $\mathbf{F}(X)$ is the function $f + g$ in $\mathbf{F}(X)$ defined by

$$(f + g)(x) = f(x) + g(x), \qquad \forall x \in X$$

and the product of a scalar $k \in \mathbf{R}$ and a function f in $\mathbf{F}(X)$ is the function kf in $\mathbf{F}(X)$ defined by

$$(kf)(x) = kf(x), \qquad \forall x \in X$$

(The symbol $\forall$ means "for every".) Then $\mathbf{F}(X)$ with the above operations is a vector space over $\mathbf{R}$.

The zero vector in $\mathbf{F}(X)$ is the zero function $\mathbf{0}$ which maps every $x \in X$ into the real number 0, that is,

$$\mathbf{0}(x) = 0, \qquad \forall x \in X$$

Also, for any function f in $\mathbf{F}(X)$, the function $-f$ in $\mathbf{F}(X)$ defined by

$$(-f)(x) = -f(x), \qquad \forall x \in X$$

is the negative of the function f.

Remark: All the above examples of vector spaces may be generalized by using an arbitrary field K rather than the real field $\mathbf{R}$. For example, $\mathbf{R}^n$ may be generalized to:

$\mathbf{C}^n$ vector space of all n-tuples of complex numbers

$\mathbf{Q}^n$ vector space of all n-tuples of rational numbers

K^n vector space of all *n-tuples* of elements in an arbitrary field K

Similarly, $\mathbf{P}(t)$, $\mathbf{P}_n(t)$, $\mathbf{M}_{m,n}$, and $\mathbf{F}(X)$ may be generalized to be vector spaces over the complex field $\mathbf{C}$, the rational field $\mathbf{Q}$, or any field K.

Fields and Subfields

Suppose a field E is an extension of a field K, that is, suppose E is a field which contains a subfield K.   Then E may be viewed as a vector space over K using the operations:

(1)   Vector addition $u + v$ in E is the usual addition in E.
(2)   Scalar multiplication ku in E, where $k \in K$ and $u \in E$, is the usual product of k and u as elements of E.

Then the eight axioms of a vector space are satisfied by E and K and the above two operations. That is, E is a vector space over its subfield K.

4.4   LINEAR COMBINATIONS

Let V be a vector space over a field K.   A vector v in V is a *linear combination* of vectors $u_1, u_2, \ldots, u_m$ in V if there exist scalars $a_1, a_2, \ldots, a_m$ in K such that

$$v = a_1 u_1 + a_2 u_2 + \cdots + a_m u_m$$

Alternately, v is a linear combination of $u_1, u_2, \ldots, u_m$ if there is a solution to the vector equation

$$v = x_1 u_1 + x_2 u_2 + \cdots + x_m u_m$$

where $x_1, x_2, \ldots, x_m$ are unknown scalars.

We illustrate this concept below for the vector spaces $\mathbf{R}^n$ and $\mathbf{P}(t)$.   Examples of linear combinations in other vector spaces, such as $\mathbf{M}_{m,n}$, appear as solved problems.

Linear Combinations in $\mathbf{R}^n$

The question of expressing one vector in $\mathbf{R}^n$ as a linear combination of other vectors in $\mathbf{R}^n$ is equivalent to solving a nonhomogeneous system of linear equations, as illustrated below.

(a)   Suppose we want to express $v = (3, 7, -4)$ as a linear combination of the vectors

$$u_1 = (1, 2, 3), \qquad u_2 = (2, 3, 7), \qquad u_3 = (3, 5, 6)$$

We seek scalars x, y, z such that $v = xu_1 + yu_2 + zu_3$, that is,

$$\begin{bmatrix} 3 \\ 7 \\ -4 \end{bmatrix} = x\begin{bmatrix} 1 \\ 2 \\ 3 \end{bmatrix} + y\begin{bmatrix} 2 \\ 3 \\ 7 \end{bmatrix} + z\begin{bmatrix} 3 \\ 5 \\ 6 \end{bmatrix} \qquad \text{or} \qquad \begin{aligned} x + 2y + 3z &= 3 \\ 2x + 3y + 5z &= 7 \\ 3x + 7y + 6z &= -4 \end{aligned}$$

(For notational convenience, we wrote the vectors in $\mathbf{R}^n$ as columns since it is then easier to find the equivalent system of linear equations.)   Reducing the system to echelon form yields

$$\begin{aligned} x + 2y + 3z &= 3 \\ -y - z &= 1 \\ y - 3z &= -13 \end{aligned} \qquad \text{and then} \qquad \begin{aligned} x + 2y + 3z &= 3 \\ -y - z &= 1 \\ -4z &= -12 \end{aligned}$$

Back-substitution yields the solution $x = 2$, $y = -4$, $z = 3$.   Thus

$$v = 2u_1 - 4u_2 + 3u_3$$

(b) Suppose we want to express $v = (1, 3, 8)$ as a linear combination of the vectors

$$u_1 = (1, 2, 3), \qquad u_2 = (2, 5, 8), \qquad u_3 = (1, 3, 5)$$

We seek scalars x, y, z such that $v = xu_1 + yu_2 + zu_3$, that is,

$$\begin{bmatrix} 1 \\ 3 \\ 8 \end{bmatrix} = x\begin{bmatrix} 1 \\ 2 \\ 3 \end{bmatrix} + y\begin{bmatrix} 2 \\ 5 \\ 8 \end{bmatrix} + z\begin{bmatrix} 1 \\ 3 \\ 5 \end{bmatrix} \qquad \text{or} \qquad \begin{aligned} x + 2y + z &= 1 \\ 2x + 5y + 3z &= 3 \\ 3x + 8y + 5z &= 8 \end{aligned}$$

Reducing the system to echelon form yields

$$\begin{aligned} x + 2y + z &= 1 \\ y + z &= 1 \\ 2y + 2z &= 5 \end{aligned} \qquad \text{and then} \qquad \begin{aligned} x + 2y + z &= 1 \\ y + z &= 1 \\ 0 &= 3 \end{aligned}$$

The system has no solution. Thus it is impossible to express v as a linear combination of u_1, u_2, u_3.

(c) The system of linear equations

$$\begin{aligned} 2x + 4y - 5z &= 5 \\ 3x + 7y - 8z &= 9 \\ 7x - 6y + z &= -4 \end{aligned}$$

can be rewritten as the following vector equation:

$$x\begin{bmatrix} 2 \\ 3 \\ 7 \end{bmatrix} + y\begin{bmatrix} 4 \\ 7 \\ -6 \end{bmatrix} + z\begin{bmatrix} -5 \\ -8 \\ 1 \end{bmatrix} = \begin{bmatrix} 5 \\ 9 \\ -4 \end{bmatrix}$$

Thus the system has a solution if and only if $v = (5, 9, -4)$ is a linear combination of the vectors

$$u_1 = (2, 3, 7), \qquad u_2 = (4, 7, -6), \qquad u_3 = (-5, -8, 1)$$

Solving the system yields the solution $x = 1$, $y = 2$, $z = 1$. Accordingly, v is a linear combination of u_1, u_2, u_3.

Linear Combinations in P(t)

Suppose we want to express the polynomial $v = 3t^2 + 5t - 5$ as a linear combination of the polynomials

$$p_1 = t^2 + 2t + 1, \qquad p_2 = 2t^2 + 5t + 4, \qquad p_3 = t^2 + 3t + 6$$

We seek scalars x, y, z such that $v = xp_1 + yp_2 + zp_3$, that is,

$$3t^2 + 5t - 5 = x(t^2 + 2t + 1) + y(2t^2 + 5t + 4) + z(t^2 + 3t + 6) \qquad (\star)$$

There are two ways to proceed from here.

(1) Expand the right side of Eq. $(\star)$, obtaining

$$3t^2 + 5t - 5 = xt^2 + 2xt + x + 2yt^2 + 5yt + 4y + zt^2 + 3zt + 6z$$
$$= (x + 2y + z)t^2 + (2x + 5y + 3z)t + (x + 4y + 6z)$$

Set coefficients of the same powers of t equal to each other and reduce the system to echelon form:

$$
\begin{array}{cc}
\begin{array}{rcr}
x + 2y + z &=& 3 \\
2x + 5y + 3z &=& 5 \\
x + 4y + 6z &=& -5
\end{array}
& \text{or} &
\begin{array}{rcr}
x + 2y + z &=& 3 \\
y + z &=& -1 \\
2y + 5z &=& -8
\end{array}
& \text{or} &
\begin{array}{rcr}
x + 2y + z &=& 3 \\
y + z &=& -1 \\
3z &=& -6
\end{array}
\end{array}
$$

The system is in triangular form and has a solution. **Back-substitution yields the solution** $x = 3,\, y = 1,\, z = -2$. Thus

$$v = 3p_1 + p_2 - 2p_3$$

(2) The Eq. ($\star$) is actually an identity in the variable t, that is, the equation holds for any value of t. We can obtain three equations in the unknowns x, y, z by setting t equal to any three values. For example,

$$
\begin{array}{ll}
\text{Set } t = 0 \text{ in } (*) \text{ to obtain} & x + 4y + 6z = -5 \\
\text{Set } t = 1 \text{ in } (*) \text{ to obtain} & 4x + 11y + 10z = 3 \\
\text{Set } t = -1 \text{ in } (*) \text{ to obtain} & y + 4z = -7
\end{array}
$$

Reduce the system to echelon form,

$$
\begin{array}{ccc}
\begin{array}{rcr}
x + 4y + 6z &=& -5 \\
-5y - 14z &=& 23 \\
y + 4z &=& -7
\end{array}
& \text{or} &
\begin{array}{rcr}
x + 4y + 6z &=& -5 \\
y + 4z &=& -7 \\
6z &=& -12
\end{array}
\end{array}
$$

(Note that we interchanged L_2 and L_3 before eliminating y in L_3.) **Back-substitution** again yields the solution $x = 3,\, y = 1,\, z = -2$. Thus (again) $v = 3p_1 + p_2 - 2p_3$.

4.5 SPANNING SETS

Let V be a vector space over a field K. Vectors $u_1, u_2, \ldots, u_m$ in V are said to *span* V or to form a *spanning set* of V if every v in V is a linear combination of the vectors $u_1, u_2, \ldots, u_m$.

EXAMPLE 4.1 Consider the vector space $V = \mathbf{R}^3$.

(a) We claim that the vectors

$$e_1 = (1, 0, 0), \qquad e_2 = (0, 1, 0), \qquad e_3 = (0, 0, 1)$$

form a spanning set of $\mathbf{R}^3$. Specifically, if $v = (a, b, c)$ is any vector in $\mathbf{R}^3$, then, clearly,

$$v = ae_1 + be_2 + ce_3$$

For example, $v = (5, -6, 2) = 5e_1 - 6e_2 + 2e_3$.

(b) Consider the vectors

$$w_1 = (1, 1, 1), \qquad w_2 = (0, 1, 1), \qquad w_3 = (0, 0, 1)$$

We show that these vectors span $\mathbf{R}^3$. Let $v = (a, b, c)$ be an arbitrary vector in $\mathbf{R}^3$. We set $v = xw_1 + yw_2 + zw_3$, or

$$
\begin{bmatrix} a \\ b \\ c \end{bmatrix} = x \begin{bmatrix} 1 \\ 1 \\ 1 \end{bmatrix} + y \begin{bmatrix} 0 \\ 1 \\ 1 \end{bmatrix} + z \begin{bmatrix} 0 \\ 0 \\ 1 \end{bmatrix}
\qquad \text{or} \qquad
\begin{array}{rcl}
x & = & a \\
x + y & = & b \\
x + y + z & = & c
\end{array}
$$

We can now solve for x, y, z, obtaining $x = a$, $y = b - a$, $z = c - b$. In other words, any vector v in $\mathbf{R}^3$ can be written as a linear combination of w_1, w_2, w_3. Specifically,

$$v = (a, b, c) = aw_1 + (b - a)w_2 + (c - b)w_3$$

Accordingly, w_1, w_2, w_3 span $\mathbf{R}^3$.

(c) Consider the vectors

$$u_1 = (1, 2, 3), \qquad u_2 = (2, 5, 8), \qquad u_3 = (1, 3, 5)$$

We showed above that $v = (1, 3, 8)$ cannot be written as a linear combination of u_1, u_2, u_3. Accordingly, u_1, u_2, u_3 do not span $\mathbf{R}^3$.

EXAMPLE 4.2 Consider the vector space $V = \mathbf{P}_n(t)$ consisting of all polynomials of degree at most n.

(a) Clearly every polynomial in $\mathbf{P}_n(t)$ can be expressed as a linear combination of the $n + 1$ polynomials

$$1, t, t^2, t^3, \ldots, t^n$$

Thus these powers of t (where $1 = t^0$) span $\mathbf{P}_n(t)$.

(b) One can also show that, for any scalar c, the following $n + 1$ powers of $t - c$,

$$1, t - c, (t - c)^2, (t - c)^3, \ldots, (t - c)^n$$

where $(t - c)^0 = 1$, also span $\mathbf{P}_n(t)$.

EXAMPLE 4.3 Consider the vector space $\mathbf{M} = \mathbf{M}_{2,2}$ consisting of all 2×2 matrices. Consider the following four matrices:

$$E_{11} = \begin{bmatrix} 1 & 0 \\ 0 & 0 \end{bmatrix}, \qquad E_{12} = \begin{bmatrix} 0 & 1 \\ 0 & 0 \end{bmatrix}, \qquad E_{21} = \begin{bmatrix} 0 & 0 \\ 1 & 0 \end{bmatrix}, \qquad E_{22} = \begin{bmatrix} 0 & 0 \\ 0 & 1 \end{bmatrix}$$

Then clearly any matrix A in $\mathbf{M}$ can be written as a linear combination of the four matrices. For example,

$$A = \begin{bmatrix} 5 & -6 \\ 7 & 8 \end{bmatrix} = 5E_{11} - 6E_{12} + 7E_{21} + 8E_{22}$$

Accordingly, the four matrices E_{11}, E_{12}, E_{21}, E_{22} span $\mathbf{M}$.

4.6 SUBSPACES

This section introduces the important notion of a subspace.

Definition: Let V be a vector space over a field K and let W be a subset of V. Then W is a *subspace* of V if W is itself a vector space over K with respect to the operations of vector addition and scalar multiplication in V.

The way one shows that any set W is a vector space is to show that W satisfies the eight axioms of a vector space. However, if W is a subset of a vector space V, then some of the axioms automatically hold in W since they already hold in V. Simple criteria for identifying subspaces (proved in Problem 4.27) follow.

Theorem 4.2:   Suppose W is a subset of a vector space V. Then W is a subspace of V if the following conditions hold:

    (i)   The zero vector 0 belongs to W.

    (ii) W is *closed under vector addition*, that is, for every $u, v \in W$, the sum $u + v \in W$.

    (iii) W is *closed under scalar multiplication*, that is, for every $u \in W$, $k \in K$, the multiple $ku \in W$.

Conditions (ii) and (iii) in Theorem 4.2 may be combined into one condition (proved in Problem 4.28) as follows.

Corollary 4.3: W is a subspace of V if the following conditions hold:

    (i) $0 \in W$.

    (ii) For every $u, v \in W$ and for every $a, b \in K$, the linear combination $au + bv \in W$.

Now let V be any vector space. Then the set $\{0\}$, consisting of the zero vector alone, and also the entire space V are examples of subspaces of V. Specific examples follow.

EXAMPLE 4.4   Consider the vector space $V = \mathbf{R}^3$.

(a)   Let U consist of all vectors in $\mathbf{R}^3$ whose entries are equal, that is,

$$U = \{(a, b, c):\ a = b = c\}$$

For example, $(1, 1, 1)$, $(-3, -3, -3)$, $(7, 7, 7)$, $(-2, -2, -2)$ are vectors in U. Geometrically, U is the line through the origin O and the point $(1, 1, 1)$, as shown in Fig. 4-1. Clearly $O = (0, 0, 0)$ belongs to U since all entries in O are equal. Further, suppose u and v are arbitrary vectors in U, say, $u = (a, a, a)$ and $v = (b, b, b)$. Then, for any scalar $k \in \mathbf{R}$,

$$u + v = (a + b, a + b, a + b) \qquad \text{and} \qquad ku = (ka, ka, ka)$$

are also vectors in U. Thus U is a subspace of $\mathbf{R}^3$.

(b)   Let W be any plane in $\mathbf{R}^3$ passing through the origin, as pictured in Fig. 4-2. Then $O = (0, 0, 0)$ belongs to W since we assumed W passes through the origin O. Further, suppose u and v are vectors in W. Then u and v may be viewed as arrows in the plane W emanating from the origin O, as in Fig. 4-2. The sum $u + v$ and any multiple ku of u also lie in the plane W. Thus W is a subspace of $\mathbf{R}^3$.

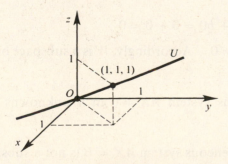

Fig. 4-1

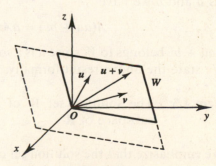

Fig. 4-2

EXAMPLE 4.5 Consider the vector space $\mathbf{M} = \mathbf{M}_{n,n}$ of $n \times n$ matrices.

(a) Let U consist of all upper triangular matrices.   Then the zero matrix 0 belongs to U.   Also, the sum and the scalar multiple of such triangular matrices are also upper triangular.   Thus U is a subspace of $\mathbf{M}$.

(b) Let W consist of all symmetric matrices.   Then the zero matrix 0 belongs to W, and W is closed under the operations of matrix addition and scalar multiplication.   Thus W is also a subspace of $\mathbf{M}$.

EXAMPLE 4.6 Consider the vector space $\mathbf{P}(t)$ of polynomials.   Then the space $\mathbf{P}_n(t)$ of polynomials of degree at most n may be viewed as a subspace of $\mathbf{P}(t)$.   Let $\mathbf{Q}(t)$ be the collection of polynomials with only even powers of t.   For example,

$$p_1 = 3 + 4\tau^2 - 5t^6 \qquad \text{and} \qquad p_2 = 6 - 7t^4 + 9t^6 + 3t^{12}$$

are polynomials in $\mathbf{Q}(t)$.   (We assume that any constant $k = kt^0$ is an even power of t.)   Then $\mathbf{Q}(t)$ is a subspace of $\mathbf{P}(t)$.

Intersection of Subspaces

Let U and W be subspaces of a vector space V.   We show that the intersection $U \cap W$ is also a subspace of V.   Clearly, $0 \in U$ and $0 \in W$ since U and W are subspaces; whence $0 \in U \cap W$.   Now suppose u and v belong to the intersection $U \cap W$.   Then $u, v \in U$ and $u, v \in W$.   Further, since U and W are subspaces, for any scalars $a, b \in R$,

$$au + bv \in U \qquad \text{and} \qquad au + bv \in W$$

whence $$au + bv \in U \cap W$$

Thus $U \cap W$ is a subspace of V.

The above result generalizes as follows.

Theorem 4.4:   The intersection of any number of subspaces of a vector space V is a subspace of V.

Solution Space of a Homogeneous System

Consider a system $AX = B$ of linear equations in n unknowns.   Then every solution u may be viewed as a vector in $\mathbf{R}^n$.   Thus the solution set of such a system is a subset of $\mathbf{R}^n$.   Now suppose the system is homogeneous, that is, it has the form $AX = 0$.   Let W be its solution set.   Since $A0 = 0$, the zero vector $0 \in W$.   Moreover, suppose u and v belong to W.   Then u and v are solutions of $AX = 0$ or, in other words, $Au = 0$ and $Av = 0$.   Therefore, for any scalars a and b we have

$$A(au + bv) = aAu + bAv = a0 + b0 = 0 + 0 = 0$$

Thus $au + bv$ belongs to W since it is a solution of $AX = 0$.   Accordingly, W is a subspace of $\mathbf{R}^n$. We state the above result formally.

Theorem 4.5:   The solution set W of a homogeneous system $AX = 0$ in n unknowns is a subspace of $\mathbf{R}^n$.

We emphasize that the solution set of a nonhomogeneous system $AX = B$ is not a subspace of $\mathbf{R}^n$.   In fact, the zero vector 0 does not belong to its solution set.

4.7 LINEAR SPANS

Suppose $u_1, u_2, \ldots, u_m$ are any vectors in a vector space V.   Recall (Section 4.4) that any vector of the form

$$a_1 u_1 + a_2 u_2 + \cdots + a_m u_m$$

where the a_i are scalars, is called a linear combination of $u_1, u_2, \ldots, u_m$.   The collection of all such linear combinations, denoted by

$$\text{span}(u_1, u_2, \ldots, u_m) \qquad \text{or} \qquad \text{span}(u_i)$$

is called the *linear span* of $u_1, u_2, \ldots, u_m$.

Clearly the zero vector 0 belongs to $\text{span}(u_i)$ since

$$0 = 0u_1 + 0u_2 + \cdots + 0u_m$$

Furthermore, suppose v and v' belong to $\text{span}(u_i)$, say,

$$v = a_1 u_1 + a_2 u_2 + \cdots + a_m u_m \qquad \text{and} \qquad v' = b_1 u_1 + b_2 u_2 + \cdots + b_m u_m$$

Then, for any scalar $k \in K$ we have

$$v + v' = (a_1 + b_1)u_1 + (a_2 + b_2)u_2 + \cdots + (a_m + b_m)u_m$$

and

$$kv = ka_1 u_1 + ka_2 u_2 + \cdots + ka_m u_m$$

Thus $v + v'$ and kv also belong to $\text{span}(u_i)$.   Accordingly, $\text{span}(u_i)$ is a subspace of V.

More generally, for any subset S of V, $\text{span}(S) = \{0\}$ when S is empty, and *span*(S) consists of all linear combinations of vectors in S.   Thus, in particular, S is a spanning set (Section 4.5) of $\text{span}(S)$.

The following theorem, which was partially proved above, applies.

Theorem 4.6:   Let S be a subset of a vector space V.

    (i)   Then $\text{span}(S)$ is a subspace of V which contains S.

    (ii)   If W is a subspace of V containing S, then $\text{span}(S) \subseteq W$.

Condition (ii) in Theorem 4.6 may be interpreted as saying that $\text{span}(S)$ is the "smallest" subspace of V containing S.

EXAMPLE 4.7   Consider the vector space $V = \mathbf{R}^3$.

(a)   Let u be any nonzero vector in $\mathbf{R}^3$.   Then $\text{span}(u)$ consists of all scalar multiples of u.   Geometrically, $\text{span}(u)$ is the line through the origin O and the endpoint of u, as shown in Fig. 4-3.

(b)   Let u and v be vectors in $\mathbf{R}^3$ which are not multiples of each other.   Then $\text{span}(u, v)$ is the plane through the origin O and the endpoints of u and v, as shown in Fig. 4-4.

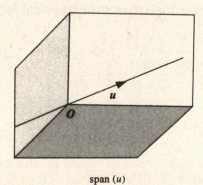

span (u)

Fig. 4-3

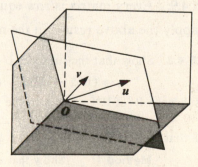

span (u, v)

Fig. 4-4

(c) Consider the vectors $e_1 = (1, 0, 0)$, $e_2 = (0, 1, 0)$, $e_3 = (0, 0, 1)$ in $\mathbf{R}^3$. Recall [Example 4.1(a)] that every vector in $\mathbf{R}^3$ is a linear combination of e_1, e_2, e_3. That is, e_1, e_2, e_3 form a spanning set of $\mathbf{R}^3$. Accordingly, span $(e_1, e_2, e_3) = \mathbf{R}^3$.

4.8 ROW SPACE OF A MATRIX

Let A be an arbitrary $m \times n$ matrix over $\mathbf{R}$, say,

$$A = \begin{bmatrix} a_{11} & a_{12} & \cdots & a_{1n} \\ a_{21} & a_{22} & \cdots & a_{2n} \\ \cdots\cdots\cdots\cdots\cdots\cdots\cdots \\ a_{m1} & a_{m2} & \cdots & a_{mn} \end{bmatrix}$$

The rows of A,

$$R_1 = (a_{11}, a_{12}, \ldots, a_{1n}), \qquad R_2 = (a_{21}, a_{22}, \ldots, a_{2n}), \ldots, R_m = (a_{m1}, a_{m2}, \ldots, a_{mn})$$

may be viewed as vectors in $\mathbf{R}^n$, and hence they span a subspace of $\mathbf{R}^n$, called the *row space* of A and denoted by rowsp (A). That is,

$$\text{rowsp } (A) = \text{span}(R_1, R_2, \ldots, R_m)$$

Analogously, the columns of A may be viewed as vectors in $\mathbf{R}^m$, called the *column space* of A and denoted by colsp (A). Observe that colsp $(A) = $ rowsp (A^T).

Now suppose we apply one of the following elementary row operations on A,

(i) $R \leftrightarrow R_j$
(ii) Multiply R_i by $k \neq 0$
(iii) Add kR_i to R_j

and obtain a matrix B. Then each row of B is clearly a row of A or a linear combination of rows of A. Hence the row space of B is contained in the row space of A. On the other hand, we can apply the inverse elementary row operations on B and obtain A. Hence the row space of A is contained in the row space of B. Accordingly, A and B have the same row space. This leads us to the following theorem.

Theorem 4.7: Row equivalent matrices have the same row space.

In particular, we prove the following fundamental results about row equivalent matrices (proved in Problems 4.32 and 4.33, respectively).

Theorem 4.8: Row canonical matrices have the same row space if and only if they have the same nonzero rows.

Theorem 4.9: Every matrix is row equivalent to a unique matrix in row canonical form.

We apply the above results in the next example.

EXAMPLE 4.8 Show that the subspace U of $\mathbf{R}^4$ spanned by the vectors

$$u_1 = (1, 2, -1, 3), \qquad u_2 = (2, 4, 1, -2), \qquad u_3 = (3, 6, 3, -7)$$

and the subspace W of $\mathbf{R}^4$ spanned by the vectors

$$v_1 = (1, 2, -4, 11), \qquad v_2 = (2, 4, -5, 14)$$

are equal, that is, $U = W$.

Method 1: Show that each u_i is a linear combination of v_1 and v_2, and show that each v_i is a linear combination of u_1, u_2, and u_3. Observe that we have to show that five systems of linear equations are consistent.

Method 2:   Form the matrix A whose rows are the u_i, and row reduce A to row canonical form:

$$A = \begin{bmatrix} 1 & 2 & -1 & 3 \\ 2 & 4 & 1 & -2 \\ 3 & 6 & 3 & -7 \end{bmatrix} \sim \begin{bmatrix} 1 & 2 & -1 & 3 \\ 0 & 0 & 3 & -8 \\ 0 & 0 & 6 & -16 \end{bmatrix} \sim \begin{bmatrix} 1 & 2 & 0 & \frac{1}{3} \\ 0 & 0 & 1 & -\frac{8}{3} \\ 0 & 0 & 0 & 0 \end{bmatrix}$$

Now form the matrix B whose rows are v_1 and v_2, and row reduce B to row canonical form:

$$B = \begin{bmatrix} 1 & 2 & -4 & 11 \\ 2 & 4 & -5 & 14 \end{bmatrix} \sim \begin{bmatrix} 1 & 2 & -4 & 11 \\ 0 & 0 & 3 & -8 \end{bmatrix} \sim \begin{bmatrix} 1 & 2 & 0 & \frac{1}{3} \\ 0 & 0 & 1 & -\frac{8}{3} \end{bmatrix}$$

Since the nonzero rows of the reduced matrices are identical, the row spaces of A and B are equal, and so $U = W$.

4.9 SUMS AND DIRECT SUMS

Let U and W be subsets of a vector space V. The sum of U and W, written $U + W$, consists of all sums $u + w$, where $u \in U$ and $w \in W$. That is,

$$U + W = \{u + w : \ u \in U, w \in W\}$$

Now suppose U and W are subspaces of a vector space V. Note that $0 = 0 + 0 \in U + W$, since $0 \in U, 0 \in W$. Furthermore, suppose $u + w$ and $u' + w'$ belong to $U + W$, with $u, u' \in U$ and $w, w' \in W$. Then

$$(u + w) + (u' + w') = (u + u') + (w + w') \in U + W$$

and, for any scalar k,

$$k(u + w) = ku + kw \in U + W$$

Thus we have proved the following theorem.

Theorem 4.10:   The sum $U + W$ of subspaces U and W of a vector space V is also a subspace of V.

EXAMPLE 4.9   Consider the vector space $\mathbf{M} = \mathbf{M}_{2,2}$ of 2×2 matrices. Let U consist of those matrices whose second row is zero, and let W consist of those matrices whose second column is zero. That is,

$$U = \left\{ \begin{bmatrix} a & b \\ 0 & 0 \end{bmatrix} \right\} \quad \text{and} \quad W = \left\{ \begin{bmatrix} a & 0 \\ c & 0 \end{bmatrix} \right\}$$

Now U and W are subspaces of $\mathbf{M}$. Note:

$$U + W = \left\{ \begin{bmatrix} a & b \\ c & 0 \end{bmatrix} \right\} \quad \text{and} \quad U \cap W = \left\{ \begin{bmatrix} a & 0 \\ 0 & 0 \end{bmatrix} \right\}$$

That is, $U + W$ consists of those matrices whose lower right entry is 0, and $U \cap W$ consists of those matrices whose second row and second column are zero.

Direct Sums

The vector space V is said to be the *direct sum* of its subspaces U and W, denoted by

$$V = U \oplus W$$

if every vector $v \in V$ can be written in one and only one way as $v = u + w$, where $u \in U$ and $w \in W$.

The following theorem (proved in Problem 4.34) characterizes such a decomposition.

Theorem 4.11:   The vector space V is the direct sum of its subspaces U and W if and only if:

(i) $V = U + W$

(ii) $U \cap W = \{0\}$.

EXAMPLE 4.10   Consider the vector space $V = \mathbf{R}^3$.

(a)   Let U be the xy plane and let W be the yz plane, that is,

$$U = \{(a, b, 0): \ a, b \in \mathbf{R}\} \qquad \text{and} \qquad W = \{(0, b, c): \ b, c \in \mathbf{R}\}$$

Then $\mathbf{R}^3 = U + W$ since every vector in $\mathbf{R}^3$ is the sum of a vector in U and a vector in W.   However, $\mathbf{R}^3$ is not the direct sum of U and W since such sums are not unique.   For example,

$$(3, 5, 7) = (3, 1, 0) + (0, 4, 7) \qquad \text{and also} \qquad (3, 5, 7) = (3, -4, 0) + (0, 9, 7)$$

(b)   Let U be the xy plane and let W be the z axis, that is,

$$U = \{(a, b, 0): \ a, b \in \mathbf{R}\} \qquad \text{and} \qquad W = \{(0, 0, c): \ c \in \mathbf{R}\}$$

Now any vector $(a, b, c) \in \mathbf{R}^3$ can be written as the sum of a vector in U and a vector in V in one and only one way:

$$(a, b, c) = (a, b, 0) + (0, 0, c)$$

Accordingly, $\mathbf{R}^3$ is the direct sum of U and W, that is, $\mathbf{R}^3 = U \oplus W$.

General Direct Sums

The notion of a direct sum is extended to more than one factor in the obvious way.   That is, V is the *direct sum* of subspaces $W_1, W_2, \ldots, W_r$, written

$$V = W_1 \oplus W_2 \oplus \cdots \oplus W_r$$

if every vector $v \in V$ can be written in one and only one way as

$$v = w_1 + w_2 + \cdots + w_r$$

where $w_1 \in W_1, w_2 \in W_2, \ldots, w_r \in W_r$.

EXAMPLE 4.11   Consider the vector space $V = \mathbf{R}^3$.   Let W_1, W_2, and W_3 be the x, y, and z axes. That is,

$$W_1 = \{(a, 0, 0): \ a \in \mathbf{R}\}, \qquad W_2 = \{(0, b, 0): \ b \in \mathbf{R}\}, \qquad W_3 = \{(0, 0, c): \ c \in \mathbf{R}\}$$

Now any vector $u = (a, b, c)$ can be written as the sum of a vector in W_1, a vector in W_2, and a vector in W_3 in exactly one way:

$$v = (a, b, c) = (a, 0, 0) + (0, b, 0) + (0, 0, c)$$

Accordingly, $\mathbf{R}^3$ is the direct sum of W_1, W_2, and W_3, that is, $\mathbf{R}^3 = W_1 \oplus W_2 \oplus W_3$.

Solved Problems

VECTOR SPACES

4.1. Suppose u and v belong to a vector space V. Simplify each expression:

(a) $E_1 = 3(2u - 4v) + 5u + 7v$

(b) $E_2 = 3u - 6(3u - 5v) + 7u$

(c) $E_3 = 2uv + 3(2u + 4v)$

(d) $E_4 = 5u - \dfrac{3}{v} + 5u$

Multiply out and collect terms.

(a) $E_1 = 6u - 12v + 5u + 7v = 11u - 5v$

(b) $E_2 = 3u - 18u + 30v + 7u = -8u + 30v$

(c) E_3 is not defined since the product uv of vectors is not defined.

(d) E_4 is not defined since division by a vector is not defined.

4.2. Show that, for any scalar k and any vectors u and v, we have $k(u - v) = ku - kv$.

Using the definition of subtraction, that $u - v = u + (-v)$, and Theorem 4.1(iv), that $k(-v) = -kv$, we have

$$k(u - v) = k[u + (-v)] = ku + k(-v) = ku + (-kv) = ku - kv$$

4.3. In the statement of axiom $[M_2]$, $(a + b)u = au + bu$, which operation does each plus sign represent?

The $+$ in $(a + b)u$ denotes the addition of the two scalars a and b; hence it represents the addition operation in field K. The $+$ in $au + bu$ denotes the addition of the two vectors au and bu; hence it represents the operation of vector addition. Thus each $+$ represents a different operation.

4.4. In the statement of axiom $[M_3]$, $(ab)u = a(bu)$, which operation does each product represent?

In $(ab)u$ the product ab of the scalars a and b denotes multiplication in field K, whereas the product of the scalar ab and the vector u denotes scalar multiplication.

In $a(bu)$ the product bu of the scalar b and the vector u denotes scalar multiplication; also, the product of the scalar a and the vector bu denotes scalar multiplication.

4.5. Show that $u + u = 2u$ for any vector u.

Using axiom $[M_4]$ and then axiom $[M_2]$, we have

$$u + u = 1u + 1u = (1 + 1)u = 2u.$$

4.6. Let V be the set of ordered pairs of real numbers. Show that V is not a vector space over R with respect to each of the following operations of addition in V and scalar multiplication on V:

(a) $(a, b) + (c, d) = (a + c, b + d)$ and $k(a, b) = (ka, b)$

(b) $(a, b) + (c, d) = (a, b)$ and $k(a, b) = (ka, kb)$

(c) $(a, b) + (c, d) = (a + c, b + d)$ and $k(a, b) = (k^2a, k^2b)$

In each case show that one of the axioms of a vector space does not hold.

(a) Let $r = 1$, $s = 2$, $v = (3, 4)$. Then

$$(r + s)v = 3(3, 4) = (9, 4)$$
$$rv + sv = 1(3, 4) + 2(3, 4) = (3, 4) + (6, 4) = (9, 8)$$

Since $(r + s)v \neq rv + sv$, axiom $[\mathbf{M}_2]$ does not hold.

(b) Let $v = (1, 2)$, $w = (3, 4)$. Then

$$v + w = (1, 2) + (3, 4) = (1, 2)$$
$$w + v = (3, 4) + (1, 2) = (3, 4)$$

Since $v + w \neq w + v$, axiom $[\mathbf{A}_4]$ does not hold.

(c) Let $r = 1$, $s = 2$, $v = (3, 4)$. Then

$$(r + s)v = 3(3, 4) = (27, 36)$$
$$rv + sv = 1(3, 4) + 2(3, 4) = (3, 4) + (12, 16) = (15, 20)$$

Thus $(r + s)v \neq rv + sv$, and so axiom $[\mathbf{M}_2]$ does not hold.

4.7. Prove Theorem 4.1: Let V be a vector space over a field K.

(i)   For any scalar $k \in K$ and $0 \in V$, $k0 = 0$.

(ii) For $0 \in K$ and any vector $u \in V$, $0u = 0$.

(iii) If $ku = 0$, where $k \in K$ and $u \in V$, then $k = 0$ or $u = 0$.

(iv) For any $k \in K$ and any $u \in V$, $(-k)u = k(-u) = -ku$.

(i) By axiom $[\mathbf{A}_2]$ with $u = 0$, we have $0 + 0 = 0$. Hence by axiom $[\mathbf{M}_1]$, we have

$$k0 = k(0 + 0) = k0 + k0$$

Adding $-k0$ to both sides gives the desired result.

(ii) For scalars, $0 + 0 = 0$. Hence by axiom $[\mathbf{M}_2]$, we have

$$0u = (0 + 0)u = 0u + 0u$$

Adding $-0u$ to both sides gives the desired result.

(iii) Suppose $ku = 0$ and $k \neq 0$. Then there exists a scalar k^{-1} such that $k^{-1}k = 1$. Thus

$$u = 1u = (k^{-1}k)u = k^{-1}(ku) = k^{-1}0 = 0$$

(iv) Using $u + (-u) = 0$, we obtain $0 = k0 = k[u + (-u)] = ku + k(-u)$. Adding $-ku$ to both sides gives $-ku = k(-u)$.

Using $k + (-k) = 0$, we obtain $0 = 0u = [k + (-k)]u = ku + (-k)u$. Adding $-ku$ to both sides yields $-ku = (-k)u$. Thus $(-k)u = k(-u) = -ku$.

LINEAR COMBINATIONS

4.8. Express $v = (1, -2, 5)$ in $\mathbf{R}^3$ as a linear combination of the vectors

$$u_1 = (1, 1, 1), \qquad u_2 = (1, 2, 3), \qquad u_3 = (2, -1, 1)$$

We seek scalars x, y, z, as yet unknown, such that $v = xu_1 + yu_2 + zu_3$. Thus we require

$$\begin{bmatrix} 1 \\ -2 \\ 5 \end{bmatrix} = x \begin{bmatrix} 1 \\ 1 \\ 1 \end{bmatrix} + y \begin{bmatrix} 1 \\ 2 \\ 3 \end{bmatrix} + z \begin{bmatrix} 2 \\ -1 \\ 1 \end{bmatrix} = \begin{bmatrix} x + y + 2z \\ x + 2y - z \\ x + 3y + z \end{bmatrix}$$

Form the equivalent system of equations by setting corresponding components equal to each other, and then reduce to echelon form:

$$\begin{array}{ll}
x + y + 2z = 1 & \\
x + 2y - z = -2 \quad \text{or} \\
x + 3y + z = 5 &
\end{array}
\qquad
\begin{array}{l}
x + y + 2z = 1 \\
y - 3z = -3 \quad \text{or} \\
2y - z = 4
\end{array}
\qquad
\begin{array}{l}
x + y + 2z = 1 \\
y - 3z = -3 \\
5z = 10
\end{array}$$

The system is consistent and has a solution. Solving by back-substitution yields the solution $x = -6$, $y = 3$, $z = 2$. Thus $v = -6u_1 + 3u_2 + 2u_3$.

Alternatively, write down the augmented matrix M of the equivalent system of linear equations, where u_1, u_2, u_3 are the first three columns of M and v is the last column, and then reduce M to echelon form:

$$M = \begin{bmatrix} 1 & 1 & 2 & 1 \\ 1 & 2 & -1 & -2 \\ 1 & 3 & 1 & 5 \end{bmatrix} \sim \begin{bmatrix} 1 & 1 & 2 & 1 \\ 0 & 1 & -3 & -3 \\ 0 & 2 & -1 & 4 \end{bmatrix} \sim \begin{bmatrix} 1 & 1 & 2 & 1 \\ 0 & 1 & -3 & -3 \\ 0 & 0 & 5 & 10 \end{bmatrix}$$

The last matrix corresponds to a triangular system, which has a solution. Solving the triangular system by back-substitution yields the solution $x = -6$, $y = 3$, $z = 2$. Thus $v = -6u_1 + 3u_2 + 2u_3$.

4.9. Express $v = (2, -5, 3)$ in $\mathbf{R}^3$ as a linear combination of the vectors

$$u_1 = (1, -3, 2), \qquad u_2 = (2, -4, -1), \qquad u_3 = (1, -5, 7)$$

We seek scalars x, y, z, as yet unknown, such that $v = xu_1 + yu_2 + zu_3$. Thus we require

$$\begin{bmatrix} 2 \\ -5 \\ 3 \end{bmatrix} = x \begin{bmatrix} 1 \\ -3 \\ 2 \end{bmatrix} + y \begin{bmatrix} 2 \\ -4 \\ -1 \end{bmatrix} + z \begin{bmatrix} 1 \\ -5 \\ 7 \end{bmatrix}$$

Form the equivalent system of equations and reduce to echelon form:

$$\begin{array}{ll}
x + 2y + z = 2 & \\
-3x - 4y - 5z = -5 \quad \text{or} \\
2x - y + 7z = 3 &
\end{array}
\qquad
\begin{array}{l}
x + 2y + z = 2 \\
2y - 2z = 1 \quad \text{or} \\
-5y + 5z = -1
\end{array}
\qquad
\begin{array}{l}
x + 2y + z = 2 \\
2y - 2z = 1 \\
0 = 3
\end{array}$$

The system is inconsistent and so has no solution. Thus v cannot be written as a linear combination of u_1, u_2, u_3.

4.10. For which value of k will the vector $u = (1, -2, k)$ in $\mathbf{R}^3$ be a linear combination of $v = (3, 0, -2)$ and $w = (2, -1, -5)$?

First set $u = xv + yw$, where x and y are unknown scalars. This yields

$$\begin{bmatrix} 1 \\ -2 \\ k \end{bmatrix} = x \begin{bmatrix} 3 \\ 0 \\ -2 \end{bmatrix} + y \begin{bmatrix} 2 \\ -1 \\ -5 \end{bmatrix}$$

Form the equivalent system of equations:

$$3x + 2y = 1, \qquad -y = -2, \qquad -2x - 5y = k$$

By the first two equations, $x = -1$, $y = 2$. Substitute into the last equation to obtain $k = -8$.

4.11. Express the polynomial $v = t^2 + 4t - 3$ in $\mathbf{P}(t)$ as a linear combination of the polynomials

$$p_1 = t^2 - 2t + 5, \qquad p_2 = 2t^2 - 3t, \qquad p_3 = t + 3$$

Set v as a linear combination of p_1, p_2, p_3 using unknowns x, y, z to obtain

$$t^2 + 4t - 3 = x(t^2 - 2t + 5) + y(2t^2 - 3t) + z(t + 3)$$

We can proceed in two ways.

Method 1: Expand the right side of Eq. $(\star)$ and express it in terms of powers of t as follows:

$$t^2 + 4t - 3 = xt^2 - 2xt + 5x + 2yt^2 - 3yt + zt + 3z$$
$$= (x + 2y)t^2 + (-2x - 3y + z)t + (5x + 3z)$$

Set coefficients of the same powers of t equal to each other and reduce the system to echelon form. This yields

$$
\begin{array}{ll}
\begin{array}{rcl}
x + 2y & = & 1 \\
-2x - 3y + z & = & 4 \\
5x + 3z & = & -3
\end{array}
&
\text{or}
\qquad
\begin{array}{rcl}
x + 2y & = & 1 \\
y + z & = & 6 \\
-10y + 3z & = & -8
\end{array}
\end{array}
$$

$$
\text{or} \qquad
\begin{array}{rcl}
x + 2y & = & 1 \\
y + z & = & 6 \\
13z & = & 52
\end{array}
$$

The system is consistent and has a solution. Solving by back-substitution yields the solution $x = -3$, $y = 2$, $z = 4$. Thus $v = -3p_1 + 2p_2 + 4p_3$.

Method 2: The Eq. $(\star)$ is an identity in t, that is, the equation holds for any value of t. Thus we can set t equal to any number to obtain equations in the unknowns.

(a) Set $t = 0$ in Eq. $(\star)$ to obtain the equation $-3 = 5x + 3z$

(b) Set $t = 1$ in Eq. $(\star)$ to obtain the equation $2 = 4x - y + 4z$

(c) Set $t = -1$ in Eq. $(\star)$ to obtain the equation $-6 = 8x + 5y + 2z$.

Solve the system of the three equations to again obtain $x = -3$, $y = 2$, $z = 4$. Thus $v = -3p_1 + 2p_2 + 4p_3$.

4.12. Express $M = \begin{bmatrix} 4 & 7 \\ 7 & 9 \end{bmatrix}$ as a linear combination of the matrices

$$A = \begin{bmatrix} 1 & 1 \\ 1 & 1 \end{bmatrix}, \qquad B = \begin{bmatrix} 1 & 2 \\ 3 & 4 \end{bmatrix}, \qquad C = \begin{bmatrix} 1 & 1 \\ 4 & 5 \end{bmatrix}$$

Set M as a linear combination of A, B, C using unknown scalars x, y, z, that is, set $M = xA + yB + zC$. This yields

$$\begin{bmatrix} 4 & 7 \\ 7 & 9 \end{bmatrix} = x\begin{bmatrix} 1 & 1 \\ 1 & 1 \end{bmatrix} + y\begin{bmatrix} 1 & 2 \\ 3 & 4 \end{bmatrix} + z\begin{bmatrix} 1 & 1 \\ 4 & 5 \end{bmatrix} = \begin{bmatrix} x+y+z & x+2y+z \\ x+3y+4z & x+4y+5z \end{bmatrix}$$

Form the equivalent system of equations by setting corresponding entries equal to each other and reduce to echelon form:

$$
\begin{array}{l}
x+\ y+\ z = 4 \\
x+2y+\ z = 7 \\
x+3y+4z = 7 \\
x+4y+5z = 9
\end{array}
\quad \text{or} \quad
\begin{array}{l}
x+\ y+\ z = 4 \\
\quad\ y\quad\ = 3 \\
2y+3z = 3 \\
3y+4z = 5
\end{array}
\quad \text{or} \quad
\begin{array}{l}
x+y+\ z = \ 4 \\
\quad\ y\quad = \ 3 \\
3z = -3 \\
4z = -4
\end{array}
$$

The last equation drops out. Solving the system by back-substitution yields $z = -1$, $y = 3$, $x = 2$. Thus $M = 2A + 3B - C$.

SUBSPACES

4.13. Let $V = \mathbf{R}^3$. Show that W is a subspace of $\mathbf{R}^3$, where:

(a) $W = \{(a, b, c): \ a = b = c\}$, that is, W consists of all vectors having three equal components.

(b) $W = \{(a, b, c): \ a + b + c = 0\}$, that is, W consists of all vectors where the sum of their components is zero.

Show that W satisfies the conditions of Corollary 4.3, that is, that $0 \in W$ and that, for any $u, v \in W$ and any scalars k, k', we have $ku + k'v \in W$.

(a) $0 = (0, 0, 0)$ belongs to W since $0 = 0 = 0$. Suppose $u = (a, b, c)$ and $v = (a', b', c')$ belong to W. Then $u = (a, a, a)$ and $v = (a', a', a')$. Then, for any scalars k and k', we have

$$ku + k'v = (ka, ka, ka) + (k'a', k'a', k'a')$$
$$= (ka + k'a', ka + k'a', ka + k'a')$$

Thus $ku + k'v$ belongs to W. Hence W is a subspace of V.

(b) $0 = (0, 0, 0)$ belongs to W since $0 + 0 + 0 = 0$. Suppose $u = (a, b, c)$ and $v = (a', b', c')$ belong to W. Then $a + b + c = 0$ and $a' + b' + c' = 0$. Then, for any scalars k and k', we have

$$ku + kv = k(a, b, c) + k'(a', b', c') = (ka, kb, kc) + (k'a', k'b', k'c')$$
$$= (ka + k'a', kb + k'b', kc + k'c')$$

Furthermore,

$$(ka + k'a') + (kb + k'b') + (kc + k'c') = k(a + b + c) + k'(a' + b' + c')$$
$$= k0 + k'0 = 0$$

Thus $ku + k'v$ belongs to W. Hence W is a subspace of V.

4.14. Let $V = \mathbf{R}^3$. Show that W is not a subspace of V, where:

(a) $W = \{(a, b, c): \ a \geq 0\}$, i.e., W consists of those vectors whose first component is nonnegative.

(b) $W = \{(a, b, c): \ a^2 + b^2 + c^2 \leq 1\}$, i.e., W consists of those vectors whose length does not exceed 1.

(c) $W = \{(a, b, c): \ a, b, c, \in \mathbf{Q}\}$, i.e., W consists of those vectors whose components are rational numbers.

   In each case, show that one of the properties of, say, Theorem 4.2 does not hold.

(a) $v = (1, 2, 3) \in W$ and $k = -5 \in \mathbf{R}$.   But $kv = -5(1, 2, 3) = (-5, -10, -15)$ does not belong to W since -5 is negative.   Hence W is not a subspace of V.

(b) $v = (1, 0, 0) \in W$ and $w = (0, 1, 0) \in W$.   But $v + w = (1, 0, 0) + (0, 1, 0) = (1, 1, 0)$ does not belong to W since $1^2 + 1^2 + 0^2 = 2 > 1$.   Hence W is not a subspace of V.

(c) $v = (1, 2, 3) \in W$ and $k = \sqrt{2} \in \mathbf{R}$.   But $kv = \sqrt{2}(1, 2, 3) = (\sqrt{2}, 2\sqrt{2}, 3\sqrt{2})$ does not belong to W since its components are not rational numbers.   Hence W is not a subspace of V.

4.15. Let V be the vector space of all 2×2 matrices over the real field $\mathbf{R}$.   Show that W is not a subspace of V, where:

(a) W consists of all matrices with zero determinant.

(b) W consists of all matrices A for which $A^2 = A$.

(a) $\left[\text{Recall that } \det \begin{bmatrix} a & b \\ c & d \end{bmatrix} = ad - bc. \right]$ The matrices $A = \begin{bmatrix} 1 & 0 \\ 0 & 0 \end{bmatrix}$ and $B = \begin{bmatrix} 0 & 0 \\ 0 & 1 \end{bmatrix}$ belong to W since $\det(A) = 0$ and $\det(B) = 0$.   But $A + B = \begin{bmatrix} 1 & 0 \\ 0 & 1 \end{bmatrix}$ does not belong to W since $\det(A + B) = 1$.   Hence W is not a subspace of V.

(b) The unit matrix $I = \begin{bmatrix} 1 & 0 \\ 0 & 1 \end{bmatrix}$ belongs to W since

$$I^2 = \begin{bmatrix} 1 & 0 \\ 0 & 1 \end{bmatrix}\begin{bmatrix} 1 & 0 \\ 0 & 1 \end{bmatrix} = \begin{bmatrix} 1 & 0 \\ 0 & 1 \end{bmatrix} = I$$

But $2I = \begin{bmatrix} 2 & 0 \\ 0 & 2 \end{bmatrix}$ does not belong to W since

$$(2I)^2 = \begin{bmatrix} 2 & 0 \\ 0 & 2 \end{bmatrix}\begin{bmatrix} 2 & 0 \\ 0 & 2 \end{bmatrix} = \begin{bmatrix} 4 & 0 \\ 0 & 4 \end{bmatrix} \neq 2I$$

Hence W is not a subspace of V.

4.16. Let $V = \mathbf{P}(t)$.   Determine whether or not W is a subspace of V, where:

(a) W consists of all polynomials with integral coefficients.

(b) W consists of all polynomials with degree ≥ 6 and the zero polynomial.

(a) No.   For example, $f(t) = 3 + 6t + 7t^2 \in W$ but $\frac{1}{2}f(t) = \frac{3}{2} + 3t + \frac{7}{2}t^2 \notin W$.

(b) Yes, since sums and scalar multiples of polynomials in W belong to W.

4.17. Let $V = \mathbf{P}(t)$, the vector space of real polynomials. Show that W is a subspace of V, where:

   (a) $W = \{f(t): \; f(1) = 0\}$, i.e., W consists of all polynomials whose value at 1 is 0.

   (b) $W = \{f(t): \; f(3) = f(1)\}$, i.e., W consists of all polynomials whose values at 3 and 1 are equal.

   Let $\hat{0}$ denote the zero polynomial, so $\hat{0}(t) = 0$ for every value of t.

   (a) $\hat{0} \in W$ since $\hat{0}(1) = 0$. Suppose f and g belong to W. Then $f(1) = 0$ and $g(1) = 0$. Thus, for any scalars k and k' we have

$$(kf + k'g)(1) = kf(1) + k'g(1) = k0 + k'0 = 0$$

   Thus $kf + k'g \in W$, and hence W is a subspace.

   (b) $\hat{0} \in W$ since $\hat{0}(3) = 0 = \hat{0}(1)$. Suppose f and g belong to W. Then $f(3) = f(1)$ and $g(3) = g(1)$. Thus, for any scalars k and k' we have

$$(kf + k'g)(3) = kf(3) + k'g(3) = kf(1) + k'g(1) = (kf + k'g)(1)$$

   Thus $kf + k'g \in W$, and hence W is a subspace.

LINEAR SPANS, ROW SPACES

4.18. Show that the vectors $u_1 = (1, 1, 1)$, $u_2 = (1, 2, 3)$, $u_3 = (1, 5, 8)$ span $\mathbf{R}^3$.

   We need to show that an arbitrary vector $v = (a, b, c)$ in $\mathbf{R}^3$ is a linear combination of u_1, u_2, u_3. Set $v = xu_1 + yu_2 + zu_3$, that is, set

$$(a, b, c) = x(1, 1, 1) + y(1, 2, 3) + z(1, 5, 8) = (x + y + z, \; x + 2y + 5z, \; x + 3y + 8z)$$

   Form the equivalent system of linear equations and reduce it to echelon form:

$$
\begin{aligned}
x + y + z &= a \\
x + 2y + 5z &= b \quad \text{or} \\
x + 3y + 8z &= c
\end{aligned}
\qquad
\begin{aligned}
x + y + z &= a \\
y + 4z &= b - a \quad \text{or} \\
2y + 7z &= c - a
\end{aligned}
\qquad
\begin{aligned}
x + y + z &= a \\
y + 4z &= b - a \\
-z &= c - 2b + a
\end{aligned}
$$

   The above system is in echelon form and is consistent. In fact,

$$x = -a + 5b - 3c, \qquad y = 3a - 7b + 4c, \qquad z = -a + 2b - c$$

   is a solution. Thus u_1, u_2, u_3 span $\mathbf{R}^3$.

4.19. Find conditions on a, b, c so that $v = (a, b, c)$ in $\mathbf{R}^3$ belongs to the subspace W spanned by $u_1 = (1, 2, 0)$, $u_2 = (-1, 1, 2)$, and $u_3 = (3, 0, -4)$.

   Set v as a linear combination of u_1, u_2, u_3 using unknowns x, y, z, that is, set

$$
\begin{bmatrix} a \\ b \\ c \end{bmatrix}
= x \begin{bmatrix} 1 \\ 2 \\ 0 \end{bmatrix}
+ y \begin{bmatrix} -1 \\ 1 \\ 2 \end{bmatrix}
+ z \begin{bmatrix} 3 \\ 0 \\ -4 \end{bmatrix}
$$

Form the equivalent system of linear equations and reduce it to echelon form:

$$
\begin{array}{llll}
x - y + 3z = a & & x - y + 3z = a & & x - y + 3z = a \\
2x + y = b & \text{or} & 3y - 6z = b - 2a & \text{or} & 3y - 6z = b - 2a \\
2y - 4z = c & & 2y - 4z = c & & 0 = 4a - 2b + 3c
\end{array}
$$

The vector $v = (a, b, c)$ belongs to W if and only if the system is consistent, and it is consistent if and only if $4a - 2b + 3c = 0$. Note, in particular, that u_1, u_2, and u_3 do not span the whole space $\mathbf{R}^3$.

4.20. Show that the vector space $V = \mathbf{P}(t)$ of real polynomials cannot be spanned by a finite number of polynomials.

Any finite set S of polynomials contains a polynomial of maximum degree, say m. Then the linear span of S cannot contain a polynomial of degree greater than m. Thus $\text{span}(S) \neq V$ for any finite set S.

4.21. Determine whether the following matrices have the same row space:

$$
A = \begin{bmatrix} 1 & 1 & 5 \\ 2 & 3 & 13 \end{bmatrix}, \qquad B = \begin{bmatrix} 1 & -1 & -2 \\ 3 & -2 & -3 \end{bmatrix}, \qquad C = \begin{bmatrix} 1 & -1 & -1 \\ 4 & -3 & -1 \\ 3 & -1 & 3 \end{bmatrix}
$$

Row reduce each matrix to row canonical form:

$$
A = \begin{bmatrix} 1 & 1 & 5 \\ 2 & 3 & 13 \end{bmatrix} \sim \begin{bmatrix} 1 & 1 & 5 \\ 0 & 1 & 3 \end{bmatrix} \sim \begin{bmatrix} 1 & 0 & 2 \\ 0 & 1 & 3 \end{bmatrix}
$$

$$
B = \begin{bmatrix} 1 & -1 & -2 \\ 3 & -2 & -3 \end{bmatrix} \sim \begin{bmatrix} 1 & -1 & -2 \\ 0 & 1 & 3 \end{bmatrix} \sim \begin{bmatrix} 1 & 0 & 1 \\ 0 & 1 & 3 \end{bmatrix}
$$

$$
C = \begin{bmatrix} 1 & -1 & -1 \\ 4 & -3 & -1 \\ 3 & -1 & 3 \end{bmatrix} \sim \begin{bmatrix} 1 & -1 & -1 \\ 0 & 1 & 3 \\ 0 & 2 & 6 \end{bmatrix} \sim \begin{bmatrix} 1 & -1 & -1 \\ 0 & 1 & 3 \\ 0 & 0 & 0 \end{bmatrix} \sim \begin{bmatrix} 1 & 0 & 2 \\ 0 & 1 & 3 \\ 0 & 0 & 0 \end{bmatrix}
$$

Since the nonzero rows of the row canonical forms of A and C are the same, A and C have the same row space. On the other hand, the nonzero rows of the row canonical form of B are not the same as the others, and so B has a different row space.

4.22. Determine whether the following matrices have the same column space:

$$
A = \begin{bmatrix} 1 & 3 & 5 \\ 1 & 4 & 3 \\ 1 & 1 & 9 \end{bmatrix}, \qquad B = \begin{bmatrix} 1 & 2 & 3 \\ -2 & -3 & -4 \\ 7 & 12 & 17 \end{bmatrix}
$$

Note that A and B have the same column space if and only if the transposes A^T and B^T have the same row space. Thus row reduce A^T and B^T to row canonical form:

$$A^T = \begin{bmatrix} 1 & 1 & 1 \\ 3 & 4 & 1 \\ 5 & 3 & 9 \end{bmatrix} \sim \begin{bmatrix} 1 & 1 & 1 \\ 0 & 1 & -2 \\ 0 & -2 & 4 \end{bmatrix} \sim \begin{bmatrix} 1 & 1 & 1 \\ 0 & 1 & -2 \\ 0 & 0 & 0 \end{bmatrix} \sim \begin{bmatrix} 1 & 0 & 3 \\ 0 & 1 & -2 \\ 0 & 0 & 0 \end{bmatrix}$$

$$B^T = \begin{bmatrix} 1 & -2 & 7 \\ 2 & -3 & 12 \\ 3 & -4 & 17 \end{bmatrix} \sim \begin{bmatrix} 1 & -2 & 7 \\ 0 & 1 & -2 \\ 0 & 2 & -4 \end{bmatrix} \sim \begin{bmatrix} 1 & -2 & 7 \\ 0 & 1 & -2 \\ 0 & 0 & 0 \end{bmatrix} \sim \begin{bmatrix} 1 & 0 & 3 \\ 0 & 1 & -2 \\ 0 & 0 & 0 \end{bmatrix}$$

Since A^T and B^T have the same row space, A and B have the same column space.

4.23. Show that $U = \text{span}(u_1, u_2, u_3)$ and $W = \text{span}(w_1, w_2)$ are identical subspaces of $\mathbf{R}^4$ where:

$$u_1 = (1, 1, 3, 2), \qquad u_2 = (3, 2, 7, 5), \qquad u_3 = (1, 3, 7, 4),$$

$$w_1 = (1, 2, 5, 3), \qquad w_2 = (3, 1, 5, 4)$$

Method 1:　Show that each u_i is a linear combination of w_1 and w_2, and show that each w_j is a linear combination of u_1, u_2, u_3. (Observe that we have to show that five systems of linear equations are consistent.)

Method 2:　Form the matrix A whose rows are u_1, u_2, u_3 and reduce A to row canonical form:

$$A = \begin{bmatrix} 1 & 1 & 3 & 2 \\ 3 & 2 & 7 & 5 \\ 1 & 3 & 7 & 4 \end{bmatrix} \sim \begin{bmatrix} 1 & 1 & 3 & 2 \\ 0 & -1 & -2 & -1 \\ 0 & 2 & 4 & 2 \end{bmatrix} \sim \begin{bmatrix} 1 & 0 & 1 & 1 \\ 0 & 1 & 2 & 1 \\ 0 & 0 & 0 & 0 \end{bmatrix}$$

Now form the matrix B whose rows are w_1 and w_2 and reduce B to row canonical form:

$$B = \begin{bmatrix} 1 & 2 & 5 & 3 \\ 3 & 1 & 5 & 4 \end{bmatrix} \sim \begin{bmatrix} 1 & 2 & 5 & 3 \\ 0 & -5 & -10 & -5 \end{bmatrix} \sim \begin{bmatrix} 1 & 0 & 1 & 1 \\ 0 & 1 & 2 & 1 \end{bmatrix}$$

Since the nonzero rows of the reduced matrices are identical, A and B have the same row spaces. Thus $U = W$.

SUMS AND DIRECT SUMS

4.24. Let U and W be subspaces of a vector space V. Show that:

(a)　U and W are each contained in $U + W$.

(b)　$U + W$ is the smallest subspace containing U and W, that is, $U + W = \text{span}(U, W)$.

(c)　$W + W = W$.

(a)　Let $u \in U$. Since W is a subspace, $0 \in W$. Hence $u = u + 0$ belongs to $U + W$. Thus $U \subseteq U + W$. Similarly, $W \subseteq U + W$.

(b)　Since $U + W$ is a subspace of V containing U and W, it must also contain the linear span of U and W, that is, $\text{span}(U, W) \subseteq U + W$.

　　On the other hand, if $v \in U + W$, then $v = u + w = 1u + 1w$, where $u \in U$ and $w \in W$. Thus v is a linear combination of elements in $U \cup W$ and so $v \in \text{span}(U, W)$. Hence $U + W \subseteq \text{span}(U, W)$. The two inclusion relations give the desired result.

(c) Since W is a subspace of V, we have that W is closed under vector addition; hence $W + W \subseteq W$. By part (a), $W \subseteq W + W$. Hence $W + W = W$.

4.25. Give an example of a subset S of $\mathbf{R}^2$ such that: (a) $S + S \subset S$ (properly contained); (b) $S \subset S + S$ (properly contained); (c) $S + S = S$ but S is not a subspace of $\mathbf{R}^2$.

(a) Let $S = \{(0, 5), (0, 6), (0, 7), \ldots\}$. Then $S + S \subset S$.

(b) Let $S = \{(0, 0), (0, 1)\}$. Then $S \subset S + S$.

(c) Let $S = \{(0, 0), (0, 1), (0, 2), (0, 3), \ldots\}$. Then $S + S = S$.

4.26. Let U and W be the following subspaces of $\mathbf{R}^3$:

$$U = \{(a, b, c): \quad a = b = c\} \qquad \text{and} \qquad W = \{(0, b, c)\}$$

(Note that W is the yz plane.)   Show that $\mathbf{R}^3 = U \oplus W$.

First we show that $U \cap W = \{0\}$. Suppose $v = (a, b, c) \in U \cap W$. Then $a = b = c$ and $a = 0$. Hence $a = 0$, $b = 0$, $c = 0$. Thus $v = 0 = (0, 0, 0)$.

Next we show that $\mathbf{R}^3 = U + W$. For if $v = (a, b, c) \in \mathbf{R}^3$, then $v = (a, a, a) + (0, b - a, c - a)$, where $(a, a, a) \in U$ and $(0, b - a, c - a) \in W$. Both conditions, $U \cap W = \{0\}$ and $U + W = \mathbf{R}^3$, imply $\mathbf{R}^3 = U \oplus W$.

PROOFS OF THEOREMS

4.27. Prove Theorem 4.2: W is a subspace of V if and only if:

  (i) $0 \in W$.

  (ii)   If $u, v \in W$ then $u + v \in W$.

  (iii)   If $u \in W$ and k is a scalar, then $ku \in W$.

For W to be a subspace, conditions (i), (ii), and (iii) are clearly necessary.   We now show them to be sufficient.   By (i), W is nonempty; and by (ii) and (iii), the operations of vector addition and scalar multiplication are well defined for W.   Moreover, the axioms $[A_1]$, $[A_4]$, $[M_1]$, $[M_2]$, $[M_3]$, and $[M_4]$ hold in W since the vectors in W belong to V.   Hence we need only show that $[A_2]$ and $[A_3]$ also hold in W.   Now $[A_2]$ obviously holds, because the zero vector of V is also the zero vector of W.   Finally, if $v \in W$, then $(-1)v = -v \in W$ and $v + (-v) = 0$, i.e., $[A_3]$ holds.

4.28. Prove Corollary 4.3: W is a subspace of V if and only if:

  (i) $0 \in W$.

  (ii)   If $u, v \in W$ and $a, b \in K$, then $au + bv \in W$.

Suppose W satisfies (i) and (ii). Then, by (i), W is nonempty. Furthermore, if $u, v \in W$, then, by (ii), $1 + v = 1u + 1w \in W$; and if $u \in W$ and $k \in K$, then, by (ii), $ku = ku + 0v \in W$. Thus by Theorem 4.2, W is a subspace of V. Conversely, if W is a subspace of V, then clearly (i) and (ii) hold in W.

4.29. Prove Theorem 4.6(ii):   If W is a subspace of V containing a set S of vectors, then $\text{span}(S) \subseteq W$.

Suppose $u_1, u_2, \ldots, u_r \in S$. Then all the u_i belong to W. Thus all multiples $a_i u_i$ belong to W, and so the sum $a_1 u_1 + a_2 u_2 + \cdots + a_r u_r \in W$. That is, W contains all linear combinations of elements in S or, in other words, $\text{span}(S) \subseteq W$, as claimed.

4.30. Suppose $u = (a_1, a_2, \ldots, a_n)$ is a linear combination of the rows $R_1, R_2, \ldots, R_m$ of a matrix $B = [b_{ij}]$, say $u = k_1 R_1 + k_2 R_2 + \cdots + k_m R_m$. Prove that

$$a_i = k_1 b_{1i} + k_2 b_{2i} + \cdots + k_m b_{mi}, \qquad i = 1, 2, \ldots, n$$

where $b_{1i}, b_{2i}, \ldots, b_{mi}$ are the entries of the ith column of B.

We are given that $u = k_1 R_1 + k_2 R_2 + \cdots + k_m R_m$. Hence

$$(a_1, a_2, \ldots, a_n) = k_1(b_{11}, \ldots, b_{1n}) + \cdots + k_m(b_{m1}, \ldots, b_{mn})$$
$$= (k_1 b_{11} + \cdots + k_m b_{m1}, \ldots, k_1 b_{1n} + k_m b_{mn})$$

Setting corresponding components equal to each other, we obtain the desired result.

4.31. Suppose $A = [a_{ij}]$ and $B = [b_{ij}]$ are echelon matrices with pivot entries

$$a_{1j_1}, a_{2j_2}, \ldots, a_{rj_r} \qquad \text{and} \qquad b_{1k_1}, b_{2k_2}, \ldots, b_{sk_s}$$

as pictured in Fig. 4-5. Suppose A and B have the same row space. Prove that the pivot entries are in the same position, that is, $j_1 = k_1, j_2 = k_2, \ldots, j_r = k_r$ and $r = s$.

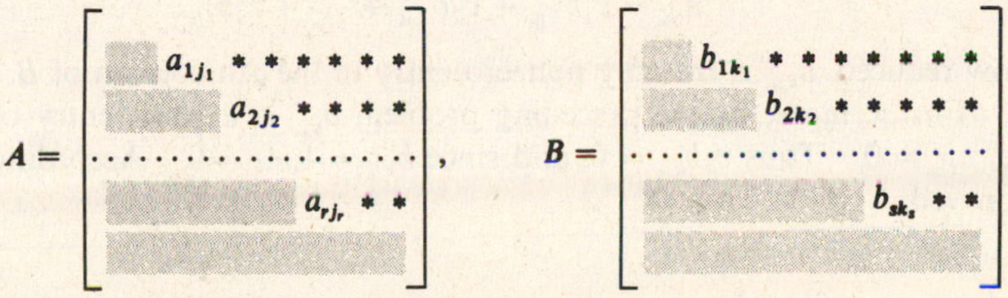

Fig. 4-5

Clearly $A = 0$ if and only if $B = 0$, and so we need only prove the theorem when $r \geq 1$ and $s \geq 1$. We first show that $j_1 = k_1$. Suppose $j_1 < k_1$. Then the j_1th column of B is zero. Since the first row R^* of A is in the row space of B, we have $R^* = c_1 R_1 + c_2 R_2 + \cdots + c_m R_m$, where the R_i are the rows of B. Since the j_1th column of B is zero, we have

$$a_{1j_1} = c_1 0 + c_2 0 + \cdots + c_m 0 = 0$$

But this contradicts the fact that the pivot entry $a_{1j_1} \neq 0$. Hence $j_1 \geq k_1$ and, similarly, $k_1 \geq j_1$. Thus $j_1 = k_1$.

Now let A' be the submatrix of A obtained by deleting the first row of A, and let B' be the submatrix of B obtained by deleting the first row of B. We prove that A' and B' have the same row space. The theorem will then follow by induction since A' and B' are also echelon matrices.

Let $R = (a_1, a_2, \ldots, a_n)$ be any row of A' and let $R_1, \ldots, R_m$ be the rows of B. Since R is in the row space of B, there exist scalars $d_1, \ldots, d_m$ such that $R = d_1 R_1 + d_2 R_2 + \cdots + d_m R_m$. Since A is in echelon form and R is not the first row of A, the j_1th entry of R is zero: $a_i = 0$ for $i = j_1 = k_1$. Furthermore, since B is in echelon form, all the entries in the k_1th column of B are 0 except the first: $b_{1k_1} \neq 0$, but $b_{2k_1} = 0, \ldots, b_{mk_1} = 0$. Thus

$$0 = a_{k_1} = d_1 b_{1k_1} + d_2 0 + \cdots + d_m 0 = d_1 b_{1k_1}$$

Now $b_{1k_1} \neq 0$ and so $d_1 = 0$. Thus R is a linear combination of $R_2, \ldots, R_m$ and so is in the row space of B'. Since R was any row of A', the row space of A' is contained in the row space of B'. Similarly, the row space of B' is contained in the row space of A'. Thus A' and B' have the same row space, and so the theorem is proved.

4.32. Prove Theorem 4.8: Row canonical matrices have the same row space if and only if they have the same nonzero rows.

Obviously, if A and B have the same nonzero rows, then they have the same row space. Thus we only have to prove the converse.

Suppose A and B have the same row space, and suppose $R \neq 0$ is the ith row of A. Then there exist scalars $c_1, \ldots, c_s$ such that

$$R = c_1 R_1 + c_2 R_2 + \cdots + c_s R_s \tag{1}$$

where the R_i are the nonzero rows of B. The theorem is proved if we show that $R = R_i$, or $c_i = 1$ but $c_k = 0$ for $k \neq i$.

Let a_{ij_i} be the pivot entry in R, i.e., the first nonzero entry of R. By Eq. (1) and Problem 4.30,

$$a_{ij_i} = c_1 b_{1j_i} + c_2 b_{2j_i} + \cdots + c_s b_{sj_i} \tag{2}$$

But by the preceding problem b_{ij_i} is a pivot entry of B, and since B is row reduced, it is the only nonzero entry in the jth column of B. Thus from Eq. (2) we obtain $a_{ij_i} = c_i b_{ij_i}$. However, $a_{ij_i} = 1$ and $b_{ij_i} = 1$ since A and B are row reduced; hence $c_i = 1$.

Now suppose $k \neq i$, and b_{kj_k} is the pivot entry in R_k. By Eq. (1) and Problem 4.30,

$$a_{ij_k} = c_1 b_{1j_k} + c_2 b_{2j_k} + \cdots + c_s b_{sj_k} \tag{3}$$

Since B is row reduced, b_{kj_k} is the only nonzero entry in the jth column of B. Hence by Eq. (3), $a_{ij_k} = c_k b_{kj_k}$. Furthermore, by the preceding problem a_{kj_k} is a pivot entry of A, and since A is row reduced, $a_{ij_k} = 0$. Thus $c_k b_{kj_k} = 0$, and since $b_{kj_k} = 1$, $c_k = 0$. Accordingly $R = R_i$, and the theorem is proved.

4.33. Prove Theorem 4.9: Every matrix is row equivalent to a unique matrix in row canonical form.

Suppose A is row equivalent to matrices A_1 and A_2, where A_1 and A_2 are in row canonical form. Then rowsp A = rowsp A_1 and rowsp A = rowsp A_2. Hence rowsp A_1 = rowsp A_2. Since A_1 and A_2 are in row canonical form, $A_1 = A_2$ by Theorem 4.8. Thus the theorem is proved.

4.34. Prove Theorem 4.11: $V = U \oplus W$ if and only if (i) $V = U + W$ and (ii) $U \cap W = \{0\}$.

Suppose $V = U \oplus W$. Then any $v \in V$ can be uniquely written in the form $v = u + w$, where $u \in U$ and $w \in W$. Thus in particular, $V = U + W$. Now suppose $v \in U \cap W$. Then

(1) $v = v + 0$, where $v \in U, 0 \in W$.
(2) $v = 0 + v$, where $0 \in U, v \in W$.

Since such a sum for v must be unique, $v = 0$. Accordingly, $U \cap W = \{0\}$.

On the other hand, suppose $V = U + W$ and $U \cap W = \{0\}$. Let $v \in V$. Since $V = U + W$, there exist $u \in U$ and $w \in W$ such that $v = u + w$. We need to show that such a sum is unique. Suppose also that $v = u' + w'$, where $u' \in U$ and $w' \in W$. Then

$$u + w = u' + w' \qquad \text{and} \qquad u - u' = w' - w$$

But $u - u' \in U$ and $w' - w \in W$.   Hence, by $U \cap W = \{0\}$,

$$u - u' = 0, \quad w' - w = 0 \qquad \text{and so} \qquad u = u', \quad w = w'$$

Thus such a sum for $v \in V$ is unique and $V = U \oplus W$.

Supplementary Problems

VECTOR SPACES

4.35. Suppose u and v belong to a vector space V.   Simplify each expression:

   (a) $E_1 = 4(5u - 6v) + 2(3u + v)$

   (b) $E_2 = 5(2u - 3) + 4(7v + 8)$

   (c) $E_3 = 6(3u + 2v) + 5u - 7v$

   (d) $E_4 = 3(5u + 2/v)$

4.36. Let V be the set of ordered pairs (a, b) of real numbers with addition in V and scalar multiplication on V defined by

$$(a, b) + (c, d) = (a + c, b + d) \qquad k(a, b) = (ka, 0)$$

   Show that V satisfies all the axioms of a vector space except $[\mathbf{M_4}]$, that is, except $1u = u$.   Hence $[\mathbf{M_4}]$ is not a consequence of the other axioms.

4.37. Show that axiom $[\mathbf{A_4}]$ of a vector space V, that is, $u + v = v + u$, can be derived from the other axioms for V.

4.38. Let V be the set of ordered pairs (a, b) of real numbers.   Show that V is not a vector space over $\mathbf{R}$ with addition in V and scalar multiplication on V defined by

   (i) $(a, b) + (c, d) = (a + d, b + c)$ and $k(a, b) = (ka, kb)$

   (ii) $(a, b) + (c, d) = (a + c, b + d)$ and $k(a, b) = (a, b)$

   (iii) $(a, b) + (c, d) = (0, 0)$ and $k(a, b) = (ka, kb)$

   (iv) $(a, b) + (c, d) = (ac, bd)$ and $k(a, b) = (ka, kb)$

4.39. Let U and W be vector spaces over a field K.   Let V be the set of ordered pairs (u, w), where $u \in U$ and $w \in W$.   Show that V is a vector space over K with addition in V and scalar multiplication on V defined by

$$(u, w) + (u', w') = (u + u', w + w') \qquad \text{and} \qquad k(u, w) = ku, kw$$

   (This space V is called the *external direct product* of U and W.)

LINEAR COMBINATIONS

4.40. Let $u_1 = (1, 1, 2)$, $u_2 = (1, 2, 4)$, $u_3 = (2, 4, 7)$ in $\mathbf{R}^3$.   Write v as a linear combination of u_1, u_2, u_3, where: (a) $v = (1, 3, 5)$; (b) $v = (3, -2, 1)$.

4.41. Consider the vectors $u = (1, 2, 3)$ and $v = (2, 3, 1)$ in $\mathbf{R}^3$.

    (a)   Write $w = (1, 3, 8)$ as a linear combination of u and v.

    (b)   Write $w = (2, 4, 5)$ as a linear combination of u and v.

    (c)   Find k so that $w = (1, k, -2)$ is a linear combination of u and v.

    (d)   Find conditions on a, b, c so that $w = (a, b, c)$ is a linear combination of u and v.

4.42. Consider the vectors $u = (1, -3, 2)$ and $v = (2, -1, 1)$ in $\mathbf{R}^3$.

    (a)   Write $(1, 7, -4)$ as a linear combination of u and v.

    (b)   Write $(2, -5, 4)$ as a linear combination of u and v.

    (c)   Find k so that $(1, k, 5)$ is a linear combination of u and v.

    (d)   Find a condition on a, b, and c so that (a, b, c) is a linear combination of u and v.

4.43. Write u as a linear combination of the polynomials $v = 2t^2 + 3t - 4$ and $w = t^2 - 2t - 3$, where:
(a) $u = 3t^2 + 8t - 5$; (b) $u = 4t^2 - 6t - 1$.

4.44. Write M as a linear combination of $A = \begin{bmatrix} 1 & 1 \\ 0 & -1 \end{bmatrix}$, $B = \begin{bmatrix} 1 & 1 \\ -1 & 1 \end{bmatrix}$, $C = \begin{bmatrix} 1 & -1 \\ 0 & 0 \end{bmatrix}$, where:

(a) $M = \begin{bmatrix} 3 & -1 \\ 1 & -3 \end{bmatrix}$; (b) $M = \begin{bmatrix} 2 & 1 \\ -1 & -2 \end{bmatrix}$.

SUBSPACES

4.45. Determine whether or not W is a subspace of $\mathbf{R}^3$, where W consists of all vectors (a, b, c) in $\mathbf{R}^3$ such that: (a) $a = 3b$; (b) $a \le b \le c$; (c) $ab = 0$.

4.46. Determine whether or not W is a subspace of $\mathbf{R}^3$, where W consists of all vectors (a, b, c) in $\mathbf{R}^3$ such that: (a) $a + b + c = 0$; (b) $b = a^2$; (c) $a = 2b = 3c$.

4.47. Consider the vector space $\mathbf{M}$ of all real 2×2 matrices $A = \begin{bmatrix} a & b \\ c & d \end{bmatrix}$. Show that W is a subspace of $\mathbf{M}$ if W consists of all matrices that are: (a) symmetric ($A^T = A$ or $b = c$); (b) (upper) triangular ($c = 0$); (c) diagonal ($b = c = 0$); (d) scalar ($a = d$, $b = c = 0$).

4.48. Let $AX = B$ be a nonhomogeneous system of linear equations in n unknowns, that is, $B \ne 0$. Show that the solution set is not a subspace of $\mathbf{R}^n$.

4.49. Suppose U and W are subspaces of V for which $U \cup W$ is a subspace. Show that $U \subseteq W$ or $W \subseteq U$.

4.50. Let V be the vector space of all functions from the real field $\mathbf{R}$ into $\mathbf{R}$. Determine whether or not W is a subspace of V in each case:

    (a) W consists of all bounded functions. [Here $f\colon \mathbf{R} \to \mathbf{R}$ is bounded if $\exists M \in \mathbf{R}$ such that, for every $x \in \mathbf{R}$, we have $|f(x)| \le M$.]

    (b) W consists of all functions $f(x) = x^k$, where k is any real scalar.

    (c) W consists of all continuous functions.

(d) W consists of the exponential function $f(x) = e^{kx}$, where k is any real scalar.

(e) W consists of all differentiable functions.

(f) W consists of all integrable functions in, say, the interval $0 \le x \le 1$.

(g) W consists of constant functions $f(x) = k$, where k is any real scalar.

LINEAR SPANS

4.51. Show that the vectors u_1, u_2, u_3 span $\mathbf{R}^3$ [that is, show that any vector $v = (a, b, c)$ in $\mathbf{R}^3$ is a linear combination of u_1, u_2, u_3] where:

    (a) $u_1 = (1, 1, 1)$, $u_2 = (0, 1, 2)$, $u_3 = (0, 1, 3)$

    (b) $u_1 = (1, 1, 0)$, $u_2 = (0, 1, 1)$, $u_3 = (0, 2, 1)$

4.52. Show that the vectors u_1, u_2, u_3 do not span $\mathbf{R}^3$. Specifically, find conditions on a, b, c so that $v = (a, b, c)$ in $\mathbf{R}^3$ is a linear combination of u_1, u_2, u_3:

    (a) $u_1 = (1, 1, 1)$, $u_2 = (1, 2, 3)$, $u_3 = (0, 1, 2)$

    (b) $u_1 = (1, 1, 0)$, $u_2 = (0, 1, 1)$, $u_3 = (1, 3, 2)$

4.53. Show that the polynomials $p_1 = (t - 1)^2$, $p_2 = t - 1$, and $p_3 = 1$ span the space $\mathbf{P}_2(t)$ of polynomials of degree ≤ 2, that is, show that any polynomial $f = at^2 + bt + c$ in $\mathbf{P}_2(t)$ is a linear combination of p_1, p_2, p_3.

4.54. Find one vector in $\mathbf{R}^3$ which spans the intersection of U and W where U is the xy plane, i.e., $U = \{(a, b, 0)\}$, and W is the space spanned by the vectors $(1, 1, 1)$ and $(1, 2, 3)$.

4.55. Prove that span(S) is the intersection of all subspaces of V containing S.

4.56. Show that span$(S) = $ span$(S \cup \{0\})$. That is, by joining or deleting the zero vector from a set, we do not change the space spanned by the set.

4.57. Show that: (a) if $S \subseteq T$, then span$(S) \subseteq$ span(T); (b) span(span$(S)) = $ span(S).

ROW SPACE OF A MATRIX

4.58. Determine which of the following matrices have the same row space:

$$A = \begin{bmatrix} 1 & -2 & -1 \\ 3 & -4 & 5 \end{bmatrix}, \qquad B = \begin{bmatrix} 1 & -1 & 2 \\ 2 & 3 & -1 \end{bmatrix}, \qquad C = \begin{bmatrix} 1 & -1 & 3 \\ 2 & -1 & 10 \\ 3 & -5 & 1 \end{bmatrix}$$

4.59. Determine which of the following matrices have the same column space:

$$A = \begin{bmatrix} 1 & 1 & 2 \\ 1 & 2 & 1 \\ 3 & 5 & 4 \end{bmatrix}, \qquad B = \begin{bmatrix} 1 & 2 & 3 \\ 3 & 3 & 2 \\ 7 & 8 & 7 \end{bmatrix}, \qquad C = \begin{bmatrix} 1 & 1 & 1 \\ 1 & 2 & 1 \\ 1 & 1 & 3 \end{bmatrix}$$

4.60. Determine which of the following subspaces of $\mathbf{R}^3$ are identical:

$$U_1 = \text{span}[(1, 1, -1), (2, 3, -1), (3, 1, -5)]$$
$$U_2 = \text{span}[(1, -1, -3), (3, -2, -8), (2, 1, -3)]$$
$$U_3 = \text{span}[(1, 1, 1), (1, -1, 3), (3, -1, 7)]$$

4.61. Determine which of the following subspaces of $\mathbf{R}^4$ are identical:

$$U_1 = \text{span}[(1, 2, 1, 4), (2, 4, 1, 5), (3, 6, 2, 9)]$$
$$U_2 = \text{span}[(1, 2, 1, 2), (2, 4, 1, 3)]$$
$$U_3 = \text{span}[(1, 2, 3, 10), (2, 4, 3, 11)]$$

4.62. Show that if any row is deleted from a matrix in echelon (row canonical) form, then the resulting matrix is still in echelon (row canonical) form.

4.63. Let A and B be matrices for which the product AB is defined. Show that the column space of AB is contained in the column space of A.

SUMS, DIRECT SUMS, INTERSECTIONS

4.64. Let S and T be arbitrary nonempty subsets (not necessarily subspaces) of a vector space V and let k be a scalar. The sum $S + T$ and the scalar product kS are defined by

$$S + T = \{u + v: \ u \in S, v \in T\}, \qquad kS = \{ku: \ u \in S\}$$

(We also write $w + S$ for $\{w\} + S$.) Let

$$S = \{(1, 2), (2, 3)\}, \qquad T = \{(1, 4), (1, 5), (2, 5)\}, \qquad w = (1, 1), \qquad k = 3$$

Find: (a) $S + T$; (b) $w + S$; (c) kS; (d) kT; (e) $kS + kT$; (f) $k(S + T)$.

4.65. Show that the above operations of $S + T$ and kS satisfy:

(a) Commutative law: $S + T = T + S$

(b) Associative law: $(S_1 + S_2) + S_3 = S_1 + (S_2 + S_3)$

(c) Distributive law: $k(S + T) = kS + kT$

(d) $S + \{0\} = \{0\} + S = S$ and $S + V = V + S = V$

4.66. Consider the following subspaces of $\mathbf{R}^3$:

$$U_1 = \{(a, b, c): \ a = c\}, \ U_2 = \{(a, b, c): \ a + b + c = 0\}, \ U_3 = \{(0, 0, c)\}$$

Show that: (a) $\mathbf{R}^3 = U_1 \oplus U_3$; (b) $\mathbf{R}^3 = U_2 \oplus U_3$; (c) $\mathbf{R}^3 = U_1 + U_2$ but $\mathbf{R}^3 \neq U_1 \oplus U_2$.

4.67. Suppose U, W_1, and W_2 are subspaces of a vector space V. Show that $(U \cap W_1) + (U \cap W_2)$ is a subspace of $U \cap (W_1 + W_2)$. Find subspaces of $\mathbf{R}^2$ for which equality does not hold.

4.68. Suppose $W_1, W_2, \ldots, W_r$ are subspaces of a vector space V. Show that:

(a) $\text{span}(W_1, W_2, \ldots, W_r) = W_1 + W_2 + \cdots + W_r$.

(b) If S_i spans W_i for $i = 1, \ldots, r$, then $S_1 \cup S_2 \cup \cdots \cup S_r$ spans $W_1 + W_2 + \cdots + W_r$.

4.69. Let V be the vector space of n-square matrices. Let U be the subspace of upper triangular matrices, and let W be the subspace of lower triangular matrices. Find: (a) $U \cap W$; (b) $U + W$.

4.70. Let V be the external direct sum of vector spaces U and W over a field K. (See Problem 4.39.) Let $\hat{U} = \{(u, 0): \ u \in U\}$ and $\hat{W} = \{(0, w): \ w \in W\}$. Show that: (a) $\hat{U}$ and $\hat{W}$ are subspaces of V; (b) $V = \hat{U} \oplus \hat{W}$.

Answers to Supplementary Problems

4.35. (a) $E_1 = 26u - 22v$; (b) the sum of the vector $7v$ and the scalar 8 is not defined; hence E_2 is not defined; (c) $E_3 = 23u + 5v$; (d) division by the vector v is not defined; hence E_4 is not defined.

4.40. (a) $v = -u_1 + u_3$; (b) $v = 8u_1 + 5u_2 - 5u_3$.

4.41. (a) $w = 3u - v$; (b) impossible; (c) $k = 1$; (d) $7a - 5b + c = 0$.

4.42. (a) $-3u + 2v$; (b) impossible; (c) $k = -8$; (d) $a - 3b - 5c = 0$.

4.43. (a) $u = 2v - w$; (b) impossible.

4.44. (a) $M = 2A - B + 2C$; (b) impossible.

4.45. (a) yes; (b) no, e.g., $(1, 2, 3) \in W$ but $-2(1, 2, 3) \notin W$; (c) no, e.g., $(1, 0, 0)$, $(0, 1, 0) \in W$, but not their sum.

4.46. (a) yes; (b) no, e.g., $(1, 1, 1) \in W$ but $2(1, 1, 1) = (2, 2, 2) \notin W$; (c) yes.

4.48. The zero vector 0 is not a solution.

4.50. (a) yes; (b) no; (c) yes; (d) no; (e) yes; (f) yes; (g) yes.

4.51. Using $v = (a, b, c) = xu_1 + yu_2 + zu_3$, we obtain: (a) $x = a$, $y = -2a + 3b - c$, $z = a - 2b + c$; (b) $x = a$, $y = a - b + 2c$, $z = -a + b - c$.

4.52. (a) $a - 2b + c = 0$; (b) $a - b + c = 0$.

4.53. Using $f = xp_1 + yp_2 + zp_3$, we get $x = a$, $y = 2a + b$, $z = a + b + c$.

4.54. $v = (2, 1, 0)$.

4.58. A and C are row equivalent to $\begin{bmatrix} 1 & 0 & 7 \\ 0 & 1 & 4 \end{bmatrix}$, but not B.

4.59. A^T and B^T are row equivalent to $\begin{bmatrix} 1 & 0 & 1 \\ 0 & 1 & 2 \end{bmatrix}$, but not C^T.

4.60. U_1 and U_2 are row equivalent to $\begin{bmatrix} 1 & 0 & -2 \\ 0 & 1 & 1 \end{bmatrix}$, but not U_3.

4.61. U_1 and U_3 are row equivalent to $\begin{bmatrix} 1 & 2 & 0 & 1 \\ 0 & 0 & 1 & 3 \end{bmatrix}$, but not U_2.

4.64. (a) $\{(2, 6), (2, 7), (3, 7), (3, 8), (4, 8)\}$; (b) $\{(2, 3), (3, 4)\}$; (c) $\{(3, 6), (6, 9)\}$; (d) $\{(3, 12), (3, 15), (6, 15)\}$; (e), (f) $\{(6, 18), (6, 21), (9, 21), (9, 24), (12, 24)\}$.

4.67. Let U = line $y = x$, W_1 = x axis, W_2 = y axis.

4.69. (a) Diagonal matrices; (b) $V = U + W$.

Chapter 5

Basis and Dimension

5.1 INTRODUCTION

Some of the fundamental results in this chapter are as follows:

(1) The dimension of a vector space V is well defined.
(2) The row rank and the column rank of a matrix A are equal.
(3) A system of linear equations has a solution if and only if the coefficient and the augmented matrices have the same rank.

These concepts and results are nontrivial and answer certain questions raised and investigated by mathematicians in the past.

The chapter begins with the definition of linear dependence and independence. This concept plays an essential role in the theory of linear algebra and in mathematics in general.

5.2 LINEAR DEPENDENCE AND INDEPENDENCE

We begin with a definition.

Definition: Let V be a vector space over a field K. We say that the vectors $v_1, v_2, \ldots, v_m$ in V are *linearly dependent* if there exist scalars $a_1, a_2, \ldots, a_m$ in K, not all of them 0, such that

$$a_1 v_1 + a_2 v_2 + \cdots + a_m v_m = 0$$

Otherwise we say that the vectors are *linearly independent*.

The above definition may be restated as follows. Consider the vector equation

$$x_1 v_1 + x_2 v_2 + \cdots + x_m v_m = 0 \qquad (\star)$$

where the x are unknown scalars. This equation always has the *zero solution* $x_1 = 0$, $x_2 = 0, \ldots, x_m = 0$. If this is the only solution, that is, if

$$x_1 v_1 + x_2 v_2 + \cdots + x_m v_m = 0 \qquad \text{implies} \qquad x_1 = 0, x_2 = 0, \ldots, x_m = 0$$

then the vectors $v_1, v_2, \ldots, v_m$ are linearly independent. On the other hand, if Eq. ($\star$) has a nonzero solution, then the vectors are linearly dependent.

A set $S = \{v_1, v_2, \ldots, v_m\}$ of vectors in V is linearly dependent or independent according to whether the vectors $v_1, v_2, \ldots, v_m$ are linearly dependent or independent. We emphasize that the set $S = \{v_1, v_2, \ldots, v_m\}$ represents a list or, in other words, a finite sequence of vectors, where the vectors are ordered and repetition is permitted.

An infinite set S of vectors is linearly dependent or independent according to whether there do or do not exist vectors $v_1, v_2, \ldots, v_k$ in S which are linearly dependent.

The following remarks follow directly from the above definition.

Remark 1: If 0 is one of the vectors $v_1, \ldots, v_m$, say $v_1 = 0$, then the vectors must be linearly dependent, for

$$1v_1 + 0v_2 + \cdots + 0v_m = 1 \cdot 0 + 0 + \cdots + 0 = 0$$

and the coefficient of v_1 is not 0.

Remark 2: Any nonzero vector v is, by itself, linearly independent, for

$$kv = 0, \ v \neq 0 \quad \text{implies} \quad k = 0$$

Remark 3: If two of the vectors $v_1, v_2, \ldots, v_m$ are equal or one is a scalar multiple of the other, say $v_1 = kv_2$, then the vectors are linearly dependent, for

$$v_1 - kv_2 + 0v_3 + \cdots + 0v_m = 0$$

and the coefficient of v_1 is not 0.

Remark 4: Two vectors v_1 and v_2 are linearly dependent if and only if one of them is a multiple of the other.

Remark 5: If the set $\{v_1, \ldots, v_m\}$ is linearly independent, then any rearrangement of the vectors $\{v_{i_1}, v_{i_2}, \ldots, v_{i_m}\}$ is also linearly independent.

Remark 6: If a set S of vectors is linearly independent, then any subset of S is linearly independent. Alternatively, if S contains a linearly dependent subset, then S is linearly dependent.

EXAMPLE 5.1

(a) The vectors $u = (1, -1, 0)$, $v = (1, 3, -1)$, and $w = (5, 3, -2)$ are linearly dependent since

$$3(1, -1, 0) + 2(1, 3, -1) - (5, 3, -2) = (0, 0, 0)$$

That is, $3u + 2v - w = 0$.

(b) We show that the vectors $u = (6, 2, 3, 4)$, $v = (0, 5, -3, 1)$, and $w = (0, 0, 7, -2)$ are linearly independent. For supposing that $xu + yv + zw = 0$, where x, y, and z are unknown scalars, then

$$(0, 0, 0, 0) = x(6, 2, 3, 4) + y(0, 5, -3, 1) + z(0, 0, 7, -2)$$

That is,

$$x \begin{bmatrix} 6 \\ 2 \\ 3 \\ 4 \end{bmatrix} + y \begin{bmatrix} 0 \\ 5 \\ -3 \\ 1 \end{bmatrix} + z \begin{bmatrix} 0 \\ 0 \\ 7 \\ -2 \end{bmatrix} = \begin{bmatrix} 0 \\ 0 \\ 0 \\ 0 \end{bmatrix} \quad \text{or} \quad \begin{aligned} 6x & & &= 0 \\ 2x + 5y & & &= 0 \\ 3x - 3y &+ 7z &= 0 \\ 4x + \ \ y &- 2z &= 0 \end{aligned}$$

The first equation yields $x = 0$; the second equation with $x = 0$ yields $y = 0$; and the third equation with $x = 0$, $y = 0$ yields $z = 0$. Thus

$$xu + yv + zw = 0 \quad \text{implies} \quad x = 0, \ y = 0, \ z = 0$$

Accordingly u, v, and w are linearly independent.

Linear Dependence in $\mathbf{R}^3$

Linear dependence in the vector space $V = \mathbf{R}^3$ can be described geometrically as follows:

(a) Any two vectors u and v in $\mathbf{R}^3$ are linearly dependent if and only if they lie on the same line through the origin O, as shown in Fig. 5-1(a).

(b) Any three vectors u, v, and w in $\mathbf{R}^3$ are linearly dependent if and only if they lie on the same plane through the origin O, as shown in Fig. 5-1(b).

Later we will be able to show that any four or more vectors in $\mathbf{R}^3$ are automatically linearly dependent.

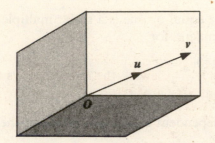 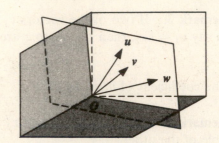

(a) u and v are linearly dependent.   (b) u, v, and w are linearly dependent.

Fig. 5-1

Linear Dependence and Linear Combinations

The notions of linear dependence and linear combinations are closely related. Specifically, for more than one vector we show that the vectors $v_1, v_2, \ldots, v_m$ are linearly dependent if and only if one of them is a linear combination of the others.

Suppose, say, v_i is a linear combination of the others,

$$v_i = a_1 v_1 + \cdots + a_{i-1} v_{i-1} + a_{i+1} v_{i+1} + \cdots + a_m v_m$$

Then by adding $-v_i$ to both sides, we obtain

$$a_1 v_1 + \cdots + a_{i-1} v_{i-1} - v_i + a_{i+1} v_{i+1} + \cdots + a_m v_m = 0$$

where the coefficient of v_i is not 0. Hence the vectors are linearly dependent. Conversely, suppose the vectors are linearly dependent, say,

$$b_1 v_1 + \cdots + b_j v_j + \cdots + b_m v_m = 0 \qquad \text{where} \qquad b_j \neq 0$$

Then

$$v_j = -b_j^{-1} b_1 v_1 - \cdots - b_j^{-1} b_{j-1} v_{j-1} - b_j^{-1} b_{j+1} v_{j+1} - \cdots - b_j^{-1} b_m v_m$$

and so v_j is a linear combination of the other vectors.

We now state a slightly stronger statement than the one above. This result has many important consequences.

Lemma 5.1: Suppose two or more nonzero vectors $v_1, v_2, \ldots, v_m$ are linearly dependent. Then one of the vectors is a linear combination of the preceding vectors, that is, there exists a $k > 1$ such that

$$v_k = c_1 v_1 + c_2 v_2 + \cdots + c_{k-1} v_{k-1}$$

Linear Dependence and Echelon Matrices

Consider the following matrix in echelon form:

$$A = \begin{bmatrix} 0 & 2 & 3 & 4 & 5 & 6 & 7 \\ 0 & 0 & 4 & -4 & 4 & -4 & 4 \\ 0 & 0 & 0 & 0 & 7 & 8 & 9 \\ 0 & 0 & 0 & 0 & 0 & 6 & -6 \\ 0 & 0 & 0 & 0 & 0 & 0 & 0 \end{bmatrix}$$

Observe that rows R_2, R_3, and R_4 have 0s in the second column (below the pivot element in R_1), and hence any linear combination of R_2, R_3, and R_4 must have a 0 as its second component. Thus R_1 cannot be a linear combination of the nonzero rows below it. Similarly, rows R_3 and R_4 have 0s in the third column below the pivot element in R_2. Hence R_2 cannot be a linear combination of the nonzero rows below it. Finally, R_3 cannot be a multiple of R_4 since R_4 has a 0 in the fifth column below the pivot in R_3. Viewing the nonzero rows from the bottom up, R_4, R_3, R_2, R_1, no row is a linear combination of the previous rows. Thus the rows are linearly independent by Lemma 5.1.

The argument used with the above echelon matrix A can be used for the nonzero rows of any echelon matrix. Thus we have the following very useful result.

Theorem 5.2: The nonzero rows of a matrix in echelon form are linearly independent.

5.3 BASIS AND DIMENSION

First we state two equivalent ways to define a basis of a vector space V. (The equivalence is proved in Problem 5.36.)

Definition A: A set $S = \{u_1, u_2, \ldots, u_n\}$ of vectors is a *basis* of V if the following two conditions hold:

    (i) $u_1, u_2, \ldots, u_n$ are linearly independent.

    (ii) $u_1, u_2, \ldots, u_n$ span V.

Definition B: A set $S = \{u_1, u_2, \ldots, u_n\}$ of vectors is a *basis* of V if every vector $v \in V$ can be written uniquely as a linear combination of the basis vectors.

The following is a fundamental result in linear algebra (proved in Problem 5.36).

Theorem 5.3: Every basis of a vector space V has the same number of elements.

A vector space V is said to be of *finite dimension n* or *n-dimensional*, written

$$\dim V = n$$

if V has such a basis with n elements. This definition of dimension is well defined in view of Theorem 5.3.

The vector space $\{0\}$ is defined to have dimension 0. If a vector space V does not have a finite basis, then V is said to be of *infinite dimension*.

The fundamental Theorem 5.3 is a consequence of the following "replacement lemma" (proved in Problem 5.34).

Lemma 5.4: Suppose $\{v_1, v_2, \ldots, v_n\}$ spans V, and suppose $\{w_1, w_2, \ldots, w_m\}$ is linearly independent. Then $m \leq n$, and V is spanned by a set of the form

$$\{w_1, \ldots, w_m, v_{i_1}, \ldots, v_{i_{n-m}}\}$$

Thus, in particular, any $n + 1$ or more vectors in V are linearly dependent.

Observe in the above lemma that we have replaced m of the vectors in the spanning set by the m independent vectors and still retained a spanning set.

Examples of Bases

This subsection presents important examples of bases of the main vector spaces appearing in this text.

(a) *Vector Space* $\mathbf{R}^n$: Consider the following n vectors in $\mathbf{R}^n$:

$$e_1 = (1, 0, 0, 0, \ldots, 0, 0)$$
$$e_2 = (0, 1, 0, 0, \ldots, 0, 0)$$
$$\ldots\ldots\ldots\ldots\ldots\ldots\ldots$$
$$e_n = (0, 0, 0, 0, \ldots, 0, 1)$$

One can easily show that the vectors are linearly independent. (For example, they form a matrix in echelon form.) Furthermore, any vector $u = (a_1, a_2, \ldots, a_n)$ in $\mathbf{R}^n$ can be written as a linear combination of the above vectors. Specifically,

$$v = a_1 e_1 + a_2 e_2 + \cdots + a_n e_n$$

Accordingly the vectors form a basis of $\mathbf{R}^n$, called the *usual* or *standard* basis of $\mathbf{R}^n$. Thus (as one might expect) $\mathbf{R}^n$ has dimension n. In particular, any other basis of $\mathbf{R}^n$ has n elements.

(b) *Vector Space* $\mathbf{M} = \mathbf{M}_{r,s}$ *of All* $r \times s$ *Matrices:* The following six matrices form a basis of the vector space $\mathbf{M}_{2,3}$ of all 2×3 matrices over $\mathbf{R}$:

$$\begin{bmatrix} 1 & 0 & 0 \\ 0 & 0 & 0 \end{bmatrix}, \begin{bmatrix} 0 & 1 & 0 \\ 0 & 0 & 0 \end{bmatrix}, \begin{bmatrix} 0 & 0 & 1 \\ 0 & 0 & 0 \end{bmatrix}, \begin{bmatrix} 0 & 0 & 0 \\ 1 & 0 & 0 \end{bmatrix}, \begin{bmatrix} 0 & 0 & 0 \\ 0 & 1 & 0 \end{bmatrix}, \begin{bmatrix} 0 & 0 & 0 \\ 0 & 0 & 1 \end{bmatrix}$$

More generally, in the vector space $\mathbf{M} = \mathbf{M}_{r,s}$ of all $r \times s$ matrices, let E_{ij} be the matrix with ij entry 1 and 0 elsewhere. Then all such matrices form a basis of $\mathbf{M}$ called the *usual* or *standard* basis of $\mathbf{M}$. Accordingly dim $\mathbf{M}_{r,s} = rs$.

(c) *Vector Space* $\mathbf{P}_n(t)$ *of All Polynomials of degree* $\leq n$: Consider the set $S = \{1, t, t^2, t^3, \ldots, t^n\}$ of polynomials in $\mathbf{P}_n(t)$. Clearly, any polynomial $f(t)$ of degree $\leq n$ can be expressed as a linear combination of the polynomials in S. Also, one can show that the polynomials in S are linearly independent. Thus S is a basis of $\mathbf{P}_n(t)$, and so dim $\mathbf{P}_n(t) = n + 1$.

(d) *Vector Space* $\mathbf{P}(t)$ *of All Polynomials:* Consider any finite set $S = \{f_1(t), f_2(t), \ldots, f_m(t)\}$ of polynomials in $\mathbf{P}(t)$. Let m denote the largest of the degrees of the polynomials in S. Then any polynomial $g(t)$ of degree greater than m cannot be expressed as a linear combination of elements of S. Thus S cannot be a basis of $\mathbf{P}(t)$. This means that the dimension of $\mathbf{P}(t)$ is infinite. We note that the infinite set $S' = \{1, t, t^2, t^3, \ldots\}$ of all powers of t spans $\mathbf{P}(t)$ and is linearly independent. Thus S' is an infinite basis of $\mathbf{P}(t)$.

Theorems on Bases

The following three theorems (proved in Problems 5.37, 5.38, and 5.39) will be used frequently.

Theorem 5.5:   Let V be a vector space of finite dimension n.   Then:

   (i)   Any $n + 1$ or more vectors in V are linearly dependent.

   (ii)   Any linearly independent set $S = \{u_1, u_2, \ldots, u_n\}$ with n elements is a basis of V.

   (iii)   Any spanning set $T = \{v_1, v_2, \ldots, v_n\}$ of V with n elements is a basis of V.

Theorem 5.6:   Suppose S spans a vector space V.   Then:

   (i)   Any maximum number of linearly independent vectors in S form a basis of V.

   (ii)   Suppose one deletes from S every vector that is a linear combination of preceding vectors in S.   Then the remaining vectors form a basis of V.

Theorem 5.7:   Let V be a vector space of finite dimension and let $S = \{u_1, u_2, \ldots, u_r\}$ be a set of linearly independent vectors in V.   Then S is part of a basis of V, that is, S may be extended to a basis of V.

EXAMPLE 5.2

(a)   Consider the following four vectors in $\mathbf{R}^4$:

$$(1, 1, 1, 1), \qquad (0, 1, 1, 1), \qquad (0, 0, 1, 1), \qquad (0, 0, 0, 1)$$

Note that the vector will form a matrix in echelon form.   Hence the vectors are linearly independent. Furthermore, since dim $\mathbf{R}^4 = 4$, the vectors form a basis of $\mathbf{R}^4$.

(b)   Consider the following $n + 1$ polynomials in $\mathbf{P}_n(t)$:

$$1, t - 1, (t - 1)^2, \ldots, (t - 1)^n$$

The degree of $(t - 1)^k$ is k.   Hence no polynomial can be a linear combination of preceding polynomials.   Thus the polynomials are linearly independent.   Furthermore, they form a basis of $\mathbf{P}_n(t)$ since dim $\mathbf{P}_n(t) = n + 1$.

(c)   Consider the following four vectors in $\mathbf{R}^3$:

$$(257, -132, 58), \qquad (43, 0, -17), \qquad (521, -317, 94), \qquad (328, -512, -731)$$

By Theorem 5.5(i), the four vectors must be linearly dependent since they come from the vector space $\mathbf{R}^3$, which has dimension 3.

5.4   DIMENSION AND SUBSPACES

The following theorem gives the basic relationship between the dimension of a vector space and the dimension of a subspace.

Theorem 5.8:   Let W be a subspace of a finite dimensional vector space V.   Then dim $W \leq$ dim V.   In particular, if $W \neq V$, then dim $W <$ dim V.

EXAMPLE 5.3 Let W be a subspace of the real space $\mathbf{R}^3$. Note that dim $\mathbf{R}^3 = 3$. Theorem 5.8 tells us that the dimension of W can only be 0, 1, 2, or 3. The following cases apply:

(a) dim $W = 0$, then $W = \{0\}$, a point.
(b) dim $W = 1$, then W is a line through the origin.
(c) dim $W = 2$, then W is a plane through the origin.
(d) dim $W = 3$, then W is the entire space $\mathbf{R}^3$.

Suppose U and W are subspaces of V. Recall that $U \cap W$ and $U + W$ are also subspaces of V. The following theorem (proved in Problem 5.42) relates their dimensions.

Theorem 5.9: Suppose U and W are finite-dimensional subspaces of a vector space V. Then $U + W$ has finite dimension and

$$\dim (U + W) = \dim U + \dim W - \dim (U \cap W)$$

EXAMPLE 5.4 Suppose U and W are the xy and yz planes, respectively, in $\mathbf{R}^3$, that is,

$$U = \{(a, b, 0)\} \qquad \text{and} \qquad W = \{(0, b, c)\}$$

Note that $\mathbf{R}^3 = U + W$; hence dim $(U + W) = 3$. Also dim $U = 2$ and dim $W = 2$. By Theorem 5.9,

$$3 = 2 + 2 - \dim (U \cap W) \qquad \text{or} \qquad \dim (U \cap W) = 1$$

This agrees with the facts that $U \cap W$ is the y axis (Fig. 5-2) and the y axis has dimension 1.

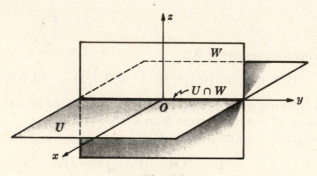

Fig. 5-2

Direct Sums

Recall that $V = W_1 \oplus W_2 \oplus \cdots \oplus W_r$, the direct sum of its subspaces $W_1, W_2, \ldots, W_r$, if every vector $v \in V$ can be written in one and only one way as

$$v = w_1 + w_2 + \cdots + w_r$$

where $w_1 \in W_1, w_2 \in W_2, \ldots, w_r \in W_r$.

The following theorems apply.

Theorem 5.10: Suppose $V = W_1 \oplus W_2 \oplus \cdots \oplus W_r$. Also, for each i suppose S_i is a linearly independent subset of W_i. Then:

   (i)   The union $S = \bigcup_i S_i$ is linearly independent in V.

   (ii) If each S_i is a basis of W_i, then $S = \bigcup_i S_i$ is a basis of V.

   (iii) dim $V = \dim W_1 + \dim W_2 + \cdots + \dim W_r$

Theorem 5.11: Suppose $V = W_1 + W_2 + \cdots + W_r$ (where V has finite dimension) and suppose

$$\dim V = \dim W_1 + \dim W_2 + \cdots + \dim W_r.$$

Then $V = W_1 \oplus W_2 \oplus \cdots \oplus W_r$.

5.5 RANK OF A MATRIX

Let A be any $m \times n$ matrix over the real field $\mathbf{R}$. Recall that the rows of A may be viewed as vectors in $\mathbf{R}^n$ and that the row space of A, written rowsp(A), is the subspace of $\mathbf{R}^n$ spanned by the rows of A. Similarly, the columns of A may be viewed as vectors in $\mathbf{R}^m$ and the column space of A, written colsp(A), is the subspace of $\mathbf{R}^m$ spanned by the columns of A.

The *row rank* of the matrix A is equal to the maximum number of linearly independent rows or, equivalently, to the dimension of the row space of A. Analogously the *column rank* of A is equal to the maximum number of linearly independent columns or, equivalently, to the dimension of the column space of A.

Although rowsp(A) is a subspace of $\mathbf{R}^n$ and colsp(A) is a subspace of $\mathbf{R}^m$, where m may not be equal to n, we have the following fundamental result (proved in Problem 5.45).

Theorem 5.12: The row rank and the column rank of any matrix A are equal.

Definition: The *rank* of a matrix A, written rank(A), is the common value of its row rank and column rank.

Thus the rank of a matrix gives the maximum number of linearly independent rows and also the maximum number of independent columns. We can easily obtain the rank of a matrix using row reduction, as illustrated in the next example.

EXAMPLE 5.5 Suppose we want to find a basis and the dimension of the row space of

$$A = \begin{bmatrix} 1 & 2 & 0 & -1 \\ 2 & 6 & -3 & -3 \\ 3 & 10 & -6 & -5 \end{bmatrix}$$

We reduce A to echelon form, using elementary row operations,

$$A \sim \begin{bmatrix} 1 & 2 & 0 & -1 \\ 0 & 2 & -3 & -1 \\ 0 & 4 & 6 & 2 \end{bmatrix} \sim \begin{bmatrix} 1 & 2 & 0 & -1 \\ 0 & 2 & -3 & -1 \\ 0 & 0 & 0 & 0 \end{bmatrix}$$

Recall that row equivalent matrices have the same row space. Thus the nonzero rows of the echelon matrix, which are independent by Theorem 5.2, form a basis of the row space of A. Thus dim rowsp(A) = 2, and so rank(A) = 2. This also means that dim colsp(A) = 2, and so any three of the columns are linearly dependent.

5.6 LINEAR EQUATIONS AND VECTOR SPACES

Consider a system of m linear equations in n unknowns, say

$$a_{11}x_1 + a_{12}x_2 + \cdots + a_{1n}x_n = b_1$$
$$a_{21}x_1 + a_{22}x_2 + \cdots + a_{2n}x_n = b_2$$
$$\cdots\cdots\cdots\cdots\cdots\cdots\cdots\cdots\cdots\cdots\cdots \qquad (1)$$
$$a_{m1}x_1 + a_{m2}x_2 + \cdots + a_{mn}x_n = b_m$$

or the equivalent matrix equation

$$AX = B$$

where $A = [a_{ij}]$ is the coefficient matrix, and $X = [x_j]$ and $B = [b_i]$ are the column vectors consisting of the unknowns and the constants, respectively. Recall that the *augmented matrix* of the system is defined to be the matrix

$$M = [A, B] = \begin{bmatrix} a_{11} & a_{12} & \cdots & a_{1n} & b_1 \\ a_{21} & a_{22} & \cdots & a_{2n} & b_2 \\ \cdots\cdots\cdots\cdots\cdots\cdots\cdots \\ a_{m1} & a_{m2} & \cdots & a_{mn} & b_m \end{bmatrix}$$

Remark 1: The linear Eqs. (1) are said to be dependent or independent according to whether the corresponding vectors, i.e., the rows of the augmented matrix, are dependent or independent.

Remark 2: Two systems of linear equations are equivalent if and only if the corresponding augmented matrices are row equivalent, i.e., have the same row space.

Remark 3: We can always replace a system of equations by a system of independent equations, such as a system in echelon form. The number of independent equations will always be equal to the rank of the augmented matrix.

Observe that the system (1) is also equivalent to the vector equation

$$x_1 \begin{bmatrix} a_{11} \\ a_{21} \\ \cdots \\ a_{m1} \end{bmatrix} + x_2 \begin{bmatrix} a_{12} \\ a_{22} \\ \cdots \\ a_{m2} \end{bmatrix} + \cdots + x_n \begin{bmatrix} a_{1n} \\ a_{2n} \\ \cdots \\ a_{mn} \end{bmatrix} = \begin{bmatrix} b_1 \\ b_2 \\ \cdots \\ b_m \end{bmatrix}$$

The above comment gives us the following basic existence theorem.

Theorem 5.13: The following three statements are equivalent.

(a) The system of linear equations $AX = B$ has a solution.
(b) B is a linear combination of the columns of A.
(c) The coefficient matrix A and the augmented matrix $M = [A, B]$ have the same rank.

EXAMPLE 5.6 For the following matrix A find those columns C_{k+1} which are linear combinations of the preceding columns $C_1, \ldots, C_k$:

$$A = \begin{bmatrix} 1 & 1 & 2 & 1 & 2 \\ 2 & 3 & 5 & 5 & 5 \\ 1 & 3 & 4 & 8 & 6 \\ 3 & 4 & 7 & 8 & 11 \end{bmatrix}$$

Let M_k be the submatrix of A consisting of the first k columns of A, that is, let $M_k = [C_1, \ldots, C_k]$. Then the coefficient matrix and the augmented matrix of the vector equation $x_1 C_1 + \cdots + x_k C_k = C_{k+1}$ are M_k and M_{k+1}, respectively. Accordingly, by Theorem 5.13, C_{k+1} is a linear combination of the preceding columns if and only if $\text{rank}(M_k) = \text{rank}(M_{k+1})$. Thus we first reduce A to an echelon form, which simultaneously reduces each submatrix M_k to an echelon form:

$$A \sim \begin{bmatrix} 1 & 1 & 2 & 1 & 2 \\ 0 & 1 & 1 & 3 & 1 \\ 0 & 2 & 2 & 7 & 4 \\ 0 & 1 & 1 & 5 & 5 \end{bmatrix} \sim \begin{bmatrix} 1 & 1 & 2 & 1 & 2 \\ 0 & 1 & 1 & 3 & 1 \\ 0 & 0 & 0 & 1 & 2 \\ 0 & 0 & 0 & 2 & 4 \end{bmatrix} \sim \begin{bmatrix} 1 & 1 & 2 & 1 & 2 \\ 0 & 1 & 1 & 3 & 1 \\ 0 & 0 & 0 & 1 & 2 \\ 0 & 0 & 0 & 0 & 0 \end{bmatrix}$$

From the echelon matrix we see that $\text{rank}(M_2) = \text{rank}(M_3) = 2$ and $\text{rank}(M_4) = \text{rank}(M_5) = 3$. Hence C_3 and C_5 are each a linear combination of the preceding columns.

Remark: The fact that the remaining columns C_1, C_2, and C_4 in the above matrix A are not linear combinations of their respective preceding columns also tells us that they are linearly independent. Thus they form a basis for the column space of A. Observe that C_1, C_2, and C_4 may also be characterized as those columns which contain the pivots in the echelon matrix.

Homogeneous Systems

Suppose that a nonhomogeneous system $AX = B$ does have a solution, that is, suppose $\text{rank}(A) = \text{rank}(A, B)$. Recall (Theorem 2.8) that the general solution of $AX = B$ is of the form

$$v_0 + W = \{v_0 + w: \ w \in W\}$$

where v_0 is one solution of $AX = B$ and W is the general solution of the homogeneous system $AX = 0$. Thus one way of presenting the general solution of $AX = B$ is to find a particular solution v_0 and then describe the solution space W of $AX = 0$.

Recall that W is a subspace of $\mathbf{R}^n$ and so has a dimension. The next theorem, whose proof is postponed until Chapter 8, applies.

Theorem 5.14: The dimension of the solution space W of a homogeneous system of linear equations $AX = 0$ is $n - r$, where n is the number of unknowns and r is the rank of the coefficient matrix A.

In case the system $AX = 0$ is in echelon form, then it has precisely $n - r$ free variables, say $x_{i_1}, x_{i_2}, \ldots, x_{i_{n-r}}$. Let v_j be the solution obtained by setting $x_{i_j} = 1$ (or any nonzero constant) and the remaining free variables equal to 0. Then the solutions $v_1, v_2, \ldots, v_{n-r}$ are linearly independent (see Problem 5.41) and hence form a basis of the solution space W.

EXAMPLE 5.7 Suppose we want to find the dimension and a basis of the solution space W of the following homogeneous system:

$$x + 2y + 2z - s + 3t = 0$$
$$x + 2y + 3z + s + t = 0$$
$$3x + 6y + 8z + s + 5t = 0$$

First reduce the system to echelon form:

$$x + 2y + 2z - s + 3t = 0 \qquad\qquad x + 2y + 2z - s + 3t = 0$$
$$z + 2s - 2t = 0 \qquad \text{or} \qquad z + 2s - 2t = 0$$
$$2z + 4s - 4t = 0$$

The system in echelon form has two (nonzero) equations in five unknowns. Hence the system has $5 - 2 = 3$ free variables, which are y, s, and t. Thus dim $W = 3$. To obtain a basis for W, set:

(1) $y = 1$, $s = 0$, $t = 0$ to obtain the solution $v_1 = (-2, 1, 0, 0, 0)$.
(2) $y = 0$, $s = 1$, $t = 0$ to obtain the solution $v_2 = (5, 0, -2, 1, 0)$.
(3) $y = 0$, $s = 0$, $t = 1$ to obtain the solution $v_3 = (-7, 0, 2, 0, 1)$.

The set $\{v_1, v_2, v_3\}$ is a basis of the solution space W.

5.7   FINDING A BASIS FOR $W = \operatorname{span}(u_1, u_2, \ldots, u_r)$

Frequently we are given vectors $u_1, u_2, \ldots, u_r$ in $\mathbf{R}^n$ and we want to find a basis for the subspace

$$W = \operatorname{span}(u_1, u_2, \ldots, u_r)$$

of $\mathbf{R}^n$, that is, the subspace of $\mathbf{R}^n$ spanned by the given vectors. The following are two such algorithms which find such a basis (and hence the dimension) of W.

Algorithm 5.7A   (Row Space Algorithm):

Step 1. Form the matrix A whose *rows* are the given vectors.

Step 2. Row reduce A to echelon form.

Step 3. Output the nonzero rows of the echelon matrix.

The above algorithm essentially already appeared in Example 5.5. However, sometimes we want to find a basis which comes from the original given vectors. The next algorithm, implicitly described in Example 5.6, accomplishes this task. Note that in Algorithm 5.7A we form a matrix whose rows are the given vectors whereas in Algorithm 5.7B we form a matrix whose columns are the given vectors.

Algorithm 5.7B   (Casting-out Algorithm):

Step 1. Form the matrix M whose *columns* are the given vectors.

Step 2. Row reduce M to echelon form.

Step 3. For each column C_k in the echelon matrix without a pivot, delete (cast out) the vector u_k from the given vectors.

Step 4. Output the remaining vectors (which correspond to columns with pivots).

EXAMPLE 5.8   Let W be the subspace of $\mathbf{R}^5$ spanned by the following vectors:

$$v_1 = (1, 2, 1, -2, 3), \qquad v_2 = (2, 5, -1, 3, -2), \qquad v_3 = (1, 3, -2, 5, -5),$$
$$v_4 = (3, 1, 2, -4, 1), \qquad v_5 = (5, 6, 1, -1, -1)$$

We use Algorithm 5.7B to find the dimension and a basis of W.

First form the matrix M whose columns are the given vectors, and reduce the matrix to echelon form:

$$M = \begin{bmatrix} 1 & 2 & 1 & 3 & 5 \\ 2 & 5 & 3 & 1 & 6 \\ 1 & -1 & -2 & 2 & 1 \\ -2 & 3 & 5 & -4 & -1 \\ 3 & -2 & -5 & 1 & -1 \end{bmatrix} \sim \begin{bmatrix} 1 & 2 & 1 & 3 & 5 \\ 0 & 1 & 1 & -5 & -4 \\ 0 & -3 & -3 & -1 & -4 \\ 0 & 7 & 7 & 2 & 9 \\ 0 & -8 & -8 & -8 & -16 \end{bmatrix}$$

$$\sim \begin{bmatrix} 1 & 2 & 1 & 3 & 5 \\ 0 & 1 & 1 & -5 & -4 \\ 0 & 0 & 0 & -16 & -16 \\ 0 & 0 & 0 & 37 & 37 \\ 0 & 0 & 0 & -48 & -48 \end{bmatrix} \sim \begin{bmatrix} 1 & 2 & 1 & 3 & 5 \\ 0 & 1 & 1 & -5 & -4 \\ 0 & 0 & 0 & 1 & 1 \\ 0 & 0 & 0 & 0 & 0 \\ 0 & 0 & 0 & 0 & 0 \end{bmatrix}$$

Observe that the pivots in the echelon matrix appear in columns C_1, C_2, and C_4. Accordingly, we "cast out" the vectors v_3 and v_5 from the original five vectors. The remaining vectors v_1, v_2, and v_4, which correspond to the columns in the echelon matrix with pivots, form a basis of W, and so dim $W = 3$.

Remark: The justification of the casting-out algorithm is as follows. The fact that column C_3 in the echelon matrix in Example 5.8 does not have a pivot means that the system $xv_1 + yv_2 = v_3$ has a solution, and hence v_3 is a linear combination of v_1 and v_2. Similarly, the fact that C_5 does not have a pivot means that v_5 is a linear combination of preceding vectors. We have therefore deleted each vector in the original spanning set which is a linear combination of preceding vectors. Thus the remaining vectors are linearly independent and form a basis of W.

Solved Problems

LINEAR DEPENDENCE

5.1. Determine whether or not u and v are linearly dependent, where:

(a) $u = (1, 2)$ and $v = (3, -5)$; (b) $u = (1, -3)$ and $v = (-2, 6)$; (c) $u = (1, 2, -3)$ and $v = (4, 5, -6)$; (d) $u = (2, 4, -8)$ and $v = (3, 6, -12)$.

Two vectors u and v are linearly dependent if and only if one is a multiple of the other.

(a) No; (b) yes; for $v = -2u$; (c) no; (d) yes, for $v = \frac{3}{2}u$.

5.2. Determine whether or not u and v are linearly dependent, where:

(a) $u = 2t^2 + 4t - 3$ and $v = 4t^2 + 8t - 6$

(b) $u = 2t^2 - 3t + 4$ and $v = 4t^2 - 3t + 2$

(c) $u = \begin{bmatrix} 1 & 3 & -4 \\ 5 & 0 & -1 \end{bmatrix}$ and $v = \begin{bmatrix} -4 & -12 & 16 \\ -20 & 0 & 4 \end{bmatrix}$

(d) $u = \begin{bmatrix} 1 & 1 & 1 \\ 2 & 2 & 2 \end{bmatrix}$ and $v = \begin{bmatrix} 2 & 2 & 2 \\ 3 & 3 & 3 \end{bmatrix}$

Two vectors u and v are linearly dependent if and only if one is a multiple of the other.

(a) Yes, for $v = 2u$; (b) no; (c) yes, for $v = -4u$; (d) no.

5.3. Determine whether or not the vectors $u = (1, 1, 2)$, $v = (2, 3, 1)$, and $w = (4, 5, 5)$ in $\mathbf{R}^3$ are linearly dependent.

Method 1: Set a linear combination of u, v, and w equal to the zero vector using unknowns x, y, and z. This yields

$$x\begin{bmatrix} 1 \\ 1 \\ 2 \end{bmatrix} + y\begin{bmatrix} 2 \\ 3 \\ 1 \end{bmatrix} + z\begin{bmatrix} 4 \\ 5 \\ 5 \end{bmatrix} = \begin{bmatrix} 0 \\ 0 \\ 0 \end{bmatrix}$$

Reduce the equivalent homogeneous system to echelon form:

$$\begin{array}{ccccc} x + 2y + 4z = 0 & & x + 2y + 4z = 0 & & x + 2y + 4z = 0 \\ x + 3y + 5z = 0 & \text{or} & y + z = 0 & \text{or} & y + z = 0 \\ 2x + y + 5z = 0 & & -3y - 3z = 0 & & \end{array}$$

The echelon system has only two nonzero equations in three unknowns. Hence it has a free variable and a nonzero solution. Thus, u, v, and w are linearly dependent.

Method 2: Form the matrix A whose columns are u, v, w and reduce to echelon form:

$$A = \begin{bmatrix} 1 & 2 & 4 \\ 1 & 3 & 5 \\ 2 & 1 & 5 \end{bmatrix} \sim \begin{bmatrix} 1 & 2 & 4 \\ 0 & 1 & 1 \\ 0 & -3 & -3 \end{bmatrix} \sim \begin{bmatrix} 1 & 2 & 4 \\ 0 & 1 & 1 \\ 0 & 0 & 0 \end{bmatrix}$$

The third column does not have a pivot. Hence the third vector w is a linear combination of the first two vectors u and v. Thus the vectors are linearly dependent. (Observe that the matrix A is also the coefficient matrix in Method 1. In other words, this method is essentially the same as the first method.)

Method 3: Form the matrix B whose rows are u, v, and w and reduce to echelon form:

$$B = \begin{bmatrix} 1 & 1 & 2 \\ 2 & 3 & 1 \\ 4 & 5 & 5 \end{bmatrix} \sim \begin{bmatrix} 1 & 1 & 2 \\ 0 & 1 & -3 \\ 0 & 1 & -3 \end{bmatrix} \sim \begin{bmatrix} 1 & 1 & 2 \\ 0 & 1 & -3 \\ 0 & 0 & 0 \end{bmatrix}$$

Since the echelon matrix has only two nonzero rows, the three vectors are linearly dependent. (The three given vectors span a space of dimension 2.)

5.4. Determine whether or not each list of vectors in $\mathbf{R}^3$ is linearly dependent:

(a) $u_1 = (1, 2, 5)$, $u_2 = (1, 3, 1)$, $u_3 = (2, 5, 7)$, $u_4 = (3, 1, 4)$

(b) $u = (1, 2, 5)$, $v = (2, 5, 1)$, $w = (1, 5, 2)$

(c) $u = (1, 2, 3)$, $v = (0, 0, 0)$, $w = (1, 5, 6)$

(a) Yes; for any four vectors in $\mathbf{R}^3$ are linearly dependent.

(b) Use Method 2, that is, form the matrix A whose columns are the given vectors and reduce the matrix to echelon form:

$$A = \begin{bmatrix} 1 & 2 & 1 \\ 2 & 5 & 5 \\ 5 & 1 & 2 \end{bmatrix} \sim \begin{bmatrix} 1 & 2 & 1 \\ 0 & 1 & 3 \\ 0 & -9 & -3 \end{bmatrix} \sim \begin{bmatrix} 1 & 2 & 1 \\ 0 & 1 & 3 \\ 0 & 0 & 24 \end{bmatrix}$$

Every column has a pivot entry. Hence no vector is a linear combination of the previous vectors. Thus the vectors are linearly independent.

(c)   Since $0 = (0, 0, 0)$ is one of the vectors, the vectors are linearly dependent.

5.5.   Determine whether or not the polynomials, u, v, and w in $\mathbf{P}(t)$ are linearly dependent, where:

$$u = t^3 + 4t^2 - 2t + 3, \qquad v = t^3 + 6t^2 - t + 4, \qquad w = 3t^3 + 8t^2 - 8t + 7$$

Set a linear combination of the polynomials u, v, and w equal to the zero polynomial using unknown scalars x, y, and z, that is, set $xu + yv + zw = 0$. Thus

$$x(t^3 + 4t^2 - 2t + 3) + y(t^3 + 6t^2 - t + 4) + z(3t^3 + 8t^2 - 8t + 7) = 0$$

or $xt^3 + 4xt^2 - 2xt + 3x + yt^3 + 6yt^2 - yt + 4y + 3zt^3 + 8zt^2 - 8zt + 7z = 0$

or $(x + y + 3z)t^3 + (4x + 6y + 8z)t^2 + (-2x - y - 8z)t + (3x + 4y + 7z) = 0$

Set the coefficients of the powers of t each equal to 0 and reduce the system to echelon form:

$$\begin{array}{ll} x + \ \ y + 3z = 0 \\ 4x + 6y + 8z = 0 \\ -2x - \ \ y - 8z = 0 \\ 3x + 4y + 7z = 0 \end{array} \quad \text{or} \quad \begin{array}{ll} x + \ \ y + 3z = 0 \\ 2y - 4z = 0 \\ y - 2z = 0 \\ y - 2z = 0 \end{array} \quad \text{or finally} \quad \begin{array}{ll} x + y + 3z = 0 \\ y - 2z = 0 \end{array}$$

The system in echelon form has a free variable and hence a nonzero solution. We have shown that $xu + yv + zw = 0$ does not imply that $x = 0$, $y = 0$, $z = 0$. Hence the polynomials are linearly dependent.

5.6.   Show that the functions $f(t) = \sin t$, $g(t) = \cos t$, and $h(t) = t$ from $\mathbf{R}$ into $\mathbf{R}$ are linearly independent.

Set a linear combination of the functions equal to the zero function 0 using unknown scalars x, y, z, that is, set $xf + yg + zh = 0$; then show that $x = 0$, $y = 0$, $z = 0$. We emphasize that $xf + yg + zh = 0$ means that, for every value of t, we have $xf(t) + yg(t) + zh(t) = 0$.
Thus in the equation $x \sin t + y \cos t + zt = 0$ substitute:

$$\begin{array}{llll} t = 0 & \text{to obtain} & x(0) + y(1) + z(0) = 0 & \text{or} & y = 0 \\[2mm] t = \dfrac{\pi}{2} & \text{to obtain} & x(1) + y(0) + \dfrac{z\pi}{2} = 0 & \text{or} & x + \dfrac{\pi z}{2} = 0 \\[2mm] t = \pi & \text{to obtain} & x(0) + y(-1) + z(\pi) = 0 & \text{or} & -y + \pi z = 0 \end{array}$$

The last three equations have only the zero solution, that is, $x = 0$, $y = 0$, $z = 0$. Thus f, g, and h are linearly independent.

5.7. Let **M** be the vector space of 2×2 real matrices.   Determine whether or not the matrices A, B, and C in **M** are linearly dependent, where

$$A = \begin{bmatrix} 1 & 1 \\ 1 & 1 \end{bmatrix}, \qquad B = \begin{bmatrix} 1 & 0 \\ 0 & 1 \end{bmatrix}, \qquad C = \begin{bmatrix} 1 & 1 \\ 0 & 0 \end{bmatrix}$$

Set a linear combination of the matrices A, B, and C equal to the zero matrix using unknown scalars x, y, and z; that is, set $xA + yB + zC = 0$.   Thus

$$x\begin{bmatrix} 1 & 1 \\ 1 & 1 \end{bmatrix} + y\begin{bmatrix} 1 & 0 \\ 0 & 1 \end{bmatrix} + z\begin{bmatrix} 1 & 1 \\ 0 & 0 \end{bmatrix} = \begin{bmatrix} 0 & 0 \\ 0 & 0 \end{bmatrix}$$

or

$$\begin{bmatrix} x+y+z & x+z \\ x & x+y \end{bmatrix} = \begin{bmatrix} 0 & 0 \\ 0 & 0 \end{bmatrix}$$

Set corresponding entries equal to each other to obtain the following equivalent system of linear equations:

$$x + y + z = 0, \qquad x + z = 0, \qquad x = 0, \qquad x + y = 0$$

Solving the above system we obtain only the zero solution, $x = 0$, $y = 0$, and $z = 0$.   We have shown that $xA + yB + zC = 0$ implies $x = 0$, $y = 0$, $z = 0$.   Hence the matrices A, B, and C are linearly independent.

5.8. Suppose the vectors u, v, and w are linearly independent.   Show that the vectors $u + v$, $u - v$, and $u - 2v + w$ are also linearly independent.

Suppose $x(u + v) + y(u - v) + z(u - 2v + w) = 0$, where x, y, and z are scalars.   Then

$$xu + xv + yu - yv + zu - 2zv + zw = 0$$

or

$$(x + y + z)u + (x - y - 2z)v + zw = 0$$

But u, v, and w are linearly independent.   Hence the coefficients in the above relation are each 0. In other words,

$$
\begin{aligned}
x + y + \ z &= 0 \\
x - y - 2z &= 0 \qquad \text{or} \\
z &= 0
\end{aligned}
\qquad
\begin{aligned}
x + \ y + \ z &= 0 \\
2y + 3z &= 0 \\
z &= 0
\end{aligned}
$$

The only solution to the above system is $x = 0$, $y = 0$, $z = 0$.   Hence $u + v$, $u - v$, and $u - 2v + w$ are linearly independent.

BASIS AND DIMENSION

5.9. Determine whether or not each of the following forms a basis of $\mathbf{R}^3$:

(a)   (1, 1, 1), (1, 0, 1)   (c)   (1, 1, 1), (1, 2, 3), (2, −1, 1)

(b)   (1, 2, 3), (1, 3, 5), (1, 0, 1), (2, 3, 0)   (d)   (1, 1, 2), (1, 2, 5), (5, 3, 4)

(a), (b)   No; for a basis of $\mathbf{R}^3$ must contain exactly three elements since dim $\mathbf{R}^3 = 3$.

(c)   The three vectors form a basis if and only if they are linearly independent.   Thus form the matrix whose rows are the given vectors and row reduce to echelon form:

$$\begin{bmatrix} 1 & 1 & 1 \\ 1 & 2 & 3 \\ 2 & -1 & 1 \end{bmatrix} \sim \begin{bmatrix} 1 & 1 & 1 \\ 0 & 1 & 2 \\ 0 & -3 & -1 \end{bmatrix} \sim \begin{bmatrix} 1 & 1 & 1 \\ 0 & 1 & 2 \\ 0 & 0 & 5 \end{bmatrix}$$

The echelon matrix has no zero rows. Hence the three vectors are linearly independent, and so they do form a basis of $\mathbf{R}^3$.

(d) Form the matrix whose rows are the given vectors and row reduce to echelon form:

$$\begin{bmatrix} 1 & 1 & 2 \\ 1 & 2 & 5 \\ 5 & 3 & 4 \end{bmatrix} \sim \begin{bmatrix} 1 & 1 & 2 \\ 0 & 1 & 3 \\ 0 & -2 & -6 \end{bmatrix} \sim \begin{bmatrix} 1 & 1 & 2 \\ 0 & 1 & 3 \\ 0 & 0 & 0 \end{bmatrix}$$

The echelon matrix has a zero row. Hence the three vectors are linearly dependent, and so they do not form a basis of $\mathbf{R}^3$.

5.10. Determine whether $(1, 1, 1, 1)$, $(1, 2, 3, 2)$, $(2, 5, 6, 4)$, $(2, 6, 8, 5)$ form a basis of $\mathbf{R}^4$.

Form the matrix whose rows are the given vectors, and row reduce to echelon form:

$$B = \begin{bmatrix} 1 & 1 & 1 & 1 \\ 1 & 2 & 3 & 2 \\ 2 & 5 & 6 & 4 \\ 2 & 6 & 8 & 5 \end{bmatrix} \sim \begin{bmatrix} 1 & 1 & 1 & 1 \\ 0 & 1 & 2 & 1 \\ 0 & 3 & 4 & 2 \\ 0 & 4 & 6 & 3 \end{bmatrix} \sim \begin{bmatrix} 1 & 1 & 1 & 1 \\ 0 & 1 & 2 & 1 \\ 0 & 0 & -2 & -1 \\ 0 & 0 & -2 & -1 \end{bmatrix} \sim \begin{bmatrix} 1 & 1 & 1 & 1 \\ 0 & 1 & 2 & 1 \\ 0 & 0 & 2 & 1 \\ 0 & 0 & 0 & 0 \end{bmatrix}$$

The echelon matrix has a zero row. Hence the four vectors are linearly dependent and do not form a basis of $\mathbf{R}^4$.

5.11. Consider the vector space $\mathbf{P}_n(t)$ of polynomials in t of degree $\leq n$. Determine whether or not $1 + t, t + t^2, t^2 + t^3, \ldots, t^{n-1} + t^n$ form a basis of $\mathbf{P}_n(t)$.

The polynomials are linearly independent since each one is of degree higher than the preceding ones. However, there are only n polynomials, and dim $\mathbf{P}_n(t) = n + 1$. Thus the polynomials do not form a basis of $\mathbf{P}_n(t)$.

5.12. Extend $\{u_1, u_2\}$ to a basis of $\mathbf{R}^4$, where:

(a) $u_1 = (1, 1, 1, 1)$, $u_2 = (0, 1, 2, 3)$;   (b) $u_1 = (1, 1, 1, 1)$, $u_2 = (2, 2, 3, 4)$

We need to find two other vectors u_3 and u_4 so that the four vectors u_1, u_2, u_3, u_4 are linearly independent. They then form a basis of $\mathbf{R}^4$ since dim $\mathbf{R}^4 = 4$.

(a) Let $u_3 = (0, 0, 1, 1)$ and $u_4 = (0, 0, 0, 1)$. Then u_1, u_2, u_3, u_4 form a matrix in echelon form and hence they are linearly independent. Hence u_1, u_2, u_3, u_4 form a basis of $\mathbf{R}^4$.

(b) First form the matrix with rows u_1 and u_2 and reduce to echelon form:

$$\begin{bmatrix} 1 & 1 & 1 & 1 \\ 2 & 2 & 3 & 4 \end{bmatrix} \sim \begin{bmatrix} 1 & 1 & 1 & 1 \\ 0 & 0 & 1 & 2 \end{bmatrix}$$

Then $w_1 = (1, 1, 1, 1)$ and $w_2 = (0, 0, 1, 2)$ span the same set of vectors as spanned by u_1 and u_2. Let $u_3 = (0, 1, 0, 0)$ and $u_4 = (0, 0, 0, 1)$. Then w_1, u_3, w_2, u_4 form a matrix in echelon form. Thus they are linearly independent and they form a basis of $\mathbf{R}^4$. Hence u_1, u_2, u_3, u_4 form a basis of $\mathbf{R}^4$.

5.13. Consider the complex field **C**, which contains the real field **R**, which in turn contains the rational field **Q**. (Thus **C** is a vector space over **R**, and **R** is a vector space over **Q**.)

(a) Show that $\{1, i\}$ is a basis of **C** over **R**. Hence **C** is a vector space of dimension 2 over **R**.

(b) Show that **R** is a vector space of infinite dimension over **Q**.

(a) For any $v \in$ **C** we have $v = a + bi = a(1) + b(i)$, where $a, b \in$ **R**. Hence $\{1, i\}$ spans **C** over **R**. Furthermore, if

$$x(1) + y(i) = 0 \text{ or } x + yi = 0, \text{ where } x, y \in \mathbf{R}, \text{ then } x = 0 \text{ and } y = 0$$

Hence $\{1, i\}$ is linearly independent over **R**. Thus $\{1, i\}$ is a basis for **C** over **R**.

(b) It can be shown that π is a transcendental number, that is, π is not a root of any polynomial over **Q**. Therefore for any n, the $n + 1$ real numbers $1, \pi, \pi^2, \ldots, \pi^n$ are linearly independent over **Q**. Thus **R** cannot be of dimension n over **Q**. Accordingly, **R** is of infinite dimension over **Q**.

DIMENSION AND SUBSPACES

5.14. Find a basis and the dimension of the subspace W of $\mathbf{R}^3$, where:

$$(a) \quad W = \{(a, b, c): \quad a + b + c = 0\}, \qquad (b) \quad W = \{(a, b, c): \quad a = b = c\}$$

$$(c) \quad W = \{(a, b, c): \quad c = 3a\}$$

(a) Note that $W \neq \mathbf{R}^3$ since, e.g.., $(1, 2, 3) \notin W$. Thus dim $W < 3$. Note that $u_1 = (1, 0, -1)$ and $u_2 = (0, 1, -1)$ are two linearly independent vectors in W. Thus dim $W = 2$, and so u_1 and u_2 form a basis of W.

(b) The vector $u = (1, 1, 1) \in W$. Any vector $w \in W$ has the form $w = (k, k, k)$. Hence $w = ku$. Thus u spans W and dim $W = 1$.

(c) $W \neq \mathbf{R}^3$ since, e.g., $(1, 1, 1) \notin W$. Thus dim $W < 3$. The two vectors $u_1 = (1, 0, 3)$ and $u_2 = (0, 1, 0)$ belong to W and are linearly independent. Thus dim $W = 2$, and u_1 and u_2 form a basis of W.

5.15. Find a basis and the dimension of the subspace W of $\mathbf{R}^4$ spanned by

$$u_1 = (1, -4, -2, 1), \qquad u_2 = (1, -3, -1, 2), \qquad u_3 = (3, -8, -2, 7)$$

Apply Algorithm 5.7A, the row space algorithm. Form a matrix where the rows are the given vectors, and row reduce it to echelon form:

$$\begin{bmatrix} 1 & -4 & -2 & 1 \\ 1 & -3 & -1 & 2 \\ 3 & -8 & -2 & 7 \end{bmatrix} \sim \begin{bmatrix} 1 & -4 & -2 & 1 \\ 0 & 1 & 1 & 1 \\ 0 & 4 & 4 & 4 \end{bmatrix} \sim \begin{bmatrix} 1 & -4 & -2 & 1 \\ 0 & 1 & 1 & 1 \\ 0 & 0 & 0 & 0 \end{bmatrix}$$

The nonzero rows in the echelon matrix form a basis of W, and so dim $W = 2$. In particular, this means that the original three vectors are linearly dependent.

5.16. Let W be the subspace of $\mathbf{R}^4$ spanned by the vectors

$$u_1 = (1, -2, 5, -3), \qquad u_2 = (2, 3, 1, -4), \qquad u_3 = (3, 8, -3, -5)$$

(a) Find a basis and the dimension of W. (b) Extend the basis of W to a basis of the whole space $\mathbf{R}^4$.

(a) Form the matrix A whose rows are the given vectors, and row reduce it to echelon form:

$$A = \begin{bmatrix} 1 & -2 & 5 & -3 \\ 2 & 3 & 1 & -4 \\ 3 & 8 & -3 & -5 \end{bmatrix} \sim \begin{bmatrix} 1 & -2 & 5 & -3 \\ 0 & 7 & -9 & 2 \\ 0 & 14 & -18 & 4 \end{bmatrix} \sim \begin{bmatrix} 1 & -2 & 5 & -3 \\ 0 & 7 & -9 & 2 \\ 0 & 0 & 0 & 0 \end{bmatrix}$$

The nonzero rows $(1, -2, 5, -3)$ and $(0, 7, -9, 2)$ of the echelon matrix form a basis of the row space of A and hence of W. Thus in particular, dim $W = 2$.

(b) We seek four linearly independent vectors which include the above two vectors. The four vectors $(1, -2, 5, -3)$, $(0, 7, -9, 2)$, $(0, 0, 1, 0)$, and $(0, 0, 0, 1)$ are linearly independent (since they form an echelon matrix), and so they form a basis of $\mathbf{R}^4$, which is an extension of the basis of W.

5.17. Let W be the subspace of $\mathbf{R}^5$ spanned by the vectors

$$u_1 = (1, 2, -1, 3, 4), \qquad u_2 = (2, 4, -2, 6, 8), \qquad u_3 = (1, 3, 2, 2, 6),$$

$$u_4 = (1, 4, 5, 1, 8), \qquad u_5 = (2, 7, 3, 3, 9)$$

Find a subset of the vectors which form a basis of W.

Method 1: Here we use Algorithm 5.7B, the casting-out algorithm. Form the matrix M whose columns are the given vectors and reduce it to echelon form:

$$M = \begin{bmatrix} 1 & 2 & 1 & 1 & 2 \\ 2 & 4 & 3 & 4 & 7 \\ -1 & -2 & 2 & 5 & 3 \\ 3 & 6 & 2 & 1 & 3 \\ 4 & 8 & 6 & 8 & 9 \end{bmatrix} \sim \begin{bmatrix} 1 & 2 & 1 & 1 & 2 \\ 0 & 0 & 1 & 2 & 3 \\ 0 & 0 & 3 & 6 & 5 \\ 0 & 0 & -1 & -2 & -3 \\ 0 & 0 & 2 & 4 & 1 \end{bmatrix}$$

$$\sim \begin{bmatrix} 1 & 2 & 1 & 1 & 2 \\ 0 & 0 & 1 & 2 & 3 \\ 0 & 0 & 0 & 0 & -4 \\ 0 & 0 & 0 & 0 & 0 \\ 0 & 0 & 0 & 0 & -5 \end{bmatrix} \sim \begin{bmatrix} 1 & 2 & 1 & 1 & 2 \\ 0 & 0 & 1 & 2 & 3 \\ 0 & 0 & 0 & 0 & -4 \\ 0 & 0 & 0 & 0 & 0 \\ 0 & 0 & 0 & 0 & 0 \end{bmatrix}$$

The pivot positions are in columns C_1, C_3, C_5. Hence the corresponding vectors u_1, u_3, u_5 form a basis of W and dim $W = 3$.

Method 2: Here we use a slight modification of Algorithm 5.7A. Form the matrix M' whose rows are the given vectors and reduce it to echelon form, but without interchanging any zero rows:

$$M = \begin{bmatrix} 1 & 2 & -1 & 3 & 4 \\ 2 & 4 & -2 & 6 & 8 \\ 1 & 3 & 2 & 2 & 6 \\ 1 & 4 & 5 & 1 & 8 \\ 2 & 7 & 3 & 3 & 9 \end{bmatrix} \sim \begin{bmatrix} 1 & 2 & -1 & 3 & 4 \\ 0 & 0 & 0 & 0 & 0 \\ 0 & 1 & 3 & -1 & 2 \\ 0 & 2 & 6 & -2 & 4 \\ 0 & 3 & 5 & -3 & 1 \end{bmatrix}$$

$$\sim \begin{bmatrix} 1 & 2 & -1 & 3 & 4 \\ 0 & 0 & 0 & 0 & 0 \\ 0 & 1 & 3 & -1 & 2 \\ 0 & 0 & 0 & 0 & 0 \\ 0 & 0 & -4 & 0 & -5 \end{bmatrix}$$

The nonzero rows are the first, third, and fifth rows. Hence u_1, u_3, u_5 form a basis of W. Thus in particular, dim $W = 3$.

5.18. Find the dimension of the subspace W spanned by:

(a) $(1, -3, 2, -1)$ and $(1, 2, 1, 2)$ in $\mathbf{R}^4$.

(b) $(3, -9, 3, -6)$ and $(-2, 6, -2, 4)$ in $\mathbf{R}^4$.

(c) $t^3 + 2t^2 - 3t + 4$ and $2t^3 + 4t^2 - 6t + 8$ in $\mathbf{P}(t)$

(d) $t^3 - 2t^2 + 3$ and $t^2 - 5t + 3$ in $\mathbf{P}(t)$

Two nonzero vectors span a subspace W of dimension 2 if they are linearly independent, and of dimension 1 if they are linearly dependent. Recall that two vectors are linearly dependent if and only if one is a multiple of the other. Thus: (a) 2; (b) 1; (c) 1; (d) 2.

RANK OF A MATRIX, ROW AND COLUMN SPACES

5.19. Find the rank of each matrix:

(a) $A = \begin{bmatrix} 1 & 2 & 0 & -1 \\ 2 & 6 & -3 & -3 \\ 3 & 10 & -6 & -5 \end{bmatrix}$; (b) $B = \begin{bmatrix} 1 & 3 & 1 & -2 & -3 \\ 1 & 4 & 3 & -1 & -4 \\ 2 & 3 & -4 & -7 & -3 \\ 3 & 8 & 1 & -7 & -8 \end{bmatrix}$.

(a)   Row reduce A to echelon form:

$$A \sim \begin{bmatrix} 1 & 2 & 0 & -1 \\ 0 & 2 & -3 & -1 \\ 0 & 4 & -6 & -2 \end{bmatrix} \sim \begin{bmatrix} 1 & 2 & 0 & -1 \\ 0 & 2 & -3 & -1 \\ 0 & 0 & 0 & 0 \end{bmatrix}$$

The nonzero rows of the echelon matrix form a basis of the row space of A, and hence the dimension of the row space of A is 2. Thus rank$(A) = 2$.

(b)   Row reduce B to echelon form:

$$B \sim \begin{bmatrix} 1 & 3 & 1 & -2 & -3 \\ 0 & 1 & 2 & 1 & -1 \\ 0 & -3 & -6 & -3 & 3 \\ 0 & -1 & -2 & -1 & 1 \end{bmatrix} \sim \begin{bmatrix} 1 & 3 & 1 & -2 & -3 \\ 0 & 1 & 2 & 1 & -1 \\ 0 & 0 & 0 & 0 & 0 \\ 0 & 0 & 0 & 0 & 0 \end{bmatrix}$$

Since the echelon matrix has two nonzero rows, rank$(B) = 2$.

5.20.   Find the rank of each matrix:

(a) $A = \begin{bmatrix} 1 & 2 & -3 \\ 2 & 1 & 0 \\ -2 & -1 & 3 \\ -1 & 4 & -2 \end{bmatrix}$; (b) $B = \begin{bmatrix} 1 & 3 \\ 0 & -2 \\ 5 & -1 \\ -2 & 3 \end{bmatrix}$.

(a)   Since row rank equals column rank, it is easier to form the transpose of A and then row reduce to echelon form:

$$A^T = \begin{bmatrix} 1 & 2 & -2 & -1 \\ 2 & 1 & -1 & 4 \\ -3 & 0 & 3 & -2 \end{bmatrix} \sim \begin{bmatrix} 1 & 2 & -2 & -1 \\ 0 & -3 & 3 & 6 \\ 0 & 6 & -3 & -5 \end{bmatrix} \sim \begin{bmatrix} 1 & 2 & -2 & -1 \\ 0 & -3 & 3 & 6 \\ 0 & 0 & 3 & 7 \end{bmatrix}$$

Thus rank$(A) = 3$.

(b)   The two columns are linearly independent since one is not a multiple of the other.   Thus rank$(B) = 2$.

5.21.   For (a) $k = 1$; (b) $k = 2$; (c) $k = 3$; (d) $k = 4$; (e) $k = 5$; (f) $k = 6$, find the number n_k of k-element linearly independent subsets of the set C of columns of the matrix

$$A = \begin{bmatrix} 1 & 1 & 0 & 2 & 2 & 2 \\ 2 & 3 & 0 & 4 & 7 & 5 \\ 1 & 2 & 0 & 2 & 5 & 4 \end{bmatrix}$$

(a)   The set $\{v\}$ with a single element is linearly independent if and only if $v \neq 0$.   Hence $n_1 = 5$ since there are five nonzero columns.

(b)   Two columns are linearly dependent if and only if one column is a multiple of the other (or one is the zero vector).   Thus $\{C_1, C_2\}$, (C_1, C_5), (C_1, C_6), (C_2, C_4), (C_2, C_5), (C_2, C_6), (C_4, C_5), (C_4, C_6), (C_5, C_6) are the only 2-element linearly independent subsets of C. Hence $n_2 = 9$.

(c)   We need only investigate 3-element subsets without multiples or the zero vector.

(1)   Reduce the submatrix $M = [C_1, C_2, C_5]^T$ to echelon form:

$$M = \begin{bmatrix} 1 & 2 & 1 \\ 1 & 3 & 2 \\ 2 & 7 & 5 \end{bmatrix} \sim \begin{bmatrix} 1 & 2 & 1 \\ 0 & 1 & 1 \\ 0 & 3 & 3 \end{bmatrix} \sim \begin{bmatrix} 1 & 2 & 1 \\ 0 & 1 & 1 \\ 0 & 0 & 0 \end{bmatrix}$$

There is a zero row.   Thus the rows of M, and hence the columns C_1, C_2, C_5, are linearly dependent.

(2) Since C_4 is a multiple of C_1, the columns C_4, C_2, C_5 are also linearly dependent.

(3) Reduce the submatrix $M = [C_1, C_2, C_6]^T$ to echelon form:

$$M = \begin{bmatrix} 1 & 2 & 1 \\ 1 & 3 & 2 \\ 2 & 5 & 4 \end{bmatrix} \sim \begin{bmatrix} 1 & 2 & 1 \\ 0 & 1 & 1 \\ 0 & 1 & 2 \end{bmatrix} \sim \begin{bmatrix} 1 & 2 & 1 \\ 0 & 1 & 1 \\ 0 & 0 & 1 \end{bmatrix}$$

There is no zero row. Thus the rows of M, and hence the columns C_1, C_2, C_6, are linearly independent.

(4) Since C_4 is a multiple of C_1, the columns C_4, C_2, C_6 are also linearly independent.

(5) Similarly, reducing the submatrix $M = [C_1, C_5, C_6]^T$ to echelon form yields no zero row. Thus the columns C_1, C_5, C_6 are linearly independent.

(6) Since C_4 is a multiple of C_1, the columns C_4, C_5, C_6 are also linearly independent.

(7) Similarly, reducing the submatrix $M = [C_2, C_5, C_6]^T$ to echelon form yields no zero row. Thus the columns C_2, C_5, C_6 are linearly independent.

Altogether there are five 3-element subsets of C which are linearly independent. Thus $n_3 = 5$.

(d), (e), (f) Since A has only three rows, $\text{rank}(A) \le 3$. Thus any four or more columns must be linearly dependent, that is, $n_4 = n_5 = n_6 = 0$.

5.22. Let $A = \begin{bmatrix} 1 & 2 & 1 & 2 & 3 & 1 \\ 2 & 4 & 3 & 7 & 7 & 4 \\ 1 & 2 & 2 & 5 & 5 & 6 \\ 3 & 6 & 6 & 15 & 14 & 15 \end{bmatrix}$. Let M_k be the submatrix of A consisting of the first k columns $C_1, C_2, \ldots, C_k$ of A.

(a) Find M_1, M_2, M_4, and M_6.

(b) Find $\text{rank}(M_k)$ for $k = 1, 2, \ldots, 6$.

(a) Since M_k consists of columns $C_1, \ldots, C_k$ we have

$$M_1 = \begin{bmatrix} 1 \\ 2 \\ 1 \\ 3 \end{bmatrix}, \quad M_2 = \begin{bmatrix} 1 & 2 \\ 2 & 4 \\ 1 & 2 \\ 3 & 6 \end{bmatrix}, \quad M_4 = \begin{bmatrix} 1 & 2 & 1 & 2 \\ 2 & 4 & 3 & 7 \\ 1 & 2 & 2 & 5 \\ 3 & 6 & 6 & 15 \end{bmatrix}, \quad M_6 = A$$

(b) Row reduce A to echelon form:

$$A \sim \begin{bmatrix} 1 & 2 & 1 & 2 & 3 & 1 \\ 0 & 0 & 1 & 3 & 1 & 2 \\ 0 & 0 & 1 & 3 & 2 & 5 \\ 0 & 0 & 3 & 9 & 5 & 12 \end{bmatrix} \sim \begin{bmatrix} 1 & 2 & 1 & 2 & 3 & 1 \\ 0 & 0 & 1 & 3 & 1 & 2 \\ 0 & 0 & 0 & 0 & 1 & 3 \\ 0 & 0 & 0 & 0 & 0 & 0 \end{bmatrix}$$

Observe that this simultaneously reduces all the matrices M_k to echelon form. For example, the first four columns of the echelon form of A are an echelon form of M_4. Since row rank equals column rank, we know that $\text{rank}(M_k)$ is equal to the number of nonzero rows in an echelon form of M_k. Thus $\text{rank}(M_1) = \text{rank}(M_2) = 1$, $\text{rank}(M_3) = \text{rank}(M_4) = 2$, $\text{rank}(M_5) = \text{rank}(M_6) = 3$.

5.23. Consider the matrix A in Problem 5.22.

(a) Which columns C_{k+1} are linear combinations of the preceding columns $C_1, \ldots, C_k$?

(b) Find columns of A which form a basis for the column space of A.

(c) Express column C_4 as a linear combination of the columns in part (b).

(a) The vector equation $x_1 C_1 + x_2 C_2 + \cdots + x_k C_k = C_{k+1}$ yields the system with coefficient matrix M_k and augmented matrix M_{k+1}. Thus C_{k+1} is a linear combination of $C_1, \ldots, C_k$ if and only if $\text{rank}(M_k) = \text{rank}(M_{k+1})$. Thus each of the columns $C_2, C_4,$ and C_6 is a linear combination of the preceding columns.

(b) In the echelon form of A, the pivots are in columns 1, 3, and 5. Hence columns $C_1, C_3,$ and C_5 of A form a basis for the column space of A. Alternately, deleting columns $C_2, C_4,$ and C_6 from the spanning set of columns (they are linear combinations of other columns) yields, again, $C_1, C_3,$ and C_5.

(c) The echelon matrix tells us that C_4 is a linear combination of columns C_1 and C_3. The augmented matrix M of the vector equation $C_4 = xC_1 + yC_3$ consists of the columns $C_1,$ $C_3,$ and C_4 which, when reduced to echelon form, yields the matrix

$$\begin{bmatrix} 1 & 1 & 2 \\ 0 & 1 & 3 \end{bmatrix} \quad \text{or} \quad \begin{array}{l} x + y = 2 \\ y = 3 \end{array} \quad \text{or} \quad x = -1, y = 3$$

Thus $C_4 = -C_1 + 3C_3 = -C_1 + 3C_3 + 0C_5$.

APPLICATIONS TO LINEAR EQUATIONS

5.24. Find the dimension and a basis of the solution space W of each homogeneous system:

$$
\begin{array}{ll}
\text{(a)} & \begin{array}{l} x + 2y + 2z - s + 3t = 0 \\ x + 2y + 3z + s + t = 0; \\ 3x + 6y + 8z + s + 5t = 0 \end{array}
\qquad
\text{(b)} & \begin{array}{l} x + 2y + z - 3t = 0 \\ 2x + 4y + 4z - t = 0. \\ 3x + 6y + 7z + t = 0 \end{array}
\end{array}
$$

(a) Reduce the system to echelon form:

$$
\begin{array}{l}
x + 2y + 2z - s + 3t = 0 \\
 z + 2s - 2t = 0 \qquad \text{or} \\
 2z + 4s - 4t = 0
\end{array}
\qquad
\begin{array}{l}
x + 2y + 2z - s + 3t = 0 \\
 z + 2s - 2t = 0
\end{array}
$$

The system in echelon form has two (nonzero) equations in five unknowns. Hence the system has $5 - 2 = 3$ free variables, which are $y, s,$ and t. Thus $\dim W = 3$. To obtain a basis for W, set:

(1) $y = 1, s = 0, t = 0$ to obtain the solution $v_1 = (-2, 1, 0, 0, 0)$.

(2) $y = 0, s = 1, t = 0$ to obtain the solution $v_2 = (5, 0, -2, 1, 0)$.

(3) $y = 0, s = 0, t = 1$ to obtain the solution $v_3 = (-7, 0, 2, 0, 1)$.

The set $\{v_1, v_2, v_3\}$ is a basis of the solution space W.

(b) Reduce the system to echelon form:

$$
\begin{array}{l}
x + 2y + z - 3t = 0 \\
 2z + 5t = 0 \qquad \text{or} \\
 4z + 10t = 0
\end{array}
\qquad
\begin{array}{l}
x + 2y + z - 3t = 0 \\
 2z + 5t = 0
\end{array}
$$

The free variables are y and t, and dim $W = 2$. Set:

(1) $y = 1$, $t = 0$ to obtain the solution $u_1 = (-2, 1, 0, 0)$.
(2) $y = 0$, $t = 2$ to obtain the solution $u_2 = (11, 0, -5, 2)$.

Then $\{u_1, u_2\}$ is a basis of W. [We could have chosen $y = 0$, $t = 1$ in (2), but such a choice would introduce fractions into the solution.]

5.25. Find the dimension and a basis of the solution space W of each homogeneous system:

$$
\begin{array}{ll}
\quad x + 2y + \ z - 2t = 0 & \quad x + \ y + 2z = 0 \\
(a)\ 2x + 4y + 4z - 3t = 0; & (b)\ 2x + 3y + 3z = 0. \\
\quad 3x + 6y + 7z - 4t = 0 & \quad x + 3y + 5z = 0
\end{array}
$$

(Here we use the matrix format of our homogeneous system.)

(a) Reduce the coefficient matrix A to echelon form:

$$
A = \begin{bmatrix} 1 & 2 & 1 & -2 \\ 2 & 4 & 4 & -3 \\ 3 & 6 & 7 & -4 \end{bmatrix} \sim \begin{bmatrix} 1 & 2 & 1 & -2 \\ 0 & 0 & 2 & 1 \\ 0 & 0 & 4 & 2 \end{bmatrix} \sim \begin{bmatrix} 1 & 2 & 1 & -2 \\ 0 & 0 & 2 & 1 \\ 0 & 0 & 0 & 0 \end{bmatrix}
$$

This corresponds to the system

$$
\begin{aligned}
x + 2y + z - 2t &= 0 \\
2z + \ t &= 0
\end{aligned}
$$

The free variables are y and t, and dim $W = 2$. Set:

(1) $y = 1$ $t = 0$ to obtain the solution $u_1 = (-2, 1, 0, 0)$.
(2) $y = 0$, $t = 2$ to obtain the solution $u_2 = (5, 0, -1, 2)$.

Then $\{u_1, u_2\}$ is a basis of W.

(b) Reduce the coefficient matrix A to echelon form:

$$
A = \begin{bmatrix} 1 & 1 & 2 \\ 2 & 3 & 3 \\ 1 & 3 & 5 \end{bmatrix} \sim \begin{bmatrix} 1 & 1 & 2 \\ 0 & 1 & -1 \\ 0 & 2 & 3 \end{bmatrix} \sim \begin{bmatrix} 1 & 1 & 2 \\ 0 & 1 & -1 \\ 0 & 0 & 5 \end{bmatrix}
$$

This corresponds to a triangular system with no free variables. Thus 0 is the only solution, that is, $W = \{0\}$. Hence dim $W = 0$.

5.26. Find a homogeneous system whose solution set W is spanned by:

$$
\{u_1, u_2, u_3\} = \{(1, -2, 0, 3), \quad (1, -1, -1, 4), \quad (1, 0, -2, 5)\}
$$

Let $v = (x, y, z, t)$.

Method 1: Form the matrix M whose first rows are the given vectors u_1, u_2, and u_3 and whose last row is v. Then row reduce M to echelon form:

$$M = \begin{bmatrix} 1 & -2 & 0 & 3 \\ 1 & -1 & -1 & 4 \\ 1 & 0 & -2 & 5 \\ x & y & z & t \end{bmatrix} \sim \begin{bmatrix} 1 & -2 & 0 & 3 \\ 0 & 1 & -1 & 1 \\ 0 & 2 & -2 & 2 \\ 0 & 2x+y & z & -3x+t \end{bmatrix}$$

$$\sim \begin{bmatrix} 1 & -2 & 0 & 3 \\ 0 & 1 & -1 & 1 \\ 0 & 0 & 2x+y+z & -5x-y+t \\ 0 & 0 & 0 & 0 \end{bmatrix}$$

The original first three rows show that W has dimension 2. Thus $v \in W$ if and only if the addition row does not increase the dimension of the row space. Hence we set the last two entries in the third row on the right equal to 0 to obtain the required homogeneous system

$$2x + y + z = 0$$
$$5x + y \quad\quad - t = 0$$

Method 2: The vector $v \in W$ if and only if v is a linear combination of the vectors u_1, u_2, u_3 which span W. Thus form the matrix M whose first columns are u_1, u_2, u_3 and whose last column is v. Then row reduce M to echelon form:

$$M = \begin{bmatrix} 1 & 1 & 1 & x \\ -2 & -1 & 0 & y \\ 0 & -1 & -2 & z \\ 3 & 4 & 5 & t \end{bmatrix} \sim \begin{bmatrix} 1 & 1 & 1 & x \\ 0 & 1 & 2 & 2x+y \\ 0 & -1 & -2 & z \\ 0 & 1 & 2 & -3x+t \end{bmatrix}$$

$$\sim \begin{bmatrix} 1 & 1 & 1 & x \\ 0 & 1 & 2 & 2x+y \\ 0 & 0 & 0 & 2x+y+z \\ 0 & 0 & 0 & -5x-y+t \end{bmatrix}$$

Then v is a linear combination of u_1, u_2, u_3 if $\text{rank}(M) = \text{rank}(A)$, where A is the submatrix without column v. Thus set the last two entries in the fourth column on the right equal to zero to obtain the required homogeneous system:

$$2x + y + z = 0$$
$$5x + y \quad\quad - t = 0$$

(Observe that the matrix M above is the transpose of the matrix M used in the first method.)

5.27. Consider the following subspaces of $\mathbf{R}^4$:

$$U = \{(a, b, c, d): \ b + c + d = 0\} \ \text{and} \ W = \{(a, b, c, d): \ a + b = 0, \ c = 2d\}$$

Find the dimension and a basis of: (a) U; (b) W; (c) $U \cap W$.

(a) We seek a basis of the set of solutions (a, b, c, d) of the equation

$$b + c + d = 0 \quad \text{or} \quad 0a + b + c + d = 0$$

The free variables are a, c, and d. Set:

(1) $a = 1$, $c = 0$, $d = 0$ to obtain the solution $u_1 = (1, 0, 0, 0)$.

(2) $a = 0$, $c = 1$, $d = 0$ to obtain the solution $u_2 = (0, -1, 1, 0)$.

(3) $a = 0$, $c = 0$, $d = 1$ to obtain the solution $u_3 = (0, -1, 0, 1)$.

The set $\{u_1, u_2, u_3\}$ is a basis of U, and dim $U = 3$.

(b)   We seek a basis of the set of solutions (a, b, c, d) of the system:

$$\begin{array}{lll} \begin{aligned} a + b &= 0 \\ c &= 2d \end{aligned} & \text{or} & \begin{aligned} a + b &= 0 \\ c - 2d &= 0 \end{aligned} \end{array}$$

The free variables are b and d. Set:

(1) $b = 1$, $d = 0$ to obtain the solution $w_1 = (-1, 1, 0, 0)$.

(2) $b = 0$, $d = 1$ to obtain the solution $w_2 = (0, 0, 2, 1)$.

The set $\{w_1, w_2\}$ is a basis of W, and dim $W = 2$.

(c) $U \cap W$ consists of those vectors (a, b, c, d) which satisfy the conditions defining U and the conditions defining W, that is, the three equations

$$\begin{array}{lll} \begin{aligned} b + c + d &= 0 \\ a + b \phantom{{}+ c + d} &= 0 \\ c \phantom{{}+ b + d} &= 2d \end{aligned} & \text{or} & \begin{aligned} a + b \phantom{{}+ c + d} &= 0 \\ b + c + d &= 0 \\ c - 2d &= 0 \end{aligned} \end{array}$$

The only free variable is d. Set $d = 1$ to obtain the solution $v = (3, -3, 2, 1)$. Thus $\{v\}$ is a basis of $U \cap W$, and dim $(U \cap W) = 1$.

SUMS AND INTERSECTIONS

5.28.   Suppose U and W are distinct four-dimensional subspaces of a vector space V, where dim $V = 6$. Find the possible dimensions of $U \cap W$.

Since U and W are distinct, $U + W$ properly contains U and W; consequently dim $(U + W) > 4$. But dim $(U + W)$ cannot be greater than 6, since dim $V = 6$. Hence we have two possibilities: (1) dim $(U + W) = 5$ or (2) dim $(U + W) = 6$. By Theorem 5.9,

$$\dim (U \cap W) = \dim U + \dim W - \dim (U + W) = 8 - \dim (U + W)$$

Thus (1) dim $(U \cap W) = 3$ or (2) dim $(U \cap W) = 2$.

5.29.   Suppose U and W are two-dimensional subspaces of $\mathbf{R}^3$. Show that $U \cap W \neq \{0\}$. In particular, find the possible dimensions of $U \cap W$.

Suppose $U = W$. Then $U \cap W = U = W$, and hence dim $(U \cap W) = 2$. Suppose $U \neq W$. Then $U + W$ properly contains U (and W). Hence dim $(U + W) > \dim U = 2$. However, $U + W \subseteq \mathbf{R}^3$, which has dimension 3. Therefore dim $(U + W) = 3$. Thus by Theorem 5.9,

$$\dim (U \cap W) = \dim U + \dim W - \dim (U + W) = 2 + 2 - 3 = 1$$

That is, $U \cap W$ is a line through the origin.

Remark: The above agrees with the well-known result in solid geometry that the intersection of two distinct planes is a line.

5.30. Consider the following subspaces of $\mathbf{R}^4$:

$$U = \text{span}\{(1, 1, 0, -1), (1, 2, 3, 0), (2, 3, 3, -1)\}$$

$$W = \text{span}\{(1, 2, 2, -2), (2, 3, 2, -3), (1, 3, 4, -3)\}$$

Find: (a) dim $(U + W)$; (b) dim $(U \cap W)$.

(a) $U + W$ is the space spanned by all six vectors.   Hence form the matrix M whose rows are the given six vectors, and then row reduce to echelon form:

$$M = \begin{bmatrix} 1 & 1 & 0 & -1 \\ 1 & 2 & 3 & 0 \\ 2 & 3 & 3 & -1 \\ 1 & 2 & 2 & -2 \\ 2 & 3 & 2 & -3 \\ 1 & 3 & 4 & -3 \end{bmatrix} \sim \begin{bmatrix} 1 & 1 & 0 & -1 \\ 0 & 1 & 3 & 1 \\ 0 & 1 & 3 & 1 \\ 0 & 1 & 2 & -1 \\ 0 & 1 & 2 & -1 \\ 0 & 2 & 4 & -2 \end{bmatrix} \sim \begin{bmatrix} 1 & 1 & 0 & -1 \\ 0 & 1 & 3 & 1 \\ 0 & 0 & -1 & -2 \\ 0 & 0 & 0 & 0 \\ 0 & 0 & 0 & 0 \\ 0 & 0 & 0 & 0 \end{bmatrix}$$

Since the echelon matrix has three nonzero rows, dim $(U + W) = 3$.

(b)   First find dim U and dim W.   Form the two matrices M_1 and M_2 whose rows span U and W, respectively, and then row reduce each to echelon form:

$$M_1 = \begin{bmatrix} 1 & 1 & 0 & -1 \\ 1 & 2 & 3 & 0 \\ 2 & 3 & 3 & -1 \end{bmatrix} \sim \begin{bmatrix} 1 & 1 & 0 & -1 \\ 0 & 1 & 3 & 1 \\ 0 & 1 & 3 & 1 \end{bmatrix} \sim \begin{bmatrix} 1 & 1 & 0 & -1 \\ 0 & 1 & 3 & 1 \\ 0 & 0 & 0 & 0 \end{bmatrix}$$

and $$M_2 = \begin{bmatrix} 1 & 2 & 2 & -2 \\ 2 & 3 & 2 & -3 \\ 1 & 3 & 4 & -3 \end{bmatrix} \sim \begin{bmatrix} 1 & 2 & 2 & -2 \\ 0 & -1 & -2 & 1 \\ 0 & 1 & 2 & -1 \end{bmatrix} \sim \begin{bmatrix} 1 & 2 & 2 & -2 \\ 0 & -1 & -2 & 1 \\ 0 & 0 & 0 & 0 \end{bmatrix}$$

Since each of the echelon matrices has two nonzero rows, dim $U = 2$ and dim $W = 2$.   Using Theorem 5.9, we have

$$\dim (U \cap W) = \dim U + \dim W - \dim (U + W) = 2 + 2 - 3 = 1$$

Remark: Theorem 5.9 does not help us to find a basis for $U \cap W$, just its dimension. Problem 5.31 will show how to find a basis for $U \cap W$.

5.31. Consider the following subspaces of $\mathbf{R}^5$:

$$U = \text{span}\{(1, 3, -2, 2, 3), (1, 4, -3, 4, 2), (2, 3, -1, -2, 9)\}$$

$$W = \text{span}\{(1, 3, 0, 2, 1), (1, 5, -6, 6, 3), (2, 5, 3, 2, 1)\}$$

Find a basis and dimension of: (a) $U + W$; (b) $U \cap W$.

(a) $U + W$ is the space spanned by all six vectors.   Hence form the matrix whose rows are the given six vectors, and then row reduce to echelon form:

$$\begin{bmatrix} 1 & 3 & -2 & 2 & 3 \\ 1 & 4 & -3 & 4 & 2 \\ 2 & 3 & -1 & -2 & 9 \\ 1 & 3 & 0 & 2 & 1 \\ 1 & 5 & -6 & 6 & 3 \\ 2 & 5 & 3 & 2 & 1 \end{bmatrix} \sim \begin{bmatrix} 1 & 3 & -2 & 2 & 3 \\ 0 & 1 & -1 & 2 & -1 \\ 0 & -3 & 3 & -6 & 3 \\ 0 & 0 & 2 & 0 & -2 \\ 0 & 2 & -4 & 4 & 0 \\ 0 & -1 & 7 & -2 & -5 \end{bmatrix} \sim \begin{bmatrix} 1 & 3 & -2 & 2 & 3 \\ 0 & 1 & -1 & 2 & -1 \\ 0 & 0 & 1 & 0 & -1 \\ 0 & 0 & 0 & 0 & 0 \\ 0 & 0 & 0 & 0 & 0 \\ 0 & 0 & 0 & 0 & 0 \end{bmatrix}$$

The set of nonzero rows of the echelon matrix

$$\{(1, 3, -2, 2, 3), (0, 1, -1, 2, -1), (0, 0, 1, 0, -1)\}$$

is a basis of $U + W$; thus dim $(U + W) = 3$.

(b) First find homogeneous systems whose solution sets are U and W, respectively. Form the matrix whose first three rows span U and whose last row is (x, y, z, s, t) and then row reduce to an echelon form:

$$\begin{bmatrix} 1 & 3 & -2 & 2 & 3 \\ 1 & 4 & -3 & 4 & 2 \\ 2 & 3 & -1 & -2 & 9 \\ x & y & z & s & t \end{bmatrix} \sim \begin{bmatrix} 1 & 3 & -2 & 2 & 3 \\ 0 & 1 & -1 & 2 & -1 \\ 0 & -3 & 3 & -6 & 3 \\ 0 & -3x+y & 2x+z & -2x+s & -3x+t \end{bmatrix}$$

$$\sim \begin{bmatrix} 1 & 3 & -2 & 2 & 3 \\ 0 & 1 & -1 & 2 & -1 \\ 0 & 0 & -x+y+z & 4x-2y+s & -6x+y+t \\ 0 & 0 & 0 & 0 & 0 \end{bmatrix}$$

Set the entries of the third row equal to 0 to obtain the homogeneous system whose solution space is U, that is,

$$-x + y + z = 0, \qquad 4x - 2y + s = 0, \qquad -6x + y + t = 0$$

Now form the matrix whose first rows span W and whose last row is (x, y, z, s, t) and then row reduce to echelon form:

$$\begin{bmatrix} 1 & 3 & 0 & 2 & 1 \\ 1 & 5 & -6 & 6 & 3 \\ 2 & 5 & 3 & 2 & 1 \\ x & y & z & s & t \end{bmatrix} \sim \begin{bmatrix} 1 & 3 & 0 & 2 & 1 \\ 0 & 2 & -6 & 4 & 2 \\ 0 & -1 & 3 & -2 & -1 \\ 0 & -3x+y & z & -2x+s & -x+t \end{bmatrix}$$

$$\sim \begin{bmatrix} 1 & 3 & 0 & 2 & 1 \\ 0 & 1 & -3 & 2 & 1 \\ 0 & 0 & -9x+3y+z & 4x-2y+s & 2x-y+t \\ 0 & 0 & 0 & 0 & 0 \end{bmatrix}$$

Set the entries of the third row equal to 0 to obtain the homogeneous system whose solution space is W, that is,

$$-9x + 3y + z = 0, \qquad 4x - 2y + s = 0, \qquad 2x - y + t = 0$$

Combine both of the above systems to obtain a homogeneous system whose solution space is $U \cap W$, and then reduce to echelon form:

$$
\begin{aligned}
-x + \ y + z \quad\quad\quad\quad &= 0 \\
4x - 2y \quad\quad + s \quad\quad &= 0 \\
-6x + \ y \quad\quad\quad\quad + t &= 0 \\
-9x + 3y + z \quad\quad\quad\quad &= 0 \\
4x - 2y \quad\quad + s \quad\quad &= 0 \\
2x - \ y \quad\quad\quad\quad + t &= 0
\end{aligned}
\qquad \text{or} \qquad
\begin{aligned}
-x + \ y + \ z \quad\quad\quad\quad &= 0 \\
2y + 4z + \ s \quad\quad &= 0 \\
8z + 5s + 2t &= 0 \\
s - 2t &= 0
\end{aligned}
$$

There is one free variable, which is t; hence dim $(U \cap W) = 1$. Setting $t = 2$, we obtain the solution $x = 1$, $y = 4$, $z = -3$, $s = 4$, $t = 2$. Thus $\{(1, 4, -3, 4, 2)\}$ is a basis of $U \cap W$.

PROOFS OF THEOREMS

5.32. Prove Lemma 5.1: Suppose two or more nonzero vectors $v_1, v_2, \ldots, v_m$ are linearly dependent.   Then one of them is a linear combination of the preceding vectors.

Since the v_i are linearly dependent, there exist scalars $a_1, \ldots, a_m$, not all 0, such that $a_1 v_1 + \cdots + a_m v_m = 0$.   Let k be the largest integer such that $a_k \neq 0$.   Then

$$ a_1 v_1 + \cdots + a_k v_k + 0v_{k+1} + \cdots + 0v_m = 0 \qquad \text{or} \qquad a_1 v_1 + \cdots + a_k v_k = 0 $$

Suppose $k = 1$; then $a_1 v_1 = 0$, $a_1 \neq 0$, and so $v_1 = 0$.   But the v_i are nonzero vectors.   Hence $k > 1$ and

$$ v_k = -a_k^{-1} a_1 v_1 - \cdots - a_k^{-1} a_{k-1} v_{k-1} $$

That is, v_k is a linear combination of the preceding vectors.

5.33. Suppose $\{v_1, \ldots, v_m\}$ spans a vector space V.   Prove:

(a)　If $w \in V$, then $\{w, v_1, \ldots, v_m\}$ is linearly dependent and spans V.

(b)　If v_i is a linear combination of vectors $(v_1, v_2, \ldots, v_{i-1})$, then $\{v_1, \ldots, v_{i-1}, v_{i+1}, \ldots, v_m\}$ spans V.

(a)　The vector w is a linear combination of the v_i since $\{v_i\}$ spans V.   Accordingly, $\{w, v_1, \ldots, v_m\}$ is linearly dependent.   Clearly, w with the v_i span V since the v_i by themselves span V, that is, $\{w, v_1, \ldots, v_m\}$ spans V.

(b)　Suppose $v_i = k_1 v_1 + \cdots + k_{i-1} v_{i-1}$.   Let $u \in V$.   Since $\{v_i\}$ spans V, u is a linear combination of the v_i, say $u = a_1 v_1 + \cdots + a_m v_m$.   Substituting for v_i, we obtain

$$
\begin{aligned}
u &= a_1 v_1 + \cdots + a_{i-1} v_{i-1} + a_i (k_1 v_1 + \cdots + k_{i-1} v_{i-1}) + a_{i+1} v_{i+1} + \cdots + a_m v_m \\
&= (a_1 + a_i k_1) v_1 + \cdots + (a_{i-1} + a_i k_{i-1}) v_{i-1} + a_{i+1} v_{i+1} + \cdots + a_m v_m
\end{aligned}
$$

Thus $\{v_1, \ldots, v_{i-1}, v_{i+1}, \ldots, v_m\}$ spans V.   In other words, we can delete v_i from the spanning set and still retain a spanning set.

5.34. Prove Lemma 5.4: Suppose $\{v_1, v_2, \ldots, v_n\}$ spans V, and suppose $\{w_1, w_2, \ldots, w_m\}$ is linearly independent.   Then $m \leq n$, and V is spanned by a set of the form

$$ \{w_1, w_2, \ldots, w_m, v_{i_1}, v_{i_2}, \ldots, v_{i_{n-m}}\} $$

Thus, in particular, any $n + 1$ or more vectors in V are linearly dependent.

It suffices to prove the lemma in the case that the v_i are all not 0.   (Prove!)   Since $\{v_i\}$ spans V, we have by Problem 5.33 that

$$\{w_1, v_1, \ldots, v_n\}$$

(1)

is linearly dependent and also spans V.   By Lemma 5.1, one of the vectors in Eq. (1) is a linear combination of the preceding vectors.   This vector cannot be w_1, so it must be one of the v's, say v_j.   Thus by Problem 5.33 we can delete v_j from the spanning set (1) and obtain the spanning set

$$\{w_1; v_1, \ldots, v_{j-1}, v_{j+1}, \ldots, v_n\}$$

(2)

Now we repeat the argument with the vector w_2.   That is, since Eq. (2) spans V, the set

$$\{w_1, w_2, v_1, \ldots, v_{j-1}, v_{j+1}, \ldots, v_n\}$$

(3)

is linearly dependent and also spans V.   Again by Lemma 5.1 one of the vectors in Eq. (3) is a linear combination of the preceding vectors.   We emphasize that this vector cannot be w_1 or w_2 since $\{w_1, \ldots, w_m\}$ is independent; hence it must be one of the v's, say v_k.   Thus by the preceding problem we can delete v_k from the spanning set (3) and obtain the spanning set

$$\{w_1, w_2, v_1, \ldots, v_{j-1}, v_{j+1}, \ldots, v_{k-1}, v_{k+1}, \ldots, v_n\}$$

We repeat the argument with w_3 and so forth.   At each step we are able to add one of the w's and delete one of the v's in the spanning set.   If $m \leq n$, then we finally obtain a spanning set of the required form:

$$\{w_1, \ldots, w_m, v_{i_1}, \ldots, v_{i_{n-m}}\}$$

Last we show that $m > n$ is not possible.   Otherwise, after n of the above steps, we obtain the spanning set $\{w_1, \ldots, w_n\}$.   This implies that w_{n+1} is a linear combination of $w_1, \ldots, w_n$, which contradicts the hypothesis that $\{w_i\}$ is linearly independent.

5.35. Show that Definition A and Definition B of a basis of a vector space V are equivalent. That is, show that if $S = \{u_1, u_2, \ldots, u_n)$ is a subset of V, then the following two conditions are equivalent:

(a) S is linearly independent and spans V.

(b)   Every vector $v \in V$ can be written uniquely as a linear combination of the vectors in S.

  Suppose (a) holds.   Since S spans V, the vector v is a linear combination of the u_i, say,

$$v = a_1 u_1 + a_2 u_2 + \cdots + a_n u_n$$

Suppose we also have

$$v = b_1 u_1 + b_2 u_2 + \cdots + b_n u_n$$

Subtracting, we get

$$0 = v - v = (a_1 - b_1)u_1 + (a_2 - b_2)u_2 + \cdots + (a_n - b_n)u_n$$

But the u_i are linearly independent.   Hence the coefficients in the above relation are each 0:

$$a_1 - b_1 = 0, \ a_2 - b_2 = 0, \ldots, a_n - b_n = 0$$

Therefore $a_1 = b_1, \ a_2 = b_2, \ldots, a_n = b_n$.   Hence the representation of v as a linear combination of the u_i is unique.   Thus (a) implies (b).

  Suppose (b) holds.   Then S spans V.   Suppose

$$0 = c_1 u_1 + c_2 u_2 + \cdots + c_n u_n$$

However, we do have

$$0 = 0u_1 + 0u_2 + \cdots + 0u_n$$

By hypothesis the representation of 0 as a linear combination of the u_i is unique. Hence each $c_i = 0$ and the u_i are linearly independent. Thus (b) implies (a).

5.36. Prove Theorem 5.3: Every basis of a vector space V has the same number of elements.

Suppose $\{u_1, u_2, \ldots, u_n\}$ is a basis of V, and suppose $\{v_1, v_2, \ldots\}$ is another basis of V. Since $\{u_i\}$ spans V, the basis $\{v_1, v_2, \ldots\}$ must contain n or less vectors, or else it is linearly dependent by Problem 5.34 (Lemma 5.4). On the other hand, if the basis $\{v_1, v_2, \ldots\}$ contains less than n elements, then $\{u_1, u_2, \ldots, u_n\}$ is linearly dependent by Problem 5.34. Thus the basis $\{v_1, v_2, \ldots\}$ contains exactly n vectors, and so the theorem is true.

5.37. Prove Theorem 5.5: Let V be a vector space of finite dimension n. Then:

(i)   Any $n + 1$ or more vectors must be linearly dependent.
(ii) Any linearly independent set $S = \{u_1, u_2, \ldots, u_n\}$ with n elements is a basis of V.
(iii) Any spanning set $T = \{v_1, v_2, \ldots, v_n\}$ of V with n elements is a basis of V.

Suppose $B = \{w_1, w_2, \ldots, w_n\}$ is a basis of V.

(i)   Since B spans V, any $n + 1$ or more vectors are linearly dependent by Lemma 5.4.
(ii) By Lemma 5.4, elements from B can be adjoined to S to form a spanning set of V with n elements. Since S already has n elements, S itself is a spanning set of V. Thus S is a basis of V.
(iii) Suppose T is linearly dependent. Then some v_i is a linear combination of the preceding vectors. By Problem 5.33, V is spanned by the vectors in T without v_i and there are $n - 1$ of them. By Lemma 5.4, the independent set B cannot have more than $n - 1$ elements. This contradicts the fact that B has n elements. Thus T is linearly independent, and hence T is a basis of V.

5.38. Prove Theorem 5.6: Suppose S spans a vector space V. Then:

(i) Any maximum number of linearly independent vectors in S form a basis of V.
(ii) Suppose one deletes from S every vector that is a linear combination of preceding vectors in S. Then the remaining vectors form a basis of V.

(i) Suppose $\{v_1, \ldots, v_m\}$ is a maximum linearly independent subset of S, and suppose $w \in S$. Accordingly $\{v_1, \ldots, v_m, w\}$ is linearly dependent. No v_k can be a linear combination of preceding vectors. Hence w is a linear combination of the v_i. Thus $w \in \text{span}\,(v_i)$ and hence $S \subseteq \text{span}\,(v_i)$. This leads to

$$V = \text{span}\,(S) \subseteq \text{span}\,(v_i) \subseteq V$$

Thus $\{v_i\}$ spans V, and since it is linearly independent, it is a basis of V.

(ii) The remaining vectors form a maximum linearly independent subset of S, and hence by part (i) it is a basis of V.

5.39. Prove Theorem 5.7: Let V be a vector space of finite dimension and let $S = \{u_1, u_2, \ldots, u_r\}$ be a set of linearly independent vectors in V. Then S is part of a basis of V, that is, S may be extended to a basis of V.

Suppose $B = \{w_1, w_2, \ldots, w_n\}$ is a basis of V. Then B spans V and hence V is spanned by

$$S \cup B = \{u_1, u_2, \ldots, u_r, w_1, w_2, \ldots, w_n\}$$

By Theorem 5.6 we can delete from $S \cup B$ each vector which is a linear combination of preceding vectors to obtain a basis B' for V. Since S is linearly independent, no u_k is a linear combination of preceding vectors. Thus B' contains every vector in S, and S is part of the basis B' for V.

5.40. Prove Theorem 5.8: Let W be a subspace of an n-dimensional vector space V. Then $\dim W \leq n$. In particular, if $\dim W = n$, then $W = V$.

Since V is of dimension n, any $n + 1$ or more vectors are linearly dependent. Furthermore, since a basis of W consists of linearly independent vectors, it cannot contain more than n elements. Accordingly, $\dim W \leq n$.

In particular, if $\{w_1, \ldots, w_n\}$ is a basis of W, then since it is an independent set with n elements, it is also a basis of V. Thus $W = V$ when $\dim W = n$.

5.41. Let $x_{i_1}, x_{i_2}, \ldots, x_{i_k}$ be the free variables of a homogeneous system of linear equations with n unknowns. Let v_j be the solution for which $x_{i_j} = 1$, and all other free variables equal 0. Show that the solutions $v_1, v_2, \ldots, v_k$ are linearly independent.

Let A be the matrix whose rows are the v_i. We interchange column 1 and column i_1, then column 2 and column $i_2, \ldots$, then column k and column i_k, and we obtain the $k \times n$ matrix

$$B = (I, C) = \begin{bmatrix} 1 & 0 & 0 & \ldots & 0 & 0 & c_{1,k+1} & \ldots & c_{1n} \\ 0 & 1 & 0 & \ldots & 0 & 0 & c_{2,k+1} & \ldots & c_{2n} \\ \cdots\cdots\cdots\cdots\cdots\cdots\cdots\cdots\cdots\cdots\cdots\cdots \\ 0 & 0 & 0 & \ldots & 0 & 1 & c_{k,k+1} & \ldots & c_{kn} \end{bmatrix}$$

The above matrix B is in echelon form, and so its rows are independent; hence rank $(B) = k$. Since A and B are column equivalent, they have the same rank, i.e., rank $(A) = k$. But A has k rows; hence these rows, i.e., the v_i, are linearly independent, as claimed.

5.42. Prove Theorem 5.9: Suppose U and V are finite-dimensional subspaces of a vector space V. Then $U + W$ has finite dimension and

$$\dim (U + W) = \dim U + \dim W - \dim (U \cap W)$$

Observe that $U \cap W$ is a subspace of both U and W. Suppose $\dim U = m$, $\dim W = n$, and $\dim (U \cap W) = r$. Suppose $\{v_1, \ldots, v_r\}$ is a basis of $U \cap W$. By Theorem 5.7 we can extend $\{v_i\}$ to a basis of U and to a basis of W, say,

$$\{v_1, \ldots, v_r, u_1, \ldots, u_{m-r}\} \quad \text{and} \quad \{v_1, \ldots, v_r, w_1, \ldots, w_{n-r}\}$$

are bases of U and W, respectively. Let

$$B = \{v_1, \ldots, v_r, u_1, \ldots, u_{m-r}, w_1, \ldots, w_{n-r}\}$$

Note that B has exactly $m + n - r$ elements. Thus the theorem is proved if we can show that B is a basis of $U + W$. Since $\{v_i, u_j\}$ spans U and $\{v_i, w_k\}$ spans W, the union $B = \{v_i, u_j, w_k\}$ spans $U + W$. Thus it suffices to show that B is independent.

Suppose

$$a_1v_1 + \cdots + a_rv_r + b_1u_1 + \cdots + b_{m-r}u_{m-r} + c_1w_1 + \cdots + c_{n-r}w_{n-r} = 0 \qquad (1)$$

where a_i, b_j, and c_k are scalars.　Let

$$v = a_1v_1 + \cdots + a_rv_r + b_1u_1 + \cdots + b_{m-r}u_{m-r} \qquad (2)$$

By Eq. (*1*) we also have

$$v = -c_1w_1 - \cdots - c_{n-r}w_{n-r} \qquad (3)$$

Since $\{v_i, u_j\} \subseteq U$, $v \in U$ by Eq. (*2*); and since $\{w_k\} \subseteq W$, $v \in W$ by Eq. (*3*).　Accordingly, $v \in U \cap W$.　Now $\{v_i\}$ is a basis of $U \cap W$, and so there exist scalars $d_1, \ldots, d_r$ for which $v = d_1v_1 + \cdots + d_rv_r$.　Thus by Eq. (*3*) we have

$$d_1v_1 + \cdots + d_rv_r + c_1w_1 + \cdots + c_{n-r}w_{n-r} = 0$$

But $\{v_i, w_k\}$ is a basis of W and so is independent.　Hence the above equation forces $c_1 = 0, \ldots, c_{n-r} = 0$.　Substituting this into Eq. (*1*), we obtain

$$a_1v_1 + \cdots + a_rv_r + b_1u_1 + \cdots + b_{m-r}u_{m-r} = 0$$

But $\{v_i, u_j\}$ is a basis of U and so is independent.　Hence the above equation forces $a_1 = 0, \ldots, a_r = 0, b_1 = 0, \ldots, b_{m-r} = 0$.

Since Eq. (*1*) implies that the a_i, b_j, and c_k are all 0, $B = \{v_i, u_j, w_k\}$ is independent and the theorem is proved.

5.43. Suppose U and W are subspaces of a vector space V, and suppose that $S = \{u_i\}$ spans U and $S' = \{w_j\}$ spans W.　Show that $S \cup S'$ spans $U + W$.　(Accordingly, by induction, if S_i spans W_i for $i = 1, 2, \ldots, n$, then $S_1 \cup \cdots \cup S_n$ spans $W_1 + \cdots + W_n$.)

Let $v \in U + W$.　Then $v = u + w$, where $u \in U$ and $w \in W$.　Since S spans U, u is a linear combination of the u_i, and since S' spans W, w is a linear combination of the w_j, say,

$$u = a_1u_{i_1} + a_2u_{i_2} + \cdots + a_nu_{i_n} \qquad \text{and} \qquad w = b_1w_{j_1} + b_2w_{j_2} + \cdots + b_mw_{j_m}$$

Thus　　　　$v = u + w = a_1u_{i_1} + a_2u_{i_2} + \cdots + a_nu_{i_n} + b_1w_{j_1} + b_2w_{j_2} + \cdots + b_mw_{j_m}$

Accordingly, $S \cup S' = \{u_i, v_j\}$ spans $U + W$.

5.44. Prove Theorem 5.10 (for two factors):　Suppose $V = U \oplus W$.　Moreover, suppose $S_1 = \{u_1, \ldots, u_m\}$ and $S_2 = \{w_1, \ldots, w_n\}$ are linearly independent subsets of U and W, respectively.　Then:

(i)　The union $S = S_1 \cup S_2$ is linearly independent in V.

(ii)　If S_1 and S_2 are bases of U and W, respectively, then $S = S_1 \cup S_2$ is a basis of V.

(iii)　$\dim V = \dim U + \dim W$.

(i)　Suppose $a_1u_1 + \cdots + a_mu_m + b_1w_1 + \cdots + b_nw_n = 0$, where a_i, b_j are scalars.　Then

$$(a_1u_1 + \cdots + a_mu_m) + (b_1w_1 + \cdots + b_nw_n) = 0 + 0 = 0$$

where $0, a_1u_1 + \cdots + a_mu_m \in U$ and $0, b_1w_1 + \cdots + b_nw_n \in W$.　Since such a sum for 0 is unique, this leads to

$$a_1u_1 + \cdots + a_mu_m = 0 \qquad \text{and} \qquad b_1w_1 + \cdots + b_nw_n = 0$$

Since S_1 is linearly independent, each $a_i = 0$, and since S_2 is linearly independent, each $b_j = 0$.　Thus $S = S_1 \cup S_2$ is linearly independent.

(ii)   By part (a), $S = S_1 \cup S_2$ is linearly independent, and, by Problem 5.84. $S = S_1 \cup S_2$ spans $V = U + W$.   Thus $S = S_1 \cup S_2$ is a basis of V.

(iii)   Follows directly from part (b).

5.45.   Prove Theorem 5.12:   The row rank and the column rank of any matrix A are equal.

Let A be an arbitrary $m \times n$ matrix:

$$A = \begin{bmatrix} a_{11} & a_{12} & \ldots & a_{1n} \\ a_{21} & a_{22} & \ldots & a_{2n} \\ \multicolumn{4}{c}{\dotfill} \\ a_{m1} & a_{m2} & \ldots & a_{mn} \end{bmatrix}$$

Let $R_1, R_2, \ldots, R_m$ denote its rows:

$$R_1 = (a_{11}, a_{12}, \ldots, a_{1n}), \ldots, R_m = (a_{m1}, a_{m2}, \ldots, a_{mn})$$

Suppose the row rank is r and that the following r vectors form a basis for the row space:

$$S_1 = (b_{11}, b_{12}, \ldots, b_{1n}), S_2 = (b_{21}, b_{22}, \ldots, b_{2n}), \ldots, S_r = (b_{r1}, b_{r2}, \ldots, b_{rn})$$

Then each of the row vectors is a linear combination of the S_i:

$$R_1 = k_{11}S_1 + k_{12}S_2 + \cdots + k_{1r}S_r$$
$$R_2 = k_{21}S_1 + k_{22}S_2 + \cdots + k_{2r}S_r$$
$$\dotfill$$
$$R_m = k_{m1}S_1 + k_{m2}S_2 + \cdots + k_{mr}S_r$$

where the k_{ij} are scalars.   Setting the ith components of each of the above vector equations equal to each other, we obtain the following system of equations, each valid for $i = 1, \ldots, n$:

$$a_{1i} = k_{11}b_{1i} + k_{12}b_{2i} + \cdots + k_{1r}b_{ri}$$
$$a_{2i} = k_{21}b_{1i} + k_{22}b_{2i} + \cdots + k_{2r}b_{ri}$$
$$\dotfill$$
$$a_{mi} = k_{m1}b_{1i} + k_{m2}b_{2i} + \cdots + k_{mr}b_{ri}$$

Thus for $i = 1, \ldots, n$,

$$\begin{bmatrix} a_{1i} \\ a_{2i} \\ \ldots \\ a_{mi} \end{bmatrix} = b_{1i}\begin{bmatrix} k_{11} \\ k_{21} \\ \ldots \\ k_{m1} \end{bmatrix} + b_{2i}\begin{bmatrix} k_{12} \\ k_{22} \\ \ldots \\ k_{m2} \end{bmatrix} + \cdots + b_{ri}\begin{bmatrix} k_{1r} \\ k_{2r} \\ \ldots \\ k_{mr} \end{bmatrix}$$

In other words, each of the columns of A is a linear combination of the r vectors,

$$\begin{bmatrix} k_{11} \\ k_{21} \\ \ldots \\ k_{m1} \end{bmatrix}, \begin{bmatrix} k_{12} \\ k_{22} \\ \ldots \\ k_{m2} \end{bmatrix}, \ldots, \begin{bmatrix} k_{1r} \\ k_{2r} \\ \ldots \\ k_{mr} \end{bmatrix}$$

Thus the column space of the matrix A has dimension at most r, i.e., column rank $\leq r$.   Hence column rank $\leq$ row rank.

Similarly (or considering the transpose matrix A^T) we obtain row rank $\leq$ column rank. Thus the row rank and the column rank are equal.

5.46. Suppose R is a row vector and A and B are matrices such that RB and AB are defined. Prove:

    (a) RB is a linear combination of the rows of B.

    (b) Row space of AB is contained in the row space of B.

    (c) Column space of AB is contained in the column space of A.

    (d) rank $(AB) \leq$ rank (B) and rank $(AB) \leq$ rank (A).

    (a) Suppose $R = (a_1, a_2, \ldots, a_m)$ and $B = [b_{ij}]$. Let $B_1, \ldots, B_m$ denote the rows of B and $B^1, \ldots, B^n$ its columns. Then

$$RB = (R \cdot B^1, R \cdot B^2, \ldots, R \cdot B^n)$$
$$= (a_1 b_{11} + a_2 b_{21} + \cdots + a_m b_{m1}, a_1 b_{12} + a_2 b_{22} + \cdots + a_m b_{m2}, \ldots, a_1 b_{1n} + a_2 b_{2n} + \cdots + a_m b_{mn})$$
$$= a_1 (b_{11}, b_{12}, \ldots, b_{1n}) + a_2 (b_{21}, b_{22}, \ldots, b_{2n}) + \cdots + a_m (b_{m1}, b_{m2}, \ldots, b_{mn})$$
$$= a_1 B_1 + a_2 B_2 + \cdots + a_m B_m$$

Thus RB is a linear combination of the rows of B, as claimed.

    (b) The rows of AB are $R_i B$, where R_i is the ith row of A. Thus by part (a), each row of AB is in the row space of B. Thus rowsp $(AB) \subseteq$ rowsp (B), as claimed.

    (c) Using part (b), we have

$$\text{colsp}\,(AB) = \text{rowsp}\,(AB)^T = \text{rowsp}\,(B^T A^T) \subseteq \text{rowsp}\,(A^T) = \text{colsp}\,(A)$$

    (d) The row space of AB is contained in the row space of B; hence rank $(AB) \leq$ rank (B). Furthermore, the column space of AB is contained in the column space of A; hence rank $(AB) \leq$ rank (A).

5.47. Let A be an n-square matrix. Show that A is invertible if and only if rank $(A) = n$.

    Note that the rows of the n-square identity matrix I_n are linearly independent since I_n is in echelon form; hence rank $(I_n) = n$. Now if A is invertible, then A is row equivalent to I_n; hence rank $A = n$. But if A is not invertible, then A is row equivalent to a matrix with a zero row; hence rank $(A) < n$, that is, A is invertible if and only if rank $(A) = n$.

Supplementary Problems

LINEAR DEPENDENCE

5.48. Determine whether or nor u and v are linearly dependent, where:

    (a) $u = (1, 2, 3)$, $v = (3, 2, 1)$,   (c) $u = (1, 2, 3, 4)$, $v = (0, 0, 0, 0)$

    (b) $u = (2, -4, 6)$, $v = (-3, 6, -9)$ (d) $u = (1, 1, 2, 2)$, $v = (2, 2, 1, 1)$

5.49. Determine whether or not u and v are linearly dependent, where:

    (a) $u = \begin{bmatrix} 4 & -2 \\ 0 & -1 \end{bmatrix}$, $v = \begin{bmatrix} -2 & 1 \\ 0 & \frac{1}{2} \end{bmatrix}$;   (c) $u = \begin{bmatrix} 1 & 0 \\ 0 & -1 \end{bmatrix}$, $v = \begin{bmatrix} 0 & -1 \\ 1 & 0 \end{bmatrix}$

    (b) $u = 2t^2 + 8t - 6$, $v = -3t^2 - 12t + 9$;   (d) $u = t^2 + t$, $v = t + 1$

5.50. Determine whether the following vectors in $\mathbf{R}^4$ are linearly dependent or independent:

   (a) $(1, 2, -3, 1)$, $(3, 7, 1, -2)$, $(1, 3, 7, -4)$;   (b) $(1, 3, 1, -2)$, $(2, 5, -1, 3)$, $(1, 3, 7, -2)$.

5.51. Determine whether the polynomials u, v, w in $\mathbf{P}(t)$ are linearly dependent or independent:

   (a) $u = t^3 - 4t^2 + 3t + 3$, $v = t^3 + 2t^2 + 4t - 1$, $w = 2t^3 - t^2 - 3t + 5$

   (b) $u = t^3 - 5t^2 - 2t + 3$, $v = t^3 - 4t^2 - 3t + 4$, $w = 2t^3 - 7t^2 - 7t + 9$

5.52. Show that the following functions f, g, and h are linearly independent:

   (a) $f(t) = e^t$, $g(t) = \sin t$, $h(t) = t^2$;   (b) $f(t) = e^t$, $g(t) = e^{2t}$, $h(t) = t$

5.53. Show that $u = (a, b)$ and $v = (c, d)$ in $\mathbf{R}^2$ are linearly dependent if and only if $ad - bc = 0$.

5.54. Suppose u, v, and w are linearly independent vectors.   Show that:

   (a) $u + v - 2w$, $u - v - w$, and $u + w$ are linearly independent.

   (b) $u - v - 3w$, $u + 3v - w$, and $v + w$ are linearly independent.

5.55. Suppose that $\{u_1, \ldots, u_r, w_1, \ldots, w_s\}$ is a linearly independent subset of a vector space V.   Show that span $(u_i) \cap$ span $(w_j) = \{0\}$.   [Recall that span (u_i) is the subspace of V spanned by the u_i.]

5.56. Suppose $v_1, v_2, \ldots, v_n$ are linearly independent vectors.   Prove the following:

   (a) $\{a_1 v_1, a_2 v_2, \ldots, a_n v_n\}$ is linearly independent, where each $a_i \neq 0$.

   (b) $\{v_1, \ldots, v_{i-1}, w, v_{i+1}, \ldots, v_n\}$ is linearly independent, where $w = b_1 v_1 + \cdots + b_i v_i + \cdots + b_n v_n$ and $b_i \neq 0$.

5.57. Suppose $(a_{i1}, a_{i2}, \ldots, a_{in})$, $i = 1, \ldots, m$, are linearly independent vectors in K^n, and suppose $v_1, \ldots, v_n$ are linearly independent vectors in a vector space V over K.   Show that the following vectors are also linearly independent:

$$w_1 = a_{11} v_1 + \cdots + a_{1n} v_n, \quad \ldots, \quad w_m = a_{m1} v_1 + \cdots + a_{mn} v_n$$

5.58. Suppose A is any n-square matrix and suppose $u_1, u_2, \ldots, u_r$ are $n \times 1$ column vectors.   Show that if $Au_1, Au_2, \ldots, Au_r$ are linearly independent (column) vectors, then $u_1, u_2, \ldots, u_r$ are linearly independent.

BASIS AND DIMENSION

5.59. Determine whether or not each of the following forms a basis for $\mathbf{R}^3$: (a) $(1, 1, 1)$ and $(1, 3, 5)$; (b) $(1, 1, 1)$, $(1, 2, 3)$, $(4, 7, 10)$; (c) $(1, 1, 1)$, $(0, 1, 5)$, $(1, 2, 6)$, $(1, 3, 5)$; (d) $(1, 1, 1)$, $(1, 2, 3)$, $(0, 1, 5)$.

5.60. Find a subset of u_1, u_2, u_3, u_4 which gives a basis for $W = $ span (u_1, u_2, u_3, u_4) of $\mathbf{R}^5$, where:

   (a) $u_1 = (1, 1, 1, 2, 3)$, $u_2 = (1, 2, -1, -2, 1)$, $u_3 = (3, 5, -1, -2, 5)$, $u_4 = (1, 2, 1, -1, 4)$

   (b) $u_1 = (1, -2, 1, 3, -1)$, $u_2 = (-2, 4, -2, -6, 2)$, $u_3 = (1, -3, 1, 2, 1)$, $u_4 = (3, -7, 3, 8, -1)$

   (c) $u_1 = (1, 0, 1, 0, 1)$, $u_2 = (1, 1, 2, 1, 0)$, $u_3 = (1, 2, 3, 1, 1)$, $u_4 = (1, 2, 1, 1, 1)$

   (d) $u_1 = (1, 0, 1, 1, 1)$, $u_2 = (2, 1, 2, 0, 1)$, $u_3 = (1, 1, 2, 3, 4)$, $u_4 = (4, 2, 5, 4, 6)$

5.61. Let U and W be the following subspaces of $\mathbf{R}^4$:

$$U = \{(a, b, c, d): \quad b - 2c + d = 0\}, \qquad W = \{(a, b, c, d): \quad a = d, b = 2c\}$$

Find a basis and the dimension of: (a) U; (b) W; (c) $U \cap W$.

5.62. Find a basis and the dimension of the solution space W of each homogeneous system:

(a) $\begin{aligned} x + 3y + 2z &= 0 \\ x + 5y + z &= 0; \\ 3x + 5y + 8z &= 0 \end{aligned}$
(b) $\begin{aligned} x - 2y + 7z &= 0 \\ 2x + 3y - 2z &= 0; \\ 2x - y + z &= 0 \end{aligned}$
(c) $\begin{aligned} x + 4y + 2z &= 0 \\ 2x + y + 5z &= 0 \end{aligned}$

5.63. Find a basis and the dimension of the solution space W of each homogeneous system:

(a) $\begin{aligned} x + 2y - 2z + 2s - t &= 0 \\ x + 2y - z + 3s - 2t &= 0; \\ 2x + 4y - 7z + s + t &= 0 \end{aligned}$
(b) $\begin{aligned} x + 2y - z + 3s - 4t &= 0 \\ 2x + 4y - 2z - s + 5t &= 0 \\ 2x + 4y - 2z + 4s - 2t &= 0 \end{aligned}$

5.64. Find a homogeneous system whose solution space is spanned by the three vectors:

$$u_1 = (1, -2, 0, 3, -1), \qquad u_2 = (2, -3, 2, 5, -3), \qquad u_3 = (1, -2, 1, 2, -2)$$

5.65. Find a homogeneous system whose solution space is spanned by the three vectors:

$$u_1 = (1, 1, 2, 1, 1), \qquad u_2 = (1, 2, 1, 4, 3), \qquad u_3 = (3, 5, 4, 9, 7)$$

5.66. Determine whether or not each of the following is a basis of the vector space $\mathbf{P}_n(t)$ of polynomials of degree $\leq n$:

(a) $\{1, 1 + t, 1 + t + t^2, 1 + t + t^2 + t^3, \ldots, 1 + t + t^2 + \cdots + t^{n-1} + t^n\}$

(b) $\{1 + t, t + t^2, t^2 + t^3, \ldots, t^{n-2} + t^{n-1}, t^{n-1} + t^n\}$

5.67. Find a basis and the dimension of the subspace W of $\mathbf{P}(t)$ spanned by the polynomials:

(a) $u = t^3 + 2t^2 - 2t + 1, v = t^3 + 3t^2 - t + 4$, and $w = 2t^3 + t^2 - 7t - 7$

(b) $u = t^3 + t^2 - 3t + 2, v = 2t^3 + t^2 + t - 4$, and $w = 4t^3 + 3t^2 - 5t + 2$

RANK OF A MATRIX, ROW AND COLUMN SPACES

5.68. Find the rank of each matrix:

(a) $\begin{bmatrix} 1 & 3 & -2 & 5 & 4 \\ 1 & 4 & 1 & 3 & 5 \\ 1 & 4 & 2 & 4 & 3 \\ 2 & 7 & -3 & 6 & 13 \end{bmatrix}$;
(b) $\begin{bmatrix} 1 & 2 & -3 & -2 & -3 \\ 1 & 3 & -2 & 0 & -4 \\ 3 & 8 & -7 & -2 & -11 \\ 2 & 1 & -9 & -10 & -3 \end{bmatrix}$;

(c) $\begin{bmatrix} 1 & 1 & 2 \\ 4 & 5 & 5 \\ 5 & 8 & 1 \\ -1 & -2 & 2 \end{bmatrix}$;
(d) $\begin{bmatrix} 2 & 1 \\ 3 & -7 \\ -6 & 1 \\ 5 & -8 \end{bmatrix}$

5.69. For $k = 1, 2, \ldots, 5$ find the number n_k of linearly independent columns of the set of columns of each matrix:

$$(a) \quad A = \begin{bmatrix} 1 & 1 & 0 & 2 & 3 \\ 1 & 2 & 0 & 2 & 5 \\ 1 & 3 & 0 & 2 & 7 \end{bmatrix}; \qquad (b) \quad B = \begin{bmatrix} 1 & 2 & 1 & 0 & 2 \\ 1 & 2 & 3 & 0 & 4 \\ 1 & 1 & 5 & 0 & 2 \end{bmatrix}$$

5.70. For each of the following matrices, find (i) columns that are linear combinations of preceding columns, and (ii) columns that form a basis for the column space:

$$(a) \quad A = \begin{bmatrix} 1 & 1 & 2 & 2 & 3 & 3 \\ 2 & 2 & 5 & 6 & 8 & 7 \\ 1 & 1 & 4 & 6 & 7 & 7 \end{bmatrix}; \qquad (b) \quad B = \begin{bmatrix} 1 & 1 & 2 & 2 & 3 & 3 \\ 2 & 3 & 5 & 8 & 10 & 7 \\ 1 & 3 & 4 & 11 & 11 & 6 \end{bmatrix}$$

In each case express the last column C_6 as a linear combination of the basis vectors obtained in (ii).

5.71. Consider the following matrix A and (column) vectors u and v.

$$A = \begin{bmatrix} 1 & -1 & -3 & 0 \\ 0 & 1 & 5 & 4 \\ -1 & 2 & 8 & 5 \\ 3 & -1 & 1 & 3 \end{bmatrix}, \qquad u = \begin{bmatrix} 0 \\ 0 \\ 1 \\ 1 \end{bmatrix}, \qquad v = \begin{bmatrix} 1 \\ 1 \\ 1 \\ 0 \end{bmatrix}$$

(a) Find columns of A which form a basis for colsp (A).

(b) Express C_4 as a linear combination of the columns in part (a).

(c) Does u or v belong to colsp (A)? If yes, express it as a linear combination of the columns in part (a).

(d) Find conditions on x, y, z, t such that $v = (x, y, z, t)^T$ belongs to colsp (A).

5.72. Find a basis for (i) the row space and (ii) the column space of each matrix M:

$$(a) \quad M = \begin{bmatrix} 0 & 0 & 3 & 1 & 4 \\ 1 & 3 & 1 & 2 & 1 \\ 3 & 9 & 4 & 5 & 2 \\ 4 & 12 & 8 & 8 & 7 \end{bmatrix}; \qquad (b) \quad M = \begin{bmatrix} 1 & 2 & 1 & 0 & 1 \\ 1 & 2 & 2 & 1 & 3 \\ 3 & 6 & 5 & 2 & 7 \\ 2 & 4 & 1 & -1 & 0 \end{bmatrix}$$

5.73. Let A and B be arbitrary $m \times n$ matrices. Show that rank $(A + B) \le$ rank$(A) +$ rank (B).

5.74. Let $r =$ rank $(A + B)$. Find 2×2 matrices A and B such that: (a) $r <$ rank (A), rank (B); (b) $r =$ rank $(A) =$ rank (B); (c) $r >$ rank (A), rank (B).

SUMS AND INTERSECTIONS

5.75. Suppose U and W are subspaces of V and that dim $U = 4$, dim $W = 5$, and dim $V = 7$. Find the possible dimensions of $U \cap W$.

5.76. Let U and W be subspaces of $\mathbf{R}^3$ for which dim $U = 1$, dim $W = 2$, and $U \not\subseteq W$. Show that $\mathbf{R}^3 = U \oplus W$.

5.77.   Consider the following subspaces of $\mathbf{R}^5$:

$$U = \text{span}\,[(1, 3, -3, -1, -4), (1, 4, -1, -2, -2), (2, 9, 0, -5, -2)]$$
$$W = \text{span}\,[(1, 6, 2, -2, 3), (2, 8, -1, -6, -5), (1, 3, -1, -5, -6)]$$

Find: (a) dim $(U + W)$; (b) dim $(U \cap W)$.

5.78.   Consider the following subspaces of $\mathbf{R}^5$:

$$U = \text{span}\,[(1, -1, -1, -2, 0), (1, -2, -2, 0, -3), (1, -1, -2, -2, 1)]$$
$$W = \text{span}\,[(1, -2, -3, 0, -2), (1, -1, -3, 2, -4), (1, -1, -2, 2, -5)]$$

(a)   Find two homogeneous systems whose solution spaces are U and W, respectively.

(b)   Find a basis and dimension of $U \cap W$.

5.79.   Suppose $V = U \oplus W$.   Show that dim V = dim U + dim W.

MISCELLANEOUS PROBLEMS

5.80.   Answer true or false.   If false, prove it with a counterexample.

(a)   If u_1, u_2, u_3 span V, then dim $V = 3$.

(b)   If A is a 4×8 matrix, then any six columns are linearly dependent.

(c)   If u_1, u_2, u_3 are linearly independent, then u_1, u_2, u_3, w are linearly dependent.

(d)   If u_1, u_2, u_3, u_4 are linearly independent, then dim $V \geq 4$.

(e)   If u_1, u_2, u_3 span V, then w, u_1, u_2, u_3 span V.

(f)   If u_1, u_2, u_3, u_4 are linearly independent, then u_1, u_2, u_3 are linearly independent.

5.81.   Answer true or false.   If false, prove it with a counterexample.

(a)   If any row is deleted from a matrix in echelon form, then the resulting matrix is still in echelon form.

(b)   If any column is deleted from a matrix in echelon form, then the resulting matrix is still in echelon form.

(c)   If any row is deleted from a matrix in row canonical form, then the resulting matrix is still in row canonical form.

(d)   If any column is deleted from a matrix in row canonical form, then the resulting matrix is still in row canonical form.

(e)   If any column without a pivot is deleted from a matrix in row canonical form, then the resulting matrix is in row canonical form.

5.82.   Determine the dimension of the vector space W of the following n-square matrices: (a) symmetric matrices; (b) antisymmetric matrices; (c) diagonal matrices; (d) scalar matrices.

5.83.   Suppose $S_1, S_2, \ldots$ are linearly independent subsets of V such that $S_1 \subseteq S_2 \subseteq \cdots$.   Show that the union $S = \bigcup_i S_i$ is also linearly independent.

5.84. Suppose $S_1, S_2, \ldots, S_r$ span, respectively, the subspaces $W_1, W_2, \ldots, W_r$. Show that $S = S_1 \cup S_2 \cup \cdots \cup S_r$ spans $W_1 + W_2 + \cdots + W_r$.

5.85 Consider a finite sequence of vectors $S = \{u_1, u_2, \ldots, u_n\}$. Let T be a sequence of vectors obtained from S by one of the following "elementary" operations:

(1) Interchange two vectors.
(2) Multiply a vector by a nonzero scalar.
(3) Add a multiple of one vector to another vector.

Show that S and T span the same subspace W. Also show that T is linearly independent if and only if S is linearly independent.

5.86. Suppose $u_1, u_2, \ldots, u_n$ belong to a vector space V. Suppose $P = [a_{ij}]$ is an n-square matrix and let

$$v_i = a_{i1}u_1 + a_{i2}u_2 + \cdots + a_{in}u_n, \qquad i = 1, 2, \ldots, n$$

(a) Suppose P is invertible. Show that $\{u_i\}$ and $\{v_i\}$ span the same subspace; hence $\{u_i\}$ is linearly independent if and only if $\{v_i\}$ is linearly independent.

(b) Suppose P is singular (not invertible). Show that $\{v_i\}$ is linearly dependent.

(c) Suppose $\{v_i\}$ is linearly independent. Show that P is invertible.

5.87. Suppose K is a subfield of L and L is a subfield of E, that is, suppose $K \subseteq L \subseteq E$. (Hence K is a subfield of E.) Suppose $\dim_L E = n$ and $\dim L_K = m$. Show that $\dim_K E = mn$. (Here $\dim_K V$ is the dimension of V as a vector space over K.)

Answers to Supplementary Problems

5.48. (a) No; (b) yes; (c) yes; (d) no

5.49. (a) Yes; (b) yes; (c) no; (d) no

5.50. (a) Dependent; (b) independent

5.51. (a) Independent; (b) dependent

5.59. (a) No; (b) no; (c) no; (d) yes

5.60. (a) u_1, u_2, u_4; (b) u_1, u_3; (c) u_1, u_2, u_3, u_4; (d) u_1, u_2, u_3

5.61. (a) $\dim U = 3$; (b) $\dim W = 2$; (c) $\dim (U \cap W) = 1$

5.62. (a) Basis: $\{(7, -1, -2)\}$, $\dim W = 1$; (b) $\dim W = 0$; (c) basis: $\{(18, -1, -7)\}$, $\dim W = 1$

5.63. (a) Basis: $\{(2, -1, 0, 0, 0), (4, 0, 1, -1, 0), (3, 0, 1, 0, 1)\}$, $\dim W = 3$
(b) basis: $\{(2, -1, 0, 0, 0), (1, 0, 1, 0, 0)\}$, $\dim W = 2$

5.64. $5x + y - z - s = 0,\ x + y - z - t = 0$

5.65. $3x - y - z = 0,\ 2x - 3y + s = 0,\ x - 2y + t = 0$

5.66. (a) Yes; (b) no; for $\dim \mathbf{P}_n(t) = n + 1$, but the set contains only n elements

5.67. (a) $\dim W = 2$; (b) $\dim W = 3$

5.68. (a) 3; (b) 2; (c) 3; (d) 2

5.69. (a) $n_1 = 4,\ n_2 = 5,\ n_3 = n_4 = n_5 = 0$; (b) $n_1 = 4,\ n_2 = 6,\ n_3 = 4,\ n_4 = n_5 = 0$

5.70. (a) (i) $C_2,\ C_4,\ C_5$; (ii) $C_1,\ C_3,\ C_6$; $C_6 = 0C_1 + 0C_3 + C_6$
(b) (i) $C_3,\ C_5,\ C_6$; (ii) $C_1,\ C_2,\ C_4$; $C_6 = 4C_1 - 3C_2 + C_4$

5.71. (a) $C_1,\ C_2,\ C_4$; (b) $C_4 = 0C_1 + 0C_2 + C_4$; (c) $v = -2C_1 - 3C_2 + C_4$; (d) $2x - 7y + 5z + t = 0$

5.72. (a) (i) $(1, 3, 1, 2, 1),\ (0, 0, 1, -1, -1),\ (0, 0, 0, 4, 7)$; (ii) $C_1,\ C_3,\ C_4$
(b) (i) $(1, 2, 1, 0, 1),\ (0, 0, 1, 1, 2)$; (ii) $C_1,\ C_3$

5.74. (a) $A = \begin{bmatrix} 1 & 1 \\ 0 & 0 \end{bmatrix},\ B = \begin{bmatrix} -1 & -1 \\ 0 & 0 \end{bmatrix}$; (b) $A = \begin{bmatrix} 1 & 0 \\ 0 & 0 \end{bmatrix},\ B = \begin{bmatrix} 0 & 2 \\ 0 & 0 \end{bmatrix}$; (c) $A = \begin{bmatrix} 1 & 0 \\ 0 & 0 \end{bmatrix},\ B = \begin{bmatrix} 0 & 0 \\ 0 & 1 \end{bmatrix}$

5.75. $\dim (U \cap W) = 2,\ 3,\ \text{or } 4$

5.77. (a) 3; (b) 2

5.78. (a) $\begin{array}{ll} 3x + 4y - z \quad\ - t = 0 & 4x + 2y \quad\ - s \quad = 0 \\ 4x + 2y \quad\ + s \quad = 0 & 9x + 2y + z \quad\ + t = 0 \end{array}$

(b) basis: $\{(1, -2, -5, 0, 0),\ (0, 0, 1, 0, -1)\},\ \dim (U \cap W) = 2$

5.80. (a) false; $(1, 1),\ (1, 2),\ (2, 1)$ span $\mathbf{R}^2$; (b) true; (c) false; $(1, 0, 0, 0),\ (0, 1, 0, 0),\ (0, 0, 1, 0)$, $w = (0, 0, 0, 1)$; (d) true; (e) true; (f) true

5.81. All true except (d).   Delete C_2 from $\begin{bmatrix} 1 & 0 & 3 \\ 0 & 1 & 2 \end{bmatrix}$.

5.82. (a) $n(n + 1)/2$; (b) $n(n - 1)/2$; (c) n; (d) 1

Chapter 6

Coordinates; Change of Basis

6.1 INTRODUCTION

First we studied in Chapter 1 the vector space $\mathbf{R}^n$ of n-tuples of real numbers. Then we used properties of $\mathbf{R}^n$ to define an abstract vector space V in Chapter 4. Here we show that if V is a real vector space (vector space over R) of finite dimension n, then "structurally" V is "identical" to $\mathbf{R}^n$ or, in other words, V is *isomorphic* to $\mathbf{R}^n$. These notions will be made precise below.

The results in this chapter are true for a vector space V over any field K. However, for pedagogical reasons, we will assume our underlying field is the real field $\mathbf{R}$.

6.2 COORDINATES

Let V be an n-dimensional vector space over the real field $\mathbf{R}$. Suppose

$$S = \{u_1, u_2, \ldots, u_n\}$$

is a basis of V. Then any vector $v \in V$ can be expressed uniquely as a linear combination of the basis vectors in S, say

$$v = a_1 u_1 + a_2 u_2 + \cdots + a_n u_n$$

These n scalars $a_1, a_2, \ldots, a_n$ are called the *coordinates* of v relative to the basis S, and they form a vector $[a_1, a_2, \ldots, a_n]$ in $\mathbf{R}^n$ called the *coordinate vector* of v relative to S. We denote this vector by $[v]_S$, or simply $[v]$ when S is understood. Thus

$$[v]_S = [a_1, a_2, \ldots, a_n]$$

For notational convenience, brackets $[\ldots]$, not parentheses $(\ldots)$, are used to denote the coordinate vector.

Remark: The above n scalars $a_1, a_2, \ldots, a_n$ also form a column vector $[a_1, a_2, \ldots, a_n]^T$ called the *coordinate column vector* of v relative to S. The choice of the column vector $[a_1, a_2, \ldots, a_n]^T$ rather than the row vector $[a_1, a_2, \ldots, a_n]$ to represent v depends on the context in which it is used. The use of such column vectors will become clear in Section 6.4.

EXAMPLE 6.1 Consider the vector space $\mathbf{P}_2(t)$ of polynomials of degree ≤ 2. The polynomials

$$p_1 = 1, \qquad p_2 = t - 1, \qquad p_3 = (t-1)^2 = t^2 - 2t + 1$$

form a basis S of $\mathbf{P}_2(t)$. Let $v = 2t^2 - 5t + 6$. The coordinate vector of v relative to the basis S is obtained as follows.

Set $v = xp_1 + yp_2 + zp_3$ using unknown scalars x, y, z and simplify:

$$2t^2 - 5t + 6 = x(1) + y(t-1) + z(t^2 - 2t + 1)$$
$$= x + yt - y + zt^2 - 2zt + z$$
$$= zt^2 + (y - 2z)t + (x - y + z)$$

222

Then set the coefficients of the same powers of t equal to each other to obtain the system:

$$x - y + z = 6$$
$$y - 2z = -5$$
$$z = 2$$

The solution of the above system is $x = 3$, $y = -1$, $z = 2$. Thus

$$v = 3p_1 - p_2 + 2p_3 \qquad \text{and so} \qquad [v] = [3, -1, 2]$$

EXAMPLE 6.2 Consider real space $\mathbf{R}^3$. The vectors $u_1 = (1, -1, 0)$, $u_2 = (1, 1, 0)$, and $u_3 = (0, 1, 1)$ form a basis S of $\mathbf{R}^3$. Let $v = (5, 3, 4)$. The coordinates of v relative to the basis S are obtained as follows.

Set $v = xu_1 + yu_2 + zu_3$, that is, set v as a linear combination of the basis vectors using unknown scalars x, y, z:

$$\begin{bmatrix} 5 \\ 3 \\ 4 \end{bmatrix} = x \begin{bmatrix} 1 \\ -1 \\ 0 \end{bmatrix} + y \begin{bmatrix} 1 \\ 1 \\ 0 \end{bmatrix} + z \begin{bmatrix} 0 \\ 1 \\ 1 \end{bmatrix}$$

The equivalent system of linear equations follows:

$$x + y = 5, \qquad -x + y + z = 3, \qquad z = 4$$

The solution of the system is $x = 3$, $y = 2$, $z = 4$. Thus

$$v = 3u_1 + 2u_2 + 4u_3 \qquad \text{and so} \qquad [v]_S = [3, 2, 4]$$

Remark 1: There is a geometrical interpretation of the coordinates of a vector v relative to a basis S for real space $\mathbf{R}^n$. We illustrate this by using the following basis of $\mathbf{R}^3$ appearing in Example 6.2:

$$S = \{u_1, u_2, u_3\} = \{(1, -1, 0), (1, 1, 0), (0, 1, 1)\}$$

First consider the space $\mathbf{R}^3$ with the usual x, y, and z axes. Then the basis vectors determine a new coordinate system of $\mathbf{R}^3$, say with x', y', and z' axes, as shown in Fig. 6.1, that is,

(1) The x' axis is in the direction of u_1.
(2) The y' axis is in the direction of u_2.
(3) The z' axis is in the direction of u_3.

Furthermore, the unit length in each of the axes will be equal to the length of the corresponding basis vector. Then each vector $v = (a, b, c)$ or, equivalently, the point $P(a, b, c)$ in $\mathbf{R}^3$ will have new coordinates with respect to the new x', y', and z' axes. These new coordinates are precisely the coordinates of v with respect to the basis S.

Remark 2: Consider the usual basis $E = \{e_1, e_2, \ldots, e_n\}$ of $\mathbf{R}^n$ defined by

$$e_1 = (1, 0, 0, \ldots, 0, 0)$$
$$e_2 = (0, 1, 0, \ldots, 0, 0)$$
$$\cdots\cdots\cdots\cdots\cdots$$
$$e_n = (0, 0, 0, \ldots, 0, 1)$$

Let $v = (a_1, a_2, \ldots, a_n)$ be any vector in $\mathbf{R}^n$. Then one can easily show that

$$v = a_1 e_1 + a_2 e_2 + \cdots + a_n e_n \qquad \text{and so} \qquad [v]_E = [a_1, a_2, \ldots, a_n]$$

That is, the coordinate vector $[v]_E$ of any vector v relative to the usual basis E of $\mathbf{R}^n$ is identical to the original vector v.

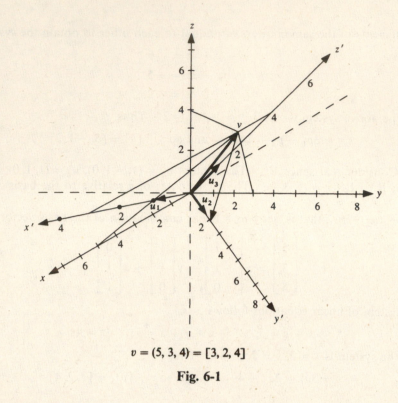

$$v = (5, 3, 4) = [3, 2, 4]$$

Fig. 6-1

6.3 ISOMORPHISM BETWEEN V AND $\mathbf{R}^n$

Let V be a real vector space of dimension n, and suppose $S = \{u_1, u_2, \ldots, u_n\}$ is a basis of V. Section 6.2 showed that to each vector $v \in V$ there corresponds a unique n-tuple (vector) in $\mathbf{R}^n$. On the other hand, for any n-tuple $[c_1, c_2, \ldots, c_n]$ in $\mathbf{R}^n$ there corresponds the vector $c_1 u_1 + c_2 u_2 + \cdots + c_n u_n$ in V. Thus the basis S induces a one-to-one correspondence between the vectors in V and the n-tuples in $\mathbf{R}^n$. Furthermore, suppose

$$v = a_1 u_1 + a_2 u_2 + \cdots + a_n u_n \qquad \text{and} \qquad w = b_1 u_1 + b_2 u_2 + \cdots + b_n u_n$$

Then

$$v + w = (a_1 + b_1)u_1 + (a_2 + b_2)u_2 + \cdots + (a_n + b_n)u_n$$
$$kv = (ka_1)u_1 + (ka_2)u_2 + \cdots + (ka_n)u_n$$

where k is a scalar. Accordingly,

$$[v + w]_S = [a_1 + b_1, \ldots, a_n + b_n] = [a_1, \ldots, a_n] + [b_1, \ldots, b_n] = [v]_S + [w]_S$$

and

$$[kv]_S = [ka_1, ka_2, \ldots, ka_n] = k[a_1, a_2, \ldots, a_n] = k[v]_S$$

Thus the above one-to-one correspondence between V and $\mathbf{R}^n$ preserves the vector space operations of vector addition and scalar multiplication. We then say that V and $\mathbf{R}^n$ are *isomorphic*, written

$$V \cong \mathbf{R}^n$$

We state this result formally.

Theorem 6.1: Let V be a real vector space of dimension n. Then V is isomorphic to $\mathbf{R}^n$.

The next example gives a practical application to the above result.

EXAMPLE 6.3 Suppose we want to determine whether or not the following matrices are linearly independent:

$$A = \begin{bmatrix} 1 & 2 & -3 \\ 4 & 0 & 1 \end{bmatrix}, \qquad B = \begin{bmatrix} 1 & 3 & -4 \\ 6 & 5 & 4 \end{bmatrix}, \qquad C = \begin{bmatrix} 3 & 8 & -11 \\ 16 & 10 & 9 \end{bmatrix}$$

The coordinate vectors of the above matrices relative to the usual basis (Section 5.3) of $\mathbf{M}_{2,3}$ are as follows:

$$[A] = [1, 2, -3, 4, 0, 1], \qquad [B] = [1, 3, -4, 6, 5, 4], \qquad [C] = [3, 8, -11, 16, 10, 9]$$

Form the matrix M whose rows are the above coordinate vectors:

$$M = \begin{bmatrix} 1 & 2 & -3 & 4 & 0 & 1 \\ 1 & 3 & -4 & 6 & 5 & 4 \\ 3 & 8 & -11 & 16 & 10 & 9 \end{bmatrix}$$

Row reduce M to echelon form:

$$M \sim \begin{bmatrix} 1 & 2 & -3 & 4 & 0 & 1 \\ 0 & 1 & -1 & 2 & 5 & 3 \\ 0 & 2 & -2 & 4 & 10 & 6 \end{bmatrix} \sim \begin{bmatrix} 1 & 2 & -3 & 4 & 0 & 1 \\ 0 & 1 & -1 & 2 & 5 & 3 \\ 0 & 0 & 0 & 0 & 0 & 0 \end{bmatrix}$$

Since the echelon matrix has only two nonzero rows, the coordinate vectors $[A]$, $[B]$, $[C]$ span a subspace of dimension 2 and so are linearly dependent. Accordingly, the original matrices A, B, C are linearly dependent.

6.4 CHANGE OF BASIS

Let V be a real vector space of dimension n. Section 6.2 showed that once we select a basis S of V, then every vector v in V can be represented by means of an n-tuple $[v]_S$. We ask the following natural question:

> How does our representation change if we select another basis?

For the answer, we must first redefine the meaning of $[v]_S$. Specifically, if $c_1, c_2, \ldots, c_n$ are the coordinates of v relative to the basis S of V, then $[v]_S$ will denote the *coordinate column vector* of v, that is,

$$[v]_S = \begin{bmatrix} c_1 \\ c_2 \\ \ldots \\ c_n \end{bmatrix} = (c_1, c_2, \ldots, c_n)^T$$

We emphasize that in this section $[v]_S$ is an $n \times 1$ matrix, not simply an element of $\mathbf{R}^n$. (The meaning of $[v]_S$ will always be clear from its context.)

Suppose $S = \{u_1, u_2, \ldots, u_n\}$ is a basis of a vector space V, and suppose $S' = \{v_1, v_2, \ldots, v_n\}$ is another basis. For reference, we will call S the "old" basis and S' the "new" basis. One can then associate two matrices with respect to the bases S and S' as follows.

(1) Since S is a basis, each vector in the new basis S' can be written uniquely as a linear

combination of the vectors in S. Say,

$$v_1 = a_{11}u_1 + a_{12}u_2 + \cdots + a_{1n}u_n$$
$$v_2 = a_{21}u_1 + a_{22}u_2 + \cdots + a_{2n}u_n$$
$$\cdots\cdots\cdots\cdots\cdots\cdots\cdots\cdots\cdots\cdots\cdots\cdots$$
$$v_n = a_{n1}u_1 + a_{n2}u_2 + \cdots + a_{nn}u_n$$

Let P be the transpose of the above matrix of coefficients

$$P = \begin{bmatrix} a_{11} & a_{21} & \cdots & a_{n1} \\ a_{12} & a_{22} & \cdots & a_{n2} \\ \cdots\cdots\cdots\cdots\cdots\cdots \\ a_{1n} & a_{2n} & \cdots & a_{nn} \end{bmatrix}$$

That is, $P = [p_{ij}]$, where $p_{ij} = a_{ji}$. Observe that P may also be viewed as the matrix whose columns are, respectively, the coordinate column vectors of the new basis vectors v_i relative to the old basis S, that is,

$$P = ([v_1]_S, [v_2]_S, \ldots, [v_n]_S)$$

Then P is called the *change-of-basis matrix*, or *transition matrix*, from the old basis S to the new basis S'.

(2) Since S' is a basis, each vector in the old basis S can be written uniquely as a linear combination of the vectors in new basis S'. Say,

$$u_1 = b_{11}v_1 + b_{12}v_2 + \cdots + b_{1n}v_n$$
$$u_2 = b_{21}v_1 + b_{22}v_2 + \cdots + b_{2n}v_n$$
$$\cdots\cdots\cdots\cdots\cdots\cdots\cdots\cdots\cdots\cdots\cdots\cdots$$
$$u_n = b_{n1}v_1 + b_{n2}v_2 + \cdots + b_{nn}v_n$$

Let Q be the transpose of the above matrix of coefficients,

$$Q = \begin{bmatrix} b_{11} & b_{21} & \cdots & b_{n1} \\ b_{12} & b_{22} & \cdots & b_{n2} \\ \cdots\cdots\cdots\cdots\cdots\cdots \\ b_{1n} & b_{2n} & \cdots & b_{nn} \end{bmatrix}$$

That is, $Q = [q_{ij}]$, where $q_{ij} = b_{ji}$. Observe that Q may also be viewed as the matrix whose columns are the coordinate column vectors of the old basis vectors u_i relative to the new basis S', that is,

$$Q = ([u_1]_{S'}, [u_2]_{S'}, \ldots, [u_n]_{S'})$$

Analogously, Q is called the *change-of-basis matrix*, or *transition matrix*, from the new basis S' to the old basis S.

Remark: Since the vectors $v_1, v_2, \ldots, v_n$ in the new basis S' are linearly independent, the matrix P is invertible (see Problem 6.20). Similarly, Q is invertible. In fact, we show (see Problem 6.17) that $Q = P^{-1}$.

EXAMPLE 6.4 Consider the following two bases of $\mathbf{R}^2$:

$$S = \{u_1, u_2\} = \{(1, 2), (3, 5)\} \qquad S' = \{v_1, v_2\} = \{(1, -1), (1, -2)\}$$

(a) Find the change-of-basis matrix P from S to the new basis S'.

Write each of the new basis vectors of S' as a linear combination of the original basis vectors u_1 and u_2 of S. We have

$$(1, -1) = x(1, 2) + y(3, 5) \quad \text{or} \quad \begin{array}{r} x + 3y = 1 \\ 2x + 5y = -1 \end{array} \quad \text{yielding} \quad x = -8, \; y = 3$$

$$(1, -2) = x(1, 2) + y(3, 5) \quad \text{or} \quad \begin{array}{r} x + 3y = 1 \\ 2x + 5y = -2 \end{array} \quad \text{yielding} \quad x = -11, \; y = 4$$

Thus

$$v_1 = -8u_1 + 3u_2$$
$$v_2 = -11u_1 + 4u_2$$

Writing the coefficients of u_1 and u_2 as columns gives us the change-of-basis matrix P from S to S', that is,

$$P = \begin{bmatrix} -8 & -11 \\ 3 & 4 \end{bmatrix}$$

(b) Find the change-of-basis matrix Q from the basis S' to the basis S. This can be done in two ways.

Method 1: Write each basis vector in S as a linear combination of the basis vectors v_1 and v_2 of S'. We have

$$(1, 2) = x(1, -1) + y(1, -2) \quad \text{or} \quad \begin{array}{r} x + y = 1 \\ -x - 2y = 2 \end{array}, \quad \text{so} \quad \begin{array}{r} x = 4 \\ y = -3 \end{array}$$

$$(3, 5) = x(1, -1) + y(1, -2) \quad \text{or} \quad \begin{array}{r} x + y = 3 \\ -x - 2y = 5 \end{array}, \quad \text{so} \quad \begin{array}{r} x = 11 \\ y = -8 \end{array}$$

Thus

$$u_1 = 4v_1 - 3v_2$$
$$u_2 = 11v_1 - 8v_2$$

Writing the coefficients of v_1 and v_2 as columns gives us the change-of-basis matrix Q from S' back to S, that is,

$$Q = \begin{bmatrix} 4 & 11 \\ -3 & -8 \end{bmatrix}$$

Method 2: Find the inverse of the 2×2 matrix P. (See Section 3.4.) Here $|P| = -32 + 33 = 1$. Thus

$$Q = P^{-1} = \begin{bmatrix} 4 & 11 \\ -3 & -8 \end{bmatrix}$$

(Here we use the fact that Q is the inverse of P.)

EXAMPLE 6.5 Consider the following two bases of $\mathbf{R}^3$:

$$E = \{e_1, e_2, e_3\} = \{(1, 0, 0), (0, 1, 0), (0, 0, 1)\}$$

$$S = \{u_1, u_2, u_3\} = \{(1, 0, 1), (2, 1, 2), (1, 2, 2)\}$$

(a) Find the change-of-basis matrix P from the basis E to the basis S.

Since E is the usual basis, we can immediately write each basis element of S as a linear combination of the basis elements of E:

$$
\begin{aligned}
u_1 &= (1, 0, 1) = e_1 +   e_3 \\
u_2 &= (2, 1, 2) = 2e_1 + e_2 + 2e_3 \\
u_3 &= (1, 2, 2) = e_1 + 2e_2 + 2e_3
\end{aligned}
$$

Writing the coefficients of e_1, e_2, e_3 as columns gives us

$$
P = \begin{bmatrix} 1 & 2 & 1 \\ 0 & 1 & 2 \\ 1 & 2 & 2 \end{bmatrix}
$$

Observe that P is simply the matrix whose columns are the basic vectors of S. This is true only because the original basis was the usual basis E.

(b) Find the change-of-basis matrix Q from the basis S to the basis E.

Find P^{-1}. Form the matrix $M = [P, I]$ and row reduce M to row canonical form:

$$
M = \begin{bmatrix} 1 & 2 & 1 & \vdots & 1 & 0 & 0 \\ 0 & 1 & 2 & \vdots & 0 & 1 & 0 \\ 1 & 2 & 2 & \vdots & 0 & 0 & 1 \end{bmatrix}
\sim
\begin{bmatrix} 1 & 2 & 1 & \vdots & 1 & 0 & 0 \\ 0 & 1 & 2 & \vdots & 0 & 1 & 0 \\ 0 & 0 & 1 & \vdots & -1 & 0 & 1 \end{bmatrix}
$$

$$
\sim
\begin{bmatrix} 1 & 2 & 0 & \vdots & 2 & 0 & -1 \\ 0 & 1 & 0 & \vdots & 2 & 1 & -2 \\ 0 & 0 & 1 & \vdots & -1 & 0 & 1 \end{bmatrix}
\sim
\begin{bmatrix} 1 & 0 & 0 & \vdots & -2 & -2 & 3 \\ 0 & 1 & 0 & \vdots & 2 & 1 & -2 \\ 0 & 0 & 1 & \vdots & -1 & 0 & 1 \end{bmatrix}
$$

Thus

$$
Q = P^{-1} = \begin{bmatrix} -2 & -2 & 3 \\ 2 & 1 & -2 \\ -1 & 0 & 1 \end{bmatrix}
$$

(Here we use the fact that Q is the inverse of P.)

The result in Example 6.5 is true for all $\mathbf{R}^n$. We state this result formally since it occurs often.

Proposition 6.2: The change-of-basis matrix from the usual basis E of $\mathbf{R}^n$ to any basis S of $\mathbf{R}^n$ is the matrix P whose columns are the basis vectors of S.

The next theorem (proved in Problem 6.21) tells us how the coordinate (column) vectors are affected by a change of basis.

Theorem 6.3: Let P be the change-of-basis matrix from a basis S to a basis S' in a vector space V. Then, for any vector $v \in V$, we have

$$
P[v]_{S'} = [v]_S \quad \text{and hence} \quad P^{-1}[v]_S = [v]_{S'}
$$

Remark 1: Although P is called the change-of-basis matrix from the old basis S to the new basis S', it is P^{-1} which transforms the coordinates of v relative to the original basis S into the coordinates of v relative to the new basis S'.

Remark 2: Because of the above theorem, many texts call $Q = P^{-1}$ the change-of-basis matrix from the old basis S to the new basis S', rather than P. Some such texts then refer to Q as the change-of-coordinates matrix.

We illustrate the above theorem in the case dim $V = 3$. Suppose P is the change-of-basis matrix from the basis $S = \{u_1, u_2, u_3\}$ to the basis $S' = \{v_1, v_2, v_3\}$, say,

$$v_1 = a_1u_1 + a_2u_2 + a_3u_3$$
$$v_2 = b_1u_1 + b_2u_2 + b_3u_3$$
$$v_3 = c_1u_1 + c_2u_2 + c_3u_3$$

Hence

$$P = \begin{bmatrix} a_1 & b_1 & c_1 \\ a_2 & b_2 & c_2 \\ a_3 & b_3 & c_3 \end{bmatrix}$$

Now suppose $v \in V$ and, say, $v = k_1v_1 + k_2v_2 + k_3v_3$. Then, substituting for v_1, v_2, v_3 from above, we obtain

$$v = k_1(a_1u_1 + a_2u_2 + a_3u_3) + k_2(b_1u_1 + b_2u_2 + b_3u_3) + k_3(c_1u_1 + c_2u_2 + c_3u_3)$$
$$= (a_1k_1 + b_1k_2 + c_1k_3)u_1 + (a_2k_1 + b_2k_2 + c_2k_3)u_2 + (a_3k_1 + b_3k_2 + c_3k_3)u_3$$

Thus

$$[v]_{S'} = \begin{bmatrix} k_1 \\ k_2 \\ k_3 \end{bmatrix} \quad \text{and} \quad [v]_S = \begin{bmatrix} a_1k_1 + b_1k_2 + c_1k_3 \\ a_2k_1 + b_2k_2 + c_2k_3 \\ a_3k_1 + b_3k_2 + c_3k_3 \end{bmatrix}$$

Accordingly,

$$P[v]_{S'} = \begin{bmatrix} a_1 & b_1 & c_1 \\ a_2 & b_2 & c_2 \\ a_3 & b_3 & c_3 \end{bmatrix}\begin{bmatrix} k_1 \\ k_2 \\ k_3 \end{bmatrix} = \begin{bmatrix} a_1k_1 + b_1k_2 + c_1k_3 \\ a_2k_1 + b_2k_2 + c_2k_3 \\ a_3k_1 + b_3k_2 + c_3k_3 \end{bmatrix} = [v]_S$$

Also, multiplying the above equation by P^{-1}, we have

$$P^{-1}[v]_S = P^{-1}P[v]_{S'} = 1[v]_{S'} = [v]_{S'}$$

EXAMPLE 6.6 Find the coordinates of $v = (5, -2)$ in $\mathbf{R}^2$ relative to the following basis of $\mathbf{R}^2$:

$$S = \{u_1, u_2\} = \{(1, 3), (1, 4)\}$$

This can be done in two ways.

Method 1: Write v as a linear combination of u_1 and u_2. We have

$$(5, -2) = x(1, 3) + y(1, 4) \quad \text{or} \quad \begin{array}{r} x + y = 5 \\ 3x + 4y = -2 \end{array}$$

yielding $x = 22$, $y = -17$. Hence $[v]_S = [22, -17]^T$.

Method 2: Let E denote the usual basis. Then $[v]_E = [5, -2]^T$. Also, the change-of-basis matrix P from the usual basis E to S is the matrix whose columns are the basis elements u_1 and u_2 of S. Thus

$$P = \begin{bmatrix} 1 & 1 \\ 3 & 4 \end{bmatrix} \quad \text{and hence} \quad P^{-1} = \begin{bmatrix} 4 & -1 \\ -3 & 1 \end{bmatrix}$$

(We used the formula for the inverse of a 2×2 matrix to find P^{-1}.)
Then, by Theorem 6.3,

$$[v]_S = P^{-1}[v]_E = \begin{bmatrix} 4 & -1 \\ -3 & 1 \end{bmatrix}\begin{bmatrix} 5 \\ -2 \end{bmatrix} = \begin{bmatrix} 22 \\ -17 \end{bmatrix}$$

Remark: Suppose $S = \{u_1, u_2, \ldots, u_n\}$ is a basis of a vector space V, and suppose $P = [p_{ij}]$ is any nonsingular matrix. Then the n vectors

$$v_i = p_{1i}u_1 + p_{2i}u_2 + \cdots + p_{ni}u_n, \qquad i = 1, 2, \ldots, n$$

are linearly independent (see Problem 6.20), and hence they form another basis S' of V. Moreover, P will be the change-of-basis matrix from S to the new basis S'.

Solved Problems

COORDINATES

6.1. Relative to the basis $S = \{u_1, u_2\} = \{(1, 1), (2, 3)\}$ of $\mathbf{R}^2$, find the coordinate vector of v, where: (a) $v = (4, -3)$; (b) $v = (a, b)$.

In each case set

$$v = xu_1 + yu_2 = x(1, 1) + y(2, 3) = (x + 2y, x + 3y)$$

and then solve for x and y.

(a) We have

$$(4, -3) = (x + 2y, x + 3y) \qquad \text{or} \qquad \begin{matrix} x + 2y = 4 \\ x + 3y = -3 \end{matrix}$$

The solution is $x = 18$, $y = -7$. Hence $[v] = [18, -7]$.

(b) We have

$$(a, b) = (x + 2y, x + 3y) \qquad \text{or} \qquad \begin{matrix} x + 2y = a \\ x + 3y = b \end{matrix}$$

The solution is $x = 3a - 2b$, $y = -a + b$. Hence $[v] = [3a - 2b, -a + b]$.

6.2. Relative to the usual basis $E = \{(1, 0, 0), (0, 1, 0), (0, 0, 1)\}$ of $\mathbf{R}^3$, find the coordinate vector $[v]_E$ of v, where: (a) $v = (3, -5, 2)$; (b) $v = (a, b, c)$.

Relative to the usual basis E, the coordinates of $[v]_E$ are the same as v itself. That is, (a) $[v]_E = [3, -5, 2]$; (b) $[v]_E = [a, b, c]$.

6.3. Repeat Problem 6.2 for the basis $S = \{u_1, u_2, u_3\} = \{(1, 1, 1), (1, 1, 0), (1, 0, 0)\}$ of $\mathbf{R}^3$.

Set v as a linear combination of u_1, u_2, u_3 using unknown scalars x, y, z, that is, set

$$v = xu_1 + yu_2 + zu_3 = x(1, 1, 1) + y(1, 1, 0) + z(1, 0, 0)$$
$$= (x + y + z, x + y, x)$$

and then solve for the solution vector $[x, y, z]$.   (The solution is unique since the vectors are linearly independent.)

(a)   We have

$$(3, -5, 2) = (x + y + z, x + y, x) \qquad \text{or} \qquad x + y + z = 3, \ x + y = -5, \ x = 2$$

Solving the system yields $x = 2$, $y = -7$, $z = 8$.   Thus $[v] = [2, -7, 8]$.

(b)   We have

$$(a, b, c) = (x + y + z, x + y, x) \qquad \text{or} \qquad x + y + z = a, \ x + y = b, \ x = c$$

Solving the system yields $x = c$, $y = b - c$, $z = a - b$.   Thus $[v] = [c, b - c, a - b]$.

6.4.   Consider the vector space $P_3(t)$ of polynomials of degree ≤ 3.

(a)   Show that $S = \{(t - 1)^3, (t - 1)^2, (t - 1), 1\}$ is a basis of $P_3(t)$.

(b)   Find the coordinate vector $[v]$ of $v = 3t^3 + 4t^2 + 2t - 5$ relative to S.

(a)   The degree of $(t - 1)^k$ is k.   Writing the polynomials of S in reverse order, we see that no polynomial is a linear combination of preceding polynomials.   Thus the polynomials are linearly independent, and since $\dim P_3(t) = 4$, they form a basis of $P_3(t)$.

(b)   Set v as a linear combination of the basis vectors using unknown scalars x, y, z, and s. We have

$$\begin{aligned}
v &= 3t^3 + 4t^2 + 2t - 5 = x(t - 1)^3 + y(t - 1)^2 + z(t - 1) + s(1) \\
&= x(t^3 - 3t^2 + 3t - 1) + y(t^2 - 2t + 1) + z(t - 1) + s(1) \\
&= xt^3 - 3xt^2 + 3xt - x + yt^2 - 2yt + y + zt - z + s \\
&= xt^3 + (-3x + y)t^2 + (3x - 2y + z)t + (-x + y - z + s)
\end{aligned}$$

Then set coefficients of the same powers of t equal to each other to obtain

$$x = 3, \qquad -3x + y = 4, \qquad 3x - 2y + z = 2, \qquad -x + y - z + s = -5$$

Solving the system yields $x = 3$, $y = 13$, $z = 19$, and $s = 4$.   Thus $[v] = [3, 13, 19, 4]$.

6.5.   Find the coordinates of $v = 3t^3 - 4t^2 + 2t - 5$ relative to the basis $E = \{t^3, t^2, t, 1\}$ of $P_3(t)$.

The (usual) basis E of $P_3(t)$ consists of the powers of t.   Hence simply write down the corresponding coefficients to obtain $[v] = [3, -4, 2, -5]$.

6.6.   In the vector space $M = M_{2,2}$ of 2×2 matrices, find the coordinate vector $[A]$ of the matrix A relative to the basis

$$S = \left\{ \begin{bmatrix} 1 & 1 \\ 1 & 1 \end{bmatrix}, \begin{bmatrix} 0 & -1 \\ 1 & 0 \end{bmatrix}, \begin{bmatrix} 1 & -1 \\ 0 & 0 \end{bmatrix}, \begin{bmatrix} 1 & 0 \\ 0 & 0 \end{bmatrix} \right\} \qquad \text{where} \qquad A = \begin{bmatrix} 2 & 3 \\ 4 & -7 \end{bmatrix}$$

Set A as a linear combination of the basis vectors using unknown scalars x, y, z, and t as follows:

$$\begin{aligned}
A = \begin{bmatrix} 2 & 3 \\ 4 & -7 \end{bmatrix} &= x \begin{bmatrix} 1 & 1 \\ 1 & 1 \end{bmatrix} + y \begin{bmatrix} 0 & -1 \\ 1 & 0 \end{bmatrix} + z \begin{bmatrix} 1 & -1 \\ 0 & 0 \end{bmatrix} + t \begin{bmatrix} 1 & 0 \\ 0 & 0 \end{bmatrix} \\
&= \begin{bmatrix} x + z + t & x - y - z \\ x + y & x \end{bmatrix}
\end{aligned}$$

Set corresponding entries equal to each other to obtain the system

$$x + z + t = 2, \qquad x - y - z = 3, \qquad x + y = 4, \qquad x = -7$$

Solving the system yields $x = -7$, $y = 11$, $z = -21$, $t = 30$. Thus $[A] = [-7, 11, -21, 30]$. (Note that the coordinate vector of A is a vector in $\mathbf{R}^4$ since dim $\mathbf{M} = 4$.)

6.7. Repeat Problem 6.6 for the usual basis E of $\mathbf{M}$, that is, for

$$E = \left\{ \begin{bmatrix} 1 & 0 \\ 0 & 0 \end{bmatrix}, \begin{bmatrix} 0 & 1 \\ 0 & 0 \end{bmatrix}, \begin{bmatrix} 0 & 0 \\ 1 & 0 \end{bmatrix}, \begin{bmatrix} 0 & 0 \\ 0 & 1 \end{bmatrix} \right\}$$

Expressing A as a linear combination of the basis matrices yields

$$\begin{bmatrix} 2 & 3 \\ 4 & -7 \end{bmatrix} = x \begin{bmatrix} 1 & 0 \\ 0 & 0 \end{bmatrix} + y \begin{bmatrix} 0 & 1 \\ 0 & 0 \end{bmatrix} + z \begin{bmatrix} 0 & 0 \\ 1 & 0 \end{bmatrix} + t \begin{bmatrix} 0 & 0 \\ 0 & 1 \end{bmatrix} = \begin{bmatrix} x & y \\ z & t \end{bmatrix}$$

Thus $x = 2$, $y = 3$, $z = 4$, $t = -7$. Hence $[A] = [2, 3, 4, -7]$, whose components are the elements of A written row by row.

Remark: This result is true in general, that is, if A is any $m \times n$ matrix in $\mathbf{M} = \mathbf{M}_{m,n}$, then the coordinates of A relative to the usual basis of $\mathbf{M}$ are the elements of A written row by row.

APPLICATIONS OF COORDINATES

6.8. In the space $\mathbf{M} = \mathbf{M}_{2,3}$ determine whether or not the following matrices are linearly dependent:

$$A = \begin{bmatrix} 1 & 2 & 3 \\ 4 & 0 & 5 \end{bmatrix}, \qquad B = \begin{bmatrix} 2 & 4 & 7 \\ 10 & 1 & 13 \end{bmatrix}, \qquad C = \begin{bmatrix} 1 & 2 & 5 \\ 8 & 2 & 11 \end{bmatrix}$$

If the matrices are linearly dependent, find the dimension and a basis of the subspace W of $\mathbf{M}$ spanned by the matrices.

The coordinate vectors of the above matrices relative to the usual basis of $\mathbf{M}$ are as follows:

$$[A] = [1, 2, 3, 4, 0, 5], \qquad [B] = [2, 4, 7, 10, 1, 13], \qquad [C] = [1, 2, 5, 8, 2, 11]$$

Form the matrix M whose rows are the above coordinate vectors,

$$M = \begin{bmatrix} 1 & 2 & 3 & 4 & 0 & 5 \\ 2 & 4 & 7 & 10 & 1 & 13 \\ 1 & 2 & 5 & 8 & 2 & 11 \end{bmatrix}$$

Row reduce M to echelon form, obtaining

$$M \sim \begin{bmatrix} 1 & 2 & 3 & 4 & 0 & 5 \\ 0 & 0 & 1 & 2 & 1 & 3 \\ 0 & 0 & 2 & 4 & 2 & 6 \end{bmatrix} \sim \begin{bmatrix} 1 & 2 & 3 & 4 & 0 & 5 \\ 0 & 0 & 1 & 2 & 1 & 3 \\ 0 & 0 & 0 & 0 & 0 & 0 \end{bmatrix}$$

Since the echelon matrix has only two nonzero rows, the coordinate vectors $[A]$, $[B]$, and $[C]$ span a space of dimension 2, and so they are linearly dependent. Thus A, B, and C are linearly dependent. Furthermore, dim $W = 2$, and the matrices

$$w_1 = \begin{bmatrix} 1 & 2 & 3 \\ 4 & 0 & 5 \end{bmatrix} \qquad \text{and} \qquad w_2 = \begin{bmatrix} 0 & 0 & 1 \\ 2 & 1 & 3 \end{bmatrix}$$

corresponding to the nonzero rows of the echelon matrix, form a basis of W.

6.9. Determine whether or not the following polynomials are linearly dependent:

$$u_1 = t^3 + 3t^2 - 2t + 4, \qquad u_2 = 2t^3 + 7t^2 - 2t + 5, \qquad u_3 = t^3 + 5t^2 + 2t - 2$$

If they are linearly dependent, find the dimension and a basis of the subspace W spanned by the polynomials.

The coordinate vectors of the polynomials relative to the basis $\{t^3, t^2, t, 1\}$ are as follows:

$$[u_1] = [1, 3, -2, 4], \qquad [u_2] = [2, 7, -2, 5], \qquad [u_3] = [1, 5, 2, -2]$$

Form the matrix M whose rows are the above coordinate vectors and row reduce to echelon form:

$$M = \begin{bmatrix} 1 & 3 & -2 & 4 \\ 2 & 7 & -2 & 5 \\ 1 & 5 & 2 & -2 \end{bmatrix} \sim \begin{bmatrix} 1 & 3 & -2 & 4 \\ 0 & 1 & 2 & -3 \\ 0 & 2 & 4 & -6 \end{bmatrix} \sim \begin{bmatrix} 1 & 3 & -2 & 4 \\ 0 & 1 & 2 & -3 \\ 0 & 0 & 0 & 0 \end{bmatrix}$$

Since the echelon matrix has only two nonzero rows, the original three polynomials span a space of dimension 2, and hence they are linearly dependent. That is, dim $W = 2$ and the polynomials

$$w_1 = t^3 + 3t^2 - 2t + 4 \qquad \text{and} \qquad w_2 = t^2 + 2t - 3$$

corresponding to the nonzero rows of the echelon matrix, form a basis of W.

6.10. In the vector space $\mathbf{M} = \mathbf{M}_{2,2}$ determine whether or not the matrices

$$A = \begin{bmatrix} 1 & 1 \\ 0 & 0 \end{bmatrix}, \qquad B = \begin{bmatrix} 0 & 1 \\ 1 & 0 \end{bmatrix}, \qquad C = \begin{bmatrix} 0 & 0 \\ 1 & 1 \end{bmatrix}, \qquad D = \begin{bmatrix} 0 & 0 \\ 0 & 1 \end{bmatrix}$$

form a basis for $\mathbf{M}$.

The coordinate vectors of the matrices relative to the usual basis of $\mathbf{M}$ are, respectively,

$$[A] = [1, 1, 0, 0], \qquad [B] = [0, 1, 1, 0], \qquad [C] = [0, 0, 1, 1], \qquad [D] = [0, 0, 0, 1]$$

The coordinate vectors form a matrix in echelon form, and hence they are linearly independent. Thus the four corresponding matrices are linearly independent. Moreover, since dim $\mathbf{M} = 4$, they form a basis of $\mathbf{M}$.

6.11. Consider the subspaces $U = \text{span}\,(u_1, u_2, u_3)$ and $W = \text{span}\,(w_1, w_2, w_3)$ of $\mathbf{P}_3(t)$, where

$$u_1 = t^3 + 2t^2 + t + 3, \qquad u_2 = 2t^3 + 5t^2 + 3t + 8, \qquad u_3 = t^3 + 4t^2 + 3t + 7$$
$$w_1 = t^3 + 3t^2 + 4t + 1, \qquad w_2 = 2t^3 + 5t^2 + 5t + 4, \qquad w_3 = t^3 + 5t^2 + 10t - 3$$

Find: (a) dim $(U + W)$; (b) dim $(U \cap W)$.

(a) First find the dimension and a basis for U using the coordinate vectors of the polynomials (relative to the basis $S = \{t^3, t^2, t, 1\}$). Specifically, form the matrix M_1 whose rows are the coordinate vectors of u_1, u_2, and u_3 and then row reduce to echelon form:

$$M_1 = \begin{bmatrix} 1 & 2 & 1 & 3 \\ 2 & 5 & 3 & 8 \\ 1 & 4 & 3 & 7 \end{bmatrix} \sim \begin{bmatrix} 1 & 2 & 1 & 3 \\ 0 & 1 & 1 & 2 \\ 0 & 2 & 2 & 4 \end{bmatrix} \sim \begin{bmatrix} 1 & 2 & 1 & 3 \\ 0 & 1 & 1 & 2 \\ 0 & 0 & 0 & 0 \end{bmatrix}$$

Thus dim $U = 2$ and $t^3 + 2t^2 + t + 3$ and $t^2 + t + 2$ form a basis of U. Repeat for the subspace W. Specifically, form the matrix M_2 whose rows are the coordinate vectors of

w_1, w_2, w_3 and then row reduce to echelon form:

$$M_2 = \begin{bmatrix} 1 & 3 & 4 & 1 \\ 2 & 5 & 5 & 4 \\ 1 & 5 & 10 & -3 \end{bmatrix} \sim \begin{bmatrix} 1 & 3 & 4 & 1 \\ 0 & -1 & -3 & 2 \\ 0 & 2 & 6 & -4 \end{bmatrix} \sim \begin{bmatrix} 1 & 3 & 4 & 1 \\ 0 & 1 & 3 & -2 \\ 0 & 0 & 0 & 0 \end{bmatrix}$$

Thus dim $W = 2$ and $t^3 + 3t^2 + 4t + 1$ and $t^2 + 3t - 2$ form a basis of W.

$U + W$ is the space spanned by the six original polynomials and also the four polynomials forming bases for U and W. Hence form the matrix M whose rows come from the basis vectors and row reduce to echelon form:

$$M = \begin{bmatrix} 1 & 2 & 1 & 3 \\ 0 & 1 & 1 & 2 \\ 1 & 3 & 4 & 1 \\ 0 & 1 & 3 & -2 \end{bmatrix} \sim \begin{bmatrix} 1 & 2 & 1 & 3 \\ 0 & 1 & 1 & 2 \\ 0 & 1 & 3 & -2 \\ 0 & 1 & 3 & -2 \end{bmatrix} \sim \begin{bmatrix} 1 & 2 & 1 & 3 \\ 0 & 1 & 1 & 2 \\ 0 & 0 & 2 & -4 \\ 0 & 0 & 0 & 0 \end{bmatrix}$$

Thus dim $(U + W) = 3$.

(b)   By Theorem 5.9, dim $(U \cap W) = $ dim $U + $ dim $W - $ dim $(U + W) = 2 + 2 - 3 = 1$.

CHANGE OF BASIS

The coordinate vector $[v]_S$ in this section will always denote a column vector, that is,

$$[v]_S = [a_1, a_2, \ldots, a_n]^T$$

6.12.   Consider the following basis of $\mathbf{R}^2$:

$$E = \{e_1, e_2\} = \{(1, 0), (0, 1)\} \qquad \text{and} \qquad S = \{u_1, u_2\} = \{(1, 3), (1, 4)\}$$

(a)   Find the change-of-basis matrix P from the usual basis E to S.

(b)   Find the change-of-basis matrix Q from S back to E.

(c)   Find the coordinate vector $[v]$ of $v = (5, -3)$ relative to S.

(a)   Since E is the usual basis of $\mathbf{R}^2$, simply write the basis vectors in S as columns, that is,

$$P = \begin{bmatrix} 1 & 1 \\ 3 & 4 \end{bmatrix}$$

(b)   **Method 1:**   Use the definition of the change-of-basis matrix. That is, express each vector in E as a linear combination of the vectors in S. We do this by first finding the coordinates of an arbitrary vector $v = (a, b)$ relative to S. We have

$$(a, b) = x(1, 3) + y(1, 4) = (x + y, 3x + 4y) \qquad \text{or} \qquad \begin{aligned} x + y &= a \\ 3x + 4y &= b \end{aligned}$$

Solve for x and y to obtain $x = 4a - b$, $y = -3a + b$. Thus

$$v = (4a - b)u_1 + (-3a + b)u_2 \qquad \text{and} \qquad [v]_S = [(a, b)]_S = [4a - b, -3a + b]^T$$

Using the above formula for $[v]_S$ and writing the coordinates of the e_i as columns yields

$$\begin{aligned} e_1 &= (1, 0) = 4u_1 - 3u_2 \\ e_2 &= (0, 1) = -u_1 + u_2 \end{aligned} \qquad \text{and} \qquad Q = \begin{bmatrix} 4 & -1 \\ -3 & 1 \end{bmatrix}$$

Method 2:   Find P^{-1}, say by using the formula for the inverse of a 2×2 matrix. We have

$$P^{-1} = \begin{bmatrix} 4 & -1 \\ -3 & 1 \end{bmatrix}$$

Then $Q = P^{-1}$.

(c) **Method 1:**   Write v as a linear combination of the vectors in S, say by using the above formula for $v = (a, b)$.   We have

$$v = (5, -3) = 23u_1 - 18u_2 \quad \text{and so} \quad [v]_S = [23, -18]^T$$

Method 2:   Use Theorem 6.3 that $[v]_S = P^{-1}[v]_E$ and the fact that $[v]_E = [5, -3]^T$. We have

$$[v]_S = P^{-1}[v]_E = \begin{bmatrix} 4 & -1 \\ -3 & 1 \end{bmatrix}\begin{bmatrix} 5 \\ -3 \end{bmatrix} = \begin{bmatrix} 23 \\ -18 \end{bmatrix}$$

6.13. The vectors $u_1 = (1, 2, 0)$, $u_2 = (1, 3, 2)$, $u_3 = (0, 1, 3)$ form a basis S of $\mathbf{R}^3$.   Find:

(a) The change-of-basis matrix P from the usual basis $E = \{e_1, e_2, e_3\}$ of $\mathbf{R}^3$ to the basis S.

(b) The change-of-basis matrix Q from the above basis S back to the usual basis E of $\mathbf{R}^3$.

(a) Since E is the usual basis, simply write the basis vectors of S as columns:

$$P = \begin{bmatrix} 1 & 1 & 0 \\ 2 & 3 & 1 \\ 0 & 2 & 3 \end{bmatrix}$$

(b) **Method 1:**   Express each basis vector of E as a linear combination of the basis vectors of S by first finding the coordinates of an arbitrary vector $v = (a, b, c)$ relative to the basis S. We have

$$\begin{bmatrix} a \\ b \\ c \end{bmatrix} = x\begin{bmatrix} 1 \\ 2 \\ 0 \end{bmatrix} + y\begin{bmatrix} 1 \\ 3 \\ 2 \end{bmatrix} + z\begin{bmatrix} 0 \\ 1 \\ 3 \end{bmatrix} \quad \text{or} \quad \begin{aligned} x + y \quad\;\; &= a \\ 2x + 3y + z &= b \\ 2y + 3z &= c \end{aligned}$$

Solve for x, y, z to get $x = 7a - 3b + c$, $y = -6a + 3b - c$, $z = 4a - 2b + c$.   Thus

$$v = (a, b, c) = (7a - 3b + c)u_1 + (-6a + 3b - c)u_2 + (4a - 2b + c)u_3$$

or $[v]_S = [(a, b, c)]_S = [7a - 3b + c, -6a + 3b - c, 4a - 2b + c]^T$

Using the above formula for $[v]_S$ and then writing the coordinates of the e_i as columns yields

$$\begin{aligned} e_1 = (1, 0, 0) &= \quad 7u_1 - 6u_2 + 4u_3 \\ e_2 = (0, 1, 0) &= -3u_1 + 3u_2 - 2u_3 \\ e_3 = (0, 0, 1) &= \quad u_1 - u_2 + u_3 \end{aligned} \quad \text{and} \quad Q = \begin{bmatrix} 7 & -3 & 1 \\ -6 & 3 & -1 \\ 4 & -2 & 1 \end{bmatrix}$$

Method 2:   Find P^{-1} by row reducing $M = [P, I]$ to the form $[I, P^{-1}]$:

$$M = \begin{bmatrix} 1 & 1 & 0 & | & 1 & 0 & 0 \\ 2 & 3 & 1 & | & 0 & 1 & 0 \\ 0 & 2 & 3 & | & 0 & 0 & 1 \end{bmatrix} \sim \begin{bmatrix} 1 & 1 & 0 & | & 1 & 0 & 0 \\ 0 & 1 & 1 & | & -2 & 1 & 0 \\ 0 & 2 & 3 & | & 0 & 0 & 1 \end{bmatrix}$$

$$\sim \begin{bmatrix} 1 & 1 & 0 & | & 1 & 0 & 0 \\ 0 & 1 & 1 & | & -2 & 1 & 0 \\ 0 & 0 & 1 & | & 4 & -2 & 1 \end{bmatrix} \sim \begin{bmatrix} 1 & 1 & 0 & | & 1 & 0 & 0 \\ 0 & 1 & 0 & | & -6 & 3 & -1 \\ 0 & 0 & 1 & | & 4 & -2 & 1 \end{bmatrix}$$

$$\sim \begin{bmatrix} 1 & 0 & 0 & | & 7 & -3 & 1 \\ 0 & 1 & 0 & | & -6 & 3 & 1 \\ 0 & 0 & 1 & | & 4 & -2 & 1 \end{bmatrix}$$

Thus $Q = P^{-1} = \begin{bmatrix} 7 & -3 & 1 \\ -6 & 3 & -1 \\ 4 & -2 & 1 \end{bmatrix}$.

6.14. Suppose the x and y axes in the plane $\mathbf{R}^2$ are rotated counterclockwise $45°$ so that the new x' and y' axes are along the lines $y = x$ and $y = -x$, respectively.   Find:

(a)   The change-of-basis matrix P.

(b)   The coordinates of the point $A(5, 6)$ under the given rotation.

(a)   The unit vectors in the direction of the new x' and y' axes are

$$u_1 = (\sqrt{2}/2, \sqrt{2}/2) \qquad \text{and} \qquad u_2 = (-\sqrt{2}/2, \sqrt{2}/2)$$

(The unit vectors in the direction of the original x and y axes are the usual basis of $\mathbf{R}^2$.) Thus write the coordinates of u_1 and u_2 as columns to obtain

$$P = \begin{bmatrix} \sqrt{2}/2 & -\sqrt{2}/2 \\ \sqrt{2}/2 & \sqrt{2}/2 \end{bmatrix}$$

(b)   Multiply the coordinates of the point by P^{-1}:

$$\begin{bmatrix} \sqrt{2}/2 & \sqrt{2}/2 \\ -\sqrt{2}/2 & \sqrt{2}/2 \end{bmatrix}\begin{bmatrix} 5 \\ 6 \end{bmatrix} = \begin{bmatrix} 11\sqrt{2}/2 \\ \sqrt{2}/2 \end{bmatrix}$$

(Since P is orthogonal, P^{-1} is simply the transpose of P.)

6.15. The vectors $u_1 = (1, 1, 0)$, $u_2 = (0, 1, 1)$, $u_3 = (1, 2, 2)$ form a basis S of $\mathbf{R}^3$.   Find the coordinates of an arbitrary vector $v = (a, b, c)$ relative to the basis S.

Method 1:   Express v as a linear combination of u_1, u_2, u_3 using unknowns x, y, z.   We have

$$(a, b, c) = x(1, 1, 0) + y(0, 1, 1) + z(1, 2, 2) = (x + z, x + y + 2z, y + 2z)$$

which yields the system

$$\begin{array}{llll} x + \quad\ z = a & & x + \quad\ z = a & & x + \quad\ z = a \\ x + y + 2z = b & \text{or} & \quad\ y + \ z = -a + b & \text{or} & \quad\ y + z = -a + b \\ \quad\ y + 2z = c & & \quad\ y + 2z = c & & \qquad\quad z = a - b + c \end{array}$$

Solving by back-substitution yields $x = b - c$, $y = -2a + 2b - c$, and $z = a - b + c$. Thus

$$[v]_S = [b - c, -2a + 2b - c, a - b + c]^T$$

Method 2:   Find P^{-1} by row reducing $M = [P, I]$ to the form $[I, P^{-1}]$, where P is the change-of-basis matrix from the usual basis E to S or, in other words, the matrix whose columns are the basis vectors of S.   We have

$$M = \begin{bmatrix} 1 & 0 & 1 & \vdots & 1 & 0 & 0 \\ 1 & 1 & 2 & \vdots & 0 & 1 & 0 \\ 0 & 1 & 2 & \vdots & 0 & 0 & 1 \end{bmatrix} \sim \begin{bmatrix} 1 & 0 & 1 & \vdots & 1 & 0 & 0 \\ 0 & 1 & 1 & \vdots & -1 & 1 & 0 \\ 0 & 1 & 2 & \vdots & 0 & 0 & 1 \end{bmatrix}$$

$$\sim \begin{bmatrix} 1 & 0 & 1 & \vdots & 1 & 0 & 0 \\ 0 & 1 & 1 & \vdots & -1 & 1 & 0 \\ 0 & 0 & 1 & \vdots & 1 & -1 & 1 \end{bmatrix} \sim \begin{bmatrix} 1 & 0 & 0 & \vdots & 0 & 1 & -1 \\ 0 & 1 & 0 & \vdots & -2 & 2 & -1 \\ 0 & 0 & 1 & \vdots & 1 & -1 & 1 \end{bmatrix} = [I, P^{-1}]$$

Thus

$$[v]_S = P^{-1}[v]_E = \begin{bmatrix} 0 & 1 & -1 \\ -2 & 2 & -1 \\ 1 & -1 & 1 \end{bmatrix} \begin{bmatrix} a \\ b \\ c \end{bmatrix} = \begin{bmatrix} b - c \\ -2a + 2b - c \\ a - b + c \end{bmatrix}$$

6.16. Consider the following bases of $\mathbf{R}^2$:

$$S = \{u_1, u_2\} = \{(1, -2), (3, -4)\} \quad \text{and} \quad S' = \{v_1, v_2\} = \{(1, 3), (3, 8)\}$$

(a)   Find the coordinates of $v = (a, b)$ relative to the basis S.

(b)   Find the change-of-basis matrix P from S to S'.

(c)   Find the coordinates of $v = (a, b)$ relative to the basis S'.

(d)   Find the change-of-basis matrix Q from S' back to S.

(e)   Verify $Q = P^{-1}$.

(f)   Show that, for any vector $v = (a, b)$ in $\mathbf{R}^2$, $P^{-1}[v]_s = [v]_{s'}$.   (See Theorem 6.3.)

(a)   Let $v = xu_1 + yu_2$ for unknowns x and y, that is,

$$\begin{bmatrix} a \\ b \end{bmatrix} = x\begin{bmatrix} 1 \\ -2 \end{bmatrix} + y\begin{bmatrix} 3 \\ -4 \end{bmatrix} \quad \text{or} \quad \begin{matrix} x + 3y = a \\ -2x - 4y = b \end{matrix} \quad \text{or} \quad \begin{matrix} x + 3y = a \\ 2y = 2a + b \end{matrix}$$

Solve for x and y in terms of a and b to get $x = -2a - \frac{3}{2}b$ and $y = a + \frac{1}{2}b$. Thus

$$(a, b) = (-2a - \tfrac{3}{2}b)u_1 + (a + \tfrac{1}{2}b)u_2 \quad \text{or} \quad [(a, b)]_S = [-2a - \tfrac{3}{2}b, a + \tfrac{1}{2}b]^T$$

(b)   Use part (a) to write each of the basis vectors v_1 and v_2 of S' as a linear combination of the basis vectors u_1 and u_2 of S, that is,

$$v_1 = (1, 3) = (-2 - \tfrac{9}{2})u_1 + (1 + \tfrac{3}{2})u_2 = -\tfrac{13}{2}u_1 + \tfrac{5}{2}u_2$$
$$v_2 = (3, 8) = (-6 - 12)u_1 + (3 + 4)u_2 = -18u_1 + 7u_2$$

Then P is the matrix whose columns are the coordinates of v_1 and v_2 relative to the basis S, that is,

$$P = \begin{bmatrix} -\tfrac{13}{2} & -18 \\ \tfrac{5}{2} & 7 \end{bmatrix}$$

(c)   Let $v = xv_1 + yv_2$ for unknown scalars x and y:

$$\begin{bmatrix} a \\ b \end{bmatrix} = x\begin{bmatrix} 1 \\ 3 \end{bmatrix} + y\begin{bmatrix} 3 \\ 8 \end{bmatrix} \quad \text{or} \quad \begin{matrix} x + 3y = a \\ 3x + 8y = b \end{matrix} \quad \text{or} \quad \begin{matrix} x + 3y = a \\ -y = b - 3a \end{matrix}$$

Solving for x and y to get $x = -8a + 3b$ and $y = 3a - b$. Thus

$$(a, b) = (-8a + 3b)v_1 + (3a - b)v_2 \quad \text{or} \quad [(a, b)]_{S'} = [-8a + 3b, 3a - b]^T$$

(d) Use part (c) to express each of the basis vectors u_1 and u_2 of S as a linear combination of the basis vectors v_1 and v_2 of S':

$$u_1 = (1, -2) = (-8 - 6)v_1 + (3 + 2)v_2 = -14v_1 + 5v_2$$
$$u_2 = (3, -4) = (-24 - 12)v_1 + (9 + 4)v_2 = -36v_1 + 13v_2$$

Write the coordinates of u_1 and u_2 relative to S' as columns to obtain $Q = \begin{bmatrix} -14 & -36 \\ 5 & 13 \end{bmatrix}$.

(e) $QP = \begin{bmatrix} -14 & -36 \\ 5 & 13 \end{bmatrix}\begin{bmatrix} -\frac{13}{2} & -18 \\ \frac{5}{2} & 7 \end{bmatrix} = \begin{bmatrix} 1 & 0 \\ 0 & 1 \end{bmatrix} = I$

(f) Use parts (a), (c), and (d) to obtain

$$P^{-1}[v]_S = Q[v]_S = \begin{bmatrix} -14 & -36 \\ 5 & 13 \end{bmatrix}\begin{bmatrix} -2a - \frac{3}{2}b \\ a + \frac{1}{2}b \end{bmatrix} = \begin{bmatrix} -8a + 3b \\ 3a - b \end{bmatrix} = [v]_{S'}$$

PROOFS

6.17. Suppose P is the change-of-basis matrix from a basis $\{u_i\}$ to a basis $\{w_i\}$, and suppose Q is the change-of-basis matrix from the basis $\{w_i\}$ back to $\{u_i\}$. Prove that P is invertible and that $Q = P^{-1}$.

Suppose, for $i = 1, 2, \ldots, n$, that

$$w_i = a_{i1}u_1 + a_{i2}u_2 + \cdots + a_{in}u_n = \sum_{j=1}^{n} a_{ij}u_j \qquad (1)$$

and, for $j = 1, 2, \ldots, n$,

$$u_j = b_{j1}w_1 + b_{j2}w_2 + \cdots + b_{jn}w_n = \sum_{k=1}^{n} b_{jk}w_k \qquad (2)$$

Let $A = [a_{ij}]$ and $B = [b_{jk}]$. Then $P = A^T$ and $Q = B^T$. Substituting Eq. (2) into Eq. (1) yields

$$w_i = \sum_{j=1}^{n} a_{ij}\left(\sum_{k=1}^{n} b_{jk}w_k\right) = \sum_{k=1}^{n}\left(\sum_{j=1}^{n} a_{ij}b_{jk}\right)w_k$$

Since $\{w_i\}$ is a basis, $\sum a_{ij}b_{jk} = \delta_{ik}$, where δ_{ik} is the Kronecker delta, that is, $\delta_{ik} = 1$ if $i = k$ but $\delta_{ik} = 0$ if $i \neq k$. Suppose $AB = [c_{ik}]$. Then $c_{ik} = \delta_{ik}$. Accordingly, $AB = I$, and so

$$QP = B^T A^T = (AB)^T = I^T = I$$

Thus $Q = P^{-1}$.

6.18. Consider a finite sequence of vectors $S = \{u_1, u_2, \ldots, u_n\}$. Let S' be the sequence of vectors obtained from S by one of the following "elementary operations":

(1) Interchange two vectors.

(2) Multiply a vector by a nonzero scalar.

(3) Add a multiple of one vector to another vector.

Show that S and S' span the same subspace W. Also, show that S' is linearly independent if and only if S is linearly independent.

Observe that, for each operation, the vectors S' are linear combinations of vectors in S. Also, since each operation has an inverse of the same type, each vector in S is a linear combination of vectors in S'. Thus S and S' span the same subspace W. Moreover, S' is linearly independent if and only if $\dim W = n$, and this is true if and only if S is linearly independent.

6.19. Let $A = [a_{ij}]$ and $B = [b_{ij}]$ be row equivalent $m \times n$ matrices over a field K, and let $v_1, v_2, \ldots, v_n$ be any vectors in a vector space V over K. For $i = 1, 2, \ldots, m$, let u_i and w_i be defined by

$$u_i = a_{i1}v_1 + a_{i2}v_2 + \cdots + a_{in}v_n \quad \text{and} \quad w_i = b_{i1}v_1 + b_{i2}v_2 + \cdots + b_{in}v_n$$

Show that $[u_i\}$ and $\{w_i\}$ span the same subspace of V.

    Applying an "elementary operation" of Problem 6.18 to $\{u_i\}$ is equivalent to applying an elementary row operation to the matrix A. Since A and B are row equivalent, B can be obtained from A by a sequence of elementary row operations. Hence $\{w_i\}$ can be obtained from $\{u_i\}$ by the corresponding sequence of operations. Accordingly, $\{u_i\}$ and $\{w_i\}$ span the same space.

6.20. Suppose $u_1, u_2, \ldots, u_n$ belong to a vector space V over a field K, and suppose $P = [a_{ij}]$ is an n-square matrix over K. For $i = 1, 2, \ldots, n$, let $v_i = a_{i1}u_1 + a_{i2}u_2 + \cdots + a_{in}u_n$.

  (a) Suppose P is invertible. Show that $\{u_i\}$ and $\{v_i\}$ span the same subspace of V. Hence $\{u_i\}$ is linearly independent if and only if $\{v_i\}$ is linearly independent.

  (b) Suppose P is singular (not invertible). Show that $\{v_i\}$ is linearly dependent.

  (c) Suppose $\{v_i\}$ is linearly independent. Show that P is invertible.

  (a) Since P is invertible, it is row equivalent to the identity matrix I. Hence by Problem 6.18, $\{v_i\}$ and $\{u_i\}$ span the same subspace of V. Thus one is linearly independent if and only if the other is linearly independent.

  (b) Since P is not invertible, it is row equivalent to a matrix with a zero row. This means $\{v_i\}$ spans a subspace that has a spanning set with less than n elements. Thus $\{v_i\}$ is linearly dependent.

  (c) This is the contrapositive of the statement of part (b), and so it follows from part (b).

6.21. Prove Theorem 6.3: Let P be the change-of-basis matrix from a basis S to a basis S' in a vector space V. Then, for any vector $v \in V$, we have $P[v]_{S'} = [v]_S$, and hence $P^{-1}[v]_S = [v]_{S'}$.

    Suppose $S = \{u_1, \ldots, u_n\}$ and $S' = \{w_1, \ldots, w_n\}$, and suppose, for $i = 1, \ldots, n$,

$$w_i = a_{i1}u_1 + a_{i2}u_2 + \cdots + a_{in}u_n = \sum_{j=1}^{n} a_{ij}u_j$$

Then P is the n-square matrix whose jth row is

$$(a_{1j}, a_{2j}, \ldots, a_{nj}) \tag{1}$$

Also suppose $v = k_1w_1 + k_2w_2 + \cdots + k_nw_n = \sum_{i=1}^{n} k_iw_i$. Then

$$[v]_{S'} = [k_{1j}, k_{2j}, \ldots, k_{nj}]^T \tag{2}$$

Substituting for w_i in the equation for v, we obtain

$$v = \sum_{i=1}^{n} k_iw_i = \sum_{i=1}^{n} k_i \left(\sum_{j=1}^{n} a_{ij}u_j \right) = \sum_{j=1}^{n} \left(\sum_{i=1}^{n} a_{ij}k_i \right) u_j$$

$$= \sum_{j=1}^{n} (a_{1j}k_1 + a_{2j}k_2 + \cdots + a_{nj}k_n)u_j$$

Accordingly, $[v]_S$ is the column vector whose jth entry is

$$a_{1j}k_1 + a_{2j}k_2 + \cdots + a_{nj}k_n \tag{3}$$

On the other hand, the jth entry of $P[v]_{S'}$ is obtained by multiplying the jth row of P by $[v]_{S'}$, that is, Eq. (1) by Eq. (2). However, the product of Eqs. (1) and (2) is Eq. (3). Hence $P[v]_{S'}$ and $[v]_S$ have the same entries. Thus $P[v]_{S'} = [v]_{S'}$, as claimed.

Furthermore, multiplying the above by P^{-1} gives $P^{-1}[v]_S = P^{-1}P[v]_{S'} = [v]_{S'}$.

Supplementary Problems

COORDINATES

6.22. The vectors $u_1 = (1, -2)$ and $u_2 = (4, -7)$ form a basis S of $\mathbf{R}^2$. Find the coordinate vector $[v]$ of v relative to S, where: (a) $v = (5, 3)$; (b) $v = (1, 1)$; (c) $v = (3, -6)$, (d) $v = (a, b)$.

6.23. The vectors $u_1 = (2, 1)$ and $u_2 = (1, -1)$ form a basis S of $\mathbf{R}^2$. Find the coordinate vector $[v]$ of v relative to S, where: (a) $v = (4, -1)$; (b) $v = (2, 3)$; (c) $v = (3, -3)$; (d) $v = (a, b)$.

6.24. The vectors $u_1 = (1, 1, 1)$, $u_2 = (1, 1, 0)$, and $u_3 = (1, 0, 0)$ form a basis of $\mathbf{R}^3$. Find the coordinate vector $[v]$ of v relative to S, where: (a) $v = (3, -4, 2)$; (b) $v = (a, b, c)$.

6.25. Consider the basis $S = \{t^3 + t^2, t^2 + t, t + 1, 1\}$ of the vector space $\mathbf{P}_3(t)$. Find the coordinate vector $[v]$ of v relative to S, where: (a) $v = 2t^3 + t^2 - 3t + 2$; (b) $v = t^2 + 2t - 3$; (c) $v = at^3 + bt^2 + ct + d$.

6.26. In the vector space $\mathbf{M} = \mathbf{M}_{2,2}$ of 2×2 matrices find the coordinate vector $[A]$ of the matrix A relative to the basis

$$S = \left\{ \begin{bmatrix} 1 & 1 \\ 1 & 1 \end{bmatrix}, \begin{bmatrix} 1 & -1 \\ 1 & 0 \end{bmatrix}, \begin{bmatrix} 1 & 1 \\ 0 & 0 \end{bmatrix}, \begin{bmatrix} 1 & 0 \\ 0 & 0 \end{bmatrix} \right\}$$

where: (a) $A = \begin{bmatrix} 3 & -5 \\ 6 & 7 \end{bmatrix}$; (b) $A = \begin{bmatrix} a & b \\ c & d \end{bmatrix}$.

APPLICATIONS

6.27. Determine whether or not the following polynomials are linearly dependent:

$$u = t^3 + 2t^2 - 3t + 4, \qquad v = 2t^3 + 5t^2 - 4t + 7, \qquad w = t^3 + 4t^2 + t + 2$$

If they are linearly dependent, find the dimension and a basis of the subspace W spanned by the polynomials.

6.28. In the space $\mathbf{M} = \mathbf{M}_{2,3}$ determine whether or not the following matrices are linearly dependent:

$$A = \begin{bmatrix} 1 & 2 & 1 \\ 3 & 1 & 2 \end{bmatrix}, \qquad B = \begin{bmatrix} 2 & 4 & 3 \\ 7 & 5 & 6 \end{bmatrix}, \qquad C = \begin{bmatrix} 1 & 2 & 3 \\ 5 & 7 & 6 \end{bmatrix}$$

If they are linearly dependent, find the dimension and a basis of the subspace W spanned by the matrices.

6.29. Consider the subspaces $U = \text{span}(u_1, u_2, u_3)$ and $W = \text{span}(w_1, w_2, w_3)$ of $\mathbf{P}_3(t)$, where:

$$u_1 = t^3 + t^2 + 2t + 2, \qquad u_2 = 2t^3 + 3t^2 + 7t + 5, \qquad u_3 = t^3 + 3t^2 + 8t + 4$$
$$w_1 = t^3 + t^2 + t + 2, \qquad w_2 = t^3 + 3t^2 + 7t + 4, \qquad w_3 = 2t^3 + 3t^2 + 6t + 5$$

Find: (a) $\dim(U + W)$; (b) $\dim(U \cap W)$.

CHANGE OF BASIS

6.30. Find the change-of-basis matrix P from the usual basis E of $\mathbf{R}^2$ to the basis S, the change-of-basis matrix Q from S back to E, and the coordinate vector $[v]$ of $v = (a, b)$ relative to S, where:

(a) $S = \{(1, 2), (3, 5)\}$;   (b) $S = \{1, -3), (3, -8)\}$;   (c) $S = \{(2, 5), (3, 7)\}$;

(d) $S = \{(2, 3), (4, 5)\}$.

6.31. Consider the bases $S = \{(1, 2), (2, 3)\}$ and $S' = \{(1, 3), (1, 4)\}$ of $\mathbf{R}^2$. Find: (a) the change-of-basis matrix P from S to S'; (b) the change-of-basis matrix Q from S' back to S.

6.32. Suppose that the x and y axes in the plane $\mathbf{R}^2$ are rotated counterclockwise $30°$ to yield new x' and y' axes for the plane. Find: (a) the unit vectors in the direction of the new x' and y' axes; (b) the change-of-basis matrix P for the new coordinate system; (c) the new coordinates of each of the following points under the new coordinate system: $A(1, 3)$, $B(2, -5)$, $C(a, b)$.

6.33. Find the change-of-basis matrix P from the usual basis E of $\mathbf{R}^3$ to the basis S, the change-of-basis matrix Q from S back to E, and the coordinate vector $[v]$ of $v = (a, b, c)$ relative to S, where S consists of the vectors: (a) $u_1 = (1, 1, 0)$, $u_2 = (0, 1, 2)$, $u_3 = (0, 1, 1)$; (b) $u_1 = (1, 0, 1)$, $u_2 = (1, 1, 2)$, $u_3 = (1, 2, 4)$; (c) $u_1 = (1, 2, 1)$, $u_2 = (1, 3, 4)$, $u_3 = (2, 5, 6)$.

6.34. Suppose S_1, S_2, and S_3 are bases of a vector space V. Suppose also that P is the change-of-basis matrix from S_1 to S_2 and Q is the change-of-basis matrix from S_2 to S_3. Prove that the product PQ is the change-of-basis matrix from S_1 to S_3.

Answers to Supplementary Problems

6.22. (a) $[-47, 13]$; (b) $[-11, 3]$; (c) $[3, 0]$; (d) $[-7a - 4b, 2a + b]$

6.23. (a) $[1, 2]$; (b) $[\frac{5}{3}, -\frac{4}{3}]$; (c) $[0, 3]$; (d) $[(a + b)/3, (a - 2b)/3]$

6.24. (a) $[2, -6, 7]$; (b) $[c, b - c, a - b]$

6.25. (a) $[2, -1, -2, 4]$; (b) $[0, 1, 1, -4]$; (c) $[a, b - a, c - b + a, d - c + b - a]$

6.26. (a) $[7, -1, -13, 10]$; (b) $[d, c - d, b + c - 2d, a - b - 2c + 2d]$

6.27. $\dim W = 2$; basis: $\{t^3 + 2t^2 - 3t + 4, t^2 + 2t - 1\}$

6.28. $\dim W = 2$; basis: $\begin{bmatrix} 1 & 2 & 1 \\ 3 & 1 & 2 \end{bmatrix}, \begin{bmatrix} 0 & 0 & 1 \\ 1 & 3 & 2 \end{bmatrix}$

6.29. (a) $\dim(U + W) = 3$, (b) $\dim(U \cap W) = 2$

6.30. (a) $P = \begin{bmatrix} 1 & 3 \\ 2 & 5 \end{bmatrix}, Q = \begin{bmatrix} -5 & 3 \\ 2 & -1 \end{bmatrix}, [v] = \begin{bmatrix} -5a + 3b \\ 2a - b \end{bmatrix}$

(b) $P = \begin{bmatrix} 1 & 3 \\ -3 & -8 \end{bmatrix}, Q = \begin{bmatrix} -8 & -3 \\ 3 & 1 \end{bmatrix}, [v] = \begin{bmatrix} -8a - 3b \\ 3a + b \end{bmatrix}$

(c) $P = \begin{bmatrix} 2 & 3 \\ 5 & 7 \end{bmatrix}, Q = \begin{bmatrix} -7 & 3 \\ 5 & -2 \end{bmatrix}, [v] = \begin{bmatrix} -7a + 3b \\ 5a - 2b \end{bmatrix}$

(d) $P = \begin{bmatrix} 2 & 4 \\ 3 & 5 \end{bmatrix}, Q = \begin{bmatrix} -\frac{5}{2} & 2 \\ \frac{3}{2} & -1 \end{bmatrix}, [v] = \begin{bmatrix} -\frac{5}{2}a + 2b \\ \frac{3}{2}a - b \end{bmatrix}$

6.31. (a) $P = \begin{bmatrix} 3 & 5 \\ -1 & -2 \end{bmatrix}$; (b) $Q = \begin{bmatrix} 2 & 5 \\ -1 & -3 \end{bmatrix}$

6.32. (a) $(\sqrt{3}/2, \frac{1}{2})$, $(-\frac{1}{2}, \sqrt{3}/2)$; (b) $P = \begin{bmatrix} \sqrt{3}/2 & -\frac{1}{2} \\ \frac{1}{2} & \sqrt{3}/2 \end{bmatrix}$; (c) $[A] = [(\sqrt{3} + 3)/2, \ (1 + 3\sqrt{3})/2]$,

$[B] = [(2\sqrt{3} - 5)/2, (2 - 5\sqrt{3})/2]$, $[C] = [(\sqrt{3}a + b)/2, (a + \sqrt{3}b)/2]$

6.33. Since E is the usual basis, simply let P be the matrix whose columns are u_1, u_2, and u_3. Then $Q = P^{-1}$ and $[v] = P^{-1}v = Qv$.

(a) $P = \begin{bmatrix} 1 & 0 & 0 \\ 1 & 1 & 1 \\ 0 & 2 & 1 \end{bmatrix}, Q = \begin{bmatrix} 1 & 0 & 0 \\ 1 & -1 & 1 \\ -2 & 2 & -1 \end{bmatrix}, [v] = \begin{bmatrix} a \\ a - b + c \\ -2a + 2b - c \end{bmatrix}$

(b) $P = \begin{bmatrix} 1 & 1 & 1 \\ 0 & 1 & 2 \\ 1 & 2 & 4 \end{bmatrix}, Q = \begin{bmatrix} 0 & -2 & 1 \\ 2 & 3 & -2 \\ -1 & -1 & 1 \end{bmatrix}, [v] = \begin{bmatrix} -2b + c \\ 2a + 3b - 2c \\ -a - b + c \end{bmatrix}$

(c) $P = \begin{bmatrix} 1 & 1 & 2 \\ 2 & 3 & 5 \\ 1 & 4 & 6 \end{bmatrix}, Q = \begin{bmatrix} -2 & 2 & -1 \\ -7 & 4 & -1 \\ 5 & -3 & 1 \end{bmatrix}, [v] = \begin{bmatrix} -2a + 2b - c \\ -7a + 4b - c \\ 5a - 3b + c \end{bmatrix}$

Chapter 7

Inner Product Spaces and Orthogonality

7.1 INTRODUCTION

The concepts of "length" and "orthogonality" did not appear in the investigation of arbitrary vector spaces V. In this chapter we place an additional structure on a vector space V to obtain an inner product space, and in this context these concepts are defined.

Although the definition of a vector space V involves an arbitrary field K of scalars, we restrict K in this chapter to be the real field $\mathbf{R}$. In this case V is called a *real vector space*. Also, as in Chapter 4, we adopt the following notation (unless otherwise stated or implied):

$$\begin{array}{ll} V & \text{given vector space} \\ u, v, w & \text{vectors in } V \\ \mathbf{R} & \text{field of scalars} \\ a, b, c, \text{ or } k & \text{scalars in } \mathbf{R} \end{array}$$

The vector spaces V in this chapter have finite dimension unless otherwise stated or implied. In fact, many of the theorems in this chapter are not valid for spaces of infinite dimension. This is illustrated by some of the examples and problems.

Although we restrict ourselves here to vector spaces over the real field $\mathbf{R}$, one can also define an analogous inner product for vector spaces over the complex field $\mathbf{C}$. Complex inner product spaces lie beyond the scope of this text. We do note, however, that inner products cannot be defined for arbitrary fields K, only for subfields of the complex field $\mathbf{C}$.

7.2 INNER PRODUCT SPACES

We begin with a definition.

Definition: Let V be a real vector space. Suppose to each pair of vectors $u, v \in V$ there is assigned a real number, denoted by $\langle u, v \rangle$. This function is called a *(real) inner product* on V if it satisfies the following axioms:

[$\mathbf{I_1}$] (*Linear Property*): $\langle au_1 + bu_2, v \rangle = a\langle u_1, v \rangle + b\langle u_2, v \rangle$.

[$\mathbf{I_2}$] (*Symmetric Property*): $\langle u, v \rangle = \langle v, u \rangle$.

[$\mathbf{I_3}$] (*Positive Definite Property*): $\langle u, u \rangle \geq 0$; and $\langle u, u \rangle = 0$ if and only if $u = 0$.

The vector space V with an inner product is called a (real) inner product space.

Using [$\mathbf{I_1}$] and the symmetry axiom [$\mathbf{I_2}$], we obtain

$$\langle u, cv_1 + dv_2 \rangle = \langle cv_1 + dv_2, u \rangle = c\langle v_1, u \rangle + d\langle v_2, u \rangle = c\langle u, v_1 \rangle + d\langle u, v_2 \rangle$$

That is, the inner product function is also linear in its second position (variable). By induction, we obtain

$$\langle a_1 u_1 + \cdots + a_r u_r, v \rangle = a_1\langle u_1, v \rangle + a_2\langle u_2, v \rangle + \cdots + a_r\langle u_r, v \rangle$$

and $$\langle u, b_1 v_1 + b_2 v_2 + \cdots + b_s v_s \rangle = b_1 \langle u, v_1 \rangle + b_2 \langle u, v_2 \rangle + \cdots + b_s \langle u, v_s \rangle$$

Combining these two properties yields the following general formula:

$$\left\langle \sum_{i=1}^{r} a_i u_i, \sum_{j=1}^{s} b_j v_j \right\rangle = \sum_{i=1}^{r} \sum_{j=1}^{s} a_i b_j \langle u_i, v_j \rangle$$

EXAMPLE 7.1   Let V be an inner product space.   Then, by the linearity property of the inner product,

$$\langle 3u_1 + 5u_2 - 6u_3, v \rangle = 3\langle u_1, v \rangle + 5\langle u_2, v \rangle - 6\langle u_3, v \rangle$$
$$\langle u, 4v_1 - 7v_2 - 2v_3 \rangle = 4\langle u, v_1 \rangle - 7\langle u, v_2 \rangle - 2\langle u, v_3 \rangle$$
$$\langle 2u - 5v, 4u + 6v \rangle = 8\langle u, u \rangle + 12\langle u, v \rangle - 20\langle v, u \rangle - 30\langle v, v \rangle$$
$$= 8\langle u, u \rangle - 8\langle u, v \rangle - 30\langle v, v \rangle$$

Observe that in the last equation we used the symmetry property that $\langle u, v \rangle = \langle v, u \rangle$.

Norm of a Vector

By the third axiom $[\mathbf{I}_3]$ of an inner product, $\langle u, u \rangle$ is nonnegative for any vector u. Thus its positive square root exists.   We use the notation

$$\|u\| = \sqrt{\langle u, u \rangle}$$

This nonnegative number is called the *norm* or *length* of u.   The relation $\|u\|^2 = \langle u, u \rangle$ will be used frequently.

Remark: If $\|u\| = 1$ or, equivalently, if $\langle u, u \rangle = 1$, then u is called a *unit vector* and is said to be *normalized*.   Every nonzero vector v in V can be multiplied by the reciprocal of its length to obtain the unit vector

$$\hat{v} = \frac{1}{\|v\|} v$$

which is a positive multiple of v. This process is called *normalizing v*.

7.3   EXAMPLES OF INNER PRODUCT SPACES

This section lists the main examples of inner product spaces used in this text.

Euclidean n-Space $\mathbf{R}^n$

Consider the vector space $\mathbf{R}^n$.   The *dot product* or *scalar product* in $\mathbf{R}^n$ is defined by

$$u \cdot v = a_1 b_1 + a_2 b_2 + \cdots + a_n b_n$$

where $u = (a_i)$ and $v = (b_i)$.   This function defines an inner product on $\mathbf{R}^n$.   The norm $\|u\|$ of the vector $u = (a_i)$ in this space follows:

$$\|u\| = \sqrt{u \cdot u} = \sqrt{a_1^2 + a_2^2 + \cdots + a_n^2}$$

On the other hand, by the Pythagorean theorem, the distance from the origin O in $\mathbf{R}^3$ to the point $P(a, b, c)$, shown in Fig. 7-1, is given by $\sqrt{a^2 + b^2 + c^2}$.   This is precisely the same as the above defined norm of the vector $v = (a, b, c)$ in $\mathbf{R}^3$.   Since the Pythagorean theorem is a

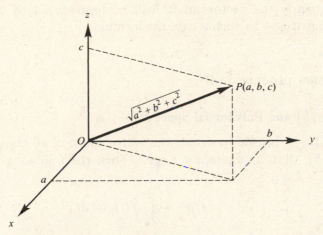

Fig. 7-1

consequence of the axioms of Euclidean geometry, the vector space $\mathbf{R}^n$ with the above inner product and norm is called *Euclidean n-space*. Although there are many ways to define an inner product on $\mathbf{R}^n$, we shall assume this as the inner product on $\mathbf{R}^n$, unless otherwise stated or implied. It is called the *usual inner product* on $\mathbf{R}^n$.

EXAMPLE 7.2 Let $u = (1, 3, -4, 2)$, $v = (4, -2, 2, 1)$, $w = (5, -1, -2, 6)$ in $\mathbf{R}^4$.

(a) By definition,

$$\langle u, w \rangle = 1(5) + 3(-1) + -4(-2) + 2(6) = 5 - 3 + 8 + 12 = 22$$

$$\langle v, w \rangle = 4(5) - 2(-1) + 2(-2) + 1(6) = 20 + 2 - 4 + 6 = 24$$

Since $u + v = (5, 1, -2, 3)$, we have

$$\langle u + v, w \rangle = 5(5) + 1(-1) - 2(-2) + 3(6) = 25 - 1 + 4 + 18 = 46$$

As expected, $\langle u + v, w \rangle = \langle u, w \rangle + \langle v, w \rangle$.

(b) By definition,

$$\|u\|^2 = 1^2 + 3^2 + (-4)^2 + 2^2 = 1 + 9 + 16 + 4 = 30 \qquad \text{hence } \|u\| = \sqrt{30}$$

$$\|v\|^2 = 16 + 4 + 4 + 1 = 25, \qquad \text{hence } \|v\| = 5$$

$$\|w\|^2 = 25 + 1 + 4 + 36 = 66, \qquad \text{hence } \|w\| = \sqrt{66}$$

(c) We normalize u, v, and w to obtain the following unit vectors $\hat{u}$, $\hat{v}$, and $\hat{w}$ in the directions of u, v, and w, respectively:

$$\hat{u} = \frac{1}{\|u\|} u = \left(\frac{1}{\sqrt{30}}, \frac{3}{\sqrt{30}}, \frac{-4}{\sqrt{30}}, \frac{2}{\sqrt{30}} \right)$$

$$\hat{v} = \frac{1}{\|v\|} v = \left(\frac{4}{5}, \frac{-2}{5}, \frac{2}{5}, \frac{1}{5} \right)$$

$$\hat{w} = \frac{1}{\|w\|} w = \left(\frac{5}{\sqrt{66}}, \frac{-1}{\sqrt{66}}, \frac{-2}{\sqrt{66}}, \frac{6}{\sqrt{66}} \right)$$

Remark: Frequently the vectors in $\mathbf{R}^n$ will be represented by column vectors, that is, by $n \times 1$ column matrices. In such a case the formula

$$\langle u, v \rangle = u^T v$$

defines the usual inner product on $\mathbf{R}^n$.

Function Space $C[a, b]$ and Polynomial Space $\mathbf{P}(t)$

The notation $C[a, b]$ is used to denote the vector space of all continuous functions on the closed interval $[a, b]$, that is, where $a \le t \le b$. Then the following is an inner product on $C[a, b]$:

$$\langle f, g \rangle = \int_a^b f(t)g(t)\, dt$$

where $f(t)$ and $g(t)$ are now continuous functions on $[a, b]$. It is called the *usual inner product* on $C[a, b]$.

The vector space $\mathbf{P}(t)$ of all polynomials is a subspace of $C[a, b]$ for any interval $[a, b]$, and hence the above is also an inner product on $\mathbf{P}(t)$.

EXAMPLE 7.3 Consider the vector space $\mathbf{P}(t)$ with inner product

$$\langle f, g \rangle = \int_0^1 f(t)g(t)\, dt$$

Let $f(t) = t + 2$ and $g(t) = 6t - 5$. Then

$$f(t)g(t) = (t + 2)(6t - 5) = 6t^2 + 7t - 10$$

Hence

$$\langle f, g \rangle = \int_0^1 (6t^2 + 7t - 10)\, dt = 2t^3 + \tfrac{7}{2}t^2 - 10t \Big|_0^1$$
$$= (2 + \tfrac{7}{2} - 10) - (0) = -4.5$$

Also, $[f(t)]^2 = f(t)f(t) = t^2 + 4t + 4$. Hence

$$\|f\|^2 = \langle f, f \rangle = \int_0^1 (t^2 + 4t + 4)\, dt = \frac{t^3}{3} + 2t^2 + 4t \Big|_0^1$$
$$= \tfrac{1}{3} + 2 + 4 = \tfrac{19}{3}$$

Thus $\|f\| = \sqrt{\tfrac{19}{3}}$. Similarly, $[g(t)]^2 = g(t)g(t) = 36t^2 - 60t + 25$. Hence

$$\|g\|^2 = \langle g, g \rangle = \int_0^1 (36t^2 - 60t + 25) = 12t^3 - 30t^2 + 25t \Big|_0^1$$
$$= (12 - 30 + 25) - (0) = 7$$

Hence $\|g\| = \sqrt{7}$.

Matrix Space $\mathbf{M} = \mathbf{M}_{m,n}$

Consider the vector space $\mathbf{M} = \mathbf{M}_{m,n}$ of all real $m \times n$ matrices. An inner product is defined on $\mathbf{M}$ by

$$\langle A, B \rangle = \operatorname{tr}(B^T A)$$

where tr stands for trace, the sum of the diagonal elements. If $A = [a_{ij}]$ and $B = [b_{ij}]$, then

$$\langle A, B \rangle = \text{tr}(B^T A) = \sum_{i=1}^{m} \sum_{j=1}^{n} a_{ij} b_{ij} \quad \text{and} \quad \|A\|^2 = \langle A, A \rangle = \sum_{i=1}^{m} \sum_{j=1}^{n} a_{ij}^2$$

That is, $\langle A, B \rangle$ is the sum of the products of corresponding entries in A and B and, in particular, $\langle A, A \rangle$ is the sum of all the squares of the entries of A.

EXAMPLE 7.4 Consider the vector space $\mathbf{M} = \mathbf{M}_{2,3}$ with inner product defined by $\langle A, B \rangle = \text{tr}(B^T A)$. Suppose

$$A = \begin{bmatrix} 4 & 5 & 6 \\ 7 & 8 & 9 \end{bmatrix}, \quad B = \begin{bmatrix} 2 & -6 & 5 \\ 1 & 4 & -3 \end{bmatrix}$$

Then

$$\langle A, B \rangle = \text{sum of products of corresponding entries}$$
$$= 4(2) + 5(-6) + 6(5) + 7(1) + 8(4) + 9(-3)$$
$$= 8 - 30 + 30 + 7 + 32 - 27 = 20$$
$$\|A\|^2 = \langle A, A \rangle = \text{sum of squares of all elements of } A$$
$$= 4^2 + 5^2 + 6^2 + 7^2 + 8^2 + 9^2 = 16 + 25 + 36 + 49 + 64 + 81 = 271$$

Thus $\|A\| = \sqrt{271}$.

Hilbert Space

Let V be the vector space of all infinite sequences of real numbers $(a_1, a_2, a_3, \ldots)$ satisfying

$$\sum_{i=1}^{\infty} a_i^2 = a_1^2 + a_2^2 + \cdots < \infty$$

that is, the sum converges. Addition and scalar multiplication are defined in V componentwise, that is, if

$$u = (a_1, a_2, \ldots) \quad \text{and} \quad v = (b_1, b_2, \ldots)$$

then $\quad u + v = (a_1 + b_1, a_2 + b_2, \ldots) \quad \text{and} \quad ku = (ka_1, ka_2, \ldots)$

An inner product is defined in V by

$$\langle u, v \rangle = a_1 b_1 + a_2 b_2 + \cdots$$

The above sum converges absolutely for any pair of points in V. Hence the inner product is well defined. This inner product space is called l_2-space or *Hilbert space*.

7.4   CAUCHY-SCHWARZ INEQUALITY, APPLICATIONS

The following formula (proved in Problem 7.35) is called the Cauchy-Schwarz inequality. It is used in many branches of mathematics.

Theorem 7.1   (Cauchy-Schwarz):   For any vectors u and v in an inner product space V,

$$\langle u, v \rangle^2 \leq \langle u, u \rangle \langle v, v \rangle \quad \text{or equivalently} \quad |\langle u, v \rangle| \leq \|u\| \, \|v\|$$

Next we examine this inequality in specific cases.

EXAMPLE 7.5

(a) Consider any real $a_1, \ldots, a_n, b_1, \ldots, b_n$. Then by the Cauchy-Schwarz inequality,

$$(a_1 b_1 + a_2 b_2 + \cdots + a_n b_n)^2 \leq (a_1^2 + \cdots + a_n^2)(b_1^2 + \cdots + b_n^2)$$

that is, $(u \cdot v)^2 \leq \|u\|^2 \|v\|^2$, where $u = (a_i)$ and $v = (b_i)$.

(b) Let f and g be any real continuous functions defined on the unit interval $0 \leq t \leq 1$. Then by the Cauchy-Schwarz inequality,

$$(\langle f, g \rangle)^2 = \left[\int_0^1 f(t)g(t)\, dt \right]^2 \leq \int_0^1 f^2(t)\, dt \int_0^1 g^2(t)\, dt = \|f\|^2 \|g\|^2$$

Here V is the inner product space $C[0, 1]$ of all continuous functions on the unit interval $0 \leq t \leq 1$.

The next theorem (proved in Problem 7.36) gives basic properties of a norm. The proof of the third property requires the Cauchy-Schwarz inequality.

Theorem 7.2:   Let V be an inner product space. Then the norm in V satisfies the following properties:

     $[N_1]$ $\|v\| \geq 0$; and $\|v\| = 0$ if and only if $v = 0$.

     $[N_2]$ $\|kv\| = |k|\, \|v\|$.

     $[N_3]$ $\|u + v\| \leq \|u\| + \|v\|$.

The property $[N_3]$ is frequently called the *triangle inequality* because if we view $u + v$ as the side of the triangle formed with u and v (as shown in Fig. 7-2), then $[N_3]$ states that the length of one side of a triangle is less than or equal to the sum of the lengths of the other two sides.

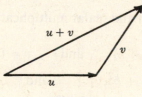

Fig. 7-2

Angle between Vectors

For any nonzero vectors u and v in an inner product space V, the *angle between u and v* is defined to be the angle θ such that $0 \leq \theta \leq \pi$ and

$$\cos \theta = \frac{\langle u, v \rangle}{\|u\|\, \|v\|}$$

By the Cauchy-Schwarz inequality, $-1 \leq \cos \theta \leq 1$ and so the angle θ always exists and is unique.

EXAMPLE 7.6

(a) Consider vectors $u = (2, 3, 5)$ and $v = (1, -4, 3)$ in $\mathbf{R}^3$. Then

$$\langle u, v \rangle = 2 - 12 + 15 = 5, \qquad \|u\| = \sqrt{4 + 9 + 25} = \sqrt{38}, \qquad \|v\| = \sqrt{1 + 16 + 9} = \sqrt{26}$$

Hence

$$\cos \theta = \frac{5}{\sqrt{38}\sqrt{26}}$$

where θ is the angle between u and v. Note that θ is an acute angle since Θ is positive.

(b) Consider the vector space $\mathbf{P}(t)$ of polynomials with inner product

$$\langle f, g \rangle = \int_0^1 f(t)g(t)\, dt$$

Let $f(t) = t + 2$ and $g(t) = 6t - 5$. By Example 7.3,

$$\langle f, g \rangle = -\frac{9}{2}, \qquad \|f\| = \frac{\sqrt{57}}{3}, \qquad \|g\| = \sqrt{7}$$

Hence

$$\cos \theta = \frac{-9/2}{(\sqrt{57}/3)(\sqrt{7})} = -\frac{27}{2\sqrt{57}\sqrt{7}}$$

where θ is the angle between f and g. Note that θ is an obtuse angle since Θ is negative.

7.5 ORTHOGONALITY

Let V be an inner product space. The vectors $u, v \in V$ are said to be *orthogonal* and u is said to be *orthogonal* to v if

$$\langle u, v \rangle = 0$$

The relation is clearly symmetric, that is, if u is orthogonal to v, then $\langle v, u \rangle = 0$, and so v is orthogonal to u. We note that $0 \in V$ is orthogonal to every $v \in V$ for

$$\langle 0, v \rangle = \langle 0v, v \rangle = 0 \langle v, v \rangle = 0$$

Conversely, if u is orthogonal to every $v \in V$, then $\langle u, u \rangle = 0$ and hence $u = 0$ by [$\mathbf{I}_3$]. Observe that u and v are orthogonal if and only if $\cos \theta = 0$, where θ is the angle between u and v, and this is true if and only if u and v are "perpendicular", i.e., $\theta = \pi/2$ (or $\theta = 90°$).

EXAMPLE 7.7

(a) Consider the vectors $u = (1, 1, 1)$, $v = (1, 2, -3)$, $w = (1, -4, 3)$ in $\mathbf{R}^3$. Then

$$\langle u, v \rangle = 1 + 2 - 3 = 0, \qquad \langle u, w \rangle = 1 - 4 + 3 = 0, \qquad \langle v, w \rangle = 1 - 8 - 9 = -16$$

Thus u is orthogonal to v and w, but v and w are not orthogonal.

(b) Consider the functions $\sin t$ and $\cos t$ in the vector space $C[-\pi, \pi]$ of continuous functions on the closed interval $[-\pi, \pi]$. Then

$$\langle \sin t, \cos t \rangle = \int_{-\pi}^{\pi} \sin t \cos t\, dt = \frac{1}{2} \sin^2 t \Big|_{-\pi}^{\pi} = 0 - 0 = 0$$

Thus $\sin t$ and $\cos t$ are orthogonal functions in the vector space $C[-\pi, \pi]$.

EXAMPLE 7.8 Suppose we want a nonzero vector w which is orthogonal to $u_1 = (1, 2, 1)$ and $u_2 = (2, 5, 4)$ in $\mathbf{R}^3$. Let $w = (x, y, z)$. Then we want

$$0 = \langle u_1, w \rangle = x + 2y + z \qquad \text{and} \qquad 0 = \langle u_2, w \rangle = 2x + 5y + 4z$$

This yields the homogeneous system

$$\begin{array}{ll} x + 2y + z = 0 & \phantom{\text{or}} \quad x + 2y + z = 0 \\ 2x + 5y + 4z = 0 & \text{or} \quad y + 2z = 0 \end{array}$$

Here z is the only free variable in the echelon system. Let $z = 1$ to obtain $y = -2$ and $x = 3$. Thus $w = (3, -2, 1)$ is a desired nonzero vector orthogonal to u_1 and u_2. (Any multiple of w will also be orthogonal to u_1 and u_2.)

Remark: Consider any vector $u = (a_1, a_2, \ldots, a_n)$ in $\mathbf{R}^n$. Then a vector $w = (x_1, x_2, \ldots, x_n)$ is orthogonal to u if

$$\langle u, w \rangle = a_1 x_1 + a_2 x_2 + \cdots + a_n x_n = 0$$

That is, w is orthogonal to u if w satisfies a homogeneous equation whose coefficients are the elements of u.

Orthogonal Complements

Let S be a subset of an inner product space V. The orthogonal complement of S, denoted by $S^\perp$ (read "S perp") consists of those vectors in V which are orthogonal to every vector $u \in S$, that is,

$$S^\perp = \{v \in V: \quad \langle v, u \rangle = 0 \text{ for every } u \in S\}$$

In particular, for a given vector u in V, we have

$$u^\perp = \{v \in V: \quad \langle v, u \rangle = 0\}$$

that is, $u^\perp$ consists of all vectors in V that are orthogonal to the given vector u.

We show that $S^\perp$ is a subspace of V. Clearly $0 \in S^\perp$ since 0 is orthogonal to every vector in V. Now suppose $v, w \in S^\perp$. Then, for any scalars a and b and any vector $u \in S$, we have

$$\langle av + bw, u \rangle = a \langle v, u \rangle + b \langle w, u \rangle = a \cdot 0 + b \cdot 0 = 0$$

Thus $av + bw \in S^\perp$, and therefore $S^\perp$ is a subspace of V.

We state this result formally.

Proposition 7.3: Let S be a subset of an inner product space V. Then $S^\perp$ is a subspace of V.

Remark 1: Suppose u is a nonzero vector in $\mathbf{R}^3$. Then there is a geometrical description of $u^\perp$. Specifically, $u^\perp$ is the plane in $\mathbf{R}^3$ through the origin O and perpendicular to the vector u, as shown in Fig. 7-3.

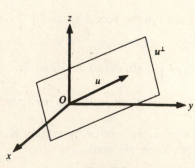

Fig. 7-3

Remark 2:   Let W be the solution space of a homogeneous system,

$$a_{11}x_1 + a_{12}x_2 + \cdots + a_{1n}x_n = 0$$
$$a_{21}x_1 + a_{22}x_2 + \cdots + a_{2n}x_n = 0$$
$$\cdots \cdots \cdots \cdots \cdots \cdots \cdots \cdots \cdots \cdots \cdots \cdots$$
$$a_{m1}x_1 + a_{m2}x_2 + \cdots + a_{mn}x_n = 0$$

Recall that W may be viewed as the solution of the equivalent matrix equation $AX = 0$, where $A = [a_{ij}]$ and $X = [x_j]$.   Now we can give another interpretation of W using the notion of orthogonality.   Specifically, each solution vector $w = (x_1, x_2, \ldots, x_n)$ is orthogonal to each row of A; and consequently W is the orthogonal complement of the row space of A.

EXAMPLE 7.9   Suppose we want to find a basis for the subspace $u^\perp$ of $\mathbf{R}^3$, where $u = (1, 3, -4)$.   Note that $u^\perp$ consists of all vectors (x, y, z) such that

$$\langle (x, y, z), (1, 3, -4) \rangle = 0 \qquad \text{or} \qquad x + 3y - 4z = 0$$

The free variables are y and z.

(1)   Set $y = -1$, $z = 0$ to obtain the solution $w_1 = (3, -1, 0)$.
(2)   Set $y = 0$, $z = 1$ to obtain the solution $w_2 = (4, 0, 1)$.

The vectors w_1 and w_2 form a basis for the solution space of the equation and hence a basis for $u^\perp$.

Suppose W is a subspace of V.   Then both W and $W^\perp$ are subspaces of V.   The next theorem, whose proof (see Problem 7.42) requires results of later sections, is a basic result in linear algebra.

Theorem 7.4:   Let W be a subspace of V.   Then V is the direct sum of W and $W^\perp$, that is, $V = W \oplus W^\perp$.

7.6   ORTHOGONAL SETS AND BASES

Consider a set $S = \{u_1, u_2, \ldots, u_r\}$ of nonzero vectors in an inner product space V.   The set S is called *orthogonal* if each pair of vectors in S are orthogonal, that is, if

$$\langle u_i, u_j \rangle = 0 \qquad \text{for} \qquad i \neq j$$

and S is called *orthonormal* if S is orthogonal and each vector in S has unit length, that is, if

$$\langle u_i, u_j \rangle = \delta_{ij} = \begin{cases} 0 & \text{for } i \neq j \\ 1 & \text{for } i = j \end{cases}$$

Normalizing an orthogonal set S refers to the process of multiplying each vector in S by the reciprocal of its length in order to transform S into an orthonormal set of vectors.

The following theorems apply.   (See Problem 7.37 for a proof of Theorem 7.5.)

Theorem 7.5:   Suppose S is an orthogonal set of nonzero vectors.   Then S is linearly independent.

Theorem 7.6   (Pythagoras):   Suppose $\{u_1, u_2, \ldots, u_r\}$ is an orthogonal set of vectors.   Then

$$\|u_1 + u_2 + \cdots + u_r\|^2 = \|u_1\|^2 + \|u_2\|^2 + \cdots + \|u_r\|^2$$

Here we prove the Pythagorean theorem in the special and familiar case for two vectors. Specifically, suppose $\langle u, v \rangle = 0$.   Then

$$\|u + v\|^2 = \langle u + v, u + v \rangle = \langle u, u \rangle + 2\langle u, v \rangle + \langle v, v \rangle = \langle u, u \rangle + \langle v, v \rangle = \|u\|^2 + \|v\|^2$$

which gives our result.

EXAMPLE 7.10

(a)   Consider the usual basis E of Euclidean space $\mathbf{R}^3$:

$$E = \{e_1, e_2, e_3\} = \{(1, 0, 0), (0, 1, 0), (0, 0, 1)\}$$

It is clear that

$$\langle e_1, e_2 \rangle = \langle e_1, e_3 \rangle = \langle e_2, e_3 \rangle = 0 \qquad \text{and} \qquad \langle e_1, e_1 \rangle = \langle e_2, e_2 \rangle = \langle e_3, e_3 \rangle = 1$$

Thus E is an orthonormal basis of $\mathbf{R}^3$.   More generally, the usual basis of $\mathbf{R}^n$ is orthonormal for every n.

(b)   Let $V = C[-\pi, \pi]$ be the vector space of continuous functions on the interval $-\pi \le t \le \pi$ with inner product defined by

$$\langle f, g \rangle = \int_{-\pi}^{\pi} f(t)g(t)\, dt$$

The following is a classical example of an orthogonal set in V:

$$\{1, \cos t, \cos 2t, \cos 3t, \ldots, \sin t, \sin 2t, \sin 3t, \ldots\}$$

This orthogonal set plays a fundamental role in the theory of Fourier series.

EXAMPLE 7.11   Let S consist of the following three vectors in $\mathbf{R}^4$:

$$u = (1, 2, -3, 4), \qquad v = (3, 4, 1, -2), \qquad w = (3, -2, 1, 1)$$

Note that

$$\langle u, v \rangle = 3 + 8 - 3 - 8 = 0, \qquad \langle u, w \rangle = 3 - 4 - 3 + 4 = 0, \qquad \langle v, w \rangle = 9 - 8 + 1 - 2 = 0$$

Thus S is orthogonal.   We normalize S to obtain an orthonormal set by first finding

$$\|u\|^2 = 1 + 4 + 9 + 16 = 30, \qquad \|v\|^2 = 9 + 16 + 1 + 4 = 30, \qquad \|w\|^2 = 9 + 4 + 1 + 1 = 15$$

Then the following form the desired orthonormal set of vectors:

$$\hat{u} = \left(\frac{1}{\sqrt{30}}, \frac{2}{\sqrt{30}}, \frac{-3}{\sqrt{30}}, \frac{4}{\sqrt{30}} \right)$$

$$\hat{v} = \left(\frac{3}{\sqrt{30}}, \frac{4}{\sqrt{30}}, \frac{1}{\sqrt{30}}, \frac{-2}{\sqrt{30}} \right)$$

$$\hat{w} = \left(\frac{3}{\sqrt{15}}, \frac{-2}{\sqrt{15}}, \frac{1}{\sqrt{15}}, \frac{1}{\sqrt{15}} \right)$$

We also have $u + v + w = (7, 4, -1, 3)$ and $\|u + v + w\|^2 = 49 + 16 + 1 + 9 = 75$.   Thus

$$\|u\|^2 + \|v\|^2 + \|w\|^2 = 30 + 30 + 15 = 75 = \|u + v + w\|^2$$

which verifies the Pythagorean theorem for the orthogonal set S.

Orthogonal Basis and Linear Combinations, Fourier Coefficients

Let S consist of the following three vectors in $\mathbf{R}^3$:

$$u_1 = (1, 2, 1), \qquad u_2 = (2, 1, -4), \qquad u_3 = (3, -2, 1)$$

Observe that

$$\langle u_1, u_2 \rangle = 2 + 2 - 4 = 0, \qquad \langle u_1, u_3 \rangle = 3 - 4 + 1 = 0, \qquad \langle u_2, u_3 \rangle = 6 - 2 - 4 = 0$$

Thus S is orthogonal, and hence linearly independent. Accordingly, S is an orthogonal basis of $\mathbf{R}^3$.

Suppose we want to write $v = (7, 1, 9)$ as a linear combination of u_1, u_2, and u_3. First set v as a linear combination of u_1, u_2, and u_3 using unknowns x, y, and z, as follows:

$$v = xu_1 + yu_2 + zu_3 \tag{$\star$}$$

or

$$(7, 1, 9) = x(1, 2, 1) + y(2, 1, -4) + z(3, -2, 1) \tag{$\star\star$}$$

We can proceed in two ways.

Method 1: Expand Eq. ($\star\star$) to obtain the system

$$x + 2y + 3z = 7, \qquad 2x + y - 2z = 1, \qquad x - 4y + z = 9$$

Solve the system by Gaussian elimination to obtain $x = 3$, $y = -1$, $z = 2$. Thus $v = 3u_1 - u_2 + 2u_3$.

Method 2: (This method uses the fact that the basis vectors are orthogonal, and the arithmetic is much simpler.) If we take the inner product of each side of Eq. ($\star$) with respect to u_1, we get

$$\langle v, u_1 \rangle = \langle xu_1 + yu_2 + zu_3, u_1 \rangle \qquad \text{or} \qquad \langle v, u_1 \rangle = x\langle u_1, u_1 \rangle$$

Here the last two terms drop out since u_1 is orthogonal to u_2 and u_3. Thus

$$x = \frac{\langle v, u_1 \rangle}{\langle u_1, u_1 \rangle} = \frac{7 + 2 + 9}{1 + 4 + 1} = \frac{18}{6} = 3$$

Similarly, taking the inner product of each side of Eq. ($\star$) with respect to u_2 we get

$$y = \frac{\langle v, u_2 \rangle}{\langle u_2, u_2 \rangle} = \frac{14 + 1 - 36}{4 + 1 + 16} = \frac{-21}{21} = -1$$

Lastly, taking the inner product of each side of Eq. ($\star$) with respect to u_3 we get

$$z = \frac{\langle v, u_3 \rangle}{\langle u_3, u_3 \rangle} = \frac{21 - 2 + 9}{9 + 4 + 1} = \frac{28}{14} = 2$$

Thus again we get $v = 3u_1 - u_2 + 2u_3$.

The procedure in Method 2 is true in general, that is,

Theorem 7.7: Suppose $\{u_1, u_2, \ldots, u_n\}$ is an orthogonal basis for V. Then, for any $v \in V$,

$$v = \frac{\langle v, u_1 \rangle}{\langle u_1, u_1 \rangle} u_1 + \frac{\langle v, u_2 \rangle}{\langle u_2, u_2 \rangle} u_2 + \cdots + \frac{\langle v, u_n \rangle}{\langle u_n, u_n \rangle} u_n$$

Remark: The above scalar,

$$k_i \equiv \frac{\langle v, u_i \rangle}{\langle u_i, u_i \rangle} = \frac{\langle v, u_i \rangle}{\|u_i\|^2}$$

is called the *Fourier coefficient* of v with respect to u_i since it is analogous to a coefficient in the Fourier series of a function. This scalar also has a geometric interpretation, which is discussed below.

Projections

Let V be an inner product space and let w be a given nonzero vector in V. Suppose v is another vector in V. We seek a scalar c such that $v' = v - cw$ is orthogonal to w, as pictured in Fig. 7-4. In order for v' to be orthogonal to w we must have that

$$\langle v - cw, w \rangle = 0 \quad \text{or} \quad \langle v, w \rangle - c\langle w, w \rangle = 0 \quad \text{or} \quad c = \frac{\langle v, w \rangle}{\langle w, w \rangle} = \frac{\langle v, w \rangle}{\|w\|^2}$$

The *projection of v along w*, as indicated by Fig. 7-4, is denoted and defined by

$$\text{proj}\,(v, w) = cw = \frac{\langle v, w \rangle}{\langle w, w \rangle} w = \frac{\langle v, w \rangle}{\|w\|^2} w$$

Such a scalar c is unique, and it is called the *Fourier coefficient* of v with respect to w or the *component* of v along w.

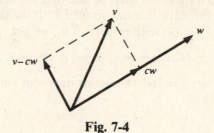

Fig. 7-4

EXAMPLE 7.12 Consider vectors $v = (1, 2, 3, 4)$ and $w = (1, -3, 6, -2)$ in $\mathbf{R}^4$. We find the Fourier coefficient c and the projection cw of v along w. First we compute

$$\langle v, w \rangle = 1 - 6 + 18 - 8 = 5 \quad \text{and} \quad \langle w, w \rangle = 1 + 9 + 36 + 4 = 50$$

Then

$$c = \tfrac{5}{50} = \tfrac{1}{10} \quad \text{and} \quad \text{proj}\,(v, w) = cw = (\tfrac{1}{10}, -\tfrac{3}{10}, \tfrac{3}{5}, -\tfrac{1}{5})$$

The above notion may be generalized as follows.

Theorem 7.8: Suppose $w_1, w_2, \ldots, w_r$ form an orthogonal set of nonzero vectors in V. Let v be any vector in V. Define:

$$v' = v - (c_1 w_1 + c_2 w_2 + \cdots + c_r w_r)$$

where

$$c_1 = \frac{\langle v, w_1 \rangle}{\|w_1\| \cdots \|^2}, \quad c_2 = \frac{\langle v, w_2 \rangle}{\|w_2\| \cdots \|^2}, \ldots, c_r = \frac{\langle v, w_r \rangle}{\|w_1\| \cdots \|^2},$$

Then v' is orthogonal to $w_1, w_2, \ldots, w_r$.

Note that each c_i in the above theorem is the component (Fourier coefficient) of v along the given w_i.

Remark: The notion of projection includes that of a vector along a subspace as follows. Suppose W is a subspace of V and $v \in V$. By Theorem 7.4, $V = W \oplus W^\perp$. Hence v can be expressed uniquely in the form

$$v = w + w' \quad \text{where} \quad w \in W, \quad w' \in W^\perp$$

We call w the *projection of v along W* and denote it by proj (v, W). (See Fig. 7-5). In particular, if $W = \text{span}(w_1, \ldots, w_r)$, where the w_i forms an orthogonal set, then

$$\text{proj}(v, W) = c_1 w_1 + c_2 w_2 + \cdots + c_r w_r$$

where c_i is the component of v along w_i, as above.

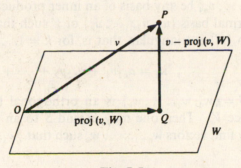

Fig. 7-5

7.7 GRAM-SCHMIDT ORTHOGONALIZATION PROCESS

Suppose $\{v_1, v_2, \ldots, v_n\}$ is a basis of an inner product space V. One can use this basis to construct an orthogonal basis $\{w_1, w_2, \ldots, w_n\}$ of V as follows. Set

$$w_1 = v_1$$

$$w_2 = v_2 - \frac{\langle v_2, w_1 \rangle}{\|w_1\|^2} w_1$$

$$w_3 = v_3 - \frac{\langle v_3, w_1 \rangle}{\|w_1\|^2} w_1 - \frac{\langle v_3, w_2 \rangle}{\|w_2\|^2} w_2$$

$$w_n = v_n - \frac{\langle v_n, w_1 \rangle}{\|w_1\|^2} w_1 - \frac{\langle v_n, w_2 \rangle}{\|w_2\|^2} w_2 - \cdots - \frac{\langle v_n, w_{n-1} \rangle}{\|w_{n-1}\|^2} w_{n-1}$$

In other words, for $k = 2, 3, \ldots, n$, we define

$$w_k = v_k - c_{k1} w_1 - c_{k2} w_2 - \cdots - c_{k,k-1} w_{k-1}$$

where $c_{ki} = \langle v_k, w_i \rangle / \|w_i\|^2$ is the component of v_k along w_i. By Theorem 7.8, each w_k is orthogonal to the preceding w. Thus $w_1, w_2, \ldots, w_n$ form an orthogonal basis for V as claimed. Normalizing each w_k will then yield an orthonormal basis for V.

The above construction is known as the *Gram-Schmidt orthogonalization process*. The following remarks are in order.

Remark 1:   Each vector w_k is a linear combination of v_k and the preceding w_s'. Hence one can easily show, by induction, that each w_k is a linear combination of $v_1, v_2, \ldots, v_k$.

Remark 2:   Since taking multiples of vectors does not affect orthogonality, it may be simpler in hand calculations to clear fractions in any new w_k by multiplying w_k by an appropriate scalar, before obtaining the next w_{k+1}.

Remark 3:   Suppose $u_1, u_2, \ldots, u_r$ are linearly independent, and so they form a basis for $U = \text{span}(u_i)$. Applying the Gram-Schmidt orthogonalization process to the u's yields an orthogonal basis for U.

The following theorems, proved in Problems 7.40 and 7.41, use the above algorithm and remarks.

Theorem 7.9:   Let $\{v_1, v_2, \ldots, v_n\}$ be any basis of an inner product space V.   Then there exists an orthonormal basis $\{u_1, u_2, \ldots, u_n\}$ of V such that the change-of-basis matrix from $\{v_i\}$ to $\{u_i\}$ is triangular, that is, for $k = 1, \ldots, n$,

$$u_k = a_{k1}v_1 + a_{k2}v_2 + \cdots + a_{kk}v_k$$

Theorem 7.10:   Suppose $S = \{w_1, w_2, \ldots, w_r\}$ is an orthogonal basis for a subspace W of a vector space V.   Then one may extend S to an orthogonal basis for V, that is, one may find vectors $w_{r+1}, \ldots, w_n$ such that $\{w_1, w_2, \ldots, w_n\}$ is an orthogonal basis for V.

EXAMPLE 7.13   Consider the subspace U of $\mathbf{R}^4$ spanned by

$$v_1 = (1, 1, 1, 1), \qquad v_2 = (1, 2, 4, 5), \qquad v_3 = (1, -3, -4, -2)$$

The Gram-Schmidt orthogonalization process is used to find an orthogonal basis for U and then an orthonormal basis for U as follows.   First set $w_1 = v_1 = (1, 1, 1, 1)$.   Next find

$$v_2 - \frac{\langle v_2, w_1 \rangle}{\|w_1\|^2} w_1 = (1, 2, 4, 5) - \frac{12}{4}(1, 1, 1, 1) = (-2, -1, 1, 2)$$

Set $w_2 = (-2, -1, 1, 2)$.   Then find

$$v_3 - \frac{\langle v_3, w_1 \rangle}{\|w_1\|^2} w_1 - \frac{\langle v_3, w_2 \rangle}{\|w_2\|^2} w_2 = (1, -3, -4, -2) - \frac{-8}{4}(1, 1, 1, 1) - \frac{-7}{10}(-2, -1, 1, 2)$$

$$= \left(\frac{8}{5}, -\frac{17}{10}, -\frac{13}{10}, \frac{7}{5} \right)$$

Clear fractions to obtain $w_3 = (16, -17, -13, 14)$.   Last, normalize the orthogonal basis

$$w_1 = (1, 1, 1, 1), \qquad w_2 = (-2, -1, 1, 2), \qquad w_3 = (16, -17, -13, 14)$$

Since $\|w_1\|^2 = 4$, $\|w_2\|^2 = 10$, $\|w_3\|^2 = 910$, the following form an orthonormal basis of U:

$$u_1 = \frac{1}{2}(1, 1, 1, 1), \qquad u_2 = \frac{1}{\sqrt{10}}(-2, -1, 1, 2), \qquad u_3 = \frac{1}{\sqrt{910}}(16, -17, -13, 14)$$

7.8   ORTHOGONAL AND POSITIVE DEFINITE MATRICES

This section discusses two types of matrices which are closely related to real inner product spaces.

Orthogonal Matrices

A real matrix P is *orthogonal* if P is nonsingular and $P^{-1} = P^T$ or, in other words, if $PP^T = P^T P = I$.   First we recall (Theorem 3.3) an important characterization of such matrices.

Theorem 7.11:   Let P be a real matrix.   Then the following three properties are equivalent:

    (i) P is orthogonal, that is, $P^T = P^{-1}$.

    (ii) The rows of P form an orthonormal set of vectors.

    (iii) The columns of P form an orthonormal set of vectors.

(The above theorem is true only using the usual inner product on $\mathbf{R}^n$.   It is not true if $\mathbf{R}^n$ is given any other inner product.)

EXAMPLE 7.14

(a) Let $P = \begin{bmatrix} 1/\sqrt{3} & 1/\sqrt{3} & 1/\sqrt{3} \\ 0 & 1/\sqrt{2} & -1/\sqrt{2} \\ 2/\sqrt{6} & -1/\sqrt{6} & -1/\sqrt{6} \end{bmatrix}$.   The rows of P are orthogonal to each other and are unit vectors.   Thus P is an orthogonal matrix.

(b) Let P be a 2×2 orthogonal matrix.   Then, for some real number θ, we have

$$P = \begin{bmatrix} \cos\theta & \sin\theta \\ -\sin\theta & \cos\theta \end{bmatrix} \quad \text{or} \quad P = \begin{bmatrix} \cos\theta & \sin\theta \\ \sin\theta & -\cos\theta \end{bmatrix}$$

The following two theorems show important relationships between orthogonal matrices and orthonormal bases of a real inner product space V.

Theorem 7.12:   Suppose $E = \{e_i\}$ and $E' = \{e_i'\}$ are orthonormal bases of V.   Let P be the change-of-basis matrix from the basis E to the basis E'.   Then P is orthogonal.

Theorem 7.13:   Let $\{e_1, \ldots, e_n\}$ be an orthonormal basis of an inner product space V.   Let $P = [a_{ij}]$ be an orthogonal matrix.   Then the following n vectors form an orthonormal basis for V:

$$e_i' = a_{1i}e_1 + a_{2i}e_2 + \cdots + a_{ni}e_n, \qquad i = 1, 2, \ldots, n$$

Positive Definite Matrices

Let A be a real symmetric matrix.   Then A is said to be *positive definite* if, for every vector $u \neq 0$ in $\mathbf{R}^n$,

$$u^T A u > 0$$

Algorithms to decide whether or not a matrix A is positive definite will be given in Chapter 12. However, for 2×2 matrices we have simple criteria, which we state formally:

Theorem 7.14: A 2×2 real symmetric matrix $A = \begin{bmatrix} a & b \\ c & d \end{bmatrix} = \begin{bmatrix} a & b \\ b & d \end{bmatrix}$ is positive definite if and only if the diagonal entries a and d are positive and the determinant $|A| = ad - bc = ad - b^2$ is positive.

EXAMPLE 7.15 Consider the following symmetric matrices:

$$A = \begin{bmatrix} 1 & 3 \\ 3 & 4 \end{bmatrix}, \qquad B = \begin{bmatrix} 1 & -2 \\ -2 & -3 \end{bmatrix}, \qquad C = \begin{bmatrix} 1 & -2 \\ -2 & 5 \end{bmatrix}$$

Then A is not positive definite since $|A| = 4 - 9 = -5$ is negative. B is not positive definite since the diagonal entry -3 is negative. However, C is positive definite since the diagonal entries 1 and 5 are positive, and the determinant $|C| = 5 - 4 = 1$ is also positive.

The following theorem applies.

Theorem 7.15: Let A be a real positive definite matrix. Then the function $\langle u, v \rangle = u^T A v$ is an inner product on $\mathbf{R}^n$.

Matrix Representation of an Inner Product

Theorem 7.15 says that every positive definite matrix A determines an inner product. The following discussion and Theorem 7.17 may be viewed as the converse of this result.

Let V be a real inner product space and let $S = \{u_1, u_2, \ldots, u_n\}$ be any basis for V. The matrix $A = [a_{ij}]$, defined by $a_{ij} = \langle u_i, u_j \rangle$, that is,

$$A = \begin{bmatrix} \langle u_1, u_1 \rangle & \langle u_1, u_2 \rangle & \ldots & \langle u_1, u_n \rangle \\ \langle u_2, u_1 \rangle & \langle u_2, u_2 \rangle & \ldots & \langle u_2, u_n \rangle \\ \ldots\ldots\ldots\ldots\ldots\ldots\ldots\ldots\ldots\ldots \\ \langle u_n, u_1 \rangle & \langle u_n, u_2 \rangle & \ldots & \langle u_n, u_n \rangle \end{bmatrix}$$

is called the *matrix representation of the inner product on V relative to the basis S.*

Observe that A is symmetric since the inner product is symmetric, that is, $\langle u_i, u_j \rangle = \langle u_j, u_i \rangle$. Also, A depends on both the inner product on V and the basis S for V. Moreover, if S is an orthogonal basis, then A is diagonal, and if S is an orthonormal basis, then A is the identity matrix.

EXAMPLE 7.16 The following three vectors form a basis S for Euclidean space $\mathbf{R}^3$:

$$u_1 = (1, 1, 0), \qquad u_2 = (1, 2, 3), \qquad u_3 = (1, 3, 5)$$

Computing each $\langle u_i, u_j \rangle = \langle u_j, u_i \rangle$ yields:

$$\langle u_1, u_1 \rangle = 1 + 1 + 0 = 2 \qquad \langle u_1, u_2 \rangle = 1 + 2 + 0 = 3 \qquad \langle u_1, u_3 \rangle = 1 + 3 + 0 = 4$$
$$\langle u_2, u_2 \rangle = 1 + 4 + 9 = 14 \qquad \langle u_2, u_3 \rangle = 1 + 6 + 15 = 22 \qquad \langle u_3, u_3 \rangle = 1 + 9 + 25 = 35$$

Thus

$$A = \begin{bmatrix} 2 & 3 & 4 \\ 3 & 14 & 22 \\ 4 & 22 & 35 \end{bmatrix}$$

is the matrix representation of the usual inner product on $\mathbf{R}^3$ relative to the basis S.

The following theorems apply.

Theorem 7.16: Let A be the matrix representation of an inner product relative to a basis S for V. Then, for any vectors $u, v \in V$, we have

$$\langle u, v \rangle = [u]^T A [v]$$

where $[u]$ and $[v]$ denote the (column) coordinate vectors relative to the basis S.

Theorem 7.17: Let A be the matrix representation of any inner product on V. Then A is a positive definite matrix.

7.9 NORMED VECTOR SPACES (OPTIONAL)

We begin with a definition.

Definition: Let V be a real or complex vector space. Suppose to each $v \in V$ there is assigned a real number, denoted by $\|v\|$. This function $\| \cdot \|$ is called a *norm* on V if it satisfies the following axioms:

[N_1] $\|v\| \geq 0$; and $\|v\| = 0$ if and only if $v = 0$.

[N_2] $\|kv\| = |k|\,\|v\|$.

[N_3] $\|u + v\| \leq \|u\| + \|v\|$.

A vector space V with a norm is called a *normed vector space*.

Suppose V is a normed vector space. The *distance* between two vectors u and v in V is denoted and defined by

$$d(u, v) = \|u - v\|$$

The following theorem is the main reason $d(u, v)$ is called the distance between u and v.

Theorem 7.18: Let V be a normed vector space. Then the function $d(u, v) = \|u - v\|$ satisfies the following three axioms of a metric space:

[M_1] $d(u, v) \geq 0$; and $d(u, v) = 0$ if and only if $u = v$.

[M_2] $d(u, v) = d(v, u)$.

[M_3] $d(u, v) \leq d(u, w) + d(w, v)$.

Normed Vector Spaces and Inner Product Spaces

Suppose V is an inner product space. Recall that the norm of a vector v in V is defined by

$$\|v\| = \sqrt{\langle v, v \rangle}$$

One can prove (Theorem 7.2) that this norm does satisfy [N_1], [N_2], and [N_3]. Thus every inner product space V is a normed vector space. On the other hand, there may be norms on a vector space V that do not come from an inner product on V.

Norms on $\mathbf{R}^n$

The following defines three important norms on $\mathbf{R}^n$:

$$\|(a_1, \ldots, a_n)\|_\infty = \max (|a_i|)$$

$$\|(a_1, \ldots, a_n)\|_1 = |a_1| + |a_2| + \cdots + |a_n|$$

$$\|(a_1, \ldots, a_n)\|_2 = \sqrt{|a_1|^2 + |a_2|^2 + \cdots + |a_n|^2}$$

(Note that subscripts are used to distinguish between the three norms.) The norms $\|\cdot\|_\infty$, $\|\cdot\|_1$, and $\|\cdot\|_2$ are called *infinity norm*, *one-norm* and *two-norm*, respectively. Observe that $\|\cdot\|_2$ is the norm on $\mathbf{R}^n$ induced by the usual inner product on $\mathbf{R}^n$. (We will let d_∞, d_1, and d_2 denote the corresponding functions.)

EXAMPLE 7.17 Consider the vectors $u = (1, -5, 3)$ and $v = (4, 2, -3)$ in $\mathbf{R}^3$.

(a) The infinity norm chooses the maximum of the absolute values of the components. Hence

$$\|u\|_\infty = 5 \qquad \text{and} \qquad \|v\|_\infty = 4$$

(b) The one-norm adds the absolute values of the components. Thus

$$\|u\|_1 = 1 + 5 + 3 = 9 \qquad \text{and} \qquad \|v\|_1 = 4 + 2 + 3 = 9$$

(c) The two-norm is equal to the square root of the sum of the squares of the components (i.e., the norm induced by the usual inner product on $\mathbf{R}^3$). Thus

$$\|u\|_2 = \sqrt{1 + 25 + 9} = \sqrt{35} \qquad \text{and} \qquad \|v\|_2 = \sqrt{16 + 4 + 9} = \sqrt{29}$$

(d) Since $u - v = (1 - 4, -5 - 2, 3 + 3) = (-3, -7, 6)$, we have

$$d_\infty(u, v) = 7, \qquad d_1(u, v) = 3 + 7 + 6 = 16, \qquad d_2(u, v) = \sqrt{9 + 49 + 36} = \sqrt{94}$$

EXAMPLE 7.18 Consider the Cartesian plane $\mathbf{R}^2$ shown in Fig. 7-6.

(a) Let D_1 be the set of points $u = (x, y)$ in $\mathbf{R}^2$ such that $\|u\|_2 = 1$. Then D_1 consists of the points (x, y) such that $\|u\|_2^2 = x^2 + y^2 = 1$. Thus D_1 is the unit circle, as shown in Fig. 7-6.

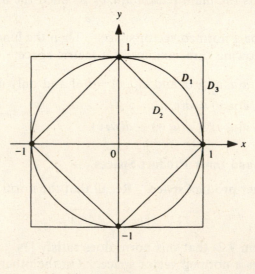

Fig. 7-6

(b)   Let D_2 be the set of points $u = (x, y)$ in $\mathbf{R}^2$ such that $\|u\|_1 = 1$. Then D_2 consists of the points (x, y) such that $\|u\|_1 = |x| + |y| = 1$. Thus D_2 is the diamond inside the unit circle, as shown in Fig. 7-6.

(c)   Let D_3 be the set of points $u = (x, y)$ in $\mathbf{R}^2$ such that $\|u\|_\infty = 1$. Then D_3 consists of the points (x, y) such that $\|u\|_\infty = \max(|x|, |y|) = 1$. Thus D_3 is the square circumscribing the unit circle, as shown in Fig. 7-6.

Norms on $C[a, b]$

Consider the vector space $V = C[a, b]$ of real continuous functions on the interval $a \le t \le b$. Recall that the following defines an inner product on V:

$$\langle f, g \rangle = \int_a^b f(t) g(t)\, dt$$

Accordingly, the above inner product defines the following norm on $V = C[a, b]$ (which is analogous to the $\|\cdot\|_2$ norm on $\mathbf{R}^n$):

$$\|f\|_2 = \sqrt{\int_a^b [f(t)]^2\, dt}$$

The following defines two other norms on $V = C[a, b]$:

$$\|f\|_1 = \int_a^b |f(t)|\, dt \qquad \text{and} \qquad \|f\|_\infty = \max(|f(t)|)$$

There are geometrical descriptions of these norms and their corresponding distance functions. Specifically, as shown in Fig. 7-7,

$$\|f\|_1 = \text{area between function } |f| \text{ and } t \text{ axis}$$
$$d_1(f, g) = \text{area between functions } f \text{ and } g$$

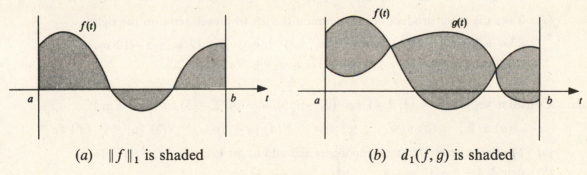

(a) $\|f\|_1$ is shaded   (b) $d_1(f, g)$ is shaded

Fig. 7-7

and, as shown in Fig. 7-8,

$$\|f\|_\infty = \text{maximum distance between } f \text{ and } t \text{ axis}$$
$$d_\infty(f, g) = \text{maximum distance between } f \text{ and } g$$

These norms are also analogous to the norms $\|\cdot\|_1$ and $\|\cdot\|_\infty$ on $\mathbf{R}^n$.

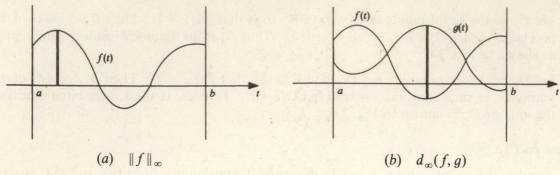

$$(a) \quad \|f\|_\infty \qquad\qquad\qquad (b) \quad d_\infty(f, g)$$

Fig. 7-8

Solved Problems

INNER PRODUCTS

7.1. Expand: (a) $\langle 5u_1 + 8u_2, 6v_1 - 7v_2 \rangle$; (b) $\langle 3u + 5v, 4u - 6v \rangle$; (c) $\|2u - 3v\|^2$;
(d) $\langle 3u_1 + 2u_2, 5v_1 - 6v_2 + 4v_3 \rangle$.

Use linearity in both positions and, when possible, symmetry, $\langle u, v \rangle = \langle v, u \rangle$.

(a) $\langle 5u_1 + 8u_2, 6v_1 - 7v_2 \rangle = \langle 5u_1, 6v_1 \rangle + \langle 5u_1, -7v_2 \rangle + \langle 8u_2, 6v_1 \rangle + \langle 8u_2, -7v_2 \rangle$
$$= 30\langle u_1, v_1 \rangle - 35\langle u_1, v_2 \rangle + 48\langle u_2, v_1 \rangle - 56\langle u_2, v_2 \rangle$$

Remark: Observe the similarity between the above expansion and the expansion of $(5a + 8b)(6c - 7d)$ in ordinary algebra.

(b) $\langle 3u + 5v, 4u - 6v \rangle = 12\langle u, u \rangle - 18\langle u, v \rangle + 20\langle v, u \rangle - 30\langle v, v \rangle$
$$= 12\langle u, u \rangle + 2\langle u, v \rangle - 30\langle v, v \rangle$$

(c) $\|2u - 3v\|^2 = \langle 2u - 3v, 2u - 3v \rangle = 4\langle u, u \rangle - 6\langle u, v \rangle - 6\langle v, u \rangle + 9\langle v, v \rangle$
$$= 4\|u\|^2 - 12\langle u, v \rangle + 9\|v\|^2$$

(d) Take the inner product of each term on the left with each term on the right:

$$\langle 3u_1 + 2u_2, 5v_1 - 6v_2 + 4v_3 \rangle = 15\langle u_1, v_1 \rangle - 18\langle u_1, v_2 \rangle + 12\langle u_1, v_3 \rangle + 10\langle u_2, v_1 \rangle$$
$$- 12\langle u_2, v_2 \rangle + 8\langle u_2, v_3 \rangle$$

7.2. Consider vectors $u = (1, 2, 4)$, $v = (2, -3, 5)$, $w = (4, 2, -3)$ in $\mathbf{R}^3$. Find:

(a) $u \cdot v$,   (b) $u \cdot w$,   (c) $v \cdot w$,   (d) $(u + v) \cdot w$,   (e) $\|u\|$,   (f) $\|v\|$

(a) Multiply corresponding components and add to get $u \cdot v = 2 - 6 + 20 = 16$.

(b) $u \cdot w = 4 + 4 - 12 = -4$.

(c) $v \cdot w = 8 - 6 - 15 = -13$.

(d) First find $u + v = (3, -1, 9)$. Then $(u + v) \cdot w = 12 - 2 - 27 = -17$. Alternatively, using $[\mathbf{I}_1]$, $(u + v) \cdot w = u \cdot w + v \cdot w = -4 - 13 = -17$.

(e) First find $\|u\|^2$ by squaring the components of u and adding:
$$\|u\|^2 = 1^2 + 2^2 + 4^2 = 1 + 4 + 16 = 21 \qquad \text{and so} \qquad \|u\| = \sqrt{21}$$

(f) $\|v\|^2 = 4 + 9 + 25 = 38$ and so $\|v\| = \sqrt{38}$.

7.3. Verify that the following defines an inner product in $\mathbf{R}^2$:

$$\langle u, v \rangle = x_1 y_1 - x_1 y_2 - x_2 y_1 + 3x_2 y_2 \qquad \text{where} \qquad u = (x_1, x_2), \ v = (y_1, y_2)$$

Method 1:   We verify the three axioms of an inner product.   Letting $w = (z_1, z_2)$, we find

$$au + bw = a(x_1, x_2) + b(z_1, z_2) = (ax_1 + bz_1, ax_2 + bz_2)$$

Thus

$$
\begin{aligned}
\langle au + bw, v \rangle &= \langle (ax_1 + bz_1, ax_2 + bz_2), (y_1, y_2) \rangle \\
&= (ax_1 + bz_1)y_1 - (ax_1 + bz_1)y_2 \\
&\quad - (ax_2 + bz_2)y_1 + 3(ax_2 + bz_2)y_2 \\
&= a(x_1 y_1 - x_1 y_2 - x_2 y_1 + 3x_2 y_2) \\
&\quad + b(z_1 y_1 - z_1 y_2 - z_2 y_1 + 3z_2 y_2) \\
&= a\langle u, v \rangle + b\langle w, v \rangle
\end{aligned}
$$

and so axiom $[I_1]$ is satisfied.   Also,

$$\langle v, u \rangle = y_1 x_1 - y_1 x_2 - y_2 x_1 + 3y_2 x_2 = x_1 y_1 - x_1 y_2 - x_2 y_1 + 3x_2 y_2 = \langle u, v \rangle$$

and axiom $[I_2]$ is satisfied.   Finally,

$$\langle u, u \rangle = x_1^2 - 2x_1 x_2 + 3x_2^2 = x_1^2 - 2x_1 x_2 + x_2^2 + 2x_2^2 = (x_1 - x_2)^2 + 2x_2^2 \geq 0$$

Also, $\langle u, u \rangle = 0$ if and only if $x_1 = 0$, $x_2 = 0$, i.e., $u = 0$.   Hence axiom $[I_3]$ is satisfied.

Method 2:   We argue via matrices, that is, we can write $\langle u, v \rangle$ in matrix notation:

$$\langle u, v \rangle = u^T A v = (x_1, x_2) \begin{bmatrix} 1 & -1 \\ -1 & 3 \end{bmatrix} \begin{bmatrix} y_1 \\ y_2 \end{bmatrix}$$

Since A is real and symmetric, we need only show that A is positive definite.   The diagonal elements 1 and 3 are positive, and the determinant $|A| = 3 - 1 = 2$ is positive.   Thus by Theorem 7.14, A is positive definite.   Accordingly, by Theorem 7.15, $\langle u, v \rangle$ is an inner product.

7.4. Consider the vectors $u = (1, 5)$ and $v = (3, 4)$ in $\mathbf{R}^2$.   Find:

(a) $\langle u, v \rangle$ with respect to the usual inner product in $\mathbf{R}^2$.

(b) $\langle u, v \rangle$ with respect to the inner product in $\mathbf{R}^2$ in Problem 7.3.

(c) $\|v\|$ using the usual inner product in $\mathbf{R}^2$.

(d) $\|v\|$ using the inner product in $\mathbf{R}^2$ in Problem 7.3.

(a) $\langle u, v \rangle = 3 + 20 = 23$.

(b) $\langle u, v \rangle = 1 \cdot 3 - 1 \cdot 4 - 5 \cdot 3 + 3 \cdot 5 \cdot 4 = 3 - 4 - 15 + 60 = 44$.

(c) $\|v\|^2 = \langle v, v \rangle = \langle (3, 4), (3, 4) \rangle = 9 + 16 = 25$; hence $\|v\| = 5$.

(d) $\|v\|^2 = \langle v, v \rangle = \langle (3, 4), (3, 4) \rangle = 9 - 12 - 12 + 48 = 33$; hence $\|v\| = \sqrt{33}$.

7.5. Consider the following polynomials in $\mathbf{P}(t)$ and inner product:

$$f(t) = t + 2, \qquad g(t) = 3t - 2, \qquad h(t) = t^2 - 2t - 3, \qquad \text{and} \qquad \langle f, g \rangle = \int_0^1 f(t) g(t) \, dt$$

(a) Find $\langle f, g \rangle$ and $\langle f, h \rangle$; (b) find $\|f\|$ and $\|g\|$; (c) normalize f and g.

(a) Integrate as follows:

$$\langle f, g \rangle = \int_0^1 (t + 2)(3t - 2) \, dt = \int_0^1 (3t^2 + 4t - 4) \, dt = [t^3 + 2t^2 - 4t]_0^1 = -1$$

$$\langle f, h \rangle = \int_0^1 (t + 2)(t^2 - 2t - 3) \, dt = \left[\frac{t^4}{4} - \frac{7t^2}{2} - 6t \right]_0^1 = -\frac{37}{4}$$

(b) $$\langle f, f \rangle = \int_0^1 (t + 2)(t + 2) \, dt = \frac{19}{3} \quad \text{and} \quad \|f\| = \sqrt{\frac{19}{3}} = \frac{\sqrt{57}}{3}$$

$$\langle g, g \rangle = \int_0^1 (3t - 2)(3t - 2) = 1; \text{ hence } \|g\| = \sqrt{1} = 1$$

(c) Since $\|f\| = \sqrt{57}/3$ and g is already a unit vector, we have

$$\hat{f} = \frac{1}{\|f\|} f = \frac{3}{\sqrt{57}} (t + 2) \qquad \text{and} \qquad \hat{g} = g = 3t - 2$$

7.6. Let $\mathbf{M} = \mathbf{M}_{2,3}$ with inner product $\langle A, B \rangle = \text{tr}\,(B^T A)$, and let

$$A = \begin{bmatrix} 9 & 8 & 7 \\ 6 & 5 & 4 \end{bmatrix}, \qquad B = \begin{bmatrix} 1 & 2 & 3 \\ 4 & 5 & 6 \end{bmatrix}, \qquad C = \begin{bmatrix} 3 & -5 & 2 \\ 1 & 0 & -4 \end{bmatrix}$$

Find: (a) $\langle A, B \rangle$, $\langle A, C \rangle$, $\langle B, C \rangle$; (b) $\langle 2A + 3B, 4C \rangle$; (c) $\|A\|$ and $\|B\|$.

(a) Use $\langle A, B \rangle = \text{tr}\,(B^T A) = \sum_{i=1}^{m} \sum_{j=1}^{n} a_{ij} b_{ij}$, the sum of the products of corresponding entries.

$$\langle A, B \rangle = 9 + 16 + 21 + 24 + 25 + 24 = 119$$
$$\langle A, C \rangle = 27 - 40 + 14 + 6 + 0 - 16 = -9$$
$$\langle B, C \rangle = 3 - 10 + 6 + 4 + 0 - 24 = -21$$

(b) Find $2A + 3B = \begin{bmatrix} 21 & 22 & 23 \\ 24 & 25 & 26 \end{bmatrix}$ and $4C = \begin{bmatrix} 12 & -20 & 8 \\ 4 & 0 & -16 \end{bmatrix}$. Then

$$\langle 2A + 3B, 4C \rangle = 252 - 440 + 184 + 96 + 0 - 416 = -324$$

Alternatively, using the linear property of inner products,

$$\langle 2A + 3B, 4C \rangle = 8\langle A, C \rangle + 12\langle B, C \rangle = 8(-9) + 12(-21) = -324$$

(c) Use $\|A\|^2 = \langle A, A \rangle = \sum_{i=1}^{m} \sum_{j=1}^{n} a_{ij}^2$, the sum of the squares of all the elements of A.

$$\|A\|^2 = \langle A, A \rangle = 9^2 + 8^2 + 7^2 + 6^2 + 5^2 + 4^2 = 271 \qquad \text{and so} \qquad \|A\| = \sqrt{271}$$
$$\|B\|^2 = \langle B, B \rangle = 1^2 + 2^2 + 3^2 + 4^2 + 5^2 + 6^2 = 91 \qquad \text{and so} \qquad \|B\| = \sqrt{91}$$

7.7. Find $\cos\theta$, where θ is the angle between:

(a) $u = (1, -3, 2)$ and $v = (2, 1, 5)$ in $\mathbf{R}^3$.

(b) $u = (1, 3, -5, 4)$ and $v = (2, -3, 4, 1)$ in $\mathbf{R}^4$.

(c) $f(t) = 2t - 1$ and $g(t) = t^2$, where $\langle f, g \rangle = \int_0^1 f(t)g(t)\,dt$.

(d) $A = \begin{bmatrix} 2 & 1 \\ 3 & -1 \end{bmatrix}$ and $B = \begin{bmatrix} 0 & -1 \\ 2 & 3 \end{bmatrix}$, where $\langle A, B \rangle = \operatorname{tr}(B^T A)$.

Use $\cos\theta = \dfrac{\langle u, v \rangle}{\|u\|\,\|v\|}$.

(a) Compute $\langle u, v \rangle = 2 - 3 + 10 = 9$, $\|u\|^2 = 1 + 9 + 4 = 14$, $\|v\|^2 = 4 + 1 + 25 = 30$. Thus

$$\cos\theta = \frac{9}{\sqrt{14}\sqrt{30}} = \frac{9}{\sqrt{105}}$$

(b) Here

$$\langle u, v \rangle = 2 - 9 - 20 + 4 = -23, \quad \|u\|^2 = 1 + 9 + 25 + 16 = 51, \quad \|v\|^2 = 4 + 9 + 16 + 1 = 30$$

Thus

$$\cos\theta = \frac{-23}{\sqrt{51}\sqrt{30}} = \frac{-23}{3\sqrt{170}}$$

(c) Compute

$$\langle f, g \rangle = \int_0^1 (2t^3 - t^2)\,dt = \left[\frac{t^4}{2} - \frac{t^3}{3}\right]_0^1 = \frac{1}{2} - \frac{1}{3} = \frac{1}{6}$$

$$\|f\|^2 = \langle f, f \rangle = \int_0^1 (4t^2 - 4t + 1)\,dt = \frac{1}{3} \quad \text{and} \quad \|g\|^2 = \langle g, g \rangle = \int_0^1 t^4\,dt = \frac{1}{5}$$

Thus

$$\cos\theta = \frac{\frac{1}{6}}{(1/\sqrt{3})(1/\sqrt{5})} = \frac{\sqrt{15}}{6}$$

(d) Compute $\langle A, B \rangle = 0 - 1 + 6 - 3 = 2$, $\|A\|^2 = 4 + 1 + 9 + 1 = 15$, $\|B\|^2 = 0 + 1 + 4 + 9 = 14$.

Thus

$$\cos\theta = \frac{2}{\sqrt{15}\sqrt{14}} = \frac{2}{\sqrt{210}}$$

7.8. Verify each of the following:

(a) Parallelogram law (Fig. 7-9): $\|u + v\|^2 + \|u - v\|^2 = 2\|u\|^2 + 2\|v\|^2$.

(b) Polar form for $\langle u, v \rangle$ (which shows that the inner product can be obtained from the norm function): $\langle u, v \rangle = \frac{1}{4}(\|u + v\|^2 - \|u - v\|^2)$.

Expand each of the following to obtain:

$$\|u + v\|^2 = \langle u + v, u + v \rangle = \|u\|^2 + 2\langle u, v \rangle + \|v\|^2 \tag{1}$$

$$\|u - v\|^2 = \langle u - v, u - v \rangle = \|u\|^2 - 2\langle u, v \rangle + \|v\|^2 \tag{2}$$

Add Eqs. (1) and (2) to get the Parallelogram law (a). Subtract Eq. (2) from Eq. (1) to obtain

$$\|u + v\|^2 - \|u - v\|^2 = 4\langle u, v \rangle$$

Divide by 4 to obtain the (real) polar form (b).

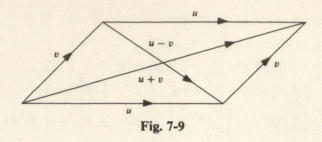

Fig. 7-9

ORTHOGONALITY, ORTHOGONAL COMPLEMENTS, ORTHOGONAL SETS

7.9. Find k so that the following pairs are orthogonal:

(a) $u = (1, 2, k, 3)$ and $v = (3, k, 7, -5)$ in $\mathbf{R}^4$.

(b) $f(t) = t + k$ and $g(t) = t^2$, where $\langle f, g \rangle = \int_0^1 f(t)g(t)\, dt$.

(a)   First find $\langle u, v \rangle = (1, 2, k, 3) \cdot (3, k, 7, -5) = 3 + 2k + 7k - 15 = 9k - 12$.   Then set $\langle u, v \rangle = 9k - 12 = 0$ to find $k = \frac{4}{3}$.

(b)   First find

$$\langle f, g \rangle = \int_0^1 (t + k)t^2\, dt = \int_0^1 (t^3 + kt^2)\, dt = \left[\frac{t^4}{4} + \frac{kt^3}{3} \right]_0^1 = \frac{1}{4} + \frac{k}{3}$$

Set $\langle f, g \rangle = \frac{1}{4} + \frac{k}{3} = 0$ to obtain $k = -\frac{3}{4}$.

7.10. Consider $u = (0, 1, -2, 5)$ in $\mathbf{R}^4$.   Find a basis for the orthogonal complement $u^\perp$ of u.

We seek all vectors (x, y, z, t) in $\mathbf{R}^4$ such that

$$\langle (x, y, z, t), (0, 1, -2, 5) \rangle = 0 \qquad \text{or} \qquad 0x + y - 2z + 5t = 0$$

The free variables are x, z, and t.   Accordingly:

(1)   Set $x = 1$, $z = 0$, $t = 0$ to obtain the solution $w_1 = (1, 0, 0, 0)$.

(2)   Set $x = 0$, $z = 1$, $t = 0$ to obtain the solution $w_2 = (0, 2, 1, 0)$.

(3)   Set $x = 0$, $z = 0$, $t = 1$ to obtain the solution $w_3 = (0, -5, 0, 1)$.

The vectors w_1, w_2, w_3 form a basis of the solution space of the equation and hence a basis for $u^\perp$.

7.11. Let W be the subspace of $\mathbf{R}^5$ spanned by $u = (1, 2, 3, -1, 2)$ and $v = (2, 4, 7, 2, -1)$.   Find a basis of the orthogonal complement $W^\perp$ of W.

We seek all vectors $w = (x, y, z, s, t)$ such that

$$\langle w, u \rangle = \ \ x + 2y + 3z - \ \ s + 2t = 0$$
$$\langle w, v \rangle = 2x + 4y + 7z + 2s - \ \ t = 0$$

Eliminating x from the second equation, we find the equivalent system

$$x + 2y + 3z - \ s + 2t = 0$$
$$z + 4s - 5t = 0$$

The free variables are y, s, and t.   Therefore

(1)   Set $y = -1$, $s = 0$, $t = 0$ to obtain the solution $w_1 = (2, -1, 0, 0, 0)$.

(2)   Set $y = 0$, $s = 1$, $t = 0$ to find the solution $w_2 = (13, 0, -4, 1, 0)$.

(3)   Set $y = 0$, $s = 0$, $t = 1$ to obtain the solution $w_3 = (-17, 0, 5, 0, 1)$.

The set $\{w_1, w_2, w_3\}$ is a basis of $W^\perp$.

7.12.   Let $w = (1, 2, 3, 1)$ be a vector in $\mathbf{R}^4$.   Find an orthogonal basis for $w^\perp$.

Find a nonzero solution of $x + 2y + 3z + t = 0$, say $v_1 = (0, 0, 1, -3)$.   Now find a nonzero solution of the system

$$x + 2y + 3z + t = 0, \qquad z - 3t = 0$$

say $v_2 = (0, -5, 3, 1)$.   Lastly, find a nonzero solution of the system

$$x + 2y + 3z + t = 0, \qquad -5y + 3z + t = 0, \qquad z - 3t = 0$$

say $v_3 = (-14, 2, 3, 1)$.   Thus v_1, v_2, v_3 form an orthogonal basis for $w^\perp$.   (Compare with Problem 7.10, where the basis need not be orthogonal.)

7.13.   Let S consist of the following vectors in $\mathbf{R}^3$:

$$u_1 = (1, 1, 1), \qquad u_2 = (1, 2, -3), \qquad u_3 = (5, -4, -1)$$

(*a*)   Show that S is orthogonal and S is a basis for $\mathbf{R}^3$.

(*b*)   Write $v = (1, 5, -7)$ as a linear combination of u_1, u_2, u_3.

(*a*)   Compute

$$\langle u_1, u_2 \rangle = 1 + 2 - 3 = 0, \qquad \langle u_1, u_3 \rangle = 5 - 4 - 1 = 0, \qquad \langle u_2, u_3 \rangle = 5 - 8 + 3 = 0$$

Since each inner product equals 0, S is orthogonal and hence S is linearly independent. Thus S is a basis for $\mathbf{R}^3$ since any three linearly independent vectors form a basis for $\mathbf{R}^3$.

(*b*)   Let $v = xu_1 + yu_2 + zu_3$ for unknown scalars x, y, z, that is,

$$(1, 5, -7) = x(1, 1, 1) + y(1, 2, -3) + z(5, -4, -1) \tag{1}$$

Method 1:   Expand Eq. (*1*), obtaining the system

$$x + y + 5z = 1, \qquad x + 2y - 4z = 5, \qquad x - 3y - z = -7$$

Solve the system to obtain $x = -\frac{1}{3}$, $y = \frac{16}{7}$, $z = -\frac{4}{21}$.

Method 2:   (This method uses the fact that the basis vectors are orthogonal, and the arithmetic is simpler).   Take the inner product of Eq. (*1*) with u_1 to get

$$(1, 5, -7) \cdot (1, 1, 1) = x(1, 1, 1) \cdot (1, 1, 1) \qquad \text{or} \qquad -1 = 3x$$

or
$$x = -\tfrac{1}{3}$$

(The two last terms drop out since u_1 is orthogonal to u_2 and to u_3.)   Take the inner product of Eq. (*1*) with u_2 to get

$$(1, 5, -7) \cdot (1, 2, -3) = y(1, 2, -3) \cdot (1, 2, -3) \qquad \text{or} \qquad 32 = 14y$$

or
$$y = \tfrac{16}{7}$$

Take the inner product of Eq. (1) with u_3 to get

$$(1, 5, -7) \cdot (5, -4, -1) = z(5, -4, -1) \cdot (5, -4, -1)$$

or $\qquad -8 = 42z \qquad$ or $\qquad z = -\frac{4}{21}$

In either case, we get $v = -\frac{1}{3}u_1 + \frac{16}{7}u_2 - \frac{4}{21}u_3$.

(The procedure in Method 2 is the content of Theorem 7.7, that is, that x, y, z are the Fourier coefficients of v with respect to u_1, u_2, u_3.)

7.14. Let S consist of the following vectors in $\mathbf{R}^4$:

$$u_1 = (1, 1, 0, -1), \qquad u_2 = (1, 2, 1, 3), \qquad u_3 = (1, 1, -9, 2), \qquad u_4 = (16, -13, 1, 3)$$

(a) Show that S is orthogonal and a basis of $\mathbf{R}^4$.

(b) Find the coordinates of an arbitrary vector $v = (a, b, c, d)$ in $\mathbf{R}^4$ relative to the basis S.

(a) Compute

$$u_1 \cdot u_2 = 1 + 2 + 0 - 3 = 0, \quad u_1 \cdot u_3 = 1 + 1 + 0 - 2 = 0, \quad u_1 \cdot u_4 = 16 - 13 + 0 - 3 = 0$$
$$u_2 \cdot u_3 = 1 + 2 - 9 + 6 = 0, \quad u_2 \cdot u_4 = 16 - 26 + 1 + 9 = 0, \quad u_3 \cdot u_4 = 16 - 13 - 9 + 6 = 0$$

Thus S is orthogonal, and hence S is linearly independent. Accordingly, S is a basis for $\mathbf{R}^4$ since any four linearly independent vectors form a basis of $\mathbf{R}^4$.

(b) Since S is orthogonal, we need only find the Fourier coefficients of v with respect to the basis vectors, as in Theorem 7.7. Thus

$$k_1 = \frac{\langle v, u_1 \rangle}{\langle u_1, u_1 \rangle} = \frac{a + b - d}{3}, \qquad k_3 = \frac{\langle v, u_3 \rangle}{\langle u_3, u_3 \rangle} = \frac{a + b - 9c + 2d}{87}$$

$$k_2 = \frac{\langle v, u_2 \rangle}{\langle u_2, u_2 \rangle} = \frac{a + 2b + c + 3d}{15}, \qquad k_4 = \frac{\langle v, u_4 \rangle}{\langle u_4, u_4 \rangle} = \frac{16a - 13b + c + 3d}{435}$$

are the coordinates of v with respect to the basis S.

7.15. Suppose S, S_1, S_2 are subsets of V. Prove the following:

(a) $S \subseteq S^{\perp\perp}$, (b) if $S_1 \subseteq S_2$, then $S_2^{\perp} \subseteq S_1^{\perp}$; (c) $S^{\perp} = \text{span}(S)^{\perp}$.

(a) Let $w \in S$. Then $\langle w, v \rangle = 0$ for every $v \in S^{\perp}$; hence $w \in S^{\perp\perp}$. Accordingly, $S \subseteq S^{\perp\perp}$.

(b) Let $w \in S_2^{\perp}$. Then $\langle w, v \rangle = 0$ for every $v \in S_2$. Since $S_1 \subseteq S_2$, $\langle w, v \rangle = 0$ for every $v \in S_1$. Thus $w \in S_1^{\perp}$, and hence $S_2^{\perp} \subseteq S_1^{\perp}$.

(c) Since $S \subseteq \text{span}(S)$, part (b) gives us span$(S)^{\perp} \subseteq S$. Suppose $u \in S^{\perp}$ and $v \in \text{span}(S)$. Then there exist $w_1, w_2, \ldots, w_k$ in S such that $v = a_1 w_1 + a_2 w_2 + \cdots + a_k w_k$. Then, using $u \in S^{\perp}$, we have

$$\langle u, v \rangle = \langle u, a_1 w_1 + a_2 w_2 + \cdots + a_k w_k \rangle = a_1 \langle u, w_1 \rangle + a_2 \langle u, w_2 \rangle + \cdots + a_k \langle u, w_k \rangle$$
$$= a_1(0) + a_2(0) + \cdots + a_k(0) = 0$$

Thus $u \in \text{span}(S)^{\perp}$. Accordingly, $S^{\perp} \subseteq \text{span}(S)^{\perp}$. Both inclusions give $S^{\perp} = \text{span}(S)^{\perp}$.

7.16. Prove Theorem 7.6 (Pythagoras): Suppose $\{u_1, u_2, \ldots, u_r\}$ is an orthogonal set of vectors. Then
$$\|u_1 + u_2 + \cdots + u_r\|^2 = \|u_1\|^2 + \|u_2\|^2 + \cdots + \|u_r\|^2$$

Expanding the inner product, we have

$$\|u_1 + u_2 + \cdots + u_r\|^2 = \langle u_1 + u_2 + \cdots + u_r, u_1 + u_2 + \cdots + u_r \rangle$$
$$= \langle u_1, u_1 \rangle + \langle u_2, u_2 \rangle + \cdots + \langle u_r, u_r \rangle + \sum_{i \neq j} \langle u_i, u_j \rangle$$

The theorem follows from the fact that $\langle u_i, u_i \rangle = \|u_i\|^2$ and $\langle u_i, u_j \rangle = 0$ for $i \neq j$.

7.17. Suppose $E = \{e_1, e_2, \ldots, e_n\}$ is an orthonormal basis of V. Prove:

(a) For any $u \in V$, we have $u = \langle u, e_1 \rangle e_1 + \langle u, e_2 \rangle e_2 + \cdots + \langle u, e_n \rangle e_n$.

(b) $\langle a_1 e_1 + \cdots + a_n e_n, b_1 e_1 + \cdots + b_n e_n \rangle = a_1 b_1 + a_2 b_2 + \cdots + a_n b_n$.

(c) For any $u, v \in V$, we have $\langle u, v \rangle = \langle u, e_1 \rangle \langle v, e_1 \rangle + \cdots + \langle u, e_n \rangle \langle v, e_n \rangle$.

(a) Suppose $u = k_1 e_1 + k_2 e_2 + \cdots + k_n e_n$. Taking the inner product of u with e_1,

$$\langle u, e_1 \rangle = \langle k_1 e_1 + k_2 e_2 + \cdots + k_n e_n, e_1 \rangle$$
$$= k_1 \langle e_1, e_1 \rangle + k_2 \langle e_2, e_1 \rangle + \cdots + k_n \langle e_n, e_1 \rangle$$
$$= k_1(1) + k_2(0) + \cdots + k_n(0) = k_1$$

Similarly, for $i = 2, \ldots, n$,

$$\langle u, e_i \rangle = \langle k_1 e_1 + \cdots + k_i e_i + \cdots + k_n e_n, e_i \rangle$$
$$= k_1 \langle e_1, e_i \rangle + \cdots + k_i \langle e_i, e_i \rangle + \cdots + k_n \langle e_n, e_i \rangle$$
$$= k_1(0) + \cdots + k_i(1) + \cdots + k_n(0) = k_i$$

Substituting $\langle u, e_i \rangle$ for k_i in the equation $u = k_1 e_1 + \cdots + k_n e_n$, we obtain the desired result.

(b) We have

$$\left\langle \sum_{i=1}^{n} a_i e_i, \sum_{j=1}^{n} b_j e_j \right\rangle = \sum_{i,j=1}^{n} a_j b_j \langle e_i, e_j \rangle = \sum_{i=1}^{n} a_i b_i \langle e_i, e_i \rangle + \sum_{i \neq 1} a_i b_j \langle e_i, e_j \rangle$$

But $\langle e_i, e_j \rangle = 0$ for $i \neq j$, and $\langle e_i, e_j \rangle = 1$ for $i = j$. Hence, as required,

$$\left\langle \sum_{i=1}^{n} a_i e_i, \sum_{j=1}^{n} b_j e_j \right\rangle = \sum_{i=1}^{n} a_i b_i = a_1 b_1 + a_2 b_2 + \cdots + a_n b_n$$

(c) By part (a) we have

$$u = \langle u, e_1 \rangle e_1 + \cdots + \langle u, e_n \rangle e_n \quad \text{and} \quad v = \langle v, e_1 \rangle e_1 + \cdots + \langle v, e_n \rangle e_n$$

Thus by part (b),

$$\langle u, v \rangle = \langle u, e_1 \rangle \langle v, e_1 \rangle + \langle u, e_2 \rangle \langle v, e_2 \rangle + \cdots + \langle u, e_n \rangle \langle v, e_n \rangle$$

PROJECTIONS, GRAM-SCHMIDT ALGORITHM, APPLICATIONS

7.18. Suppose $w \neq 0$. Let v be any vector in V. Show that

$$c = \frac{\langle v, w \rangle}{\langle w, w \rangle} = \frac{\langle v, w \rangle}{\|w\|^2}$$

is the unique scalar such that $v' = v - cw$ is orthogonal to w.

In order for v' to be orthogonal to w we must have

$$\langle v - cw, w \rangle = 0 \qquad \text{or} \qquad \langle v, w \rangle - c\langle w, w \rangle = 0 \qquad \text{or} \qquad \langle v, w \rangle = c\langle w, w \rangle$$

Thus $c = \dfrac{\langle v, w \rangle}{\langle w, w \rangle}$. Conversely, suppose $c = \dfrac{\langle v, w \rangle}{\langle w, w \rangle}$. Then

$$\langle v - cw, w \rangle = \langle v, w \rangle - c\langle w, w \rangle = \langle v, w \rangle - \frac{\langle v, w \rangle}{\langle w, w \rangle}\langle w, w \rangle = 0$$

7.19. Find the Fourier coefficient c and the projection of $v = (1, -2, 3, -4)$ along $w = (1, 2, 1, 2)$ in $\mathbf{R}^4$.

Compute $\langle v, w \rangle = 1 - 4 + 3 - 8 = -8$ and $\|w\|^2 = 1 + 4 + 1 + 4 = 10$. Then

$$c = -\tfrac{8}{10} = -\tfrac{4}{5} \qquad \text{and} \qquad \text{proj}\,(v, w) = cw = (-\tfrac{4}{5}, -\tfrac{8}{5}, -\tfrac{4}{5}, -\tfrac{8}{5})$$

7.20. Consider the subspace U of $\mathbf{R}^4$ spanned by the vectors:

$$v_1 = (1, 1, 1, 1), \qquad v_2 = (1, 1, 2, 4), \qquad v_3 = (1, 2, -4, -3)$$

Find (a) an orthogonal basis of U; (b) an orthonormal basis of U.

(a)   Use the Gram-Schmidt algorithm. Begin by setting $w_1 = v_1 = (1, 1, 1, 1)$. Next find

$$v_2 - \frac{\langle v_2, w_1 \rangle}{\|w_1\|^2}\, w_1 = (1, 1, 2, 4) - \frac{8}{4}(1, 1, 1, 1) = (-1, -1, 0, 2)$$

Set $w_2 = (-1, -1, 0, 2)$. Then find

$$v_3 - \frac{\langle v_3, w_1 \rangle}{\|w_1\|^2}\, w_1 - \frac{\langle v_3, w_2 \rangle}{\|w_2\|^2}\, w_2 = (1, 2, -4, -3) - \frac{(-4)}{4}(1, 1, 1, 1) - \frac{(-9)}{6}(-1, -1, 0, 2)$$

$$= (\tfrac{1}{2}, \tfrac{3}{2}, -3, 1)$$

Clear fractions to obtain $w_3 = (1, 3, -6, 2)$. Then w_1, w_2, w_3 form an orthogonal basis of U.

(b)   Normalize the orthogonal basis consisting of w_1, w_2, w_3. Since $\|w_1\|^2 = 4$, $\|w_2\|^2 = 6$, and $\|w_3\|^2 = 50$, the following vectors form an orthonormal basis of U:

$$u_1 = \frac{1}{2}(1, 1, 1, 1), \qquad u_2 = \frac{1}{\sqrt{6}}(-1, -1, 0, 2), \qquad u_3 = \frac{1}{5\sqrt{2}}(1, 3, -6, 2)$$

7.21. Consider the vector space $\mathbf{P}(t)$ with inner product $\langle f, g \rangle = \int_0^1 f(t)g(t)\,dt$. Apply the Gram-Schmidt algorithm to the set $\{1, t, t^2\}$ to obtain an orthogonal set $\{f_0, f_1, f_2\}$ with integer coefficients.

First set $f_0 = 1$. Then find

$$t - \frac{\langle t, 1 \rangle}{\langle 1, 1 \rangle} \cdot 1 = t - \frac{\tfrac{1}{2}}{1} \cdot 1 = t - \frac{1}{2}$$

Clear fractions to obtain $f_1 = 2t - 1$. Then find

$$t^2 - \frac{\langle t^2, 1 \rangle}{\langle 1, 1 \rangle}(1) - \frac{\langle t^2, 2t - 1 \rangle}{\langle 2t - 1, 2t - 1 \rangle}(2t - 1) = t^2 - \frac{\tfrac{1}{3}}{1}(1) - \frac{\tfrac{1}{6}}{\tfrac{1}{3}}(2t - 1) = t^2 - t + \frac{1}{6}$$

Clear fractions to obtain $f_2 = 6t^2 - 6t + 1$. Thus $\{1, 2t - 1, 6t^2 - 6t + 1\}$ is the required orthogonal set.

7.22. Suppose $v = (1, 3, 5, 7)$.   Find the projection of v onto W or, in other words, find $w \in W$ which minimizes $\|v - w\|$, where W is the subspace of $\mathbf{R}^4$ spanned by:

(a) $u_1 = (1, 1, 1, 1)$ and $u_2 = (1, -3, 4, -2)$,   (b) $v_1 = (1, 1, 1, 1)$ and $v_2 = (1, 2, 3, 2)$

(a) Since u_1 and u_2 are orthogonal, we need only compute the Fourier coefficients:

$$c_1 = \frac{\langle v, u_1 \rangle}{\|u_1\|^2} = \frac{1 + 3 + 5 + 7}{1 + 1 + 1 + 1} = \frac{16}{4} = 4$$

$$c_2 = \frac{\langle v, u_2 \rangle}{\|u_2\|^2} = \frac{1 - 9 + 20 - 14}{1 + 9 + 16 + 4} = \frac{-2}{30} = \frac{-1}{15}$$

Then $w = \text{proj}(v, W) = c_1 u_1 + c_2 u_2 = 4(1, 1, 1, 1) - \frac{1}{15}(1, -3, 4, -2) = (\frac{59}{15}, \frac{63}{15}, \frac{56}{15}, \frac{62}{15})$.

(b) Since v_1 and v_2 are not orthogonal, first apply the Gram-Schmidt algorithm to find an orthogonal basis for W.   Set $w_1 = v_1 = (1, 1, 1, 1)$.   Then find

$$v_2 - \frac{\langle v_2, w_1 \rangle}{w_1^2} w_1 = (1, 2, 3, 2) - \frac{8}{4}(1, 1, 1, 1) = (-1, 0, 1, 0)$$

Set $w_2 = (-1, 0, 1, 0)$.   Now compute

$$c_1 = \frac{\langle v, w_1 \rangle}{\|w_1\|^2} = \frac{1 + 3 + 5 + 7}{1 + 1 + 1 + 1}$$

$$c_2 = \frac{\langle v, w_2 \rangle}{\|w_2\|^2} = \frac{-1 + 0 + 5 + 0}{1 + 0 + 1 + 0} = \frac{4}{2} = 2$$

Then $w = \text{proj}(v, W) = c_1 w_1 + c_2 w_2 = 4(1, 1, 1, 1) + 2(-1, 0, 1, 0) = (2, 4, 6, 4)$

7.23. Suppose w_1 and w_2 are nonzero orthogonal vectors.   Let v be any vector in V.   Find c_1 and c_2 so that v' is orthogonal to w_1 and w_2, where $v' = v - c_1 w_1 - c_2 w_2$.

If v' is orthogonal to w_1, then

$$0 = \langle v - c_1 w_1 - c_2 w_2, w_1 \rangle = \langle v, w_1 \rangle - c_1 \langle w_1, w_1 \rangle - c_2 \langle w_2, w_1 \rangle$$
$$= \langle v, w_1 \rangle - c_1 \langle w_1, w_1 \rangle - c_2 0 = \langle v, w_1 \rangle - c_1 \langle w_1, w_1 \rangle$$

Thus $c_1 = \langle v, w_1 \rangle / \langle w_1, w_1 \rangle$.   (That is, c_1 is the component of v along w_1.)   Similarly, if v' is orthogonal to w_2, then

$$0 = \langle v - c_1 w_1 - c_2 w_2, w_2 \rangle = \langle v, w_2 \rangle - c_2 \langle w_2, w_2 \rangle$$

Thus $c_2 = \langle v, w_2 \rangle / \langle w_2, w_2 \rangle$.   (That is, c_2 is the component of v along w_2.)

ORTHOGONAL MATRICES

7.24.   Find an orthogonal matrix P whose first row is $u_1 = (\frac{1}{3}, \frac{2}{3}, \frac{2}{3})$.

First find a nonzero vector $w_2 = (x, y, z)$ which is orthogonal to u_1, i.e., for which

$$0 = \langle u_1, w_2 \rangle = \frac{x}{3} + \frac{2y}{3} + \frac{2z}{3} = 0 \quad \text{or} \quad x + 2y + 2z = 0$$

One such solution is $w_2 = (0, 1, -1)$.   Normalize w_2 to obtain the second row of P, i.e., $u_2 = (0, 1/\sqrt{2}, -1/\sqrt{2})$.

Next find a nonzero vector $w_3 = (x, y, z)$ which is orthogonal to both u_1 and u_2, i.e., for which

$$0 = \langle u_1, w_3 \rangle = \frac{x}{3} + \frac{2y}{3} + \frac{2z}{3} = 0 \qquad \text{or} \qquad x + 2y + 2z = 0$$

$$0 = \langle u_2, w_3 \rangle = \frac{y}{\sqrt{2}} - \frac{z}{\sqrt{2}} = 0 \qquad \text{or} \qquad y - z = 0$$

Set $z = -1$ and find the solution $w_3 = (4, -1, -1)$. Normalize w_3 and obtain the third row of P, that is, $u_3 = (4/\sqrt{18}, -1/\sqrt{18}, -1/\sqrt{18})$. Thus

$$P = \begin{bmatrix} \frac{1}{3} & \frac{2}{3} & \frac{2}{3} \\ 0 & 1/\sqrt{2} & -1/\sqrt{2} \\ 4/3\sqrt{2} & -1/3\sqrt{2} & -1/3\sqrt{2} \end{bmatrix}$$

We emphasize that the above matrix P is not unique.

7.25. Let $A = \begin{bmatrix} 1 & 1 & -1 \\ 1 & 3 & 4 \\ 7 & -5 & 2 \end{bmatrix}$. Determine whether or not: (a) the rows of A are orthogonal; (b) A is an orthogonal matrix; (c) the columns of A are orthogonal.

(a) Yes, since $(1, 1, -1) \cdot (1, 3, 4) = 1 + 3 - 4 = 0$, $(1, 1, -1) \cdot (7, -5, 2) = 7 - 5 - 2 = 0$, and $(1, 3, 4) \cdot (7, -5, 2) = 7 - 15 + 8 = 0$.

(b) No, since the rows of A are not unit vectors, e.g., $(1, 1, -1)^2 = 1 + 1 + 1 = 3$.

(c) No, e.g., $(1, 1, 7) \cdot (1, 3, -5) = 1 + 3 - 35 = -31 \neq 0$.

7.26. Let B be the matrix obtained by normalizing each row of A in Problem 7.25. (a) Find B; (b) is B an orthogonal matrix?; (c) are the columns of B orthogonal?

(a) We have

$$\|(1, 1, -1)\|^2 = 1 + 1 + 1 = 3 \qquad \|(1, 3, 4)\|^2 = 1 + 9 + 16 = 26$$

$$\|(7, -5, 2)\|^2 = 49 + 25 + 4 = 78$$

Thus

$$B = \begin{bmatrix} 1/\sqrt{3} & 1/\sqrt{3} & -1/\sqrt{3} \\ 1/\sqrt{26} & 3/\sqrt{26} & 4/\sqrt{26} \\ 7/\sqrt{78} & -5/\sqrt{78} & 2/\sqrt{78} \end{bmatrix}$$

(b) Yes, since the rows of B are still orthogonal and are now unit vectors.

(c) Yes, since the rows of B form an orthonormal set of vectors. Then, by Theorem 7.11, the columns of B must automatically form an orthonormal set.

7.27. Prove each of the following:

(a) P is orthogonal if and only if P^T is orthogonal.

(b) If P is orthogonal, then P^{-1} is orthogonal.

(c) If P and Q are orthogonal, then PQ is orthogonal.

(a)   We have $(P^T)^T = P$.   Thus P is orthogonal if and only if $PP^T = I$ if and only if $P^{TT}P^T = I$ if and only if P^T is orthogonal.

(b)   We have $P^T = P^{-1}$ since P is orthogonal.   Thus by part (a), P^{-1} is orthogonal.

(c)   We have $P^T = P^{-1}$ and $Q^T = Q^{-1}$.   Thus $(PQ)(PQ)^T = PQQ^TP^T = PQQ^{-1}P^{-1} = I$. Therefore $(PQ)^T = (PQ)^{-1}$, and so PQ is orthogonal.

7.28.   Suppose P is an orthogonal matrix.   Show that:

(a) $\langle Pu, Pv \rangle = \langle u, v \rangle$ for any $u, v \in V$;   (b) $\|Pu\| = \|u\|$ for every $u \in V$.

Use $P^T P = I$ and $\langle u, v \rangle = u^T v$.

(a) $\langle Pu, Pv \rangle = (Pu)^T(Pv) = u^T P^T P v = u^T v = \langle u, v \rangle$

(b)   We have

$$\|Pu\|^2 = \langle Pu, Pu \rangle = u^T P^T P u = u^T u = \langle u, u \rangle = \|u\|^2$$

Taking the square root of both sides gives our result.

INNER PRODUCTS AND POSITIVE DEFINITE MATRICES

7.29.   Which of the following symmetric matrices are positive definite?

(a) $A = \begin{bmatrix} 3 & 4 \\ 4 & 5 \end{bmatrix}$;   (b) $B = \begin{bmatrix} 8 & -3 \\ -3 & 2 \end{bmatrix}$;   (c) $C = \begin{bmatrix} 2 & 1 \\ 1 & -3 \end{bmatrix}$;   (d) $D = \begin{bmatrix} 3 & 5 \\ 5 & 9 \end{bmatrix}$.

Use Theorem 7.14 that a 2×2 real symmetric matrix is positive definite if its diagonal entries are positive and if its determinant is positive.

(a) No, since $|A| = 15 - 16 = -1$ is negative; (b) yes; (c) no, since the diagonal entry -3 is negative; (d) yes.

7.30.   Find the values of k which make each matrix positive definite:

(a) $A = \begin{bmatrix} 2 & -4 \\ -4 & k \end{bmatrix}$;   (b) $B = \begin{bmatrix} 4 & k \\ k & 9 \end{bmatrix}$;   (c) $C = \begin{bmatrix} k & 5 \\ 5 & -2 \end{bmatrix}$.

(a)   First k must be positive.   Also, $|A| = 2k - 16$ must be positive, that is, $2k - 16 > 0$.   Hence $k > 8$.

(b)   We need $|B| = 36 - k^2$ positive, that is, $36 - k^2 > 0$.   Hence $k^2 < 36$ or $-6 < k < 6$.

(c) C can never be positive definite since C has a negative diagonal entry -2.

7.31.   Find the matrix A which represents the usual inner product on $\mathbf{R}^2$ relative to each of the following bases of $\mathbf{R}^2$:

(a) $\{v_1 = (1, 3), v_2 = (2, 5)\}$,   (b) $\{w_1 = (1, 2), w_2 = (4, -2)\}$

(a)   Compute $\langle v_1, v_1 \rangle = 1 + 9 = 10$, $\langle v_1, v_2 \rangle = 2 + 15 = 17$, and $\langle v_2, v_2 \rangle = 4 + 25 = 29$.   Thus

$$A = \begin{bmatrix} 10 & 17 \\ 17 & 29 \end{bmatrix}.$$

(b)   Compute $\langle w_1, w_1 \rangle = 1 + 4 = 5$, $\langle w_1, w_2 \rangle = 4 - 4 = 0$, $\langle w_2, w_2 \rangle = 16 + 4 = 20$.   Thus

$$A = \begin{bmatrix} 5 & 0 \\ 0 & 20 \end{bmatrix}.$$ (Since the basis vectors are orthogonal, the matrix A is diagonal.)

7.32. Consider the vector space $P_2(t)$ with inner product $\langle f, g \rangle = \int_{-1}^{1} f(t)g(t) \, dt$.

    (a)   Find $\langle f, g \rangle$, where $f(t) = t + 2$ and $g(t) = t^2 - 3t + 4$.

    (b)   Find the matrix A of the inner product with respect to the basis $\{1, t, t^2\}$ of V.

    (c)   Verify Theorem 7.16 by showing that $\langle f, g \rangle = [f]^T A [g]$ with respect to the basis $\{1, t, t^2\}$.

    (a) $\langle f, g \rangle = \int_{-1}^{1} (t+2)(t^2 - 3t + 4) \, dt = \int_{-1}^{1} (t^3 - t^2 - 2t + 8) \, dt = \left[\dfrac{t^4}{4} - \dfrac{t^3}{3} - t^2 + 8t \right]_{-1}^{1} = \dfrac{46}{3}$

    (b)   Here we use the fact that, if $r + s = n$,

$$\langle t^r, t^s \rangle = \int_{-1}^{1} t^n \, dt = \left[\frac{t^{n+1}}{n+1} \right]_{-1}^{1} = \begin{cases} 2/(n+1) & \text{if } n \text{ is even} \\ 0 & \text{if } n \text{ is odd} \end{cases}$$

Then $\langle 1, 1 \rangle = 2$, $\langle 1, t \rangle = 0$, $\langle 1, t^2 \rangle = \frac{2}{3}$, $\langle t, t \rangle = \frac{2}{3}$, $\langle t, t^2 \rangle = 0$, $\langle t^2, t^2 \rangle = \frac{2}{5}$. Thus

$$A = \begin{bmatrix} 2 & 0 & \frac{2}{3} \\ 0 & \frac{2}{3} & 0 \\ \frac{2}{3} & 0 & \frac{2}{5} \end{bmatrix}$$

    (c)   We have $[f]^T = (2, 1, 0)$ and $[g]^T = (4, -3, 1)$ relative to the given basis. Then

$$[f]^T A [g] = (2, 1, 0) \begin{bmatrix} 2 & 0 & \frac{2}{3} \\ 0 & \frac{2}{3} & 0 \\ \frac{2}{3} & 0 & \frac{2}{5} \end{bmatrix} \begin{bmatrix} 4 \\ -3 \\ 1 \end{bmatrix} = (4, \tfrac{2}{3}, \tfrac{4}{3}) \begin{bmatrix} 4 \\ -3 \\ 1 \end{bmatrix} = \tfrac{46}{3} = \langle f, g \rangle$$

NORMED VECTOR SPACES

7.33. Consider vectors $u = (1, 3, -6, 4)$ and $v = (3, -5, 1, -2)$ in $\mathbf{R}^4$. Find:

    (a) $\|u\|_\infty$ and $\|v\|_\infty$,   (c) $\|u\|_2$ and $\|v\|_2$

    (b) $\|u\|_1$ and $\|v\|_1$,   (d) $d_\infty(u, v)$, $d_1(u, v)$, and $d_2(u, v)$.

    (a)   The infinity norm chooses the maximum of the absolute values of the components. Hence

$$\|u\|_\infty = 6 \qquad \text{and} \qquad \|v\|_\infty = 5$$

    (b)   The one-norm adds the absolute values of the components. Thus

$$\|u\|_1 = 1 + 3 + 6 + 4 = 14, \qquad \|v\|_1 = 3 + 5 + 1 + 2 = 11$$

    (c)   The two-norm is equal to the square root of the sum of the squares of the components (i.e., the norm induced by the usual inner product on $\mathbf{R}^3$). Thus

$$\|u\|_2 = \sqrt{1 + 9 + 36 + 16} = \sqrt{62} \qquad \text{and} \qquad \|v\|_2 = \sqrt{9 + 25 + 1 + 4} = \sqrt{39}$$

    (d)   First find $u - v = (-2, 8, -7, 6)$. Then

$$d_\infty(u, v) = \|u - v\|_\infty = 8$$
$$d_1(u, v) = \|u - v\|_1 = 2 + 8 + 7 + 6 = 23$$
$$d_2(u, v) = \|u - v\|_2 = \sqrt{4 + 64 + 49 + 36} = \sqrt{153}$$

7.34. Consider the function $f(t) = t^2 - 4t$ in $C[0, 3]$.   (a) Find $\|f\|_\infty$; (b) plot $f(t)$ in the plane $\mathbf{R}^2$; (c) find $\|f\|_1$; (d) find $\|f\|_2$.

(a)   We seek $\|f\|_\infty = \max(|f(t)|)$.   Since $f(t)$ is differentiable on $[0, 3]$, $|f(t)|$ has a maximum at a critical point of $f(t)$, i.e., when the derivative $f'(t) = 0$, or at an endpoint of $[0, 3]$.   Since $f'(t) = 2t - 4$, we set $2t - 4 = 0$ and obtain $t = 2$ as a critical point.   Compute

$$f(2) = 4 - 8 = -4, \qquad f(0) = 0 - 0 = 0, \qquad f(3) = 9 - 12 = -3$$

Thus $\|f\|_\infty = |f(2)| = |-4| = 4$.

(b)   Compute $f(t)$ for various values of t in $[0, 3]$, e.g.,

t	0	1	2	3
$f(t)$	0	-3	-4	-3

Plot the points in $\mathbf{R}^2$ and then draw a continuous curve through the points, as shown in Fig. 7-10.

(c)   We seek $\|f\|_1 = \int_0^3 |f(t)|\, dt$.   As indicated by Fig. 7-10, $f(t)$ is negative in $[0, 3]$; hence $|f(t)| = -(t^2 - 4t) = 4t - t^2$.   Thus

$$\|f\|_1 = \int_0^3 (4t - t^2)\, dt = \left[2t^2 - \frac{t^3}{3}\right]_0^3 = 18 - 9 = 9$$

(d) $\|f\|_2^2 = \int_0^3 [f(t)]^2\, dt = \int_0^3 (t^4 - 8t^3 + 16t^2)\, dt = \left[\frac{t^5}{5} - 2t^4 + \frac{16t^3}{3}\right]_0^3 = \frac{153}{5}$.
Thus $\|f\|_2 = \sqrt{\frac{153}{5}}$.

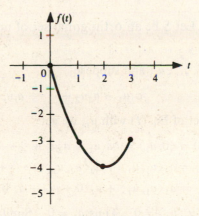

Fig. 7-10

PROOF OF THEOREMS

7.35. Prove Theorem 7.1 (Cauchy-Schwarz):   For any vectors u and v in a real inner product space V,

$$\langle u, v \rangle^2 \le \langle u, u \rangle \langle v, v \rangle \qquad \text{or equivalently} \qquad |\langle u, v \rangle| \le \|u\|\, \|v\|$$

For any real number t,

$$\langle tu + v, tu + v \rangle = t^2 \langle u, u \rangle + 2t\langle u, v \rangle + \langle v, v \rangle = t^2 \|u\|^2 + 2t\langle u, v \rangle + \|v\|^2$$

Let $a = \|u\|^2$, $b = 2\langle u, v\rangle$, and $c = \|v\|^2$. Since $\|tu + v\|^2 \geq 0$, we have

$$at^2 + bt + c \geq 0$$

for every value of t. This means that the quadratic polynomial cannot have two real roots, which implies that $b^2 - 4ac \leq 0$ or $b^2 \leq 4ac$. Thus

$$4\langle u, v\rangle^2 \leq 4\|u\|^2 \|v\|^2$$

Dividing by 4 gives our result.

7.36. Prove Theorem 7.2:   The norm in an inner product space V satisfies:

(a)   [N_1] $\|v\| \geq 0$; and $\|v\| = 0$ if and only if $v = 0$.

(b)   [N_2] $\|kv\| = |k|\,\|v\|$.

(c)   [N_3] $\|u + v\| \leq \|u\| + \|v\|$.

(a)   If $v \neq 0$, then $\langle v, v\rangle > 0$ and hence $\|v\| = \sqrt{\langle v, v\rangle} > 0$. If $v = 0$, then $\langle 0, 0\rangle = 0$. Consequently $\|0\| = \sqrt{0} = 0$. Thus [N_1] is true.

(b)   We have $\|kv\|^2 = \langle kv, kv\rangle = k^2\langle v, v\rangle = k^2\|v\|^2$. Taking the square root of both sides gives [N_2].

(c)   Using the Cauchy-Schwarz inequality, we obtain

$$\|u + v\|^2 = \langle u + v, u + v\rangle = \langle u, u\rangle + \langle u, v\rangle + \langle u, v\rangle + \langle v, v\rangle$$
$$\leq \|u\|^2 + 2\|u\|\,\|v\| + \|v\|^2 = (\|u\| + \|v\|)^2$$

Taking the square root of both sides yields [N_3].

7.37. Prove Theorem 7.5:   Let S be an orthogonal set of nonzero vectors. Then S is linearly independent.

Suppose $S = \{u_1, u_2, \ldots, u_r\}$ and suppose

$$a_1u_1 + a_2u_2 + \cdots + a_ru_r = 0 \qquad\qquad (1)$$

Taking the inner product of Eq. (1) with u_1, we get

$$0 = \langle 0, u_1\rangle = \langle a_1u_1 + a_2u_2 + \cdots + a_ru_r, u_1\rangle$$
$$= a_1\langle u_1, u_1\rangle + a_2\langle u_2, u_1\rangle + \cdots + a_r\langle u_r, u_1\rangle$$
$$= a_1\langle u_1, u_1\rangle + a_2\cdot 0 + \cdots + a_r\cdot 0 = a_1\langle u_1, u_1\rangle$$

Since $u_1 \neq 0$, we have $\langle u_1, u_1\rangle \neq 0$. Thus $a_1 = 0$. Similarly, for $i = 2, \ldots, r$, taking the inner product for Eq. (1) with u_i,

$$0 = \langle 0, u_i\rangle = \langle a_1u_1 + \cdots + a_ru_r, u_i\rangle$$
$$= a_1\langle u_1, u_i\rangle + \cdots + a_i\langle u_i, u_i\rangle + \cdots + a_r\langle u_r, u_i\rangle = a_i\langle u_i, u_i\rangle$$

But $\langle u_i, u_i\rangle \neq 0$, and hence $a_i = 0$. Thus S is linearly independent.

7.38. Prove Theorem 7.7:   Let $\{u_1, u_2, \ldots, u_n\}$ be an orthogonal basis of V. Then for any $v \in V$,

$$v = \frac{\langle v, u_1\rangle}{\langle u_1, u_1\rangle}u_1 + \frac{\langle v, u_2\rangle}{\langle u_2, u_2\rangle}u_2 + \cdots + \frac{\langle v, u_n\rangle}{\langle u_n, u_n\rangle}u_n$$

Suppose $v = k_1 u_1 + k_2 u_2 + \cdots + k_n u_n$. Taking the inner product of both sides with u_1 yields

$$\begin{aligned}
\langle v, u_1 \rangle &= \langle k_1 u_1 + k_2 u_2 + \cdots + k_n u_n, u_1 \rangle \\
&= k_1 \langle u_1, u_1 \rangle + k_2 \langle u_2, u_1 \rangle + \cdots + k_n \langle u_n, u_1 \rangle \\
&= k_1 \langle u_1, u_1 \rangle + k_2 \cdot 0 + \cdots + k_n \cdot 0 = k_1 \langle u_1, u_1 \rangle
\end{aligned}$$

Thus $k_1 = \dfrac{\langle v, u_1 \rangle}{\langle u_1, u_1 \rangle}$. Similarly, for $i = 2, \ldots, n$,

$$\begin{aligned}
\langle v, u_1 \rangle &= \langle k_1 u_1 + k_2 u_2 + \cdots + k_n u_n, u_i \rangle \\
&= k_1 \langle u_1, u_i \rangle + k_2 \langle u_2, u_i \rangle + \cdots + k_n \langle u_n, u_i \rangle \\
&= k_1 \cdot 0 + \cdots + k_i \langle u_i, u_i \rangle + \cdots + k_n \cdot 0 = k_i \langle u_i, u_i \rangle
\end{aligned}$$

Thus $k_i = \dfrac{\langle v, u_i \rangle}{\langle u_i, u_i \rangle}$. Substituting for k_i in the equation $u = k_1 u_1 + \cdots + k_n u_n$, we obtain the desired result.

7.39. Prove Theorem 7.8:   Suppose $w_1, w_2, \ldots, w_r$ form an orthogonal set of nonzero vectors in V.   Let $v \in V$.   Define

$$v' = v - (c_1 w_1 + c_2 w_2 + \cdots + c_r w_r) \qquad \text{where} \qquad c_i = \frac{\langle v, w_i \rangle}{\|w_i\|^2}$$

Then v' is orthogonal to $w_1, w_2, \ldots, w_r$.

For $i = 1, 2, \ldots, r$ and using $\langle w_i, w_j \rangle = 0$ for $i \neq j$, we have

$$\begin{aligned}
\langle v - c_1 w_1 - c_2 w_2 - \cdots - c_r w_r, w_i \rangle &= \langle v, w_i \rangle - c_1 \langle w_1, w_i \rangle - \cdots - c_i \langle w_i, w_i \rangle - \cdots - c_r \langle w_r, w_i \rangle \\
&= \langle v, w_i \rangle - c_1 \cdot 0 - \cdots - c_i \langle w_i, w_i \rangle - \cdots - c_r \cdot 0 \\
&= \langle v, w_i \rangle - c_i \langle w_i, w_i \rangle = \langle v, w_i \rangle - \frac{\langle v, w_i \rangle}{\langle w_i, w_i \rangle} \langle w_i, w_i \rangle = 0
\end{aligned}$$

Thus the theorem is proved.

7.40. Prove Theorem 7.9:   Let $\{v_1, v_2, \ldots, v_n\}$ be any basis of an inner product space V.   Then there exists an orthonormal basis $\{u_1, u_2, \ldots, u_n\}$ of V such that the change-of-basis matrix from $\{v_i\}$ to $\{u_i\}$ is triangular, that is, for $k = 1, 2, \ldots, n$,

$$u_k = a_{k1} v_1 + a_{k2} v_2 + \cdots + a_{kk} v_k$$

The proof uses the Gram-Schmidt algorithm and Remarks 1 and 2 of Section 7.7.   That is, apply the algorithm to $\{v_i\}$ to obtain an orthogonal basis $\{w_i, \ldots, w_n\}$, and then normalize $\{w_i\}$ to obtain an orthonormal basis $\{u_i\}$ of V.   The specific algorithm guarantees that each w_k is a linear combination of $v_1, \ldots, v_k$, and hence each u_k is a linear combination of $v_1, \ldots, v_k$.

7.41. Prove Theorem 7.10:   Suppose $S = \{w_1, w_2, \ldots, w_r\}$ is an orthogonal basis for a subspace W of V.   Then one may extend S to an orthogonal basis for V, that is, one may find vectors $w_{r+1}, \ldots, w_r$ such that $\{w_1, w_2, \ldots, w_n\}$ is an orthogonal basis for V.

Extend S to a basis $S' = \{w_1, \ldots, w_r, v_{r+1}, \ldots, v_n\}$ for V.   Applying the Gram-Schmidt algorithm to S', we first obtain $w_1, w_2, \ldots, w_r$ since S is orthogonal, and then we obtain vectors $w_{r+1}, \ldots, w_n$, where $\{w_1, w_2, \ldots, w_n\}$ is an orthogonal basis for V.   Thus the theorem is proved.

7.42. Prove Theorem 7.4: Let W be a subspace of V. Then $V = W \oplus W^\perp$.

By Theorem 7.9 there exists an orthogonal basis $\{u_1, \ldots, u_r\}$ of W, and by Theorem 7.10 we can extend it to an orthogonal basis $\{u_1, u_2, \ldots, u_n\}$ of V. Hence $u_{r+1}, \ldots, u_n \in W^\perp$. If $v \in V$, then

$$v = a_1 u_1 + \cdots + a_n u_n \quad \text{where} \quad a_1 u_1 + \cdots + a_r u_r \in W \quad \text{and} \quad a_{r+1} u_{r+1} + \cdots + a_n u_n \in W^\perp$$

Accordingly, $V = W + W^\perp$.

On the other hand, if $w \in W \cap W^\perp$, then $\langle w, w \rangle = 0$. This yields $w = 0$. Hence $W \cap W^\perp = \{0\}$.

The two conditions, $V = W + W^\perp$ and $W \cap W^\perp = \{0\}$, give the desired result $V = W \oplus W^\perp$.

Note that we have proved the theorem for the case that V has finite dimension. We remark that the theorem also holds for spaces of arbitrary dimension.

7.43. Suppose W is a subspace of a finite-dimensional space V. Prove that $W = W^{\perp\perp}$.

By Theorem 7.4, $V = W \oplus W^\perp$ and also, $V = W^\perp \oplus W^{\perp\perp}$. Hence

$$\dim W = \dim V - \dim W^\perp \quad \text{and} \quad \dim W^{\perp\perp} = \dim V - \dim W^\perp$$

This yields $\dim W = \dim W^{\perp\perp}$. But $W \subseteq W^{\perp\perp}$ (see Problem 7.15). Hence $W = W^{\perp\perp}$, as required.

7.44. Prove Theorem 7.12: Suppose $E = \{e_i\}$ and $E' = \{e_i'\}$ are orthonormal bases of V. Let P be the change-of-basis matrix from E to E'. Then P is orthogonal.

Suppose

$$e_i' = b_{i1} e_1 + b_{i2} + b_{i2} e_2 + \cdots + b_{in} e_n, \qquad i = 1, \ldots, n \tag{1}$$

Using Problem 7.17(b) and the fact that E' is orthonormal, we get

$$\delta_{ij} = \langle e_i', e_j' \rangle = b_{i1} b_{j1} + b_{i2} b_{j2} + \cdots + b_{in} b_{jn} \tag{2}$$

Let $B = [b_{ij}]$ be the matrix of the coefficients in Eq. (1). (Then $P = B^T$.) Suppose $BB^T = [c_{ij}]$. Then

$$c_{ij} = b_{i1} b_{j1} + b_{i2} b_{j2} + \cdots + b_{in} b_{jn} \tag{3}$$

By Eqs. (2) and (3) we have $c_{ij} = \delta_{ij}$. Thus $BB^T = I$. Accordingly, B is orthogonal, and hence $P = B^T$ is orthogonal.

7.45. Prove Theorem 7.13: Let $\{e_1, \ldots, e_n\}$ be an orthonormal basis of an inner product space V. Let $P = [a_{ij}]$ be an orthogonal matrix. Then the following n vectors form an orthonormal basis for V:

$$e_i' = a_{1i} e_1 + a_{2i} e_2 + \cdots + a_{ni} e_n, \qquad i = 1, 2, \ldots, n$$

Since $\{e_i\}$ is orthonormal, we get, by Problem 7.17(b),

$$\langle e_i', e_j' \rangle = a_{1i} a_{1j} + a_{2i} a_{2j} + \cdots + a_{ni} a_{nj} = \langle C_i, C_j \rangle$$

where C_i denotes the ith column of the orthogonal matrix $P = [a_{ij}]$. Since P is orthogonal, its columns form an orthonormal set. This implies $\langle e_i', e_j' \rangle = \langle C_i, C_j \rangle = \delta_{ij}$. Thus $\{e_i'\}$ is an orthonormal basis.

7.46. Prove Theorem 7.14: $A = \begin{bmatrix} a & b \\ b & d \end{bmatrix}$ is positive definite if and only if a and d are positive and $|A| = ad - b^2$ is positive.

Let $u = [x, y]^T$.   Then

$$f(u) = u^TAu = [x, y]\begin{bmatrix} a & b \\ b & d \end{bmatrix}\begin{bmatrix} x \\ y \end{bmatrix} = ax^2 + 2bxy + dy^2$$

Suppose $f(u) > 0$ for every $u \neq 0$.   Then $f(1, 0) = a > 0$ and $f(0, 1) = d > 0$.   Also, we have $f(b, -a) = a(ad - b^2) > 0$.   Since $a > 0$, we get $ad - b^2 > 0$.

Conversely, suppose $a > 0$, $b > 0$, and $ad - b^2 > 0$.   Completing the square gives us

$$f(u) = a\left(x^2 + \frac{2b}{a}xy + \frac{b^2}{a_2}y^2\right) + dy^2 - \frac{b^2}{a}y^2$$

$$= a\left(x + \frac{by}{a}\right)^2 + \frac{ad - b^2}{a}y^2$$

Accordingly, $f(u) > 0$ for every $u \neq 0$.

7.47. Prove Theorem 7.15:   Let A be a real positive definite matrix.   Then the function $\langle u, v \rangle = u^TAv$ is an inner product on $\mathbf{R}^n$.

For any vectors u_1, u_2, and v,

$$\langle v_1 + u_2, v \rangle = (u_1 + u_2)^TAv = (u_1^T + u_2^T)Av = u_1^TAv + u_2^TAv = \langle u_1, v \rangle + \langle u_2, v \rangle$$

and, for any scalar k and vectors u, v,

$$\langle ku, v \rangle = (ku)^TAv = ku^TAv = k\langle u, v \rangle$$

Thus $[\mathbf{I}_1]$ is satisfied.

Since u^TAv is a scalar, $(u^TAv)^T = u^TAv$.   Also, $A^T = A$ since A is symmetric.   Therefore,

$$\langle u, v \rangle = u^TAv = (u^TAv)^T = v^TA^Tt^{TT} = v^TAu = \langle v, u \rangle$$

Thus $[\mathbf{I}_2]$ is satisfied.

Lastly, since A is positive definite, $X^TAX > 0$ for any nonzero $X \in \mathbf{R}^n$.   Thus for any nonzero vector v, $\langle v, v \rangle = v^TAv > 0$.   Also, $\langle 0, 0 \rangle = 0^TA0 = 0$.   Thus $[\mathbf{I}_3]$ is satisfied.   Accordingly, the function $\langle u, v \rangle = u^TAv$ is an inner product.

7.48. Prove Theorem 7.16:   Let A be the matrix representation of an inner product relative to a basis S of V.   Then, for any vectors $u, v \in V$, we have

$$\langle u, v \rangle = [u]^TA[v]$$

Suppose $S = \{w_1, w_2, \ldots, w_n\}$ and $A = [k_{ij}]$.   Hence $k_{ij} = \langle w_i, w_j \rangle$.   Suppose

$$u = a_1w_1 + a_2w_2 + \cdots + a_nw_n \qquad \text{and} \qquad v = b_1w_1 + b_2w_2 + \cdots + b_nw_n$$

Then
$$\langle u, v \rangle = \sum_{i=1}^{n} \sum_{j=1}^{n} a_ib_j\langle w_i, w_j \rangle \tag{1}$$

On the other hand,

$$[u]^T A[v] = (a_1, a_2, \ldots, a_n) \begin{bmatrix} k_{11} & k_{12} & \ldots & k_{1n} \\ k_{21} & k_{22} & \ldots & k_{2n} \\ \cdots\cdots\cdots\cdots\cdots\cdots\cdots \\ k_{n1} & k_{n2} & \ldots & k_{nn} \end{bmatrix} \begin{bmatrix} b_1 \\ b_2 \\ \vdots \\ b_n \end{bmatrix}$$

$$= \left(\sum_{i=1}^{n} a_i k_{i1}, \sum_{i=1}^{n} a_i k_{i2}, \ldots, \sum_{i=1}^{n} a_i k_{in} \right) \begin{bmatrix} b_1 \\ b_2 \\ \vdots \\ b_n \end{bmatrix} = \sum_{j=1}^{n} \sum_{i=1}^{n} a_i b_j k_{ij} \qquad (2)$$

Equations (1) and (2) give us our result.

7.49. Prove Theorem 7.17: Let A be the matrix representation of any inner product on V. Then A is a positive definite matrix.

Since $\langle w_i, w_j \rangle = \langle w_j, w_i \rangle$ for any basis vectors w_i and w_j, the matrix A is symmetric. Let X be any nonzero vector in $\mathbf{R}^n$. Then $[u] = X$ for some nonzero vector $u \in V$. Theorem 7.16 tells us $X^T A X = [u]^T A[u] = \langle u, u \rangle > 0$. Thus A is positive definite.

7.50. Prove Theorem 7.18: Let V be a normed vector space. Let $d(u, v) = \|u - v\|$. Then the function $d(u, v)$ satisfies the following three axioms of a metric space:

[$\mathbf{M}_1$] $d(u, v) \geq 0$; and $d(u, v) = 0$ if and only if $u = v$.

[$\mathbf{M}_2$] $d(u, v) = d(v, u)$.

[$\mathbf{M}_3$] $d(u, v) \leq d(u, w) + d(w, v)$.

If $u \neq v$, then $u - v \neq 0$, and hence $d(u, v) = \|u - v\| > 0$. Also, $d(u, u) = \|u - u\| = \|0\| = 0$. Thus [$\mathbf{M}_1$] is satisfied. We also have

$$d(u, v) = \|u - v\| = \| -1(v - u)\| = |-1| \, \|v - u\| = \|v - u\| = d(v, u)$$

and $\qquad d(u, v) = \|u - v\| = \|(u - w) + (w - v)\| \leq \|u - w\| + \|w - v\| = d(u, w) + d(w, v)$

Thus [$\mathbf{M}_2$] and [$\mathbf{M}_3$] are satisfied.

7.51. Prove: Suppose $w_1, w_2, \ldots, w_r$ form an orthogonal set of nonzero vectors in V. Let v be any vector in V and let c_i be the component of v along w_i. Then, for any scalars $a_1, \ldots, a_r$, we have

$$\left\| v - \sum_{k=1}^{r} c_k w_k \right\| \leq \left\| v - \sum_{k=1}^{r} a_k w_k \right\|$$

That is, $\sum c_i w_i$ is the closest approximation to v as a linear combination of $w_1, \ldots, w_r$.

By Theorem 7.8, $v - \sum c_k w_k$ is orthogonal to every w_i and hence orthogonal to any linear combination of $w_1, w_2, \ldots, w_r$. Therefore using the Pythagorean theorem and summing from $k = 1$ to r,

$$\left\| v - \sum a_k w_k \right\|^2 = \left\| v - \sum c_k w_k + \sum (c_k - a_k) w_k \right\|^2 = \left\| v - \sum c_k w_k \right\|^2 + \left\| \sum (c_k - a_k) w_k \right\|^2$$

$$\geq \left\| v - \sum c_k w_k \right\|^2$$

The square root of both sides gives our theorem.

7.52. Suppose $\{e_1, e_2, \ldots, e_r\}$ is an orthonormal set of vectors in V.   Let v be any vector in V and let c_i be the Fourier coefficient of v with respect to u_i.   Prove Bessel's inequality:

$$\sum_{k=1}^{r} c_k^2 \leq \|v\|^2$$

Note that $c_i = \langle v, e_i \rangle$ since $\|e_i\| = 1$.   Then, using $\langle e_i, e_j \rangle = 0$ for $i \neq j$ and summing from $k = 1$ to r, we get

$$0 \leq \left\langle v - \sum c_k e_k, \ v - \sum c_k, e_k \right\rangle = \langle v, v \rangle - 2\left\langle v, \sum c_k e_k \right\rangle + \sum c_k^2$$

$$= \langle v, v \rangle - \sum 2c_k \langle v, e_k \rangle + \sum c_k^2 = \langle v, v \rangle - \sum 2c_k^2 + \sum c_k^2$$

$$= \langle v, v \rangle - \sum c_k^2$$

This gives our inequality.

Supplementary Problems

INNER PRODUCTS

7.53. Verify that the following is an inner product on $\mathbf{R}^2$, where $u = (x_1, x_2)$ and $v = (y_1, y_2)$:

$$f(u, v) = x_1 y_1 - 2x_1 y_2 - 2x_2 y_1 + 5x_2 y_2$$

7.54. Find the values of k so that the following is an inner product on $\mathbf{R}^2$, where $u = (x_1, x_2)$ and $v = (y_1, y_2)$:

$$f(u, v) = x_1 y_1 - 3x_1 y_2 - 3x_2 y_1 + kx_2 y_2$$

7.55. Consider the vectors $u = (1, -3)$ and $v = (2, 5)$ in $\mathbf{R}^2$.   Find:

(a) $\langle u, v \rangle$ with respect to the usual inner product in $\mathbf{R}^2$.

(b) $\langle u, v \rangle$ with respect to the inner product in $\mathbf{R}^2$ in Problem 7.53.

(c) $\|v\|$ using the usual inner product in $\mathbf{R}^2$.

(d) $\|v\|$ using the inner product in $\mathbf{R}^2$ in Problem 7.53.

7.56. Show that each of the following is not an inner product on $\mathbf{R}^3$, where $u = (x_1, x_2, x_3)$ and $v = (y_1, y_2, y_3)$:

(a) $\langle u, v \rangle = x_1 y_1 + x_2 y_2$; (b) $\langle u, v \rangle = x_1 y_2 x_3 + y_1 x_2 y_3$.

7.57. Let V be the vector space of $m \times n$ matrices over $\mathbf{R}$.   Show that $\langle A, B \rangle = \text{tr}\,(B^T A)$ defines an inner product in V.

7.58. Suppose $|\langle u, v \rangle| = \|u\|\,\|v\|$.   (That is, the Cauchy-Schwarz inequality reduces to an equality.) Show that u and v are linearly dependent.

7.59. Suppose $f(u, v)$ and $g(u, v)$ are inner products on a vector space V over **R**. Prove:

(a) The sum $f + g$ is an inner product on V, where $(f + g)(u, v) = f(u, v) + g(u, v)$.

(b) The scalar product kf, for $k > 0$, is an inner product on V, where $(kf)(u, v) = kf(u, v)$.

ORTHOGONALITY, ORTHOGONAL COMPLEMENTS, ORTHOGONAL SETS

7.60. Let V be the vector space of polynomials over **R** of degree ≤ 2 with inner product defined by $\langle f, g \rangle = \int_0^1 f(t)g(t)\, dt$. Find a basis of the subspace W orthogonal to $h(t) = 2t + 1$.

7.61. Find a basis of the subspace W of $\mathbf{R}^4$ orthogonal to $u_1 = (1, -2, 3, 4)$ and $u_2 = (3, -5, 7, 8)$.

7.62. Find a basis for the subspace W of $\mathbf{R}^5$ orthogonal to the vectors $u_1 = (1, 1, 3, 4, 1)$ and $u_2 = (1, 2, 1, 2, 1)$.

7.63. Let $w = (1, -2, -1, 3)$ be a vector in $\mathbf{R}^4$. Find: (a) an orthogonal and (b) an orthonormal basis for $w^\perp$.

7.64. Let W be the subspace of $\mathbf{R}^4$ orthogonal to $u_1 = (1, 1, 2, 2)$ and $u_2 = (0, 1, 2, -1)$. Find: (a) an orthogonal and (b) an orthonormal basis for W. (Compare with Problem 7.61.)

7.65. Let S consist of the following vectors in $\mathbf{R}^4$:

$$u_1 = (1, 1, 1, 1), \qquad u_2 = (1, 1, -1, -1), \qquad u_3 = (1, -1, 1, -1), \qquad u_4 = (1, -1, -1, 1)$$

(a) Show that S is orthogonal and a basis of $\mathbf{R}^4$.

(b) Write $v = (1, 3, -5, 6)$ as a linear combination of u_1, u_2, u_3, u_4.

(c) Find the coordinates of an arbitrary vector $v = (a, b, c, d)$ in $\mathbf{R}^4$ relative to the basis S.

(d) Normalize S to obtain an orthonormal basis of $\mathbf{R}^4$.

7.66. Let $\mathbf{M} = \mathbf{M}_{2,2}$ with inner product $\langle A, B \rangle = \operatorname{tr}(B^T A)$. Show that the following is an orthonormal basis for $\mathbf{M}$:

$$\left\{ \begin{bmatrix} 1 & 0 \\ 0 & 0 \end{bmatrix}, \begin{bmatrix} 0 & 1 \\ 0 & 0 \end{bmatrix}, \begin{bmatrix} 0 & 0 \\ 1 & 0 \end{bmatrix}, \begin{bmatrix} 0 & 0 \\ 0 & 1 \end{bmatrix} \right\}$$

7.67. Let $\mathbf{M} = \mathbf{M}_{2,2}$ with inner product $\langle A, B \rangle = \operatorname{tr}(B^T A)$. Find an orthogonal basis for the orthogonal complement of: (a) diagonal matrices; (b) symmetric matrices.

7.68. Suppose $\{u_1, u_2, \ldots, u_r\}$ is an orthogonal set of vectors. Show that $\{k_1 u_1, k_2 u_2, \ldots, k_r u_r\}$ is an orthogonal set for any scalars $k_1, k_2, \ldots, k_r$.

7.69. Let U and W be subspaces of a finite-dimensional inner product space V. Show that:

(a) $(U + W)^\perp = U^\perp \cap W^\perp$; (b) $(U \cap W)^\perp = U^\perp + W^\perp$.

PROJECTIONS, GRAM-SCHMIDT ALGORITHM, APPLICATIONS

7.70. Find the Fourier coefficient c and the projection cw of v along w, where:

(a) $v = (2, 3, -5)$ and $w = (1, -5, 2)$ in $\mathbf{R}^3$.

(b) $v = (1, 3, 1, 2)$ and $w = (1, -2, 7, 4)$ in $\mathbf{R}^4$.

(c) $v = t^2$ and $w = t + 3$ in $\mathbf{P}(t)$, with inner product $\langle f, g \rangle = \int_0^1 f(t)g(t)\, dt$.

(d) $v = \begin{bmatrix} 1 & 2 \\ 3 & 4 \end{bmatrix}$ and $w = \begin{bmatrix} 1 & 1 \\ 5 & 5 \end{bmatrix}$ in $\mathbf{M} = \mathbf{M}_{2,2}$ with inner product $\langle A, B \rangle = \text{tr}\,(B^T A)$.

7.71. Let U be the subspace of $\mathbf{R}^4$ spanned by:

$$v_1 = (1, 1, 1, 1), \qquad v_2 = (1, -1, 2, 2), \qquad v_3 = (1, 2, -3, -4)$$

(a) Apply the Gram-Schmidt algorithm to find an orthogonal and an orthonormal basis for U.

(b) Find the projection of $v = (1, 2, -3, 4)$ onto U.

7.72. Suppose $v = (1, 2, 3, 4, 6)$. Find the projection of v onto W or, in other words, find $w \in W$ which minimizes $\|v - w\|$, where W is the subspace of $\mathbf{R}^5$ spanned by:

(a) $u_1 = (1, 2, 1, 2, 1)$ and $u_2 = (1, -1, 2, -1, 1)$; (b) $v_1 = (1, 2, 1, 2, 1)$ and $v_2 = (1, 0, 1, 5, -1)$.

7.73. Consider the subspace $W = \mathbf{P}_2(t)$ of $\mathbf{P}(t)$ with inner product $\langle f, g \rangle = \int_0^1 f(t)g(t)\, dt$. Find the projection of $f(t) = t^3$ onto W. (Hint: Use the orthogonal polynomials $1, 2t - 1, 6t^2 - 6t + 1$ obtained in Problem 7.21.)

7.74. Consider $\mathbf{P}(t)$ with inner product $\langle f, g \rangle = \int_{-1}^1 f(t)g(t)\, dt$.

(a) Find an orthogonal basis for the subspace $W = \mathbf{P}_3(t)$ by applying the Gram-Schmidt algorithm to $\{1, t, t^2, t^3\}$.

(b) Find the projection of $f(t) = t^5$ onto W.

ORTHOGONAL MATRICES

7.75. Find the number and exhibit all 2×2 orthogonal matrices of the form $\begin{bmatrix} \frac{1}{3} & x \\ y & z \end{bmatrix}$.

7.76. Find a 3×3 orthogonal matrix P whose first two rows are multiples of $u = (1, 1, 1)$ and $v = (1, -2, 3)$, respectively.

7.77. Find a symmetric orthogonal matrix P whose first row is $(\frac{1}{3}, \frac{2}{3}, \frac{2}{3})$. (Compare with Problem 7.24.)

7.78. Real matrices A and B are said to be *orthogonally equivalent* if there exists an orthogonal matrix P such that $B = P^T A P$. Show that this relation is an equivalence relation.

POSITIVE DEFINITE MATRICES AND INNER PRODUCTS

7.79. Find the matrix A which represents the usual inner product on $\mathbf{R}^2$ relative to each of the following bases:

(a) $\{v_1 = (1, 4), v_2 = (2, -3)\}$; (b) $\{w_1 = (1, -3), w_2 = (6, 2)\}$.

7.80. Consider the following inner product on $\mathbf{R}^2$:

$$f(u, v) = x_1 y_1 - 2x_1 y_2 - 2x_2 y_1 + 5x_2 y_2 \qquad \text{where} \qquad u = (x_1, x_2), \qquad v = (y_1, y_2)$$

Find the matrix B which represents this inner product on $\mathbf{R}^2$ relative to each basis in Problem 7.79.

7.81. Find the matrix C which represents the usual inner product on $\mathbf{R}^3$ relative to the basis S of $\mathbf{R}^3$ consisting of the vectors $u_1 = (1, 1, 1)$, $u_2 = (1, 2, 1)$, and $u_3 = (1, -1, 3)$.

7.82. Consider $\mathbf{P}_2(t)$ with inner product $\langle f, g \rangle = \int_0^1 f(t)g(t)\, dt$.

    (a) Find $\langle f, g \rangle$, where $f(t) = t + 2$ and $g(t) = t^2 - 3t + 4$.

    (b) Find the matrix A of the inner product with respect to the basis $\{1, t, t^2\}$ of V.

    (c) Verify Theorem 7.16 that $\langle f, g \rangle = [f]^T A[g]$ with respect to the basis $\{1, t, t^2\}$.

7.83. Determine which of the following matrices are positive definite:

$$(a)\ \begin{bmatrix} 1 & 3 \\ 3 & 5 \end{bmatrix};\ (b)\ \begin{bmatrix} 3 & 4 \\ 4 & 7 \end{bmatrix};\ (c)\ \begin{bmatrix} 4 & 2 \\ 2 & 1 \end{bmatrix};\ (d)\ \begin{bmatrix} 6 & -7 \\ -7 & 9 \end{bmatrix}.$$

7.84. Suppose A and B are positive definite matrices. Show that: (a) $A + B$ is positive definite; (b) kA is positive definite for $k > 0$.

7.85. Suppose B is a real nonsingular matrix. Show that: (a) $B^T B$ is symmetric; (b) $B^T B$ is positive definite.

NORMED VECTOR SPACES

7.86. Consider vectors $u = (1, -3, 4, 1, -2)$ and $v = (3, 1, -2, -3, 1)$ in $\mathbf{R}^5$. Find:

    (a) $\|u\|_\infty$ and $\|v\|_\infty$,   (c) $\|u\|_2$ and $\|v\|_2$

    (b) $\|u\|_1$ and $\|v\|_1$,   (d) $d_\infty(u, v)$, $d_1(u, v)$, and $d_2(u, v)$

7.87. Consider the functions $f(t) = 5t - t^2$ and $g(t) = 3t - t^2$ in $C[0, 4]$. Find: (a) $d_\infty(f, g)$: (b) $d_1(f, g)$; (c) $d_2(f, g)$.

7.88. Prove that: (a) $\|\cdot\|_1$ is a norm on $\mathbf{R}^n$; (b) $\|\cdot\|_\infty$ is a norm on $\mathbf{R}^n$.

Answers to Supplementary Problems

7.54. $k > 9$

7.55. (a) -13; (b) -71; (c) $\sqrt{29}$; (d) $\sqrt{89}$

7.56. Let $u = (0, 0, 1)$. Then $\langle u, u \rangle = 0$ in both cases.

7.60. $\{7t^2 - 5t, 12t^2 - 5\}$

7.61. $\{(1, 2, 1, 0), (4, 4, 0, 1)\}$

7.62. $(-1, 0, 0, 0, 1), (-6, 2, 0, 1, 0), (-5, 2, 1, 0, 0)$

7.63. (a) $(0,0,3,1)$, $(0,3,-3,1)$, $(13,-2,1,-3)$; (b) $(0,0,3,1)/\sqrt{10}$, $(0,3,-3,1)/\sqrt{19}$, $(13,-2,1,-3)/\sqrt{183}$ [answer is not unique.]

7.64. (a) $(0,2,-1,0)$, $(-15,1,2,5)$; (b) $(0,2,-1,0)/\sqrt{5}$, $(-15,1,2,5)/\sqrt{255}$

7.65. (b) $v = (5u_1 + 3u_2 - 13u_3 + 9u_4)/4$;
(c) $[v] = [a+b+c+d, a+b-c-d, a-b+c-d, a-b-c+d]/4$

7.67. (a) $\begin{bmatrix} 0 & 1 \\ 0 & 0 \end{bmatrix}$, $\begin{bmatrix} 0 & 0 \\ 1 & 0 \end{bmatrix}$; (b) $\begin{bmatrix} 0 & -1 \\ 1 & 0 \end{bmatrix}$

7.70. (a) $c = -\frac{23}{30}$; (b) $c = \frac{1}{7}$; (c) $c = \frac{15}{148}$; (d) $c = \frac{19}{26}$

7.71. (a) $w_1 = (1,1,1,1)$, $w_2 = (0,-2,1,1)$, $w_3 = (12,-4,-1,-7)$;
(b) proj $(v, U) = (-1, 12, 3, 6)/5$

7.72. (a) proj $(v, W) = (13, 25, 30, 25, 23)/8$
(b) First find an orthogonal basis for W; say, $w_1 = (1, 2, 1, 2, 1)$ and $w_2 = (0, 2, 0, -3, 2)$.
Then proj $(v, W) = (34, 76, 34, 56, 42)/17$

7.73. proj $(f, W) = 3t^2/2 - 3t/5 + \frac{1}{20}$

7.74. (a) $\{1, t, 3t^2 - 1, 5t^3 - 3t\}$; (b) proj $(f, W) = 10t^3/9 - 5t/21$

7.75. Four: $\begin{bmatrix} \frac{1}{3} & \sqrt{8}/3 \\ \sqrt{8}/3 & -\frac{1}{3} \end{bmatrix}$, $\begin{bmatrix} \frac{1}{3} & \sqrt{8}/3 \\ -\sqrt{8}/3 & \frac{1}{3} \end{bmatrix}$, $\begin{bmatrix} \frac{1}{3} & -\sqrt{8}/3 \\ \sqrt{8}/3 & \frac{1}{3} \end{bmatrix}$, $\begin{bmatrix} \frac{1}{3} & -\sqrt{8}/3 \\ -\sqrt{8}/3 & -\frac{1}{3} \end{bmatrix}$

7.76. $P = \begin{bmatrix} 1/\sqrt{3} & 1/\sqrt{3} & 1/\sqrt{3} \\ 1/\sqrt{14} & -2/\sqrt{14} & 3/\sqrt{14} \\ 5/\sqrt{38} & -2/\sqrt{38} & -3/\sqrt{38} \end{bmatrix}$

7.77. $\begin{bmatrix} \frac{1}{3} & \frac{2}{3} & \frac{2}{3} \\ \frac{2}{3} & -\frac{2}{3} & \frac{1}{3} \\ \frac{2}{3} & \frac{1}{3} & -\frac{2}{3} \end{bmatrix}$

7.79. (a) $\begin{bmatrix} 17 & -10 \\ -10 & 13 \end{bmatrix}$; (b) $\begin{bmatrix} 10 & 0 \\ 0 & 40 \end{bmatrix}$

7.80. (a) $\begin{bmatrix} 65 & -68 \\ -68 & 73 \end{bmatrix}$; (b) $\begin{bmatrix} 58 & 8 \\ 8 & 8 \end{bmatrix}$

7.81. $\begin{bmatrix} 3 & 4 & 3 \\ 4 & 6 & 2 \\ 3 & 2 & 11 \end{bmatrix}$

7.82. (a) $\frac{83}{12}$; (b) $\begin{bmatrix} 1 & \frac{1}{2} & \frac{1}{3} \\ \frac{1}{2} & \frac{1}{3} & \frac{1}{4} \\ \frac{1}{3} & \frac{1}{4} & \frac{1}{5} \end{bmatrix}$

7.83. (a) No; (b) yes; (c) no; (d) yes

7.86. (a) 4 and 3; (b) 11 and 10; (c) $\sqrt{31}$ and $\sqrt{24}$; (d) 6, 19, and 9

7.87. (a) 8; (b) 16; (c) $\sqrt{\frac{256}{3}}$

Chapter 8

Linear Mappings

8.1 INTRODUCTION

The main subject matter of linear algebra is the study of linear mappings and their representation by means of matrices. This chapter introduces us to these linear maps and the next chapter shows how they can be represented by matrices. First, however, we begin with a study of mappings in general.

8.2 MAPPINGS, FUNCTIONS

Let A and B be arbitrary nonempty sets. Suppose to each element in A there is assigned a unique element of B; the collection f of such assignments is called a *mapping* or *map* from A into B and is denoted by

$$f: A \rightarrow B$$

The set A is called the *domain* of the mapping, and B is called the *codomain*. We write $f(a)$ (read "f of a") for the unique element of B that f assigns to $a \in A$.

Remark: The term *function* is used synonymously with the word mapping, although some texts reserve the word function for a real-valued or complex-valued mapping.

Consider a mapping $f: A \rightarrow B$. If A' is any subset of A, then $f(A')$ denotes the set of images of elements of A'; and if B' is any subset of B, then $f^{-1}(B')$ denotes the set of elements of A each of whose image lies in B':

$$f(A') = \{f(a): a \in A'\} \quad \text{and} \quad f^{-1}(B') = \{a \in A: f(a) \in B'\}$$

We call $f(A')$ the *image* of A' and $f^{-1}(B')$ the *inverse image* or *preimage* of B'. In particular, the set of all images, i.e., $f(A)$, is called the image or *range* of f.

To each mapping $f: A \rightarrow B$ there corresponds the subset of $A \times B$ given by $\{(a, f(a)): a \in A\}$. We call this set the *graph* of f. Two mappings $f: A \rightarrow B$ and $g: A \rightarrow B$ are defined to be *equal*, written $f = g$, if $f(a) = g(a)$ for every $a \in A$, that is, if they have the same graph. Thus we do not distinguish between a function and its graph. The negation of $f = g$ is written $f \neq g$ and is the statement:

> There exists an $a \in A$ for which $f(a) \neq g(a)$.

Sometimes the "barred" arrow $\mapsto$ is used to denote the image of an arbitrary element $x \in A$ under a mapping $f: A \rightarrow B$ by writing

$$x \mapsto f(x)$$

This is illustrated in the following example.

EXAMPLE 8.1

(a) Let $A = \{a, b, c, d\}$ and $B = \{x, y, z, t\}$. Then the diagram in Fig. 8-1 defines a mapping f from A into B. Specifically,

$$f(a) = y, \qquad f(b) = x, \qquad f(c) = z, \qquad f(d) = y$$

and the graph of f is the set

$$\{(a, y), (b, x), (c, z), (d, y)\}$$

Also,

$$f(\{a, b, d\}) = \{f(a), f(b), f(d)\} = \{y, x, y\} = \{x, y\}$$

Furthermore, $f(A) = \{x, y, z\}$ is the image of f.

(b) Let $f: \mathbf{R} \to \mathbf{R}$ be the function that assigns to each real number its square x^2. We can denote this function by writing

$$f(x) = x^2 \qquad \text{or} \qquad x \mapsto x^2$$

The image of -3 is 9, so here we may write $f(-3) = 9$. However, $f^{-1}(9) = \{3, -3\}$. Also, $f(\mathbf{R}) = [0, \infty) = \{x: x \geq 0\}$ is the image of f.

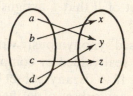

Fig. 8-1

EXAMPLE 8.2   Consider the vector space $V = \mathbf{P}(t)$ of polynomials over $\mathbf{R}$, and suppose $p(t) = 3t^2 - 5t + 2$.

(a) The derivative defines a mapping $\mathbf{D}: V \to V$, where, for any polynomial $f(t)$, we have $\mathbf{D}(f) = df/dt$. Thus

$$\mathbf{D}(p) = \mathbf{D}(3t^2 - 5t + 2) = 6t - 5$$

(b) The integral, say from 0 to 1, defines a mapping $\mathbf{J}: V \to \mathbf{R}$, where for any polynomial $f(t)$, we let

$$\mathbf{J}(f) = \int_0^1 f(t) \, dt.$$

Thus

$$\mathbf{J}(p) = \int_0^1 (3t^2 - 5t + 2) = \tfrac{1}{2}$$

Observe that the mapping in part (b) is from the vector space V into the scalar field $\mathbf{R}$, whereas the mapping in part (a) is from the vector space V into itself.

Matrix Mappings

Consider a real $m \times n$ matrix A. Then A determines a mapping from $F_A: \mathbf{R}^n \to \mathbf{R}^m$ by the assignment

$$F_A(u) = Au$$

where the vectors in $\mathbf{R}^n$ and $\mathbf{R}^m$ are written as columns.   For example, suppose

$$A = \begin{bmatrix} 1 & -4 & 5 \\ 2 & 3 & -6 \end{bmatrix}$$

Then for any (column) vector u in $\mathbf{R}^3$, say $u = (1, 3, -5)^T$, we have

$$F_A(u) = Au = \begin{bmatrix} 1 & -4 & 5 \\ 2 & 3 & -6 \end{bmatrix} \begin{bmatrix} 1 \\ 3 \\ -5 \end{bmatrix} = \begin{bmatrix} -36 \\ 41 \end{bmatrix}$$

We emphasize that all vectors must be written as columns for this mapping to be defined.

Remark: For convenience, we shall frequently denote the mapping F_A by the letter A, the same symbol as that used for the matrix.

Composition of Mappings

Consider two mappings $f: A \to B$ and $g: B \to C$, illustrated below:

$$\textcircled{A} \xrightarrow{\ f\ } \textcircled{B} \xrightarrow{\ g\ } \textcircled{C}$$

Let $a \in A$; then $f(a) \in B$, the domain of g.   Hence we can obtain the image of $f(a)$ under the mapping g, that is, $g(f(a))$.   This map

$$a \mapsto g(f(a))$$

from A into C is called the *composition* or *product* of f and g, and is denoted by $g \circ f$.   In other words, $(g \circ f): A \to C$ is the mapping defined by

$$(g \circ f)(a) = g(f(a))$$

Our first theorem tells us that the composition of mappings satisfies the associative law.

Theorem 8.1:   Let $f: A \to B$, $g: B \to C$, and $h: C \to D$.   Then $h \circ (g \circ f) = (h \circ g) \circ f$.

We prove this theorem now.   If $a \in A$, then

$$(h \circ (g \circ f))(a) = h((g \circ f)(a)) = h(g(f(a)))$$

and

$$((h \circ g) \circ f)(a) = (h \circ g)(f(a)) = h(g(f(a)))$$

Thus $(h \circ (g \circ f))(a) = ((h \circ g) \circ f)(a)$ for every $a \in A$, and so $h \circ (g \circ f) = (h \circ g) \circ f$.

One-to-One and Onto Mappings

We formally introduce some special types of mappings.

Definition: A mapping $f: A \to B$ is said to be *one-to-one* (or *one-one* or *1-1*) or *injective* if different elements of A have distinct images, that is,

$$\text{if } a \neq a' \quad \text{implies} \quad f(a) \neq f(a')$$

or, equivalently, $\quad$ if $f(a) = f(a')$ implies $a = a'$

Definition: A mapping $f: A \to B$ is said to be *onto* (or f maps A *onto* B) or *surjective* if every $b \in B$ is the image of at least one $a \in A$.

Definition: A mapping $f: A \rightarrow B$ is said to be a *one-to-one correspondence* between A and B or *bijective* if f is both one-to-one and onto.

EXAMPLE 8.3 Let $f: \mathbf{R} \rightarrow \mathbf{R}$, $g: \mathbf{R} \rightarrow \mathbf{R}$, and $h: \mathbf{R} \rightarrow \mathbf{R}$ be defined by $f(x) = 2^x$, $g(x) = x^3 - x$, and $h(x) = x^2$. The graphs of these mappings are shown in Fig. 8-2. The mapping f is one-to-one. Geometrically this means that each horizontal line does not contain more than one point of f. The mapping g is onto. Geometrically this means that each horizontal line contains at least one point of g. The mapping h is neither one-to-one nor onto. For example, 2 and -2 have the same image 4, and -16 is not the image of any element of $\mathbf{R}$.

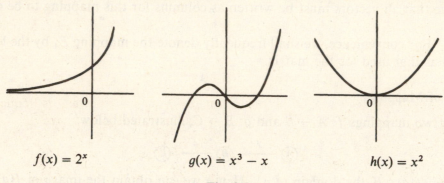

$$f(x) = 2^x \qquad\qquad g(x) = x^3 - x \qquad\qquad h(x) = x^2$$

Fig. 8-2

Identity and Inverse Mappings

Let A be any nonempty set. The mapping $f: A \rightarrow A$, defined by $f(a) = a$, that is, it assigns to each element in A itself, is called *identity mapping*. It is usually denoted by $\mathbf{1}_A$ or $\mathbf{1}$ or I. Thus for any $a \in A$,

$$\mathbf{1}_A(a) = a$$

Now let $f: A \rightarrow B$. We call $g: B \rightarrow A$ the inverse of f, written f^{-1}, if

$$f \circ g = \mathbf{1}_B \qquad \text{and} \qquad g \circ f = \mathbf{1}_A$$

We emphasize that f has an inverse if and only if f is a one-to-one correspondence between A and B, that is, f is one-to-one and onto (see Problem 8.11). Also, if $b \in B$, then $f^{-1}(b) = a$, where a is the unique element of A for which $f(a) = b$.

8.3 LINEAR MAPPINGS (TRANSFORMATIONS)

We begin with a definition.

Definition: Let V and U be vector spaces over the same field K. A mapping $F: V \rightarrow U$ is called a *linear mapping* or *linear transformation* if it satisfies the following two conditions:

    (1)   For any vectors $v, w \in V$, $F(v + w) = F(v) + F(w)$.
    (2)   For any scalar k and vector $v \in V$, $F(kv) = kF(v)$.

In other words, $F: V \rightarrow U$ is linear if it "preserves" the two basic operations of a vector space, that of vector addition and that of scalar multiplication.

Substituting $k = 0$ into condition (2) we obtain $F(0) = 0$. That is, every linear mapping takes the zero vector into the zero vector.

Now for any scalars $a, b \in K$ and any vectors $v, w \in V$ we obtain, by applying both conditions of linearity,

$$F(av + bw) = F(av) + F(bw) = aF(v) + bF(w)$$

More generally, for any scalars $a_i \in K$ and any vectors $v_i \in V$ we obtain the basic property of linear mappings:

$$F(a_1 v_1 + a_2 v_2 + \cdots + a_n v_n) = a_1 F(v_1) + a_2 F(v_2) + \cdots + a_n F(v_n)$$

Remark 1: A linear mapping $F: V \to U$ is completely characterized by the condition

$$F(av + bw) = aF(v) + bF(w) \tag{$\star$}$$

and so this condition is sometimes used as its definition.

Remark 2: The term linear transformation rather than linear mapping is frequently used for linear mappings of the form $F: \mathbf{R}^n \to \mathbf{R}^m$, that is, between Euclidean spaces.

EXAMPLE 8.4

(a) Let $F: \mathbf{R}^3 \to \mathbf{R}^3$ be the "projection" mapping into the xy plane, that is, F is the mapping defined by $F(x, y, z) = (x, y, 0)$. We show that F is linear. Let $v = (a, b, c)$ and $w = (a', b', c')$. Then

$$F(v + w) = F(a + a', b + b', c + c') = (a + a', b + b', 0)$$
$$= (a, b, 0) + (a', b', 0) = F(v) + F(w)$$

and, for any scalar k.

$$F(kv) = F(ka, kb, kc) = (ka, kb, 0) = k(a, b, 0) = kF(v)$$

Thus F is linear.

(b) Let $G: \mathbf{R}^2 \to \mathbf{R}^2$ be the "translation" mapping defined by $G(x, y) = (x + 1, y + 2)$. [That is, G adds the vector $(1, 2)$ to any vector $v = (x, y)$ in $\mathbf{R}^2$.] Note that

$$G(0) = G(0, 0) = (1, 2) \neq 0$$

Thus the zero vector is not mapped into the zero vector. Hence G cannot be linear.

EXAMPLE 8.5 (Derivative and Integral Mappings)

Consider the vector space $V = \mathbf{P}(t)$ of polynomials over the real field $\mathbf{R}$. Let $u(t)$ and $v(t)$ be any polynomials in V and let k be any scalar.

(a) Let $\mathbf{D}: V \to V$ be the derivative mapping. One proves in calculus that

$$\frac{d(u + v)}{dt} = \frac{du}{dt} + \frac{dv}{dt} \quad \text{and} \quad \frac{d(ku)}{dt} = k\frac{du}{dt}$$

That is, $\mathbf{D}(u + v) = \mathbf{D}(u) + \mathbf{D}(v)$ and $\mathbf{D}(ku) = k\mathbf{D}(u)$. Thus the derivative mapping is linear.

(b) Let $\mathbf{J}: V \to \mathbf{R}$ be an integral mapping, say

$$\mathbf{J}(f(t)) = \int_0^1 f(t)\, dt$$

One also proves in calculus that

$$\int_0^1 [u(t) + v(t)]\, dt = \int_0^1 u(t)\, dt + \int_0^1 v(t)\, dt \quad \text{and} \quad \int_0^1 ku(t)\, dt = k \int_0^1 u(t)\, dt$$

That is, $\mathbf{J}(u + v) = \mathbf{J}(u) + \mathbf{J}(v)$ and $\mathbf{J}(ku) = k\mathbf{J}(u)$. Thus the integral mapping is linear.

EXAMPLE 8.6 (Zero and Identity Mappings)

(a) Let $F: V \to U$ be the mapping that assigns the zero vector $0 \in U$ to every vector $v \in V$. Then, for any vectors $v, w \in V$ and any scalar $k \in K$, we have

$$F(v + w) = 0 = 0 + 0 = F(v) + F(w) \quad \text{and} \quad F(kv) = 0 = k0 = kF(v)$$

Thus F is linear. We call F the *zero mapping*, and we shall usually denote it by $\mathbf{0}$.

(b) Consider the identity mapping $I: V \to V$, which maps each $v \in V$ into itself. Then, for any vectors $v, w \in V$ and any scalars a, b in K, we have

$$I(av + bw) = av + bw = aI(v) + bI(w)$$

Thus I is linear.

Our next theorem (proved in Problem 8.45) gives us an abundance of examples of linear mappings. In particular, it tells us that a linear mapping is completely determined by its values on the elements of a basis.

Theorem 8.2: Let V and U be vector spaces over a field K. Let $\{v_1, v_2, \ldots, v_n\}$ be a basis of V and let $u_1, u_2, \ldots, u_n$ be any vectors in U. Then there exists a unique linear mapping $F: V \to U$ such that $F(v_1) = u_1$, $F(v_2) = u_2$, $\ldots$, $F(v_n) = u_n$.

We emphasize that the vectors $u_1, \ldots, u_n$ in Theorem 8.2 are completely arbitrary; they may be linearly dependent or they may even be equal to each other.

Matrices as Linear Mappings

Let A be any real $m \times n$ matrix. Recall that A determines a mapping $F_A: \mathbf{R}^n \to \mathbf{R}^m$ by $F_A(u) = Au$ (where the vectors in $\mathbf{R}^n$ and $\mathbf{R}^m$ are written as columns). We show that F_A is linear. By matrix multiplication,

$$F_A(v + w) = A(v + w) = Av + Aw = F_A(v) + F_A(w)$$
$$F_A(kv) = A(kv) = k(Av) = kF_A(v)$$

In other words, using A to represent the mapping, we have

$$A(v + w) = Av + Aw \quad \text{and} \quad A(kv) = k(Av)$$

Thus the matrix mapping A is linear.

Vector Space Isomorphism

The notion of two vector spaces being isomorphic was defined in Chapter 6 when we investigated the coordinates of a vector relative to a basis. We now redefine this concept.

Definition: Two vector spaces V and U over K are said to be *isomorphic*, written $V \simeq U$, if there exists a bijective linear mapping $F: V \to U$. The mapping F is then called an *isomorphism* between V and U.

Consider any vector space V of dimension n and let S be any basis of V. Then the mapping

$$v \mapsto [v]_S$$

which maps each vector $v \in V$ into its coordinate vector $[v]_S$, is an isomorphism between V and K^n.

8.4   KERNEL AND IMAGE OF A LINEAR MAPPING

We begin by defining two concepts.

Definition: Let $F: V \to U$ be a linear mapping. The *kernel* of F, written Ker F, is the set of elements in V which map into the zero vector 0 in U, that is,

$$\text{Ker } F = \{v \in V: F(v) = 0\}$$

The *image* or *range* of F, written Im F, is the set of image points in $\mathbf{U}$, that is,

$$\text{Im } F = \{u \in U: \text{there exists } v \in V \text{ for which } F(v) = u\}$$

The following theorem is easily proved (see Problem 8.46).

Theorem 8.3:   Let $F: V \to U$ be a linear mapping. Then

   (i)   The image of F is a subspace of U.

   (ii)   The kernel of F is a subspace of V.

Now suppose that the vectors $v_1, \ldots, v_n$ span V and that $F: V \to U$ is linear. We show that the vectors $F(v_1), \ldots, F(v_n) \in U$ span Im F. If we let $u \in$ Im F, then $F(v) = u$ for some vector $v \in V$. Since the v_i span V and since $v \in V$, there exist scalars $a_1, \ldots, a_n$ for which

$$v = a_1 v_1 + a_2 v_2 + \cdots + a_n v_n$$

Accordingly,

$$u = F(v) = F(a_1 v_1 + a_2 v_2 + \cdots + a_n v_n) = a_1 F(v_1) + a_2 F(v_2) + \cdots + a_n F(v_n)$$

and hence the vectors $F(v_1), \ldots, F(v_n)$ span Im F.

We formally state the above useful result.

Proposition 8.4:   Suppose $v_1, v_2, \ldots, v_n$ span a vector space V and $F: V \to U$ is linear. Then $F(v_1), F(v_2), \ldots, F(v_n)$ span Im F.

EXAMPLE 8.7

(a)   Let $F: \mathbf{R}^3 \to \mathbf{R}^3$ be the projection of a vector v into the xy plane (as pictured in Fig. 8-3), that is,

$$F(x, y, z) = (x, y, 0)$$

Clearly the image of F is the entire xy plane, i.e., points of the form $(x, y, 0)$, and the kernel of F is the z axis, i.e., points of the form $(0, 0, c)$, since these points and only these points map into the zero vector $0 = (0, 0, 0)$. In other words,

$$\text{Im } F = \{(a, b, c): c = 0\} \quad \text{and} \quad \text{Ker } F = \{(a, b, c): a = 0, b = 0\}$$

(b)   Let $G: \mathbf{R}^3 \to \mathbf{R}^3$ be the linear mapping which rotates a vector v about the z axis through an angle θ (as pictured in Fig. 8-4), that is,

$$G(x, y, z) = (x \cos \theta - y \sin \theta, x \sin \theta + y \cos \theta, z)$$

Observe that the distance of a vector v from the origin O does not change under the rotation, and so only the zero vector 0 is mapped into the zero vector 0. Thus Ker $G = \{0\}$. On the other hand, every vector u in $\mathbf{R}^3$ is the image of a vector v in $\mathbf{R}^3$, which can be obtained by rotating u back by an angle θ. Thus Im $G = \mathbf{R}^3$, the entire space.

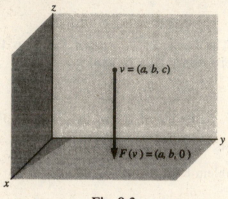

Fig. 8-3

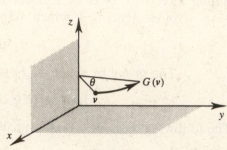

Fig. 8-4

EXAMPLE 8.8   Consider the vector space $V = \mathbf{P}(t)$ of polynomials over the real field $\mathbf{R}$, and let $H: V \to V$ be the third derivative operator, that is,

$$H[f(t)] = \frac{d^3 f}{dt^3}$$

(Sometimes the notation $H = \mathbf{D}^3$ is used, where D is the derivative operator.)   Then

$$\text{Ker } H = \{\text{polynomials of degree} \le 2\} = \mathbf{P}_2(t)$$

since $H(at^2 + bt + c) = 0$ but $H(t^n) \ne 0$ for $n \ge 3$.   On the other hand,

$$\text{Im } H = V$$

since every polynomial $g(t)$ in V is the third derivative of some polynomial $f(t)$ [which could be obtained by taking the antiderivative of $g(t)$ three times].

Kernel and Image of Matrix Mappings

Consider any matrix A, say the 4×3 matrix

$$A = \begin{bmatrix} a_1 & a_2 & a_3 \\ b_1 & b_2 & b_3 \\ c_1 & c_2 & c_3 \\ d_1 & d_2 & d_3 \end{bmatrix}$$

Recall that we view A as a linear mapping $A: \mathbf{R}^3 \to \mathbf{R}^4$, where the vectors in $\mathbf{R}^3$ and $\mathbf{R}^4$ are viewed as column vectors.   Now the usual basis $\{e_1, e_2, e_3\}$ of $\mathbf{R}^3$ spans $\mathbf{R}^3$, and so their values Ae_1, Ae_2, Ae_3 under A span the image of A. But the vectors Ae_1, Ae_2, Ae_3 are precisely the columns of A,

$$Ae_1 = \begin{bmatrix} a_1 & a_2 & a_3 \\ b_1 & b_2 & b_3 \\ c_1 & c_2 & c_3 \\ d_1 & d_2 & d_3 \end{bmatrix} \begin{bmatrix} 1 \\ 0 \\ 0 \end{bmatrix} = \begin{bmatrix} a_1 \\ b_1 \\ c_1 \\ d_1 \end{bmatrix}, \qquad Ae_2 = \begin{bmatrix} a_1 & a_2 & a_3 \\ b_1 & b_2 & b_3 \\ c_1 & c_2 & c_3 \\ d_1 & d_2 & d_3 \end{bmatrix} \begin{bmatrix} 0 \\ 1 \\ 0 \end{bmatrix} = \begin{bmatrix} a_2 \\ b_2 \\ c_2 \\ d_2 \end{bmatrix}$$

$$Ae_3 = \begin{bmatrix} a_1 & a_2 & a_3 \\ b_1 & b_2 & b_3 \\ c_1 & c_2 & c_3 \\ d_1 & d_2 & d_3 \end{bmatrix} \begin{bmatrix} 0 \\ 0 \\ 1 \end{bmatrix} = \begin{bmatrix} a_3 \\ b_3 \\ c_3 \\ d_3 \end{bmatrix}$$

Thus the image of A is precisely the column space of A.

On the other hand, the kernel of A consists of all vectors v for which $Av = 0$. This means that the kernel of A is the solution space of the homogeneous system $AX = 0$.

We state the above result formally.

Proposition 8.5: Let A be any $m \times n$ matrix over a field K viewed as a linear map $A: K^n \to K^m$. Then

$$\text{Ker } A = \text{nullsp}(A) \qquad \text{and} \qquad \text{Im } A = \text{colsp}(A)$$

Here colsp(A) denotes the *column space* of A, and nullsp(A) denotes the *null space* of A, that is, the solution space of the homogeneous system $AX = 0$.

8.5 RANK AND NULLITY OF A LINEAR MAPPING

So far we have not related the notion of dimension to that of a linear mapping $F: V \to U$. In the case that V is of finite dimension, we have the following fundamental relationship (proved in Problem 8.47).

Theorem 8.6: Let V be of finite dimension, and let $F: V \to U$ be a linear mapping. Then

$$\dim V = \dim (\text{Ker } F) + \dim (\text{Im } F)$$

That is, the sum of the dimensions of the image and the kernel of a linear mapping is equal to the dimension of its domain.

Remark: Let $F: V \to U$ be a linear mapping. Then the *rank* of F is defined to be the dimension of its image, and the *nullity* of F is defined to be the dimension of its kernel, that is,

$$\text{rank}(F) = \dim (\text{Im } F) \qquad \text{and} \qquad \text{nullity}(F) = \dim (\text{Ker } F)$$

Thus Theorem 8.6 yields the following formula for F when V has finite dimension:

$$\text{rank}(F) + \text{nullity}(F) = \dim V$$

Recall that the rank of a matrix A was originally defined to be the dimensions of its column space and its row space. Observe that if we now view A as a linear mapping, then both definitions correspond since the image of A is precisely its column space.

EXAMPLE 8.9   Let $F: \mathbf{R}^4 \to \mathbf{R}^3$ be the linear mapping defined by

$$F(x, y, z, t) = (x - y + z + t, 2x - 2y + 3z + 4t, 3x - 3y + 4z + 5t)$$

(a)   Find a basis and the dimension of the image of F.
    Find the image of the usual basis vectors of $\mathbf{R}^4$,

$$F(1, 0, 0, 0) = (1, 2, 3), \qquad\qquad F(0, 0, 1, 0) = (1, 3, 4)$$
$$F(0, 1, 0, 0) = (-1, -2, -3), \qquad F(0, 0, 0, 1) = (1, 4, 5)$$

By Proposition 8.4, the image vectors span Im F.   Hence form the matrix M whose rows are these image vectors and row reduce to echelon form:

$$M = \begin{bmatrix} 1 & 2 & 3 \\ -1 & -2 & -3 \\ 1 & 3 & 4 \\ 1 & 4 & 5 \end{bmatrix} \sim \begin{bmatrix} 1 & 2 & 3 \\ 0 & 0 & 0 \\ 0 & 1 & 1 \\ 0 & 2 & 2 \end{bmatrix} \sim \begin{bmatrix} 1 & 2 & 3 \\ 0 & 1 & 1 \\ 0 & 0 & 0 \\ 0 & 0 & 0 \end{bmatrix}$$

Thus $(1, 2, 3)$ and $(0, 1, 1)$ form a basis of Im F.   Hence dim (Im F) = 2 and rank (F) = 2.

(b)   Find a basis and the dimension of the kernel of the map F.
    Set $F(v) = 0$, where $v = (x, y, z, t)$,

$$F(x, y, z, t) = (x - y + z + t, 2x - 2y + 3z + 4t, 3x - 3y + 4z + 5t) = (0, 0, 0)$$

Set corresponding components equal to each other to form the following homogeneous system whose solution space is Ker F:

$$\begin{array}{llll} x - y + z + t = 0 & & x - y + z + t = 0 & \\ 2x - 2y + 3z + 4t = 0 & \text{or} & z + 2t = 0 & \text{or} \quad \begin{array}{l} x - y + z + t = 0 \\ z + 2t = 0 \end{array} \\ 3x - 3y + 4z + 5t = 0 & & z + 2t = 0 & \end{array}$$

The free variables are y and t.   Hence dim (Ker F) = 2 or nullity (F) = 2.   Set:

(i) $y = 1$, $t = 0$ to obtain the solution $(1, 1, 0, 0)$.

(ii) $y = 0$, $t = 1$ to obtain the solution $(1, 0, -2, 1)$.

Thus $(1, 1, 0, 0)$ and $(1, 0, -2, 1)$ form a basis for Ker F.

Application to Systems of Linear Equations

Consider a system of m linear equations in n unknowns which is equivalent to the matrix equation

$$Ax = b$$

where $A = [a_{ij}]$ is the $m \times n$ coefficient matrix, and $x = [\psi_j]$ and $b = [b_i]$ are the column vectors of the unknowns and constants, respectively.   Now the matrix A may be viewed as the linear mapping

$$A: \mathbf{R}^n \to \mathbf{R}^m$$

Thus the solution of the equation $Ax = b$ may be viewed as the preimage of the vector $b \in \mathbf{R}^m$ under the linear mapping A.

Consider now the associated homogeneous system

$$Ax = 0$$

Its solution may be viewed as the kernel of the linear mapping $A: \mathbf{R}^n \to \mathbf{R}^m$. Applying Theorem 8.6 to this homogeneous system yields

$$\dim (\text{Ker } A) = \dim \mathbf{R}^n - \dim (\text{Im } A) = n - \text{rank } (A)$$

But n is exactly the number of unknowns in the homogeneous system $Ax = 0$. Thus we have recovered Theorem 5.14, which we restate.

Theorem 8.7: The dimension of the solution space W of the homogeneous system of linear equations $AX = 0$ is $n - r$, where n is the number of unknowns and r is the rank of the coefficient matrix A.

8.6 NONSINGULAR LINEAR MAPPINGS

Consider a linear mapping $F: V \to U$. Then the image of the zero vector 0 under F must be 0, that is, $F(0) = 0$. The linear mapping F is said to be *singular* if the image of some nonzero vector v under F is 0, that is, if there exists $v \neq 0$ such that $F(v) = 0$. Thus $F: V \to U$ is *nonsingular* if the zero vector 0 is the only vector in V whose image under F is 0. In other words, F is nonsingular if the kernel of F only consists of the zero vector, that is, if Ker $F = \{0\}$.

EXAMPLE 8.10 Consider the projection map $F: \mathbf{R}^3 \to \mathbf{R}^3$ in Fig. 8-3, and the rotation map $G: \mathbf{R}^3 \to \mathbf{R}^3$ in Fig. 8-4. (See Example 8.7.) Since the kernel of F is the z axis, F is singular. On the other hand, the kernel of G consists only of the zero vector 0. Thus G is nonsingular.

Suppose a linear mapping $F: V \to U$ is one-to-one. Then only $0 \in V$ can map into $0 \in U$, and so F is nonsingular. The converse is also true. For suppose F is nonsingular and $F(v) = F(w)$, then $F(v - w) = F(v) - F(w) = 0$, and hence $v - w = 0$ or $v = w$. Thus $F(v) = F(w)$ implies $v = w$, that is, F is one-to-one. Thus we have proved the following proposition.

Proposition 8.8: A linear mapping $F: V \to U$ is one-to-one if and only if it is nonsingular.

Nonsingular linear mappings may also be characterized as those mappings which carry linearly independent sets into linearly independent sets. Specifically, we prove (see Problem 8.48) the following theorem.

Theorem 8.9: Suppose a linear mapping $F: V \to U$ is nonsingular. Then the image of any linearly independent set is linearly independent.

8.7 OPERATIONS WITH LINEAR MAPPINGS

We are able to combine linear mappings in various ways to obtain new linear mappings. These operations are very important and shall be used throughout the text.

Suppose $F: V \to U$ and $G: V \to U$ are linear mappings of vector spaces over a field K. We define the sum $F + G$ to be the mapping from V into U, which assigns $F(v) + G(v)$ to $v \in V$, that is,

$$(F + G)(v) = F(v) + G(v)$$

Furthermore, for any scalar $k \in K$, we define the product kF to be the mapping from V into U which assigns $kF(v)$ to $v \in V$, that is,

$$(kF)(v) = kF(v)$$

We now show that if F and G are linear, then $F + G$ and kF are also linear. We have, for any vectors $v, w \in V$ and any scalars $a, b \in K$,

$$
\begin{aligned}
(F + G)(av + bw) &= F(av + bw) + G(av + bw) \\
&= aF(v) + bF(w) + aG(v) + bG(w) \\
&= a[F(v) + G(v)] + b[F(w) + G(w)] \\
&= a(F + G)(v) + b(F + G)(w)
\end{aligned}
$$

and

$$
\begin{aligned}
(kF)(av + bw) &= kF(av + bw) = k[aF(v) + bF(w)] \\
&= akF(v) + bkF(w) = a(kF)(v) + b(kF)(w)
\end{aligned}
$$

Thus $F + G$ and kF are linear.

The following theorem applies.

Theorem 8.10: Let V and U be vector spaces over a field K. Then the collection of all linear mappings from V into U with the above operations of addition and scalar multiplication forms a vector space over K.

The vector space of linear mappings in Theorem 8.10 is usually denoted by

$$\text{Hom}\,(V, U)$$

Here Hom comes from the word homomorphism. Note that the proof of Theorem 8.10 reduces to showing that Hom (V, U) does satisfy the eight axioms of a vector space. The zero element of Hom (V, U) is the *zero mapping* from V into U, denoted by **0** and defined by

$$\mathbf{0}(v) = 0$$

for every vector $v \in V$.

Suppose V and U are of finite dimension. Then we have the following theorem.

Theorem 8.11: Suppose dim $V = m$ and dim $U = n$. Then dim Hom $(V, U) = mn$.

Composition of Linear Mappings

Now suppose V, U, and W are vector spaces over the same field K, and suppose $F\colon V \to U$ and $G\colon U \to W$ are linear mappings. We picture these mappings as follows:

$$\textcircled{V} \xrightarrow{\ F\ } \textcircled{U} \xrightarrow{\ G\ } \textcircled{W}$$

Recall that the composition function $G \circ F$ is the mapping from V into W defined by $(G \circ F)(v) = G(F(v))$. We show that $G \circ F$ is linear whenever F and G are linear. We have, for any vectors $v, w \in V$ and any scalars $a, b \in K$,

$$
\begin{aligned}
(G \circ F)(av + bw) &= G(F(av + bw)) = G(aF(v) + bF(w)) \\
&= aG(F(v)) + bG(F(w)) = a(G \circ F)(v) + b(G \circ F)(w)
\end{aligned}
$$

that is, $G \circ F$ is linear.

The composition of linear mappings and the operations of addition and scalar multiplication are related as follows.

Theorem 8.12: Let V, U, and W be vector spaces over K. Let F and F' be linear mappings from V into U, let G and G' be linear mappings from U into W, and let $k \in K$. Then

    (i) $G \circ (F + F') = G \circ F + G \circ F'$

    (ii) $(G + G') \circ F = G \circ F + G' \circ F$

    (iii) $k(G \circ F) = (kG) \circ F = G \circ (kF)$

8.8 ALGEBRA $A(V)$ OF LINEAR OPERATORS

Let V be a vector space over a field K. We now consider the special case of linear mappings $F: V \to V$, i.e., from V into itself. They are also called *linear operators* or *linear transformations* on V. We will write $A(V)$, instead of Hom (V, V), for the space of all such mappings.

By Theorem 8.10, $A(V)$ is a vector space over K. Also, if dim $V = n$, then dim $A(V) = n^2$. Now if F, $G \in A(V)$, then the composition $G \circ F$ exists and is also a linear mapping from V into itself, i.e., $G \circ F \in A(V)$. Thus we have a "multiplication" defined in $A(V)$. [We shall write GF for $G \circ F$ in the space $A(V)$.]

Remark: An *algebra* A over a field K is a vector space over K in which an operation of multiplication is defined satisfying, for every F, G, $H \in A$ and every $k \in K$,

  (i) $F(G + H) = FG + FH$

  (ii) $(G + H)F = GF + HF$

 (iii) $k(GF) = (kG)F = G(kF)$

If the associative law also holds for the multiplication, i.e., if for every F, G, $H \in A$,

 (iv) $(FG)H = F(GH)$

then the algebra A is said to be *associative*.

The above definition of an algebra and Theorems 8.10, 8.11, and 8.12 give us the following basic result.

Theorem 8.13: Let V be a vector space over K. Then $A(V)$ is an associative algebra over K with respect to composition of mappings. If dim $V = n$, then dim $A(V) = n^2$.

In view of Theorem 8.13, $A(V)$ is frequently called the *algebra of linear operators* on V.

Polynomials and Linear Operators

Observe that the identity mapping $I: V \to V$ belongs to $A(V)$. Also, for any linear mapping $F \in A(V)$, we have $FI = IF = F$. We note that we can also form "powers" of F. Specifically we use the notation

$$F^2 = F \circ F, \qquad F^3 = F^2 \circ F = F \circ F \circ F, \qquad F^4 = F^3 \circ F, \qquad \cdots$$

Furthermore, for any polynomial

$$p(x) = a_0 + a_1 x + a_2 x^2 + \cdots + a_s x^s$$

where $a_i \in K$, we can form the operator $p(F)$ defined by

$$p(F) = a_0 I + a_1 F + a_2 F^2 + \cdots + a_s F^s$$

(For any scalar k, the operator kI is frequently denoted simply by k.)   In particular, if $p(F) = 0$, the zero mapping, then F is said to be a *zero* of the polynomial $p(x)$.

EXAMPLE 8.11   Let $F: \mathbf{R}^3 \to \mathbf{R}^3$ be defined by $F(x, y, z) = (0, x, y)$.   Consider any element (a, b, c) in $\mathbf{R}^3$.   Then

$$(F + I)(a, b, c) = (0, a, b) + (a, b, c) = (a, a + b, b + c)$$
$$F^3(a, b, c) = F^2(0, a, b) = F(0, 0, a) = (0, 0, 0)$$

Thus $F^3 = 0$, the zero mapping in $A(V)$.   Thus F is a zero of the polynomial $p(x) = x^3$.

Square Matrices as Linear Operators

Consider the collection $\mathbf{M} = \mathbf{M}_{n,n}$ of all real square $n \times n$ matrices.   Recall that any matrix A in $\mathbf{M}$ defines a linear mapping $F_A: \mathbf{R}^n \to \mathbf{R}^n$ by

$$F_A(u) = Au$$

(where the vectors in $\mathbf{R}^n$ are written as columns).   Since the mapping is from $\mathbf{R}^n$ into itself, the square matrix A is a linear operator, not simply a linear mapping.

Suppose A and B are matrices in $\mathbf{M}$.   Then the matrix product AB is defined.   Furthermore, for any (column) vector u in $\mathbf{R}^n$ we have

$$F_{AB}(u) = AB(u) = A(B(u)) = AF_B(u) = F_A(F_B(u)) = F_A \circ F_B(u)$$

In other words, the matrix product AB corresponds to the composition of A and B as mappings. Similarly, the matrix sum $A + B$ corresponds to the sum of A and B as mappings, and the scalar product kA corresponds to the scalar product of A as a mapping.

8.9   INVERTIBLE OPERATORS

A linear operator $F: V \to V$ is said to be *invertible* if it has an inverse, that is, if there exists F^{-1} in $A(V)$ such that $FF^{-1} = F^{-1}F = I$.   Now F is invertible if and only if F is one-to-one and onto.   Thus in particular, if F is invertible, then only $0 \in V$ can map into itself and so F is nonsingular.   The converse is not true, as seen by the following example.

EXAMPLE 8.12   Consider the vector space $V = \mathbf{P}(t)$ of polynomials.   Let F be the mapping on V which increases by 1 the exponent of t in each term of a polynomial, that is,

$$F(a_0 + a_1 t + a_2 t^2 + \cdots + a_s t^s) = a_0 t + a_1 t^2 + a_2 t^3 + \cdots + a_s t^{s+1}$$

Then F is a linear mapping and F is nonsingular.   However, F is not onto, and so F is not invertible.

The vector space $V = \mathbf{P}(t)$ in the above example has infinite dimension.   The situation changes significantly when V has finite dimension.   Specifically, the following theorem applies.

Theorem 8.14:   Suppose F is a linear operator on a finite-dimensional vector space V.   Then the following four conditions are equivalent:

    (i) F is nonsingular, i.e., Ker $F = \{0\}$.

    (ii) F is one-to-one.

(iii) F is an onto mapping.

(iv) F is invertible, i.e., one-to-one and onto.

The proof of the above theorem follows directly from previous results.   Specifically, we mainly use Theorem 8.6, which tells us that

$$\dim V = \dim (\text{Ker } F) + \dim (\text{Im } F)$$

(Theorem 8.6 holds here since V has finite dimension.)   By Proposition 8.8, (i) and (ii) are equivalent.   Thus to prove the theorem, we need only show that (i) and (iii) are equivalent. This we do below.

(a)   Suppose (i) holds.   Then $\dim (\text{Ker } F) = 0$, and so the above equation tells us that $\dim V = \dim (\text{Im } F)$.   This means $V = \text{Im } F$ or, in other words, F is an onto mapping. Thus (i) implies (iii).

(b)   Suppose (iii) holds.   Then $V = \text{Im } F$, and so $\dim V = \dim (\text{Im } F)$.   Therefore the above equation tells us that $\dim (\text{Ker } F) = 0$ and so F is nonsingular.   Therefore (iii) implies (i).

Accordingly, all four conditions are equivalent.

Remark: Suppose A is a square matrix, say of order n.   Then A may be viewed as a linear operator on $\mathbf{R}^n$.   Since $\mathbf{R}^n$ has finite dimension, Theorem 8.14 holds for the square matrix A. This is the reason why the terms "nonsingular" and "invertible" are used interchangeably when applied to square matrices.

EXAMPLE 8.13   Let F be the linear operator on $\mathbf{R}^2$ defined by

$$F(x, y) = (2x + y, 3x + 2y)$$

(a)   Show that F is nonsingular.
      Set $F(x, y) = (0, 0)$ to obtain the homogeneous system

$$2x + y = 0 \quad \text{and} \quad 3x + 2y = 0$$

Solve for x and y to get $x = 0$, $y = 0$.   Hence F is nonsingular.

(b)   Show that F is invertible.
      Since F is nonsingular and $\mathbf{R}^2$ has finite dimension, F is automatically invertible.

(c)   Find a formula for F^{-1}.
      Set $F(x, y) = (s, t)$ and so $F^{-1}(s, t) = (x, y)$.   We have

$$(2x + y, 3x + 2y) = (s, t) \quad \text{or} \quad \begin{array}{l} 2x + y = s \\ 3x + 2y = t \end{array}$$

Solve for x and y in terms of s and t to obtain $x = 2s - t$, $y = -3s + 2t$.   Thus

$$F^{-1}(s, t) = (2s - t, -3s + 2t) \quad \text{or} \quad F^{-1}(x, y) = (2x - y, -3x + 2y)$$

where we rewrite the formula for F^{-1} using x and y instead of s and t.

Solved Problems

MAPPINGS

8.1. State whether or not each diagram in Fig. 8-5 defines a mapping from $A = \{a, b, c\}$ into $B = \{x, y, z\}$.

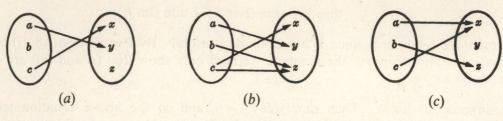

(a)   (b)   (c)

Fig. 8-5

    (a) No. There is nothing assigned to the element $b \in A$.

    (b) No. Two elements, x and z, are assigned to $c \in A$.

    (c) Yes.

8.2. Use a formula to define each of the following functions from **R** into **R**.

    (a) To each number let f assign its cube.

    (b) To each number let g assign the number 5.

    (c) To each positive number let h assign its square, and to each nonpositive number let h assign the number 6.

Also, find the value of each function at 4, -2, and 0.

    (a) Since f assigns to any number x its cube x^3, we can define f by $f(x) = x^3$. Also

$$f(4) = 4^3 = 64, \qquad f(-2) = (-2)^3 = -8, \qquad f(0) = 0^3 = 0$$

    (b) Since g assigns 5 to any number x, we can define g by $g(x) = 5$. Thus the value of g at each of the numbers, 4, -2, and 0 is 5,

$$g(4) = 5, \qquad g(-2) = 5, \qquad g(0) = 5$$

    (c) Two different rules are used to define h as follows:

$$h(x) = \begin{cases} x^2 & \text{if } x > 0 \\ 6 & \text{if } x \le 0 \end{cases}$$

    Since $4 > 0$, $h(4) = 4^2 = 16$. On the other hand, $-2, 0 \le 0$, and so $h(-2) = 6$ and $h(0) = 6$.

8.3. Let $A = \{1, 2, 3, 4, 5\}$ and let $f: A \to A$ be the mapping defined by Fig. 8-6. Find: (a) the image of f; (b) the graph of f.

    (a) The image $f(A)$ of the mapping f consists of all the points assigned to elements of A. Now only 2, 3, and 5 appear as the image of any elements of A. Hence $f(A) = \{2, 3, 5\}$.

    (b) The graph of f consists of the ordered pairs $(a, f(a))$, where $a \in A$. Now $f(1) = 3$, $f(2) = 5$, $f(3) = 5$, $f(4) = 2$, $f(5) = 3$. Hence the graph of $f = \{(1, 3), (2, 5), (3, 5), (4, 2), (5, 3)\}$.

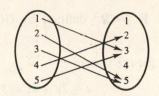

Fig. 8-6

8.4. Let $f: A \to B$ and $g: B \to C$ be defined by Fig. 8-7. Find: (a) the composition mapping $(g \circ f): A \to C$; (b) the image of the mappings f, g, and $g \circ f$.

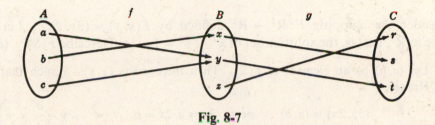

Fig. 8-7

(a) We use the definition of the composition mapping to compute

$$(g \circ f)(a) = g(f(a)) = g(y) = t$$
$$(g \circ f)(b) = g(f(b)) = g(x) = s$$
$$(g \circ f)(c) = g(f(c)) = g(y) = t$$

Observe that we arrive at the same answer if we "follow the arrows" in Fig. 8-7,

$$a \to y \to t, \qquad b \to x \to s, \qquad c \to y \to t$$

(b) By Fig. 8-7 the image values under the mapping f are x and y, and the image values under g are r, s, and t.   Hence

$$\text{Im } f = \{x, y\} \qquad \text{and} \qquad \text{Im } g = \{r, s, t\}$$

Also by part (a), the image values under the composition mapping $g \circ f$ are t and s; accordingly, $\text{Im } (g \circ f) = \{s, t\}$.   Note that the images of g and $g \circ f$ are different.

8.5. Consider the mapping $F: \mathbf{R}^3 \to \mathbf{R}^2$ defined by $F(x, y, z) = (yz, x^2)$.   Find: (a) $F(2, 3, 4)$; (b) $F(5, -2, 7)$; (c) $F^{-1}(0, 0)$, i.e., all vectors $v \in \mathbf{R}^3$ such that $F(v) = 0$.

(a) Substitute in the formula for F to get $F(2, 3, 4) = (3 \cdot 4, 2^2) = (12, 4)$.

(b) $F(5, -2, 7) = (-2 \cdot 7, 5^2) = (-14, 25)$.

(c) Set $F(v) = 0$, where $v = (x, y, z)$, and then solve for x, y, z:

$$F(x, y, z) = (yz, x^2) = (0, 0) \qquad \text{or} \qquad \begin{aligned} yz &= 0 \\ x^2 &= 0 \end{aligned}$$

Thus $x = 0$ and either $y = 0$ or $z = 0$.   In other words, $x = 0$, $y = 0$ or $x = 0$, $z = 0$. That is, the z axis and the y axis.

8.6. Consider the mapping $G: \mathbf{R}^3 \to \mathbf{R}^2$ defined by $G(x, y, z) = (x + 2y - 4z, 2x + 3y + z)$. Find $G^{-1}(3, 4)$.

Set $G(x, y, z) = (3, 4)$ to get the system

$$
\begin{array}{ccc}
\begin{array}{l} x + 2y - 4z = 3 \\ 2x + 3y + z = 4 \end{array}
\quad \text{or} \quad
\begin{array}{l} x + 2y - 4z = 3 \\ -y + 9z = -2 \end{array}
\quad \text{or} \quad
\begin{array}{l} x + 2y - 4z = 3 \\ y - 9z = 2 \end{array}
\end{array}
$$

Here z is a free variable. Set $z = a$, $a \in \mathbf{R}$ to obtain the general solution

$$x = -14a - 1, \qquad y = 9a + 2, \qquad z = a$$

In other words, $G^{-1}(3, 4) = \{(-14a - 1, 9a + 2, a)\}$.

8.7. Consider the mapping $F: \mathbf{R}^2 \to \mathbf{R}^2$ defined by $F(x, y) = (3y, 2x)$. Let S be the unit circle in $\mathbf{R}^2$, that is, the solution set of $x^2 + y^2 = 1$. (a) Describe $F(S)$. (b) Find $F^{-1}(S)$.

(a) Let (a, b) be an element of $F(S)$. Then there exists $(x, y) \in S$ such that $F(x, y) = (a, b)$. Hence

$$(3y, 2x) = (a, b) \qquad \text{or} \qquad 3y = a, 2x = b \qquad \text{or} \qquad y = \frac{a}{3}, x = \frac{b}{2}$$

Since $(x, y) \in S$, that is, $x^2 + y^2 = 1$, we have

$$\left(\frac{b}{2}\right)^2 + \left(\frac{a}{3}\right)^2 = 1 \qquad \text{or} \qquad \frac{a^2}{9} + \frac{b^2}{4} = 1$$

Thus $F(S)$ is an ellipse.

(b) Let $F(x, y) = (a, b)$, where $(a, b) \in S$. Then $(3y, 2x) = (a, b)$ or $3y = a$, $2x = b$. Since $(a, b) \in S$, we have $a^2 + b^2 = 1$. Thus $(3y)^2 + (2x)^2 = 1$. Accordingly, $F^{-1}(S)$ is the ellipse $4x^2 + 9y^2 = 1$.

8.8. Let the mappings f and g be defined by $f(x) = 2x + 1$ and $g(x) = x^2 - 2$. (a) Find $(g \circ f)(5)$ and $(f \circ g)(5)$. (b) Find formulas defining the composition functions $g \circ f$, $f \circ g$, and $g \circ g$ (sometimes denoted by g^2).

(a) $f(5) = 2(5) + 1 = 10 + 1 = 11$. Hence $(g \circ f)(5) = g(f(5)) = g(11) = 11^2 - 2 = 119$.
$g(5) = 5^2 - 2 = 25 - 2 = 23$. Hence $(f \circ g)(5) = f(g(5)) = f(23) = 2(23) + 1 = 47$.

(b) Compute the formula for $g \circ f$ as follows:

$$(g \circ f)(x) = g(f(x)) = g(2x + 1) = (2x + 1)^2 - 2 = 4x^2 + 4x - 1$$

Observe that the same answer can be found by writing

$$y = f(x) = 2x + 1 \qquad \text{and} \qquad z = g(y) = y^2 - 2$$

and then eliminating y as follows: $z = y^2 - 2 = (2x + 1)^2 - 2 = 4x^2 + 4x - 1$. Also,

$$(f \circ g)(x) = f(g(x)) = f(x^2 - 2) = 2(x^2 - 2) + 1 = 2x^2 - 3$$
$$(g \circ g)(x) = g(g(x)) = g(x^2 - 2) = (x^2 - 2)^2 - 2 = x^4 - 4x^2 + 2$$

8.9. Let the mappings $f: A \to B$, $g: B \to C$, and $h: C \to D$ be defined by Fig. 8-8. Determine whether or not each function is: (a) one-to-one; (b) onto; (c) invertible, i.e., has an inverse.

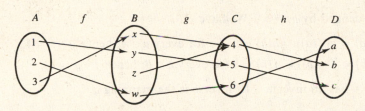

Fig. 8-8

(a) The mapping $f: A \to B$ is one-to-one since each element of A has a different image. The mapping $g: B \to C$ is not one-to-one since x and z both have the same image, 4. The mapping $h: C \to D$ is one-to-one.

(b) The mapping $f: A \to B$ is not onto since $z \in B$ is not the image of any element of A. The mapping $g: B \to C$ is onto since each element of C is the image of some element of B. The mapping $h: C \to D$ is also onto.

(c) A mapping has an inverse if and only if it is one-to-one and onto. Hence only h has an inverse.

8.10. Suppose $f: A \to B$ and $g: B \to C$. Hence the composition $(g \circ f): A \to C$ exists. Prove:

(a) If f and g are one-to-one, then $g \circ f$ is one-to-one.

(b) If f and g are onto mappings, then $g \circ f$ is an onto mapping.

(c) If $g \circ f$ is one-to-one, then f is one-to-one.

(d) If $g \circ f$ is an onto mapping, then g is an onto mapping.

(a) Suppose $(g \circ f)(x) = (g \circ f)(y)$. Then $g(f(x)) = g(f(y))$. Since g is one-to-one, $f(x) = f(y)$. Since f is one-to-one, $x = y$. We have proven that $(g \circ f)(x) = (g \circ f)(y)$ implies $x = y$; hence $g \circ f$ is one-to-one.

(b) Suppose $c \in C$. Since g is onto, there exists $b \in B$ for which $g(b) = c$. Since f is onto, there exists $a \in A$ for which $f(a) = b$. Thus $(g \circ f)(a) = g(f(a)) = g(b) = c$. Hence $g \circ f$ is onto.

(c) Suppose f is not one-to-one. Then there exist distinct elements $x, y \in A$ for which $f(x) = f(y)$. Thus $(g \circ f)(x) = g(f(x)) = g(f(y)) = (g \circ f)(y)$. Hence $g \circ f$ is not one-to-one. Therefore if $g \circ f$ is one-to-one, then f must be one-to-one.

(d) If $a \in A$, then $(g \circ f)(a) = g(f(a)) \in g(B)$. Hence $(g \circ f)(A) \subseteq g(B)$. Suppose g is not onto. Then $g(B)$ is properly contained in C and so $(g \circ f)(A)$ is properly contained in C; thus $g \circ f$ is not onto. Accordingly if $g \circ f$ is onto, then g must be onto.

8.11. Prove that a mapping $f: A \to B$ has an inverse if and only if it is one-to-one and onto.

Suppose f has an inverse, i.e., there exists a function $f^{-1}: B \to A$ for which $f^{-1} \circ f = 1_A$ and $f \circ f^{-1} = 1_B$. Since 1_A is one-to-one, f is one-to-one by Problem 8.10(c), and since 1_B is onto, f is onto by Problem 8.10(d), that is, f is both one-to-one and onto.

Now suppose f is both one-to-one and onto. Then each $b \in B$ is the image of a unique element in A, say $\hat{b}$. Thus if $f(a) = b$, then $a = \hat{b}$; hence $f(\hat{b}) = b$. Now let g denote the mapping from B to A defined by $b \mapsto \hat{b}$. We have

(i) $(g \circ f)(a) = g(f(a)) = g(b) = \hat{b} = a$ for every $a \in A$; hence $g \circ f = \mathbf{1}_A$.

(ii) $(f \circ g)(b) = f(g(b)) = f(\hat{b}) = b$ for every $b \in B$; hence $f \circ g = \mathbf{1}_B$.

Accordingly, f has an inverse. Its inverse is the mapping g.

8.12. Let $f: \mathbf{R} \to \mathbf{R}$ be defined by $f(x) = 2x - 3$. Now f is one-to-one and onto. Hence f has an inverse mapping f^{-1}. Find a formula for f^{-1}.

Let y be the image of x under the mapping f; that is, $y = f(x) = 2x - 3$. Thus x will be the image of y under the inverse mapping f^{-1}. Thus solve for x in terms of y in the above equation to obtain $x = (y + 3)/2$. Then the formula defining the inverse function is $f^{-1}(y) = (y + 3)/2$ or, using x instead of y, $f^{-1}(x) = (x + 3)/2$.

LINEAR MAPPINGS

8.13. Suppose the mapping $F: \mathbf{R}^2 \to \mathbf{R}^2$ is defined by $F(x, y) = (x + y, x)$. Show that F is linear.

We need to show that $F(v + w) = F(v) + F(w)$ and $F(kv) = kF(v)$, where v and w are any elements of $\mathbf{R}^2$ and k is any scalar. Let $v = (a, b)$ and $w = (a', b')$. Then

$$v + w = (a + a', b + b') \qquad \text{and} \qquad kv = (ka, kb)$$

We have $F(v) = (a + b, a)$ and $F(w) = (a' + b', a')$. Thus

$$F(v + w) = F(a + a', b + b') = (a + a' + b + b', a + a')$$
$$= (a + b, a) + (a' + b', a') = F(v) + F(w)$$

and
$$F(kv) = F(ka, kb) = (ka + kb, ka) = k(a + b, a) = kF(v)$$

Since v, w, and k were arbitrary, F is linear.

8.14. Suppose $F: \mathbf{R}^3 \to \mathbf{R}^2$ is defined by $F(x, y, z) = (x + y + z, 2x - 3y + 4z)$. Show that F is linear.

Method 1:   Let $v = (a, b, c)$ and $w = (a', b', c')$. Then

$$v + w = (a + a', b + b', c + c') \qquad \text{and} \qquad kv = (ka, kb, kc)$$

where k is a scalar. Then

$$F(v) = (a + b + c, 2a - 3b + 4c)$$

and
$$F(w) = (a' + b' + c', 2a' - 3b' + 4c')$$

Thus

$$F(v + w) = F(a + a', b + b', c + c')$$
$$= (a + a' + b + b' + c + c', 2a + 2a' - 3b - 3b' + 4c + 4c')$$
$$= ((a + b + c) + (a' + b' + c'), (2a - 3b + 4c) + (2a' - 3b' + 4c'))$$
$$= (a + b + c, 2a - 3b + 4c) + (a' + b' + c', 2a' - 3b' + 4c')$$
$$= F(v) + F(w)$$

and

$$F(kv) = F(ka, kb, kc) = (ka + kb + kc, 2ka - 3kb + 4kc)$$

$$= (k(a + b + c), k(2a - 3b + 4c)) = k(a + b + c, 2a - 3b + 4c) = kF(v)$$

Thus F is linear.

Method 2:　　We argue via matrices.　Writing vectors as columns, the mapping F may be written in the form $F(v) = Av$, where $v = [x, y, z]^T$ and

$$A = \begin{bmatrix} 1 & 1 & 1 \\ 2 & -3 & 4 \end{bmatrix}$$

Then, using properties of matrices, we have

$$F(v + w) = A(v + w) = Av + Aw = F(v) + F(w)$$

and　　　　　　　　　$$F(kv) = A(kv) = k(Av) = kF(v)$$

Thus F is linear.

8.15. Show that the following mappings are not linear:

(a)　$F: \mathbf{R}^2 \to \mathbf{R}^2$ defined by $F(x, y) = (xy, x)$.

(b)　$F: \mathbf{R}^2 \to \mathbf{R}^3$ defined by $F(x, y) = (x + 3, 2y, x + y)$.

(c)　$F: \mathbf{R}^3 \to \mathbf{R}^2$ defined by $F(x, y, z) = (|x|, y + z)$.

(a)　Let $v = (1, 2)$ and $w = (3, 4)$, then $v + w = (4, 6)$.　Then

$$F(v) = (1(2), 1) = (2, 1), \qquad F(w) = (3(4), 3) = (12, 3)$$

Hence　　　　　　$$F(v + w) = (4(6), 4) = (24, 4) \neq F(v) + F(w)$$

(b)　Since $F(0, 0) = (3, 0, 0) \neq (0, 0, 0)$, F cannot be linear.

(c)　Let $v = (1, 2, 3)$ and $k = -3$.　Then $kv = (-3, -6, -9)$.　We have $F(v) = (1, 5)$ and $kF(v) = -3(1, 5) = (-3, -15)$.　Thus

$$F(kv) = F(-3, -6, -9) = (3, -15) \neq kF(v)$$

Accordingly F is not linear.

8.16. Let V be the vector space of n-square real matrices.　Let M be an arbitrary but fixed matrix in V.　Let $F: V \to V$ be defined by $F(A) = AM + MA$, where A is any matrix in V.　Show that F is linear.

For any matrices A and B in V and any scalar k we have

$$F(A + B) = (A + B)M + M(A + B) = AM + BM + MA + MB$$

$$= (AM + MA) + (BM + MB) = F(A) + F(B)$$

and

$$F(kA) = (kA)M + M(kA) = k(AM) + k(MA) = k(AM + MA) + kF(A)$$

Thus F is linear.

8.17. Let $F: \mathbf{R}^2 \to \mathbf{R}^2$ be the linear mapping for which

$$F(1, 2) = (2, 3) \qquad \text{and} \qquad F(0, 1) = (1, 4)$$

[Since $(1, 2)$ and $(0, 1)$ form a basis of $\mathbf{R}^2$, such a linear map F exists and is unique by Theorem 8.2.]   Find a formula for F, that is, find $F(a, b)$.

Write (a, b) as a linear combination of $(1, 2)$ and $(0, 1)$ using unknowns x and y,

$$(a, b) = x(1, 2) + y(0, 1) = (x, 2x + y) \qquad \text{so} \qquad a = x, \quad b = 2x + y$$

Solve for x and y in terms of a and b to get $x = a$, $y = -2a + b$.   Then

$$F(a, b) = xF(1, 2) + yF(0, 1) = a(2, 3) + (-2a + b)(1, 4) = (b, -5a + 4b)$$

8.18. Let $V = \mathbf{P}(t)$, the vector space of real polynomials.   Let $T: V \to V$ be the mapping defined by

$$T(a_0 + a_1 t + \cdots + a_n t^n) = a_0 t + a_1 t^2 + \cdots + a_n t^{n+1}$$

[Note that T multiplies a polynomial by t, that is, $T(f(t)) = tf(t)$.]   Show that T is linear.

For any polynomials $f(t)$ and $g(t)$ and scalar k, we have

$$T(f(t) + g(t)) = t(f(t) + g(t)) = tf(t) + tg(t) = T(f(t)) + T(g(t))$$

and
$$T(kf(t)) = t(kf(t)) = k(tf(t)) = kT(f(t))$$

Thus T is linear.

8.19. Let $T: V \to U$ be linear, and suppose $v_1, \ldots, v_n \in V$ have the property that their images $T(v_1), \ldots, T(v_n)$ are linearly independent.   Show that the vectors $v_1, \ldots, v_n$ are also linearly independent.

Suppose that, for scalars $a_1, \ldots, a_n$, $a_1 v_1 + a_2 v_2 + \cdots + a_n v_n = 0$.   Then

$$0 = T(0) = T(a_1 v_1 + a_2 v_2 + \cdots + a_n v_n) = a_1 T(v_1) + a_2 T(v_2) + \cdots + a_n T(v_n)$$

Since the $T(v_i)$ are linearly independent, all the $a_i = 0$.   Thus the vectors $v_1, \ldots, v_n$ are linearly independent.

8.20. Suppose the linear mapping $F: V \to U$ is one-to-one and onto.   Show that the inverse mapping $F^{-1}: U \to V$ is also linear.

Suppose $u, u' \in U$.   Since F is one-to-one and onto, there exist unique vectors $v, v' \in V$ for which $F(v) = u$ and $F(v') = u'$.   Since F is linear, we also have

$$F(v + v') = F(v) + F(v') = u + u' \qquad \text{and} \qquad F(kv) = kF(v) = ku$$

By definition of the inverse mapping, $F^{-1}(u) = v$, $F^{-1}(u') = v'$, $F^{-1}(u + u') = v + v'$, and $F^{-1}(ku) = kv$.   Then

$$F^{-1}(u + u') = v + v' = F^{-1}(u) + F^{-1}(u') \qquad \text{and} \qquad F^{-1}(ku) = kv = kF^{-1}(u)$$

and thus F^{-1} is linear.

KERNEL AND IMAGE OF LINEAR MAPPINGS

8.21. Let $F: \mathbf{R}^4 \to \mathbf{R}^3$ be the linear mapping defined by

$$F(x, y, z, t) = (x - y + z + t,\ x + 2z - t,\ x + y + 3z - 3t)$$

Find a basis and the dimension of: (a) the image of F; (b) the kernel of F.

(a) Find the images of the usual basis of $\mathbf{R}^4$:

$$F(1, 0, 0, 0) = (1, 1, 1), \qquad F(0, 0, 1, 0) = (1, 2, 3)$$
$$F(0, 1, 0, 0) = (-1, 0, 1), \qquad F(0, 0, 0, 1) = (1, -1, -3)$$

By Proposition 8.4, the image vectors span Im F. Hence form the matrix whose rows are these image vectors, and row reduce to echelon form:

$$\begin{bmatrix} 1 & 1 & 1 \\ -1 & 0 & 1 \\ 1 & 2 & 3 \\ 1 & -1 & -3 \end{bmatrix} \sim \begin{bmatrix} 1 & 1 & 1 \\ 0 & 1 & 2 \\ 0 & 1 & 2 \\ 0 & -2 & -4 \end{bmatrix} \sim \begin{bmatrix} 1 & 1 & 1 \\ 0 & 1 & 2 \\ 0 & 0 & 0 \\ 0 & 0 & 0 \end{bmatrix}$$

Thus $(1, 1, 1)$ and $(0, 1, 2)$ form a basis for Im F; hence $\dim(\text{Im } F) = 2$.

(b) Set $F(v) = 0$, where $v = (x, y, z, t)$, that is,

$$F(x, y, z, t) = (x - y + z + t, x + 2z - t, x + y + 3z - 3t) = (0, 0, 0)$$

Set corresponding entries equal to each other to form the following homogeneous system whose solution space is Ker F:

$$\begin{array}{l} x - y + z + t = 0 \\ x \quad\ \ + 2z - \ t = 0 \\ x + y + 3z - 3t = 0 \end{array} \quad \text{or} \quad \begin{array}{l} x - y + \ z + \ t = 0 \\ y + \ z - 2t = 0 \\ 2y + 2z - 4t = 0 \end{array} \quad \text{or} \quad \begin{array}{l} x - y + z + \ t = 0 \\ y + z - 2t = 0 \end{array}$$

The free variables are z and t. Hence $\dim (\text{Ker } F) = 2$.

(i) Set $z = -1$, $t = 0$ to obtain the solution $(2, 1, -1, 0)$.

(ii) Set $z = 0$, $t = 1$ to obtain the solution $(1, 2, 0, 1)$.

Thus $(2, 1, -1, 0)$ and $(1, 2, 0, 1)$ form a basis of Ker F.
    [As expected, $\dim (\text{Im } F) + \dim (\text{Ker } F) = 2 + 2 = 4 = \dim R^4$, the domain of F.]

8.22. Let $G: \mathbf{R}^3 \to \mathbf{R}^3$ be the linear mapping defined by

$$G(x, y, z) = (x + 2y - z,\ y + z,\ x + y - 2z)$$

Find a basis and the dimension of: (a) the image of G; (b) the kernel of G.

(a) Find the images of the usual basis of $\mathbf{R}^3$:

$$G(1, 0, 0) = (1, 0, 1), \qquad G(0, 1, 0) = (2, 1, 1), \qquad G(0, 0, 1) = (-1, 1, -2)$$

By Proposition 8.4, the image vectors span Im G. Hence form the matrix M whose rows are these image vectors, and row reduce to echelon form:

$$M = \begin{bmatrix} 1 & 0 & 1 \\ 2 & 1 & 1 \\ -1 & 1 & -2 \end{bmatrix} \sim \begin{bmatrix} 1 & 0 & 1 \\ 0 & 1 & -1 \\ 0 & 1 & -1 \end{bmatrix} \sim \begin{bmatrix} 1 & 0 & 1 \\ 0 & 1 & -1 \\ 0 & 0 & 0 \end{bmatrix}$$

Thus $(1, 0, 1)$ and $(0, 1, -1)$ form a basis for Im G; hence $\dim (\text{Im } G) = 2$.

(b)   Set $G(v) = 0$, where $v = (x, y, z)$, that is,

$$G(x, y, z) = (x + 2y - z, y + z, x + y - 2z) = (0, 0, 0)$$

Set corresponding entries equal to each other to form the following homogeneous system whose solution space is Ker G:

$$\begin{array}{llll}
x + 2y - z = 0 & & x + 2y - z = 0 & \\
\quad\; y + z = 0 & \text{or} & \quad\; y + z = 0 & \text{or} \quad \begin{array}{l} x + 2y - z = 0 \\ \quad\; y + z = 0 \end{array} \\
x + \;\; y - 2z = 0 & & \quad\; -y - z = 0 &
\end{array}$$

The only free variable is z; hence dim (Ker G) = 1. Set $z = 1$; then $y = -1$ and $x = 3$. Thus $(3, -1, 1)$ forms a basis of Ker G.
   [As expected, dim (Im G) + dim (Ker G) = 2 + 1 = 3 = dim R^3, the domain of G.]

8.23. Consider the matrix mapping $A: \mathbf{R}^4 \to \mathbf{R}^3$, where $A = \begin{bmatrix} 1 & 2 & 3 & 1 \\ 1 & 3 & 5 & -2 \\ 3 & 8 & 13 & -3 \end{bmatrix}$. Find a basis and the dimension of: (a) the image of A; (b) the kernel of A.

(a)   The column space of A is equal to Im A.   Now reduce A^T to echelon form:

$$A^T = \begin{bmatrix} 1 & 1 & 3 \\ 2 & 3 & 8 \\ 3 & 5 & 13 \\ 1 & -2 & -3 \end{bmatrix} \sim \begin{bmatrix} 1 & 1 & 3 \\ 0 & 1 & 2 \\ 0 & 2 & 4 \\ 0 & -3 & -6 \end{bmatrix} \sim \begin{bmatrix} 1 & 1 & 3 \\ 0 & 1 & 2 \\ 0 & 0 & 0 \\ 0 & 0 & 0 \end{bmatrix}$$

Thus $\{(1, 1, 3), (0, 1, 2)\}$ is a basis of Im A and dim (Im A) = 2.

(b)   Here Ker A is the solution space of the homogeneous system $AX = 0$, where $X = (x, y, z, t)^T$. Thus reduce the matrix A of coefficients to echelon form:

$$\begin{bmatrix} 1 & 2 & 3 & 1 \\ 0 & 1 & 2 & -3 \\ 0 & 2 & 4 & -6 \end{bmatrix} \sim \begin{bmatrix} 1 & 2 & 3 & 1 \\ 0 & 1 & 2 & -3 \\ 0 & 0 & 0 & 0 \end{bmatrix} \quad \text{or} \quad \begin{array}{l} x + 2y + 3z + \;\; t = 0 \\ \quad\; y + 2z - 3t = 0 \end{array}$$

The free variables are z and t.   Thus dim (Ker A) = 2.

(i)   Set $z = 1$, $t = 0$ to get the solution $(1, -2, 1, 0)$.

(ii)   Set $z = 0$, $t = 1$ to get the solution $(-7, 3, 0, 1)$.

Thus $(1, -2, 1, 0)$ and $(-7, 3, 0, 1)$ form a basis for Ker A.

8.24. Consider the matrix map $B: \mathbf{R}^3 \to \mathbf{R}^3$, where $B = \begin{bmatrix} 1 & 2 & 5 \\ 3 & 5 & 13 \\ -2 & -1 & -4 \end{bmatrix}$. Find the dimension and a basis for: (a) the kernel of B; (b) the image of B.

(a)   Reduce B to echelon form to get the homogeneous system corresponding to Ker B,

$$B = \begin{bmatrix} 1 & 2 & 5 \\ 3 & 5 & 13 \\ -2 & -1 & -4 \end{bmatrix} \sim \begin{bmatrix} 1 & 2 & 5 \\ 0 & -1 & -2 \\ 0 & 3 & 6 \end{bmatrix} \sim \begin{bmatrix} 1 & 2 & 5 \\ 0 & 1 & 2 \\ 0 & 0 & 0 \end{bmatrix} \quad \text{or} \quad \begin{array}{l} x + 2y + 5z = 0 \\ \quad\; y + 2z = 0 \end{array}$$

There is one free variable z, so dim (Ker B) = 1. Set $z = 1$ to get the solution $(-1, -2, 1)$, which forms a basis of Ker B.

(b) Reduce B^T to echelon form,

$$B^T = \begin{bmatrix} 1 & 3 & -2 \\ 2 & 5 & -1 \\ 5 & 13 & -4 \end{bmatrix} \sim \begin{bmatrix} 1 & 3 & -2 \\ 0 & -1 & 3 \\ 0 & -2 & 6 \end{bmatrix} \sim \begin{bmatrix} 1 & 3 & -2 \\ 0 & 1 & -3 \\ 0 & 0 & 0 \end{bmatrix}$$

Thus, $(1, 3, -2)$ and $(0, 1, -3)$ form a basis of Im B and dim(dm B) = 2.

8.25. Find a linear map $F: \mathbf{R}^3 \to \mathbf{R}^4$ whose image is spanned by $(1, 2, 0, -4)$ and $(2, 0, -1, -3)$.

Method 1: Consider the usual basis of $\mathbf{R}^3$, that is, $e_1 = (1, 0, 0)$, $e_2 = (0, 1, 0)$, $e_3 = (0, 0, 1)$. Set

$$F(e_1) = (1, 2, 0, -4), \qquad F(e_2) = (2, 0, -1, -3), \qquad F(e_3) = (0, 0, 0, 0)$$

By Theorem 8.2, such a linear map F exists and is unique. Furthermore the image of F is spanned by the $F(e_i)$; hence F has the required property. We find a general formula for $F(x, y, z)$:

$$\begin{aligned} F(x, y, z) = F(xe_1 + ye_2 + ze_3) &= xF(e_1) + yF(e_2) + zF(e_3) \\ &= x(1, 2, 0, -4) + y(2, 0, -1, -3) + z(0, 0, 0, 0) \\ &= (x + 2y, 2x, -y, -4x - 3y) \end{aligned}$$

Method 2: Form a 4×3 matrix A whose columns consist only of the given vectors, say

$$A = \begin{bmatrix} 1 & 2 & 2 \\ 2 & 0 & 0 \\ 0 & -1 & -1 \\ -4 & -3 & -3 \end{bmatrix}$$

Recall that A determines a linear map $A: \mathbf{R}^3 \to \mathbf{R}^4$ whose image is spanned by the columns of A. Thus A satisfies the required condition.

8.26. Let $V = \mathbf{M}_{2,2}$, the vector space of real 2×2 matrices, and let $M = \begin{bmatrix} 1 & 2 \\ 0 & 3 \end{bmatrix}$. Let $F: V \to V$ be the linear map defined by $F(A) = AM - MA$. Find a basis and the dimension of the kernel W of F.

We seek the set of $\begin{bmatrix} x & y \\ s & t \end{bmatrix}$ such that $F\begin{bmatrix} x & y \\ s & t \end{bmatrix} = \begin{bmatrix} 0 & 0 \\ 0 & 0 \end{bmatrix}$,

$$\begin{aligned} F\begin{bmatrix} x & y \\ s & t \end{bmatrix} &= \begin{bmatrix} x & y \\ s & t \end{bmatrix}\begin{bmatrix} 1 & 2 \\ 0 & 3 \end{bmatrix} - \begin{bmatrix} 1 & 2 \\ 0 & 3 \end{bmatrix}\begin{bmatrix} x & y \\ s & t \end{bmatrix} \\ &= \begin{bmatrix} x & 2x + 3y \\ s & 2s + 3t \end{bmatrix} - \begin{bmatrix} x + 2s & y + 2t \\ 3s & 3t \end{bmatrix} \\ &= \begin{bmatrix} -2s & 2x + 2y - 2t \\ -2s & 2s \end{bmatrix} = \begin{bmatrix} 0 & 0 \\ 0 & 0 \end{bmatrix} \end{aligned}$$

Thus
$$\begin{aligned} 2x + 2y - 2t &= 0 \\ 2s &= 0 \end{aligned} \quad \text{or} \quad \begin{aligned} x + y - t &= 0 \\ s &= 0 \end{aligned}$$

The free variables are y and t; hence dim $W = 2$. To obtain a basis of W,

(i)   Set $y = -1$, $t = 0$ to obtain the solution $x = 1$, $y = -1$, $s = 0$, $t = 0$.

(ii) Set $y = 0$, $t = 1$ to obtain the solution $x = 1$, $y = 0$, $s = 0$, $t = 1$.

Thus $\left\{ \begin{bmatrix} 1 & -1 \\ 0 & 0 \end{bmatrix}, \begin{bmatrix} 1 & 0 \\ 0 & 1 \end{bmatrix} \right\}$ is a basis of W.

8.27. Suppose $f: V \to U$ is linear with kernel W, and that $f(v) = u$. Show that the "coset" $v + W = \{v + w : w \in W\}$ is the preimage of u, that is, $f^{-1}(u) = v + W$.

We must prove that (i) $f^{-1}(u) \subseteq v + W$ and (ii) $v + W \subseteq f^{-1}(u)$. We first prove (i). Suppose $v' \in f^{-1}(u)$. Then $f(v') = u$, and so

$$f(v' - v) = f(v') - f(v) = u - u = 0$$

that is, $v' - v \in W$. Thus $v' = v + (v' - v) \in v + W$, and hence $f^{-1}(u) \subseteq v + W$.

Now we prove (ii). Suppose $v' \in v + W$. Then $v' = v + w$, where $w \in W$. Since W is the kernel of f, $f(w) = 0$. Accordingly,

$$f(v') = f(v + w) + f(v) + f(w) = f(v) + 0 = f(v) = u$$

Thus $v' \in f^{-1}(u)$, and so $v + W \subseteq f^{-1}(u)$.

Both inclusions imply $f^{-1}(u) = v + W$.

8.28. Suppose $F: V \to U$ and $G: U \to W$ are linear. Prove: (a) rank $(G \circ F) \leq$ rank (G); (b) rank $(G \circ F) \leq$ rank (F).

(a)   Since $F(V) \subseteq U$, we also have $G(F(V)) \subseteq G(U)$, and so dim $(G(F(V))) \leq$ dim $(G(U))$. Then

$$\text{rank } (G \circ F) = \text{dim } ((G \circ F)(V)) = \text{dim } (G(F(V))) \leq \text{dim } (G(U)) = \text{rank } (G)$$

(b)   We have dim $(G(F(V))) \leq$ dim $(F(V))$. Hence

$$\text{rank } (G \circ F) = \text{dim } ((G \circ F)(V)) = \text{dim } (G(F(V))) \leq \text{dim } (F(V)) = \text{rank } (F)$$

SINGULAR AND NONSINGULAR LINEAR MAPS, ISOMORPHISMS

8.29. Determine whether or not each linear map is nonsingular. If not, find a nonzero vector v whose image is 0.

(a) $F: \mathbf{R}^2 \to \mathbf{R}^2$ defined by $F(x, y) = (x - y, x - 2y)$.

(b) $G: \mathbf{R}^2 \to \mathbf{R}^2$ defined by $G(x, y) = (2x - 4y, 3x - 6y)$.

(a)   Find Ker F by setting $F(v) = 0$, where $v = (x, y)$,

$$(x - y, x - 2y) = (0, 0) \qquad \text{or} \qquad \begin{matrix} x - y = 0 \\ x - 2y = 0 \end{matrix} \qquad \text{or} \qquad \begin{matrix} x - y = 0 \\ - y = 0 \end{matrix}$$

The only solution is $x = 0$, $y = 0$. Hence F is nonsingular.

(b)   Set $G(x, y) = (0, 0)$ to find Ker G,

$$(2x - 4y, 3x - 6y) = (0, 0) \qquad \text{or} \qquad \begin{matrix} 2x - 4y = 0 \\ 3x - 6y = 0 \end{matrix} \qquad \text{or} \qquad x - 2y = 0$$

The system has nonzero solutions since y is a free variable. Hence G is singular. Let $y = 1$ to obtain the solution $v = (2, 1)$, which is a nonzero vector, such that $G(v) = 0$.

8.30. The linear map $F: \mathbf{R}^2 \to \mathbf{R}^2$ defined by $F(x, y) = (x - y, x - 2y)$ is nonsingular by Problem 8.29. Find a formula for F^{-1}.

Set $F(x, y) = (a, b)$, so that $F^{-1}(a, b) = (x, y)$. We have

$$(x - y, x - 2y) = (a, b) \quad \text{or} \quad \begin{array}{l} x - y = a \\ x - 2y = b \end{array} \quad \text{or} \quad \begin{array}{l} x - y = a \\ -y = b - a \end{array}$$

Solve for x and y in terms of a and b to get $x = 2a - b$ and $y = a - b$. Thus

$$F^{-1}(a, b) = (2a - b, a - b) \quad \text{or} \quad F^{-1}(x, y) = (2x - y, x - y)$$

where we replace a and b by x and y.

8.31. Let $G: \mathbf{R}^2 \to \mathbf{R}^3$ be defined by $G(x, y) = (x + y, x - 2y, 3x + y)$. (a) Show that G is nonsingular. (b) Find a formula for G^{-1}.

(a) Set $G(x, y) = (0, 0, 0)$ to find Ker G. We have

$$(x + y, x - 2y, 3x + y) = (0, 0, 0)$$

or $\qquad x + y = 0, \qquad x - 2y = 0, \qquad 3x + y = 0$

The only solution is $x = 0$, $y = 0$. Hence G is nonsingular.

(b) Although G is nonsingular, it is not invertible since $\mathbf{R}^2$ and $\mathbf{R}^3$ have different dimensions. (Thus Theorem 8.14 does not apply.) Accordingly G^{-1} does not exist.

8.32. Let $H: \mathbf{R}^3 \to \mathbf{R}^3$ be defined by $H(x, y, z) = (x + y - 2z, x + 2y + z, 2x + 2y - 3z)$. (a) Show that H is nonsingular. (b) Find a formula for H^{-1}.

(a) Set $H(x, y, z) = (0, 0, 0)$, that is,

$$(x + y - 2z, x + 2y + z, 2x + 2y - 3z) = (0, 0, 0)$$

This yields the homogeneous system

$$\begin{array}{l} x + y - 2z = 0 \\ x + 2y + z = 0 \\ 2x + 2y - 3z = 0 \end{array} \quad \text{or} \quad \begin{array}{l} x + y - 2z = 0 \\ y + 3z = 0 \\ z = 0 \end{array}$$

The echelon system is in triangular form, so the only solution is $x = 0$, $y = 0$, $z = 0$. Thus H is nonsingular.

(b) Set $H(x, y, z) = (a, b, c)$ and then solve for x, y, z in terms of a, b, c,

$$\begin{array}{l} x + y - 2z = a \\ x + 2y + z = b \\ 2x + 2y - 3z = c \end{array} \quad \text{or} \quad \begin{array}{l} x + y - 2z = a \\ y + 3z = b - a \\ z = c - 2a \end{array}$$

Solving for x, y, z yields $x = -8a - b + 5c$, $y = 5a + b - 3c$, $z = -2a + c$. Thus

$$H^{-1}(a, b, c) = (-8a - b + 5c, 5a + b - 3c, -2a + c)$$

or $\qquad H^{-1}(x, y, z) = (-8x - y + 5z, 5x + y - 3z, -2x + z)$

8.33. Suppose $F: V \to U$ is linear and that V is of finite dimension. Show that V and the image of F have the same dimension if and only if F is nonsingular. Determine all nonsingular linear mappings $T: \mathbf{R}^4 \to \mathbf{R}^3$.

By Theorem 8.6, $\dim V = \dim (\operatorname{Im} F) + \dim (\operatorname{Ker} F)$. Hence V and $\operatorname{Im} F$ have the same dimension if and only if $\dim (\operatorname{Ker} F) = 0$ or $\operatorname{Ker} F = \{0\}$, i.e., if and only if F is nonsingular.

Since $\dim \mathbf{R}^3$ is less than $\dim \mathbf{R}^4$, we have $\dim (\operatorname{Im} T)$ is less than the dimension of the domain $\mathbf{R}^4$ of T. Accordingly no linear mapping $T: \mathbf{R}^4 \to \mathbf{R}^3$ can be nonsingular.

OPERATIONS WITH LINEAR MAPS, ALGEBRA OF LINEAR MAPS

8.34. Define $F: \mathbf{R}^3 \to \mathbf{R}^2$ and $G: \mathbf{R}^3 \to \mathbf{R}^2$ by $F(x, y, z) = (2x, y + z)$ and $G(x, y, z) = (x - z, y)$. Find formulas defining the maps: (a) $F + G$; (b) $3F$; (c) $2F - 5G$.

(a) $(F + G)(x, y, z) = F(x, y, z) + G(x, y, z)$
$$= (2x, y + z) + (x - z, y) = (3x - z, 2y + z)$$

(b) $(3F)(x, y, z) = 3F(x, y, z) = 3(2x, y + z) = (6x, 3y + 3z)$

(c) $(2F - 5G)(x, y, z) = 2F(x, y, z) - 5G(x, y, z) = 2(2x, y + z) - 5(x - z, y)$
$$= (4x, 2y + 2z) + (-5x + 5z, -5y) = (-x + 5z, -3y + 2z)$$

8.35. Let $F: \mathbf{R}^3 \to \mathbf{R}^2$ and $G: \mathbf{R}^2 \to \mathbf{R}^2$ be defined by $F(x, y, z) = (2x, y + z)$ and $G(x, y) = (y, x)$. Derive formulas defining the mappings: (a) $G \circ F$; (b) $F \circ G$.

(a) $(G \circ F)(x, y, z) = G(F(x, y, z)) = G(2x, y + z) = (y + z, 2x)$

(b) The mapping $F \circ G$ is not defined since the image of G is not contained in the domain of F.

8.36. Let F and G be the linear operators on $\mathbf{R}^2$ defined by $F(x, y) = (y, x)$ and $G(x, y) = (0, x)$. Find formulas defining the operators: (a) $F + G$; (b) $2F - 3G$; (c) FG; (d) GF; (e) F^2; (f) G^2.

(a) $(F + G)(x, y) = F(x, y) + G(x, y) = (y, x) + (0, x) = (y, 2x)$

(b) $(2F - 3G)(x, y) = 2F(x, y) - 3G(x, y) = 2(y, x) - 3(0, x) = (2y, -x)$

(c) $(FG)(x, y) = F(G(x, y)) = F(0, x) = (x, 0)$

(d) $(GF)(x, y) = G(F(x, y)) = G(y, x) = (0, y)$

(e) $F^2(x, y) = F(F(x, y)) = F(y, x) = (x, y)$ (Note $F^2 = I$, the identity mapping.)

(f) $G^2(x, y) = G(G(x, y)) = G(0, x) = (0, 0)$ (Note $G^2 = \mathbf{0}$, the zero mapping.)

8.37. Consider the linear operator T on $\mathbf{R}^3$ defined by $T(x, y, z) = (2x, 4x - y, 2x + 3y - z)$. (a) Show that T is invertible. Find formulas for: (b) T^{-1}; (c) T^2; (d) T^{-2}.

(a) Let $W = \operatorname{Ker} T$. We need only show that T is nonsingular, i.e., that $W = \{0\}$. Set $T(x, y, z) = (0, 0, 0)$, which yields
$$T(x, y, z) = (2x, 4x - y, 2x + 3y - z) = (0, 0, 0)$$

Thus W is the solution space of the homogeneous system
$$2x = 0, \qquad 4x - y = 0, \qquad 2x + 3y - z = 0$$

which has only the trivial solution $(0, 0, 0)$. Thus $W = \{0\}$. Hence T is nonsingular, and so T is invertible.

(b)   Set $T(x, y, z) = (r, s, t)$ [and so $T^{-1}(r, s, t) = (x, y, z)$].   We have

$$(2x, 4x - y, 2x + 3y - z) = (r, s, t) \qquad \text{or} \qquad 2x = r, \quad 4x - y = s, \quad 2x + 3y - z = t$$

Solve for x, y, z in terms of r, s, t to get $x = \tfrac{1}{2}r, \ y = 2r - s, \ z = 7r - 3s - t$.   Thus

$$T^{-1}(r, s, t) = (\tfrac{1}{2}r, 2r - s, 7r - 3s - t) \qquad \text{or} \qquad T^{-1}(x, y, z) = (\tfrac{1}{2}x, 2x - y, 7x - 3y - z)$$

(c)   Apply T twice to get

$$\begin{aligned}
T^2(x, y, z) &= T(2x, 4x - y, 2x + 3y - z) \\
&= [4x, 4(2x) - (4x - y), 2(2x) + 3(4x - y) - (2x + 3y - z)] \\
&= (4x, 4x + y, 14x - 6y + z)
\end{aligned}$$

(d)   Apply T^{-1} twice to get

$$\begin{aligned}
T^{-2}(x, y, z) &= T^{-2}(\tfrac{1}{2}x, 2x - y, 7x - 3y - z) \\
&= [\tfrac{1}{4}x, 2(\tfrac{1}{2}x) - (2x - y), 7(\tfrac{1}{2}x) - 3(2x - y) - (7x - 3y - z)] \\
&= (\tfrac{1}{4}x, -x + y, -\tfrac{19}{2}x + 6y + z)
\end{aligned}$$

8.38.   Consider the linear operator T on $\mathbf{R}^2$ defined by $T(x, y) = (2x + 4y, 3x + 6y)$.   Find:
(a) Formula for T^{-1}.   (b) $T^{-1}(8, 12)$.   (c) $T^{-1}(1, 2)$.   (d) Is T an onto mapping?

(a) T is singular, e.g., $T(-2) = (0, 0)$.   Hence the linear operator $T^{-1} : \mathbf{R}^2 \to \mathbf{R}^2$ does not exist.

(b) $T^{-1}(8, 12)$ means the preimage of $(8, 12)$ under T.   Set $T(x, y) = (8, 12)$ to get the system

$$\begin{array}{ll}
2x + 4y = 8 \\
3x + 6y = 12
\end{array} \qquad \text{or} \qquad x + 2y = 4$$

Here y is a free variable.   Set $y = a$, where a is a parameter, to get the solution $x = -2a + 4$, $y = a$.   Thus $T^{-1}(8, 12) = \{(-2a + 4, a) : a \in \mathbf{R}\}$.

(c)   Set $T(x, y) = (1, 2)$ to get the system

$$2x + 4y = 1, \qquad 3x + 6y = 2$$

The system has no solution.   Thus $T^{-1}(1, 2) = \varnothing$, the empty set.

(d)   No since, e.g., $(1, 2)$ has no preimage.

8.39.   Let F and G be linear operators on $\mathbf{R}^2$ defined by $F(x, y) = (0, x)$ and $G(x, y) = (x, 0)$.   Show that: (a) $GF = \mathbf{0}$, the zero mapping, but $FG \neq \mathbf{0}$; (b) $G^2 = G$.

(a) $(GF)(x, y) = G(F(x, y)) = G(0, x) = (0, 0)$.   Since GF assigns $(0, 0)$ to every vector (x, y) in $\mathbf{R}^2$, it is the zero mapping, that is, $GF = \mathbf{0}$.
  On the other hand, $(FG)(x, y) = F(G(x, y)) = F(x, 0) = (0, x)$.   For example, $(FG)(2, 3) = (0, 2)$.   Thus $FG \neq \mathbf{0}$, since it does not assign $0 = (0, 0)$ to every vector in $\mathbf{R}^2$.

(b)   For any vector (x, y) in $\mathbf{R}^2$ we have $G^2(x, y) = G(G(x, y)) = G(x, 0) = (x, 0) = G(x, y)$.   Hence $G^2 = G$.

8.40.   Prove: (a) The zero mapping $\mathbf{0}$, defined by $\mathbf{0}(v) = 0 \in U$ for every $v \in V$, is the zero element of $\operatorname{Hom}(V, U)$.   (b) The negative of $F \in \operatorname{Hom}(V, U)$ is the mapping $(-1)F$, i.e., $-F = (-1)F$.

(a)   Let $F \in \operatorname{Hom}(V, U)$.   Then, for every $v \in V$,

$$(F + \mathbf{0})(v) = F(v) + \mathbf{0}(v) = F(v) + 0 = F(v)$$

Since $(F + \mathbf{0})(v) = F(v)$ for every $v \in V$, $F + \mathbf{0} = F$.

(b)   For every $v \in V$,

$$(F + (-1)F)(v) = F(v) + (-1)F(v) = F(v) - F(v) = 0 = \mathbf{0}(v)$$

Since $(F + (-1)F)(v) = \mathbf{0}(v)$ for every $v \in V$, $F + (-1)F = \mathbf{0}$.   Thus $(-1)F$ is the negative of F.

8.41.   Consider linear mappings $F: \mathbf{R}^3 \rightarrow \mathbf{R}^2$, $G: \mathbf{R}^3 \rightarrow \mathbf{R}^2$, $H: \mathbf{R}^3 \rightarrow \mathbf{R}^2$ defined by

$$F(x, y, z) = (x + y + z, x + y), \qquad G(x, y, z) = (2x + z, x + y), \qquad H(x, y, z) = (2y, x)$$

Show that F, G, H are linearly independent [as elements of Hom $(\mathbf{R}^3, \mathbf{R}^2)$].

Suppose, for scalars $a, b, c \in K$,

$$aF + bG + cH = \mathbf{0} \tag{1}$$

(Here $\mathbf{0}$ is the zero mapping.)   For $e_1 = (1, 0, 0) \in \mathbf{R}^3$, we have $\mathbf{0}(e_1) = (0, 0)$ and

$$(aF + bG + cH)(e_1) = aF(1, 0, 0) + bG(1, 0, 0) + cH(1, 0, 0)$$
$$= a(1, 1) + b(2, 1) + c(0, 1) = (a + 2b, a + b + c)$$

Thus by Eq. (1), $(a + 2b, a + b + c) = (0, 0)$ and so

$$a + 2b = 0 \qquad \text{and} \qquad a + b + c = 0 \tag{2}$$

Similarly for $e_2 = (0, 1, 0) \in \mathbf{R}^3$, we have $\mathbf{0}(e_2) = (0, 0)$ and

$$(aF + bG + cH)(e_2) = aF(0, 1, 0) + bG(0, 1, 0) + cH(0, 1, 0)$$
$$= a(1, 1) + b(0, 1) + c(2, 0) = (a + 2c, a + b)$$

Thus $$a + 2c = 0 \qquad \text{and} \qquad a + b = 0 \tag{3}$$

Using Eqs. (2) and (3) we obtain

$$a = 0, \qquad b = 0, \qquad c = 0 \tag{4}$$

Since Eq. (1) implies Eq. (4), the mappings F, G, and H are linearly independent.

8.42.   Let k be a nonzero scalar.   Show that a linear map T is singular if and only if kT is singular.   Hence T is singular if and only if $-T$ is singular.

Suppose T is singular.   Then $T(v) = 0$ for some vector $v \neq 0$.   Hence

$$(kT)(v) = kT(v) = k0 = 0$$

and so kT is singular.

Now suppose kT is singular.   Then $(kT)(w) = 0$ for some vector $w \neq 0$.   Hence

$$T(kw) = kT(w) = (kT)(w) = 0$$

But $k \neq 0$ and $w \neq 0$ implies $kw \neq 0$.   Thus T is also singular.

8.43.   Find the dimension d of: (a) Hom $(\mathbf{R}^3, \mathbf{R}^4)$; (b) Hom $(\mathbf{R}^5, \mathbf{R}^3)$; (c) Hom $(\mathbf{P}_3(t), \mathbf{R}^2)$; (d) Hom $(\mathbf{M}_{2,3}, \mathbf{R}^4)$.

Use dim $(\text{Hom }(V, U)) = mn$, where dim $V = m$ and dim $U = n$.

(a) $d = 3(4) = 12$

(b) $d = 5(3) = 15$

(c)   Since dim $(\mathbf{P}_3(t)) = 4$, $d = 4(2) = 8$.

(d)   Since dim $\mathbf{M}_{2,3} = 6$, $d = 6(4) = 24$.

8.44. Find the dimension of: (a) $A(\mathbf{R}^4)$; (b) $A(\mathbf{P}_2(t))$; (c) $A(\mathbf{M}_{2,3})$.

Use dim $(A(V)) = n^2$, where dim $V = n$.   Hence:

(a) dim $(A(\mathbf{R}^4)) = 4^2 = 16$; (b) dim $(\mathbf{P}_2(t)) = 3^2 = 9$; (c) dim $\mathbf{M}_{2,3} = 6^2 = 36$

PROOFS OF THEOREMS

8.45. Prove Theorem 8.2:   Let V and U be vector spaces over a field K.   Let $\{v_1, v_2, \ldots, v_n\}$ be a basis of V and let $u_1, u_2, \ldots, u_n$ be any vectors in U.   Then there exists a unique linear mapping $F: V \to U$ such that $F(v_1) = u_1$, $F(v_2) = u_2, \ldots, F(v_n) = u_n$.

There are three steps to the proof of the theorem: (1) Define the mapping $F: V \to U$ such that $F(v_i) = u_i$, $i = 1, \ldots, n$.   (2) Show that F is linear.   (3) Show that F is unique.

Step 1.   Let $v \in V$.   Since $\{v_1, \ldots, v_n\}$ is a basis of V, there exist unique scalars $a_1, \ldots, a_n \in K$ for which $v = a_1v_1 + a_2v_2 + \cdots + a_nv_n$.   We define $F: V \to U$ by

$$F(v) = a_1u_1 + a_2u_2 + \cdots + a_nu_n$$

(Since the a_i are unique, the mapping F is well-defined.)   Now, for $i = 1, \ldots, n$,

$$v_i = 0v_1 + \cdots + 1v_i + \cdots + 0v_n$$

Hence $F(v_i) = 0u_1 + \cdots + 1u_i + \cdots + 0u_n = u_i$

Thus the first step of the proof is complete.

Step 2.   Suppose $v = a_1v_1 + a_2v_2 + \cdots + a_nv_n$ and $w = b_1v_1 + b_2v_2 + \cdots + b_nv_n$.   Then

$$v + w = (a_1 + b_1)v_1 + (a_2 + b_2)v_2 + \cdots + (a_n + b_n)v_n$$

and, for any $k \in K$, $kv = ka_1v_1 + ka_2v_2 + \cdots + ka_nv_n$.   By definition of the mapping F,

$$F(v) = a_1u_1 + a_2u_2 + \cdots + a_nv_n \quad \text{and} \quad F(w) = b_1v_1 + b_2v_2 + \cdots + b_nv_n$$

Hence $F(v + w) = (a_1 + b_1)u_1 + (a_2 + b_2)u_2 + \cdots + (a_n + b_n)u_n$

$$= (a_1u_1 + a_2u_2 + \cdots + a_nu_n) + (b_1u_1 + b_2u_2 + \cdots + b_nu_n)$$

$$= F(v) + F(w)$$

and $F(kv) = k(a_1u_1 + a_2u_2 + \cdots + a_nu_n) = kF(v)$

Thus F is linear.

Step 3.   Suppose $G: V \to U$ is linear and $G(v_i) = u_i$, $i = 1, \ldots, n$.   If

$$v = a_1v_1 + a_2v_2 + \cdots + a_nv_n$$

then $G(v) = G(a_1v_1 + a_2v_2 + \cdots + a_nv_n) = a_1G(v_1) + a_2G(v_2) + \cdots + a_nG(v_n)$

$$= a_1u_1 + a_2u_2 + \cdots + a_nu_n = F(v)$$

Since $G(v) = F(v)$ for every $v \in V$, $G = F$.   Thus F is unique and the theorem is proved.

8.46. Prove Theorem 8.3:   Let $F: V \to U$ be a linear mapping.   Then

(i)   The image of F is a subspace of U.

(ii) The kernel of F is a subspace of V.

(i) Since $F(0) = 0$, $0 \in \text{Im } F$. Now suppose $u, u' \in \text{Im } F$ and $a, b \in K$. Since u and u' belong to the image of F, there exist vectors $v, v' \in V$ such that $F(v) = u$ and $F(v') = u'$. Then

$$F(av + bv') = aF(v) + bF(v') + au + bu' \in \text{Im } F$$

Thus the image of F is a subspace of U.

(ii) Since $F(0) = 0$, $0 \in \text{Ker } F$. Now suppose $v, w \in \text{Ker } F$ and $a, b \in K$. Since v and w belong to the kernel of F, $F(v) = 0$ and $F(w) = 0$. Thus

$$F(av + bw) = aF(v) + bF(w) = a0 + b0 = 0 + 0 = 0 \qquad \text{and so} \qquad av + bw \in \text{Ker } F$$

Thus the kernel of F is a subspace of V.

8.47. Prove Theorem 8.6: Let V be of finite dimension, and let $F: V \to U$ be a linear mapping. Then

$$\dim V = \dim (\text{Ker } F) + \dim (\text{Im } F)$$

Suppose $\dim (\text{Ker } F) = r$ and $\{w_1, \ldots, w_r\}$ is a basis of Ker F, and suppose $\dim (\text{Im } F) = s$ and $\{u_1, \ldots, u_s\}$ is a basis of Im F. (By Proposition 8.4, Im F has finite dimension.) Since $u_j \in \text{Im } F$, there exist vectors $v_1, \ldots, v_s$ in V such that $F(v_1) = u_1, \ldots, F(v_s) = u_s$. We claim that the set

$$B = \{w_1, \ldots, w_r, v_1, \ldots, v_s\}$$

is a basis of V, that is, (i) B spans V, and (ii) B is linearly independent. Once we prove (i) and (ii), then $\dim V = r + s = \dim (\text{Ker } F) + \dim (\text{Im } F)$.

(i) B spans V. Let $v \in V$. Then $F(v) \in \text{Im } F$. Since the u_j span Im F, there exist scalars $a_1, \ldots, a_s$ such that $F(v) = a_1 u_1 + \cdots + a_s u_s$. Set $\hat{v} = a_1 v_1 + \cdots + a_s v_s - v$. Then

$$F(\hat{v}) = F(a_1 v_1 + \cdots + a_s v_s - v) = a_1 F(v_1) + \cdots + a_s F(v_s) - F(v)$$
$$= a_1 u_1 + \cdots + a_s u_s - F(v) = 0$$

Thus $\hat{v} \in \text{Ker } F$. Since the w_i span Ker F, there exist scalars $b_1, \ldots, b_r$ such that

$$\hat{v} = b_1 w_1 + \cdots + b_r w_r = a_1 v_1 + \cdots + a_s v_s - v$$

Accordingly

$$v = a_1 v_1 + \cdots + a_s v_s - b_1 w_1 - \cdots - b_r w_r$$

Thus B spans V.

(ii) B is linearly independent. Suppose

$$x_1 w_1 + \cdots + x_r w_r + y_1 v_1 + \cdots + y_s v_s = 0 \tag{1}$$

where $x_i, y_j \in K$. Then

$$0 = F(0) = F(x_1 w_1 + \cdots + x_r w_r + y_1 v_1 + \cdots + y_s v_s)$$
$$= x_1 F(w_1) + \cdots + x_r F(w_r) + y_1 F(v_1) + \cdots + y_s F(v_s) \tag{2}$$

But $F(w_i) = 0$ since $w_i \in \text{Ker } F$, and $F(v_j) = u_j$. Substituting into Eq. (2) we will obtain $y_1 u_1 + \cdots + y_s u_s = 0$. Since the u_j are linearly independent, each $y_j = 0$. Substitution into Eq. (1) gives $x_1 w_1 + \cdots + x_r w_r = 0$. Since the w_i are linearly independent, each $x_i = 0$. Thus B is linearly independent.

8.48. Prove Theorem 8.9: Suppose a linear mapping $F: V \to U$ is nonsingular. Then the image of any linearly independent set is linearly independent.

Suppose $v_1, v_2, \ldots, v_n$ are linearly independent vectors in V. We claim that $F(v_1), F(v_2), \ldots, F(v_n)$ are also linearly independent. Suppose $a_1 F(v_1) + a_2 F(v_2) + \cdots + a_n F(v_n) = 0$, where $a_i \in K$. Since F is linear, $F(a_1 v_1 + a_2 v_2 + \cdots + a_n v_n) = 0$. Hence

$$a_1 v_1 + a_2 v_2 + \cdots + a_n v_n \in \text{Ker } F$$

But F is nonsingular, i.e., Ker $F = \{0\}$. Hence $a_1 v_1 + a_2 v_2 + \cdots + a_n v_n = 0$. Since the v_i are linearly independent, all the a_i are 0. Accordingly, the $F(v_i)$ are linearly independent. Thus the theorem is proved.

8.49. Prove Theorem 8.12: Let V, U, and W be vector spaces over K. Let F and F' be linear mappings from V into U, let G and G' be linear mappings from U into W, and let $k \in K$. Then

(i)　$G \circ (F + F') = G \circ F + G \circ F'$

(ii)　$(G + G') \circ F = G \circ F + G' \circ F$

(iii)　$k(G \circ F) = (kG) \circ F = G \circ (kF)$

(i)　For every $v \in V$,

$$(G \circ (F + F'))(v) = G((F + F')(v)) = G(F(v) + F'(v))$$
$$= G(F(v)) + G(F'(v)) = (G \circ F)(v) + (G \circ F')(v) = (G \circ F + G \circ F')(v)$$

Thus $G \circ (F + F') = G \circ F + G \circ F'$

(ii)　For every $v \in V$,

$$((G + G') \circ F)(v) = (G + G')(F(v)) = G(F(v)) + G'(F(v))$$
$$= (G \circ F)(v) + (G' \circ F)(v) = (G \circ F + G' \circ F)(v)$$

Thus $(G + G') \circ F = G \circ F + G' \circ F$.

(iii)　For every $v \in V$,

$$(k(G \circ F))(v) = k(G \circ F)(v) = k(G(F(v))) = (kG)(F(v)) = (kG \circ F)(v)$$

and　　$(k(G \circ F))(v) = k(G \circ F)(v) = k(G(F(v))) = G(kF(v)) = G((kF)(v)) = (G \circ kF)(v)$

Accordingly $k(G \circ F) = (kG) \circ F = G \circ (kF)$. (We emphasize that two mappings are shown to be equal by showing that they assign the same image to each point in the domain.)

8.50. Let E be a linear operator on V for which $E^2 = E$. (Such an operator is called a *projection*.) Let U be the image of E, and let W be the kernel. Prove:

(a)　If $u \in U$, then $E(u) = u$, i.e., E is the identity mapping on U.

(b)　If $E \neq I$, then E is singular, i.e., $E(v) = 0$ for some $v \neq 0$.

(c)　$V = U \oplus W$.

(a)　If $u \in U$, the image of E, then $E(v) = u$ for some $v \in V$. Hence using $E^2 = E$, we have

$$u = E(v) = E^2(v) = E(E(v)) = E(u)$$

(b)　If $E \neq I$, then for some $v \in V$, $E(v) = u$, where $v \neq u$. By (i), $E(u) = u$. Thus

$$E(v - u) = E(v) - E(u) = u - u = 0 \quad \text{where} \quad v - u \neq 0$$

(c)　We first show that $V = U + W$. Let $v \in V$. Set $u = E(v)$ and $w = v - E(v)$. Then

$$v = E(v) + v - E(v) = u + w$$

By definition, $u = E(v) \in U$, the image of E.   We now show that $w \in W$, the kernel of E,

$$E(w) = E(v - E(v)) = E(v) - E^2(v) = E(v) - E(v) = 0$$

and thus $w \in W$.   Hence $V = U + W$.

   We next show that $U \cap W = \{0\}$.   Let $v \in U \cap W$.   Since $v \in U$, $E(v) = v$ by part (a). Since $v \in W$, $E(v) = 0$.   Thus $v = E(v) = 0$ and so $U \cap W = \{0\}$.

   The above two properties imply that $V = U \oplus W$.

Supplementary Problems

MAPPINGS

8.51.   Determine the number of different mappings from $\{a, b\}$ into $\{1, 2, 3\}$.

8.52.   Let the mapping g assign to each name in the set $\{$Betty, Martin, David, Alan, Rebecca$\}$ the number of different letters needed to spell the name.   Find: (a) the graph of g; (b) the image of g.

8.53.   Figure 8-9 is a diagram of maps:

$$f: A \to B, \; g: B \to A, \; h: C \to B, \; F: B \to C, \; G: A \to C$$

Determine whether each of the following defines a mapping, and if it does, find its domain and codomain: (a) $g \circ f$; (b) $h \circ f$; (c) $F \circ f$; (d) $G \circ f$; (e) $g \circ h$; (f) $h \circ G \circ g$.

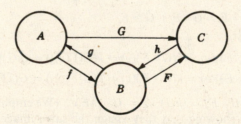

Fig. 8-9

8.54.   Let $f: \mathbf{R} \to \mathbf{R}$ and $g: \mathbf{R} \to \mathbf{R}$ be defined by $f(x) = x^2 + 3x + 1$ and $g(x) = 2x - 3$. Find formulas defining the composition mappings: (a) $f \circ g$; (b) $g \circ f$; (c) $g \circ g$; (d) $f \circ f$.

8.55.   For each of the following mappings $f: \mathbf{R} \to \mathbf{R}$ find a formula for the inverse mapping: (a) $f(x) = 3x - 7$; (b) $f(x) = x^3 + 2$.

8.56.   For any mapping $f: A \to B$ show that $\mathbf{1}_B \circ f = f = f \circ \mathbf{1}_A$.

LINEAR MAPPINGS

8.57.   Show that the following mappings are linear:

   (a) $F: \mathbf{R}^3 \to \mathbf{R}^2$ defined by $F(x, y, z) = (x + 2y - 3z, 4x - 5y + 6z)$.

   (b) $F: \mathbf{R}^2 \to \mathbf{R}^2$ defined by $F(x, y) = (ax + by, cx + dy)$, where a, b, c, d belong to $\mathbf{R}$.

8.58. Show that the following mappings are not linear:

    (a) $F: \mathbf{R}^2 \to \mathbf{R}^2$ defined by $F(x, y) = (x^2, y^2)$.

    (b) $F: \mathbf{R}^3 \to \mathbf{R}^2$ defined by $F(x, y, z) = (x + 1, y + z)$.

    (c) $F: \mathbf{R}^2 \to \mathbf{R}^2$ defined by $F(x, y) = (xy, y)$.

    (d) $F: \mathbf{R}^3 \to \mathbf{R}^2$ defined by $F(x, y, z) = (|x|, y + z)$.

8.59. Find $F(a, b)$, where the linear map $F: \mathbf{R}^2 \to \mathbf{R}^2$ is defined by $F(1, 2) = (3, -1)$ and $F(0, 1) = (2, 1)$.

8.60. Find a 2×2 matrix A which maps:

    (a) $(1, 3)^T$ and $(1, 4)^T$ into $(-2, 5)^T$ and $(3, -1)^T$, respectively.

    (b) $(2, -4)^T$ and $(-1, 2)^T$ into $(1, 1)^T$ and $(1, 3)^T$, respectively.

8.61. Find a 2×2 singular matrix B which maps $(1, 1)^T$ into $(1, 3)^T$.

8.62. Let V be the vector space of real n-square matrices, and let M be a fixed nonzero matrix in V. Show that the first two mappings $T: V \to V$ are linear, but the third is not: (a) $T(A) = MA$; (b) $T(A) = AM - MA$; (c) $T(A) = M + A$.

8.63. Give an example of a nonlinear map $F: \mathbf{R}^2 \to \mathbf{R}^2$ such that $F^{-1}(0) = \{0\}$ but F is not one-to-one.

8.64. Let $F: \mathbf{R}^2 \to \mathbf{R}^2$ be defined by $F(x, y) = (3x + 5y, 2x + 3y)$, and let S be the unit circle in $\mathbf{R}^2$. (S consists of all points satisfying $x^2 + y^2 = 1$.) Find: (a) the image $F(S)$; (b) the preimage $F^{-1}(S)$.

8.65. Consider the linear map $G: \mathbf{R}^3 \to \mathbf{R}^3$ defined by $G(x, y, z) = (x + y + z, y - 2z, y - 3z)$ and the unit sphere S_2 in $\mathbf{R}^3$, which consists of the points satisfying $x^2 + y^2 + z^2 = 1$. Find: (a) $G(S_2)$; (b) $G^{-1}(S_2)$.

8.66. Let H be the plane $x + 2y - 3z = 4$ in $\mathbf{R}^3$ and let G be the linear map in Problem 8.65. Find: (a) $G(H)$; (b) $G^{-1}(H)$.

8.67. Let W be a subspace of V. The *inclusion* map denoted by $i: W \hookrightarrow V$ is defined by $i(w) = w$ for every $w \in W$. Show that the inclusion map is linear.

8.68. Suppose $F: V \to U$ is linear. Show that $F(-v) = -F(v)$.

8.69. Let V be of finite dimension and let $T: V \to V$ be linear. Suppose there is a linear mapping $S: V \to V$ such that $TS = I$, the identity mapping on V. (We call S a *right inverse* of T.) (a) Show that T is invertible. (b) Show that $S = T^{-1}$. (c) Give an example to show that the above need not be true if V has infinite dimension.

KERNEL AND IMAGE OF LINEAR MAPPINGS

8.70. For each of the following linear maps F find a basis as well as the dimension of the kernel and the image of F:

    (a) $F: \mathbf{R}^3 \to \mathbf{R}^3$ defined by $F(x, y, z) = (x + 2y - 3z, 2x + 5y - 4z, x + 4y + z)$.

    (b) $F: \mathbf{R}^4 \to \mathbf{R}^3$ defined by $F(x, y, z, t) = (x + 2y + 3z + 2t, 2x + 4y + 7z + 5t, x + 2y + 6z + 5t)$.

8.71. For each of the following linear maps G find a basis as well as the dimension of the kernel and the image of G:

    (a) $G: \mathbf{R}^3 \to \mathbf{R}^2$ defined by $G(x, y, z) = (x + y + z, 2x + 2y + 2z)$.

    (b) $G: \mathbf{R}^3 \to \mathbf{R}^2$ defined by $G(x, y, z) = (x + y, y + z)$.

    (c) $G: \mathbf{R}^5 \to \mathbf{R}^3$ defined by $G(x, y, z, s, t) = (x + 2y + 2z + s + t, x + 2y + 3z + 2s - t,$
        $3x + 6y + 8z + 5s - t)$.

8.72. Each of the following matrices determines a linear map from $\mathbf{R}^4$ into $\mathbf{R}^3$:

$$(a)\ A = \begin{bmatrix} 1 & 2 & 0 & 1 \\ 2 & -1 & 2 & -1 \\ 1 & -3 & 2 & -2 \end{bmatrix};\ (b)\ B = \begin{bmatrix} 1 & 0 & 2 & -1 \\ 2 & 3 & -1 & 1 \\ -2 & 0 & -5 & 3 \end{bmatrix}$$

Find a basis as well as the dimension of the kernel and the image of each linear map.

8.73. Find a linear mapping $F: \mathbf{R}^3 \to \mathbf{R}^3$ whose image is spanned by $(1, 2, 3)$ and $(4, 5, 6)$.

8.74. Find a linear mapping $G: \mathbf{R}^4 \to \mathbf{R}^3$ whose kernel is spanned by $(1, 2, 3, 4)$ and $(0, 1, 1, 1)$.

8.75. Let $V = \mathbf{P}_{10}(t)$, the vector space of polynomials of degree ≤ 10. Consider the linear map $\mathbf{D}^4: V \to V$, where $\mathbf{D}^4$ denotes the fourth derivative of $d^4 f/dt^4$. Find a basis and the dimension of: (a) the image of $\mathbf{D}^4$; (b) the kernel of $\mathbf{D}^4$.

8.76. Suppose $F: V \to U$ is linear. Show that: (a) the image of any subspace of V is a subspace of U; (b) the preimage of any subspace of U is a subspace of V.

8.77. Show that if $F: V \to U$ is onto, then $\dim U \leq \dim V$. Determine all linear maps $F: \mathbf{R}^3 \to \mathbf{R}^4$ which are onto.

8.78. Consider the zero mapping $\mathbf{0}: V \to U$ defined by $\mathbf{0}(v) = 0$ for every v in V. Find the kernel and the image of $\mathbf{0}$.

OPERATIONS WITH LINEAR MAPPINGS

8.79. Let $F: \mathbf{R}^3 \to \mathbf{R}^2$ and $G: \mathbf{R}^3 \to \mathbf{R}^2$ be defined by $F(x, y, z) = (y, x + z)$ and $G(x, y, z) = (2z, x - y)$. Find formulas defining the mappings $F + G$ and $3F - 2G$.

8.80. Let $H: \mathbf{R}^2 \to \mathbf{R}^2$ be defined by $H(x, y) = (y, 2x)$. Using the maps F and G in Problem 8.79, find formulas defining the mappings: (a) $H \circ F$ and $H \circ G$; (b) $F \circ H$ and $G \circ H$; (c) $H \circ (F + G)$ and $H \circ F + H \circ G$.

8.81. Show that the following mappings F, G, and H are linearly independent:

    (a) $F, G, H \in \text{Hom}(\mathbf{R}^2, \mathbf{R}^2)$ defined by $F(x, y) = (x, 2y)$, $G(x, y) = (y, x + y)$, $H(x, y) = (0, x)$.

    (b) $F, G, H \in \text{Hom}(\mathbf{R}^3, \mathbf{R})$ defined by $F(x, y, z) = x + y + z$, $G(x, y, z) = y + z$, $H(x, y, z) = x - z$.

8.82. For $F, G \in \text{Hom}(V, U)$ show that $\text{rank}(F + G) \leq \text{rank}(F) + \text{rank}(G)$. (Here V has finite dimension.)

8.83. Let $F: V \to U$ and $G: U \to V$ be linear. Show that if F and G are nonsingular, then $G \circ F$ is nonsingular. Give an example where $G \circ F$ is nonsingular but G is not.

8.84. Find the dimension d of: (a) Hom $(\mathbf{R}^2, \mathbf{R}^8)$; (b) Hom $(\mathbf{P}_4(t), \mathbf{R}^3)$; (c) Hom $(\mathbf{M}_{2,4}, \mathbf{P}_2(t))$.

8.85. Determine whether or not each linear map is nonsingular. If not, find a nonzero vector v whose image is 0; otherwise find a formula for the inverse map:

    (a) $F: \mathbf{R}^3 \to \mathbf{R}^3$ defined by $F(x, y, z) = (x + y + z, 2x + 3y + 5z, x + 3y + 7z)$.

    (b) $G: \mathbf{R}^3 \to \mathbf{P}_2(t)$ defined by $G(x, y, z) = (x + y)t^2 + (x + 2y + 2z)t + y + z$.

    (c) $H: \mathbf{R}^2 \to \mathbf{P}_2(t)$ defined by $H(x, y) = (x + 2y)t^2 + (x - y)t + x + y$.

8.86. When can dim (Hom (V, U)) = dim V?

8.87. Prove Theorem 8.10; that is, that Hom (V, U) does satisfy all the required axioms of a vector space.

8.88. Prove Theorem 8.11; that is, that if dim $V = m$ and dim $U = n$, then dim (Hom (V, U)) = mn.

ALGEBRA OF LINEAR OPERATORS

8.89. Let F and G be the linear operators on $\mathbf{R}^2$ defined by $F(x, y) = (x + y, 0)$ and $G(x, y) = (-y, x)$. Find formulas defining the linear operators: (a) $F + G$; (b) $5F - 3G$; (c) FG; (d) GF; (e) F^2; (f) G^2.

8.90. Show that each linear operator T on $\mathbf{R}^2$ is nonsingular and find a formula for T^{-1}, where: (a) $T(x, y) = (x + 2y, 2x + 3y)$; (b) $T(x, y) = (2x - 3y, 3x - 4y)$.

8.91. Show that each linear operator T on $\mathbf{R}^3$ is nonsingular and find a formula for T^{-1}, where: (a) $T(x, y, z) = (x - 3y - 2z, y - 4z, z)$; (b) $T(x, y, z) = (x + z, x - y, y)$.

8.92. Find the dimension of $A(V)$, where: (a) $V = \mathbf{R}^7$; (b) $V = \mathbf{P}_5(t)$; (c) $V = \mathbf{M}_{3,4}$.

8.93. Which of the following integers can be the dimension of an algebra $A(V)$ of linear maps: 5, 9, 12, 25, 28, 36, 45, 64, 88, 100?

8.94. Let T be the linear operator on $\mathbf{R}^2$ defined by $T(x, y) = (x + 2y, 3x + 4y)$. Find a formula for $f(T)$, where: (a) $f(t) = t^2 + 2t - 3$; (b) $f(t) = t^2 - 5t - 2$.

MISCELLANEOUS PROBLEMS

8.95. Suppose $F: V \to U$ is linear and k is a nonzero scalar. Prove that the maps F and kF have the same kernel and the same image.

8.96. Suppose F and G are linear operators on V and that F is nonsingular. Assume that V has finite dimension. Show that rank (FG) = rank (GF) = rank (G).

8.97. Let $F: V \to U$ be linear and let W be a subspace of V. The *restriction* of F to W is the map $F|W: W \to U$ defined by $F|W(v) = F(v)$ for every v in W. Prove the following: (a) $F|W$ is linear; (b) Ker $(F|W)$ = (Ker F) $\cap$ W; (c) Im $(F|W)$ = $F(W)$.

8.98. Suppose V has finite dimension. Suppose T is a linear operator on V such that rank $(T^2) =$ rank (T). Show that Ker $T \cap$ Im $T = \{0\}$.

8.99. Suppose $V = U \oplus W$. Let E_1 and E_2 be the linear operators on V defined by $E_1(v) = u$, $E_2(v) = w$, where $v = u + w$, $u \in U$, $w \in W$. Show that: (a) $E_1^2 = E_1$ and $E_2^2 = E_2$, i.e., that E_1 and E_2 are projections; (b) $E_1 + E_2 = I$, the identity mapping; (c) $E_1 E_2 = 0$ and $E_2 E_1 = 0$.

8.100. Let E_1 and E_2 be linear operators on V satisfying parts (a), (b), and (c) of Problem 8.99. Prove: $V = \text{Im } E_1 \oplus \text{Im } E_2$.

8.101. Let v and w be elements of a real vector space V. The *line segment* L from v to $v + w$ is defined to be the set of vectors $v + tw$ for $0 \le t \le 1$. (See Fig. 8-10.)

 (a) Show that the line segment L between vectors v and u consists of the points: (i) $(1 - t)v + tu$ for $0 \le t \le 1$, and (ii) $t_1 v + t_2 u$ for $t_1 + t_2 = 1$, $t_1 \ge 0$, $t_2 \ge 0$.

 (b) Let $F: V \to U$ be linear. Show that the image $F(L)$ of a line segment L in V is a line segment in U.

8.102. A subset X of a vector space V is said to be *convex* if the line segment L between any two points (vectors) $P, Q \in X$ is contained in X. (a) Show that the intersection of convex sets is convex; (b) suppose $F: V \to U$ is linear and X is convex. Show that $F(X)$ is convex.

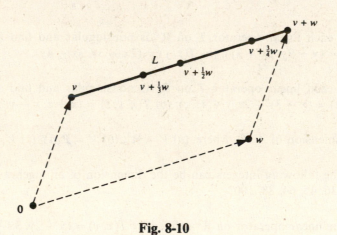

Fig. 8-10

Answers to Supplementary Problems

8.51. Nine.

8.52. (a) $\{(\text{Betty}, 4), (\text{Martin}, 6), (\text{David}, 4), (\text{Alan}, 3), (\text{Rebecca}, 5)\}$; (b) image of $g = \{3, 4, 5, 6\}$

8.53. (a) $(g \circ f): A \to A$; (b) no; (c) $(F \circ f): A \to C$; (d) no; (e) $(g \circ h): C \to A$;
  (f) $(h \circ G \circ g): B \to B$.

8.54. (a) $(f \circ g)(x) = 4x^2 - 6x + 1$; (b) $(g \circ f)(x) = 2x^2 + 6x - 1$; (c) $(g \circ g)(x) = 4x - 9$;
(d) $(f \circ f)(x) = x^4 + 6x^3 + 14x^2 + 15x + 5$

8.55. (a) $f^{-1}(x) = (x + 7)/3$; (b) $f^{-1}(x) = \sqrt[3]{x - 2}$

8.57. $F(x, y, z) = A(x, y, z)^T$, where: (a) $A = \begin{bmatrix} 1 & 2 & -3 \\ 4 & -5 & 6 \end{bmatrix}$; (b) $A = \begin{bmatrix} a & b \\ c & d \end{bmatrix}$

8.58. (a) $u = (2, 2)$, $k = 3$; then $F(ku) = (36, 36)$ but $kF(u) = (12, 12)$; (b) $F(0) \neq 0$; (c) $u = (1, 2)$, $v = (3, 4)$; then $F(u + v) = (24, 6)$ but $F(u) + F(v) = (14, 6)$; (d) $u = (1, 2, 3)$, $k = -2$; then $F(ku) = (2, -10)$ but $kF(u) = (-2, -10)$.

8.59. $F(a, b) = (-a + 2b, -3a + b)$

8.60. (a) $A = \begin{bmatrix} -17 & 5 \\ 23 & -6 \end{bmatrix}$; (b) no such matrix exists since $(2, -4)$ and $(-1, 2)$ are linearly dependent but $(1, 1)$ and $(1, 3)$ are not.

8.61. $B = \begin{bmatrix} 1 & 0 \\ 3 & 0 \end{bmatrix}$. [Hint: Send $(0, 1)^T$ into $(0, 0)^T$.]

8.63. $F(x, y) = (x^2, y^2)$

8.64. (a) $13x^2 - 42xy + 34y^2 = 1$; (b) $13x^2 + 42xy + 34y^2 = 1$

8.65. (a) $x^2 - 8xy + 26y^2 + 6xz - 38yz + 14z^2 = 1$; (b) $x^2 + 2xy + 3y^2 + 2xz - 8yz + 14z^2 = 1$

8.66. (a) $x - y + 2z = 4$; (b) $x + 6z = 4$

8.69. (c) For $p(t) = a_0 + a_1 t + a_2 t^2 + \cdots + a_n t^n$ in $P(t)$, define $T(p(t)) = a_1 + a_2 t + \cdots + a_n t^{n-1}$ and $S(p(t)) = a_0 t + a_1 t^2 + \cdots + a_n t^{n+1}$

8.70. (a) dim (Ker F) = 1, $\{(7, -2, 1)\}$; dim (Im F) = 2, $\{(1, 2, 1), (0, 1, 2)\}$
(b) dim (Ker F) = 2, $\{(-2, 1, 0, 0), (1, 0, -1, 1)\}$; dim (Im F) = 2, $\{(1, 2, 1), (0, 1, 3)\}$

8.71. (a) dim (Ker G) = 2, $\{(1, 0, -1), (1, -1, 0)\}$; dim (Im G) = 1, $\{(1, 2)\}$
(b) dim (Ker G) = 1, $\{(1, -1, 1)\}$; (Im G) = $\mathbf{R}^2$, $\{(1, 0), (0, 1)\}$
(c) dim (Ker G) = 3, $\{(-2, 1, 0, 0, 0), (1, 0, -1, 1, 0), (-5, 0, 2, 0, 1)\}$; dim (Im G) = 2, $\{(1, 1, 3), (0, 1, 2)\}$

8.72. (a) dim (Ker A) = 2, $\{(4, -2, -5, 0), (1, -3, 0, 5)\}$; dim (Im A) = 2, $\{(1, 2, 1), (0, 1, 1)\}$
(b) dim (Ker B) = 1, $\{(-1, \frac{2}{3}, 1, 1)\}$; (Im B) = $\mathbf{R}^3$

8.73. $F(x, y, z) = (x + 4y, 2x + 5y, 3x + 6y)$

8.74. $G(x, y, z, t) = (x + y - z, 2x + y - t, 0)$

8.75. (a) $\{1, t, t^2, \ldots, t^6\}$; (b) $\{1, t, t^2, t^3\}$

8.77. None since $\dim \mathbf{R}^4 > \dim \mathbf{R}^3$

8.78. $\operatorname{Ker} \mathbf{0} = V$; $\operatorname{Im} \mathbf{0} = \{0\}$

8.79. $(F + G)(x, y, z) = (y + 2z, 2x - y + z)$; $(3F - 2G)(x, y, z) = (3y - 4z, x + 2y + 3z)$

8.80. (a) $(H \circ F)(x, y, z) = (x + z, 2y)$, $(H \circ G)(x, y, z) = (x - y, 4z)$; (b) not defined;
(c) $(H \circ (F + G))(x, y, z) = (H \circ F + H \circ G)(x, y, z) = (2x - y + z, 2y + 4z)$

8.83. $F(x, y) = (x, y, y)$, $G(x, y, z) = (x, y)$

8.84. (a) 16; (b) 15; (c) 24

8.85. (a) $v = (2, -3, 1)$; (b) $G^{-1}(at^2 + bt + c) = (b - 2c, a - b + 2c, -a + b - c)$; (c) H is nonsingular, but not invertible since $\dim \mathbf{P}_2(t) > \dim \mathbf{R}^2$.

8.86. $\dim U = 1$, that is, $U = K$.

8.89. (a) $(F + G)(x, y) = (x, x)$; (b) $(5F - 3G)(x, y) = (5x + 8y, -3x)$; (c) $(FG)(x, y) = (x - y, 0)$;
(d) $(GF)(x, y) = (0, x + y)$; (e) $F^2(x, y) = (x + y, 0)$ (Note $F^2 = F$.); (f) $G^2(x, y) = (-x, -y)$.
[Note $G^2 + I = 0$, hence G is a zero of $f(t) = t^2 + 1$.]

8.90. (a) $T^{-1}(x, y) = (-3x + 2y, 2x - y)$; (b) $T^{-1}(x, y) = (-4x + 3y, -3x + 2y)$

8.91. (a) $T^{-1}(x, y, z) = (x + 3y + 14z, y - 4z, z)$; (b) $T^{-1}(x, y, z) = (y + z, y, x - y - z)$

8.92. (a) 49; (b) 36; (c) 144

8.93. Squares: 9, 25, 36, 64, 100

8.94. (a) $f(T(x, y)) = (6x + 14y, 21x + 27y)$; (b) $T(x, y) = (0, 0)$, i.e., $f(T) = 0$

Chapter 9

Linear Mappings and Matrix Representations

9.1 INTRODUCTION

Consider a basis $S = \{u_1, u_2, \ldots, u_n\}$ of a vector space V over a field K. For any vector $v \in V$, suppose

$$v = a_1 u_1 + a_2 u_2 + \cdots + a_n u_n$$

Then the coordinate vector of v relative to the basis S, which we write as a column vector unless otherwise stated or implied, is denoted and defined by

$$[v]_S = \begin{bmatrix} a_1 \\ a_2 \\ \cdots \\ a_n \end{bmatrix} = [a_1, a_2, \ldots, a_n]^T$$

Recall (Section 6.3) that the mapping $v \mapsto [v]_S$, determined by the basis S, is an isomorphism between V and K^n.

This chapter shows that there is also an isomorphism, determined by the basis S, between the algebra $A(V)$ of linear operators on V and the algebra $\mathbf{M}$ of n-square matrices over K. Thus every linear mapping $F: V \to V$ will correspond to an n-square matrix $[F]_S$ determined by the basis S. We will also show how our matrix representation changes when we choose another basis.

9.2 MATRIX REPRESENTATION OF A LINEAR OPERATOR

Let T be a linear operator (transformation) from a vector space V into itself, and suppose $S = \{u_1, u_2, \ldots, u_n\}$ is a basis of V. Now $T(u_1), T(u_2), \ldots, T(u_n)$ are vectors in V, and so each is a linear combination of the vectors in the basis S, say

$$T(u_1) = a_{11} u_1 + a_{12} u_2 + \cdots + a_{1n} u_n$$
$$T(u_2) = a_{21} u_1 + a_{22} u_2 + \cdots + a_{2n} u_n$$
$$\cdots\cdots\cdots\cdots\cdots\cdots\cdots\cdots\cdots\cdots\cdots\cdots\cdots$$
$$T(u_n) = a_{n1} u_1 + a_{n2} u_2 + \cdots + a_{nn} u_n$$

The following definition applies.

Definition: The transpose of the above matrix of coefficients, denoted by $m_S(T)$ or $[T]_S$, is called the *matrix representation* of T relative to the basis S, or simply the matrix

327

of T in the basis S, that is,

$$m_S(T) = [T]_S = \begin{bmatrix} a_{11} & a_{21} & \cdots & a_{n1} \\ a_{12} & a_{22} & \cdots & a_{n2} \\ \cdots\cdots\cdots\cdots\cdots\cdots \\ a_{1n} & a_{2n} & \cdots & a_{nn} \end{bmatrix}$$

(The subscript S may be omitted if the basis S is understood.)

Remark: Using the coordinate (column) vector notation, the matrix representation of T may also be written in the form

$$m(T) = [T] = ([T(u_1)], [T(u_2)], \ldots, [T(u_n)])$$

that is, the columns of $m(T)$ are the coordinate vectors $[T(u_1)], \ldots, [T(u_n)]$.

EXAMPLE 9.1 Consider the following linear mapping $F: \mathbf{R}^2 \to \mathbf{R}^2$ and bases S and E of $\mathbf{R}^2$:

$$F\left(\begin{bmatrix} x \\ y \end{bmatrix}\right) = \begin{bmatrix} 2x + 3y \\ 4x - 5y \end{bmatrix}, \qquad S = \{u_1, u_2\} = \left\{\begin{bmatrix} 1 \\ 2 \end{bmatrix}, \begin{bmatrix} 2 \\ 5 \end{bmatrix}\right\}, \qquad E = \{e_1, e_2\} = \left\{\begin{bmatrix} 1 \\ 0 \end{bmatrix}, \begin{bmatrix} 0 \\ 1 \end{bmatrix}\right\}$$

(a)   Find the matrix representation of F relative to the basis S.

First find $F(u_1)$, and then write $F(u_1)$ as a linear combination of u_1 and u_2. We have

$$F(u_1) = F\left(\begin{bmatrix} 1 \\ 2 \end{bmatrix}\right) = \begin{bmatrix} 8 \\ -6 \end{bmatrix} = x\begin{bmatrix} 1 \\ 2 \end{bmatrix} + y\begin{bmatrix} 2 \\ 5 \end{bmatrix} \qquad \text{and} \qquad \begin{matrix} x + 2y = 8 \\ 2x + 5y = -6 \end{matrix}$$

Solve the system to obtain $x = 52$, $y = -22$. Accordingly,

$$F(u_1) = 52u_1 - 22u_2$$

Next find $F(u_2)$ and then write $F(u_2)$ as a linear combination of u_1 and u_2. We have

$$F(u_2) = F\left(\begin{bmatrix} 2 \\ 5 \end{bmatrix}\right) = \begin{bmatrix} 19 \\ -17 \end{bmatrix} = x\begin{bmatrix} 1 \\ 2 \end{bmatrix} + y\begin{bmatrix} 2 \\ 5 \end{bmatrix} \qquad \text{and} \qquad \begin{matrix} x + 2y = 19 \\ 2x + 5y = -17 \end{matrix}$$

Solve the system to get $x = 129$, $y = -55$. Thus

$$F(u_2) = 129u_1 - 55u_2$$

Accordingly,

$$[F]_S = \begin{bmatrix} 52 & 129 \\ -22 & -55 \end{bmatrix}$$

(b)   Find the matrix representation of F relative to the basis E.

Find $F(e_1)$ and then write $F(e_1)$ as a linear combination of e_1 and e_2, and then repeat the process for $F(e_2)$. We have

$$F(e_1) = \left(\begin{bmatrix} 1 \\ 0 \end{bmatrix}\right) = \begin{bmatrix} 2 \\ 4 \end{bmatrix} = 2e_1 + 4e_2 \qquad \text{and} \qquad F(e_2) = \left(\begin{bmatrix} 0 \\ 1 \end{bmatrix}\right) = \begin{bmatrix} 3 \\ -5 \end{bmatrix} = 3e_1 - 5e_2$$

Accordingly,

$$[F]_E = \begin{bmatrix} 2 & 3 \\ 4 & -5 \end{bmatrix}$$

(Observe that the arithmetic is much simpler using the usual basis of $\mathbf{R}^2$.)

EXAMPLE 9.2 Let V be the vector space of polynomials in t over $\mathbf{R}$ of degree ≤ 3, and let $\mathbf{D}: V \to V$ be the differential operator defined by $\mathbf{D}(p(t)) = d(p(t))/dt$. We compute the matrix of $\mathbf{D}$ in the basis $\{1, t, t^2, t^3\}$, as follows:

$$
\begin{aligned}
\mathbf{D}(1) &= 0 = 0 + 0t + 0t^2 + 0t^3 \\
\mathbf{D}(t) &= 1 = 1 + 0t + 0t^2 + 0t^3 \\
\mathbf{D}(t^2) &= 2t = 0 + 2t + 0t^2 + 0t^3 \\
\mathbf{D}(t^3) &= 3t^2 = 0 + 0t + 3t^2 + 0t^3
\end{aligned}
\qquad \text{and} \qquad
[\mathbf{D}] =
\begin{bmatrix}
0 & 1 & 0 & 0 \\
0 & 0 & 2 & 0 \\
0 & 0 & 0 & 3 \\
0 & 0 & 0 & 0
\end{bmatrix}
$$

[Note that the coordinate vectors of $\mathbf{D}(1)$, $\mathbf{D}(t)$, $\mathbf{D}(t^2)$, $\mathbf{D}(t^3)$ are the columns, not the rows, of $[\mathbf{D}]$.]

Matrix Mappings and Their Matrix Representation

Consider the square matrix $A = \begin{bmatrix} 3 & -2 \\ 4 & -5 \end{bmatrix}$, which may be viewed as a linear mapping from $\mathbf{R}^2$ into itself, and consider the following bases of $\mathbf{R}^2$:

$$
S = \{u_1, u_2\} = \left\{ \begin{bmatrix} 1 \\ 2 \end{bmatrix}, \begin{bmatrix} 2 \\ 5 \end{bmatrix} \right\}, \qquad
E = \{e_1, e_2\} = \left\{ \begin{bmatrix} 1 \\ 0 \end{bmatrix}, \begin{bmatrix} 0 \\ 1 \end{bmatrix} \right\}
$$

We find the matrix representation of A relative to the basis S. First we write $A(u_1)$ as a linear combination of u_1 and u_2. We have

$$
A(u_1) = \begin{bmatrix} 3 & -2 \\ 4 & -5 \end{bmatrix} \begin{bmatrix} 1 \\ 2 \end{bmatrix} = \begin{bmatrix} -1 \\ -6 \end{bmatrix} = x \begin{bmatrix} 1 \\ 2 \end{bmatrix} + y \begin{bmatrix} 2 \\ 5 \end{bmatrix}
\qquad \text{and so} \qquad
\begin{aligned}
x + 2y &= -1 \\
2x + 5y &= -6
\end{aligned}
$$

Solving the system yields $x = 7$, $y = -4$. Thus

$$
A(u_1) = 7u_1 - 4u_2
$$

Next we write $A(u_2)$ as a linear combination of u_1 and u_2. We have

$$
A(u_2) = \begin{bmatrix} 3 & -2 \\ 4 & -5 \end{bmatrix} \begin{bmatrix} 2 \\ 5 \end{bmatrix} = \begin{bmatrix} -4 \\ -17 \end{bmatrix} = x \begin{bmatrix} 1 \\ 2 \end{bmatrix} + y \begin{bmatrix} 2 \\ 5 \end{bmatrix}
\qquad \text{and so} \qquad
\begin{aligned}
x + 2y &= -4 \\
2x + 5y &= -17
\end{aligned}
$$

Solving the system yields $x = 14$, $y = -9$. Thus

$$
A(u_2) = 14u_1 - 9u_2
$$

Writing the coordinates of $A(u_1)$ and $A(u_2)$ as columns gives us the following matrix representation of A:

$$
[A]_S = \begin{bmatrix} 7 & 14 \\ -4 & -9 \end{bmatrix}
$$

Now we find the matrix representation of A relative to the usual basis E of $\mathbf{R}^2$. We have

$$
A(e_1) = \begin{bmatrix} 3 & -2 \\ 4 & -5 \end{bmatrix} \begin{bmatrix} 1 \\ 0 \end{bmatrix} = \begin{bmatrix} 3 \\ 4 \end{bmatrix} = 3e_1 + 4e_2
$$

$$
A(e_2) = \begin{bmatrix} 3 & -2 \\ 4 & -5 \end{bmatrix} \begin{bmatrix} 0 \\ 1 \end{bmatrix} = \begin{bmatrix} -2 \\ -5 \end{bmatrix} = -2e_1 - 5e_2
$$

Thus
$$
[A]_E = \begin{bmatrix} 3 & -2 \\ 4 & -5 \end{bmatrix}
$$

which is the original matrix A.   This result is true in general.   That is,

> The matrix representation of any square matrix A relative to the usual basis E is the matrix A itself, that is,
>
> $$[A]_E = A$$

Algorithm for Finding Matrix Representation

Next follows a formal algorithm for finding the matrix representation of an arbitrary linear operator.   The first step, Step 0, is optional.   It may be useful to use it in Step 1(b), which is repeated for each basis vector.

Algorithm 9.2:   The input is a linear operator T on a vector space V and a basis $S = \{u_1, u_2, \ldots, u_n\}$.   The output is the matrix representation $[T]_S$.

Step 0.   Find a formula for the coordinates of an arbitrary vector v relative to the basis S.

Step 1.   Repeat for each basis vector u_k in S:

    (a)   Find $T(u_k)$.

    (b)   Write $T(u_k)$ as a linear combination of the basis vectors $u_1, \ldots, u_n$ to obtain the coordinates of $T(u_k)$ in the basis S.

Step 2.   Form the matrix $[T]_S$ whose columns are the coordinate vectors $[T(u_k)]_S$ obtained in Step 1(b).

Step 3.   Exit.

EXAMPLE 9.3   Find the matrix representation $[F]_S$ of the linear operator $F: \mathbf{R}^2 \to \mathbf{R}^2$ defined by $F(x, y) = (2x + 3y, 4x - 5y)$ relative to the basis $S = \{u_1, u_2\} = \{(1, -2), (2, -5)\}$.

(*Step 0*)   First we find the coordinates of an arbitrary vector $(a, b) \in \mathbf{R}^2$ relative to the basis S. We have

$$\begin{bmatrix} a \\ b \end{bmatrix} = x \begin{bmatrix} 1 \\ -2 \end{bmatrix} + y \begin{bmatrix} 2 \\ -5 \end{bmatrix} \quad \text{or} \quad \begin{array}{l} x + 2y = a \\ -2x - 5y = b \end{array} \quad \text{or} \quad \begin{array}{l} x + 2y = a \\ -y = 2a + b \end{array}$$

Solving for x and y in terms of a and b yields $x = 5a + 2b$, $y = -2a - b$.   Thus

$$(a, b) = (5a + 2b)u_1 + (-2a - b)u_2$$

(*Step 1*)   Now we find $F(u_1)$ and write it as a linear combination of u_1 and u_2 using the above formula for (a, b), and then we repeat the process for $F(u_2)$.   We have

$$F(u_1) = F(1, -2) = (-4, 14) \;\; = \;\; 8u_1 - \;\; 6u_2$$
$$F(u_2) = F(2, -5) = (-11, 33) = 11u_1 - 11u_2$$

(*Step 2*)   Lastly, we write the coordinates of $F(u_1)$ and $F(u_2)$ as columns to obtain the required matrix

$$[F]_S = \begin{bmatrix} 8 & 11 \\ -6 & -11 \end{bmatrix}$$

9.3   PROPERTIES OF MATRIX REPRESENTATIONS

This section gives the main properties of the matrix representations of linear operators T on a vector space V.   We emphasize that we are always given a particular basis S of V.

Our first theorem, proved in Problem 9.21, tells us that the "action" of an operator T on a vector v is preserved by its matrix representation.

Theorem 9.1:   Let $S = \{u_1, u_2, \ldots, u_n\}$ be a basis for V and let T be any linear operator on V. Then, for any vector $v \in V$, $[T]_S[v]_S = [T(v)]_S$.

That is, if we multiply the coordinate vector of v by the matrix representation of T, then we obtain the coordinate vector of $T(v)$.

EXAMPLE 9.4

(a)   Consider the differential operator $\mathbf{D} : V \to V$, where $V = \mathbf{P}_3(t)$, the vector space of polynomials of degree ≤ 3.   Let
$$f(t) = 3 + 5t - 4t^2 + 2t^3 \quad \text{and so} \quad \mathbf{D}(f) = 5 - 8t + 6t^2$$
Hence relative to the basis $\{1, t, t^2, t^3\}$,
$$[f] = [3, 5, -4, 2]^T \quad \text{and} \quad [\mathbf{D}(f)] = [5, -8, 6, 0]^T$$
Using the matrix representation of $\mathbf{D}$ obtained in Example 9.2, we show that Theorem 9.1 does hold here for the polynomial f:
$$[\mathbf{D}][f] = \begin{bmatrix} 0 & 1 & 0 & 0 \\ 0 & 0 & 2 & 0 \\ 0 & 0 & 0 & 3 \\ 0 & 0 & 0 & 0 \end{bmatrix} \begin{bmatrix} 3 \\ 5 \\ -4 \\ 2 \end{bmatrix} = \begin{bmatrix} 5 \\ -8 \\ 6 \\ 0 \end{bmatrix} = [\mathbf{D}(f)]$$

(b)   Consider the linear operator $F(x, y) = (2x + 3y, 4x - 5y)$ and the basis
$$S = \{u_1, u_2\} = \{(1, -2), (2, -5)\}$$
of $\mathbf{R}^2$ in Example 9.3.   Let
$$v = (5, -7) \quad \text{and so} \quad F(v) = (-11, 55)$$
Using the formula from Example 9.3, we get
$$[v] = [11, -3]^T \quad \text{and} \quad [F(v)] = [55, -33]^T$$
We show that Theorem 9.1 holds here for the vector v (where $[F]$ is obtained from Example 9.3):
$$[F][v] = \begin{bmatrix} 8 & 11 \\ -6 & -11 \end{bmatrix} \begin{bmatrix} 11 \\ -3 \end{bmatrix} = \begin{bmatrix} 55 \\ -33 \end{bmatrix} = [F(v)]$$

Given a basis S of a vector space V, we have associated a matrix $[T]$ to each T in $A(V)$, the algebra of linear operators on V.   Theorem 9.1 told us that the "action" of an individual linear operator T is preserved by this representation.   The next two theorems (proved in Problems 9.22 and 9.23) tell us that the three basic operations with these operators, (i) addition, (ii) scalar multiplication, and (iii) composition, are also preserved.

Theorem 9.2:   Let $S = \{u_1, u_2, \ldots, u_n\}$ be a basis for a vector space V over K, and let $\mathbf{M}$ be the algebra of n-square matrices over K.   Then the mapping $m : A(V) \to \mathbf{M}$ defined by $m(T) = [T]_S$ is a vector space isomorphism.   That is, for any $F, G \in A(V)$ and any $k \in K$, we have

(i) $m(F + G) = m(F) + m(G)$ or $[F + G] = [F] + [G]$

(ii) $m(kF) = km(F)$ or $[kF] = k[F]$

(iii) m is one-to-one and onto.

Theorem 9.3:   For any linear operators $G, F \in A(v)$,

$$m(G \circ F) = m(G)m(F) \qquad \text{or} \qquad [G \circ F] = [G][F]$$

(Here $G \circ F$ denotes the composition of the maps G and F.)

9.4 CHANGE OF BASIS AND MATRIX REPRESENTATION OF LINEAR OPERATORS

The above discussion shows that we can represent a linear operator by a matrix once we have chosen a basis.   We ask the following natural question: How does our representation change if we select another basis?   In order to answer this question, we first recall a definition and some facts.

Definition: Let $S = \{u_1, u_2, \ldots, u_n\}$ be a basis of V and let $S' = \{v_1, v_2, \ldots, v_n\}$ be another basis.   Suppose, for $i = 1, 2, \ldots, n$,

$$v_i = a_{i1}u_1 + a_{i2}u_2 + \cdots + a_{in}u_n$$

The transpose P of the above matrix of coefficients is termed the change-of-basis (or transition) matrix from the "old" basis S to the "new" basis S'.

Fact 1:   The above change-of-basis matrix P is invertible, and its inverse P^{-1} is the change-of-basis matrix from S' back to S.

Fact 2:   Let P be the change-of-basis matrix from the usual basis E of K^n to another basis S.   Then P is the matrix whose columns are precisely the elements of S.

Fact 3:   Let P be the change-of-basis matrix from a basis S to a basis S' in V.   Then (Theorem 6.3) for any vector $v \in V$,

$$P[v]_{S'} = [v]_S \qquad \text{and} \qquad P^{-1}[v]_S = [v]_{S'}$$

(Thus P^{-1} transforms the coordinates of v in the old basis S to the new basis S'.)

The following theorem, proved in Problem 9.25, answers the above question, that is, shows how the matrix representation of a linear operator is affected by a change of basis.

Theorem 9.4:   Let P be the change-of-basis matrix from a basis S to a basis S' in a vector space V.   Then, for any linear operator T on V,

$$[T]_{S'} = P^{-1}[T]_S P$$

In other words, if A is the matrix representing T in a basis S, then $B = P^{-1}AP$ is the matrix that represents T in a new basis S', where P is the change-of-basis matrix from S to S'.

EXAMPLE 9.5   Consider the following bases of $\mathbf{R}^2$:

$$E = \{e_1, e_2\} = \{(1, 0), (0, 1)\} \qquad \text{and} \qquad S = \{u_1, u_2\} = \{(1, -2), (2, -5)\}$$

Since E is the usual basis of $\mathbf{R}^2$, we write the basis vectors in S as columns to obtain the change-of-basis matrix P from E to S.   Thus

$$P = \begin{bmatrix} 1 & 2 \\ -2 & -5 \end{bmatrix} \qquad \text{and so} \qquad P^{-1} = \begin{bmatrix} 5 & 2 \\ -2 & -1 \end{bmatrix}$$

(where we obtain P^{-1} by using the formula for the inverse of a 2×2 matrix in Section 3.4).   Consider the linear operator F on $\mathbf{R}^2$ defined by $F(x, y) = (2x + 3y, 4x - 5y)$.   We have

$$F(e_1) = F(1, 0) = (2, 4) \quad = 2e_1 + 4e_2$$
$$F(e_2) = F(0, 1) = (3, -5) = 3e_1 - 5e_2 \quad \text{and so} \quad A = \begin{bmatrix} 2 & 3 \\ 4 & -5 \end{bmatrix}$$

is the matrix representation of F relative to the usual basis E.   By Theorem 9.4,

$$B = P^{-1}AP = \begin{bmatrix} 5 & 2 \\ -2 & -1 \end{bmatrix} \begin{bmatrix} 2 & 3 \\ 4 & -5 \end{bmatrix} \begin{bmatrix} 1 & 2 \\ -2 & -5 \end{bmatrix} = \begin{bmatrix} 8 & 11 \\ -6 & -11 \end{bmatrix}$$

is the matrix representation of F relative to the basis S.   Observe that this agrees with the direct calculation of $B = [F]_S$ in Example 9.3.

Remark: Suppose $P = [a_{ij}]$ is any n-square invertible matrix over a field K, and suppose $S = \{u_1, u_2, \ldots, u_n\}$ is a basis for a vector space V over K.   Then the n vectors

$$v_i = a_{1i}u_1 + a_{2i}u_2 + \cdots + a_{ni}u_n, \quad i = 1, 2, \ldots, n$$

are linearly independent, and hence they form another basis S' for V.   Furthermore, P is the change-of-basis matrix from the basis S to the basis S'.   Accordingly if A is any matrix representation of a linear operator T on V, then the matrix $B = P^{-1}AP$ is also a matrix representation of T.

9.5 SIMILARITY AND LINEAR OPERATORS

Suppose A and B are square matrices for which there exists an invertible matrix P such that $B = P^{-1}AP$.   Then B is said to be *similar* to A, or B is said to be obtained from A by a *similarity transformation*.   We note (see Problem 9.14) that similarity is an equivalence relation.

By Theorem 9.4 and the above remark we have the following basic result.

Theorem 9.5:   Two matrices represent the same linear operator if and only if the matrices are similar.

That is, all the matrix representations of a linear operator T form an equivalence class of similar matrices.

Functions and Similar Matrices

Suppose f is a function on square matrices which assigns the same value to similar matrices, that is, $f(A) = f(B)$ whenever A is similar to B.   Then f induces a function, also denoted by f, on linear operators T in the following natural way.   We define

$$f(T) = f([T]_S)$$

where S is any basis.   The function is well-defined by Theorem 9.5.

The determinant (Chapter 10) is perhaps the most important example of such a function.   The trace (Section 3.2) is another important example of such a function.

EXAMPLE 9.6   Let F be the linear operator on $\mathbf{R}^2$ defined by $F(x, y) = (2x + 3y, 4x - 5y)$. By Example 9.5, the matrix representations of F relative to the usual basis E and the basis $S = \{(1, -2), (2, -5)\}$ are

$$A = \begin{bmatrix} 2 & 3 \\ 4 & -5 \end{bmatrix}, \qquad B = \begin{bmatrix} 8 & 11 \\ -6 & -11 \end{bmatrix}$$

Using matrix A, we have

(i)   det (F) = det $(A) = -10 - 12 = -22$ is the determinant of F.

(ii)   tr (F) = tr $(A) = 2 - 5 = -3$ is the trace of F.

Using matrix B, we have

(i)   det (F) = det $(B) = -88 + 66 = -22$ is the determinant of F.

(ii)   tr (F) = tr $(B) = 8 - 11 = -3$ is the trace of F.

As expected, both matrices yield the same result.

9.6   MATRICES AND GENERAL LINEAR MAPPINGS

Lastly we consider the general case of linear mappings from one vector space into another. Suppose V and U are vector spaces over the same field $\mathbf{K}$ and, say, dim $V = m$ and dim $U = n$. Furthermore, suppose

$$S = \{v_1, v_2, \ldots, v_m\} \qquad \text{and} \qquad S' = \{u_1, u_2, \ldots, u_n\}$$

are arbitrary but fixed bases of V and U, respectively.

Suppose $F: \; V \to U$ is a linear mapping. Then the vectors $F(v_1), F(v_2), \ldots, F(v_m)$ belong to U, and so each is a linear combination of the basis vectors in S', say

$$F(v_1) = a_{11}u_1 + a_{12}u_2 + \cdots + a_{1n}u_n$$
$$F(v_2) = a_{21}u_1 + a_{22}u_2 + \cdots + a_{2n}u_n$$
$$\cdots\cdots\cdots\cdots\cdots\cdots\cdots\cdots\cdots\cdots\cdots$$
$$F(v_m) = a_{m1}u_1 + a_{m2}u_2 + \cdots + a_{mn}u_n$$

The transpose of the above matrix of coefficients, denoted by $m_{S, S'}(F)$ or $[F]_{S, S'}$, is called the *matrix representation* of F relative to the bases S and S', that is,

$$m_{S, S'}(F) = [F]_{S, S'} = \begin{bmatrix} a_{11} & a_{21} & \ldots & a_{m1} \\ a_{12} & a_{22} & \ldots & a_{m2} \\ \cdots\cdots\cdots\cdots\cdots\cdots\cdots \\ a_{1n} & a_{2n} & \ldots & a_{mn} \end{bmatrix}$$

(We will use the simple notation $m(F)$ and $[F]$ when the bases are understood.)

The following theorem is analogous to Theorem 9.1 for linear operators.

Theorem 9.6:   For any vector $v \in V$, $[F]_{S, S'}[v]_S = [F(v)]_{S'}$.

That is, multiplying the coordinate vector of v (relative to the basis S of V) by $[F]$, we obtain the coordinate vector of $F(v)$ (relative to the basis S' of U).

Recall that for any vector spaces V and U, the collection of all linear mappings from V into U is a vector space and is denoted by Hom(V, U). Recall also that we let $\mathbf{M} = \mathbf{M}_{m, n}$ denote the vector space of all $m \times n$ matrices. The following theorem is analogous to the above Theorem 9.2 for linear operators.

Theorem 9.7:   The mapping m: Hom $(V, U) \to$ **M** defined by $m(F) = [F]$ is an isomorphism. That is, for any $F, G \in$ Hom(V, U) and any scalar k,

 (i) $m(F + G) = m(F) + m(G)$ or $[F + G] = [F] + [G]$.

 (ii) $m(kF) = km(F)$ or $[kF] = k[F]$.

 (iii)   The mapping m is one-to-one and onto.

Our last theorem (proved in Problem 9.26) shows that any linear mapping from one vector space V into another vector space U can be represented by a very simple matrix.   This theorem is analogous to Theorem 3.14 for $m \times n$ matrices.

Theorem 9.8:   Let $F: V \to U$ be linear and, say, rank $(F) = r$.   Then there exist bases of V and of U such that the matrix representation of F has the form

$$A = \begin{bmatrix} I_r & 0 \\ 0 & 0 \end{bmatrix}$$

where I_r is the r-square identity matrix.

The above matrix A is called the *normal* or *canonical* form of the linear map F.

Solved Problems

MATRIX REPRESENTATION OF LINEAR OPERATORS

9.1.   Consider the linear mapping $F: \mathbf{R}^2 \to \mathbf{R}^2$ defined by $F(x, y) = (3x + 4y, 2x - 5y)$ and the following bases of $\mathbf{R}^2$:

$$E = \{e_1, e_2\} = \{(1, 0), (0, 1)\} \quad \text{and} \quad S = \{u_1, u_2\} = \{(1, 2), (2, 3)\}$$

(a)   Find the matrix A representing F relative to the basis E.

(b)   Find the matrix B representing F relative to the basis S.

(c)   Verify $B = P^{-1}AP$, where P is the change-of-basis matrix from the basis E to S.

(a)   Since E is the usual basis, the rows of A are simply the coefficients in the components of $F(x, y)$, that is, using $(a, b) = ae_1 + be_2$, we have

$$\begin{aligned} F(e_1) &= F(1, 0) = (3, 2) &= 3e_1 + 2e_2 \\ F(e_2) &= F(0, 1) = (4, -5) = 4e_1 - 5e_2 \end{aligned} \quad \text{and so} \quad A = \begin{bmatrix} 3 & 4 \\ 2 & -5 \end{bmatrix}$$

Note that the coefficients of the basis vectors are written as columns in the matrix representation.

(b)   First find $F(u_1)$ and write it as a linear combination of the basis vectors u_1 and u_2. We have

$$F(u_1) = F(1, 2) = (11, -8) = x(1, 2) + y(2, 3) \quad \text{and so} \quad \begin{aligned} x + 2y &= 11 \\ 2x + 3y &= -8 \end{aligned}$$

Solve the system to obtain $x = -49, y = 30$.   Therefore

$$F(u_1) = -49u_1 + 30u_2$$

Next find $F(u_2)$ and write it as a linear combination of the basis vectors u_1 and u_2. We have

$$F(u_2) = F(2, 3) = (18, -11) = x(1, 2) + y(2, 3) \qquad \text{and so} \qquad \begin{aligned} x + 2y &= 18 \\ 2x + 3y &= -11 \end{aligned}$$

Solve for x and y to obtain $x = -76$, $y = 47$. Hence

$$F(u_2) = -76u_1 + 47u_2$$

Write the coefficients of u_1 and u_2 as columns to obtain

$$B = \begin{bmatrix} -49 & -76 \\ 30 & 47 \end{bmatrix}$$

(b')   Alternately, one can first find the coordinates of an arbitrary vector (a, b) in $\mathbf{R}^2$ relative to the basis S. We have

$$(a, b) = x(1, 2) + y(2, 3) = (x + 2y, 2x + 3y) \qquad \text{and so} \qquad \begin{aligned} x + 2y &= a \\ 2x + 3y &= b \end{aligned}$$

Solve for x and y in terms of a and b to get $x = -3a + 2b$, $y = 2a - b$. Thus

$$(a, b) = (-3a + 2b)u_1 + (2a - b)u_2$$

Then use the formula for (a, b) to find the coordinates of $F(u_1)$ and $F(u_2)$ relative to S,

$$\begin{aligned} F(u_1) &= F(1, 2) = (11, -8) = -49u_1 + 30u_2 \\ F(u_2) &= F(2, 3) = (18, -11) = -76u_1 + 47u_2 \end{aligned} \qquad \text{and so} \qquad B = \begin{bmatrix} -49 & -76 \\ 30 & 47 \end{bmatrix}$$

(c)   Since P is the change-of-basis matrix from the usual basis E to S, write the vectors in S as the columns of P and use the formula for the inverse of a 2×2 matrix to obtain P^{-1}. Thus

$$P = \begin{bmatrix} 1 & 2 \\ 2 & 3 \end{bmatrix} \qquad \text{and} \qquad P^{-1} = \begin{bmatrix} -3 & 2 \\ 2 & -1 \end{bmatrix}$$

Then

$$P^{-1}AP = \begin{bmatrix} -3 & 2 \\ 2 & -1 \end{bmatrix} \begin{bmatrix} 3 & 4 \\ 2 & -5 \end{bmatrix} \begin{bmatrix} 1 & 2 \\ 2 & 3 \end{bmatrix} = \begin{bmatrix} -49 & -76 \\ 30 & 47 \end{bmatrix} = B$$

(as expected by Theorem 9.4).

9.2.   Consider the following linear operators G on $\mathbf{R}^2$ and basis S:

$$G(x, y) = (2x - 7y, 4x + 3y) \qquad \text{and} \qquad S = \{u_1, u_2\} = \{(1, 3), (2, 5)\}$$

(a)   Find the matrix representation $[G]_S$ of G relative to S.

(b)   Verify $[G]_S[v]_S = [G(v)]_S$ for the vector $v = (4, -3)$ in $\mathbf{R}^2$.

First find the coordinates of an arbitrary vector $v = (a, b)$ in $\mathbf{R}^2$ relative to the basis S. We have

$$\begin{bmatrix} a \\ b \end{bmatrix} = x \begin{bmatrix} 1 \\ 3 \end{bmatrix} + y \begin{bmatrix} 2 \\ 5 \end{bmatrix} \qquad \text{and so} \qquad \begin{aligned} x + 2y &= a \\ 3x + 5y &= b \end{aligned}$$

Solve for x and y in terms of a and b to get $x = -5a + 2b$, $y = 3a - b$. Thus

$$(a, b) = (-5a + 2b)u_1 + (3a - b)u_2 \qquad \text{and so} \qquad [v] = [-5a + 2b, 3a - b]^T$$

(a)   Using the formula for (a, b) and $G(x, y) = (2x - 7y, 4x + 3y)$, we have

$$G(u_1) = G(1, 3) = (-19, 13) = 121u_1 - 70u_2$$
$$G(u_2) = G(2, 5) = (-31, 23) = 201u_1 - 116u_2$$

and so $[G]_S = \begin{bmatrix} 121 & 201 \\ -70 & -116 \end{bmatrix}$

(We emphasize that the coefficients of u_1 and u_2 are written as columns, not rows, in the matrix representation.)

(b)   Use the formula $(a, b) = (-5a + 2b)u_1 + (3a - b)u_2$ to get

$$v = (4, -3) = -26u_1 + 15u_2$$
$$G(v) = G(4, -3) = (29, 7) = -131u_1 + 80u_2$$

Then

$$[v]_S = [-26, 15]^T \quad \text{and} \quad [G(v)]_S = [-131, 80]^T$$

Accordingly,

$$[G]_S[v]_S = \begin{bmatrix} 121 & 201 \\ -70 & -116 \end{bmatrix} \begin{bmatrix} -26 \\ 15 \end{bmatrix} = \begin{bmatrix} -131 \\ 80 \end{bmatrix} = [G(v)]_S$$

(as expected by Theorem 9.1).

9.3.   Consider the following 2×2 matrix A and basis S of $\mathbf{R}^2$:

$$A = \begin{bmatrix} 2 & 4 \\ 5 & 6 \end{bmatrix} \quad \text{and} \quad S = \{u_1, u_2\} = \left\{ \begin{bmatrix} 1 \\ -2 \end{bmatrix}, \begin{bmatrix} 3 \\ -7 \end{bmatrix} \right\}$$

The matrix A defines a linear operator on $\mathbf{R}^2$. Find the matrix B that represents the mapping A relative to the basis S.

Method 1:   First find the coordinates of an arbitrary vector $(a, b)^T$ with respect to the basis S.   We have

$$\begin{bmatrix} a \\ b \end{bmatrix} = x \begin{bmatrix} 1 \\ -2 \end{bmatrix} + y \begin{bmatrix} 3 \\ -7 \end{bmatrix} \quad \text{or} \quad \begin{array}{c} x + 3y = a \\ -2x - 7y = b \end{array}$$

Solve for x and y in terms of a and b to obtain $x = 7a + 3b$, $y = -2a - b$. Thus

$$(a, b)^T = (7a + 3b)u_1 + (-2a - b)u_2$$

Then use the formula for $(a, b)^T$ to find the coordinates of Au_1 and Au_2 relative to the basis S:

$$Au_1 = \begin{bmatrix} 2 & 4 \\ 5 & 6 \end{bmatrix} \begin{bmatrix} 1 \\ -2 \end{bmatrix} = \begin{bmatrix} -6 \\ -7 \end{bmatrix} = -63u_1 + 19u_2$$

$$Au_2 = \begin{bmatrix} 2 & 4 \\ 5 & 6 \end{bmatrix} \begin{bmatrix} 3 \\ -7 \end{bmatrix} = \begin{bmatrix} -22 \\ -27 \end{bmatrix} = -235u_1 + 71u_2$$

Writing the coordinates as columns yields

$$B = \begin{bmatrix} -63 & -235 \\ 19 & 71 \end{bmatrix}$$

Method 2:   By Theorem 9.4, $B = P^{-1}AP$, where P is the change-of-basis matrix from the usual basis E to S.   Write the vectors in S as columns to get P, and use the formula for the inverse of a 2×2 matrix to get P^{-1}. Thus

$$P = \begin{bmatrix} 1 & 3 \\ -2 & -7 \end{bmatrix} \quad \text{and} \quad P^{-1} = \begin{bmatrix} 7 & 3 \\ -2 & -1 \end{bmatrix}$$

Then

$$B = P^{-1}AP = \begin{bmatrix} 7 & 3 \\ -2 & -1 \end{bmatrix}\begin{bmatrix} 2 & 4 \\ 5 & 6 \end{bmatrix}\begin{bmatrix} 1 & 3 \\ -2 & -7 \end{bmatrix} = \begin{bmatrix} -63 & -235 \\ 19 & 71 \end{bmatrix}$$

9.4. Find the matrix representation of each linear operator F on $\mathbf{R}^3$ relative to the usual basis $E = \{e_1, e_2, e_3\}$ of $\mathbf{R}^3$, that is, find $[F] = [F]_E$:

(a) F defined by $F(x, y, z) = (x + 2y - 3z, 4x - 5y - 6z, 7x + 8y + 9z)$.

(b) F defined by the 3×3 matrix $A = \begin{bmatrix} 1 & 1 & 1 \\ 2 & 3 & 4 \\ 5 & 5 & 5 \end{bmatrix}$.

(c) F defined by $F(e_1) = (1, 3, 5)$, $F(e_2) = (2, 4, 6)$, $F(e_3) = (7, 7, 7)$.   (Theorem 8.2 states that a linear map is completely defined by its action on the vectors in a basis.)

(a)   Since E is the usual basis, simply write the coefficients of the components of $F(x, y, z)$ as rows:

$$[F] = \begin{bmatrix} 1 & 2 & -3 \\ 4 & -5 & -6 \\ 7 & 8 & 9 \end{bmatrix}$$

(b)   Since E is the usual basis, $[F] = A$, the matrix A itself.

(c)   Here $\begin{aligned} F(e_1) &= (1, 3, 5) = e_1 + 3e_2 + 5e_3 \\ F(e_2) &= (2, 4, 6) = 2e_1 + 4e_2 + 6e_3 \\ F(e_3) &= (7, 7, 7) = 7e_1 + 7e_2 + 7e_3 \end{aligned}$ and so $[F] = \begin{bmatrix} 1 & 2 & 7 \\ 3 & 4 & 7 \\ 5 & 6 & 7 \end{bmatrix}$

That is, the columns of $[F]$ are the images of the usual basis vectors.

9.5. Let G be the linear operator on $\mathbf{R}^3$ defined by $G(x, y, z) = (2y + z, x - 4y, 3x)$.

(a)   Find the matrix representation of G relative to the basis

$$S = \{w_1, w_2, w_3\} = \{(1, 1, 1), (1, 1, 0), (1, 0, 0)\}$$

(b)   Verify that $[G][v] = [G(v)]$ for any vector v in $\mathbf{R}^3$.

First find the coordinates of an arbitrary vector $(a, b, c) \in \mathbf{R}^3$ with respect to the basis S. Write (a, b, c) as a linear combination of w_1, w_2, w_3 using unknown scalars x, y, and z:

$$(a, b, c) = x(1, 1, 1) + y(1, 1, 0) + z(1, 0, 0) = (x + y + z, x + y, x)$$

Set corresponding components equal to each other to obtain the system of equations

$$x + y + z = a, \qquad x + y = b, \qquad x = c$$

Solve the system for x, y, and z in terms of a, b, and c to find $x = c$, $y = b - c$, $z = a - b$. Thus

$$(a, b, c) = cw_1 + (b - c)w_2 + (a - b)w_3 \qquad \text{or equivalently} \qquad [(a, b, c)] = [c, b - c, a - b]^T$$

(a)   Since $G(x, y, z) = (2y + z, x - 4y, 3x)$,

$$G(w_1) = G(1, 1, 1) = (3, -3, 3) = 3w_1 - 6w_2 + 6w_3$$
$$G(w_2) = G(1, 1, 0) = (2, -3, 3) = 3w_1 - 6w_2 + 5w_3$$
$$G(w_3) = G(1, 0, 0) = (0, 1, 3) = 3w_1 - 2w_2 - w_3$$

Write the coordinates $G(w_1)$, $G(w_2)$, $G(w_3)$ as columns to get

$$[G] = \begin{bmatrix} 3 & 3 & 3 \\ -6 & -6 & -2 \\ 6 & 5 & -1 \end{bmatrix}$$

(b)   Write $G(v)$ as a linear combination of w_1, w_2, w_3, where $v = (a, b, c)$ is an arbitrary vector in $\mathbf{R}^3$,

$$G(v) = G(a, b, c) = (2b + c, a - 4b, 3a) = 3aw_1 + (-2a - 4b)w_2 + (-a + 6b + c)w_3$$

or, equivalently,

$$[G(v)] = [3a, -2a - 4b, -a + 6b + c]^T$$

Accordingly,

$$[G][v] = \begin{bmatrix} 3 & 3 & 3 \\ -6 & -6 & -2 \\ 6 & 5 & -1 \end{bmatrix} \begin{bmatrix} c \\ b - c \\ a - b \end{bmatrix} = \begin{bmatrix} 3a \\ -2a - 4b \\ -a + 6b + c \end{bmatrix} = [G(v)]$$

9.6.   Consider the following 3×3 matrix A and basis S of $\mathbf{R}^3$:

$$A = \begin{bmatrix} 1 & -2 & 1 \\ 3 & -1 & 0 \\ 1 & 4 & 2 \end{bmatrix} \quad \text{and} \quad S = \{u_1, u_2, u_3\} = \left\{ \begin{bmatrix} 1 \\ 1 \\ 1 \end{bmatrix}, \begin{bmatrix} 0 \\ 1 \\ 1 \end{bmatrix}, \begin{bmatrix} 0 \\ 0 \\ 1 \end{bmatrix} \right\}$$

The matrix A defines a linear operator on $\mathbf{R}^3$.   Find the matrix B which represents the mapping A relative to the basis S.   (Recall that A represents itself relative to the usual basis of $\mathbf{R}^3$.)

Method 1:   First find the coordinates of an arbitrary vector (a, b, c) in $\mathbf{R}^3$ with respect to the basis S.   We have

$$\begin{bmatrix} a \\ b \\ c \end{bmatrix} = x \begin{bmatrix} 1 \\ 1 \\ 1 \end{bmatrix} + y \begin{bmatrix} 0 \\ 1 \\ 1 \end{bmatrix} + z \begin{bmatrix} 0 \\ 0 \\ 1 \end{bmatrix} \quad \text{or} \quad \begin{array}{l} x = a \\ x + y = b \\ x + y + z = c \end{array}$$

Solve for x, y, z in terms of a, b, c to get $x = a$, $y = b - a$, $z = c - b$.   Then

$$(a, b, c)^T = au_1 + (b - a)u_2 + (c - b)u_3$$

Then use the formula for $(a, b, c)^T$ to find the coordinates of Au_1, Au_2, Au_3 relative to the basis S:

$$\begin{array}{lll} A(u_1) = A(1, 1, 1)^T = (0, 2, 7)^T & = 0u_1 + 2u_2 + 5u_3 & \\ A(u_2) = A(0, 1, 1)^T = (-1, -1, 6)^T & = -u_1 - 0u_2 + 7u_3 & \text{so} \quad B = \begin{bmatrix} 0 & -1 & 1 \\ 2 & 0 & -1 \\ 5 & 7 & 2 \end{bmatrix} \\ A(u_3) = A(0, 0, 1)^T = (1, 0, 2)^T & = u_1 - u_2 + 2u_3 & \end{array}$$

Method 2:   Use $B = P^{-1}AP$, where $P = \begin{bmatrix} 1 & 0 & 0 \\ 1 & 1 & 0 \\ 1 & 1 & 1 \end{bmatrix}$ is the change-of-basis matrix

from the usual basis E to S.   First find P^{-1} by reducing $M = [P, I]$ to row canonical form.   We have

$$M = \begin{bmatrix} 1 & 0 & 0 & \vdots & 1 & 0 & 0 \\ 1 & 1 & 0 & \vdots & 0 & 1 & 0 \\ 1 & 1 & 1 & \vdots & 0 & 0 & 1 \end{bmatrix} \sim \begin{bmatrix} 1 & 0 & 0 & \vdots & 1 & 0 & 0 \\ 0 & 1 & 0 & \vdots & -1 & 1 & 0 \\ 0 & 1 & 1 & \vdots & -1 & 0 & 1 \end{bmatrix}$$

$$\sim \begin{bmatrix} 1 & 0 & 0 & \vdots & 1 & 0 & 0 \\ 0 & 1 & 0 & \vdots & -1 & 1 & 0 \\ 0 & 0 & 1 & \vdots & 0 & -1 & 1 \end{bmatrix} \quad \text{so} \quad P^{-1} = \begin{bmatrix} 1 & 0 & 0 \\ -1 & 1 & 0 \\ 0 & -1 & 1 \end{bmatrix}$$

Then

$$B = P^{-1}AP = \begin{bmatrix} 1 & 0 & 0 \\ -1 & 1 & 0 \\ 0 & -1 & 1 \end{bmatrix}\begin{bmatrix} 1 & -2 & 1 \\ 3 & -1 & 0 \\ 1 & 4 & 2 \end{bmatrix}\begin{bmatrix} 1 & 0 & 0 \\ 1 & 1 & 0 \\ 1 & 1 & 1 \end{bmatrix} = \begin{bmatrix} 0 & -1 & 1 \\ 2 & 0 & -1 \\ 5 & 7 & 2 \end{bmatrix}$$

9.7.   For each of the following linear transformations (operators) L on $\mathbf{R}^2$, find the matrix A which represents L (relative to the usual basis of $\mathbf{R}^2$):

(a) L is defined by $L(1, 0) = (2, 4)$ and $L(0, 1) = (5, 8)$.

(b) L is the rotation in $\mathbf{R}^2$ counterclockwise by $90°$.

(c) L is the reflection in $\mathbf{R}^2$ about the line $y = -x$.

(a)   Since $(1, 0)$ and $(0, 1)$ do form the usual basis of $\mathbf{R}^2$, write their images under L as columns to get

$$A = \begin{bmatrix} 2 & 5 \\ 4 & 8 \end{bmatrix}$$

(b)   Under the rotation L, we have $L(1, 0) = (0, 1)$ and $L(0, 1) = (-1, 0)$.   Thus $A = \begin{bmatrix} 0 & -1 \\ 1 & 0 \end{bmatrix}$.

(c)   Under the reflection L, we have $L(1, 0) = (0, -1)$ and $L(0, 1) = (-1, 0)$.   Thus $A = \begin{bmatrix} 0 & -1 \\ -1 & 0 \end{bmatrix}$.

9.8.   Consider the basis $S = \{u_1, u_2\} = \{(1, 1), (1, 2)\}$ of $\mathbf{R}^2$.   Let $L: \mathbf{R}^2 \to \mathbf{R}^2$ be defined by $L(1, 1) = (4, 7)$ and $L(1, 2) = (1, 6)$.   Find the matrix representing L relative to the basis S.

First find the coordinates of an arbitrary vector (a, b) in $\mathbf{R}^2$ relative to the basis S. We have

$$\begin{bmatrix} a \\ b \end{bmatrix} = x \begin{bmatrix} 1 \\ 1 \end{bmatrix} + y \begin{bmatrix} 1 \\ 2 \end{bmatrix} \qquad \text{and so} \qquad \begin{array}{c} x + y = a \\ x + 2y = b \end{array}$$

Solve for x and y in terms of a and b to get $x = 2a - b$, $y = -a + b$. Thus

$$(a, b) = (2a - b)u_1 + (-a + b)u_2$$

Then use the formula for (a, b) to obtain

$$\begin{array}{ll} L(u_1) = L(1, 1) = (4, 7) = u_1 + 3u_2 \\ L(u_2) = L(1, 2) = (1, 6) = -4u_1 + 5u_2 \end{array} \qquad \text{and so} \qquad [L] = \begin{bmatrix} 1 & -4 \\ 3 & 5 \end{bmatrix}$$

9.9. The set $S = \{e^{3t}, te^{3t}, t^2e^{3t}\}$ is a basis of a vector space V of functions $f: \mathbf{R} \to \mathbf{R}$. Let $\mathbf{D}$ be the differential operator on V, that is, $\mathbf{D}(f) = df/dt$. Find the matrix representation of $\mathbf{D}$ relative to the basis S.

Find the image of each basis function:

$$\begin{array}{lll} \mathbf{D}(e^{3t}) & = 3e^{3t} & = 3(e^{3t}) + 0(te^{3t}) + 0(t^2e^{3t}) \\ \mathbf{D}(te^{3t}) & = e^{3t} + 3te^{3t} & = 1(e^{3t}) + 3(te^{3t}) + 0(t^2e^{3t}) \\ \mathbf{D}(t^2e^{3t}) & = 2te^{3t} + 3t^2e^{3t} & = 0(e^{3t}) + 2(te^{3t}) + 3(t^2e^{3t}) \end{array} \qquad \text{and thus} \qquad [\mathbf{D}] = \begin{bmatrix} 3 & 1 & 0 \\ 0 & 3 & 2 \\ 0 & 0 & 3 \end{bmatrix}$$

9.10. Let $V = \mathbf{M}_{2,2}$, the vector space of 2×2 matrices, with the *usual basis*

$$\left\{ E_1 = \begin{bmatrix} 1 & 0 \\ 0 & 0 \end{bmatrix}, E_2 = \begin{bmatrix} 0 & 1 \\ 0 & 0 \end{bmatrix}, E_3 = \begin{bmatrix} 0 & 0 \\ 1 & 0 \end{bmatrix}, E_4 = \begin{bmatrix} 0 & 0 \\ 0 & 1 \end{bmatrix} \right\}$$

Let $M = \begin{bmatrix} 1 & 2 \\ 3 & 4 \end{bmatrix}$ and T be the linear operator on V defined by $T(A) = MA$. Find the matrix representation of T relative to the above usual basis of V.

We have

$$T(E_1) = ME_1 = \begin{bmatrix} 1 & 2 \\ 3 & 4 \end{bmatrix}\begin{bmatrix} 1 & 0 \\ 0 & 0 \end{bmatrix} = \begin{bmatrix} 1 & 0 \\ 3 & 0 \end{bmatrix} = 1E_1 + 0E_2 + 3E_3 + 0E_4$$

$$T(E_2) = ME_2 = \begin{bmatrix} 1 & 2 \\ 3 & 4 \end{bmatrix}\begin{bmatrix} 0 & 1 \\ 0 & 0 \end{bmatrix} = \begin{bmatrix} 0 & 1 \\ 0 & 3 \end{bmatrix} = 0E_1 + 1E_2 + 0E_3 + 3E_4$$

$$T(E_3) = ME_3 = \begin{bmatrix} 1 & 2 \\ 3 & 4 \end{bmatrix}\begin{bmatrix} 0 & 0 \\ 1 & 0 \end{bmatrix} = \begin{bmatrix} 2 & 0 \\ 4 & 0 \end{bmatrix} = 2E_1 + 0E_2 + 4E_3 + 0E_4$$

$$T(E_4) = ME_4 = \begin{bmatrix} 1 & 2 \\ 3 & 4 \end{bmatrix}\begin{bmatrix} 0 & 0 \\ 0 & 1 \end{bmatrix} = \begin{bmatrix} 0 & 2 \\ 0 & 4 \end{bmatrix} = 0E_1 + 2E_2 + 0E_3 + 4E_4$$

Hence

$$[T] = \begin{bmatrix} 1 & 0 & 2 & 0 \\ 0 & 1 & 0 & 2 \\ 3 & 0 & 4 & 0 \\ 0 & 3 & 0 & 4 \end{bmatrix}$$

(Since dim $V = 4$, any matrix representation of a linear operator on V must be a 4-square matrix.)

SIMILARITY OF MATRICES, CHANGE OF BASIS

9.11. Consider the linear transformation F on $\mathbf{R}^2$ defined by $F(x, y) = (5x - y, 2x + y)$ and the following bases of $\mathbf{R}^2$:

$$E = \{e_1, e_2\} = \{(1, 0), (0, 1)\} \quad \text{and} \quad S = \{u_1, u_2\} = \{(1, 4), (2, 7)\}$$

(a) Find the change-of-basis matrix P from E to S and the change-of-basis matrix Q from S back to E, and verify that $Q = P^{-1}$.

(b) Find the matrix A that represents F in the basis E and the matrix B that represents F in the basis S, and verify that $B = P^{-1}AP$.

(c) Find the trace and the determinant of F, that is, tr (F) and det (F).

(a) Since E is the usual basis, write the vectors in S as columns to obtain the change-of-basis matrix

$$P = \begin{bmatrix} 1 & 2 \\ 4 & 7 \end{bmatrix}$$

Now find the coordinates of an arbitrary vector (a, b) in $\mathbf{R}^2$ relative to the basis S. We have

$$\begin{bmatrix} a \\ b \end{bmatrix} = x \begin{bmatrix} 1 \\ 4 \end{bmatrix} + y \begin{bmatrix} 2 \\ 7 \end{bmatrix} \quad \text{and so} \quad \begin{matrix} x + 2y = a \\ 4x + 7y = b \end{matrix}$$

Solve for x and y in terms of a and b to get $x = -7a + 2b$, $y = 4a - b$. Then

$$(a, b) = (-7a + 2b)u_1 + (4a - b)u_2$$

Then use the formula for (a, b) to find the coordinates of e_1 and e_2 relative to S,

$$\begin{matrix} e_1 = (1, 0) = -7u_1 + 4u_2 \\ e_2 = (0, 1) = 2u_1 - u_2 \end{matrix} \quad \text{and thus} \quad Q = \begin{bmatrix} -7 & 2 \\ 4 & -1 \end{bmatrix}$$

We have

$$PQ = \begin{bmatrix} 1 & 2 \\ 4 & 7 \end{bmatrix}\begin{bmatrix} -7 & 2 \\ 4 & -1 \end{bmatrix} = \begin{bmatrix} 1 & 0 \\ 0 & 1 \end{bmatrix} = I$$

(b) Write the coefficients of x and y in $F(x, y) = (5x - y, 2x + y)$ as rows to get

$$A = \begin{bmatrix} 5 & -1 \\ 2 & 1 \end{bmatrix}$$

Use the formula $(a, b) = (-7a + 2b)u_1 + (4a - b)u_2$ to find the coordinates of $F(u_1)$ and $F(u_2)$ relative to S. That is,

$$\begin{matrix} F(u_1) = F(1, 4) = (1, 6) = 5u_1 - 2u_2 \\ F(u_2) = F(2, 7) = (3, 11) = u_1 + u_2 \end{matrix} \quad \text{and so} \quad B = \begin{bmatrix} 5 & 1 \\ -2 & 1 \end{bmatrix}$$

We have

$$P^{-1}AP = \begin{bmatrix} -7 & 2 \\ 4 & -1 \end{bmatrix}\begin{bmatrix} 5 & -1 \\ 2 & 1 \end{bmatrix}\begin{bmatrix} 1 & 2 \\ 4 & 7 \end{bmatrix} = \begin{bmatrix} 5 & 1 \\ -2 & 1 \end{bmatrix} = B$$

(c) Use A (or B) to obtain tr $(F) =$ tr $(A) = 5 + 1 = 6$ and det $(F) =$ det $(A) = 5 + 2 = 7$.

9.12. Let $A = \begin{bmatrix} 4 & -2 \\ 3 & 6 \end{bmatrix}$ and $P = \begin{bmatrix} 1 & 2 \\ 3 & 4 \end{bmatrix}$. (a) Find $B = P^{-1}AP$; (b) verify tr $(B) =$ tr (A); (c) verify det $(B) =$ det (A).

(a) First find P^{-1} using the formula for the inverse of a 2 × 2 matrix,

$$P^{-1} = \begin{bmatrix} -2 & 1 \\ \frac{3}{2} & -\frac{1}{2} \end{bmatrix}$$

Then

$$B = P^{-1}AP = \begin{bmatrix} -2 & 1 \\ \frac{3}{2} & -\frac{1}{2} \end{bmatrix}\begin{bmatrix} 4 & -2 \\ 3 & 6 \end{bmatrix}\begin{bmatrix} 1 & 2 \\ 3 & 4 \end{bmatrix} = \begin{bmatrix} 25 & 30 \\ -\frac{27}{2} & -15 \end{bmatrix}$$

(b) tr $(A) = 4 + 6 = 10$ and tr $(B) = 25 - 15 = 10$. Hence tr $(B) =$ tr (A).

(c) det $(A) = 4(6) - (-2)(3) = 24 + 6 = 30$ and

$$\text{det } (B) = 25(-15) - 30(-\tfrac{27}{2}) = -375 + 405 = 30$$

Thus det $(B) =$ det (A).

9.13. Find the trace of each of the linear transformations F on $\mathbf{R}^3$ in Problem 9.4.

Find the trace (sum of the diagonal elements) of any matrix representation of F such as the matrix representation $[F] = [F]_E$ of F relative to the usual basis E given in Problem 9.4.

(a) tr $(F) =$ tr $([F]) = 1 - 5 + 9 = 5$ (b) tr $(F) =$ tr $([F]) = 1 + 3 + 5 = 9$; (c) tr $(F) =$ tr $([F]) = 1 + 4 + 7 = 12$.

9.14. Write $A \simeq B$ if A is similar to B, that is, if there exists an invertible matrix P such that $A = P^{-1}BP$. Prove that $\simeq$ is an equivalence relation (on square matrices), that is, prove: (a) $A \simeq A$, for every A; (b) if $A \simeq B$, then $B \simeq A$; (c) if $A \simeq B$ and $B \simeq C$, then $A \simeq C$.

(a) The identity matrix I is invertible, and $I^{-1} = I$. Since $A = I^{-1}AI$, we have $A \simeq A$.

(b) Since $A \simeq B$, there exists an invertible matrix P such that $A = P^{-1}BP$. P^{-1} is invertible and $B = PAP^{-1} = (P^{-1})^{-1}AP^{-1}$. Thus $B \simeq A$.

(c) Since $A \simeq B$, there exists an invertible matrix P such that $A = P^{-1}BP$, and since $B \simeq C$, there exists an invertible matrix Q such that $B = Q^{-1}CQ$. Thus

$$A = P^{-1}BP = P^{-1}(Q^{-1}CQ)P = (P^{-1}Q^{-1})C(QP) = (QP)^{-1}C(QP)$$

and QP is invertible. Thus $A \simeq C$.

9.15. Suppose B is similar to A, say $B = P^{-1}AP$.

(a) Show that $B^n = P^{-1}A^nP$, and so B^n is similar to A^n.

(b) Show that $f(B) = P^{-1}f(A)P$ for any polynomial $f(x)$, and so $f(B)$ is similar to $f(A)$.

(c) Show that B is a root of a polynomial $g(x)$ if and only if A is a root of $g(x)$.

(a) The proof is by induction on n. The result holds for $n = 1$ by hypothesis. Suppose $n > 1$ and the result holds for $n - 1$. Then

$$B^n = BB^{n-1} = (P^{-1}AP)(P^{-1}A^{n-1}P) = P^{-1}A^nP$$

(b) Suppose $f(x) = a_n x^n + \cdots + a_1 x + a_0$. Using the left and right distributive laws and part (a), we have

$$P^{-1}f(A)P = P^{-1}(a_n A^n + \cdots + a_1 A + a_0 I)P$$
$$= P^{-1}(a_n A^n)P + \cdots + P^{-1}(a_1 A)P + P^{-1}(a_0 I)P$$
$$= a_n(P^{-1}A^n P) + \cdots + a_1(P^{-1}AP) + a_0(P^{-1}IP)$$
$$= a_n B^n + \cdots + a_1 B + a_0 I = f(B)$$

(c) By part (b), $g(B) = 0$ if and only if $P^{-1}g(A)P = 0$ if and only if $g(A) = P0P^{-1} = 0$.

MATRIX REPRESENTATIONS OF GENERAL LINEAR MAPPINGS

9.16. Let $F: \mathbf{R}^3 \to \mathbf{R}^2$ be the linear mapping defined by $F(x, y, z) = (3x + 2y - 4z, x - 5y + 3z)$.

(a) Find the matrix of F in the following bases of $\mathbf{R}^3$ and $\mathbf{R}^2$:

$$S = \{w_1, w_2, w_3\} = \{(1, 1, 1), (1, 1, 0), (1, 0, 0)\} \qquad \text{and} \qquad S' = \{u_1, u_2\} = \{(1, 3), (2, 5)\}$$

(b) Verify Theorem 9.6 that the action of F is preserved by its matrix representation, that is, for any v in $\mathbf{R}^3$, we have $[F]_{S, S'}[v]_S = [F(v)]_{S'}$.

(a) From Problem 9.2, $(a, b) = (-5a + 2b)u_1 + (3a - b)u_2$. Thus

$$F(w_1) = F(1, 1, 1) = (1, -1) = -7u_1 + 4u_2$$
$$F(w_2) = F(1, 1, 0) = (5, -4) = -33u_1 + 19u_2$$
$$F(w_3) = F(1, 0, 0) = (3, 1) = -13u_1 + 8u_2$$

Write the coordinates of $F(w_1)$, $F(w_2)$, $F(w_3)$ as columns to get

$$[F]_{S, S'} = \begin{bmatrix} -7 & -33 & -13 \\ 4 & 19 & 8 \end{bmatrix}$$

(b) If $v = (x, y, z)$, then, by Problem 9.5, $v = zw_1 + (y - z)w_2 + (x - y)w_3$. Also,

$$F(v) = (3x + 2y - 4z, x - 5y + 3z) = (-13x - 20y + 26z)u_1 + (8x + 11y - 15z)u_2$$

Hence $[v]_S = (z, y - z, x - y)^T$ and $[F(v)]_{S'} = \begin{bmatrix} -13x - 20y + 26z \\ 8x + 11y - 15z \end{bmatrix}$

Thus

$$[F]_{S, S'}[v]_S = \begin{bmatrix} -7 & -33 & -13 \\ 4 & 19 & 8 \end{bmatrix} \begin{bmatrix} z \\ y - z \\ x - y \end{bmatrix} = \begin{bmatrix} -13x - 20y + 26z \\ 8x + 11y - 15z \end{bmatrix} = [F(v)]_{S'}$$

9.17. Let $F: \mathbf{R}^n \to \mathbf{R}^m$ be the linear mapping defined by

$$F(x_1, x_2, \ldots, x_n) = (a_{11}x_1 + \cdots + a_{1n}x_n, a_{21}x_1 + \cdots + a_{2n}x_n, \ldots, a_{m1}x_1 + \cdots + a_{mn}x_n)$$

(a) Show that the rows of the matrix $[F]$ representing F relative to the usual basis of $\mathbf{R}^n$ and $\mathbf{R}^m$ are the coefficients of the x_i in the components of $F(x_1, \ldots, x_n)$.

(b) Find the matrix representation of each of the following linear mappings relative to the usual bases of $\mathbf{R}^n$:

(1) $F: \mathbf{R}^2 \to \mathbf{R}^3$ defined by $F(x, y) = (3x - y, 2x + 4y, 5x - 6y)$.

(2) $F: \mathbf{R}^4 \to \mathbf{R}^2$ defined by $F(x, y, s, t) = (3x - 4y + 2s - 5t, 5x + 7y - s - 2t)$.

(3) $F: \mathbf{R}^3 \to \mathbf{R}^4$ defined by $F(x, y, z) = (2x + 3y - 8z, x + y + z, 4x - 5z, 6y)$.

(a) We have

$$F(1, 0, \ldots, 0) = (a_{11}, a_{21}, \ldots, a_{m1})$$
$$F(0, 1, \ldots, 0) = (a_{12}, a_{22}, \ldots, a_{m2})$$
$$\ldots\ldots\ldots\ldots\ldots\ldots\ldots\ldots\ldots$$
$$F(0, 0, \ldots, 1) = (a_{1n}, a_{2n}, \ldots, a_{mn})$$

and thus

$$[F] = \begin{bmatrix} a_{11} & a_{12} & \cdots & a_{1n} \\ a_{21} & a_{22} & \cdots & a_{2n} \\ \cdots\cdots\cdots\cdots\cdots\cdots \\ a_{m1} & a_{m2} & \cdots & a_{mn} \end{bmatrix}$$

(b) By part (a), we need only look at the coefficients of the unknown $x, y, \ldots$ in $F(x, y, \ldots)$. Thus

$$(1)\ [F] = \begin{bmatrix} 3 & -1 \\ 2 & 4 \\ 5 & -6 \end{bmatrix};\ (2)\ [F] = \begin{bmatrix} 3 & -4 & 2 & -5 \\ 5 & 7 & -1 & -2 \end{bmatrix};\ (3)\ [F] = \begin{bmatrix} 2 & 3 & -8 \\ 1 & 1 & 1 \\ 4 & 0 & -5 \\ 0 & 6 & 0 \end{bmatrix}$$

9.18. Let $A = \begin{bmatrix} 2 & 5 & -3 \\ 1 & -4 & 7 \end{bmatrix}$. Recall that A determines a mapping $F: \mathbf{R}^3 \to \mathbf{R}^2$ defined by $F(v) = Av$, where vectors are written as columns. Find the matrix $[F]$ which represents the mapping relative to the following bases of $\mathbf{R}^3$ and $\mathbf{R}^2$:

(a) Usual bases E of $\mathbf{R}^3$ and E' of $\mathbf{R}^2$.

(b) $S = \{w_1, w_2, w_3\} = \{(1, 1, 1), (1, 1, 0), (1, 0, 0)\}$ and $S' = \{u_1, u_2\} = \{(1, 3), (2, 5)\}$.

(a) Relative to the usual bases, $[F]$ is the matrix A itself.

(b) From Problem 9.2, $(a, b) = (-5a + 2b)u_1 + (3a - b)u_2$. Thus

$$F(w_1) = \begin{bmatrix} 2 & 5 & -3 \\ 1 & -4 & 7 \end{bmatrix} \begin{bmatrix} 1 \\ 1 \\ 1 \end{bmatrix} = \begin{bmatrix} 4 \\ 4 \end{bmatrix} = -12u_1 + 8u_2$$

$$F(w_2) = \begin{bmatrix} 2 & 5 & -3 \\ 1 & -4 & 7 \end{bmatrix} \begin{bmatrix} 1 \\ 1 \\ 0 \end{bmatrix} = \begin{bmatrix} 7 \\ -3 \end{bmatrix} = -41u_1 + 24u_2$$

$$F(w_3) = \begin{bmatrix} 2 & 5 & -3 \\ 1 & -4 & 7 \end{bmatrix} \begin{bmatrix} 1 \\ 0 \\ 0 \end{bmatrix} = \begin{bmatrix} 2 \\ 1 \end{bmatrix} = -8u_1 + 5u_2$$

Writing the coefficients of $F(w_1)$, $F(w_2)$, $F(w_3)$ as columns yields

$$[F] = \begin{bmatrix} -12 & -41 & -8 \\ 8 & 24 & 5 \end{bmatrix}$$

9.19. Consider the linear transformation T on $\mathbf{R}^2$ defined by $T(x, y) = (2x - 3y, x + 4y)$ and the following bases of $\mathbf{R}^2$:

$$E = \{e_1, e_2\} = \{(1, 0), (0, 1)\} \quad \text{and} \quad S = \{u_1, u_2\} = \{(1, 3), (2, 5)\}$$

(a) Find the matrix A representing T relative to the bases E and S.

(b) Find the matrix B representing T relative to the bases S and E.

(We can view T as a linear mapping from one space into another, each having its own basis.)

(a)   From Problem 9.2, $(a, b) = (-5a + 2b)u_1 + (3a - b)u_2$.   Hence

$$T(e_1) = T(1, 0) = (2, 1) \quad = -8u_1 + 5u_2$$
$$T(e_2) = T(0, 1) = (-3, 4) = 23u_1 - 13u_2$$

and so $A = \begin{bmatrix} -8 & 23 \\ 5 & -13 \end{bmatrix}$

(b)   We have

$$T(u_1) = T(1, 3) = (-7, 13) \quad = -7e_1 + 13e_2$$
$$T(u_2) = T(2, 5) = (-11, 22) = -11e_1 + 22e_2$$

and so $B = \begin{bmatrix} -7 & -11 \\ 13 & 22 \end{bmatrix}$

9.20. Let V be the vector space of functions that have $S = \{\sin \theta, \cos \theta\}$ as a basis.   Let **D** be the differential operator on V.

(a)   Find the matrix representation $A = [\mathbf{D}]_S$.

(b)   Show that **D** is a zero of $f(t) = t^2 + 1$.

(a)   We have

$$\mathbf{D}(\sin \theta) = \cos \theta = 0 \sin \theta + \cos \theta$$
$$\mathbf{D}(\cos \theta) = -\sin \theta = -\sin \theta + 0 \cos \theta$$

and so $A = \begin{bmatrix} 0 & -1 \\ 1 & 0 \end{bmatrix}$

(b)   Apply $(f)(\mathbf{D})$ to each basis vector:

$$f(\mathbf{D})(\sin \theta) = (\mathbf{D}^2 + I)(\sin \theta) = \mathbf{D}^2(\sin \theta) + I(\sin \theta) = -\sin \theta + \sin \theta = 0$$
$$f(\mathbf{D})(\cos \theta) = (\mathbf{D}^2 + I)(\cos \theta) = \mathbf{D}^2(\cos \theta) + I(\cos \theta) = -\cos \theta + \cos \theta = 0$$

Since each basis vector is mapped into 0, every vector v in V is mapped into 0 by $f(\mathbf{D})$. Thus $f(\mathbf{D}) = 0$.

Alternately, show that $f(A) = 0$.   We have

$$f(A) = A^2 + I = \begin{bmatrix} -1 & 0 \\ 0 & -1 \end{bmatrix} + \begin{bmatrix} 1 & 0 \\ 0 & 1 \end{bmatrix} = \begin{bmatrix} 0 & 0 \\ 0 & 0 \end{bmatrix} = 0$$

Since $f(A) = 0$, by Problem 9.24, $f(\mathbf{D}) = 0$.

PROOFS OF THEOREMS

9.21. Prove Theorem 9.1:   Let $S = \{u_1, u_2, \ldots, u_n\}$ be a basis for V and let T be any linear operator on V.   Then, for any vector $v \in V$, $[T]_S[v]_S = [T(v)]_S$.

Suppose, for $i = 1, \ldots, n$,

$$T(u_i) = a_{i1}u_1 + a_{i2}u_2 + \cdots + a_{in}u_n = \sum_{j=1}^{n} a_{ij}u_j$$

Then $[T]_S$ is the n-square matrix whose jth row is

$$(a_{1j}, a_{2j}, \ldots, a_{nj}) \tag{1}$$

Now suppose

$$v = k_1u_1 + k_2u_2 + \cdots + k_nu_n = \sum_{i=1}^{n} k_iu_i$$

Writing a column vector as the transpose of a row vector, we have

$$[v]_S = (k_1, k_2, \ldots, k_n)^T \tag{2}$$

Furthermore, using the linearity of T,

$$T(v) = T\left(\sum_{i=1}^{n} k_i u_i\right) = \sum_{i=1}^{n} k_i T(u_i) = \sum_{i=1}^{n} k_i \left(\sum_{j=1}^{n} a_{ij} u_j\right)$$

$$= \sum_{j=1}^{n} \left(\sum_{i=1}^{n} a_{ij} k_i\right) u_j = \sum_{j=1}^{n} (a_{1j} k_1 + a_{2j} k_2 + \cdots + a_{nj} k_n) u_j$$

Thus $[T(v)]_s$ is the column vector whose jth entry is

$$a_{1j} k_1 + a_{2j} k_2 + \cdots + a_{nj} k_n \tag{3}$$

On the other hand, the jth entry of $[T]_S [v]_S$ is obtained by multiplying the jth row of $[T]_S$ by $[v]_S$, i.e., Eq. (1) by Eq. (2). But the product of Eqs. (1) and (2) is Eq. (3). Hence $[T]_S [v]_S$ and $[T(v)]_S$ have the same entries. Thus $[T]_S [v]_S = [T(v)]_S$.

9.22. Prove Theorem 9.2: Let $S = \{u_1, u_2, \ldots, u_n\}$ be a basis for V over K, and let $\mathbf{M}$ be the algebra of n-square matrices over K. Then the mapping $m:\ A(V) \to \mathbf{M}$ defined by $m(T) = [T]_S$ is a vector space isomorphism. That is, for any $F, G \in A(V)$ and any $k \in K$ we have

(i) $[F + G] = [F] + [G]$.

(ii) $[kF] = k[F]$.

(iii) m is one-to-one and onto.

Suppose, for $i = 1, \ldots, n$,

$$F(u_i) \sum_{j=1}^{n} a_{ij} u_j \qquad \text{and} \qquad G(u_i) = \sum_{j=1}^{n} b_{ij} u_j$$

Consider the matrices $A = [a_{ij}]$ and $B = [b_{ij}]$. Then $[F] = A^T$ and $[G] = B^T$. We have, for $i = 1, \ldots, n$,

$$(F + G)(u_i) = F(u_i) + G(u_i) = \sum_{j=1}^{n} (a_{ij} + b_{ij}) u_j$$

Since $A + B$ is the matrix $(a_{ij} + b_{ij})$, we have

$$[F + G] = (A + B)^T = A^T + B^T = [F] + [G]$$

Also, for $i = 1, \ldots, n$,

$$(kF)(u_i) = kF(u_i) = k \sum_{j=1}^{n} a_{ij} u_j = \sum_{j=1}^{n} (ka_{ij}) u_j$$

Since kA is the matrix (ka_{ij}), we have

$$[kF] = (kA)^T = kA^T = k[F]$$

Lastly, m is one-to-one since a linear mapping is completely determined by its values on a basis, and m is onto since each matrix $A = [a_{ij}]$ in $\mathbf{M}$ is the image of the linear operator,

$$F(u_i) = \sum_{j=1}^{n} a_{ij} u_j, \qquad i = 1, \ldots, n$$

Thus the theorem is proved.

9.23. Prove Theorem 9.3:   For any linear operators $G, F \in A(V)$,

$$[G \circ F] = [G][F]$$

Using the notation in Problem 9.22, we have

$$(G \circ F)(u_i) = G(F(u_i)) = G\left(\sum_{j=1}^n a_{ij}u_j\right) = \sum_{j=1}^n a_{ij}G(u_j)$$

$$= \sum_{j=1}^n a_{ij}\left(\sum_{k=1}^n b_{jk}u_k\right) = \sum_{k=1}^n \left(\sum_{j=1}^n a_{ij}b_{jk}\right)u_k$$

Recall that AB is the matrix $AB = [c_{ik}]$, where $c_{ik} = \sum_{j=1}^n a_{ij}b_{jk}$.   Accordingly,

$$[G \circ F] = (AB)^T = B^TA^T = [G][F]$$

Thus the theorem is proved.

9.24. Let A be a matrix representation of a linear operator T.   Prove that, for any polynomial $f(t)$, we have that $f(A)$ is the matrix representation of $f(T)$.   [Thus $f(T) = 0$ if and only if $f(A) = 0$.]

Let ϕ be the mapping $T \mapsto A$, i.e., which sends the operator T into its matrix representation A. We need to prove that $\phi(f(T)) = f(A)$.   Suppose $f(t) = a_n t^n + \cdots + a_1 t + a_0$.   The proof is by induction on n, the degree of $f(t)$.

Suppose $n = 0$.   Recall that $\phi(I') = I$, where I' is the identity mapping and I is the identity matrix.   Thus

$$\phi(f(T)) = \phi(a_0 I') = a_0\phi(I') = a_0 I = f(A)$$

and so the theorem holds for $n = 0$.

Now assume the theorem holds for polynomials of degree less than n.   Then, since ϕ is an algebra isomorphism,

$$\phi(f(T)) = \phi(a_n T^n + a_{n-1}T^{n-1} + \cdots + a_1 T + a_0 I')$$

$$= a_n\phi(T)\phi(T^{n-1}) + \phi(a_{n-1}T^{n-1} + \cdots + a_1 T + a_0 I')$$

$$= a_n AA^{n-1} + (a_{n-1}A^{n-1} + \cdots + a_1 A + a_0 I) = f(A)$$

and the theorem is proved.

9.25. Prove Theorem 9.4:   Let P be the change-of-basis matrix from a basis S to a basis S' in a vector space V.   Then, for any linear operator T on V,

$$[T]_{S'} = P^{-1}[T]_S P$$

Let v be any vector in V.   Then, by Theorem 6.3, $P[v]_{S'} = [v]_S$.   Therefore,

$$P^{-1}[T]_S P[v]_{S'} = P^{-1}[T]_S[v]_S = P^{-1}[T(v)]_S = [T(v)]_{S'}$$

But $[T]_{S'}[v]_{S'} = [T(v)]_{S'}$.   Hence

$$P^{-1}[T]_S P[v]_{S'} = [T]_{S'}[v]_{S'}$$

Since the mapping $v \mapsto [v]_{S'}$ is onto K^n, we have $P^{-1}[T]_S PX = [T]_{S'}X$ for every $X \in K^n$.   Thus $P^{-1}[T]_S P = [T]_{S'}$, as claimed.

9.26. Prove Theorem 9.8:   Let $F: V \to U$ be linear and, say, rank $(F) = r$.   Then there exist bases of V and U such that the matrix representation of F has the form

$$A = \begin{bmatrix} I_r & 0 \\ 0 & 0 \end{bmatrix}$$

where I_r is the r-square identity matrix.

Suppose dim $V = m$ and dim $U = n$.   Let W be the kernel of F and U' the image of F. We are given that rank $(F) = r$.   Hence the dimension of the kernel of F is $m - r$.   Let $\{w_1, \ldots, w_{m-r}\}$ be a basis of the kernel of F and extend this to a basis of V,

$$\{v_1, \ldots, v_r, w_1, \ldots, w_{m-r}\}$$

Set
$$u_1 = F(v_1), u_2 = F(v_2), \ldots, u_r = F(v_r)$$

Then $\{u_1, \ldots, u_r\}$ is a basis of U', the image of F.   Extend this to a basis of U, say

$$\{u_1, \ldots, u_r, u_{r+1}, \ldots, u_n\}$$

Observe that

$$
\begin{aligned}
F(v_1) &= u_1 = 1u_1 + 0u_2 + \cdots + 0u_r + 0u_{r+1} + \cdots + 0u_n \\
F(v_2) &= u_2 = 0u_1 + 1u_2 + \cdots + 0u_r + 0u_{r+1} + \cdots + 0u_n \\
&\cdots\cdots\cdots\cdots\cdots\cdots\cdots\cdots\cdots\cdots\cdots\cdots \\
F(v_r) &= u_r = 0u_1 + 0u_2 + \cdots + 1u_r + 0u_{r+1} + \cdots + 0u_n \\
F(w_1) &= 0 = 0u_1 + 0u_2 + \cdots + 0u_r + 0u_{r+1} + \cdots + 0u_n \\
&\cdots\cdots\cdots\cdots\cdots\cdots\cdots\cdots\cdots\cdots\cdots\cdots \\
F(w_{m-r}) &= 0 = 0u_1 + 0u_2 + \cdots + 0u_r + 0u_{r+1} + \cdots + 0u_n
\end{aligned}
$$

Thus the matrix of F in the above bases has the required form.

Supplementary Problems

MATRICES AND LINEAR OPERATORS

9.27. Let $F: \mathbf{R}^2 \to \mathbf{R}^2$ be defined by $F(x, y) = (4x + 5y, 2x - y)$.

    (a) Find the matrix A representing F in the usual basis E.

    (b) Find the matrix B representing F in the basis

$$S = \{u_1, u_2\} = \{(1, 4), (2, 9)\}$$

    (c) Find P such that $B = P^{-1}AP$.

    (d) For $v = (a, b)$, find $[v]_S$ and $[F(v)]_S$.   Verify that $[F]_S[v]_S = [F(v)]_S$.

9.28. Let $A: \mathbf{R}^2 \to \mathbf{R}^2$ be defined by the matrix $A = \begin{bmatrix} 5 & -1 \\ 2 & 4 \end{bmatrix}$.

    (a) Find the matrix B representing A relative to the basis

$$S = \{u_1, u_2\} = \{(1, 3), (2, 8)\}$$

    (Recall that A represents A relative to the usual basis E.)

    (b) For $v = (a, b)$, find $[v]_S$ and $[A(v)]_S$.

9.29. For each of the following linear transformations L on $\mathbf{R}^2$, find the matrix A representing L (relative to the usual basis of $\mathbf{R}^2$):

(a) L is the rotation in $\mathbf{R}^2$ counterclockwise by $45°$.

(b) L is the reflection in $\mathbf{R}^2$ about the line $y = x$.

(c) L is defined by $L(1, 0) = (3, 5)$ and $L(0, 1) = (7, -2)$.

(d) L is defined by $L(1, 1) = (3, 7)$ and $L(1, 2) = (5, -4)$.

9.30. Find the matrix representing each of the following linear transformations T on $\mathbf{R}^3$ relative to the usual basis of $\mathbf{R}^3$:

(a) $T(x, y, z) = (x, y, 0)$

(b) $T(x, y, z) = (2x - 7y - 4z, 3x + y + 4z, 6x - 8y + z)$

(c) $T(x, y, z) = (z, y + z, x + y + z)$

9.31. Find the matrix representation of each linear transformation T in Problem 9.30 with respect to the basis

$$S = \{u_1, u_2, u_3\} = \{(1, 1, 0), (1, 2, 3), (1, 3, 5)\}$$

9.32. Let L be the linear transformation in $\mathbf{R}^3$ defined by $L(1, 0, 0) = (1, 1, 1)$, $L(0, 1, 0) = (1, 3, 5)$, $L(0, 0, 1) = (2, 2, 2)$.

(a)   Find the matrix A representing L relative to the usual basis of $\mathbf{R}^3$.

(b)   Find the matrix B representing L relative to the basis S in Problem 9.31.

9.33. Let $\mathbf{D}$ denote the differential operator, that is, $\mathbf{D}(f(t)) = df/dt$. Each of the following sets is a basis of a vector space V of functions. Find the matrix representing $\mathbf{D}$ in each basis: (a) $\{e^t, e^{2t}, te^{2t}\}$; (b) $\{1, t, \sin 3t, \cos 3t\}$; (c) $\{e^{5t}, te^{5t}, t^2 e^{5t}\}$.

9.34. Let V be the vector space of real 2×2 matrices and let $M = \begin{bmatrix} a & b \\ c & d \end{bmatrix}$. Find the matrix representing each of the following linear operators T on V relative to the usual basis of V (defined in Problem 9.10).   (a) $T(A) = MA$; (b) $T(A) = AM$; (c) $T(A) = MA - AM$.

9.35. Let $\mathbf{1}_V$ and $\mathbf{0}_V$ denote the identity and zero operators, respectively, on a vector space V. Show that, for any basis S of V: (a) $[\mathbf{1}_V]_S = I$, the identity matrix; (b) $[\mathbf{0}_V]_S = 0$, the zero matrix.

SIMILARITY OF MATRICES, CHANGE OF BASIS

9.36. Consider the linear operator T on $\mathbf{R}^2$ defined by $T(x, y) = (5x + y, 3x - 2y)$, and the following bases of $\mathbf{R}^2$:

$$S = \{(1, 2), (2, 3)\} \quad \text{and} \quad S' = \{(1, 3), (1, 4)\}$$

(a)   Find the matrix A representing T relative to the basis S.

(b)   Find the matrix B representing T relative to the basis S'.

(c)   Find the change-of-basis matrix P from S to S' and the change-of-basis matrix Q from S' back to S.   Verify $Q = P^{-1}$.

(d)   Verify that $B = P^{-1}AP$.

9.37. Find the trace and the determinant of each linear map on $\mathbf{R}^2$:

$$(a)\ F(x, y) = (2x - 3y, 5x + 4y);\ (b)\ G(x, y) = (ax + by, cx + dy)$$

9.38. Find the trace of each linear map on $\mathbf{R}^3$:

$$(a)\ F(x, y, z) = (x + 3y, 3x - 2z, x - 4y - 3z);\ (b)\ G(x, y, z) = (y + 3z, 2x - 4z, 5x + 7y)$$

9.39. Suppose $S = \{u_1, u_2\}$ is a basis of V and $T: V \to V$ is defined by $T(u_1) = 3u_1 - 2u_2$ and $T(u_2) = u_1 + 4u_2$. Suppose $S' = \{w_1, w_2\}$ is a basis of V for which $w_1 = u_1 + u_2$ and $w_2 = 2u_1 + 3u_2$.

(a)   Find the matrices A and B representing T relative to the bases S and S', respectively.

(b)   Find the matrix P such that $B = P^{-1}AP$.

9.40. Let A be a 2×2 matrix such that only A is similar to itself. Show that A has the form

$$A = \begin{bmatrix} a & 0 \\ 0 & a \end{bmatrix}.$$

9.41. Show that all matrices similar to an invertible matrix are invertible.   More generally, show that similar matrices have the same rank.

MATRIX REPRESENTATIONS OF GENERAL LINEAR MAPPINGS

9.42. Find the matrix representation of each linear map relative to the usual bases for $\mathbf{R}^n$:

(a) $F: \mathbf{R}^3 \to \mathbf{R}^2$ defined by $F(x, y, z) = (2x - 4y + 9z, 5x + 3y - 2z)$.

(b) $F: \mathbf{R}^2 \to \mathbf{R}^4$ defined by $F(x, y) = (3x + 4y, 5x - 2y, x + 7y, 4x)$.

(c) $F: \mathbf{R}^4 \to \mathbf{R}$ defined by $F(x, y, z, t) = 2x + 3y - 7z - t$.

9.43. Let $G: \mathbf{R}^3 \to \mathbf{R}^2$ be defined by $G(x, y, z) = (2x + 3y - z, 4x - y + 2z)$.

(a)   Find the matrix A representing G relative to the bases

$$S = \{(1, 1, 0), (1, 2, 3), (1, 3, 5)\} \quad \text{and} \quad S' = \{(1, 2), (2, 3)\}$$

(b)   For any $v = (a, b, c)$ in $\mathbf{R}^3$, find $[v]_S$ and $[G(v)]_{S'}$.

(c)   Verify that $A[v]_s = [G(v)]_{S'}$.

9.44. Consider the linear mapping $H: \mathbf{R}^2 \to \mathbf{R}^2$ defined by $H(x, y) = (2x + 7y, x - 3y)$ and the following bases of $\mathbf{R}^2$:

$$S = \{(1, 1), (1, 2)\} \quad \text{and} \quad S' = \{(1, 4), (1, 5)\}$$

(a)   Find the matrix A representing H relative to the bases S and S'.

(b)   Find the matrix B representing H relative to the bases S' and S.

9.45. Let $F: \mathbf{R}^3 \to \mathbf{R}^2$ be defined by $F(x, y, z) = (2x + y - z, 3x - 2y + 4z)$.

(a)   Find the matrix A representing G relative to the bases

$$S = \{(1, 1, 1), (1, 1, 0), (1, 0, 0)\} \quad \text{and} \quad S' = \{(1, 3), (1, 4)\}$$

(b)   Verify that, for any $v = (a, b, c)$ in $\mathbf{R}^3$, $A[v]_S = [F(v)]_{S'}$.

9.46. Let S and S' be bases of V, and let $\mathbf{1}_V$ be the identity mapping on V. Show that the matrix A representing $\mathbf{1}_V$ relative to the bases S and S' is the inverse of the change-of-basis matrix P from S to S', that is, $A = P^{-1}$.

9.47. Prove Theorem 9.6: For any vector $v \in V$, $[F]_{S,S'}[v]_S = [F(v)]_{S'}$. (Hint: See Problem 9.21.)

9.48. Prove Theorem 9.7: The mapping $m: \text{Hom}(V, U) \to \mathbf{M}$ defined by $m(F) = [F]$ is an isomorphism. (Hint: See Problem 9.22.)

9.49. Prove: Let $F: V \to U$ be linear. Let A represent F relative to bases S_1 and S_2 of V and U, respectively, and let B represent F relative to bases S_1' and S_2' of V and U, respectively. Then

$$B = Q^{-1}AP$$

where P is the change-of-basis matrix from S_1 to S_1' in V, and Q is the change-of-basis matrix from S_2 to S_2' in U. (Hint: See Problem 9.25.)

Answers to Supplementary Problems

9.27. (a) $A = \begin{bmatrix} 4 & 5 \\ 2 & -1 \end{bmatrix}$; (b) $B = \begin{bmatrix} 220 & 487 \\ -98 & -217 \end{bmatrix}$; (c) $P = \begin{bmatrix} 1 & 2 \\ 4 & 9 \end{bmatrix}$; (d) $[v]_S = [9a - 2b, -4a + b]^T$ and $[F(v)] = [32a + 47b, -14a - 21b]^T$

9.28. (a) $B = \begin{bmatrix} -6 & -28 \\ 4 & 15 \end{bmatrix}$; (b) $[v] = \left[4a - b, \dfrac{-3a}{2} + \dfrac{b}{2}\right]^T$ and $[A(v)]_S = \left[18a - 8b, \dfrac{-13a + 7b}{2}\right]^T$

9.29. (a) $\begin{bmatrix} \sqrt{2}/2 & -\sqrt{2}/2 \\ \sqrt{2}/2 & \sqrt{2}/2 \end{bmatrix}$; (b) $\begin{bmatrix} 0 & 1 \\ 1 & 0 \end{bmatrix}$; (c) $\begin{bmatrix} 3 & 7 \\ 5 & -2 \end{bmatrix}$; (d) $\begin{bmatrix} 1 & 2 \\ 18 & -11 \end{bmatrix}$

9.30. (a) $\begin{bmatrix} 1 & 0 & 0 \\ 0 & 1 & 0 \\ 0 & 0 & 0 \end{bmatrix}$; (b) $\begin{bmatrix} 2 & -7 & -4 \\ 3 & 1 & 4 \\ 6 & -8 & 1 \end{bmatrix}$; (c) $\begin{bmatrix} 0 & 0 & 1 \\ 0 & 1 & 1 \\ 1 & 1 & 1 \end{bmatrix}$

9.31. (a) $\begin{bmatrix} 1 & 3 & 5 \\ 0 & -5 & -10 \\ 0 & 3 & 6 \end{bmatrix}$; (b) $\begin{bmatrix} 15 & 65 & 104 \\ -49 & -219 & -351 \\ 29 & 130 & 208 \end{bmatrix}$; (c) $\begin{bmatrix} 0 & 1 & 2 \\ -1 & 2 & 3 \\ 1 & 0 & 0 \end{bmatrix}$

9.32. (a) $A = \begin{bmatrix} 1 & 1 & 2 \\ 1 & 3 & 2 \\ 1 & 5 & 2 \end{bmatrix}$; (b) $B = \begin{bmatrix} 0 & 0 & 0 \\ 2 & 14 & 22 \\ 0 & -5 & -8 \end{bmatrix}$

9.33. (a) $\begin{bmatrix} 1 & 0 & 0 \\ 0 & 2 & 1 \\ 0 & 0 & 2 \end{bmatrix}$; (b) $\begin{bmatrix} 0 & 1 & 0 & 0 \\ 0 & 0 & 0 & 0 \\ 0 & 0 & 0 & -3 \\ 0 & 0 & 3 & 0 \end{bmatrix}$; (c) $\begin{bmatrix} 5 & 1 & 0 \\ 0 & 5 & 2 \\ 0 & 0 & 5 \end{bmatrix}$

9.34. (a) $\begin{bmatrix} a & 0 & b & 0 \\ 0 & a & 0 & b \\ c & 0 & d & 0 \\ 0 & c & 0 & d \end{bmatrix}$; (b) $\begin{bmatrix} a & c & 0 & 0 \\ b & d & 0 & 0 \\ 0 & 0 & a & c \\ 0 & 0 & b & d \end{bmatrix}$; (c) $\begin{bmatrix} 0 & -c & b & 0 \\ -b & a-d & 0 & b \\ c & 0 & d-a & -c \\ 0 & c & -b & 0 \end{bmatrix}$

9.36. (a) $A = \begin{bmatrix} -23 & -39 \\ 13 & 26 \end{bmatrix}$; (b) $B = \begin{bmatrix} 35 & 41 \\ -27 & -32 \end{bmatrix}$; (c) $P = \begin{bmatrix} 3 & 5 \\ -1 & -2 \end{bmatrix}$, $Q = \begin{bmatrix} 2 & 5 \\ -1 & -3 \end{bmatrix}$

9.37. (a) tr $(F) = 6$, det $(F) = 23$; (b) tr $(G) = a + d$, det $(G) = ab - bc$

9.38. (a) tr $(F) = -2$; (b) tr $(G) = 0$

9.39. (a) $A = \begin{bmatrix} 3 & 1 \\ -2 & 4 \end{bmatrix}$, $B = \begin{bmatrix} 8 & 11 \\ -2 & -1 \end{bmatrix}$; (b) $P = \begin{bmatrix} 1 & 2 \\ 1 & 3 \end{bmatrix}$

9.42. (a) $\begin{bmatrix} 2 & -4 & 9 \\ 5 & 3 & -2 \end{bmatrix}$; (b) $[\cdots]^T$; (c) $[2, 3, -7, -1]$

9.43. (a) $A = \begin{bmatrix} -9 & 1 & 4 \\ 7 & 2 & 1 \end{bmatrix}$; (b) $[v]_S = [-a + 2b - c, 5a - 5b + 2c, -3a + 3b - c]^T$ and
$[G(v)]_{S'} = [2a - 11b + 7c, 7b - 4c]^T$

9.44. (a) $A = \begin{bmatrix} 47 & 85 \\ -38 & -69 \end{bmatrix}$; (b) $B = \begin{bmatrix} 71 & 88 \\ -41 & -51 \end{bmatrix}$

9.45. (a) $A = \begin{bmatrix} 3 & 11 & 5 \\ -1 & -8 & -3 \end{bmatrix}$

Chapter 10

Determinants

10.1 INTRODUCTION

Each n-square matrix $A = [a_{ij}]$ is assigned a special scalar called the *determinant* of A, denoted by det (A) or $|A|$ or

$$\begin{vmatrix} a_{11} & a_{12} & \cdots & a_{1n} \\ a_{21} & a_{22} & \cdots & a_{2n} \\ \cdots\cdots\cdots\cdots\cdots\cdots \\ a_{n1} & a_{n2} & \cdots & a_{nn} \end{vmatrix}$$

We emphasize that an $n \times n$ array of scalars enclosed by straight lines, called a *determinant of order n*, is not a matrix but denotes the determinant of the enclosed array of scalars, i.e., the enclosed matrix.

The determinant function was first discovered during the investigation of systems of linear equations. We shall see that the determinant is an indispensable tool in investigating and obtaining properties of square matrices.

The definition of the determinant and most of its properties also apply in the case where the entries of a matrix come from a ring.

We begin with a special case of determinants of order 1, 2, and 3. Then we define a determinant of arbitrary order. This general definition is preceded by a discussion of permutations, which is necessary for our general definition of the determinant.

10.2 DETERMINANTS OF ORDER 1 AND 2

The determinants of order 1 and 2 are defined as follows:

$$|a_{11}| = a_{11}$$

$$\begin{vmatrix} a_{11} & a_{12} \\ a_{21} & a_{22} \end{vmatrix} = a_{11}a_{22} - a_{12}a_{21}$$

Thus the determinant of a 1×1 matrix $A = [a_{11}]$ is the scalar a_{11} itself, that is, det $(A) = |a_{11}| = a_{11}$. The determinant of order two may easily be remembered by using the following diagram:

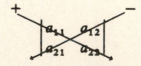

That is, the determinant is equal to the product of the elements along the plus-labeled arrow minus the product of the elements along the minus-labeled arrow. (There is an analogous diagram for determinants of order 3, but not for higher-order determinants.)

354

EXAMPLE 10.1

(a)   Since the determinant of order 1 is the scalar itself, we have

$$\det(27) = 27, \qquad \det(-7) = -7, \qquad \det(t-3) = t-3$$

(b) $\begin{vmatrix} 5 & 3 \\ 4 & 6 \end{vmatrix} = 5(6) - 3(4) = 30 - 12 = 18$ and $\begin{vmatrix} 3 & 2 \\ -5 & 7 \end{vmatrix} = 3(7) - 2(-5) = 21 + 10 = 31.$

Application to Linear Equations

Consider two linear equations in two unknowns, say

$$a_1 x + b_1 y = c_1$$
$$a_2 x + b_2 y = c_2$$

The system has a unique solution if and only if

$$D = a_1 b_2 - a_2 b_1 \neq 0$$

and that solution is

$$x = \frac{b_2 c_1 - b_1 c_2}{a_1 b_2 - a_2 b_1}, \qquad y = \frac{a_1 c_2 - a_2 c_1}{a_1 b_2 - a_2 b_1}$$

The solution may be expressed completely in terms of determinants:

$$x = \frac{N_x}{D} = \frac{b_2 c_1 - b_1 c_2}{a_1 b_2 - a_2 b_1} = \frac{\begin{vmatrix} c_1 & b_1 \\ c_2 & b_2 \end{vmatrix}}{\begin{vmatrix} a_1 & b_1 \\ a_2 & b_2 \end{vmatrix}}, \qquad y = \frac{N_y}{D} = \frac{a_1 c_2 - a_2 c_1}{a_1 b_2 - a_2 b_1} = \frac{\begin{vmatrix} a_1 & c_1 \\ a_2 & c_2 \end{vmatrix}}{\begin{vmatrix} a_1 & b_1 \\ a_2 & b_2 \end{vmatrix}}$$

Here D, the determinant of the matrix of coefficients, appears in the denominator of both quotients. The numerators N_x and N_y of the quotients for x and y can be obtained by substituting the column of constant terms in place of the column of coefficients of the given unknown in the matrix of coefficients.

EXAMPLE 10.2   Solve by determinants: $\begin{cases} 4x - 3y = 15 \\ 2x + 5y = 1 \end{cases}$.

The determinant D of the matrix of coefficients is

$$D = \begin{vmatrix} 4 & -3 \\ 2 & 5 \end{vmatrix} = 4(5) - (-3)(2) = 20 + 6 = 26$$

Since $D \neq 0$, the system has a unique solution. To obtain the numerator N_x, simply replace, in the matrix of coefficients, the coefficients of x by the constant terms, obtaining

$$N_x = \begin{vmatrix} 15 & -3 \\ 1 & 5 \end{vmatrix} = 15(5) - (-3)(1) = 75 + 3 = 78$$

To obtain the numerator N_y, simply replace, in the matrix of coefficients, the coefficients of y by the constant terms, obtaining

$$N_y = \begin{vmatrix} 4 & 15 \\ 2 & 1 \end{vmatrix} = 4(1) - 15(2) = 4 - 30 = -26$$

Then the unique solution of the system is

$$x = \frac{N_x}{D} = \frac{78}{26} = 3, \qquad y = \frac{N_y}{D} = \frac{-26}{26} = -1$$

10.3 DETERMINANTS OF ORDER 3

Consider an arbitrary 3×3 matrix $A = [a_{ij}]$. The determinant of A is defined as follows:

$$\det(A) = \begin{vmatrix} a_{11} & a_{12} & a_{13} \\ a_{21} & a_{22} & a_{23} \\ a_{31} & a_{32} & a_{33} \end{vmatrix} = a_{11}a_{22}a_{33} + a_{12}a_{23}a_{31} + a_{13}a_{21}a_{32} - a_{13}a_{22}a_{31} - a_{12}a_{21}a_{33} - a_{11}a_{23}a_{32}$$

Observe that there are six products, each product consisting of three elements of the original matrix. Three of the products are plus-labeled (keep their sign) and three of the products are minus-labeled (change their sign).

The diagrams in Fig. 10-1 may help to remember the above six products in $\det(A)$. That is, the determinant is equal to the sum of the products of the elements along the three plus-labeled arrows in Fig. 10-1 plus the sum of the negatives of the products of the elements along the three minus-labeled arrows. We emphasize that there are no such diagrammatic devices to remember determinants of higher order.

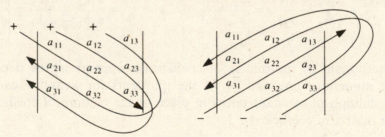

Fig. 10-1

EXAMPLE 10.3 Use Fig. 10-1.

$$\begin{vmatrix} 2 & 1 & 1 \\ 0 & 5 & -2 \\ 1 & -3 & 4 \end{vmatrix} = 2(5)(4) + 1(-2)(1) + 1(-3)(0) - 1(5)(1) - (-3)(-2)(2) - 4(1)(0)$$

$$= 40 - 2 + 0 - 5 - 12 - 0 = 21$$

$$\begin{vmatrix} 3 & 2 & 1 \\ -4 & 5 & -1 \\ 2 & -3 & 4 \end{vmatrix} = 3(5)(4) + 2(-1)(2) + 1(-3)(-4) - 2(5)(1) - (-3)(-1)(3) - 4(2)(-4)$$

$$= 60 - 4 + 12 - 10 - 9 + 32 = 81$$

Alternate Form for a Determinant of Order 3

The determinant of the 3×3 matrix $A = [a_{ij}]$ may be rewritten as follows:

$$\det(A) = a_{11}(a_{22}a_{33} - a_{23}a_{32}) - a_{12}(a_{21}a_{33} - a_{23}a_{31}) + a_{13}(a_{21}a_{32} - a_{22}a_{31})$$

$$= a_{11}\begin{vmatrix} a_{22} & a_{23} \\ a_{32} & a_{33} \end{vmatrix} - a_{12}\begin{vmatrix} a_{21} & a_{23} \\ a_{31} & a_{33} \end{vmatrix} + a_{13}\begin{vmatrix} a_{21} & a_{22} \\ a_{31} & a_{32} \end{vmatrix}$$

which is a linear combination of three determinants of order 2 whose coefficients (with alternating signs) form the first row of the given matrix. This linear combination may be indicated in the form

$$a_{11}\begin{vmatrix} a_{11} & a_{12} & a_{13} \\ a_{21} & a_{22} & a_{23} \\ a_{31} & a_{32} & a_{33} \end{vmatrix} - a_{12}\begin{vmatrix} a_{11} & a_{12} & a_{13} \\ a_{21} & a_{22} & a_{23} \\ a_{31} & a_{32} & a_{33} \end{vmatrix} + a_{13}\begin{vmatrix} a_{11} & a_{12} & a_{13} \\ a_{21} & a_{22} & a_{23} \\ a_{31} & a_{32} & a_{33} \end{vmatrix}$$

Note that each 2×2 matrix can be obtained by deleting, in the original matrix, the row and column containing its coefficient.

EXAMPLE 10.4

$$\begin{vmatrix} 1 & 2 & 3 \\ 4 & -2 & 3 \\ 0 & 5 & -1 \end{vmatrix} = 1\begin{vmatrix} 1 & 2 & 3 \\ 4 & -2 & 3 \\ 0 & 5 & -1 \end{vmatrix} - 2\begin{vmatrix} 1 & 2 & 3 \\ 4 & -2 & 3 \\ 0 & 5 & -1 \end{vmatrix} + 3\begin{vmatrix} 1 & 2 & 3 \\ 4 & -2 & 3 \\ 0 & 5 & -1 \end{vmatrix}$$

$$= 1\begin{vmatrix} -2 & 3 \\ 5 & -1 \end{vmatrix} - 2\begin{vmatrix} 4 & 3 \\ 0 & -1 \end{vmatrix} + 3\begin{vmatrix} 4 & -2 \\ 0 & 5 \end{vmatrix}$$

$$= 1(2 - 15) - 2(-4 + 0) + 3(20 + 0) = -13 + 8 + 60 = 55$$

10.4 PERMUTATIONS

A permutation σ of the set $\{1, 2, \ldots, n\}$ is a one-to-one mapping of the set onto itself or, equivalently, a rearrangement of the numbers $1, 2, \ldots, n$. Such a permutation σ is denoted by

$$\sigma = \begin{pmatrix} 1 & 2 & \cdots & n \\ j_1 & j_2 & \cdots & j_n \end{pmatrix} \qquad \text{or} \qquad \sigma = j_1 j_2 \cdots j_n, \qquad \text{where } j_i = \sigma(i)$$

The set of all such permutations is denoted by S_n, and the number of such permutations is $n!$. If $\sigma \in S_n$, then the inverse mapping $\sigma^{-1} \in S_n$; and if $\sigma, \tau \in S_n$, then the composition mapping $\sigma \circ \tau \in S_n$. Also, the identity mapping $\varepsilon = \sigma \circ \sigma^{-1} \in S_n$. (In fact, $\varepsilon = 123 \cdots n$.)

EXAMPLE 10.5

(a) There are $2! = 2 \cdot 1 = 2$ permutations in S_2, and they are

$$12 \text{ and } 21$$

(b) There are $3! = 3 \cdot 2 \cdot 1 = 6$ permutations in S_3 and they are

$$123, 132, 213, 231, 312, 321$$

Sign (Parity) of a Permutation

Consider an arbitrary permutation σ in S_n, say $\sigma = j_1 j_2 \cdots j_n$. We say σ is an even or odd permutation, according to whether there is an even or odd number of inversions in σ. By an *inversion* in σ we mean a pair of integers (i, k) such that $i > k$, but i precedes k in σ. We then define the sign or parity of σ, written sgn σ, by

$$\text{sgn } \sigma = \begin{cases} 1 & \text{if } \sigma \text{ is even} \\ -1 & \text{if } \sigma \text{ is odd} \end{cases}$$

EXAMPLE 10.6

(a) Consider the permutation $\sigma = 35142$ in S_5. For each element, count the number of elements smaller than it and to the right of it. Thus:

$$3 \text{ produces the inversions } (3, 1) \text{ and } (3, 2).$$
$$5 \text{ produces the inversions } (5, 1), (5, 4), (5, 2).$$
$$4 \text{ produces the inversion } (4, 2).$$

(Note that 1 and 2 produce no inversions.) Since there are, in all, six inversions, σ is even and sgn $\sigma = 1$.

(b) The identity permutation $\varepsilon = 123 \cdots n$ is even because there are no inversions in ε.

(c) In S_2 the permutation 12 is even and 21 is odd. In S_3 the permutations 123, 231, and 312 are even, and the permutations 132, 213, and 321 are odd.

(d) Let τ be the permutation which interchanges two numbers i and j and leaves the other numbers fixed, that is,

$$\tau(i) = j, \qquad \tau(j) = i, \qquad \tau(k) = k, \qquad k \neq i, j$$

We call τ a transposition. If $i < j$, then

$$\tau = 12 \cdots (i - 1)j(i + 1) \cdots (j - 1)i(j + 1) \cdots n$$

There are $2(j - i - 1) + 1$ inversions in τ as follows:

$$(j, i), (j, x), (x, i), \qquad \text{where } x = i + 1, \ldots, j - 1$$

Thus the transposition τ is odd.

10.5 DETERMINANTS OF ARBITRARY ORDER

Let $A = [a_{ij}]$ be an n-square matrix over a field K, that is,

$$A = \begin{bmatrix} a_{11} & a_{12} & \cdots & a_{1n} \\ a_{21} & a_{22} & \cdots & a_{2n} \\ \cdots\cdots\cdots\cdots\cdots\cdots \\ a_{n1} & a_{n2} & \cdots & a_{nn} \end{bmatrix}$$

Consider a product of n elements of A such that one and only one element comes from each row and one and only one element comes from each column. Such a product can be written in the form

$$a_{1j_1} a_{2j_2} \cdots a_{nj_n}$$

that is, where the factors come from successive rows, and so the first subscripts are in the natural order $1, 2, \ldots, n$.   Now since the factors come from different columns, the sequence of second subscripts forms a permutation $\sigma = j_1 j_2 \cdots j_n$ in S_n.   Conversely, each permutation in S_n determines a product of the above form.   Thus the matrix A contains $n!$ such products.

Definition: The determinant of $A = [a_{ij}]$, denoted by $\det(A)$ or $|A|$, is the sum of all the above $n!$ products, where each such product is multiplied by $\operatorname{sgn} \sigma$.   That is,

$$|A| = \sum_\sigma (\operatorname{sgn} \sigma) a_{1j_1} a_{2j_2} \cdots a_{nj_n}$$

or

$$|A| = \sum_{\sigma \in S_n} (\operatorname{sgn} \sigma) a_{1\sigma(1)} a_{2\sigma(2)} \cdots a_{n\sigma(n)}$$

The determinant of the n-square matrix A is said to be of order n.

The next example shows that the above definition agrees with the previous definition of determinants of order 1, 2, and 3.

EXAMPLE 10.7

(a)   Let $A = [a_{11}]$ be a 1×1 matrix.   Since S_1 has only one permutation which is even, $\det(A) = a_{11}$, the number itself.

(b)   Let $A = [a_{ij}]$ be a 2×2 matrix.   In S_2 the permutation 12 is even, and the permutation 21 is odd.   Hence

$$\det(A) = \begin{vmatrix} a_{11} & a_{12} \\ a_{21} & a_{22} \end{vmatrix} = a_{11}a_{22} - a_{12}a_{21}$$

(c)   Let $A = [a_{ij}]$ be a 3×3 matrix.   In S_3 the permutations 123, 231, and 312 are even, and the permutations 321, 213, and 132 are odd.   Hence

$$\det(A) = \begin{vmatrix} a_{11} & a_{12} & a_{13} \\ a_{21} & a_{22} & a_{23} \\ a_{31} & a_{32} & a_{33} \end{vmatrix} = a_{11}a_{22}a_{33} + a_{12}a_{23}a_{31} + a_{13}a_{21}a_{32} - a_{13}a_{22}a_{31} - a_{12}a_{21}a_{33} - a_{11}a_{23}a_{32}$$

Remark: As n increases, the number of terms in the determinant becomes astronomical.   Accordingly, we use indirect methods to evaluate determinants rather than the definition of the determinant.   In fact, we prove a number of properties about determinants which will permit us to shorten the computation considerably. In particular, we show that a determinant of order n is equal to a linear combination of determinants of order $n - 1$, as in the case $n = 3$ above.

10.6   PROPERTIES OF DETERMINANTS

We now list basic properties of the determinant.

Theorem 10.1:   The determinants of a matrix A and its transpose A^T are equal; that is, $|A| = |A^T|$.

By this theorem, proved in Problem 10.35, any theorem about the determinant of a matrix A which concerns the rows of A will have an analogous theorem concerning the columns of A.

The next theorem, proved in Problem 10.37, gives certain cases for which the determinant can be obtained immediately.

Theorem 10.2:   Let A be a square matrix.

   (i)   If A has a row (column) of zeros, then $|A| = 0$.

   (ii)   If A has two identical rows (columns), then $|A| = 0$.

   (iii)   If A is triangular, i.e., A has zeros above or below the diagonal, then $|A| =$ product of diagonal elements.   Thus in particular, $|I| = 1$, where I is the identity matrix.

The next theorem, proved in Problem 10.38, shows how the determinant of a matrix is affected by the elementary row and column operations.

Theorem 10.3:   Suppose B is obtained from A by an elementary row (column) operation.

   (i)   If two rows (columns) of A were interchanged, then $|B| = -|A|$.

   (ii)   If a row (column) of A were multiplied by a scalar k, then $|B| = k|A|$.

   (iii)   If a multiple of a row (column) of A were added to another row (column) of A, then $|B| = |A|$.

We now state two of the most important and useful theorems on determinants.

Theorem 10.4:   The determinant of a product of two matrices A and B is the product of their determinants, that is,

$$\det (AB) = \det (A) \det (B)$$

The above theorem says that the determinant is a multiplicative function.

Theorem 10.5:   Let A be an n-square matrix.   Then the following are equivalent:

   (i) A is invertible, that is, A has an inverse A^{-1}.

   (ii) $AX = 0$ has only the zero solution.

   (iii)   The determinant of A is not zero, that is, $\det (A) \neq 0$.

   Remark: Depending on the author and the text, a nonsingular matrix A is defined to be an invertible matrix A, or a matrix A for which $|A| \neq 0$, or a matrix A for which $AX = 0$ has only the zero solution.   The above theorem shows that all such definitions are equivalent.

We shall prove the above two theorems (see Problems 10.42 and 10.41) using the theory of elementary matrices and the following lemma, which is a special case of Theorem 10.4.

Lemma 10.6:   Let E be an elementary matrix.   Then, for any matrix A,

$$|EA| = |E||A|$$

Recall that matrices A and B are similar if there exists a nonsingular matrix P such that $B = P^{-1}AP$.   Using the multiplicative property of the determinant (Theorem 10.4), one can easily prove the following theorem.

Theorem 10.7:   Suppose A and B are similar matrices.   Then $|A| = |B|$.

10.7 MINORS AND COFACTORS

Consider an n-square matrix $A = [a_{ij}]$. Let M_{ij} denote the $(n-1)$-square submatrix of A obtained by deleting its ith row and jth column. The determinant $|M_{ij}|$ is called the *minor* of the element a_{ij} of A, and we define the *cofactor* of a_{ij}, denoted by A_{ij}, to be the "signed" minor:

$$A_{ij} = (-1)^{i+j}|M_{ij}|$$

Note that the "signs" $(-1)^{i+j}$ accompanying the minors form a chessboard pattern with $+$'s on the main diagonal:

$$\begin{bmatrix} + & - & + & - & \cdots \\ - & + & - & + & \cdots \\ + & - & + & - & \cdots \\ \multicolumn{5}{c}{\cdots\cdots\cdots\cdots\cdots} \end{bmatrix}$$

We emphasize that M_{ij} denotes a matrix whereas A_{ij} denotes a scalar.

Remark: The sign $(-1)^{i+j}$ of the cofactor A_{ij} is frequently obtained using the checkerboard pattern. Specifically, beginning with $+$ and alternating signs, i.e., $+$, $-$, $+$, $-$, $\ldots$, count from the main diagonal to the appropriate square.

EXAMPLE 10.8 Consider the matrix $A = \begin{bmatrix} 1 & 2 & 3 \\ 4 & 5 & 6 \\ 7 & 8 & 9 \end{bmatrix}$. Then

$$|M_{23}| = \begin{bmatrix} 1 & 2 & 3 \\ 4 & 5 & 6 \\ 7 & 8 & 9 \end{bmatrix} = \begin{vmatrix} 1 & 2 \\ 7 & 8 \end{vmatrix} = 8 - 14 = -6 \quad \text{and so} \quad A_{23} = (-1)^{2+3}|M_{23}| = -(-6) = 6$$

$$|M_{31}| = \begin{bmatrix} 1 & 2 & 3 \\ 4 & 5 & 6 \\ 7 & 8 & 9 \end{bmatrix} = \begin{vmatrix} 2 & 3 \\ 5 & 6 \end{vmatrix} = 12 - 15 = -3 \quad \text{and so} \quad A_{31} = (-1)^{3+1}|M_{31}| = +(-3) = -3$$

Laplace Expansion

The following theorem (proved in Problem 10.45) applies.

Theorem 10.8 Laplace: The determinant of a square matrix $A = [a_{ij}]$ is equal to the sum of the products obtained by multiplying the elements of a row (column) by their respective cofactors,

$$|A| = a_{i1}A_{i1} + a_{i2}A_{i2} + \cdots + a_{in}A_{in} = \sum_{j=1}^{n} a_{ij}A_{ij}$$

$$|A| = a_{1j}A_{1j} + a_{2j}A_{2j} + \cdots + a_{nj}A_{nj} = \sum_{i=1}^{n} a_{ij}A_{ij}$$

The above formulas for $|A|$ are called the *Laplace expansions* of the determinant of A by the ith row and the jth column. Together with the elementary row (column) operations, they offer a method of simplifying the computation of $|A|$, as described below.

10.8 EVALUATION OF DETERMINANTS

The following algorithm reduces the evaluation of a determinant of order n to the evaluation of a determinant of order $n - 1$.

Algorithm 10.8 **(Reduction of the Order of a Determinant):** The input is a nonzero n-square matrix $A = [a_{ij}]$ with $n > 1$.

Step 1. Choose an element $a_{ij} = 1$ or, if lacking, $a_{ij} \neq 0$.

Step 2. Using a_{ij} as a pivot, apply elementary row (column) operations to put 0s in all the other positions in the column (row) containing a_{ij}.

Step 3. Expand the determinant by the column (row) containing a_{ij}.

The following remarks are in order.

Remark 1: Algorithm 10.8 is usually used for determinants of order 4 or more. With determinants of order less than 4, one uses the specific formulas for the determinant.

Remark 2: Gaussian elimination or, equivalently, repeated use of Algorithm 10.8 together with row interchanges can be used to transform a matrix A into an upper triangular matrix whose determinant is the product of its diagonal entries. However, one must keep track of the number of row interchanges since each row interchange changes the sign of the determinant. (See Problems 10.10 and 10.11.)

EXAMPLE 10.9 Compute the determinant of $A = \begin{bmatrix} 5 & 4 & 2 & 1 \\ 2 & 3 & 1 & -2 \\ -5 & -7 & -3 & 9 \\ 1 & -2 & -1 & 4 \end{bmatrix}$ by Algorithm 10.8.

Use $a_{23} = 1$ as a pivot to put 0s in the other positions of the third column, that is, apply the row operations "Add $-2R_2$ to R_1", "Add $3R_2$ to R_3", and "Add R_2 to R_4". By Theorem 10.3(iii), the value of the determinant does not change by these operations. Thus

$$|A| = \begin{vmatrix} 5 & 4 & 2 & 1 \\ 2 & 3 & 1 & -2 \\ -5 & -7 & -3 & 9 \\ 1 & -2 & -1 & 4 \end{vmatrix} = \begin{vmatrix} 1 & -2 & 0 & 5 \\ 2 & 3 & 1 & -2 \\ 1 & 2 & 0 & 3 \\ 3 & 1 & 0 & 2 \end{vmatrix}$$

Now if we expand by the third column, we may neglect all terms which contain 0. Thus

$$|A| = (-1)^{2+3} \begin{vmatrix} 1 & -2 & 0 & 5 \\ 2 & 3 & 1 & -2 \\ 1 & 2 & 0 & 3 \\ 3 & 1 & 0 & 2 \end{vmatrix} = -\begin{vmatrix} 1 & -2 & 5 \\ 1 & 2 & 3 \\ 3 & 1 & 2 \end{vmatrix}$$

$$= -(4 - 18 + 5 - 30 - 3 + 4) = -(-38) = 38$$

10.9   CLASSICAL ADJOINT

Consider an *n*-square matrix $A = [a_{ij}]$ over a field K. The *classical adjoint* (traditionally, just *adjoint*) of A, denoted by adj A, is the transpose of the matrix of cofactors of A,

$$\text{adj } A = \begin{bmatrix} A_{11} & A_{21} & \dots & A_{n1} \\ A_{12} & A_{22} & \dots & A_{n2} \\ \multicolumn{4}{c}{\dotfill} \\ A_{1n} & A_{2n} & \dots & A_{nn} \end{bmatrix}$$

We say classical adjoint instead of simply adjoint because the term adjoint is currently used for an entirely different concept.

EXAMPLE 10.10   Let $A = \begin{bmatrix} 2 & 3 & -4 \\ 0 & -4 & 2 \\ 1 & -1 & 5 \end{bmatrix}$. The cofactors of the nine elements of A are

$$A_{11} = + \begin{vmatrix} -4 & 2 \\ -1 & 5 \end{vmatrix} = -18, \qquad A_{12} = - \begin{vmatrix} 0 & 2 \\ 1 & 5 \end{vmatrix} = 2, \qquad A_{13} = + \begin{vmatrix} 0 & -4 \\ 1 & -1 \end{vmatrix} = 4$$

$$A_{21} = - \begin{vmatrix} 3 & -4 \\ -1 & 5 \end{vmatrix} = -11, \qquad A_{22} = + \begin{vmatrix} 2 & -4 \\ 1 & 5 \end{vmatrix} = 14, \qquad A_{23} = - \begin{vmatrix} 2 & 3 \\ 1 & -1 \end{vmatrix} = 5$$

$$A_{31} = + \begin{vmatrix} 3 & -4 \\ -4 & 2 \end{vmatrix} = -10, \qquad A_{32} = - \begin{vmatrix} 2 & -4 \\ 0 & 2 \end{vmatrix} = -4, \qquad A_{33} = + \begin{vmatrix} 2 & 3 \\ 0 & -4 \end{vmatrix} = -8$$

The transpose of the above matrix of cofactors yields the classical adjoint of A, that is,

$$\text{adj } A = \begin{bmatrix} -18 & -11 & -10 \\ 2 & 14 & -4 \\ 4 & 5 & -8 \end{bmatrix}$$

The following theorem (proved in Problem 10.47) applies.

Theorem 10.9:   For any square matrix A,

$$A \cdot (\text{adj } A) = (\text{adj } A) \cdot A = |A|I$$

where I is the identity matrix. Thus if $|A| \neq 0$,

$$A^{-1} = \frac{1}{|A|} (\text{adj } A)$$

EXAMPLE 10.11   Consider the matrix A in Example 10.10. We have

$$\det (A) = -40 + 6 + 0 - 16 + 4 + 0 = -46$$

Also,

$$A(\text{adj } A) = \begin{bmatrix} 2 & 3 & -4 \\ 0 & -4 & 2 \\ 1 & -1 & 5 \end{bmatrix} \begin{bmatrix} -18 & -11 & -10 \\ 2 & 14 & -4 \\ 4 & 5 & -8 \end{bmatrix} = \begin{bmatrix} -46 & 0 & 0 \\ 0 & -46 & 0 \\ 0 & 0 & -46 \end{bmatrix} = -46 \begin{bmatrix} 1 & 0 & 0 \\ 0 & 1 & 0 \\ 0 & 0 & 1 \end{bmatrix}$$

$$= -46I = |A|I$$

Accordingly, by Theorem 10.9,

$$A^{-1} = \frac{1}{|A|}(\text{adj } A) = -\frac{1}{46}\begin{bmatrix} -18 & -11 & -10 \\ 2 & 14 & -4 \\ 4 & 5 & -8 \end{bmatrix} = \begin{bmatrix} \frac{9}{23} & \frac{11}{46} & \frac{5}{23} \\ -\frac{1}{23} & -\frac{7}{23} & \frac{2}{23} \\ -\frac{2}{23} & -\frac{5}{46} & \frac{4}{23} \end{bmatrix}$$

10.10 APPLICATIONS TO LINEAR EQUATIONS, CRAMER'S RULE

Consider a system $AX = B$ of n linear equations in n unknowns. Here $A = [a_{ij}]$ is the (square) matrix of coefficients and $B = [b_i]$ is the column vector of constants. Let A_i be the matrix obtained from A by replacing the ith column of A by the column vector B. Let

$$D = \det(A), \qquad N_1 = \det(A_1), \qquad N_2 = \det(A_2), \dots, N_n = \det(A_n)$$

The fundamental relationship between determinants and the solution of the system $AX = B$ follows.

Theorem 10.10:   The (square) system $AX = B$ has a unique solution if and only if $D \neq 0$. In this case the solution is given by

$$x_1 = \frac{N_1}{D}, \qquad x_2 = \frac{N_2}{D}, \dots, x_n = \frac{N_n}{D}$$

The above theorem, proved in Problem 10.48, is known as *Cramer's rule* for solving systems of linear equations. We emphasize that the theorem only refers to a system with the same number of equations as unknowns, and that it only gives the solution when $D \neq 0$. In fact, if $D = 0$ the theorem does not tell whether or not the system has a solution. However, in the case of a homogeneous system we have the following useful result (Problem 10.67).

Theorem 10.11:   The homogeneous system $AX = 0$ has a nonzero solution if and only if $D = |A| = 0$.

EXAMPLE 10.12   Solve, using determinants: $\begin{cases} 2x + y - z = 3 \\ x + y + z = 1. \\ x - 2y - 3z = 4 \end{cases}$

First compute the determinant D of the matrix of coefficients:

$$D = \begin{vmatrix} 2 & 1 & -1 \\ 1 & 1 & 1 \\ 1 & -2 & -3 \end{vmatrix} = -6 + 1 + 2 + 1 + 4 + 3 = 5$$

Since $D \neq 0$, the system has a unique solution. To compute N_x, N_y, and N_z, replace the coefficients of

x, y, and z in the matrix of coefficients by the constant terms. This yields

$$N_x = \begin{vmatrix} 3 & 1 & -1 \\ 1 & 1 & 1 \\ 4 & -2 & -3 \end{vmatrix} = 10, \qquad N_y = \begin{vmatrix} 2 & 3 & -1 \\ 1 & 1 & 1 \\ 1 & 4 & -3 \end{vmatrix} = -5, \qquad N_z = \begin{vmatrix} 2 & 1 & 3 \\ 1 & 1 & 1 \\ 1 & -2 & 4 \end{vmatrix} = 0$$

Thus the unique solution of the system is $x = N_x/D = 2$, $y = N_y/D = -1$, $z = N_z/D = 0$, that is, the vector $u = (2, -1, 0)$.

10.11　SUBMATRICES, MINORS, PRINCIPAL MINORS

Consider an n-square matrix $A = [a_{ij}]$. Any set of r rows and r columns or, equivalently, any set $I = (i_1, i_2, \ldots, i_r)$ of r row indices and $J = (j_1, j_2, \ldots, j_r)$ of r column indices defines the following submatrix of A of order r:

$$A(I; J) = \begin{bmatrix} a_{i_1, j_1} & a_{i_1, j_2} & \cdots & a_{i_1, j_r} \\ a_{i_2, j_1} & a_{i_2, j_2} & \cdots & a_{i_2, j_r} \\ \cdots\cdots\cdots\cdots\cdots\cdots \\ a_{i_r, j_1} & a_{i_r, j_2} & \cdots & a_{i_r, j_r} \end{bmatrix}$$

The determinant $|(A(I; J)|$ is called a *minor* of A of order r and

$$(-1)^{i_1 + i_2 + \cdots + i_r + j_1 + j_2 + \cdots + j_r} |A(I; J)|$$

is the corresponding *signed minor*. (Note that a minor of order $n - 1$ is a minor in the sense of Section 10.7, and the corresponding signed minor is a cofactor.)

Consider, for example, a 5-square matrix $A = [a_{ij}]$. The row subscripts 1, 2, 4 and the column subscripts 2, 3, 5 define the submatrix

$$M = A(1, 2, 4; 2, 3, 5) = \begin{bmatrix} a_{12} & a_{13} & a_{15} \\ a_{22} & a_{23} & a_{25} \\ a_{42} & a_{43} & a_{45} \end{bmatrix}$$

Then the determinant $|M|$ is the minor, and

$$(-1)^{1 + 2 + 4 + 2 + 3 + 5} |M| = -|M|$$

is the signed minor.

Principal Minors

A minor is a *principal minor* if the row and column indices are the same or, equivalently, if the diagonal elements of the minor come from the diagonal of the matrix. We note that the sign of a principal minor is always $+1$ since the sum of the identical row and column subscripts must always be even.

EXAMPLE 10.13　Find the sums C_1, C_2, and C_3 of the principal minors of orders 1, 2, and 3 of the matrix

$$A = \begin{bmatrix} 1 & 2 & -1 \\ 3 & 5 & 4 \\ -3 & 1 & -2 \end{bmatrix}$$

(a) There are three principal minors of order 1. These are

$$|1| = 1, \quad |5| = 5, \quad |-2| = -2, \qquad \text{and so} \qquad C_1 = 1 + 5 - 2 = 4$$

Note that C_1 is simply the trace of A.

(b) There are three ways to choose two of the three diagonal elements, and each choice gives a minor of order 2. These are

$$\begin{vmatrix} 1 & 2 \\ 3 & 5 \end{vmatrix} = -1, \qquad \begin{vmatrix} 1 & -1 \\ -3 & -2 \end{vmatrix} = -5 \qquad \begin{vmatrix} 5 & 4 \\ 1 & -2 \end{vmatrix} = -14$$

(Note that these minors of order 2 are the cofactors A_{33}, A_{22}, and A_{11} of A.) Thus

$$C_2 = -1 - 5 - 14 = -20$$

(c) There is only one way to choose three of the three diagonal elements. Thus the only minor of order 3 is the determinant of A, that is,

$$|A| = -10 - 24 - 3 - 15 - 4 + 12 = -44$$

Accordingly, $C_3 = -44$.

10.12 BLOCK MATRICES AND DETERMINANTS

The following is the main result of this section.

Theorem 10.12: Suppose M is an upper (lower) triangular block matrix with the diagonal blocks $A_1, A_2, \ldots, A_n$. Then

$$\det(M) = \det(A_1) \det(A_2) \cdots \det(A_n)$$

EXAMPLE 10.14 Find $|M|$, where $M = \begin{bmatrix} 2 & 3 & 4 & 7 & 8 \\ -1 & 5 & 3 & 2 & 1 \\ 0 & 0 & 2 & 1 & 5 \\ 0 & 0 & 3 & -1 & 4 \\ 0 & 0 & 5 & 2 & 6 \end{bmatrix}$

Note that M is an upper triangular block matrix. Evaluate the determinant of each diagonal block:

$$\begin{vmatrix} 2 & 3 \\ -1 & 5 \end{vmatrix} = 10 + 3 = 13, \qquad \begin{vmatrix} 2 & 1 & 5 \\ 3 & -1 & 4 \\ 5 & 2 & 6 \end{vmatrix} = -12 + 20 + 30 + 25 - 16 - 18 = 29$$

Then $|M| = 13(29) = 377$.

Remark: Suppose $M = \begin{bmatrix} A & B \\ C & D \end{bmatrix}$, where A, B, C, and D are square matrices. Then it is not generally true that $|M| = |A||D| - |B||C|$. (See Problem 10.81.)

10.13 DETERMINANTS AND VOLUME

Determinants are related to the notions of area and volume as follows. Let $u_1, u_2, \ldots, u_n$ be vectors in $\mathbf{R}^n$. Let S be the (solid) parallelepiped determined by the vectors, that is,

$$S = \{a_1 u_1 + a_2 u_2 + \cdots + a_n u_n : \ 0 \le a_i \le 1 \text{ for } i = 1, \ldots, n\}$$

(When $n = 2$, S is a parallelogram.)   Let $V(S)$ denote the volume of S (or area of S when $n = 2$).   Then

$$V(S) = \text{absolute value of det }(A)$$

where A is the matrix with rows $u_1, u_2, \ldots, u_n$.   In general, $V(S) = 0$ if and only if the vectors $u_1, \ldots, u_n$ do not form a coordinate system for $\mathbf{R}^n$, i.e., if and only if the vectors are linearly dependent.

EXAMPLE 10.15   Find the volume $V(S)$ of the parallelepiped S in $\mathbf{R}^3$ (Fig. 10-2) determined by the vectors

$$u_1 = (1, 1, 0), \qquad u_2 = (1, 1, 1), \qquad u_3 = (0, 2, 3)$$

Evaluate the determinant of the matrix whose rows are u_1, u_2, u_3:

$$\begin{vmatrix} 1 & 1 & 0 \\ 1 & 1 & 1 \\ 0 & 2 & 3 \end{vmatrix} = 3 + 0 + 0 - 0 - 2 - 3 = -2$$

Hence $V(S) = |-2| = 2$.

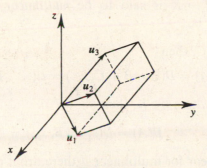

Fig. 10-2

10.14   DETERMINANT OF A LINEAR OPERATOR

Let F be a linear operator on a vector space V with finite dimension.   Let A be the matrix representation of F relative to some basis S of V.   Then we define the determinant of F, written det (F), by

$$\det (F) = |A|$$

If B were another matrix representation of F relative to another basis S' of V, then A and B are similar matrices (Theorem 9.5) and hence $|B| = |A|$ by Theorem 10.7.   In other words, the above definition of det (F) is independent of the particular basis S of V.   (We say that the definition is *well-defined*.)

The next theorem follows from analogous theorems on matrices.

Theorem 10.13:   Let F and G be linear operators on a vector space V.   Then

(i) $\det (F \circ G) = \det (F) \cdot \det (G)$.

(ii) F is invertible if and only if $\det (F) \neq 0$.

EXAMPLE 10.16   Let T be the linear transformation on $\mathbf{R}^3$ defined by

$$T(x, y, z) = (2x - 4y + z, \; x - 2y + 3z, \; 5x + y - z)$$

The matrix A representing T relative to the usual basis of $\mathbf{R}^3$ is

$$A = \begin{bmatrix} 2 & -4 & 1 \\ 1 & -2 & 3 \\ 5 & 1 & -1 \end{bmatrix}$$

Then

$$\det(T) = |A| = 4 - 60 + 1 + 10 - 6 - 4 = -55$$

10.15   MULTILINEARITY AND DETERMINANTS

Let V be a vector space over a field K.   Let $\mathscr{A} = V^n$, that is, $\mathscr{A}$ consists of all the n-tuples

$$A = (A_1, A_2, \ldots, A_n)$$

where the A_i are vectors in V.   The following definitions apply.

Definition: A function $D \colon \mathscr{A} \to K$ is said to be *multilinear* if it is linear in each of the components, that is,

(i)   If $A_i = B + C$, then

$$D(A) = D(\ldots, B + C, \ldots) = D(\ldots, B, \ldots,) + D(\ldots, C, \ldots)$$

(ii)   If $A_i = kB$, where $k \in K$, then

$$D(A) = D(\ldots, kB, \ldots) = kD(\ldots, B, \ldots)$$

We also say n-linear for multilinear if there are n components.

Definition: A function $D \colon \mathscr{A} \to K$ is said to be *alternating* if $D(A) = 0$ whenever A has two identical elements, that is,

$$D(A_1, A_2, \ldots, A_n) = 0 \qquad \text{whenever} \qquad A_i = A_j, \;\; i \neq j$$

Now let $\mathbf{M}$ denote the set of all n-square matrices A over a field K.   We may view A as an n-tuple consisting of its row vectors $A_1, A_2, \ldots, A_n$, that is, we may view A in the form $A = (A_1, A_2, \ldots, A_n)$.

The following basic result (proved in Problem 10.50) applies (where I denotes the identity matrix).

Theorem 10.14:   There exists a unique function $D \colon \mathbf{M} \to K$ such that

    (i) D is multilinear.

    (ii) D is alternating.

    (iii) $D(I) = 1$.

This function D is none other than the determinant function, that is, for any matrix $A \in \mathbf{M}$, $D(A) = |A|$.

Solved Problems

COMPUTATION OF DETERMINANTS OF ORDER 2 AND 3

10.1. Evaluate the determinant of each matrix:

$$(a)\ A = \begin{bmatrix} 6 & 5 \\ 2 & 3 \end{bmatrix};\ (b)\ B = \begin{bmatrix} 2 & -3 \\ 4 & 7 \end{bmatrix};\ (c)\ C = \begin{bmatrix} 4 & -5 \\ -1 & -2 \end{bmatrix}.$$

Use the formula $\begin{vmatrix} a & b \\ c & d \end{vmatrix} = ad - bc.$

(a) $|A| = 6(3) - 5(2) = 18 - 10 = 8$

(b) $|B| = 14 + 12 = 26$

(c) $|C| = -8 - 5 = -13$

10.2. Compute the determinant of each matrix:

$$(a)\ A = \begin{bmatrix} a - b & b \\ b & a + b \end{bmatrix};\ (b)\ B = \begin{bmatrix} a - b & a \\ a & a + b \end{bmatrix};\ (c)\ C = \begin{bmatrix} t - 5 & 6 \\ 3 & t + 2 \end{bmatrix}$$

(a) $|A| = (a - b)(a + b) - b^2 = a^2 - b^2 - b^2 = a^2 - 2b^2$

(b) $|B| = (a - b)(a + b) - a^2 = a^2 - b^2 - a^2 = -b^2$

(c) $|C| = (t - 5)(t + 2) - 18 = t^2 - 3t - 10 - 18 = t^2 - 3t - 28$

10.3. Find those values of t for which: $(a)\ \begin{vmatrix} t & t \\ 4 & 2t \end{vmatrix} = 0;\ \ (b)\ \begin{vmatrix} t - 3 & 1 \\ 2 & t - 4 \end{vmatrix} = 0.$

(a)   First find $\begin{vmatrix} t & t \\ 4 & 2t \end{vmatrix} = 2t^2 - 4t.$ Then set $2t^2 - 4t = 0$ or $2t(t - 2) = 0.$ Hence $t = 0$ and $t = 2.$ That is, if $t = 0$ or $t = 2,$ then the determinant is zero.

(b)   First find $\begin{vmatrix} t - 3 & 1 \\ 2 & t - 4 \end{vmatrix} = t^2 - 7t + 12 - 2 = t^2 - 7t + 10.$ Then set $t^2 - 7t + 10 = 0$ or $(t - 5)(t - 2) = 0.$ Thus the determinant is zero if $t = 5$ or $t = 2.$

10.4. Evaluate the determinant of each matrix:

$$(a)\ A = \begin{bmatrix} 2 & 3 & 4 \\ 5 & 4 & 3 \\ 1 & 2 & 1 \end{bmatrix};\ (b)\ B = \begin{bmatrix} 1 & -2 & 3 \\ 2 & 4 & -1 \\ 1 & 5 & -2 \end{bmatrix};\ (c)\ C = \begin{bmatrix} a_1 & b_1 & c_1 \\ a_2 & b_2 & c_2 \\ a_3 & b_3 & c_3 \end{bmatrix}.$$

Use the diagrams in Fig. 10-1.

(a) $|A| = 2(4)(1) + 3(3)(1) + 4(2)(5) - 1(4)(4) - 2(3)(2) - 1(3)(5)$
$\qquad = 8 + 9 + 40 - 16 - 12 - 15 = 14$

(b) $|B| = -8 + 2 + 30 - 12 + 5 - 8 = 9$

(c) $|C| = a_1 b_2 c_3 + b_1 c_2 a_3 + c_1 b_3 a_2 - a_3 b_2 c_1 - b_3 c_2 a_1 - c_3 b_1 a_2$

10.5. Compute the determinant of each matrix:

$$(a)\ A = \begin{bmatrix} 1 & 2 & 3 \\ 2 & 5 & -1 \\ 4 & -2 & 3 \end{bmatrix};\ (b)\ B = \begin{bmatrix} 1 & 0 & 0 \\ 3 & 2 & -4 \\ 4 & 1 & 3 \end{bmatrix};\ (c)\ C = \begin{bmatrix} a & b & c \\ c & a & b \\ b & c & a \end{bmatrix}.$$

(a) $|A| = 15 - 8 - 12 - 60 - 2 - 12 = -79$

(b)   Here expand by the first row, omitting zero products,

$$|B| = 1 \begin{vmatrix} 2 & -4 \\ 1 & 3 \end{vmatrix} = 6 + 4 = 10$$

(c) $|C| = a^3 + b^3 + c^3 - abc - abc - abc = a^3 + b^3 + c^3 - 3abc$

10.6. Compute the determinant of each matrix:

$$(a)\ A = \begin{bmatrix} 2 & 3 & 4 \\ 5 & 6 & 7 \\ 8 & 9 & 1 \end{bmatrix};\ (b)\ B = \begin{bmatrix} \frac{1}{2} & -1 & -\frac{1}{3} \\ \frac{3}{4} & \frac{1}{2} & -1 \\ 1 & -4 & 1 \end{bmatrix}.$$

(a)   One can simplify the entries by first subtracting twice the first row from the second row, that is, by applying the row operation "Add $-2R_1$ to R_2".   Then

$$|A| = \begin{vmatrix} 2 & 3 & 4 \\ 5 & 6 & 7 \\ 8 & 9 & 1 \end{vmatrix} = \begin{vmatrix} 2 & 3 & 4 \\ 1 & 0 & -1 \\ 8 & 9 & 1 \end{vmatrix} = 0 - 24 + 36 - 0 + 18 - 3 = 27$$

(b)   The arithmetic is simpler if fractions are eliminated.   Hence first multiply the first row R_1 by 6 and the second row R_2 by 4.   Then

$$6(4)|B| = 24|B| = \begin{vmatrix} 3 & -6 & -2 \\ 3 & 2 & -4 \\ 1 & -4 & 1 \end{vmatrix} = 6 + 24 + 24 + 4 - 48 + 18 = 28$$

Hence $|B| = \dfrac{28}{24} = \dfrac{7}{6}$.

COMPUTATION OF DETERMINANTS OF ARBITRARY ORDER

10.7. Compute the determinant of each matrix:

$$(a)\ A = \begin{bmatrix} 2 & 5 & -3 & -2 \\ -2 & -3 & 2 & -5 \\ 1 & 3 & -2 & 2 \\ -1 & -6 & 4 & 3 \end{bmatrix};\ (b)\ B = \begin{bmatrix} 1 & 2 & 2 & 3 \\ 1 & 0 & -2 & 0 \\ 3 & -1 & 1 & -2 \\ 4 & -3 & 0 & 2 \end{bmatrix}.$$

(a)   Use a_{31} as a pivot and apply the row operations "Add $-2R_3$ to R_1", "Add $2R_3$ to R_2", and "Add R_3 to R_4".   Then

$$|A| = \begin{vmatrix} 2 & 5 & -3 & -2 \\ -2 & -3 & 2 & -5 \\ 1 & 3 & -2 & 2 \\ -1 & -6 & 4 & 3 \end{vmatrix} = \begin{vmatrix} 0 & -1 & 1 & -6 \\ 0 & 3 & -2 & -1 \\ 1 & 3 & -2 & 2 \\ 0 & -3 & 2 & 5 \end{vmatrix} = \begin{vmatrix} -1 & 1 & -6 \\ 3 & -2 & -1 \\ -3 & 2 & 5 \end{vmatrix}$$

$$= 10 + 3 - 36 + 36 - 2 - 15 = -4$$

(b) Use $b_{21} = 1$ as a pivot and apply the column operation "Add $2C_1$ to C_3". Then

$$|B| = \begin{vmatrix} 1 & 2 & 4 & 3 \\ 1 & 0 & 0 & 0 \\ 3 & -1 & 7 & -2 \\ 4 & -3 & 8 & 2 \end{vmatrix} = - \begin{vmatrix} 2 & 4 & 3 \\ -1 & 7 & -2 \\ -3 & 8 & 2 \end{vmatrix} = -(28 + 24 - 24 + 63 + 32 + 8) = -131$$

10.8. Find the determinant of $C = \begin{bmatrix} 6 & 2 & 1 & 0 & 5 \\ 2 & 1 & 1 & -2 & 1 \\ 1 & 1 & 2 & -2 & 3 \\ 3 & 0 & 2 & 3 & -1 \\ -1 & -1 & -3 & 4 & 2 \end{bmatrix}$.

First reduce $|C|$ to a determinant of order 4, then to a determinant of order 3, for which we can use Fig. 10-1. First use $c_{22} = 1$ as a pivot and apply the row operations "Add $-2R_2$ to R_1", "Add $-R_2$ to R_3", and "Add R_2 to R_5". Then

$$|C| = \begin{vmatrix} 2 & 0 & -1 & 4 & 3 \\ 2 & 1 & 1 & -2 & 1 \\ -1 & 0 & 1 & 0 & 2 \\ 3 & 0 & 2 & 3 & -1 \\ 1 & 0 & -2 & 2 & 6 \end{vmatrix} = \begin{vmatrix} 2 & -1 & 4 & 3 \\ -1 & 1 & 0 & 2 \\ 3 & 2 & 3 & -1 \\ 1 & -2 & 2 & 3 \end{vmatrix} = \begin{vmatrix} 1 & -1 & 4 & 5 \\ 0 & 1 & 0 & 0 \\ 5 & 2 & 3 & -5 \\ -1 & -2 & 2 & 7 \end{vmatrix}$$

$$= \begin{vmatrix} 1 & 4 & 5 \\ 5 & 3 & -5 \\ -1 & 2 & 7 \end{vmatrix} = 21 + 20 + 50 + 15 + 10 - 140 = -24$$

10.9. Find the determinant of each matrix:

(a) $A = \begin{bmatrix} 5 & 6 & 7 & 8 \\ 0 & 0 & 0 & 0 \\ 1 & -3 & 5 & -7 \\ 8 & 4 & 2 & 6 \end{bmatrix}$; (b) $B = \begin{bmatrix} 5 & 6 & 7 & 6 \\ 1 & -3 & 5 & -3 \\ 4 & 9 & -3 & 9 \\ 2 & 7 & 8 & 7 \end{bmatrix}$; (c) $C = \begin{bmatrix} 2 & 3 & 4 & 5 \\ 0 & -3 & 7 & -8 \\ 0 & 0 & 5 & 6 \\ 0 & 0 & 0 & 4 \end{bmatrix}$

(a) Since A has a row of zeros, det $(A) = 0$.

(b) Since the second and fourth columns of B are equal, det $(B) = 0$.

(c) Since C is triangular, det (C) is equal to the product of the diagonal entries. Hence det $(C) = -120$.

10.10. Describe the Gaussian partial pivoting algorithm for calculating the determinant of an n-square matrix $A = [a_{ij}]$.

The algorithm uses Gaussian elimination to transform A into an upper triangular matrix (whose determinant is the product of its diagonal elements). Since the algorithm involves exchanging rows, which changes the sign of the determinant, one must keep track of such changes using some variable, say SIGN. The algorithm will also use "partial pivoting", that is, the element with the greatest absolute value in the column will be used as the pivot. The algorithm follows.

Algorithm 10.10P: Finds the determinant of an input matrix $A = [a_{ij}]$.

Step 1. Set SIGN = 0. (This initializes the variable SIGN.)

Step 2. Find in the first column the entry a_{i1} with greatest absolute value.

    (a) If $a_{i1} = 0$, then set $\det(A) = 0$ and EXIT.

    (b) If $i \neq 1$, then interchange the first and ith rows and set SIGN = SIGN + 1.

Step 3. Use a_{11} as a pivot and elementary row operations of the form "Add kR_q to R_p" to put 0s below a_{11}.

Step 4. Repeat Steps 2 and 3 with the submatrix obtained by omitting the first row and the first column.

Step 5. Continue the above process until A is an upper triangular matrix.

Step 6. Set $\det(A) = (-1)^{\text{SIGN}} a_{11} a_{22} \cdots a_{nn}$, and EXIT.

Note that the elementary row operation "Multiply R_i by $k \neq 0$", which is permitted in the Gaussian algorithm for a system of linear equations, is barred here because it changes the value of the determinant.

10.11. Use the Gaussian algorithm, Algorithm 10.10P, to find the determinant of

$$A = \begin{bmatrix} 3 & 8 & 6 \\ -2 & -3 & 1 \\ 5 & 10 & 15 \end{bmatrix}.$$

First row reduce the matrix to an upper triangular form, keeping track of the number of row interchanges:

$$A \sim \begin{bmatrix} 5 & 10 & 15 \\ -2 & -3 & 1 \\ 3 & 8 & 6 \end{bmatrix} \sim \begin{bmatrix} 5 & 10 & 15 \\ 0 & 1 & 7 \\ 0 & 2 & -3 \end{bmatrix} \sim \begin{bmatrix} 5 & 10 & 15 \\ 0 & 2 & -3 \\ 0 & 1 & 7 \end{bmatrix} \sim \begin{bmatrix} 5 & 10 & 15 \\ 0 & 2 & -3 \\ 0 & 0 & \frac{17}{2} \end{bmatrix}$$

Matrix A is now in triangular form and SIGN = 2 since there were two interchanges of rows. Hence

$$\det(A) = (-1)^{\text{SIGN}} (5)(2)(\tfrac{17}{2}) = 85$$

COFACTORS, CLASSICAL ADJOINTS, MINORS, PRINCIPAL MINORS

10.12. Let $A = \begin{bmatrix} 2 & 1 & -3 & 4 \\ 5 & -4 & 7 & -2 \\ 4 & 0 & 6 & -3 \\ 3 & -2 & 5 & 2 \end{bmatrix}.$

(a) Find A_{23}, the cofactor (signed minor) of the 7 in A.

(b) Find A_{44}, the cofactor of the 2 in the last column of A.

(c)　Find the minor and the signed minor of the submatrix $M = A(2, 4; 2, 3)$.

(d)　Find the principal minor determined by the first and third diagonal entries, that is, by $M = A(1, 3; 1, 3)$.

(a)　Take the determinant of the submatrix of A obtained by deleting row 2 and column 3 (which contain the 7), and multiply the determinant by $(-1)^{2+3}$,

$$A_{23} = (-1)^{2+3} \begin{vmatrix} 2 & 1 & -3 & 4 \\ 5 & -4 & 7 & -2 \\ 4 & 0 & 6 & -3 \\ 3 & -2 & 5 & 2 \end{vmatrix} = - \begin{vmatrix} 2 & 1 & 4 \\ 4 & 0 & -3 \\ 3 & -2 & 2 \end{vmatrix}$$

$$= -(0 - 9 - 32 - 0 - 12 - 8) = -(-61) = 61$$

The exponent $2 + 3$ comes from the subscripts of A_{23}, that is, from the fact that 7 appears in row 2 and column 3.

(b)　We have

$$A_{44} = (-1)^{4+4} \begin{vmatrix} 2 & 1 & -3 & 4 \\ 5 & -4 & 7 & -2 \\ 4 & 0 & 6 & -3 \\ 3 & -2 & 5 & 2 \end{vmatrix} = \begin{vmatrix} 2 & 1 & -3 \\ 5 & -4 & 7 \\ 4 & 0 & 6 \end{vmatrix}$$

$$= -48 + 28 + 0 - 48 - 0 - 30 = -98$$

(c)　The row subscripts are 2 and 4 and the column subscripts are 2 and 3. Hence the minor is the determinant

$$|M| = \begin{vmatrix} a_{22} & a_{23} \\ a_{42} & a_{43} \end{vmatrix} = \begin{vmatrix} -4 & 7 \\ -2 & 5 \end{vmatrix} = -20 + 14 = -6$$

and the signed minor is

$$(-1)^{2+4+2+3}|M| = -|M| = -(-6) = 6$$

(d)　The principal minor is the determinant

$$|M| = \begin{vmatrix} a_{11} & a_{13} \\ a_{31} & a_{33} \end{vmatrix} = \begin{vmatrix} 2 & -3 \\ 4 & 6 \end{vmatrix} = 12 + 12 = 24$$

Note that now the diagonal entries of the submatrix are diagonal entries of the original matrix. Also, the sign of the principal minor is positive.

10.13. Let $B = \begin{bmatrix} 1 & 1 & 1 \\ 2 & 3 & 4 \\ 5 & 8 & 9 \end{bmatrix}$. Find: (a) $|B|$; (b) adj B; (c) B^{-1} using adj B.

(a)　$|B| = 27 + 20 + 16 - 15 - 32 - 18 = -2$

(b) Take the transpose of the matrix of cofactors,

$$\text{adj } B = \begin{bmatrix} \begin{vmatrix} 3 & 4 \\ 8 & 9 \end{vmatrix} & -\begin{vmatrix} 2 & 4 \\ 5 & 9 \end{vmatrix} & \begin{vmatrix} 2 & 3 \\ 5 & 8 \end{vmatrix} \\[2mm] -\begin{vmatrix} 1 & 1 \\ 8 & 9 \end{vmatrix} & \begin{vmatrix} 1 & 1 \\ 5 & 9 \end{vmatrix} & -\begin{vmatrix} 1 & 1 \\ 5 & 8 \end{vmatrix} \\[2mm] \begin{vmatrix} 1 & 1 \\ 3 & 4 \end{vmatrix} & -\begin{vmatrix} 1 & 1 \\ 2 & 4 \end{vmatrix} & \begin{vmatrix} 1 & 1 \\ 2 & 3 \end{vmatrix} \end{bmatrix}^T = \begin{bmatrix} -5 & 2 & 1 \\ -1 & 4 & -3 \\ 1 & -2 & 1 \end{bmatrix}^T = \begin{bmatrix} -5 & -1 & 1 \\ 2 & 4 & -2 \\ 1 & -3 & 1 \end{bmatrix}$$

(c) Since $|B| \neq 0$,

$$B^{-1} = \frac{1}{|B|} (\text{adj } B) = \frac{1}{-2} \begin{bmatrix} -5 & -1 & 1 \\ 2 & 4 & -2 \\ 1 & -3 & 1 \end{bmatrix} = \begin{bmatrix} \frac{5}{2} & \frac{1}{2} & -\frac{1}{2} \\ -1 & -2 & 1 \\ -\frac{1}{2} & \frac{3}{2} & -\frac{1}{2} \end{bmatrix}$$

10.14. Consider an arbitrary 2-square matrix $A = \begin{bmatrix} a & b \\ c & d \end{bmatrix}$. (a) Find adj A. (b) Show that adj (adj A) = A.

(a) $\text{adj } A = \begin{bmatrix} +|d| & -|c| \\ -|b| & +|a| \end{bmatrix}^T = \begin{bmatrix} d & -c \\ -b & a \end{bmatrix}^T = \begin{bmatrix} d & -b \\ -c & a \end{bmatrix}$

(b) $\text{adj (adj } A) = \text{adj} \begin{bmatrix} d & -b \\ -c & a \end{bmatrix} = \begin{bmatrix} +|a| & -|-c| \\ -|-b| & +|d| \end{bmatrix}^T = \begin{bmatrix} a & c \\ b & d \end{bmatrix}^T = \begin{bmatrix} a & b \\ c & d \end{bmatrix} = A$

10.15. Let $A = \begin{bmatrix} 1 & 2 & 3 \\ 4 & 5 & 6 \\ 0 & 7 & 8 \end{bmatrix}$, and let S_k denote the sum of its principal minors of order k.

Find S_k for: (a) $k = 1$; (b) $k = 2$; (c) $k = 3$.

(a) The principal minors of order 1 are the diagonal elements. Thus S_1 is the trace of A, that is,

$$S_1 = \text{tr}(A) = 1 + 5 + 8 = 14$$

(b) The principal minors of order 2 are the cofactors of the diagonal elements. Thus

$$S_2 = A_{11} + A_{22} + A_{33} = \begin{vmatrix} 5 & 6 \\ 7 & 8 \end{vmatrix} + \begin{vmatrix} 1 & 3 \\ 0 & 8 \end{vmatrix} + \begin{vmatrix} 1 & 2 \\ 4 & 5 \end{vmatrix}$$

$$= -2 + 8 - 3 = 3$$

(c) There is only one principal minor of order 3, the determinant of A. Then

$$S_3 = |A| = 40 + 0 + 84 - 0 - 42 - 64 = 18$$

10.16. For the matrix $A = \begin{bmatrix} 1 & 3 & 0 & -1 \\ -4 & 2 & 5 & 1 \\ 1 & 0 & 3 & -2 \\ 3 & -2 & 1 & 4 \end{bmatrix}$ find the number N_k and the sum S_k of all

principal minors of order: (a) $k = 1$; (b) $k = 2$; (c) $k = 3$; (d) $k = 4$.

Each (nonempty) subset of the diagonal (or equivalently, each nonempty subset of $\{1, 2, 3, 4\}$) determines a principal minor of A, and $N_k = \binom{n}{k} = \dfrac{n!}{k!(n-k)!}$ of them are of order k.

(a) $N_1 = \binom{4}{1} = 4$ and

$$S_1 = |1| + |2| + |3| + |4| = 1 + 2 + 3 + 4 = 10$$

(b) $N_2 = \binom{4}{2} = 6$ and

$$S_2 = \begin{vmatrix} 1 & 3 \\ -4 & 2 \end{vmatrix} + \begin{vmatrix} 1 & 0 \\ 1 & 3 \end{vmatrix} + \begin{vmatrix} 1 & -1 \\ 3 & 4 \end{vmatrix} + \begin{vmatrix} 2 & 5 \\ 0 & 3 \end{vmatrix} + \begin{vmatrix} 2 & 1 \\ -2 & 4 \end{vmatrix} + \begin{vmatrix} 3 & -2 \\ 1 & 4 \end{vmatrix}$$

$$= 14 + 3 + 7 + 6 + 10 + 14 = 54$$

(c) $N_3 = \binom{4}{3} = 4$ and

$$S_3 = \begin{vmatrix} 1 & 3 & 0 \\ -4 & 2 & 5 \\ 1 & 0 & 3 \end{vmatrix} + \begin{vmatrix} 1 & 3 & -1 \\ -4 & 2 & 1 \\ 3 & -2 & 4 \end{vmatrix} + \begin{vmatrix} 1 & 0 & -1 \\ 1 & 3 & -2 \\ 3 & 1 & 4 \end{vmatrix} + \begin{vmatrix} 2 & 5 & 1 \\ 0 & 3 & -2 \\ -2 & 1 & 4 \end{vmatrix}$$

$$= 57 + 65 + 22 + 54 = 198$$

(d) $N_4 = 1$ and $S_4 = \det(A) = 378$

DETERMINANTS AND SYSTEMS OF LINEAR EQUATIONS

10.17. Solve each system using determinants:

(a) $\begin{aligned} 2x + \ y &= 7 \\ 3x - 5y &= 4 \end{aligned}$;   (b) $\begin{aligned} ax - 2by &= \ c \\ 3ax - 5by &= 2c \end{aligned}$ where $ab \neq 0$.

(a)   First find $D = \begin{vmatrix} 2 & 1 \\ 3 & -5 \end{vmatrix} = -10 - 3 = -13$.   Since $D \neq 0$, the system has a unique solution.

Next find $N_x = \begin{vmatrix} 7 & 1 \\ 4 & -5 \end{vmatrix} = -39$ and $N_y = \begin{vmatrix} 2 & 7 \\ 3 & 4 \end{vmatrix} = -13$.   Thus $x = N_x/D = 3$ and $y = N_y/D = 1$.

(b)   First find $D = \begin{vmatrix} a & -2b \\ 3a & -5b \end{vmatrix} = -5ab + 6ab = ab$.   Since $D = ab \neq 0$, the system has a unique

solution.   Next find $N_x = \begin{vmatrix} c & -2b \\ 2c & -5b \end{vmatrix} = -5bc + 4bc = -bc$ and

$$N_y = \begin{vmatrix} a & c \\ 3a & 2c \end{vmatrix} = 2ac - 3ac = -ac$$

Then $x = N_x/D = -bc/ab = -c/a$ and $y = N_y/D = -ac/ab = -c/b$.

10.18. Solve using determinants: $\begin{aligned} 3y + 2x &= z + 1 \\ 3x + 2z &= 8 - 5y \\ 3z - 1 \ &= x - 2y \end{aligned}$

First arrange the equations in standard form, and then compute the determinant D of the matrix of coefficients,

$$
\begin{array}{l}
2x + 3y - z = 1 \\
3x + 5y + 2z = 8 \qquad \text{and} \qquad D = \begin{vmatrix} 2 & 3 & -1 \\ 3 & 5 & 2 \\ 1 & -2 & -3 \end{vmatrix} = -30 + 6 + 6 + 5 + 8 + 27 = 22 \\
x - 2y - 3z = -1
\end{array}
$$

Since $D \neq 0$, the system has a unique solution. To compute N_x, N_y, and N_z, replace the corresponding coefficients of the unknown in the matrix of coefficients by the constant terms

$$
N_x = \begin{vmatrix} 1 & 3 & -1 \\ 8 & 5 & 2 \\ -1 & -2 & -3 \end{vmatrix} = -15 - 6 + 16 - 5 + 4 + 72 = 66
$$

$$
N_y = \begin{vmatrix} 2 & 1 & -1 \\ 3 & 8 & 2 \\ 1 & -1 & -3 \end{vmatrix} = -48 + 2 + 3 + 8 + 4 + 9 = -22
$$

$$
N_z = \begin{vmatrix} 2 & 3 & 1 \\ 3 & 5 & 8 \\ 1 & -2 & -1 \end{vmatrix} = -10 + 24 - 6 - 5 + 32 + 9 = 44
$$

Hence

$$
x = \frac{N_x}{D} = \frac{66}{22} = 3, \qquad y = \frac{N_y}{D} = \frac{-22}{22} = -1, \qquad z = \frac{N_z}{D} = \frac{44}{22} = 2
$$

10.19. Use determinants to find those values of k for which the system has a unique solution:

$$
\begin{array}{l}
kx + y + z = 1 \\
x + ky + z = 1 \\
x + y + kz = 1
\end{array}
$$

The system has a unique solution when $D \neq 0$, where D is the determinant of the matrix of coefficients. Compute

$$
D = \begin{vmatrix} k & 1 & 1 \\ 1 & k & 1 \\ 1 & 1 & k \end{vmatrix} = k^3 + 1 + 1 - k - k - k = k^3 - 3k + 2 = (k-1)^2(k+2)
$$

Thus the system has a unique solution when $(k-1)^2(k+2) \neq 0$, that is, when $k \neq 1$ and $k \neq -2$. (Gaussian elimination indicates that the system has no solution when $k = -2$, and the system has an infinite number of solutions when $k = 1$.)

MISCELLANEOUS PROBLEMS

10.20. Without expanding the determinant, show that $\begin{vmatrix} 1 & a & b+c \\ 1 & b & c+a \\ 1 & c & a+b \end{vmatrix} = 0$.

Add the second column to the third column, and remove the common factor from the third column. This yields

$$
\begin{vmatrix} 1 & a & b+c \\ 1 & b & c+a \\ 1 & c & a+b \end{vmatrix} = \begin{vmatrix} 1 & a & a+b+c \\ 1 & b & a+b+c \\ 1 & c & a+b+c \end{vmatrix} = (a+b+c)\begin{vmatrix} 1 & a & 1 \\ 1 & b & 1 \\ 1 & c & 1 \end{vmatrix} = (a+b+c)(0) = 0
$$

(We use the fact that a determinant with two identical columns is zero.)

10.21. Find the volume $V(S)$ of the parallelepiped S in $\mathbf{R}^3$ determined by the vectors:

    (a) $u_1 = (1, 1, 1)$, $u_2 = (1, 3, -4)$, $u_3 = (1, 2, -5)$.

    (b) $u_1 = (1, 2, 4)$, $u_2 = (2, 1, -3)$, $u_3 = (5, 7, 9)$.

      $V(S)$ is the absolute value of the determinant of the matrix M whose rows are the given vectors. Thus

$$(a)\quad |M| = \begin{vmatrix} 1 & 1 & 1 \\ 1 & 3 & -4 \\ 1 & 2 & -5 \end{vmatrix} = -15 - 4 + 2 - 3 + 8 + 5 = -7. \quad \text{Hence } V(S) = |-7| = 7.$$

$$(b)\quad |M| = \begin{vmatrix} 1 & 2 & 4 \\ 2 & 1 & -3 \\ 5 & 7 & 9 \end{vmatrix} = 9 - 30 + 56 - 20 + 21 - 36 = 0. \quad \text{Thus } V(S) = 0 \text{ or, in other words,}$$

u_1, u_2, u_3 lie in a plane and are linearly dependent.

10.22. Find the volume $V(S)$ of the parallelepiped S in $\mathbf{R}^4$ determined by the vectors:

$$u_1 = (2, -1, 4, -3), \quad u_2 = (-1, 1, 0, 2), \quad u_3 = (3, 2, 3, -1), \quad u_4 = (1, -2, 2, 3)$$

Evaluate the following determinant, using a_{22} as a pivot and applying the elementary column operations "Add C_2 to C_1" and "Add $-2C_2$ to C_4":

$$\begin{vmatrix} 2 & -1 & 4 & -3 \\ -1 & 1 & 0 & 2 \\ 3 & 2 & 3 & -1 \\ 1 & -2 & 2 & 3 \end{vmatrix} = \begin{vmatrix} 1 & -1 & 4 & -1 \\ 0 & 1 & 0 & 0 \\ 5 & 2 & 3 & -5 \\ -1 & -2 & 2 & 7 \end{vmatrix} = \begin{vmatrix} 1 & 4 & -1 \\ 5 & 3 & -5 \\ -1 & 2 & 7 \end{vmatrix}$$

$$= 21 + 20 - 10 - 3 + 10 - 140 = -102$$

Hence $V(S) = 102$.

10.23. Find det (M), where $M = \begin{bmatrix} 3 & 4 & 0 & 0 & 0 \\ 2 & 5 & 0 & 0 & 0 \\ 0 & 9 & 2 & 0 & 0 \\ 0 & 5 & 0 & 6 & 7 \\ 0 & 0 & 4 & 3 & 4 \end{bmatrix}$.

    Partition M into a (lower) triangular block matrix as follows:

$$M = \left[\begin{array}{cc|c|cc} 3 & 4 & 0 & 0 & 0 \\ 2 & 5 & 0 & 0 & 0 \\ \hline 0 & 9 & 2 & 0 & 0 \\ \hline 0 & 5 & 0 & 6 & 7 \\ 0 & 0 & 4 & 3 & 4 \end{array}\right]$$

Evaluate the determinant of each diagonal block:

$$\begin{vmatrix} 3 & 4 \\ 2 & 5 \end{vmatrix} = 15 - 8 = 7, \qquad |2| = 2, \qquad \begin{vmatrix} 6 & 7 \\ 3 & 4 \end{vmatrix} = 24 - 21 = 3$$

Hence $|M| = 7(2)(3) = 42$.

10.24. Find the determinant of each linear mapping:

(a) $F: \mathbf{R}^3 \to \mathbf{R}^3$ defined by $F(x, y, z) = (x + 3y - 4z, 2y + 7z, x + 5y - 3z)$.

(b) $\mathbf{D}: \mathbf{P}_2(t) \to \mathbf{P}_2(t)$ defined by $\mathbf{D}(f(t)) = df/dt$.

(c) $G: \mathbf{R}^3 \to \mathbf{R}^2$ defined by $G(x, y, z) = (x + 5y - 6z, 2x + 4y + 7z)$.

The determinant of a linear operator is equal to the determinant of any matrix A which represents the linear operator.   Thus:

(a) Find the matrix A which represents F relative, say, to the usual basis.   Then

$$A = \begin{bmatrix} 1 & 3 & -4 \\ 0 & 2 & 7 \\ 1 & 5 & -3 \end{bmatrix} \quad \text{and so} \quad \det(F) = |A| = -6 + 21 + 0 + 8 - 35 - 0 = -12$$

(b) Find the matrix A which represents the differential operator $\mathbf{D}$ relative, say, to the basis $\{t^2, t, 1\}$.   We have

$$\mathbf{D}(t^2) = 2t = 0t^2 + 2t + 0(1)$$

$$\mathbf{D}(t) = 1 = 0t^2 + 0t + 1(1) \quad \text{and so} \quad A = \begin{bmatrix} 0 & 0 & 0 \\ 2 & 0 & 0 \\ 0 & 1 & 0 \end{bmatrix}.$$

$$\mathbf{D}(1) = 0 = 0t^2 + 0t + 0(1)$$

Thus $\det(\mathbf{D}) = |A| = 0$.

(c) G is not a linear operator, that is, G does not map a vector space into itself.   Thus the determinant of G is not defined.

10.25. Consider the polynomial $g = g(x_1, \ldots, x_n) = \prod_{i<j} (x_i - x_j)$.   Write out explicitly the polynomial $g = g(x_1, x_2, x_3, x_4)$.

The symbol $\prod$ is used for a product of terms in the same way that the symbol $\sum$ is used for a sum of terms.   That is, $\prod_{i<j} (x_i - x_j)$ means the product of all terms $(x_i - x_j)$ for which $i < j$. Hence

$$g = g(x_1, \ldots, x_4) = (x_1 - x_2)(x_1 - x_3)(x_1 - x_4)(x_2 - x_3)(x_2 - x_4)(x_3 - x_4)$$

10.26. Show that the difference product $g(x_1, x_2, \ldots, x_n)$ of Problem 10.25 can be represented by means of the *Vandermonde determinant* of $x_1, x_2, \ldots, x_{n-1}, x$, which is defined by

$$V_{n-1}(x) \equiv \begin{vmatrix} 1 & 1 & \ldots & 1 & 1 \\ x_1 & x_2 & \ldots & x_{n-1} & x \\ x_1^2 & x_2^2 & \ldots & x_{n-1}^2 & x^2 \\ \cdots\cdots\cdots\cdots\cdots\cdots\cdots\cdots \\ x_1^{n-1} & x_2^{n-1} & \ldots & x_{n-1}^{n-1} & x^{n-1} \end{vmatrix}$$

This is a polynomial in x of degree $n - 1$, of which the roots are $x_1, x_2, \ldots, x_{n-1}$.   Moreover, the leading coefficient (the cofactor of x^{n-1}) is equal to $V_{n-2}(x_{n-1})$.   Thus from algebra,

$$V_{n-1}(x) = (x - x_1)(x - x_2) \cdots (x - x_{n-1}) V_{n-2}(x_{n-1})$$

so that, by recursion,

$$V_{n-1}(x) = [(x - x_1) \cdots (x - x_{n-1})][(x_{n-1} - x_1) \cdots (x_{n-1} - x_{n-2})]V_{n-3}(x_{n-2})$$

$$= [(x - x_1) \cdots (x - x_{n-1})][(x_{n-1} - x_1) \cdots (x_{n-1} - x_{n-2})] \cdots [(x_2 - x_1)]$$

It follows that

$$V_{n-1}(x_n) = \prod_{n \geq i > j \geq 1} (x_i - x_j) = (-1)^{n(n-1)/2} \prod_{1 \leq i < j \leq n} (x_i - x_j)$$

(where $x = x_n$).   Thus $g(x_1, \ldots, x_n) = (-1)^{n(n-1)/2} V_{n-1}(x_n)$.

10.27. Let V be the vector space of 2×2 matrices $M = \begin{bmatrix} a & b \\ c & d \end{bmatrix}$ over **R**.   Determine whether or not $D: V \to \mathbf{R}$ is 2-linear (with respect to the rows), where: (a) $D(M) = a + d$; (b) $D(M) = ad$.

(a)   No.   For example, suppose $A = (1, 1)$ and $B = (3, 3)$.   Then

$$D(A, B) = D\begin{bmatrix} 1 & 1 \\ 3 & 3 \end{bmatrix} = 4 \quad \text{and} \quad D(2A, B) = D\begin{bmatrix} 2 & 2 \\ 3 & 3 \end{bmatrix} = 5 \neq 2D(A, B)$$

(b)   Yes.   Let $A = (a_1, a_2)$, $B = (b_1, b_2)$, and $C = (c_1, c_2)$.   Then

$$D(A, C) = D\begin{bmatrix} a_1 & a_2 \\ c_1 & c_2 \end{bmatrix} = a_1 c_2 \quad \text{and} \quad D(B, C) = D\begin{bmatrix} b_1 & b_2 \\ c_1 & c_2 \end{bmatrix} = b_1 c_2$$

Hence for any scalars $s, t \in \mathbf{R}$,

$$D(sA + tB, C) = D\begin{bmatrix} sa_1 + tb_1 & sa_2 + tb_2 \\ c_1 & c_2 \end{bmatrix} = (sa_1 + tb_1)c_2$$

$$= s(a_1 c_2) + t(b_1 c_2) = sD(A, C) + tD(B, C)$$

That is, D is linear with respect to the first row.
        Furthermore,

$$D(C, A) = D\begin{bmatrix} c_1 & c_2 \\ a_1 & a_2 \end{bmatrix} = c_1 a_2 \quad \text{and} \quad D(C, B) = D\begin{bmatrix} c_1 & c_2 \\ b_1 & b_2 \end{bmatrix} = c_1 b_2$$

Hence for any scalars, $s, t \in \mathbf{R}$,

$$D(C, sA + tB) = D\begin{bmatrix} c_1 & c_2 \\ sa_1 + tb_1 & sa_2 + tb_2 \end{bmatrix} = c_1(sa_2) + tb_2)$$

$$= s(c_1 a_2) + t(c_1 b_2) = sD(C, A) + tD(C, B)$$

That is, D is linear with respect to the second row.
        Both linearity conditions imply that D is 2-linear.

10.28. Let D be a 2-linear, alternating function.   Show that $D(A, B) = -D(B, A)$.   More generally, show that if D is multilinear and alternating, then

$$D(\ldots, A, \ldots, B, \ldots) = -D(\ldots, B, \ldots, A, \ldots)$$

that is, the sign is changed whenever two components are interchanged.

Since D is alternating, $D(A + B, A + B) = 0$.   Furthermore, since D is multilinear,

$$0 = D(A + B, A + B) = D(A, A + B) + D(B, A + B)$$
$$= D(A, A) + D(A, B) + D(B, A) + D(B, B)$$

But $D(A, A) = 0$ and $D(B, B) = 0$.   Hence

$$0 = D(A, B) + D(B, A) \qquad \text{or} \qquad D(A, B) = -D(B, A)$$

Similarly,

$$0 = D(\ldots, A + B, \ldots, A + B, \ldots)$$
$$= D(\ldots, A, \ldots, A, \ldots) + D(\ldots, A, \ldots, B, \ldots) + D(\ldots, B, \ldots, A, \ldots) + D(\ldots, B, \ldots, B, \ldots)$$
$$= D(\ldots, A, \ldots, B, \ldots) + D(\ldots, B, \ldots, A, \ldots)$$

and thus $D(\ldots, A, \ldots, B, \ldots) = -D(\ldots, B, \ldots, A, \ldots)$.

PERMUTATIONS

10.29. Determine the parity of $\sigma = 364152$.

Method 1: We need to obtain the number of pairs (i, j) for which $i > j$ but i precedes j in σ.   There are:

> 3 numbers (3, 6, 4) greater than and preceding 1
>
> 4 numbers (3, 6, 4, 5) greater than and preceding 2
>
> 0 numbers greater than and preceding 3
>
> 1 number (6) greater than and preceding 4
>
> 1 number (6) greater than and preceding 5
>
> 0 numbers greater than and preceding 6

Since $3 + 4 + 0 + 1 + 1 + 0 = 9$ is odd, σ is an odd permutation, and so sgn $\sigma = -1$.

Method 2: The above procedure can be accomplished geometrically as follows:

That is, first, as in (a), we bring 1 to the first position to obtain the permutation 136452.   Then, as in (b), we bring 2 to the second position to obtain 123645.   Note 3 is now in the correct third position.   Next, as in (c), we bring 4 to the fourth position to obtain 123465.   Finally, we bring 5 to the correct fifth position to obtain the identity permutation 123456.

Now we count the number of numbers "jumped": $3 + 4 + 1 + 1 = 9$.   Since 9 is odd, σ is an odd permutation.

10.30. Let $\sigma = 24513$ and $\tau = 41352$ be permutations in S_5.   Find: (a) the composition permutations $\tau \circ \sigma$ and $\sigma \circ \tau$; (b) σ^{-1}.

Recall that $\sigma = 24513$ and $\tau = 41352$ are short ways of writing

$$\sigma = \begin{pmatrix} 1 & 2 & 3 & 4 & 5 \\ 2 & 4 & 5 & 1 & 3 \end{pmatrix} \quad \text{and} \quad \tau = \begin{pmatrix} 1 & 2 & 3 & 4 & 5 \\ 4 & 1 & 3 & 5 & 2 \end{pmatrix}$$

which means

$$\sigma(1) = 2, \quad \sigma(2) = 4, \quad \sigma(3) = 5, \quad \sigma(4) = 1, \quad \sigma(5) = 3$$

and

$$\tau(1) = 4, \quad \tau(2) = 1, \quad \tau(3) = 3, \quad \tau(4) = 5, \quad \tau(5) = 2$$

(*a*) The effect of σ and then τ on $1, 2, \ldots, 5$ is pictured in Fig. 10-3(*a*). Thus $\tau \circ \sigma = 15243$. The effect of τ and then σ on $1, 2, \ldots, 5$ is pictured in Fig. 10-3(*b*). Thus $\sigma \circ \tau = 12534$.

$$\begin{array}{cccccc} & 1 & 2 & 3 & 4 & 5 \\ \sigma & \downarrow & \downarrow & \downarrow & \downarrow & \downarrow \\ & 2 & 4 & 5 & 1 & 3 \\ \tau & \downarrow & \downarrow & \downarrow & \downarrow & \downarrow \\ & 1 & 5 & 2 & 4 & 3 \end{array} \qquad\qquad \begin{array}{cccccc} & 1 & 2 & 3 & 4 & 5 \\ \tau & \downarrow & \downarrow & \downarrow & \downarrow & \downarrow \\ & 4 & 1 & 3 & 5 & 2 \\ \sigma & \downarrow & \downarrow & \downarrow & \downarrow & \downarrow \\ & 1 & 2 & 5 & 3 & 4 \end{array}$$

(*a*) (*b*)

Fig. 10-3

(*b*) By definition, $\sigma^{-1}(j) = k$ if and only if $\sigma(k) = j$. Hence

$$\sigma^{-1} = \begin{pmatrix} 2 & 4 & 5 & 1 & 3 \\ 1 & 2 & 3 & 4 & 5 \end{pmatrix} = \begin{pmatrix} 1 & 2 & 3 & 4 & 5 \\ 4 & 1 & 5 & 2 & 3 \end{pmatrix} \quad \text{or} \quad \sigma^{-1} = 41523$$

10.31. Consider any permutation $\sigma = j_1 j_2 \cdots j_n$. Show that, for each inversion (i, k) in σ, there is a pair (i^*, k^*) such that

$$i^* < k^* \quad \text{and} \quad \sigma(i^*) > \sigma(k^*) \tag{1}$$

and vice versa. Thus σ is even or odd according to whether there is an even or an odd number of pairs satisfying Eq. (*1*).

Choose i^* and k^* so that $\sigma(i^*) = i$ and $\sigma(k^*) = k$. Then $i > k$ if and only if $\sigma(i^*) > \sigma(k^*)$, and i precedes k in σ if and only if $i^* < k^*$.

10.32. Consider the polynomials $g = g(x_1, \ldots, x_n)$ and $\sigma(g)$, defined by

$$g = g(x_1, \ldots, x_n) = \prod_{i<j} (x_i - x_j) \quad \text{and} \quad \sigma(g) = \prod_{i<j} (x_{\sigma(i)} - x_{\sigma(j)})$$

(See Problem 10.25.) Show that $\sigma(g) = g$ when σ is an even permutation, but $\sigma(g) = -g$ when σ is an odd permutation.

Since σ is one-to-one and onto,

$$\sigma(g) = \prod_{i<j} (x_{\sigma(i)} - x_{\sigma(j)}) = \prod_{i<j \text{ or } i>j} (x_i - x_j)$$

Thus $\sigma(g) = g$ or $\sigma(g) = -g$ according to whether there is an even or an odd number of terms of the form $(x_i - x_j)$, where $i > j$. Note that for each pair (i, j) for which

$$i < j \quad \text{and} \quad \sigma(i) > \sigma(j) \tag{1}$$

there is a term $(x_{\sigma(i)} - x_{\sigma(j)})$ in $\sigma(g)$ for which $\sigma(i) > \sigma(j)$. Since σ is even if and only if there is an even number of pairs satisfying Eq. (*1*), we have $\sigma(g) = g$ if and only if σ is even. Hence $\sigma(g) = -g$ if and only if σ is odd.

10.33. Let $\sigma, \tau \in S_n$. Show that sgn $(\tau \circ \sigma) = (\text{sgn } \tau)(\text{sgn } \sigma)$. Thus the product of two even or two odd permutations is even, and the product of an odd and an even permutation is odd.

Using Problem 10.32, we have

$$\text{sgn } (\tau \circ \sigma)g = (\tau \circ \sigma)(g) = \tau(\sigma(g)) = \tau((\text{sgn } \sigma)g) = (\text{sgn } \tau)(\text{sgn } \sigma)g$$

Accordingly sgn $(\tau \circ \sigma) = (\text{sgn } \tau)(\text{sgn } \sigma)$.

10.34. Consider the permutation $\sigma = j_1 j_2 \cdots j_n$. Show that sgn $\sigma^{-1} = \text{sgn } \sigma$ and, for scalars a_{ij}, show that

$$a_{j_1 1} a_{j_2 2} \cdots a_{j_n n} = a_{1 k_1} a_{2 k_2} \cdots a_{n k_n}$$

where $\sigma^{-1} = k_1 k_2 \cdots k_n$.

We have $\sigma^{-1} \circ \sigma = \varepsilon$, the identity permutation. Since ε is even, σ^{-1} and σ are both even or both odd. Hence sgn $\sigma^{-1} = \text{sgn } \sigma$.

Since $\sigma = j_1 j_2 \cdots j_n$ is a permutation, $a_{j_1 1} a_{j_2 2} \cdots a_{j_n n} = a_{1 k_1} a_{2 k_2} \cdots a_{n k_n}$. Then $k_1, k_2, \ldots, k_n$ have the property that

$$\sigma(k_1) = 1, \sigma(k_2) = 2, \ldots, \sigma(k_n) = n$$

Let $\tau = k_1 k_2 \cdots k_n$. Then for $i = 1, \ldots, n$,

$$(\sigma \circ \tau)(i) = \sigma(\tau(i)) = \sigma(k_i) = i$$

Thus $\sigma \circ \tau = \varepsilon$, the identity permutation. Hence $\tau = \sigma^{-1}$.

PROOFS OF THEOREMS

10.35. Prove Theorem 10.1: $|A^T| = |A|$.

If $A = [a_{ij}]$, then $A^T = [b_{ij}]$, with $b_{ij} = a_{ji}$. Hence

$$|A^T| = \sum_{\sigma \in S_n} (\text{sgn } \sigma) b_{1\sigma(2)} b_{2\sigma(2)} \cdots b_{n\sigma(n)} = \sum_{\sigma \in S_n} (\text{sgn } \sigma) a_{\sigma(1),1} a_{\sigma(2),2} \cdots a_{\sigma(n),n}$$

Let $\tau = \sigma^{-1}$. By Problem 10.34, sgn $\tau = \text{sgn } \sigma$, and $a_{\sigma(1),1} a_{\sigma(2),2} \cdots a_{\sigma(n),n} = a_{1\tau(1)} a_{2\tau(2)} \cdots a_{n\tau(n)}$. Hence

$$|A^T| = \sum_{\sigma \in S_n} (\text{sgn } \tau) a_{1\tau(1)} a_{2\tau(2)} \cdots a_{n\tau(n)}$$

However, as σ runs through all the elements of S_n, $\tau = \sigma^{-1}$ also runs through all the elements of S_n. Thus $|A^T| = |A|$.

10.36. Prove Theorem 10.3(i):   If two rows (columns) of A were interchanged, then $|B| = -|A|$.

We prove the theorem for the case that two columns are interchanged. Let τ be the transposition which interchanges the two numbers corresponding to the two columns of A that are interchanged. If $A = [a_{ij}]$ and $B = [b_{ij}]$, then $b_{ij} = a_{i\tau(j)}$. Hence, for any permutation σ,

$$b_{1\sigma(1)} b_{2\sigma(2)} \cdots b_{n\sigma(n)} = a_{1\tau\sigma(1)} a_{2\tau\sigma(2)} \cdots a_{n\tau\sigma(n)}$$

Thus

$$|B| = \sum_{\sigma \in S_n} (\text{sgn } \sigma) b_{1\sigma(1)} b_{2\sigma(2)} \cdots b_{n\sigma(n)} = \sum_{\sigma \in S_n} (\text{sgn } \sigma) a_{1\tau\sigma(1)} a_{2\tau\sigma(2)} \cdots a_{n\tau\sigma(n)}$$

Since the transposition τ is an odd permutation, $\operatorname{sgn} \tau\sigma = \operatorname{sgn} \tau \cdot \operatorname{sgn} \sigma = -\operatorname{sgn} \sigma$. Thus $\operatorname{sgn} \sigma = -\operatorname{sgn} \tau\sigma$, and so

$$|B| = -\sum_{\sigma \in S_n} (\operatorname{sgn} \tau\sigma) a_{1\tau\sigma(1)} a_{2\tau\sigma(2)} \cdots a_{n\tau\sigma(n)}$$

But as σ runs through all the elements of S_n, $\tau\sigma$ also runs through all the elements of S_n. Hence $|B| = -|A|$.

10.37. Prove Theorem 10.2:

  (i)   If A has a row (column) of zeros, then $|A| = 0$.

  (ii) If A has two identical rows (columns), then $|A| = 0$.

 (iii) If A is triangular, then $|A| = $ product of diagonal elements. Thus $|I| = 1$.

  (i)   Each term in $|A|$ contains a factor from every row, and so from the row of zeros. Thus each term of $|A|$ is zero, and so $|A| = 0$.

  (ii) Suppose $1 + 1 \neq 0$ in K. If we interchange the two identical rows of A, we still obtain the matrix A. Hence, by Problem 10.36, $|A| = -|A|$, and so $|A| = 0$.

       Now suppose $1 + 1 = 0$ in K. Then $\operatorname{sgn} \sigma = 1$ for every $\sigma \in S_n$. Since A has two identical rows, we can arrange the terms of A into pairs of equal terms. Since each pair is 0, the determinant of A is zero.

 (iii) Suppose $A = [a_{ij}]$ is lower triangular, that is, the entries above the diagonal are all zero: $a_{ij} = 0$ whenever $i < j$. Consider a term t of the determinant of A,

$$t = (\operatorname{sgn} \sigma) a_{1i_1} a_{2i_2} \cdots a_{ni_n} \qquad \text{where} \qquad \sigma = i_1 i_2 \cdots i_n$$

Suppose $i_1 \neq 1$. Then $1 < i_1$ and so $a_{1i_1} = 0$; hence $t = 0$. That is, each term for which $i_1 \neq 1$ is zero.

       Now suppose $i_1 = 1$ but $i_2 \neq 2$. Then $2 < i_2$, and so $a_{2i_2} = 0$; hence $t = 0$. Thus each term for which $i_1 \neq 1$ or $i_2 \neq 2$ is zero.

       Similarly we obtain that each term for which $i_1 \neq 1$ or $i_2 \neq 2$ or $\cdots$ or $i_n \neq n$ is zero. Accordingly, $|A| = a_{11} a_{22} \cdots a_{nn} = $ product of diagonal elements.

10.38. Prove Theorem 10.3: Suppose B is obtained from A by an elementary row (column) operation.

  (i)   If two rows (columns) of A were interchanged, then $|B| = -|A|$.

  (ii) If a row (column) of A were multiplied by a scalar k, then $|B| = k|A|$.

 (iii) If a multiple of a row (column) of A were added to another row (column) of A, then $|B| = |A|$.

  (i)   This result was proved in Problem 10.36.

  (ii) If the jth row of A is multiplied by k, then every term in $|A|$ is multiplied by k, and so $|B| = k|A|$. That is,

$$|B| = \sum_{\sigma} (\operatorname{sgn} \sigma) a_{1i_1} a_{2i_2} \cdots (ka_{ji_j}) \cdots a_{ni_n} = k \sum_{\sigma} (\operatorname{sgn} \sigma) a_{1i_1} a_{2i_2} \cdots a_{ni_n} = k|A|$$

 (iii) Suppose c times the kth row is added to the jth row of A. Using the symbol $\frown$ to denote the jth position in a determinant term, we have

$$|B| = \sum_{\sigma} (\operatorname{sgn} \sigma) a_{1i_1} a_{2i_2} \cdots \overbrace{(ca_{ki_k} + a_{ji_j})} \cdots a_{ni_n}$$

$$= c \sum_{\sigma} (\operatorname{sgn} \sigma) a_{1i_1} a_{2i_2} \cdots \overbrace{a_{ki_k}} \cdots a_{ni_n} + \sum_{\sigma} (\operatorname{sgn} \sigma) a_{1i_1} a_{2i_2} \cdots \overbrace{a_{ji_j}} \cdots a_{ni_n}$$

The first sum is the determinant of a matrix whose kth and jth rows are identical. Hence, by Theorem 10.2(ii), the sum is zero. The second sum is the determinant of A. Thus $|B| = c \cdot 0 + |A| = |A|$.

10.39. Prove Lemma 10.6:   Let E be an elementary matrix.   Then $|EA| = |E||A|$.

Consider the following elementary row operations:

(i)   Multiply a row by a constant $k \neq 0$.

(ii)   Interchange two rows.

(iii)   Add a multiple of one row to another.

Let E_1, E_2, and E_3 be the corresponding elementary matrices.   That is, E_1, E_2, and E_3 are obtained by applying the above operations to the identity matrix I.   By Problem 10.37,

$$|E_1| = k|I| = k, \qquad |E_2| = -|I| = -1, \qquad |E_3| = |I| = 1$$

Recall (Theorem 3.6) that $E_i A$ is identical to the matrix obtained by applying the corresponding operation to A.   Thus, by Theorem 10.3,

$$|E_1 A| = k|A| = |E_1||A|, \qquad |E_2 A| = -|A| = |E_2||A|, \qquad |E_3 A| = |A| = 1|A| = |E_3||A|$$

and the lemma is proved.

10.40. Suppose B is row equivalent to a square matrix A.   Prove that $|B| = 0$ if and only if $|A| = 0$.

By Theorem 10.3, the effect of an elementary row operation is to change the sign of the determinant or to multiply the determinant by a nonzero scalar.   Hence $|B| = 0$ if and only if $|A| = 0$.

10.41. Prove Theorem 10.5:   Let A be an n-square matrix.   Then the following are equivalent:

(i) A is invertible.

(ii) $AX = 0$ has only the zero solution.

(iii) $\det (A) \neq 0$.

The proof is by the Gaussian algorithm.   If A is invertible, it is row equivalent to I.   But $|I| \neq 0$.   Hence, by Problem 10.40, $|A| \neq 0$.   If A is not invertible, it is row equivalent to a matrix with a zero row.   Hence $\det (A) = 0$.   Thus (i) and (iii) are equivalent.

If $AX = 0$ has only the solution $X = 0$, then A is row equivalent to I and A is invertible. Conversely, if A is invertible with inverse A^{-1}, then

$$X = IX = (A^{-1}A)X = A^{-1}(AX) = A^{-1}0 = 0$$

is the only solution of $AX = 0$.   Thus (i) and (ii) are equivalent.

10.42. Prove Theorem 10.4: $|AB| = |A||B|$.

If A is singular, then AB is also singular, and so $|AB| = 0 = |A||B|$.   On the other hand, if A is nonsingular, then $A = E_n \cdots E_2 E_1$, a product of elementary matrices.   Then, using Lemma 10.6 and induction, we obtain

$$|AB| = |E_n \cdots E_2 E_1 B| = |E_n| \cdots |E_2||E_1||B| = |A||B|$$

10.43. Suppose P is invertible.   Prove that $|P^{-1}| = |P|^{-1}$.

$P^{-1}P = I$.   Hence $1 = |I| = |P^{-1}P| = |P^{-1}||P|$, and so $|P^{-1}| = |P|^{-1}$.

10.44. Prove Theorem 10.7:   Suppose A and B are similar matrices.   Then $|A| = |B|$.

Since A and B are similar, there exists an invertible matrix P such that $B = P^{-1}AP$.   Then by Problem 10.43, $|B| = |P^{-1}AP| = |P^{-1}||A||P| = |A||P^{-1}||P| = |A|$.

We remark that although the matrices P^{-1} and A may not commute, their determinants $|P^{-1}|$ and $|A|$ do commute since they are scalars in the field K.

10.45. Prove Theorem 10.8 (LaPlace):   Let $A = [a_{ij}]$, and let A_{ij} denote the cofactor of a_{ij}.   Then, for any i or j

$$|A| = a_{i1}A_{i1} + \cdots + a_{in}A_{in} \qquad \text{and} \qquad |A| = a_{1j}A_{1j} + \cdots + a_{nj}A_{nj}$$

Since $|A| = |A^T|$, we need only prove one of the expansions, say, the first one in terms of rows of A.   Each term in $|A|$ contains one and only one entry of the ith row $(a_{i1}, a_{i2}, \ldots, a_{in})$ of A. Hence we can write $|A|$ in the form

$$|A| = a_{i1}A_{i1}^* + a_{i2}A_{i2}^* + \cdots + a_{in}A_{in}^*$$

(Note that A_{ij}^* is a sum of terms involving no entry of the ith row of A.)   Thus the theorem is proved if we can show that

$$A_{ij}^* = A_{ij} = (-1)^{i+j}|M_{ij}|$$

where M_{ij} is the matrix obtained by deleting the row and column containing the entry a_{ij}. (Historically the expression A_{ij}^* was defined as the cofactor of a_{ij}, and so the theorem reduces to showing that the two definitions of the cofactor are equivalent.)   First we consider the case that $i = n, j = n$.   Then the sum of terms in $|A|$ containing a_{nn} is

$$a_{nn}A_{nn}^* = a_{nn} \sum_{\sigma} (\text{sgn } \sigma) a_{1\sigma(1)} a_{2\sigma(2)} \cdots a_{n-1, \sigma(n-1)}$$

where we sum over all permutations $\sigma \in S_n$ for which $\sigma(n) = n$.   However, this is equivalent (prove!) to summing over all permutations of $\{1, \ldots, n-1\}$.   Thus $A_{nn}^* = |M_{nn}| = (-1)^{n+n}|M_{nn}|$.

Now we consider any i and j.   We interchange the ith row with each succeeding row until it is last, and we interchange the jth column with each succeeding column until it is last. Note that the determinant $|M_{ij}|$ is not affected since the relative positions of the other rows and columns are not affected by these interchanges.   However, the "sign" of $|A|$ and of A_{ij}^* is changed $n - i$ and then $n - j$ times.   Accordingly,

$$A_{ij}^* = (-1)^{n-i+n-j}|M_{ij}| = (-1)^{i+j}|M_{ij}|$$

10.46. Let $A = [a_{ij}]$ and let B be the matrix obtained from A by replacing the ith row of A by the row vector $(b_{i1}, \ldots, b_{in})$.   Show that

$$|B| = b_{i1}A_{i1} + b_{i2}A_{i2} + \cdots + b_{in}A_{in}$$

Furthermore show that, for $j \neq i$,

$$a_{j1}A_{i1} + a_{j2}A_{i2} + \cdots + a_{jn}A_{in} = 0 \qquad \text{and} \qquad a_{1j}A_{1i} + a_{2j}A_{2i} + \cdots + a_{nj}A_{ni} = 0$$

Let $B = [b_{ij}]$.   By Theorem 10.8,

$$|B| = b_{i1}B_{i1} + b_{i2}B_{i2} + \cdots + b_{in}B_{in}$$

Since B_{ij} does not depend on the ith row of B, $B_{ij} = A_{ij}$ for $j = 1, \ldots, n$.   Hence

$$|B| = b_{i1}A_{i1} + b_{i2}A_{i2} + \cdots + b_{in}A_{in}$$

Now let A' be obtained from A by replacing the ith row of A by the jth row of A.   Since A' has two identical rows, $|A'| = 0$.   Thus by the above result,

$$|A'| = a_{j1}A_{i1} + a_{j2}A_{i2} + \cdots + a_{jn}A_{in} = 0$$

Using $|A^T| = |A|$, we also obtain that $a_{1j}A_{1i} + a_{2j}A_{2i} + \cdots + a_{nj}A_{ni} = 0$.

10.47. Prove Theorem 10.9: $A \cdot (\text{adj } A) = (\text{adj } A) \cdot A = |A|I$.

Let $A = [a_{ij}]$ and let $A \cdot (\text{adj } A) = [b_{ij}]$.   The ith row of A is

$$(a_{i1}, a_{i2}, \ldots, a_{in}) \tag{1}$$

Since adj A is the transpose of the matrix of cofactors, the jth column of adj A is the transpose of the cofactors of the jth row of A, that is,

$$(A_{j1}, A_{j2}, \ldots, A_{jn})^T \tag{2}$$

Now b_{ij}, the ij entry in $A \cdot (\text{adj } A)$, is obtained by multiplying expressions (1) and (2),

$$b_{ij} = a_{i1}A_{j1} + a_{i2}A_{j2} + \cdots + a_{in}A_{jn}$$

By Theorem 10.8 and Problem 10.46,

$$b_{ij} = \begin{cases} |A| & \text{if } i = j \\ 0 & \text{if } i \neq j \end{cases}$$

Accordingly, $A \cdot (\text{adj } A)$ is the diagonal matrix with each diagonal element $|A|$.   In other words, $A \cdot (\text{adj } A) = |A|I$.   Similarly, $(\text{adj } A) \cdot A = |A|I$.

10.48. Prove Theorem 10.10:   The (square) system $AX = B$ has a unique solution if and only if $D \neq 0$.   In this case the solution is $x_i = N_i/D$ for each i.

By previous results, $AX = B$ has a unique solution if and only if A is invertible, and A is invertible if and only if $D = |A| \neq 0$.

Now suppose $D \neq 0$.   By Theorem 10.9, $A^{-1} = (1/D)(\text{adj } A)$.   Multiplying $AX = B$ by A^{-1} we obtain

$$X = A^{-1}AX = (1/D)(\text{adj } A)B \tag{1}$$

Note that the ith row of $(1/D)(\text{adj } A)$ is $(1/D)(A_{1i}, A_{2i}, \ldots, A_{ni})$.   If $B = (b_1, b_2, \ldots, b_n)^T$, then, by Eq. (1),

$$x_i = (1/D)(b_1A_{1i} + b_2A_{2i} + \cdots + b_nA_{ni})$$

However, as in Problem 10.46, $b_1A_{1i} + b_2A_{2i} + \cdots + b_nA_{ni} = N_i$, the determinant of the matrix obtained by replacing the ith column of A by the column vector B.   Thus $x_i = (1/D)N_i$, as required.

10.49. Prove Theorem 10.12:   Suppose M is an upper (lower) triangular block matrix with diagonal blocks $A_1, A_2, \ldots, A_n$.   Then

$$\det (M) = \det (A_1) \det (A_2) \cdots \det (A_n)$$

We need only prove the theorem for $n = 2$, that is, when M is a square block matrix of the form $M = \begin{bmatrix} A & C \\ 0 & B \end{bmatrix}$.   The proof of the general theorem follows easily by induction.

Suppose $A = [a_{ij}]$ is r-square, $B = [b_{ij}]$ is s-square, and $M = [m_{ij}]$ is n-square, where $n = r + s$.   By definition,

$$\det (M) = \sum_{\sigma \in S_n} (\text{sgn } \sigma) m_{1\sigma(1)} m_{2\sigma(2)} \cdots m_{n\sigma(n)}$$

If $i > r$ and $j \leq r$, then $m_{ij} = 0$.   Thus we need only consider those permutations σ such that

$$\sigma\{r + 1, r + 2, \ldots, r + s\} = \{r + 1, r + 2, \ldots, r + s\} \qquad \text{and} \qquad \sigma\{1, 2, \ldots, r\} = \{1, 2, \ldots, r\}$$

Let $\sigma_1(k) = \sigma(k)$ for $k \leq r$, and let $\sigma_2(k) = \sigma(r + k) - r$ for $k \leq s$.   Then

$$(\text{sgn } \sigma) m_{1\sigma(1)} m_{2\sigma(2)} \cdots m_{n\sigma(n)} = (\text{sgn } \sigma_1) a_{1\sigma_1(1)} a_{2\sigma_1(2)} \cdots a_{r\sigma_1(r)} (\text{sgn } \sigma_2) b_{1\sigma_2(1)} b_{2\sigma_2(2)} \cdots b_{s\sigma_2(s)}$$

which implies $\det (M) = \det (A) \det (B)$.

10.50. Prove Theorem 10.14:   There exists a unique function D: **M** $\to K$ such that

(i) D is multilinear.

(ii) D is alternating.

(iii) $D(I) = 1$.

This function D is the determinant function, that is, $D(A) = |A|$.

Let D be the determinant function, $D(A) = |A|$.   We must show that D satisfies (i), (ii), and (iii), and that D is the only function satisfying (i), (ii), and (iii).

By Theorem 10.2, D satisfies (ii) and (iii).   Hence we now show that it is multilinear. Suppose the ith row of $A = [a_{ij}]$ has the form $(b_{i1} + c_{i1}, b_{i2} + c_{i2}, \ldots, b_{in} + c_{in})$.   Then

$$D(A) = D(A_1, \ldots, B_i + C_i, \ldots, A_n)$$
$$= \sum_{S_n} (\text{sgn } \sigma) a_{1\sigma(1)} \cdots a_{i-1, \sigma(i-1)} (b_{i\sigma(i)} + c_{i\sigma(i)}) \cdots a_{n\sigma(n)}$$
$$= \sum_{S_n} (\text{sgn } \sigma) a_{1\sigma(1)} \cdots b_{i\sigma(i)} \cdots a_{n\sigma(n)} + \sum_{S_n} (\text{sgn } \sigma) a_{1\sigma(1)} \cdots c_{i\sigma(i)} \cdots a_{n\sigma(n)}$$
$$= D(A_1, \ldots, B_i, \ldots, A_n) + D(A_1, \ldots, C_i, \ldots, A_n)$$

Also, by Theorem 10.3(ii),

$$D(A_1, \ldots, kA_i, \ldots, A_n) = kD(A_1, \ldots, A_i, \ldots, A_n)$$

Thus D is multilinear, i.e., D satisfies (i).

We next must prove the uniqueness of D.   Suppose D satisfies (i), (ii), and (iii).   If $\{e_1, \ldots, e_n\}$ is the usual basis of K^n, then by (iii), $D(e_1, e_2, \ldots, e_n) = D(I) = 1$.   Using (ii) we also have that

$$D(e_{i_1}, e_{i_2}, \ldots, e_{i_n}) = \text{sgn } \sigma \qquad \text{where} \qquad \sigma = i_1 i_2 \cdots i_n \qquad\qquad (1)$$

Now suppose $A = [a_{ij}]$.   Observe that the kth row A_k of A is

$$A_k = (a_{k1}, a_{k2}, \ldots, a_{kn}) = a_{k1} e_1 + a_{k2} e_2 + \cdots + a_{kn} e_n$$

Thus

$$D(A) = D(a_{11}e_1 + \cdots + a_{1n}e_n, a_{21}e_1 + \cdots + a_{2n}e_n, \ldots, a_{n1}e_1 + \cdots + a_{nn}e_n)$$

Using the multilinearity of D, we can write $D(A)$ as a sum of terms of the form

$$D(A) = \sum D(a_{1i_1}e_{i_1}, a_{2i_2}e_{i_2}, \ldots, a_{ni_n}e_{i_n})$$
$$= \sum (a_{1i_1}a_{2i_2} \cdots a_{ni_n})D(e_{i_1}, e_{i_2}, \ldots, e_{i_n}) \tag{2}$$

where the sum is summed over all sequences $i_1 i_2 \cdots i_n$, where $i_k \in \{1, \ldots, n\}$. If two of the indices are equal, say $i_j = i_k$ but $j \neq k$, then by (ii),

$$D(e_{i_1}, e_{i_2}, \ldots, e_{i_n}) = 0$$

Accordingly, the sum in Eq. (2) need only be summed over all permutations $\sigma = i_1 i_2 \cdots i_n$. Using Eq. (1), we finally have that

$$D(A) = \sum_\sigma (a_{1i_1}a_{2i_2} \cdots a_{ni_n})D(e_{i_1}, e_{i_2}, \ldots, e_{i_n})$$

$$= \sum_\sigma (\mathrm{sgn}\ \sigma)a_{1i_1}a_{2i_2} \cdots a_{ni_n} \qquad \text{where} \qquad \sigma = i_1 i_2 \cdots i_n$$

Hence D is the determinant function, and so the theorem is proved.

Supplementary Problems

COMPUTATION OF DETERMINANTS

10.51. Evaluate: $(a)\ \begin{vmatrix} 2 & 6 \\ 4 & 1 \end{vmatrix}$; $(b)\ \begin{vmatrix} 5 & 1 \\ 3 & -2 \end{vmatrix}$; $(c)\ \begin{vmatrix} -2 & 8 \\ -5 & -3 \end{vmatrix}$; $(d)\ \begin{vmatrix} 4 & 9 \\ 1 & -3 \end{vmatrix}$; $(e)\ \begin{vmatrix} a+b & a \\ b & a+b \end{vmatrix}$.

10.52. Find all t such that: $(a)\ \begin{vmatrix} t-4 & 3 \\ 2 & t-9 \end{vmatrix} = 0$; $(b)\ \begin{vmatrix} t-1 & 4 \\ 3 & t-2 \end{vmatrix} = 0$.

10.53. Compute the determinant of each matrix:

$(a)\ \begin{bmatrix} 2 & 1 & 1 \\ 0 & 5 & -2 \\ 1 & -3 & 4 \end{bmatrix}$; $(b)\ \begin{bmatrix} 3 & -2 & -4 \\ 2 & 5 & -1 \\ 0 & 6 & 1 \end{bmatrix}$; $(c)\ \begin{bmatrix} -2 & -1 & 4 \\ 6 & -3 & -2 \\ 4 & 1 & 2 \end{bmatrix}$; $(d)\ \begin{bmatrix} 7 & 6 & 5 \\ 1 & 2 & 1 \\ 3 & -2 & 1 \end{bmatrix}$.

10.54. Evaluate the determinant of each matrix: $(a)\ \begin{bmatrix} 1 & 2 & 2 & 3 \\ 1 & 0 & -2 & 0 \\ 3 & -1 & 1 & -2 \\ 4 & -3 & 0 & 2 \end{bmatrix}$; $(b)\ \begin{bmatrix} 2 & 1 & 3 & 2 \\ 3 & 0 & 1 & -2 \\ 1 & -1 & 4 & 3 \\ 2 & 2 & -1 & 1 \end{bmatrix}$.

10.55. Evaluate: $(a)\ \begin{vmatrix} 2 & -1 & 3 & -4 \\ 2 & 1 & -2 & 1 \\ 3 & 3 & -5 & 4 \\ 5 & 2 & -1 & 4 \end{vmatrix}$; $(b)\ \begin{vmatrix} 2 & -1 & 4 & -3 \\ -1 & 1 & 0 & 2 \\ 3 & 2 & 3 & -1 \\ 1 & -2 & 2 & -3 \end{vmatrix}$; $(c)\ \begin{vmatrix} 1 & -2 & 3 & -1 \\ 1 & 1 & -2 & 0 \\ 2 & 0 & 4 & -5 \\ 1 & 4 & 4 & -6 \end{vmatrix}$.

10.56. Evaluate each determinant:

$$(a)\ \begin{vmatrix} 1 & 2 & -1 & 3 & 1 \\ 2 & -1 & 1 & -2 & 3 \\ 3 & 1 & 0 & 2 & -1 \\ 5 & 1 & 2 & -3 & 4 \\ -2 & 3 & -1 & 1 & -2 \end{vmatrix};\ (b)\ \begin{vmatrix} 1 & 3 & 5 & 7 & 9 \\ 2 & 4 & 2 & 4 & 2 \\ 0 & 0 & 1 & 2 & 3 \\ 0 & 0 & 5 & 6 & 2 \\ 0 & 0 & 2 & 3 & 1 \end{vmatrix};\ (c)\ \begin{vmatrix} 1 & 2 & 3 & 4 & 5 \\ 5 & 4 & 3 & 2 & 1 \\ 0 & 0 & 6 & 5 & 1 \\ 0 & 0 & 0 & 7 & 4 \\ 0 & 0 & 0 & 2 & 3 \end{vmatrix}.$$

COFACTORS, CLASSICAL ADJOINTS, INVERSES

10.57. Consider the matrix $A = \begin{bmatrix} 1 & 2 & -2 & 3 \\ 3 & -1 & 5 & 0 \\ 4 & 0 & 2 & 1 \\ 1 & 7 & 2 & -3 \end{bmatrix}$. Find the cofactor: (a) A_{31}; (b) A_{23}; (c) A_{42}.

10.58. Find det (A), adj A, and A^{-1}, where:

$(a)\ A = \begin{bmatrix} 1 & 1 & 0 \\ 1 & 1 & 1 \\ 0 & 2 & 1 \end{bmatrix}$; $(b)\ A = \begin{bmatrix} 1 & 2 & 2 \\ 3 & 1 & 0 \\ 1 & 1 & 1 \end{bmatrix}$

10.59. Find the classical adjoint of each matrix in Problem 10.54.

10.60. Determine the general 2×2 matrix A for which $A = \text{adj } A$.

10.61. Suppose A is diagonal and B is triangular, say

$$A = \begin{bmatrix} a_1 & 0 & \dots & 0 \\ 0 & a_2 & \dots & 0 \\ \multicolumn{4}{c}{\dotfill} \\ 0 & 0 & \dots & a_n \end{bmatrix} \quad \text{and} \quad B = \begin{bmatrix} b_1 & c_{12} & \dots & c_{1n} \\ 0 & b_2 & \dots & c_{2n} \\ \multicolumn{4}{c}{\dotfill} \\ 0 & 0 & \dots & b_n \end{bmatrix}$$

(a) Show that adj A is diagonal and adj B is triangular.
(b) Show that B is invertible if and only if all $b_i \neq 0$. Hence A is invertible if and only if all $a_i \neq 0$.
(c) Show that the inverses of A and B (if either exists) are of the form

$$A^{-1} = \begin{bmatrix} a_1^{-1} & 0 & \dots & 0 \\ 0 & a_2^{-1} & \dots & 0 \\ \multicolumn{4}{c}{\dotfill} \\ 0 & 0 & \dots & a_n^{-1} \end{bmatrix}, \quad B^{-1} = \begin{bmatrix} b_1^{-1} & d_{12} & \dots & d_{1n} \\ 0 & b_2^{-1} & \dots & d_{2n} \\ \multicolumn{4}{c}{\dotfill} \\ 0 & 0 & \dots & b_n^{-1} \end{bmatrix}$$

That is, the diagonal elements of A^{-1} and B^{-1} are the reciprocals of the corresponding diagonal elements of A and B.

MINORS, PRINCIPAL MINORS

10.62. Let $A = \begin{bmatrix} 1 & 2 & 3 & 2 \\ 1 & 0 & -2 & 3 \\ 3 & -1 & 2 & 5 \\ 4 & -3 & 0 & -1 \end{bmatrix}$ and $B = \begin{bmatrix} 1 & 3 & -1 & 5 \\ 2 & -3 & 1 & 4 \\ 0 & -5 & 2 & 1 \\ 3 & 0 & 5 & -2 \end{bmatrix}$. Find the minor and the signed minor corresponding to the submatrix: (a) $A(1, 4; 3, 4)$; (b) $B(1, 4; 3, 4)$; (c) $A(2, 3; 2, 4)$; (d) $B(2, 3; 2, 4)$.

10.63. For $k = 1, 2, 3$ find the sum S_k of all principal minors of order k for:

$$(a)\ A = \begin{bmatrix} 1 & 3 & 2 \\ 2 & -4 & 3 \\ 5 & -2 & 1 \end{bmatrix}; \quad (b)\ B = \begin{bmatrix} 1 & 5 & -4 \\ 2 & 6 & 1 \\ 3 & -2 & 0 \end{bmatrix}; \quad (c)\ C = \begin{bmatrix} 1 & -4 & 3 \\ 2 & 1 & 5 \\ 4 & -7 & 11 \end{bmatrix}.$$

10.64. For $k = 1, 2, 3, 4$ find the sum S_k of all principal minors of order k for:

$$(a)\ A = \begin{bmatrix} 1 & 2 & 3 & -1 \\ 1 & -2 & 0 & 5 \\ 0 & 1 & -2 & 2 \\ 4 & 0 & -1 & -3 \end{bmatrix}; \quad (b)\ B = \begin{bmatrix} 1 & 2 & 1 & 2 \\ 0 & 1 & 2 & 3 \\ 1 & 3 & 0 & 4 \\ 2 & 7 & 4 & 5 \end{bmatrix}.$$

DETERMINANTS AND LINEAR EQUATIONS

10.65. Solve by determinants: (a) $\begin{array}{l} 3x + 5y = 8 \\ 4x - 2y = 1 \end{array}$; (b) $\begin{array}{l} 2x - 3y = -1 \\ 4x + 7y = -1 \end{array}$.

10.66. Solve by determinants: (a) $\begin{array}{l} 2x - 5y + 2z = 7 \\ x + 2y - 4z = 3 \\ 3x - 4y - 6z = 5 \end{array}$; (b) $\begin{array}{l} 2z + 3 = y + 3x \\ x - 3z = 2y + 1 \\ 3y + z = 2 - 2x \end{array}$.

10.67. Prove Theorem 10.11: The homogeneous system $AX = 0$ has a nonzero solution if and only if $D = |A| = 0$.

PERMUTATIONS

10.68. Find the parity of the permutations $\sigma = 32154$, $\tau = 13524$, and $\pi = 42531$ in S_5.

10.69. For the permutations in Problem 10.68, find: (a) $\tau \circ \sigma$; (b) $\pi \circ \sigma$; (c) σ^{-1}; (d) τ^{-1}.

10.70. Let $\tau \in S_n$. Show that $\tau \circ \sigma$ runs through S_n as σ runs through S_n, that is, $S_n = \{\tau \circ \sigma : \sigma \in S_n\}$.

10.71. Let $\sigma \in S_n$ have the property that $\sigma(n) = n$. Let $\sigma^* \in S_{n-1}$ be defined by $\sigma^*(x) = \sigma(x)$. (a) Show that sgn $\sigma^* =$ sgn σ. (b) Show that as σ runs through S_n, where $\sigma(n) = n$, σ^* runs through S_{n-1}, that is, $S_{n-1} = \{\sigma^* : \sigma \in S_n, \sigma(n) = n\}$.

10.72. Consider a permutation $\sigma = j_1 j_2 \cdots j_n$. Let $\{e_i\}$ be the usual basis of K^n, and let A be the matrix whose ith row is e_{ji}, i.e., $A = (e_{j_1}, e_{j_2}, \ldots, e_{j_n})$. Show that $|A| =$ sgn σ.

DETERMINANT OF LINEAR OPERATORS

10.73. Find the determinant of each linear transformation:

(a) $T: \mathbf{R}^2 \to \mathbf{R}^2$ defined by $T(x, y) = (2x - 9y, 3x - 5y)$.

(b) $T: \mathbf{R}^3 \to \mathbf{R}^3$ defined by $T(x, y, z) = (3x - 2z, 5y + 7z, x + y + z)$.

(c) $T: \mathbf{R}^3 \to \mathbf{R}^2$ defined by $T(x, y, z) = (2x + 7y - 4z, 5x - 6y + 2z)$.

10.74. Let $\mathbf{D}: V \to V$ be the differential operator, that is, $\mathbf{D}(f(t)) = df/dt$. Find $\det(T)$ if V is the vector space of functions with bases: (a) $\{1, t, \ldots, t^5\}$; (b) $\{e^t, e^{2t}, e^{3t}\}$; (c) $\{\sin t, \cos t\}$.

10.75. Prove Theorem 10.13: Let F and G be linear operators on a vector space V. Then:

(i) $\det(F \circ G) = \det(F)\det(G)$.

(ii) F is invertible if and only if $\det(F) \neq 0$.

10.76. Prove: (a) $\det(\mathbf{1}_V) = 1$, where $\mathbf{1}_V$ is the identity operator; (b) $\det(T^{-1}) = \det(T)^{-1}$ when T is invertible.

MISCELLANEOUS PROBLEMS

10.77. Find the volume $V(S)$ of the parallelepiped S in $\mathbf{R}^3$ determined by the vectors: (a) $u_1 = (1, 2, -3)$, $u_2 = (3, 4, -1)$, $u_3 = (2, -1, 5)$; (b) $u_1 = (1, 1, 3)$, $u_2 = (1, -2, -4)$, $u_3 = (4, 1, 2)$.

10.78. Find the volume $V(S)$ of the parallelepiped S in $\mathbf{R}^4$ determined by the vectors:

$$u_1 = (1, -2, 5, -1), \quad u_2 = (2, 1, -2, 1), \quad u_3 = (3, 0, 1, -2), \quad u_4 = (1, -1, 4, -1).$$

10.79. Let V be the space of 2×2 matrices $M = \begin{bmatrix} a & b \\ c & d \end{bmatrix}$ over $\mathbf{R}$. Determine whether or not $D: V \to \mathbf{R}$ is 2-linear (with respect to the rows), where: (a) $D(M) = ac - bd$; (b) $D(M) = ab - cd$; (c) $D(M) = 0$; (d) $D(M) = 1$.

10.80. Let A be an n-square matrix. Prove $|kA| = k^n|A|$.

10.81. Let A, B, C, and D be commuting n-square matrices. Consider the $2n$-square block matrix $M = \begin{bmatrix} A & B \\ C & D \end{bmatrix}$. Prove that $|M| = |A||D| - |B||C|$. Show that the result may not be true if the matrices do not commute.

10.82. Suppose A is orthogonal, that is, $A^T A = I$. Show that $\det(A) = \pm 1$.

10.83. Let V be the space of m-square matrices viewed as m-tuples of row vectors. Suppose $D: V \to K$ is m-linear and alternating. Show that if $A_1, A_2, \ldots, A_m$ are linearly dependent, then $D(A_1, \ldots, A_m) = 0$.

10.84. Let V be the space of m-square matrices (as above), and suppose $D: V \to K$. Show that the following weaker statement is equivalent to D being alternating:

$$D(A_1, A_2, \ldots, A_n) = 0 \quad \text{whenever} \quad A_i = A_{i+1} \text{ for some } i$$

10.85. Let V be the space of n-square matrices over K. Suppose $B \in V$ is invertible and so $\det(B) \neq 0$. Define $D: V \to K$ by $D(A) = \det(AB)/\det(B)$, where $A \in V$. Hence

$$D(A_1, A_2, \ldots, A_n) = \det(A_1 B, A_2 B, \ldots, A_n B)/\det(B)$$

where A_i is the ith row of A, and so $A_i B$ is the ith row of AB. Show that D is multilinear and alternating, and that $D(I) = 1$. (This method is used by some texts to prove $|AB| = |A||B|$.)

10.86. Let A be an n-square matrix. The *determinantal rank* of A is the order of the largest square submatrix of A (obtained by deleting rows and columns of A) whose determinant is not zero. Show that the determinantal rank of A is equal to its rank, i.e., the maximum number of linearly independent rows (or columns).

10.87. Let $|A| = \begin{vmatrix} a_1 & b_1 & c_1 \\ a_2 & b_2 & c_2 \\ a_3 & b_3 & c_3 \end{vmatrix} = 3$. Find: (a) $|A^2|$ and $|A^T|$; (b) $\begin{vmatrix} a_1 & b_1 & 2c_1 \\ a_2 & b_2 & 2c_2 \\ a_3 & b_3 & 2c_3 \end{vmatrix}$, $\begin{vmatrix} a_1 & b_1 & c_1 \\ a_3 & b_3 & c_3 \\ a_2 & b_2 & c_2 \end{vmatrix}$, and $\begin{vmatrix} a_1 & 5a_1 + b_1 & c_1 \\ a_2 & 5a_2 + b_2 & c_2 \\ a_3 & 5a_3 + b_3 & c_3 \end{vmatrix}$.

Answers to Supplementary Problems

10.51. (a) -22; (b) -13; (c) 46; (d) -21; (e) $a^2 + ab + b^2$

10.52. (a) 3, 10; (b) 5, -2

10.53. (a) 21; (b) -11; (c) 100; (d) 0

10.54. (a) -131; (b) -55

10.55. (a) 33; (b) 0; (c) 45

10.56. (a) -32; (b) -14; (c) -468

10.57. (a) -135; (b) -103; (c) -31

10.58. (a) $|A| = -2$ adj $A = \begin{bmatrix} -1 & -1 & 1 \\ -1 & 1 & -1 \\ 2 & -2 & 0 \end{bmatrix}$; (b) $|A| = -1$, adj $A = \begin{bmatrix} 1 & 0 & -2 \\ -3 & -1 & 6 \\ 2 & 1 & -5 \end{bmatrix}$

Also $A^{-1} = (\text{adj } A)/|A|$.

10.59. (a) $\begin{bmatrix} -16 & -29 & -26 & -2 \\ -30 & -38 & -16 & 29 \\ -8 & 51 & -13 & -1 \\ -13 & 1 & 28 & -18 \end{bmatrix}$; (b) $\begin{bmatrix} 21 & -14 & -17 & -19 \\ -44 & 11 & 33 & 11 \\ -29 & 1 & 13 & 21 \\ 17 & 7 & -19 & -18 \end{bmatrix}$

10.60. $A = \begin{bmatrix} k & 0 \\ 0 & k \end{bmatrix}$

10.62. (a) $-3, -3$; (b) $-23, -23$; (c) $3, -3$; (d) $17, -17$

10.63. (a) $-2, -17, 73$; (b) 7, 10, 105; (c) 13, 54, 0

10.64. (a) $-6, 13, 58, -219$; (b) $7, -37, 30, 20$

10.65. (a) $x = \frac{21}{26}$, $y = \frac{29}{26}$; (b) $x = -\frac{5}{13}$, $y = \frac{1}{13}$

10.66. (a) $x = 5$, $y = 1$, $z = 1$; (b) since $D = 0$, the system cannot be solved by determinants.

10.68. sgn $\sigma = 1$, $sgn\ \tau = -1$, sgn $\pi = -1$

10.69. (a) $\tau \circ \sigma = 53142$; (b) $\pi \circ \sigma = 52413$; (c) $\sigma^{-1} = 32154$; (d) $\tau^{-1} = 14235$

10.73. (a) det $(T) = 17$; (b) det $(T) = 4$; (c) not defined

10.74. (a) 0; (b) 6; (c) 1

10.77. (a) 18; (b) 9

10.78. 17

10.79. (a) Yes; (b) no; (c) yes; (d) no

10.87. (a) 9 and 3; (b) 6, -3, and 3

Chapter 11

Diagonalization: Eigenvalues and Eigenvectors

11.1 INTRODUCTION

The ideas in this chapter can be discussed from two points of view.

Matrix Point of View

Suppose an n-square matrix A is given. The matrix A is said to be *diagonalizable* if there exists a nonsingular matrix P such that

$$B = P^{-1}AP$$

is diagonal. This chapter discusses the diagonalization of a matrix A. In particular, an algorithm is given to find the matrix P when it exists.

Linear Operator Point of View

Suppose a linear operator $T: V \to V$ is given. The linear operator T is said to be diagonalizable if there exists a basis S of V such that the matrix representation of T relative to the basis S is a diagonal matrix D. This chapter discusses conditions under which the linear operator T is diagonalizable.

> The above are two ways of describing the same thing.

Specifically, a square matrix A may be viewed as a linear operator F defined by

$$F(X) = AX$$

where X is a column vector, and $B = P^{-1}AP$ represents F relative to a new coordinate system (basis) S whose elements are the columns of P. On the other hand, any linear operator T can be represented by a matrix A relative to one basis, and when a second basis is chosen, T is represented by the matrix

$$B = P^{-1}AP$$

where P is the change-of-basis matrix.

Most theorems will be stated in two ways, once in terms of matrices A and again in terms of mappings T. The proofs, however, will only be given once, usually in terms of the mappings T.

The underlying number field K did not play any special role in our previous discussions on vector spaces and linear mappings. However, the diagonalization of a matrix A or a linear operator T will depend on the roots of a polynomial $\Delta(t)$ over K, and these roots do depend on K. For example, suppose $\Delta(t) = t^2 + 1$. Then $\Delta(t)$ has no roots if $K = \mathbf{R}$, the real field; but $\Delta(t)$ has roots $\pm i$ if $K = \mathbf{C}$, the complex field. Furthermore, finding the roots of a polynomial with degree greater than 2 is a subject unto itself (frequently discussed in a course in numerical analysis). Accordingly, our examples will usually lead to those polynomials $\Delta(t)$ whose roots can be easily determined.

11.2 POLYNOMIALS OF MATRICES

Consider a polynomial $f(t)$, say

$$f(t) = a_n t^n + \cdots + a_1 t + a_0$$

Recall (Section 3.3) that if A is any square matrix, then we define

$$f(A) = a_n A^n + \cdots + a_1 A + a_0 I$$

where I is the identity matrix.   In particular we say that A is a root of $f(t)$ if $f(A) = 0$, the zero matrix.

EXAMPLE 11.1 Let $A = \begin{bmatrix} 1 & 2 \\ 3 & 4 \end{bmatrix}$. Then $A^2 = \begin{bmatrix} 7 & 10 \\ 15 & 22 \end{bmatrix}$. Suppose

$$f(t) = 2t^2 - 3t + 5 \qquad \text{and} \qquad g(t) = t^2 - 5t - 2$$

Then

$$f(A) = 2A^2 - 3A + 5I = \begin{bmatrix} 14 & 20 \\ 30 & 44 \end{bmatrix} + \begin{bmatrix} -3 & -6 \\ -9 & -12 \end{bmatrix} + \begin{bmatrix} 5 & 0 \\ 0 & 5 \end{bmatrix} = \begin{bmatrix} 16 & 14 \\ 21 & 37 \end{bmatrix}$$

and

$$g(A) = A^2 - 5A - 2I = \begin{bmatrix} 7 & 10 \\ 15 & 22 \end{bmatrix} + \begin{bmatrix} -5 & -10 \\ -15 & -20 \end{bmatrix} + \begin{bmatrix} -2 & 0 \\ 0 & -2 \end{bmatrix} = \begin{bmatrix} 0 & 0 \\ 0 & 0 \end{bmatrix}$$

Thus A is a zero of $g(t)$.

The following theorem applies.

Theorem 11.1: Let f and g be polynomials, and let A be an n-square matrix.   Then

   (i) $(f + g)(A) = f(A) + g(A)$.

   (ii) $(fg)(A) = f(A)g(A)$.

   (iii) $(kf)(A) = kf(A)$ for any scalar k.

   (iv) $f(A)g(A) = g(A)f(A)$.

By (iv), any two polynomials in A commute.

Matrices and Linear Operators

Now suppose $T: V \to V$ is a linear operator on a vector space V.   Powers of T are defined by the composition operation, that is,

$$T^2 = T \circ T, \ T^3 = T^2 \circ T, \ldots$$

Also, for any polynomial

$$f(t) = a_n t^n + \cdots + a_1 t + a_0$$

we define $f(T)$ in the same way as we did for matrices, that is,

$$f(T) = a_n T^n + \cdots + a_1 T + a_0 I$$

where I is now the identity mapping.   We also say that T is a *zero* or *root* of $f(t)$ if $f(T) = 0$, the zero mapping.   We note that the relations in Theorem 11.1 hold for linear operators as they do for matrices.

Remark: If A is a matrix representation of a linear operator T, then $f(A)$ is the matrix representation of $f(T)$. In particular, $f(T) = 0$ if and only if $f(A) = 0$.

11.3 CHARACTERISTIC POLYNOMIAL, CAYLEY-HAMILTON THEOREM

Consider an n-square matrix A, say

$$A = \begin{bmatrix} a_{11} & a_{12} & \cdots & a_{1n} \\ a_{21} & a_{22} & \cdots & a_{2n} \\ \cdots\cdots\cdots\cdots\cdots\cdots \\ a_{n1} & a_{n2} & \cdots & a_{nn} \end{bmatrix}$$

The matrix $tI_n - A$, where I_n is the n-square identity matrix and t is an indeterminate, is called the *characteristic matrix* of A, that is,

$$tI_n - A = \begin{bmatrix} t - a_{11} & -a_{12} & \cdots & -a_{1n} \\ -a_{21} & t - a_{22} & \cdots & -a_{2n} \\ \cdots\cdots\cdots\cdots\cdots\cdots\cdots\cdots\cdots \\ -a_{n1} & -a_{n2} & \cdots & t - a_{nn} \end{bmatrix}$$

Its determinant

$$\Delta_A(t) = \det(tI_n - A)$$

which is a polynomial in t, is called the *characteristic polynomial* of A. We also call

$$\Delta_A(t) = \det(tI_n - A) = 0$$

the *characteristic equation* of A.

Now each term in the determinant contains one and only one entry from each row and from each column. Hence the above characteristic polynomial is of the form

$$\Delta_A(t) = (t - a_{11})(t - a_{22}) \cdots (t - a_{nn}) + \text{terms with at most } n - 2 \text{ factors of the form } t - a_{ii}$$

Accordingly,

$$\Delta_A(t) = t^n - (a_{11} + a_{22} + \cdots + a_{nn})t^{n-1} + \text{terms of lower degree}$$

Recall that the trace of A is the sum of its diagonal elements. Thus the characteristic polynomial $\Delta_A(t) = \det(tI_n - A)$ of A is a monic polynomial of degree n, and the coefficient of t^{n-1} is the negative of the trace of A. (A polynomial is *monic* if its leading coefficient is 1.)

Furthermore if we set $t = 0$ in $\Delta_A(t)$, we obtain

$$\Delta_A(0) = |-A| = (-1)^n |A|$$

But $\Delta_A(0)$ is the constant term of the polynomial $\Delta_A(t)$. Thus the constant term of the characteristic polynomial of the matrix A is $(-1)^n |A|$, where n is the order of A.

We now state one of the most important theorems in linear algebra (which is proved in Problem 11.42).

Theorem 11.2 (Cayley-Hamilton): Every matrix A is a zero of its characteristic polynomial $\Delta(t)$.

Remark: Suppose $A = [a_{ij}]$ is a triangular matrix. Then $tI - A$ is a triangular matrix with diagonal elements $t - a_{ii}$; and hence

$$\Delta(t) = \det(tI - A) = (t - a_{11})(t - a_{22}) \cdots (t - a_{nn})$$

Observe that the roots of $\Delta(t)$ are the diagonal elements of A.

EXAMPLE 11.2   Consider the matrices

$$A = \begin{bmatrix} 1 & 3 \\ 4 & 5 \end{bmatrix} \quad \text{and} \quad B = \begin{bmatrix} 4 & 1 & 5 & 2 \\ 0 & 3 & 6 & 9 \\ 0 & 0 & 1 & 3 \\ 0 & 0 & 0 & 2 \end{bmatrix}$$

(a)   The characteristic polynomial of A is

$$\Delta(t) = |tI - A| = \begin{vmatrix} t - 1 & -3 \\ -4 & t - 5 \end{vmatrix} = (t - 1)(t - 5) - 12 = t^2 - 6t - 7$$

As expected from the Cayley-Hamilton theorem, A is a root of $\Delta(t)$, that is,

$$\Delta(A) = A^2 - 6A - 7I = \begin{bmatrix} 13 & 18 \\ 24 & 37 \end{bmatrix} + \begin{bmatrix} -6 & -18 \\ -24 & -30 \end{bmatrix} + \begin{bmatrix} -7 & 0 \\ 0 & -7 \end{bmatrix} = \begin{bmatrix} 0 & 0 \\ 0 & 0 \end{bmatrix}$$

(b)   Note that B is triangular with diagonal elements 4, 3, 1, and 2. Hence its characteristic polynomial is

$$\Delta(t) = (t - 4)(t - 3)(t - 1)(t - 2)$$

Now suppose A and B are similar matrices, say $B = P^{-1}AP$, where P is invertible. We show that A and B have the same characteristic polynomial. Using $tI = P^{-1}tIP$, we have

$$\Delta_B(t) = \det(tI - B) = \det(tI - P^{-1}AP) = \det(P^{-1}tIP - P^{-1}AP)$$

$$= \det[P^{-1}(tI - A)P] = \det(P^{-1})\det(tI - A)\det(P)$$

Using the fact that determinants are scalars and commute and that $\det(P^{-1})\det(P) = 1$, we finally obtain

$$\Delta_B(t) = \det(tI - A) = \Delta_A(t)$$

Thus we have proved the following theorem.

Theorem 11.3:   Similar matrices have the same characteristic polynomial.

Characteristic Polynomials of Degree 2 and 3

Let A be a matrix of order 2 or 3. Then there is an easy formula for its characteristic polynomial $\Delta(t)$. Specifically,

(a)   Suppose $A = \begin{bmatrix} a_{11} & a_{12} \\ a_{21} & a_{22} \end{bmatrix}$. Then

$$\Delta(t) = t^2 - (a_{11} + a_{22})t + \begin{vmatrix} a_{11} & a_{12} \\ a_{21} & a_{22} \end{vmatrix} = t^2 - \operatorname{tr}(A)t + \det(A)$$

[Here $\operatorname{tr}(A)$ denotes the trace of A, that is, the sum of the diagonal elements of A.]

(b) Suppose $A = \begin{bmatrix} a_{11} & a_{12} & a_{13} \\ a_{21} & a_{22} & a_{23} \\ a_{31} & a_{32} & a_{33} \end{bmatrix}$. Then

$$\Delta(t) = t^3 - (a_{11} + a_{22} + a_{33})t^2 + \left(\begin{vmatrix} a_{22} & a_{23} \\ a_{32} & a_{33} \end{vmatrix} + \begin{vmatrix} a_{11} & a_{13} \\ a_{31} & a_{33} \end{vmatrix} + \begin{vmatrix} a_{11} & a_{12} \\ a_{21} & a_{22} \end{vmatrix} \right) t$$

$$- \begin{vmatrix} a_{11} & a_{12} & a_{13} \\ a_{21} & a_{22} & a_{23} \\ a_{31} & a_{32} & a_{33} \end{vmatrix}$$

$$= t^3 - \text{tr}\,(A)t^2 + (A_{11} + A_{22} + A_{33})t - \det(A)$$

(Here A_{11}, A_{22}, and A_{33} denote the cofactors of the diagonal elements a_{11}, a_{22}, and a_{33}, respectively.)

EXAMPLE 11.3 Find the characteristic polynomial of each matrix:

$$(a)\ A = \begin{bmatrix} 5 & 3 \\ 2 & 10 \end{bmatrix}; \qquad (b)\ B = \begin{bmatrix} 7 & -1 \\ 6 & 2 \end{bmatrix}; \quad (c)\ C = \begin{bmatrix} 5 & -2 \\ 4 & -4 \end{bmatrix}.$$

(a) We have tr $(A) = 5 + 10 = 15$ and $|A| = 50 - 6 = 44$. Hence $\Delta(t) = t^2 - 15t + 44$.

(b) We have tr $(B) = 7 + 2 = 9$ and $|B| = 14 + 6 = 20$. Hence $\Delta(t) = t^2 - 9t + 20$.

(c) We have tr $(C) = 5 - 4 = 1$ and $|C| = -20 + 8 = -12$. Hence $\Delta(t) = t^2 - t - 12$.

EXAMPLE 11.4 Find the characteristic polynomial of $A = \begin{bmatrix} 1 & 1 & 2 \\ 0 & 3 & 2 \\ 1 & 3 & 9 \end{bmatrix}$.

We have tr $(A) = 1 + 3 + 9 = 13$. The principal minors of order 2 are as follows:

$$A_{11} = \begin{vmatrix} 3 & 2 \\ 3 & 9 \end{vmatrix} = 21, \qquad A_{22} = \begin{vmatrix} 1 & 2 \\ 1 & 9 \end{vmatrix} = 7, \qquad A_{33} = \begin{vmatrix} 1 & 1 \\ 0 & 3 \end{vmatrix} = 3$$

Thus $A_{11} + A_{22} + A_{33} = 31$. Also, $|A| = 27 + 2 + 0 - 6 - 6 - 0 = 17$. Accordingly,

$$\Delta(t) = t^3 - 13t^2 + 31t - 17$$

Remark: Observe that the coefficients of the characteristic polynomial $\Delta(t)$ of the 3-square matrix A are, with alternating signs, as follows:

$$S_1 = \text{tr}\,(A), \qquad S_2 = A_{11} + A_{22} + A_{33}, \qquad S_3 = \det(A)$$

On the other hand, each S_k is the sum of all principal minors of A of order k. The next theorem, whose proof lies beyond the scope of this text, tells us that this result is true in general.

Theorem 11.4: Let A be an n-square matrix. Then its characteristic polynomial is

$$\Delta(t) = t^n - S_1 t^{n-1} + S_2 t^{n-2} + \cdots + (-1)^n S_n$$

where S_k is the sum of the principal minors of order k.

Characteristic Polynomial of a Linear Operator

Now suppose $T: V \to V$ is a linear operator on a vector space V of finite dimension. We define the *characteristic polynomial* $\Delta(t)$ of T to be the characteristic polynomial of any matrix representation of T. Recall that if A and B are matrix representations of T, then $B = P^{-1}AP$, where P is a change-of-basis matrix. Thus A and B are similar and, by Theorem 11.3, A and B have the same characteristic polynomial. Accordingly, the characteristic polynomial of T is independent of the particular basis in which the matrix representation of T is computed.

Since $f(T) = 0$ if and only if $f(A) = 0$, where $f(t)$ is any polynomial and A is any matrix representation of T, we have the following analogous theorem for linear operators.

Theorem 11.2 (Cayley-Hamilton): A linear operator T is a zero of its characteristic polynomial.

11.4 DIAGONALIZATION, EIGENVALUES, AND EIGENVECTORS

Let A be any n-square matrix. Section 9.2 indicates that A can be be represented by (or is similar to) a diagonal matrix $D = \text{diag}(k_1, k_2, \ldots, k_n)$ if there exists a basis S consisting of (column) vectors $u_1, u_2, \ldots, u_n$ such that

$$Au_1 = k_1 u_1$$
$$Au_2 = k_2 u_2$$
$$\cdots\cdots\cdots\cdots\cdots$$
$$Au_n = k_n u_n$$

In such a case A is said to be *diagonalizable*. Furthermore $D = P^{-1}AP$, where P is the nonsingular matrix whose columns are the basis vectors $u_1, u_2, \ldots, u_n$.

The above observation leads us to the following important definition.

Definition: Let A be any square matrix. A scalar λ is called an *eigenvalue* of A if there exists a nonzero (column) vector v such that

$$Av = \lambda v$$

Every vector satisfying this relation is called an *eigenvector* of A belonging to the eigenvalue λ.

We note that each scalar multiplier kv of an eigenvector v belonging to λ is also an eigenvector since

$$A(kv) = k(Av) = k(\lambda v) = \lambda(kv)$$

The set E_λ of all such eigenvectors is a subspace of V (Problem 11.24), called the *eigenspace* of λ. (If dim $E_\lambda = 1$, then E_λ is called an *eigenline* and λ is called a *scaling factor*.)

The terms *characteristic value* and *characteristic vector*, or *proper value* and *proper vector*, are sometimes used instead of eigenvalue and eigenvector.

The above observation and definitions give us the following theorem.

Theorem 11.5:   An n-square matrix A is similar to a diagonal matrix D if and only if A has n linearly independent eigenvectors. In this case the diagonal elements of D are the corresponding eigenvalues and $D = P^{-1}AP$, where P is the matrix whose columns are the eigenvectors.

Suppose a matrix A can be diagonalized as above, say $P^{-1}AP = D$, where D is diagonal. Then A has the extremely useful *diagonal factorization*

$$A = PDP^{-1}$$

Using this factorization, the algebra of A reduces to the algebra of the diagonal matrix D, which can be easily calculated. Specifically, suppose $D = \text{diag}(k_1, k_2, \ldots, k_n)$. Then

$$A^m = (PDP^{-1})^m = PD^mP^{-1} = P\,\text{diag}(k_1^m, \ldots, k_n^m)P^{-1}$$

and, more generally, for any polynomial $f(t)$,

$$f(A) = f(PDP^{-1}) = Pf(D)P^{-1} = P\,\text{diag}(f(k_1), \ldots, f(k_n))P^{-1}$$

Furthermore, if the diagonal entries of D are nonnegative, then the following matrix B is a square root of A:

$$B = P\,\text{diag}(\sqrt{k_1}, \ldots, \sqrt{k_n})P^{-1}$$

that is, $B^2 = A$.

EXAMPLE 11.5 Let $A = \begin{bmatrix} 3 & 1 \\ 2 & 2 \end{bmatrix}$, $v_1 = \begin{bmatrix} 1 \\ -2 \end{bmatrix}$, and $v_2 = \begin{bmatrix} 1 \\ 1 \end{bmatrix}$. Then

$$Av_1 = \begin{bmatrix} 3 & 1 \\ 2 & 2 \end{bmatrix}\begin{bmatrix} 1 \\ -2 \end{bmatrix} = \begin{bmatrix} 1 \\ -2 \end{bmatrix} = v_1 \qquad Av_2 = \begin{bmatrix} 3 & 1 \\ 2 & 2 \end{bmatrix}\begin{bmatrix} 1 \\ 1 \end{bmatrix} = \begin{bmatrix} 4 \\ 4 \end{bmatrix} = 4v_2$$

Thus v_1 and v_2 are eigenvectors of A belonging to the eigenvalues $\lambda_1 = 1$ and $\lambda_2 = 4$, respectively. Observe that v_1 and v_2 are linearly independent and hence form a basis of $\mathbf{R}^2$. Accordingly, A is diagonalizable. Furthermore let P be the matrix whose columns are the eigenvectors v_1 and v_2. That is, let

$$P = \begin{bmatrix} 1 & 1 \\ -2 & 1 \end{bmatrix} \qquad \text{and so} \qquad P^{-1} = \begin{bmatrix} \frac{1}{3} & -\frac{1}{3} \\ \frac{2}{3} & \frac{1}{3} \end{bmatrix}$$

Then A is similar to the diagonal matrix

$$D = P^{-1}AP = \begin{bmatrix} \frac{1}{3} & -\frac{1}{3} \\ \frac{2}{3} & \frac{1}{3} \end{bmatrix}\begin{bmatrix} 3 & 1 \\ 2 & 2 \end{bmatrix}\begin{bmatrix} 1 & 1 \\ -2 & 1 \end{bmatrix} = \begin{bmatrix} 1 & 0 \\ 0 & 4 \end{bmatrix}$$

As expected, the diagonal elements 1 and 4 in D are the eigenvalues corresponding to the eigenvectors v_1 and v_2, respectively, which are the columns of P. In particular, A has the factorization

$$A = PDP^{-1} = \begin{bmatrix} 1 & 1 \\ -2 & 1 \end{bmatrix}\begin{bmatrix} 1 & 0 \\ 0 & 4 \end{bmatrix}\begin{bmatrix} \frac{1}{3} & -\frac{1}{3} \\ \frac{2}{3} & \frac{1}{3} \end{bmatrix}$$

Accordingly,

$$A^4 = \begin{bmatrix} 1 & 1 \\ -2 & 1 \end{bmatrix}\begin{bmatrix} 1 & 0 \\ 0 & 256 \end{bmatrix}\begin{bmatrix} \frac{1}{3} & -\frac{1}{3} \\ \frac{2}{3} & \frac{1}{3} \end{bmatrix} = \begin{bmatrix} 171 & 85 \\ 170 & 86 \end{bmatrix}$$

Moreover, suppose $f(t) = t^3 - 5t^2 + 3t + 6$. Hence $f(1) = 5$ and $f(4) = 2$. Then

$$f(A) = Pf(D)P^{-1} = \begin{bmatrix} 1 & 1 \\ -2 & 1 \end{bmatrix}\begin{bmatrix} 5 & 0 \\ 0 & 2 \end{bmatrix}\begin{bmatrix} \frac{1}{3} & -\frac{1}{3} \\ \frac{2}{3} & \frac{1}{3} \end{bmatrix} = \begin{bmatrix} 3 & -1 \\ -2 & 4 \end{bmatrix}$$

Lastly we obtain a positive square root of A. Specifically, using $\sqrt{1} = 1$ and $\sqrt{4} = 2$, we obtain the matrix

$$B = P\sqrt{D}P^{-1} = \begin{bmatrix} 1 & 1 \\ -2 & 1 \end{bmatrix}\begin{bmatrix} 1 & 0 \\ 0 & 2 \end{bmatrix}\begin{bmatrix} \frac{1}{3} & -\frac{1}{3} \\ \frac{2}{3} & \frac{1}{3} \end{bmatrix} = \begin{bmatrix} \frac{5}{3} & \frac{1}{3} \\ \frac{2}{3} & \frac{4}{3} \end{bmatrix}$$

where $B^2 = A$ and where B has positive eigenvalues.

Remark: Throughout this chapter we use the fact that the inverse of the matrix $P = \begin{bmatrix} a & b \\ c & d \end{bmatrix}$ is the matrix $P^{-1} = \begin{bmatrix} d/|P| & -b/|P| \\ -c/|P| & a/|P| \end{bmatrix}$, that is, P^{-1} is obtained by interchanging the diagonal elements a and d of P, taking the negatives of the nondiagonal elements b and c, and dividing each element by the determinant $|P|$.

Properties of Eigenvalues and Eigenvectors

Example 11.5 indicates advantages of a diagonal representation (factorization) of a square matrix. Here we list properties that help us find such a representation.

Theorem 11.6:   Let A be a square matrix. Then the following are equivalent.

    (i)   A scalar λ is an eigenvalue of A.

    (ii)   The matrix $\lambda I - A$ is singular.

    (iii)   The scalar λ is a root of the characteristic polynomial $\Delta(t)$ of A.

The eigenspace E_λ of an eigenvalue λ is the solution space of the homogeneous system $(\lambda I - A)X = 0$. Sometimes it is more convenient to solve the homogeneous system $(A - \lambda I)X = 0$. Both systems, of course, yield the same solution space.

Some matrices have no eigenvalues and hence no eigenvectors. However, Theorem 11.6 and the Fundamental Theorem of Algebra (every polynomial over the complex field **C** has a root) gives us the following result.

Theorem 11.7:   Let A be a square matrix over the complex field **C**. Then A has at least one eigenvalue.

The following theorems will be used subsequently.

Theorem 11.8:   Suppose $v_1, v_2, \ldots, v_n$ are nonzero eigenvectors of a matrix A belonging to distinct eigenvalues $\lambda_1, \lambda_2, \ldots, \lambda_n$. Then $v_1, v_2, \ldots, v_n$ are linearly independent.

Theorem 11.9:   Suppose the characteristic polynomial $\Delta(t)$ of an n-square matrix A is a product of n distinct factors, say $\Delta(t) = (t - a_1)(t - a_2) \cdots (t - a_n)$. Then A is similar to the diagonal matrix $D = \text{diag}(a_1, a_2, \ldots, a_n)$.

Now suppose λ is an eigenvalue of a matrix A. The *algebraic multiplicity* of λ is defined to be the multiplicity of λ as a root of the characteristic polynomial of A. The *geometric multiplicity* of λ is defined to be the dimension of its eigenspace.

The following theorem (essentially proved in Problem 11.46) applies.

Theorem 11.10:   Let λ be an eigenvalue of a matrix A. Then the geometric multiplicity of λ does not exceed its algebraic multiplicity.

Diagonalization of Linear Operators

Consider a linear operator $T: V \to V$. Then T is said to be *diagonalizable* if it can be represented by a diagonal matrix D. Thus T is diagonalizable if and only if there exists a basis $S = \{u_1, u_2, \ldots, u_n\}$ of V for which

$$T(u_1) = k_1 u_1$$
$$T(u_2) = \qquad k_2 u_2$$
$$\cdots\cdots\cdots\cdots\cdots$$
$$T(u_n) = \qquad\qquad k_n u_n$$

In such a case T is represented by the diagonal matrix

$$D = \mathrm{diag}\,(k_1, k_2, \ldots, k_n)$$

relative to the basis S.

The above observation leads us to the following definitions and theorems, which are analogous to the definitions and theorems for matrices discussed above.

Definition: Let T be a linear operator. A scalar λ is called an *eigenvalue* of T if there exists a nonzero vector v such that

$$T(v) = \lambda v$$

Every vector satisfying this relation is called an *eigenvector* of T *belonging* to the eigenvalue λ.

The set E_λ of all eigenvectors belonging to an eigenvalue λ is a subspace of V, called the *eigenspace of λ*. (Alternately, λ is an eigenvalue of T if $\lambda I - T$ is singular and, in this case, E_λ is the kernel of $\lambda I - T$.)

The following theorems apply to a linear operator T on a vector space V of finite dimension.

Theorem 11.5': T can be represented by a diagonal matrix D if and only if there exists a basis S of V consisting of eigenvectors of T. In this case the diagonal elements of D are the corresponding eigenvalues.

Theorem 11.6':   Let T be a linear operator. Then the following are equivalent.

    (i)   A scalar λ is an eigenvalue of T.

    (ii)   The linear operator $\lambda I - T$ is singular.

    (iii)   The scalar λ is a root of the characteristic polynomial $\Delta(t)$ of T.

Theorem 11.7':   Suppose V is a complex vector space. Then T has at least one eigenvalue.

Theorem 11.8':   Suppose $v_1, v_2, \ldots, v_n$ are nonzero eigenvectors of a linear operator T belonging to distinct eigenvalues $\lambda_1, \lambda_2, \ldots, \lambda_n$. Then $v_1, v_2, \ldots, v_n$ are linearly independent.

Theorem 11.9':   Suppose the characteristic polynomial $\Delta(t)$ of T is a product of n distinct factors, say $\Delta(t) = (t - a_1)(t - a_2) \cdots (t - a_n)$. Then T can be represented by the diagonal matrix $D = \mathrm{diag}\,(a_1, a_2, \ldots, a_n)$.

Theorem 11.10':   The geometric multiplicity of an eigenvalue λ of T does not exceed its algebraic multiplicity.

Remark: The following theorem reduces the investigation of the diagonalization of a linear operator T to the diagonalization of a matrix A.

Theorem 11.11:   Suppose A is a matrix representation of T.   Then T is diagonalizable if and only if A is diagonalizable.

11.5   COMPUTING EIGENVALUES AND EIGENVECTORS, DIAGONALIZING MATRICES

This section gives an algorithm for computing eigenvalues and eigenvectors for a given square matrix A and for determining whether or not a nonsingular matrix P exists such that $P^{-1}AP$ is diagonal.

Diagonalization Algorithm 11.5:   The input is an n-square matrix A.

Step 1.   Find the characteristic polynomial $\Delta(t)$ of A.

Step 2.   Find the roots of $\Delta(t)$ to obtain the eigenvalues of A.

Step 3.   Repeat (a) and (b) for each eigenvalue λ of A:

(a)   Form $M = A - \lambda I$ by subtracting λ down the diagonal of A, or form $M' = \lambda I - A$ by substituting $t = \lambda$ in $tI - A$.

(b)   Find a basis for the solution space of the homogeneous system $MX = 0$.   (These basis vectors are linearly independent eigenvectors of A belonging to λ.)

Step 4.   Consider the collection $S = \{v_1, v_2, \ldots, v_m\}$ of all eigenvectors obtained in Step 3:

(a)   If $m \neq n$, then A is not diagonalizable.

(b)   If $m = n$, let P be the matrix whose columns are the eigenvectors $v_1, v_2, \ldots, v_n$. Then

$$D = P^{-1}AP = \text{diag}\,(\lambda_1, \lambda_2, \ldots, \lambda_n)$$

where λ_i is the eigenvalue corresponding to the eigenvector v_i.

EXAMPLE 11.6   The diagonalization algorithm is applied to $A = \begin{bmatrix} 4 & 2 \\ 3 & -1 \end{bmatrix}$.

(a)   The characteristic polynomial $\Delta(t)$ of A is computed.   We have

$$\text{tr}\,(A) = 4 - 1 = 3, \qquad |A| = -4 - 6 = -10; \qquad \text{so} \qquad \Delta(t) = t^2 - 3t - 10 = (t - 5)(t + 2)$$

(b)   Set $\Delta(t) = (t - 5)(t + 2) = 0$.   The root $\lambda_1 = 5$ and $\lambda_2 = -2$ are the eigenvalues of A.

(c)   (i)   We find an eigenvector v_1 of A belonging to the eigenvalue $\lambda_1 = 5$.   Subtract $\lambda_1 = 5$ down the diagonal of A to obtain the matrix $M = \begin{bmatrix} -1 & 2 \\ 3 & -6 \end{bmatrix}$.   The eigenvectors belonging to $\lambda_1 = 5$ form the solution of the homogeneous system $MX = 0$, that is,

$$\begin{bmatrix} -1 & 2 \\ 3 & -6 \end{bmatrix}\begin{bmatrix} x \\ y \end{bmatrix} = \begin{bmatrix} 0 \\ 0 \end{bmatrix} \qquad \text{or} \qquad \begin{matrix} -x + 2y = 0 \\ 3x - 6y = 0 \end{matrix} \qquad \text{or} \qquad -x + 2y = 0$$

The system has only one free variable.   Thus a nonzero solution, for example, $v_1 = (2, 1)$, is an eigenvector which spans the eigenspace of $\lambda_1 = 5$.

(ii)   We find an eigenvector v_2 of A belonging to the eigenvalue $\lambda_2 = -2$.   Subtract -2 (or add 2) down the diagonal of A to obtain $M = \begin{bmatrix} 6 & 2 \\ 3 & 1 \end{bmatrix}$ which yields the homogeneous system

$$\begin{matrix} 6x + 2y = 0 \\ 3x + \ y = 0 \end{matrix} \qquad \text{or} \qquad 3x + y = 0$$

The system has only one free variable, thus a nonzero solution, say $v_2 = (-1, 3)$, is an eigenvector which spans the eigenspace of $\lambda_2 = -2$.

(d) Let P be the matrix whose columns are the eigenvectors v_1 and v_2.   Then

$$P = \begin{bmatrix} 2 & -1 \\ 1 & 3 \end{bmatrix} \quad \text{and so} \quad P^{-1} = \begin{bmatrix} \frac{3}{7} & \frac{1}{7} \\ -\frac{1}{7} & \frac{2}{7} \end{bmatrix}$$

Accordingly, $D = P^{-1}AP$ is the diagonal matrix whose diagonal entries are the corresponding eigenvalues, that is,

$$D = P^{-1}AP = \begin{bmatrix} \frac{3}{7} & \frac{1}{7} \\ -\frac{1}{7} & \frac{2}{7} \end{bmatrix} \begin{bmatrix} 4 & 2 \\ 3 & -1 \end{bmatrix} \begin{bmatrix} 2 & -1 \\ 1 & 3 \end{bmatrix} = \begin{bmatrix} 5 & 0 \\ 0 & -2 \end{bmatrix}$$

EXAMPLE 11.7   Consider the matrix $B = \begin{bmatrix} 5 & -1 \\ 1 & 3 \end{bmatrix}$.   We have

$$\text{tr}\,(B) = 5 + 3 = 8, \qquad |B| = 15 + 1 = 16; \qquad \text{so} \qquad \Delta(t) = t^2 - 8t + 16 = (t - 4)^2$$

is the characteristic polynomial of B.   Accordingly, $\lambda = 4$ is the only eigenvalue of B.

Subtract $\lambda = 4$ down the diagonal of B to obtain the matrix $M = \begin{bmatrix} 1 & -1 \\ 1 & -1 \end{bmatrix}$ and the homogeneous system

$$\begin{matrix} x - y = 0 \\ x - y = 0 \end{matrix} \quad \text{or} \quad x - y = 0$$

The system has only one free variable and $v = (1, 1)$ is a nonzero solution.   Thus $v = (1, 1)$ and its multiples are the only eigenvectors of B.   Accordingly B is not diagonalizable since there exists no basis consisting of eigenvectors of B.

EXAMPLE 11.8   Consider the matrix $A = \begin{bmatrix} 3 & -5 \\ 2 & -3 \end{bmatrix}$.   Here $\text{tr}\,(A) = 3 - 3 = 0$ and $|A| = -9 + 10 = 1$. Thus $\Delta(t) = t^2 + 1$ is the characteristic polynomial of A.   We consider two cases:

(a) A is a matrix over the real field **R**.   Then $\Delta(t)$ has no (real) roots.   Thus A has no eigenvalues and no eigenvectors, and so A is not diagonalizable.

(b) A is a matrix over the complex field **C**.   Then $\Delta(t) = (t - i)(t + i)$ has two roots, i and $-i$.   Thus A has two distinct eigenvalues i and $-i$, and hence A has two independent eigenvectors.   Accordingly there exists a nonsingular matrix P over the complex field **C** for which

$$P^{-1}AP = \begin{bmatrix} i & 0 \\ 0 & -i \end{bmatrix}$$

Therefore A is diagonalizable (over **C**).

11.6 DIAGONALIZING REAL SYMMETRIC MATRICES

There are many real matrices A that are not diagonalizable.   In fact, some real matrices may not have any (real) eigenvalues.   However, if A is a real symmetric matrix, then these problems do not exist.   Namely

Theorem 11.12:   Let A be a real symmetric matrix.   Then each root λ of its characteristic polynomial is real.

Theorem 11.13:   Let A be a real symmetric matrix.   Suppose u and v are nonzero eigenvectors of A belonging to distinct eigenvalues λ_1 and λ_2.   Then u and v are orthogonal, i.e., $\langle u, v \rangle = 0$.

The above two theorems give us the following fundamental result:

Theorem 11.14:   Let A be a real symmetric matrix.   Then there exists an orthogonal matrix P such that $D = P^{-1}AP$ is diagonal.

We can choose the columns of the above matrix P to be normalized orthogonal eigenvectors of A.   Then the diagonal entries of D are the corresponding eigenvalues.

EXAMPLE 11.9   Consider the real symmetric matrix $A = \begin{bmatrix} 2 & -2 \\ -2 & 5 \end{bmatrix}$.   We find an orthogonal matrix P such that $P^{-1}AP$ is diagonal.   We have

$$\text{tr}\,(A) = 2 + 5 = 7, \qquad |A| = 10 - 4 = 6, \qquad \text{so} \qquad \Delta(t) = t^2 - 7t + 6 = (t - 6)(t - 1)$$

is the characteristic polynomial of A.   Accordingly, $\lambda_1 = 6$ and $\lambda_2 = 1$ are the eigenvalues of A.
    Subtracting $\lambda_1 = 6$ down the diagonal of A yields the matrix

$$M = \begin{bmatrix} -4 & -2 \\ -2 & -1 \end{bmatrix} \quad \text{or the homogeneous system} \quad \begin{matrix} -4x - 2y = 0 \\ -2x - y = 0 \end{matrix} \quad \text{or} \quad 2x + y = 0$$

A nonzero solution is $u_1 = (1, -2)$.
    Subtracting $\lambda_2 = 1$ down the diagonal of A yields the matrix

$$M = \begin{bmatrix} 1 & -2 \\ -2 & 4 \end{bmatrix} \quad \text{or the homogeneous system} \quad x - 2y = 0$$

(The second equation drops out as it is a multiple of the first equation.)   A nonzero solution is $u_2 = (2, 1)$.
    As expected from Theorem 11.13, u_1 and u_2 are orthogonal.   Normalizing u_1 and u_2 yields the orthonormal vectors

$$\hat{u}_1 = 1/\sqrt{5} - 2/\sqrt{5}), \qquad \hat{u}_2 = (2/\sqrt{5}, 1/\sqrt{5})$$

Finally let P be the matrix whose columns are $\hat{u}_1$ and $\hat{u}_2$, respectively.   Then

$$P = \begin{bmatrix} 1/\sqrt{5} & 2/\sqrt{5} \\ -2/\sqrt{5} & 1/\sqrt{5} \end{bmatrix} \quad \text{and} \quad P^{-1}AP = \begin{bmatrix} 6 & 0 \\ 0 & 1 \end{bmatrix}$$

As expected, the diagonal entries of $P^{-1}AP$ are the eigenvalues corresponding to the columns of P.

The procedure in Example 11.9 is formalized in the following algorithm, which finds an orthogonal matrix P such that $P^{-1}AP$ is diagonal.

Orthogonal Diagonalization Algorithm 11.6:   The input is a real symmetric matrix A.

Step 1.   Find the characteristic polynomial $\Delta(t)$ of A.

Step 2.   Find the eigenvalues of A, which are the roots of $\Delta(t)$.

Step 3.   For each eigenvalue λ of A in Step 2, find an orthogonal basis of its eigenspace.

Step 4.   Normalize all eigenvectors in Step 3, which then forms an orthonormal basis of $\mathbf{R}^n$.

Step 5.   Let P be the matrix whose columns are the normalized eigenvectors in Step 4.

11.7 MINIMUM POLYNOMIAL

Let A be any square matrix. Let $J(A)$ denote the collection of all polynomials $f(t)$ for which A is a root, i.e., for which $f(A) = 0$. The set $J(A)$ is not empty since the Cayley-Hamilton Theorem 11.2, tells us that the characteristic polynomial $\Delta_A(t)$ of A belongs to $J(A)$. Let $m(t)$ denote the monic polynomial of minimal degree in $J(A)$. [Such a polynomial $m(t)$ exists and is unique.] We call $m(t)$ the *minimal polynomial* of the matrix A.

Theorem 11.15: The minimum polynomial $m(t)$ of a matrix (linear operator) A divides every polynomial that has A as a zero. In particular, $m(t)$ divides the characteristic polynomial $\Delta(t)$ of A.

There is an even stronger relationship between $m(t)$ and $\Delta(t)$.

Theorem 11.16: The characteristic polynomial $\Delta(t)$ and the minimum polynomial $m(t)$ of a matrix A have the same irreducible factors.

This theorem (proved in Problem 11.48) does not say that $m(t) = \Delta(t)$, only that any irreducible factor of one must divide the other. In particular, since a linear factor is irreducible, $m(t)$ and $\Delta(t)$ have the same linear factors. Hence they have the same roots. Thus we have

Theorem 11.17: A scalar λ is an eigenvalue of the matrix A if and only if λ is a root of the minimum polynomial of A.

EXAMPLE 11.10 Find the minimal polynomial $m(t)$ of $A = \begin{bmatrix} 2 & 2 & -5 \\ 3 & 7 & -15 \\ 1 & 2 & -4 \end{bmatrix}$.

First find the characteristic polynomial $\Delta(t)$ of A. We have

$$\text{tr}(A) = 5, \quad A_{11} + A_{22} + A_{33} = 2 - 3 + 8 = 7, \quad |A| = 3$$

Hence

$$\Delta(t) = t^3 - 5t^2 + 7t - 3 = (t - 1)^2(t - 3)$$

The minimum polynomial $m(t)$ must divide $\Delta(t)$. Also, each irreducible factor of $\Delta(t)$, that is, $t - 1$ and $t - 3$, must also be a factor of $m(t)$. Thus $m(t)$ is exactly one of the following:

$$f(t) = (t - 3)(t - 1) \quad \text{or} \quad g(t) = (t - 3)(t - 1)^2$$

We know, by the Cayley-Hamilton theorem, that $g(A) = \Delta(A) = 0$. Hence we need only test $f(t)$. We have

$$f(A) = (A - I)(A - 3I) = \begin{bmatrix} 1 & 2 & -5 \\ 3 & 6 & -15 \\ 1 & 2 & -5 \end{bmatrix}\begin{bmatrix} -1 & 2 & -5 \\ 3 & 4 & -15 \\ 1 & 2 & -7 \end{bmatrix} = \begin{bmatrix} 0 & 0 & 0 \\ 0 & 0 & 0 \\ 0 & 0 & 0 \end{bmatrix}$$

Thus $f(t) = m(t) = (t - 1)(t - 3) = t^2 - 4t + 3$ is the minimum polynomial of A.

EXAMPLE 11.11   Consider the r-square matrix

$$A = \begin{bmatrix} \lambda & a & 0 & \cdots & 0 & 0 \\ 0 & \lambda & a & \cdots & 0 & 0 \\ \cdots & \cdots & \cdots & \cdots & \cdots & \cdots \\ 0 & 0 & 0 & \cdots & \lambda & a \\ 0 & 0 & 0 & \cdots & 0 & \lambda \end{bmatrix}$$

where $a \neq 0$.   That is, A has the λ on the diagonal, the a's on the *superdiagonal* (consisting of the entries above the diagonal), where $a \neq 0$, and 0s elsewhere.   Since A is triangular,

$$f(t) = (t - \lambda)^r$$

is the characteristic polynomial of A.   We show (see Problem 11.34) that $f(t)$ is also the minimum polynomial of A.

Remark: The above matrix A with $a = 1$ is called a *Jordan block* matrix.   Thus $f(t) = (t - \lambda)^r$ is the characteristic and minimum polynomial of an r-square Jordan block matrix.

EXAMPLE 11.12   Consider an arbitrary monic polynomial

$$f(t) = t^n + a_{n-1}t^{n-1} + \cdots + a_1 t + a_0$$

Let A be the n-square matrix with 1s on the *subdiagonal* (consisting of the entries below the diagonal entries), the negatives of the coefficients in the last column, and 0s elsewhere, as follows:

$$A = \begin{bmatrix} 0 & 0 & \cdots & 0 & -a_0 \\ 1 & 0 & \cdots & 0 & -a_1 \\ 0 & 1 & \cdots & 0 & -a_2 \\ \cdots & \cdots & \cdots & \cdots & \cdots \\ 0 & 0 & \cdots & 1 & -a_{n-1} \end{bmatrix}$$

Then A is called the *companion matrix* of the polynomial $f(t)$.   Moreover, the minimum polynomial $m(t)$ and the characteristic polynomial $\Delta(t)$ of the above companion matrix A are both equal to $f(t)$.

Minimum Polynomial of a Linear Operator

The *minimum polynomial* $m(t)$ of a linear operator T is defined to be the monic polynomial of lowest degree for which T is a root.   However, for any polynomial $f(t)$ we have

$$f(T) = 0 \qquad \text{if and only if} \qquad f(A) = 0$$

where A is any matrix representation of T.   Accordingly, T and A have the same minimal polynomials.   Thus the above theorems on the minimal polynomial of a matrix also hold for the minimal polynomial of a linear operator.

Theorem 11.15′:   The minimal polynomial $m(t)$ of a linear operator T divides every polynomial that has T as a root.   In particular, $m(t)$ divides the characteristic polynomial $\Delta(t)$ of T.

Theorem 11.16′:   The characteristic and minimal polynomials of a linear operator T have the same irreducible factors.

Theorem 11.17':   A scalar λ is an eigenvalue of a linear operator T if and only if λ is a root of the minimal polynomial $m(t)$ of T.

11.8 CHARACTERISTIC AND MINIMAL POLYNOMIALS OF BLOCK MATRICES

This section discusses the relationship of the characteristic polynomial and the minimal polynomial to certain (square) block matrices.

Characteristic Polynomial and Block Triangular Matrices

Suppose M is a block triangular matrix, say $M = \begin{bmatrix} A_1 & B \\ 0 & A_2 \end{bmatrix}$, where A_1 and A_2 are square matrices.   Then $tI - M$ is also a block triangular matrix with diagonal blocks $tI - A_1$ and $tI - A_2$.   Thus

$$|tI - M| = \begin{vmatrix} tI - A_1 & -B \\ 0 & tI - A_2 \end{vmatrix} = |tI - A_1||tI - A_2|$$

That is, the characteristic polynomial of M is the product of the characteristic polynomials of the diagonal blocks A_1 and A_2.

By induction, we obtain the following useful result.

Theorem 11.18:   Suppose M is a block triangular matrix with diagonal blocks $A_1, A_2, \ldots, A_r$. Then the characteristic polynomial of M is the product of the characteristic polynomials of the diagonal blocks A_i, that is,

$$\Delta_M(t) = \Delta_{A_1}(t)\Delta_{A_2}(t)\cdots\Delta_{A_r}(t)$$

EXAMPLE 11.13   Consider the matrix $M = \begin{bmatrix} 9 & -1 & 5 & 7 \\ 8 & 3 & 2 & -4 \\ 0 & 0 & 3 & 6 \\ 0 & 0 & -1 & 8 \end{bmatrix}$.

Then M is a block triangular matrix with diagonal blocks $A = \begin{bmatrix} 9 & -1 \\ 8 & 3 \end{bmatrix}$ and $B = \begin{bmatrix} 3 & 6 \\ -1 & 8 \end{bmatrix}$.   Here

$$\text{tr}\,(A) = 9 + 3 = 12, \quad \det\,(A) = 27 + 8 = 35 \quad \text{and so} \quad \Delta_A(t) = t^2 - 12t + 35 = (t - 5)(t - 7)$$

$$\text{tr}\,(B) = 3 + 8 = 11, \quad \det\,(B) = 24 + 6 = 30 \quad \text{and so} \quad \Delta_B(t) = t^2 - 11t + 30 = (t - 5)(t - 6)$$

Accordingly, the characteristic polynomial of M is the product

$$\Delta_M(t) = \Delta_A(t)\Delta_B(t) = (t - 5)^2(t - 6)(t - 7)$$

Minimum Polynomial and Block Diagonal Matrices

The following theorem applies.

Theorem 11.19:   Suppose M is a block diagonal matrix with diagonal blocks $A_1, A_2, \ldots, A_r$. Then the minimum polynomial of M is equal to the least common multiple (LCM) of the minimum polynomials of the diagonal blocks A_i.

Remark: We emphasize that this theorem applies to block diagonal matrices, whereas the analogous Theorem 11.18 on characteristic polynomials applies to block triangular matrices.

EXAMPLE 11.14 Find the characteristic polynomial $\Delta(t)$ and the minimal polynomial $m(t)$ of the matrix

$$A = \begin{bmatrix} 2 & 5 & 0 & 0 & 0 \\ 0 & 2 & 0 & 0 & 0 \\ 0 & 0 & 4 & 2 & 0 \\ 0 & 0 & 3 & 5 & 0 \\ 0 & 0 & 0 & 0 & 7 \end{bmatrix}$$

Note that A is a block diagonal matrix with diagonal blocks $A_1 = \begin{bmatrix} 2 & 5 \\ 0 & 2 \end{bmatrix}$, $A_2 = \begin{bmatrix} 4 & 2 \\ 3 & 5 \end{bmatrix}$, and

$A_3 = [7]$. Then $\Delta(t)$ is the product of the characteristic polynomials $\Delta_1(t)$, $\Delta_2(t)$, and $\Delta_3(t)$ of A_1, A_2, and A_3, respectively. Since A_1 and A_3 are triangular, $\Delta_1(t) = (t-2)^2$ and $\Delta_3(t) = (t-7)$. Also,

$$\Delta_2(t) = t^2 - \text{tr}\,(A_2)t + |A_2| = t^2 - 9t + 14 = (t-2)(t-7)$$

Thus $\Delta(t) = (t-2)^3(t-7)^2$. [As expected, deg $\Delta(t) = 5$.]

The minimum polynomials $m_1(t)$, $m_2(t)$, and $m_3(t)$ of the diagonal blocks A_1, A_2, and A_3, respectively, are equal to the characteristic polynomials, that is,

$$m_1(t) = (t-2)^2, \qquad m_2(t) = (t-2)(t-7), \qquad m_3(t) = t-7$$

But $m(t)$ is equal to the least common multiple of $m_1(t)$, $m_2(t)$, $m_3(t)$. Thus $m(t) = (t-2)^2(t-7)$.

11.9 JORDAN NORMAL FORM

Let A be an arbitrary square matrix. Then A may not be diagonalizable, that is, A may not be similar to a diagonal matrix D. However, it still may be possible to "simplify" the matrix representation of A in a number of ways. We discuss one of these ways, called the Jordan normal form, in this section. This simplification is only possible when the characteristic and minimal polynomials of A can be factored into linear polynomials. This is always true if the base field K is the complex field $\mathbf{C}$, but it need not be true if K is the real field $\mathbf{R}$. There is another normal form, called the rational canonical form, which exists for any matrix. However, a discussion of such a canonical form lies beyond the scope of this text.

The following theorem applies. (The proof of this theorem also lies beyond the scope of this text.)

Theorem 11.20: Let A be a matrix whose characteristic polynomial and minimal polynomial are, respectively,

$$\Delta(t) = (t-\lambda_1)^{n_1}\cdots(t-\lambda_r)^{n_r} \qquad \text{and} \qquad m(t) = (t-\lambda_1)^{m_1}\cdots(t-\lambda_r)^{m_r}$$

where the λ_i are distinct scalars. Then A is similar to a block diagonal matrix J_A whose diagonal entries are of the form

$$J_{ij} = \begin{bmatrix} \lambda_i & 1 & 0 & \dots & 0 & 0 \\ 0 & \lambda_i & 1 & \dots & 0 & 0 \\ \hdotsfor{6} \\ 0 & 0 & 0 & \dots & \lambda_i & 1 \\ 0 & 0 & 0 & \dots & 0 & \lambda_i \end{bmatrix}$$

For each λ_i the corresponding blocks J_{ij} have the following properties:

(i)   There is at least one J_{ij} of order m_i; all other J_{ij} are of order $\leq m_i$.

(ii)   The sum of the orders of the J_{ij} is n_i.

(iii) The number of J_{ij} equals the geometric multiplicity of λ_i.

(iv)   The number of J_{ij} of each possible order is uniquely determined by A.

The matrix J_A appearing in the above theorem is called the *Jordan normal form* of the matrix A. We emphasize that the Jordan normal form of A is unique except for the order of the blocks. Any diagonal block J_{ij} is called a *Jordan block* belonging to the eigenvalue λ_i.

EXAMPLE 11.15 Suppose the characteristic and minimal polynomials of a matrix A are, respectively,

$$\Delta(t) = (t - 2)^4(t - 3)^3 \quad \text{and} \quad m(t) = (t - 2)^2(t - 3)^2$$

Then the Jordan normal form of A is one of the following (except for the order of the blocks):

$$\begin{bmatrix} 2 & 1 & & & & & \\ 0 & 2 & & & & & \\ & & 2 & 1 & & & \\ & & 0 & 2 & & & \\ & & & & 3 & 1 & \\ & & & & 0 & 3 & \\ & & & & & & 3 \end{bmatrix} \quad \text{or} \quad \begin{bmatrix} 2 & 1 & & & & & \\ 0 & 2 & & & & & \\ & & 2 & & & & \\ & & & 2 & & & \\ & & & & 3 & 1 & \\ & & & & 0 & 3 & \\ & & & & & & 3 \end{bmatrix}$$

The first matrix occurs if A has two independent eigenvectors belonging to the eigenvalue $\lambda = 2$. The second matrix occurs if A has three independent eigenvectors belonging to $\lambda = 2$.

Jordan Normal Form and Linear Operators

There is an analogous Theorem 11.20 for linear operators. That is, every linear operator T on a finite dimensional vector space V can be represented by a matrix in Jordan normal form if the characteristic and minimal polynomials of T factor into linear polynomials. Again, this is always true if the base field K is the complex field **C**, but it need not be true if the base field K is the real field **R**.

Solved Problems

POLYNOMIAL IN MATRICES, CHARACTERISTIC POLYNOMIAL

11.1. Let $A = \begin{bmatrix} 1 & -2 \\ 4 & 5 \end{bmatrix}$. Find $f(A)$, where: (a) $f(t) = t^2 - 3t + 7$; (b) $f(t) = t^2 - 6t + 13$.

(a) $f(A) = A^2 - 3A + 7I = \begin{bmatrix} 1 & -2 \\ 4 & 5 \end{bmatrix}^2 - 3\begin{bmatrix} 1 & -2 \\ 4 & 5 \end{bmatrix} + 7\begin{bmatrix} 1 & 0 \\ 0 & 1 \end{bmatrix}$

$= \begin{bmatrix} -7 & -12 \\ 24 & 17 \end{bmatrix} + \begin{bmatrix} -3 & 6 \\ -12 & -15 \end{bmatrix} + \begin{bmatrix} 7 & 0 \\ 0 & 7 \end{bmatrix} = \begin{bmatrix} -3 & -6 \\ 12 & 9 \end{bmatrix}$

(b) $f(A) = A^2 - 6A + 13I = \begin{bmatrix} -7 & -12 \\ 24 & 17 \end{bmatrix} + \begin{bmatrix} -6 & 12 \\ -24 & -30 \end{bmatrix} + \begin{bmatrix} 13 & 0 \\ 0 & 13 \end{bmatrix} = \begin{bmatrix} 0 & 0 \\ 0 & 0 \end{bmatrix}$

[Thus A is a root of $f(t)$.]

11.2. Find the characteristic polynomial $\Delta(t)$ of each matrix:

(a) $A = \begin{bmatrix} 2 & 5 \\ 4 & 1 \end{bmatrix}$; (b) $B = \begin{bmatrix} 7 & -3 \\ 5 & -2 \end{bmatrix}$; (c) $C = \begin{bmatrix} 3 & -2 \\ 9 & -3 \end{bmatrix}$.

Use the formula $\Delta(t) = t^2 - \text{tr}(M)t + |M|$ for a 2×2 matrix M.

(a)   tr $(A) = 2 + 1 = 3$, $|A| = 2 - 20 = -18$, so $\Delta(t) = t^2 - 3t - 18$.

(b)   tr $(B) = 7 - 2 = 5$, $|B| = -14 + 15 = 1$, so $\Delta(t) = t^2 - 5t + 1$.

(c)   tr $(C) = 3 - 3 = 0$, $|C| = -9 + 18 = 9$, so $\Delta(t) = t^2 + 9$.

11.3. Find the characteristic polynomial $\Delta(t)$ of each matrix:

(a) $A = \begin{bmatrix} 1 & 2 & 3 \\ 3 & 0 & 4 \\ 6 & 4 & 5 \end{bmatrix}$; (b) $B = \begin{bmatrix} 1 & 6 & -2 \\ -3 & 2 & 0 \\ 0 & 3 & -4 \end{bmatrix}$.

Use the formula $\Delta(t) = t^3 - \text{tr}(A)t^2 + (A_{11} + A_{22} + A_{33})t - |A|$, where A_{ii} is the cofactor of a_{ii} in a 3×3 matrix $A = [a_{ij}]$.

(a)   tr $(A) = 1 + 0 + 5 = 6$

$$A_{11} = \begin{vmatrix} 0 & 4 \\ 4 & 5 \end{vmatrix} = -16, \qquad A_{22} = \begin{vmatrix} 1 & 3 \\ 6 & 5 \end{vmatrix} = -13, \qquad A_{33} = \begin{vmatrix} 1 & 2 \\ 3 & 0 \end{vmatrix} = -6$$

$A_{11} + A_{22} + A_{33} = -35$, and $|A| = 48 + 36 - 16 - 30 = 38$.   Thus

$$\Delta(t) = t^3 - 6t^2 - 35t - 38$$

(b)   tr $(B) = 1 + 2 - 4 = -1$

$$B_{11} = \begin{vmatrix} 2 & 0 \\ 3 & -4 \end{vmatrix} = -8, \qquad B_{22} = \begin{vmatrix} 1 & -2 \\ 0 & -4 \end{vmatrix} = -4, \qquad B_{33} = \begin{vmatrix} 1 & 6 \\ -3 & 2 \end{vmatrix} = 20$$

$B_{11} + B_{22} + B_{33} = 8$, and $|B| = -8 + 18 - 72 = -62$.   Thus

$$\Delta(t) = t^3 + t^2 + 8t + 62$$

11.4. Find the characteristic polynomial $\Delta(t)$ of each matrix:

(a) $A = \begin{bmatrix} 2 & 5 & 1 & 1 \\ 1 & 4 & 2 & 2 \\ 0 & 0 & 6 & -5 \\ 0 & 0 & 2 & 3 \end{bmatrix}$; (b) $B = \begin{bmatrix} 1 & 1 & 2 & 2 \\ 0 & 3 & 3 & 4 \\ 0 & 0 & 5 & 5 \\ 0 & 0 & 0 & 6 \end{bmatrix}$.

(a)   Note that A is block triangular with diagonal blocks $A_1 = \begin{bmatrix} 2 & 5 \\ 1 & 4 \end{bmatrix}$ and $A_2 = \begin{bmatrix} 6 & -5 \\ 2 & 3 \end{bmatrix}$.

Thus

$$\Delta(t) = \Delta_{A_1}(t)\Delta_{A_2}(t) = (t^2 - 6t + 3)(t^2 - 9t + 28)$$

(b)   Since B is triangular, $\Delta(t) = (t - 1)(t - 3)(t - 5)(t - 6)$.

11.5. For each matrix find a polynomial having the matrix as a root:

$$(a)\ A = \begin{bmatrix} 2 & 5 \\ 1 & -3 \end{bmatrix}; \quad (b)\ B = \begin{bmatrix} 2 & -3 \\ 7 & -4 \end{bmatrix}; \quad (c)\ C = \begin{bmatrix} 5 & 4 & 3 \\ 0 & 3 & 1 \\ 0 & 2 & -1 \end{bmatrix}.$$

By the Cayley-Hamilton theorem, every matrix is a root of its characteristic polynomial. Therefore, in each case, find the characteristic polynomial $\Delta(t)$.

(a) $\text{tr}\,(A) = -1$ and $|A| = -11$, so $\Delta(t) = t^2 + t - 11$.

(b) $\text{tr}\,(B) = -2$ and $|B| = -8 + 21 = 13$, so $\Delta(t) = t^2 + 2t + 13$.

(c) C is block triangular with diagonal blocks $[5]$ and $\begin{bmatrix} 3 & 1 \\ 2 & -1 \end{bmatrix}$.   Hence

$$\Delta(t) = (t - 5)(t^2 - 2t - 5)$$

11.6. Find the characteristic polynomial $\Delta(t)$ of each linear operator:

(a) $F: \mathbf{R}^2 \to \mathbf{R}^2$ defined by $F(x, y) = (3x + 5y, 2x - 7y)$.

(b) $\mathbf{D}: V \to V$ defined by $\mathbf{D}(f) = df/dt$, where V is the vector space of functions with basis $S = \{\sin t, \cos t\}$.

The characteristic polynomial $\Delta(t)$ of a linear operator is equal to the characteristic polynomial of any matrix A which represents the linear operator.

(a) Find the matrix A that represents T relative to the usual basis of $\mathbf{R}^2$.   We have $A = \begin{bmatrix} 3 & 5 \\ 2 & -7 \end{bmatrix}$.
Then $\Delta(t) = t^2 - \text{tr}\,(A)t + |A| = t^2 + 4t - 31$.

(b) Find the matrix A representing the differential operator $\mathbf{D}$ relative to the basis S.   We have

$$\begin{aligned} \mathbf{D}(\sin t) = \quad \cos t = \quad 0(\sin t) + 1(\cos t) \\ \mathbf{D}(\cos t) = -\sin t = -1(\sin t) + 0(\cos t) \end{aligned} \quad \text{and so} \quad A = \begin{bmatrix} 0 & -1 \\ 1 & 0 \end{bmatrix}$$

Therefore $\Delta(t) = t^2 - \text{tr}\,(A)t + |A| = t^2 + 1$.

11.7. Show that a matrix A and its transpose A^T have the same characteristic polynomial.

By the transpose operation, $(tI - A)^T = tI^T - A^T = tI - A^T$.   Since a matrix and its transpose have the same determinant,

$$\Delta_A(t) = |tI - A| = |(tI - A)^T| = |tI - A^T| = \Delta_{A^T}(t)$$

11.8. Let $\mathbf{D}: V \to V$ be defined by $\mathbf{D}(f) = df/dt$, where V is the vector space of functions with basis $\{\sin t, \cos t\}$.   Show that $\mathbf{D}$ is a root of the polynomial $f(t) = t^2 + 1$.

Method 1:   Apply $f(\mathbf{D}) = \mathbf{D}^2 + I$ to each basis vector.   First we have

$$\mathbf{D}^2(\sin t) = \mathbf{D}(\mathbf{D}(\sin t)) = \mathbf{D}(\cos t) = -\sin t$$
$$\mathbf{D}^2(\cos t) = \mathbf{D}(\mathbf{D}(\cos t)) = \mathbf{D}(-\sin t) = -\cos t$$

Then

$$f(\mathbf{D})(\sin t) = (\mathbf{D}^2 + I)(\sin t) = \mathbf{D}^2(\sin t) + I(\sin t) = -\sin t + \sin t = 0$$
$$f(\mathbf{D})(\cos t) = (\mathbf{D}^2 + I)(\cos t) = \mathbf{D}^2(\cos t) = I(\cos t) = -\cos t + \cos t = 0$$

Since each basis vector is mapped into 0, every vector v in V is mapped into 0.   Thus $f(\mathbf{D}) = 0$.

Method 2:   By Problem 11.6, $A = \begin{bmatrix} 0 & -1 \\ 1 & 0 \end{bmatrix}$ is a matrix representation of **D**. Furthermore,

$$f(A) = A^2 + I = \begin{bmatrix} -1 & 0 \\ 0 & -1 \end{bmatrix} + \begin{bmatrix} 1 & 0 \\ 0 & 1 \end{bmatrix} = \begin{bmatrix} 0 & 0 \\ 0 & 0 \end{bmatrix} = 0$$

Thus $f(\mathbf{D}) = 0$ since $f(A) = 0$.

EIGENVALUES AND EIGENVECTORS OF 2 × 2 MATRICES

11.9. Consider the matrix $A = \begin{bmatrix} 3 & -4 \\ 2 & -6 \end{bmatrix}$.

(a) Find all eigenvalues and corresponding eigenvectors.

(b) Find matrices P and D such that P is nonsingular and $D = P^{-1}AP$ is diagonal.

(a) First find the characteristic polynomial $\Delta(t)$ of A:

$$\Delta(t) = t^2 - \operatorname{tr}(A)t + |A| = t^2 + 3t - 10 = (t - 2)(t + 5)$$

The roots $\lambda = 2$ and $\lambda = -5$ of $\Delta(t)$ are the eigenvalues of A. We find corresponding eigenvectors.

(i) Subtract $\lambda = 2$ down the diagonal of A to obtain the matrix $M = A - 2I$, where the corresponding homogeneous system $MX = 0$ yields the eigenvectors corresponding to $\lambda = 2$. We have

$$M = \begin{bmatrix} 1 & -4 \\ 2 & -8 \end{bmatrix} \quad \text{corresponding to} \quad \begin{matrix} x - 4y = 0 \\ 2x - 8y = 0 \end{matrix} \quad \text{or} \quad x - 4y = 0$$

The system has only one free variable and $v_1 = (4, 1)$ is a nonzero solution. Thus $v_1 = (4, 1)$ is an eigenvector belonging to (and spanning the eigenspace of) $\lambda = 2$.

(ii) Subtract $\lambda = -5$ (or, equivalently, add 5) down the diagonal of A to obtain

$$M = \begin{bmatrix} 8 & -4 \\ 2 & -1 \end{bmatrix} \quad \text{corresponding to} \quad \begin{matrix} 8x - 4y = 0 \\ 2x - y = 0 \end{matrix} \quad \text{or} \quad 2x - y = 0$$

The system has only one free variable and $v_2 = (1, 2)$ is a nonzero solution. Thus $v_2 = (1, 2)$ is an eigenvector belonging to $\lambda = 5$.

(b) Let P be the matrix whose columns are v_1 and v_2. Then

$$P = \begin{bmatrix} 4 & 1 \\ 1 & 2 \end{bmatrix} \quad \text{and} \quad D = P^{-1}AP = \begin{bmatrix} 2 & 0 \\ 0 & -5 \end{bmatrix}$$

Note that D is the diagonal matrix whose diagonal entries are the eigenvalues of A corresponding to the eigenvectors appearing in P.

Remark: Here P is the change-of-basis matrix from the usual basis of $\mathbf{R}^2$ to the basis $S = \{v_1, v_2\}$, and D is the matrix that represents (the matrix function) A relative to the new basis S.

11.10. Consider the matrix $B = \begin{bmatrix} 1 & 4 \\ 2 & 3 \end{bmatrix}$.

(a)   Find all eigenvalues and corresponding eigenvectors.

(b)   Find a nonsingular matrix P such that $D = P^{-1}BP$ is diagonal.

(c)   Find B^5 and $f(B)$, where $f(t) = t^4 - 3t^3 - 7t^2 + 6t - 15$.

(a)   First find the characteristic polynomial $\Delta(t)$ of B:

$$\Delta(t) = t^2 - \text{tr}(B)t + |B| = t^2 - 4t - 5 = (t - 5)(t + 1)$$

The roots $\lambda = 5$ and $\lambda = -1$ of $\Delta(t)$ are the eigenvalues of B. We find corresponding eigenvectors.

(i)   Subtract $\lambda = 5$ down the diagonal of B to obtain

$$M = \begin{bmatrix} -4 & 4 \\ 2 & -2 \end{bmatrix} \quad \text{corresponding to} \quad \begin{aligned} -4x + 4y = 0 \\ 2x - 2y = 0 \end{aligned} \quad \text{or} \quad x - y = 0$$

The system has only one free variable with nonzero solution $x = 1$, $y = 1$. Thus $v_1 = (1, 1)$ is an eigenvector belonging to $\lambda = 5$.

(ii)   Subtract $\lambda = -1$ (or, equivalently, add 1) down the diagonal of B to obtain

$$M = \begin{bmatrix} 2 & 4 \\ 2 & 4 \end{bmatrix} \quad \text{corresponding to} \quad \begin{aligned} 2x + 4y = 0 \\ 2x + 4y = 0 \end{aligned} \quad \text{or} \quad x + 2y = 0$$

The system has only one free variable and $x = 2$, $y = -1$ is a nonzero solution. Thus $v_2 = (2, -1)$ is an eigenvector belonging to $\lambda = -1$.

(b)   Let P be the matrix whose columns are v_1 and v_2. Then

$$P = \begin{bmatrix} 1 & 2 \\ 1 & -1 \end{bmatrix} \quad \text{and} \quad D = P^{-1}BP = \begin{bmatrix} \frac{1}{3} & \frac{2}{3} \\ \frac{1}{3} & -\frac{1}{3} \end{bmatrix} \begin{bmatrix} 1 & 4 \\ 2 & 3 \end{bmatrix} \begin{bmatrix} 1 & 2 \\ 1 & -1 \end{bmatrix} = \begin{bmatrix} 5 & 0 \\ 0 & -1 \end{bmatrix}$$

(c)   From $D = P^{-1}BP$ we obtain the diagonal factorization $B = PDP^{-1}$. Then, using $5^5 = 3125$ and $(-1)^5 = -1$, we get

$$B^5 = PD^5P^{-1} = \begin{bmatrix} 1 & 2 \\ 1 & -1 \end{bmatrix} \begin{bmatrix} 3125 & 0 \\ 0 & -1 \end{bmatrix} \begin{bmatrix} \frac{1}{3} & \frac{2}{3} \\ \frac{1}{3} & -\frac{1}{3} \end{bmatrix} = \begin{bmatrix} 1041 & 2084 \\ 1042 & 2083 \end{bmatrix}$$

Also, since $f(5) = 90$ and $f(-1) = -24$,

$$f(B) = Pf(D)P^{-1} = \begin{bmatrix} 1 & 2 \\ 1 & -1 \end{bmatrix} \begin{bmatrix} 90 & 0 \\ 0 & -24 \end{bmatrix} \begin{bmatrix} \frac{1}{3} & \frac{2}{3} \\ \frac{1}{3} & -\frac{1}{3} \end{bmatrix} = \begin{bmatrix} 14 & 76 \\ 38 & 52 \end{bmatrix}$$

11.11. Consider the matrix $A = \begin{bmatrix} 2 & 2 \\ 1 & 3 \end{bmatrix}$.

(a)   Find all eigenvalues and corresponding eigenvectors.

(b)   Find a nonsingular matrix P such that $D = P^{-1}AP$ is diagonal.

(c)   Find A^6 and a *positive square root* of A, that is, a matrix B such that $B^2 = A$ and B has positive eigenvalues.

(a) First find the characteristic polynomial $\Delta(t)$ of A:

$$\Delta(t) = t^2 - \text{tr}\,(A)t + |A| = t^2 - 5t + 4 = (t - 1)(t - 4)$$

The roots $\lambda = 1$ and $\lambda = 4$ of $\Delta(t)$ are the eigenvalues of A. We find corresponding eigenvectors.

(i) Subtract $\lambda = 1$ down the diagonal of A to obtain the matrix $M = A - \lambda I$, where the corresponding homogeneous system $MX = 0$ yields the eigenvectors belonging to $\lambda = 1$. We have

$$M = \begin{bmatrix} 1 & 2 \\ 1 & 2 \end{bmatrix} \quad \text{corresponding to} \quad \begin{array}{l} x + 2y = 0 \\ x + 2y = 0 \end{array} \quad \text{or} \quad x + 2y = 0$$

The system has only one free variable and $x = 2$, $y = -1$ is a nonzero solution. Thus $v_1 = (2, -1)$ is an eigenvector belonging to (and spanning the eigenspace) of $\lambda = 1$.

(ii) Subtract $\lambda = 4$ down the diagonal of A to obtain

$$M = \begin{bmatrix} -2 & 2 \\ 1 & -1 \end{bmatrix} \quad \text{corresponding to} \quad \begin{array}{r} -2x + 2y = 0 \\ x - y = 0 \end{array} \quad \text{or} \quad x - y = 0$$

The system has only one free variable and $x = 1$, $y = 1$ is a nonzero solution. Thus $v_2 = (1, 1)$ is an eigenvector belonging to $\lambda = 4$.

(b) Let P be the matrix whose columns are v_1 and v_2. Then

$$P = \begin{bmatrix} 2 & 1 \\ -1 & 1 \end{bmatrix} \quad \text{and} \quad D = P^{-1}AP = \begin{bmatrix} 1 & 0 \\ 0 & 4 \end{bmatrix} \quad \text{where} \quad P^{-1} = \begin{bmatrix} \frac{1}{3} & -\frac{1}{3} \\ \frac{1}{3} & \frac{2}{3} \end{bmatrix}$$

(c) Using the diagonal factorization $A = PDP^{-1}$, and $1^6 = 1$ and $4^6 = 4096$, we get

$$A^6 = PD^6P^{-1} = \begin{bmatrix} 2 & 1 \\ -1 & 1 \end{bmatrix} \begin{bmatrix} 1 & 0 \\ 0 & 4096 \end{bmatrix} \begin{bmatrix} \frac{1}{3} & -\frac{1}{3} \\ \frac{1}{3} & \frac{2}{3} \end{bmatrix} = \begin{bmatrix} 1366 & 2730 \\ 1365 & 2731 \end{bmatrix}$$

Also, $\begin{bmatrix} \pm 1 & 0 \\ 0 & \pm 2 \end{bmatrix}$ are square roots of D. Hence

$$B = P\sqrt{D}P^{-1} = \begin{bmatrix} 2 & 1 \\ -1 & 1 \end{bmatrix} \begin{bmatrix} 1 & 0 \\ 0 & 2 \end{bmatrix} \begin{bmatrix} \frac{1}{3} & -\frac{1}{3} \\ \frac{1}{3} & \frac{2}{3} \end{bmatrix} = \begin{bmatrix} \frac{4}{3} & \frac{2}{3} \\ \frac{1}{3} & \frac{5}{3} \end{bmatrix}$$

is the positive square root of A.

11.12. Consider the linear transformation $B: \mathbf{R}^2 \to \mathbf{R}^2$ defined by the matrix $B = \begin{bmatrix} 1 & 3 \\ 5 & 3 \end{bmatrix}$. Find a basis $S = \{v_1, v_2\}$ of $\mathbf{R}^2$, where B is represented by a diagonal matrix D.

The basis S must consist of eigenvectors of B. First find the characteristic polynomial $\Delta(t)$ of B:

$$\Delta(t) = t^2 - \text{tr}\,(B)t + |B| = t^2 - 4t - 12 = (t - 6)(t + 2)$$

The roots of $\lambda = 6$ and $\lambda = -2$ of $\Delta(t)$ are the eigenvalues of B. We find corresponding eigenvectors.

(i) Subtract $\lambda = 6$ down the diagonal of B to obtain

$$M = \begin{bmatrix} -5 & 3 \\ 5 & -3 \end{bmatrix} \quad \text{corresponding to} \quad \begin{array}{r} -5x + 3y = 0 \\ 5x - 3y = 0 \end{array} \quad \text{or} \quad 5x - 3y = 0$$

Here $v_1 = (3, 5)$ is a nonzero solution.

(ii) Subtract $\lambda = -2$ (or, add 2) down the diagonal of B to obtain

$$M = \begin{bmatrix} 3 & 3 \\ 5 & 5 \end{bmatrix} \qquad \text{corresponding to} \qquad \begin{array}{l} 3x + 3y = 0 \\ 5x + 5y = 0 \end{array} \qquad \text{or} \qquad x + y = 0$$

Here $v_2 = (1, -1)$ is a nonzero solution.   Thus $S = \{v_1, v_2\} = \{(3, 5), (1, -1)\}$ is a basis of $\mathbf{R}^2$ in which B is represented by the diagonal matrix $D = \text{diag}(6, -2)$.

11.13. For each of the following real matrices, which define a linear transformation on $\mathbf{R}^2$, find all eigenvalues and a maximum set S of linearly independent eigenvectors:

(a) $A = \begin{bmatrix} 5 & 6 \\ 3 & -2 \end{bmatrix}$; (b) $B = \begin{bmatrix} 1 & -1 \\ 2 & -1 \end{bmatrix}$; (c) $C = \begin{bmatrix} 5 & -1 \\ 1 & 3 \end{bmatrix}$.

Which of these linear operators are diagonalizable, that is, can be represented by a diagonal matrix?

(a) First find $\Delta(t) = t^2 - 3t - 28 = (t - 7)(t + 4)$.   The roots $\lambda = 7$ and $\lambda = -4$ are the eigenvalues of A.   We find corresponding eigenvectors.

(i) Subtract $\lambda = 7$ down the diagonal of A to obtain

$$M = \begin{bmatrix} -2 & 6 \\ 3 & -9 \end{bmatrix} \qquad \text{corresponding to} \qquad \begin{array}{l} -2x + 6y = 0 \\ 3x - 9y = 0 \end{array} \qquad \text{or} \qquad x - 3y = 0$$

Here $v_1 = (3, 1)$ is a nonzero solution.

(ii) Subtract $\lambda = -4$ (or add 4) down the diagonal of A to obtain

$$M = \begin{bmatrix} 9 & 6 \\ 3 & 2 \end{bmatrix} \qquad \text{corresponding to} \qquad \begin{array}{l} 9x + 6y = 0 \\ 3x + 2y = 0 \end{array} \qquad \text{or} \qquad 3x + 2y = 0$$

Here $v_2 = (2, -3)$ is a nonzero solution.
Then $S = \{v_1, v_2\} = \{(3, 1), (2, -3)\}$ is a maximal set of linearly independent eigenvectors. Since S is a basis of $\mathbf{R}^2$, A is diagonalizable.   Using the basis S, A is represented by the diagonal matrix $D = \text{diag}(7, -4)$.

(b) First find the characteristic polynomial $\Delta(t) = t^2 + 1$.   There are no real roots.   Thus B, a real matrix representing a linear transformation on $\mathbf{R}^2$, has no eigenvalues and no eigenvectors.   Hence, in particular, B is not diagonalizable.

(c) First find $\Delta(t) = t^2 - 8t + 16 = (t - 4)^2$.   Thus $\lambda = 4$ is the only eigenvalue of C.   Subtract $\lambda = 4$ down the diagonal of C to obtain

$$M = \begin{bmatrix} 1 & -1 \\ 1 & -1 \end{bmatrix} \qquad \text{corresponding to} \qquad x - y = 0$$

The homogeneous system has only one free variable and $x = 1$, $y = 1$ is a nonzero solution. Thus $v = (1, 1)$ is an eigenvector of C.   Furthermore, since there are no other eigenvalues, the singleton set $S = \{v\} = \{(1, 1)\}$ is a maximal set of linearly independent eigenvectors of C.   Furthermore since S is not a basis of $\mathbf{R}^2$, C is not diagonalizable.

11.14. Suppose the matrix B in Problem 11.13 represents a linear operator on complex space $\mathbf{C}^2$. In such a case show that B is diagonalizable by finding a basis S of $\mathbf{C}^2$ consisting of eigenvectors of B.

The characteristic polynomial of B is still $\Delta(t) = t^2 + 1$.   (It does not depend on the field K.) As a polynomial over $\mathbf{C}$, $\Delta(t)$ does factor; specifically, $\Delta(t) = (t - i)(t + i)$.   Thus $\lambda = i$ and $\lambda = -i$ are the eigenvalues of B.

(i)   Subtract $\lambda = i$ down the diagonal of B to obtain the homogeneous system

$$\begin{aligned} (1-i)x - \qquad\quad y &= 0 \\ 2x + (-1-i)y &= 0 \end{aligned} \qquad \text{or} \qquad (1-i)x - y = 0$$

The system has only one independent solution, for example, $x = 1$, $y = 1 - i$. Thus $v_1 = (1, 1 - i)$ is an eigenvector which spans the eigenspace of $\lambda = i$.

(ii) Subtract $\lambda = -i$ (or , add i) down the diagonal of B to obtain the homogeneous system

$$\begin{aligned} (1+i)x - \qquad\quad y &= 0 \\ 2x + (-1+i)y &= 0 \end{aligned} \qquad \text{or} \qquad (1+i)x - y = 0$$

The system has only one independent solution, for example, $x = 1$, $y = 1 + i$. Thus $v_1 = (1, 1 + i)$ is an eigenvector which spans the eigenspace of $\lambda = -i$.

As a complex matrix B is diagonalizable. Specifically, $S = \{v_1, v_2\} = \{(1, 1-i), (1, 1+i)\}$ is a basis of $\mathbf{C}^2$ consisting of eigenvectors of B. Using this basis S, B is represented by the diagonal matrix $D = \text{diag}(i, -i)$.

11.15. Let $F: \mathbf{R}^2 \to \mathbf{R}^2$ be defined by $F(x, y) = (6x - y, 3x + 2y)$. Find eigenvalues and linearly independent eigenvectors of F and, if F is diagonalizable, find a diagonal representation D.

First find the matrix A that represents F in the usual basis of $\mathbf{R}^2$ by writing down the coefficients of x and y as rows,

$$A = \begin{bmatrix} 6 & -1 \\ 3 & 2 \end{bmatrix}$$

The characteristic polynomial $\Delta(t)$ of F is then

$$\Delta(t) = t^2 - \text{tr}(A)t + |A| = t^2 - 8t + 15 = (t-3)(t-5)$$

Thus $\lambda_1 = 3$ and $\lambda_2 = 5$ are eigenvalues of F. We find the corresponding eigenvectors as follows:

(i)   Subtract $\lambda_1 = 3$ down the diagonal of A to obtain

$$M = \begin{bmatrix} 3 & -1 \\ 3 & -1 \end{bmatrix} \qquad \text{corresponding to} \qquad 3x - y = 0$$

This is a homogeneous system with one free variable. Here $v_1 = (1, 3)$ is a nonzero solution and hence an eigenvector of F belonging to $\lambda_1 = 3$.

(ii) Subtract $\lambda_2 = 5$ down the diagonal of A to obtain

$$M = \begin{bmatrix} 1 & -1 \\ 3 & -3 \end{bmatrix} \qquad \text{corresponding to} \qquad x - y = 0$$

Here $v_2 = (1, 1)$ is a nonzero solution and hence an eigenvector of F belonging to $\lambda_2 = 5$.

Then $S = \{v_1, v_2\}$ is a basis of $\mathbf{R}^2$ consisting of eigenvectors of F. Thus F is diagonalizable, with the matrix representation $D = \begin{bmatrix} 3 & 0 \\ 0 & 5 \end{bmatrix}$.

11.16. Let L be the linear transformation on $\mathbf{R}^2$ that reflects points across the line $y = kx$, where $k > 0$. (See Fig. 11-1.)

(a)   Show that $v_1 = (1, k)$ and $v_2 = (k, -1)$ are eigenvectors of L.

(b)   Show that L is diagonalizable, and find such a diagonal representation D.

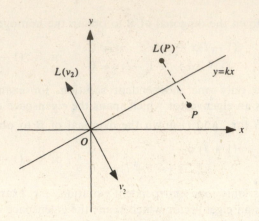

Fig. 11-1

(a) The vector $v_1 = (1, k)$ lies on the line $y = kx$ and hence is left fixed by L, that is, $L(v_1) = v_1$. Thus v_1 is an eigenvector of L belonging to the eigenvalue $\lambda_1 = 1$. The vector $v_2 = (k, -1)$ is perpendicular to the line $y = kx$, and hence L reflects v_2 into its negative, that is, $L(v_2) = -v_2$. Thus v_2 is an eigenvector of L belonging to the eigenvalue $\lambda_2 = -1$.

(b) Here $S = \{v_1, v_2\}$ is a basis of $\mathbf{R}^2$ consisting of eigenvectors of L. Thus L is diagonalizable with the diagonal representation (relative to S) $D = \begin{bmatrix} 1 & 0 \\ 0 & -1 \end{bmatrix}$.

EIGENVALUES AND EIGENVECTORS

11.17. Suppose $A = \begin{bmatrix} 4 & 1 & -1 \\ 2 & 5 & -2 \\ 1 & 1 & 2 \end{bmatrix}$.

(a) Find all eigenvalues of A.

(b) Find a maximum set S of linearly independent eigenvectors of A.

(c) Is A diagonalizable? If yes, find P such that $D = P^{-1}AP$ is diagonal.

(a) First find the characteristic polynomial $\Delta(t)$ of A. We have

$$\text{tr}\,(A) = 4 + 5 + 2 = 11 \qquad \text{and} \qquad |A| = 40 - 2 - 2 + 5 + 8 - 4 = 45$$

Also

$$A_{11} = \begin{vmatrix} 5 & -2 \\ 1 & 2 \end{vmatrix} = 12, \qquad A_{22} = \begin{vmatrix} 4 & -1 \\ 1 & 2 \end{vmatrix} = 9, \qquad A_{33} = \begin{vmatrix} 4 & 1 \\ 2 & 5 \end{vmatrix} = 18$$

Hence

$$\Delta(t) = t^3 - \text{tr}\,(A)t^2 + (A_{11} + A_{22} + A_{33})t - |A| = t^3 - 11t^2 + 39t - 45$$

where A_{ii} is the cofactor of a_{ii} in A.

Alternately,

$$\Delta(t) = |tI - A| = \begin{vmatrix} t-4 & -1 & 1 \\ -2 & t-5 & 2 \\ -1 & -1 & t-2 \end{vmatrix} = t^3 - 11t^2 + 39t - 45$$

Assuming $\Delta(t)$ has an integral root, it must be among $\pm 1, \pm 3, \pm 5, \pm 9, \pm 15, \pm 45$. Testing by synthetic division we get

$$
\begin{array}{r|rrrr}
3 & 1 - 11 + 39 - 45 \\
  &   \;\;\; 3 - 24 + 45 \\
\hline
  & 1 - \;\; 8 + 15 + \;\; 0
\end{array}
$$

Thus $t = 3$ is a root of $\Delta(t)$ and $t - 3$ is a factor, giving

$$\Delta(t) = (t - 3)(t^2 - 8t + 15) = (t - 3)(t - 5)(t - 3) = (t - 3)^2(t - 5)$$

Accordingly, $\lambda = 3$ and $\lambda = 5$ are the eigenvalues of A.

(b) Find linearly independent eigenvectors for each eigenvalue of A.

(i) Subtract $\lambda = 3$ down the diagonal of A to obtain the matrix

$$M = \begin{bmatrix} 1 & 1 & -1 \\ 2 & 2 & -2 \\ 1 & 1 & -1 \end{bmatrix} \quad \text{corresponding to} \quad x + y - z = 0$$

Here y and z are free variables, and $u = (1, -1, 0)$ and $v = (1, 0, 1)$ are linearly independent solutions.

(ii) Subtract $\lambda = 5$ down the diagonal of A to obtain

$$M = \begin{bmatrix} -1 & 1 & -1 \\ 2 & 0 & -2 \\ 1 & 1 & -3 \end{bmatrix} \quad \text{corresponding to} \quad \begin{array}{rcl} -x + y - \;\; z &=& 0 \\ 2x \quad\;\; - 2z &=& 0 \\ x + y - 3z &=& 0 \end{array} \quad \text{or} \quad \begin{array}{rcl} x - \quad\;\; z &=& 0 \\ y - 2z &=& 0 \end{array}$$

Only z is a free variable. Here $w = (1, 2, 1)$ is a solution.

Thus $S = \{u, v, w\} = \{(1, -1, 0), (1, 0, 1), (1, 2, 1)\}$ is a maximal set of linearly independent eigenvectors of A.

Remark: The vectors u and v were chosen so that they were linearly independent solutions of the system $x + y - z = 0$. On the other hand, w is automatically linearly independent of u and v since w belongs to a different eigenvalue of A. Thus the three vectors are linearly independent.

(c) A is diagonalizable since it has three linearly independent eigenvectors. Let P be the matrix with columns u, v, and w. Then

$$P = \begin{bmatrix} 1 & 1 & 1 \\ -1 & 0 & 2 \\ 0 & 1 & 1 \end{bmatrix} \quad \text{and} \quad D = P^{-1}AP = \begin{bmatrix} 3 & & \\ & 3 & \\ & & 5 \end{bmatrix}$$

11.18. Repeat Problem 11.17 for the matrix $B = \begin{bmatrix} 3 & -1 & 1 \\ 7 & -5 & 1 \\ 6 & -6 & 2 \end{bmatrix}$.

(a) First find the characteristic polynomial $\Delta(t)$ of B. We have

$$\Delta(t) = |tI - B| = \begin{vmatrix} t - 3 & 1 & -1 \\ -7 & t + 5 & -1 \\ -6 & 6 & t - 2 \end{vmatrix} = t^3 - 12t + 16$$

Therefore $\Delta(t) = (t - 2)^2(t + 4)$. Thus $\lambda_1 = 2$ and $\lambda_2 = -4$ are the eigenvalues of B.

(b) Find a basis for the eigenspace of each eigenvalue of B.

(i) Subtract $\lambda_1 = 2$ down the diagonal of B to obtain

$$M = \begin{bmatrix} 1 & -1 & 1 \\ 7 & -7 & 1 \\ 6 & -6 & 0 \end{bmatrix} \quad \text{corresponding to} \quad \begin{array}{l} x - y + z = 0 \\ 7x - 7y + z = 0 \\ 6x - 6y = 0 \end{array} \quad \text{or} \quad \begin{array}{l} x - y + z = 0 \\ z = 0 \end{array}$$

Only y is a free variable. Here $x = 1$, $y = 1$, $z = 0$ is a nonzero solution. Thus $u = (1, 1, 0)$ forms a basis for the eigenspace of $\lambda_1 = 2$.

(ii) Subtract $\lambda_2 = -4$ (or, add 4) down the diagonal of B to obtain

$$M = \begin{bmatrix} 7 & -1 & 1 \\ 7 & -1 & 1 \\ 6 & -6 & 6 \end{bmatrix} \quad \text{corresponding to} \quad \begin{array}{l} 7x - y + z = 0 \\ 7x - y + z = 0 \\ 6x - 6y + 6z = 0 \end{array} \quad \text{or} \quad \begin{array}{l} x - y + z = 0 \\ 6y - 6z = 0 \end{array}$$

Only z is a free variable, and $x = 0$, $y = 1$, $z = 1$ is a nonzero solution. Thus $v = (0, 1, 1)$ forms a basis for the eigenspace of $\lambda_2 = -4$.

Thus $S = \{u, v\}$ is a maximal set of linearly independent eigenvectors of B.

(c) Since B has at most two linearly independent eigenvectors, B is not similar to a diagonal matrix, that is, B is not diagonalizable.

11.19. Find the algebraic and geometric multiplicities of the eigenvalue $\lambda_1 = 2$ of the matrix B in Problem 11.18.

The algebraic multiplicity of $\lambda_1 = 2$ is 2 since $t - 2$ appears with exponent 2 in $\Delta(t)$. However, the geometric multiplicity of $\lambda_1 = 2$ is 1 since dim $E_{\lambda_1} = 1$ (where E_{λ_1} is the eigenspace of λ_1).

11.20. Repeat Problem 11.17 for the matrix $C = \begin{bmatrix} 0 & 1 & -2 \\ -1 & 2 & -4 \\ -1 & 1 & 4 \end{bmatrix}$.

(a) First find the characteristic polynomial $\Delta(t)$ of C. We have

$$\text{tr}\,(C) = 0 + 2 + 4 = 6 \quad \text{and} \quad |C| = 0 + 4 + 2 - 4 + 0 + 4 = 6$$

Also

$$C_{11} = \begin{vmatrix} 2 & -4 \\ 1 & 4 \end{vmatrix} = 12, \quad C_{22} = \begin{vmatrix} 0 & -2 \\ -1 & 4 \end{vmatrix} = -2, \quad C_{33} = \begin{vmatrix} 0 & 1 \\ -1 & 2 \end{vmatrix} = 1$$

(where C_{ii} is the cofactor of c_{ii} in C). Thus

$$C_{11} + C_{22} + C_{33} = 11 \quad \text{and} \quad \Delta(t) = t^3 - 6t^2 + 11t - 6 = (t - 1)(t - 2)(t - 3)$$

Thus $\lambda = 1$, $\lambda = 2$, and $\lambda = 3$ are the eigenvalues of C. In particular, we know that we can find three linearly independent eigenvectors of C, one for each eigenvalue, and so C is diagonalizable. However, we need to find the eigenvectors in order to obtain the matrix P (or basis S) which diagonalizes C.

(b) Find eigenvectors corresponding to the eigenvalues of C.

(i) Subtract $\lambda = 1$ down the diagonal of C to obtain the matrix

$$M = \begin{bmatrix} -1 & 1 & -2 \\ -1 & 1 & -4 \\ -1 & 1 & 3 \end{bmatrix} \quad \text{corresponding to} \quad \begin{array}{l} -x + y - 2z = 0 \\ -x + y - 4z = 0 \\ -x + y + 3z = 0 \end{array} \quad \text{or} \quad \begin{array}{l} -x + y - 2z = 0 \\ z = 0 \end{array}$$

Only y is a free variable. Here $u = (1, 1, 0)$ is a nonzero solution.

(ii) Subtract $\lambda = 2$ down the diagonal of C to obtain the matrix

$$M = \begin{bmatrix} -2 & 1 & -2 \\ -1 & 0 & -4 \\ -1 & 1 & 2 \end{bmatrix} \quad \text{corresponding to} \quad \begin{array}{l} -2x + y - 2z = 0 \\ -x \quad\;\; - 4z = 0 \\ -x + y + 2z = 0 \end{array} \quad \text{or} \quad \begin{array}{l} x + 4z = 0 \\ y + 6z = 0 \end{array}$$

Only z is a free variable. Here $v = (-4, -6, 1)$ is a nonzero solution.

(iii) Subtract $\lambda = 3$ down the diagonal of C to obtain the matrix

$$M = \begin{bmatrix} -3 & 1 & -2 \\ -1 & -1 & -4 \\ -1 & 1 & 1 \end{bmatrix} \quad \text{corresponding to} \quad \begin{array}{l} -3x + y - 2z = 0 \\ -x - y - 4z = 0 \\ -x + y + z = 0 \end{array} \quad \text{or} \quad \begin{array}{l} x - y - z = 0 \\ 2y + 5z = 0 \end{array}$$

Only z is a free variable. Here $w = (3, 5, -2)$ is a nonzero solution.

(c) As noted above, C is diagonalizable. Let P be the matrix with columns u, v, w. Then

$$P = \begin{bmatrix} 1 & -4 & 3 \\ 1 & -6 & 5 \\ 0 & 1 & -2 \end{bmatrix} \quad \text{and} \quad D = P^{-1}CP = \begin{bmatrix} 1 & & \\ & 2 & \\ & & 3 \end{bmatrix}$$

11.21. Determine whether or not A is diagonalizable, where $A = \begin{bmatrix} 1 & 2 & 3 \\ 0 & 2 & 3 \\ 0 & 0 & 3 \end{bmatrix}$.

Since A is triangular, the eigenvalues of A are the diagonal elements 1, 2, and 3. Since they are distinct, A has three linearly independent eigenvectors which must form a basis of $\mathbf{R}^3$. Thus A is similar to a diagonal matrix $D = \text{diag}\,(1, 2, 3)$. (We emphasize that we do not need to compute eigenvectors to tell that A is diagonalizable. However, we will have to compute eigenvectors if we want to find P such that $D = P^{-1}AP$.)

11.22. Let $T: \mathbf{R}^3 \to \mathbf{R}^3$ be defined by $T(x, y, z) = (2x + y - 2z,\ 2x + 3y - 4z,\ x + y - z)$. Find all eigenvalues of T, and find a basis of each eigenspace. Is T diagonalizable? If so, find the basis S of $\mathbf{R}^3$ which diagonalizes T and the diagonal representation D.

First find the matrix A that represents T relative to the usual basis of $\mathbf{R}^3$ by writing down the coefficients of x, y, z as rows:

$$A = [T] = \begin{bmatrix} 2 & 1 & -2 \\ 2 & 3 & -4 \\ 1 & 1 & -1 \end{bmatrix}$$

Next find the characteristic polynomial of A (and T). Here $\text{tr}\,(A) = 4$, $|A| = 2$, and $A_{11} = 1$, $A_{22} = 0$, $A_{33} = 4$. Hence

$$\Delta(t) = t^3 - 4t^2 + 5t - 2 = (t - 1)^2(t - 2)$$

Thus $\lambda = 1$ and $\lambda = 2$ are the eigenvalues of A (and T). We next find linearly independent eigenvectors for each eigenvalue of A.

(i) Subtract $\lambda = 1$ down the diagonal of A to obtain the matrix

$$M = \begin{bmatrix} 1 & 1 & -2 \\ 2 & 2 & -4 \\ 1 & 1 & -2 \end{bmatrix} \qquad \text{corresponding to} \qquad x + y - 2z = 0$$

Here y and z are free variables, and so there are two linearly independent eigenvectors belonging to $\lambda = 1$. For example, $u = (1, -1, 0)$ and $v = (2, 0, 1)$ are two such eigenvectors.

(ii) Subtract $\lambda = 2$ down the diagonal of A to obtain

$$M = \begin{bmatrix} 0 & 1 & -2 \\ 2 & 1 & -4 \\ 1 & 1 & -3 \end{bmatrix} \qquad \text{corresponding to} \qquad \begin{matrix} y - 2z = 0 \\ 2x + y - 4z = 0 \\ x + y - 3z = 0 \end{matrix} \qquad \text{or} \qquad \begin{matrix} x + y - 3z = 0 \\ y - 2z = 0 \end{matrix}$$

Only z is a free variable. Here $w = (1, 2, 1)$ is a nonzero solution.

Thus T is diagonalizable since it has three independent eigenvectors. Specifically, choosing $S = \{u, v, w\} = \{(1, -1, 0), (2, 0, 1), (1, 2, 1)\}$ as a basis, T is represented by the diagonal matrix $D = \text{diag}\,(1, 1, 2)$.

11.23. Prove the following for a linear operator (matrix) T:

(a) The scalar 0 is an eigenvalue of T if and only if T is singular.

(b) If λ is an eigenvalue of T, where T is invertible, then λ^{-1} is an eigenvalue of T^{-1}.

(a) We have 0 as an eigenvalue of T if and only if there is a vector $v \neq 0$ such that $T(v) = 0v$, i.e., if and only if T is singular.

(b) Since T is invertible, it is nonsingular. Hence, by part (a), $\lambda \neq 0$. By definition of an eigenvalue, there exists a nonzero vector v for which $T(v) = \lambda v$. Applying T^{-1} to both sides, we obtain $v = T^{-1}(\lambda v) = \lambda T^{-1}(v)$. Hence $T^{-1}(v) = \lambda^{-1}v$, that is, λ^{-1} is an eigenvalue of T^{-1}.

11.24. Let λ be an eigenvalue of a linear operator $T: V \rightarrow V$, and let E_λ be the eigenspace of λ, that is, E_λ consists of all the eigenvectors belonging to λ. Prove that E_λ is a subspace of V. Specifically, prove that:

(a) If $u \in E_\lambda$, then $ku \in E_\lambda$ for any scalar k.

(b) If $u, v \in E_\lambda$, then $u + v \in E_\lambda$.

(a) Since $u \in E_\lambda$, we have $T(u) = \lambda u$. Then

$$T(ku) = kT(u) = k(\lambda u) = \lambda(ku) \qquad \text{and so} \qquad ku \in E_\lambda$$

(We allow the zero vector $0 \in V$ to serve as the eigenvector corresponding to $k = 0$ in order for E_λ to be a subspace of V.)

(b) Since $u, v \in E_\lambda$, we have $T(u) = \lambda u$ and $T(v) = \lambda v$. Then

$$T(u + v) = T(u) + T(v) = \lambda u + \lambda v = \lambda(u + v) \qquad \text{and so} \qquad u + v \in E_\lambda$$

DIAGONALIZING REAL SYMMETRIC MATRICES

11.25. Let $A = \begin{bmatrix} 3 & 2 \\ 2 & 3 \end{bmatrix}$. Find a (real) orthogonal matrix P such that $D = P^{-1}AP$ is diagonal.

First find the characteristic polynomial $\Delta(t)$ of A. We have

$$\Delta(t) = t^2 - \operatorname{tr}(A)t + |A| = t^2 - 6t + 5 = (t-5)(t-1)$$

Thus the eigenvalues of A are $\lambda = 5$ and $\lambda = 1$. We next find corresponding eigenvectors.
Subtract $\lambda = 5$ down the diagonal of A to obtain the corresponding homogeneous system

$$\begin{aligned} -2x + 2y &= 0 \\ 2x - 2y &= 0 \end{aligned} \quad \text{or} \quad x - y = 0$$

A nonzero solution is $u_1 = (1, 1)$.
Subtract $\lambda = 1$ down the diagonal of A to obtain the corresponding homogeneous system

$$\begin{aligned} 2x + 2y &= 0 \\ 2x + 2y &= 0 \end{aligned} \quad \text{or} \quad x + y = 0$$

A nonzero solution is $u_2 = (1, -1)$.
As expected, since A is symmetric, the eigenvectors u_1 and u_2 are orthogonal. Normalize u_1 and u_2 to obtain the unit vectors $\hat{u}_1 = (1/\sqrt{2}, 1/\sqrt{2})$ and $\hat{u}_2 = (1/\sqrt{2}, -1/\sqrt{2})$.
Finally let P be the matrix whose columns are the unit vectors $\hat{u}_1$ and $\hat{u}_2$. Then

$$P = \begin{bmatrix} 1/\sqrt{2} & 1/\sqrt{2} \\ 1/\sqrt{2} & -1/\sqrt{2} \end{bmatrix} \quad \text{and} \quad D = P^{-1}AP = \begin{bmatrix} 5 & 0 \\ 0 & 1 \end{bmatrix}$$

As expected, the diagonal entries of D are the eigenvalues of A.

11.26. Let $B = \begin{bmatrix} 7 & 3 \\ 3 & -1 \end{bmatrix}$. Find an orthogonal matrix P such that $D = P^{-1}BP$ is diagonal.

First find the characteristic polynomial $\Delta(t)$ of B. We have

$$\Delta(t) = t^2 - \operatorname{tr}(B)t + |B| = t^2 - 6t - 16 = (t-8)(t+2)$$

Thus the eigenvalues of B are $\lambda = 8$ and $\lambda = -2$. We next find corresponding eigenvectors.
Subtract $\lambda = 8$ down the diagonal of B to obtain the corresponding homogeneous system

$$\begin{aligned} -x + 3y &= 0 \\ 3x - 9y &= 0 \end{aligned} \quad \text{or} \quad x - 3y = 0$$

A nonzero solution is $u_1 = (3, 1)$.
Subtract $\lambda = -2$ (or, add 2) down the diagonal of B to obtain the corresponding homogeneous system

$$\begin{aligned} 9x + 3y &= 0 \\ 3x + y &= 0 \end{aligned} \quad \text{or} \quad 3x + y = 0$$

A nonzero solution is $u_2 = (1, -3)$.
As expected, since B is symmetric, the eigenvectors u_1 and u_2 are orthogonal. Normalize u_1 and u_2 to obtain the unit vectors $\hat{u}_1 = (3/\sqrt{10}, 1/\sqrt{10})$ and $\hat{u}_2 = (1/\sqrt{10}, -3/\sqrt{10})$.

Finally let P be the matrix whose columns are the unit vectors $\hat{u}_1$ and $\hat{u}_2$. Then

$$P = \begin{bmatrix} 3/\sqrt{10} & 1/\sqrt{10} \\ 1/\sqrt{10} & -3/\sqrt{10} \end{bmatrix} \quad \text{and} \quad D = P^{-1}BP = \begin{bmatrix} 8 & 0 \\ 0 & -2 \end{bmatrix}$$

As expected, the diagonal entries of D are the eigenvalues of B.

11.27. Let A be a 2×2 symmetric matrix with eigenvalues $\lambda = 1$ and $\lambda = 9$. Suppose $u = (1, 3)^T$ is an eigenvector belonging to $\lambda = 1$.

(a) Find an eigenvector v belonging to $\lambda = 9$.

(b) Find A and a square root of A, i.e., a matrix B such that $B^2 = A$.

(a) Since A is symmetric, v must be orthogonal to u. Set $v = (-3, 1)^T$.

(b) Let P be the matrix whose columns are the eigenvectors u and v. Then, by the diagonal factorization of A, we have

$$A = PDP^{-1} = \begin{bmatrix} 1 & -3 \\ 3 & 1 \end{bmatrix} \begin{bmatrix} 1 & 0 \\ 0 & 9 \end{bmatrix} \begin{bmatrix} \frac{1}{10} & \frac{3}{10} \\ -\frac{3}{10} & \frac{1}{10} \end{bmatrix} = \begin{bmatrix} \frac{41}{5} & -\frac{12}{5} \\ -\frac{12}{5} & \frac{9}{5} \end{bmatrix}$$

(Alternatively, A is the matrix for which $Au = u$ and $Av = 9v$.) Use the diagonal factorization of A to obtain

$$B = P\sqrt{D}P^{-1} = \begin{bmatrix} 1 & -3 \\ 3 & 1 \end{bmatrix} \begin{bmatrix} 1 & 0 \\ 0 & 3 \end{bmatrix} \begin{bmatrix} \frac{1}{10} & \frac{3}{10} \\ -\frac{3}{10} & \frac{1}{10} \end{bmatrix} = \begin{bmatrix} \frac{14}{5} & -\frac{3}{5} \\ -\frac{3}{5} & \frac{6}{5} \end{bmatrix}$$

11.28. Let $A = \begin{bmatrix} 3 & 1 & 1 \\ 1 & 3 & 1 \\ 1 & 1 & 3 \end{bmatrix}$.

(a) Find the characteristic polynomial $\Delta(t)$ and all eigenvalues of A.

(b) Find a maximal set S of nonzero orthogonal eigenvectors of A.

(c) Find an orthogonal matrix P such that $D = P^{-1}AP$ is diagonal.

(a) Note that tr$(A) = 9$, $|A| = 20$, and $A_{11} = A_{22} = A_{33} = 8$. Hence

$$\Delta(t) = t^3 - \text{tr}(A)t^2 + (A_{11} + A_{22} + A_{33})t - |A| = t^3 - 9t^2 + 24t - 20$$

If $\Delta(t)$ has a rational root, it must divide the constant 20 or, in other words, it must be among $\pm 1, \pm 2, \pm 4, \pm 5, \pm 10, \pm 20$. Testing $t = 2$, we get

$$\begin{array}{r|rrrr} 2 & 1 & -9 & +24 & -20 \\ & & 2 & -14 & +20 \\ \hline & 1 & -7 & +10 & +0 \end{array}$$

Thus $t - 2$ is a factor of $\Delta(t)$, and we find

$$\Delta(t) = (t - 2)(t^2 - 7t + 10) = (t - 2)^2(t - 5)$$

Hence the eigenvalues of A are 2 (with multiplicity 2) and 5 (with multiplicity 1).

(b) Find an orthogonal basis for each eigenspace. Subtract $\lambda = 2$ down the diagonal of A to obtain the corresponding homogeneous system

$$x + y + z = 0, \qquad x + y + z = 0, \qquad x + y + z = 0$$

That is, $x + y + z = 0$. The system has two independent solutions. One such solution is $v_1 = (0, 1, -1)$. We seek a second solution $v_2 = (a, b, c)$, which is orthogonal to v_1, that is, such that

$$a + b + c = 0 \qquad \text{and also} \qquad b - c = 0$$

For example, $v_2 = (2, -1, -1)$. Thus $v_1 = (0, 1, -1)$, $v_2 = (2, -1, -1)$ form an orthogonal basis for the eigenspace of $\lambda = 2$.

Subtract $\lambda = 5$ down the diagonal of A to obtain the corresponding homogeneous system

$$-2x + y + z = 0, \qquad x - 2y + z = 0, \qquad x + y - 2z = 0$$

This system yields a nonzero solution $v_3 = (1, 1, 1)$. (As expected from Theorem 11.13, the eigenvector v_3 is orthogonal to v_1 and v_2.)

Then v_1, v_2, v_3 form a maximal set of nonzero orthogonal eigenvectors of A.

(c) Normalize v_1, v_2, v_3 to obtain the orthonormal basis

$$u_1 = (0, 1/\sqrt{2}, -1/\sqrt{2}), \qquad u_2 = (2/\sqrt{6}, -1/\sqrt{6}, -1/\sqrt{6}), \qquad u_3 = (1/\sqrt{3}, 1/\sqrt{3}, 1/\sqrt{3})$$

Let P be the matrix whose columns are u_1, u_2, and u_3. Then

$$P = \begin{bmatrix} 0 & 2/\sqrt{6} & 1/\sqrt{3} \\ 1/\sqrt{2} & -1/\sqrt{6} & 1/\sqrt{3} \\ -1/\sqrt{2} & -1/\sqrt{6} & 1/\sqrt{3} \end{bmatrix} \qquad \text{and} \qquad D = P^{-1}AP = \begin{bmatrix} 2 & & \\ & 2 & \\ & & 5 \end{bmatrix}$$

11.29. Repeat Problem 11.28 for the matrix $B = \begin{bmatrix} 11 & -8 & 4 \\ -8 & -1 & -2 \\ 4 & -2 & -4 \end{bmatrix}$.

(a) Note that $\text{tr}(B) = 6$, $|B| = 400$, and $B_{11} = 0$, $B_{22} = -60$, $B_{33} = -75$. Hence

$$\Delta(t) = t^3 - \text{tr}(B)t^2 + (B_{11} + B_{22} + B_{33})t - |B| = t^3 - 6t^2 - 135t - 400$$

If $\Delta(t)$ has a rational root, it must divide 400. Testing $t = -5$, we get

$$\begin{array}{r|rrrr} -5 & 1 - & 6 - & 135 - & 400 \\ & & -5 + & 55 + & 400 \\ \hline & 1 - & 11 - & 80 + & 0 \end{array}$$

Thus $t + 5$ is a factor of $\Delta(t)$ and

$$\Delta(t) = (t + 5)(t^2 - 11t - 80) = (t + 5)^2(t - 16)$$

Accordingly, the eigenvalues of B are $\lambda = -5$ (with multiplicity 2) and $\lambda = 16$ (with multiplicity 1).

(b) Find an orthogonal basis for each eigenspace. Subtract $\lambda = -5$ (or, add 5) down the diagonal of B to obtain the homogeneous system

$$16x - 8y + 4z = 0, \qquad -8x + 4y - 2z = 0, \qquad 4x - 2y + z = 0$$

That is, $4x - 2y + z = 0$. The system has two independent solutions. One solution is $v_1 = (0, 1, 2)$. We seek a second solution $v_2 = (a, b, c)$, which is orthogonal to v_1, i.e., such that

$$4a - 2b + c = 0, \qquad \text{and also} \qquad b + 2c = 0$$

One such solution is $v_2 = (-5, -8, 4)$.

Subtract $\lambda = 16$ down the diagonal of B to obtain the homogeneous system

$$-5x - 8y + 4z = 0, \qquad -8x - 17y - 2z = 0, \qquad 4x - 2y - 20z = 0$$

This system yields a nonzero solution $v_3 = (4, -2, 1)$. (As expected from Theorem 11.13, the eigenvector v_3 is orthogonal to v_1 and v_2.)

Then v_1, v_2, v_3 form a maximal set of nonzero orthogonal eigenvectors of B.

(c)   Normalize v_1, v_2, v_3 to obtain the orthonormal basis

$$u_1 = (0, 1/\sqrt{5}, 2/\sqrt{5}), \qquad u_2 = (-5/\sqrt{105}, -8/\sqrt{105}, 4/\sqrt{105}),$$
$$u_3 = (4/\sqrt{21}, -2/\sqrt{21}, 1/\sqrt{21})$$

Then P is the matrix whose columns are u_1, u_2, and u_3. Thus

$$P = \begin{bmatrix} 0 & -5/\sqrt{105} & 4/\sqrt{21} \\ 1/\sqrt{5} & -8/\sqrt{105} & -2/\sqrt{21} \\ 2/\sqrt{5} & 4/\sqrt{105} & 1/\sqrt{21} \end{bmatrix} \qquad \text{and} \qquad D = P^{-1}BP = \begin{bmatrix} -5 & & \\ & -5 & \\ & & 16 \end{bmatrix}$$

11.30. Repeat Problem 11.28 for the matrix $C = \begin{bmatrix} 0 & 0 & 2 \\ 0 & 2 & 0 \\ 2 & 0 & -3 \end{bmatrix}$.

(a)   Note that $\operatorname{tr}(C) = -1$, $|C| = -8$, and $C_{11} = -6$, $C_{22} = -4$, $C_{33} = 0$. Hence

$$\Delta(t) = t^3 + t^2 - 10t + 8 = (t - 1)(t + 4)(t - 2)$$

Then the eigenvalues of C are $\lambda = 1$, $\lambda = -4$, and $\lambda = 2$.

(b)   Find corresponding eigenvectors. Subtract $\lambda = 1$ down the diagonal of C to obtain the corresponding homogeneous system

$$-x + 2z = 0, \qquad y = 0, \qquad 2x - 4y = 0$$

A nonzero solution is $u_1 = (2, 0, 1)$.

Subtract $\lambda = -4$ (or, add 4) down the diagonal of C to obtain the corresponding homogeneous system

$$4x + 2z = 0, \qquad 6y = 0, \qquad 2x + y = 0$$

A nonzero solution is $u_2 = (1, 0, -2)$.

Subtract $\lambda = 2$ down the diagonal of C to obtain the corresponding homogeneous system

$$-2x + 2z = 0, \qquad 0 = 0, \qquad 2x - 5y = 0$$

A nonzero solution is $u_3 = (0, 1, 0)$.

Then $S = \{u_1, u_2, u_3\}$ is a maximal set of nonzero orthogonal eigenvectors of C.

(c)   Normalize u_1, u_2, u_3 to obtain the orthonormal basis

$$u_1 = (2/\sqrt{5}, 0, 1/\sqrt{5}), \qquad u_2 = (1/\sqrt{5}, 0, -2/\sqrt{5}), \qquad u_3 = (0, 1, 0)$$

Let P be the matrix whose columns are u_1, u_2, and u_3. Then P is orthogonal and $D = P^{-1}CP = \operatorname{diag}(1, -4, 2)$.

MINIMAL POLYNOMIAL

11.31. Find the minimum polynomial $m(t)$ of each matrix:

$$(a)\ A = \begin{bmatrix} 4 & -2 & 2 \\ 6 & -3 & 4 \\ 3 & -2 & 3 \end{bmatrix};\ (b)\ B = \begin{bmatrix} 3 & -2 & 2 \\ 4 & -4 & 6 \\ 2 & -3 & 5 \end{bmatrix}$$

(a) First find the characteristic polynomial $\Delta(t)$ of A. Note that $\text{tr}\,(A) = 4$, $|A| = 2$, and $A_{11} = -1$, $A_{22} = 6$, $A_{33} = 0$. Hence

$$\Delta(t) = t^3 - 4t^2 + 5t - 2 = (t - 2)(t - 1)^2$$

The minimal polynomial $m(t)$ must divide $\Delta(t)$. Also, each factor of $\Delta(t)$, that is, $t - 2$ and $t - 1$, must also be a factor of $m(t)$. Thus $m(t)$ must be exactly one of the following:

$$f(t) = (t - 2)(t - 1) \qquad \text{or} \qquad g(t) = (t - 2)(t - 1)^2$$

We know by the Cayley-Hamilton theorem that $g(A) = \Delta(A) = 0$. Hence we need only test $f(t)$. We have

$$f(A) = (A - 2I)(A - I) = \begin{bmatrix} 2 & -2 & 2 \\ 6 & -5 & 4 \\ 3 & -2 & 1 \end{bmatrix}\begin{bmatrix} 3 & -2 & 2 \\ 6 & -4 & 4 \\ 3 & -2 & 2 \end{bmatrix} = \begin{bmatrix} 0 & 0 & 0 \\ 0 & 0 & 0 \\ 0 & 0 & 0 \end{bmatrix}$$

Thus $m(t) = f(t) = (t - 2)(t - 1) = t^2 - 3t + 2$ is the minimal polynomial of A.

(b) First find the characteristic polynomial $\Delta(t)$ of B. Note that $\text{tr}\,(B) = 4$, $|B| = 2$, and $B_{11} = -2$, $B_{22} = 11$, $B_{33} = -4$. Hence

$$\Delta(t) = t^3 - 4t^2 + 5t - 2 = (t - 2)(t - 1)^2$$

As in part (a), the minimum polynomial $m(t)$ is exactly one of the following:

$$f(t) = (t - 2)(t - 1) \qquad \text{or} \qquad g(t) = (t - 2)(t - 1)^2$$

Testing $f(t)$ we get

$$f(B) = (B - 2I)(B - I) = \begin{bmatrix} 1 & -2 & 2 \\ 4 & -6 & 6 \\ 2 & -3 & 3 \end{bmatrix}\begin{bmatrix} 2 & -2 & 2 \\ 4 & -5 & 6 \\ 2 & -3 & 4 \end{bmatrix} = \begin{bmatrix} -2 & 2 & -2 \\ -4 & 4 & -4 \\ -2 & 2 & -2 \end{bmatrix} \neq 0$$

Thus $m(t) \neq f(t)$. Accordingly, $m(t) = g(t) = (t - 2)(t - 1)^2$ is the minimum polynomial of B. [We do not need to compute $g(B)$; we know that $g(B) = 0$ from the Cayley-Hamilton theorem.]

11.32. Find the minimum polynomial $m(t)$ of each matrix:

$$(a)\ A = \begin{bmatrix} 5 & 1 \\ 3 & 7 \end{bmatrix};\ (b)\ B = \begin{bmatrix} 1 & 2 & 3 \\ 0 & 2 & 3 \\ 0 & 0 & 3 \end{bmatrix};\ (c)\ C = \begin{bmatrix} 4 & -1 \\ 1 & 2 \end{bmatrix}$$

(a) The characteristic polynomial of A is $\Delta(t) = t^2 - 12t + 32 = (t - 4)(t - 8)$. Since $\Delta(t)$ has distinct factors, the minimal polynomial $m(t) = \Delta(t) = t^2 - 12t + 32$.

(b) Since B is diagonal, its eigenvalues are the diagonal elements 1, 2, and 3; and so its characteristic polynomial is $\Delta(t) = (t - 1)(t - 2)(t - 3)$. Since $\Delta(t)$ has distinct factors, $m(t) = \Delta(t)$.

(c)   The characteristic polynomial of C is $\Delta(t) = t^2 - 6t + 9 = (t - 3)^2$.   Hence the minimum polynomial of C is $f(t) = t - 3$ or $g(t) = (t - 3)^2$.   However, $f(C) \neq 0$, that is, $C - 3I \neq 0$. Hence $m(t) = g(t) = \Delta(t) = (t - 3)^2$.

11.33. Let $S = \{u_1, u_2, \ldots, u_n\}$ be a basis of V.   Suppose F and G are linear operators on V represented by the following matrices:

$$[F] = \begin{bmatrix} 0 & a & 0 & \ldots & 0 \\ 0 & 0 & a & \ldots & 0 \\ \cdots\cdots\cdots\cdots\cdots\cdots \\ 0 & 0 & 0 & \ldots & a \\ 0 & 0 & 0 & \ldots & 0 \end{bmatrix}, \qquad [G] = \begin{bmatrix} 0 & a_{21} & a_{31} & \ldots & a_{n1} \\ 0 & 0 & a_{32} & \ldots & a_{n2} \\ \cdots\cdots\cdots\cdots\cdots\cdots\cdots \\ 0 & 0 & 0 & \ldots & a_{n,n-1} \\ 0 & 0 & 0 & \ldots & 0 \end{bmatrix}$$

where $a \neq 0$.   That is, $[F]$ has $a \neq 0$ on the superdiagonal and zeros elsewhere, and $[G]$ has zeros on the diagonal and below the diagonal.   Show that:

(a) $F^{n-1} \neq 0$, but $F^n = 0$; and hence $[F]^{n-1} \neq 0$, but $[F]^n = 0$.

(b) $G^n = 0$, and so $[G]^n = 0$.

(a)   We have $F(u_1) = 0$ and $F(u_i) = au_{i-1}$ for $i > 1$.   Hence $F^r(u_i) = a^r u_{i-r}$ for $r < i$ and $F^r(u_i) = 0$ for $r \geq i$.   Thus $F^{n-1}(u_n) = a^{n-1} u_1 \neq 0$.   Hence $F^{n-1} \neq 0$.   On the other hand, $F^n(u_i) = 0$ for every basis vector u_i.   Hence $F^n = 0$.

(b)   We have $G(u_1) = 0$ and, for $i > 1$,

$$G(u_i) = a_{i1}u_1 + a_{i2}u_2 + \cdots + a_{i,i-1}u_{i-1}$$

We need only show that $G^r(u_r) = 0$ for each r.   In such a case, it would then follow that $G^n(u_r) = G^{n-r}(G^r(u_r)) = G^{n-r}(0) = 0$, and so $G^n = 0$.   The proof is by induction on r.   The case $r = 1$ is true by hypothesis.   By induction, for $r > 1$,

$$G^r(u_r) = G^{r-1}(G(u_r)) = G^{r-1}(a_{r1}u_1 + a_{r2}u_2 + \cdots + a_{r,r-1}u_{r-1})$$

$$= a_{r1}G^{r-1}(u_1) + a_{r2}G^{r-1}(u_2) + \cdots + a_{r,r-1}G^{r-1}(u_{r-1})$$

$$= a_{r1}0 + a_{r2}0 + \cdots + a_{r,r-1}0 = 0$$

Accordingly, $G^n = 0$.

11.34. Show that $f(t) = (t - \lambda)^n$ is the minimum polynomial of the n-square matrix

$$A = \begin{bmatrix} \lambda & a & 0 & \ldots & 0 & 0 \\ 0 & \lambda & a & \ldots & 0 & 0 \\ \cdots\cdots\cdots\cdots\cdots\cdots\cdots \\ 0 & 0 & 0 & \ldots & \lambda & a \\ 0 & 0 & 0 & \ldots & 0 & \lambda \end{bmatrix}$$

Since A is triangular with λ on the diagonal, $\Delta(t) = f(t) = (t - \lambda)^n$ is its characteristic polynomial.   Thus $m(t)$ is a power of $t - \lambda$.   By Problem 11.33, $(A - \lambda I)^{n-1} \neq 0$.   Hence $m(t) = \Delta(t) = (t - \lambda)^n$.

11.35. Find the characteristic polynomial $\Delta(t)$ and the minimal polynomial $m(t)$ of each matrix:

$$(a)\ M = \begin{bmatrix} 4 & 1 & 0 & 0 & 0 \\ 0 & 4 & 1 & 0 & 0 \\ 0 & 0 & 4 & 0 & 0 \\ 0 & 0 & 0 & 4 & 1 \\ 0 & 0 & 0 & 0 & 4 \end{bmatrix}; \quad (b)\ M' = \begin{bmatrix} 2 & 7 & 0 & 0 \\ 0 & 2 & 0 & 0 \\ 0 & 0 & 1 & 1 \\ 0 & 0 & -2 & 4 \end{bmatrix}.$$

(a) Here M is block diagonal with diagonal blocks

$$A = \begin{bmatrix} 4 & 1 & 0 \\ 0 & 4 & 1 \\ 0 & 0 & 4 \end{bmatrix} \quad \text{and} \quad B = \begin{bmatrix} 4 & 1 \\ 0 & 4 \end{bmatrix}$$

The characteristic and minimum polynomial of A is $f(t) = (t-4)^3$ and the characteristic and minimal polynomial of B is $g(t) = (t-4)^2$. Then

$$\Delta(t) = f(t)g(t) = (t-4)^5 \quad \text{but} \quad m(t) = \text{LCM}[f(t), g(t)] = (t-4)^3$$

(where LCM means least common multiple). [Note that the exponent in $m(t)$ is the size of the largest block.]

(b) Here M' is block diagonal with diagonal blocks

$$A' = \begin{bmatrix} 2 & 7 \\ 0 & 2 \end{bmatrix} \quad \text{and} \quad B' = \begin{bmatrix} 1 & 1 \\ -2 & 4 \end{bmatrix}$$

The characteristic and minimum polynomial of A' is $f(t) = (t-2)^2$. The characteristic polynomial of B' is $g(t) = t^2 - 5t + 6 = (t-2)(t-3)$, which has distinct factors; hence $g(t)$ is also the minimal polynomial of B. Accordingly,

$$\Delta(t) = f(t)g(t) = (t-2)^3(t-3) \quad \text{but} \quad m(t) = \text{LCM}[f(t), g(t)] = (t-2)^2(t-3)$$

11.36. Find a matrix A whose minimum polynomial is: (a) $f(t) = t^3 - 8t^2 + 5t + 7$; (b) $f(t) = t^4 - 3t^3 - 4t^2 + 5t + 6$.

Let A be the companion matrix of $f(t)$ (defined in Example 11.12). Then

$$(a)\ A = \begin{bmatrix} 0 & 0 & -7 \\ 1 & 0 & -5 \\ 0 & 1 & 8 \end{bmatrix}; \quad (b)\ A = \begin{bmatrix} 0 & 0 & 0 & -6 \\ 1 & 0 & 0 & -5 \\ 0 & 1 & 0 & 4 \\ 0 & 0 & 1 & 3 \end{bmatrix}.$$

Remark: The polynomial $f(t)$ is also the characteristic polynomial of A.

11.37. Show that the minimum polynomial of a matrix A exists and is unique.

By the Cayley-Hamilton theorem, the matrix A is a zero of some nonzero polynomial. Let n be the lowest degree for which a polynomial $f(t)$ exists such that $f(A) = 0$. Dividing $f(t)$ by its leading coefficient, we obtain a monic polynomial $m(t)$ of degree n which has A as a zero. Suppose $m'(t)$ is another monic polynomial of degree n for which $m'(A) = 0$. Then the difference $m(t) - m'(t)$ is a nonzero polynomial of degree less than n which has A as a zero. This contradicts the original assumption on n; hence $m(t)$ is the unique minimum polynomial.

JORDAN CANONICAL FORM

11.38. Consider the following matrix M in Jordan canonical form:

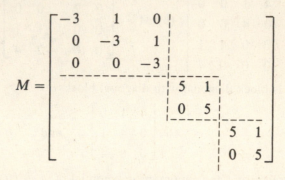

(a) Find all Jordan matrices *equivalent* to M (that is, obtained from M by rearranging the diagonal blocks).

(b) Find the characteristic polynomial $\Delta(t)$ and eigenvalues of M.

(c) Find the minimal polynomial of M.

(d) Find a maximal set S of linearly independent eigenvectors of M.

(a) There are exactly two other ways of arranging the blocks on the diagonal as follows:

$$\begin{bmatrix} 5 & 1 & & & & & \\ 0 & 5 & & & & & \\ & & -3 & 1 & 0 & & \\ & & 0 & -3 & 1 & & \\ & & 0 & 0 & -3 & & \\ & & & & & 5 & 1 \\ & & & & & 0 & 5 \end{bmatrix} \quad \text{and} \quad \begin{bmatrix} 5 & 1 & & & & & \\ 0 & 5 & & & & & \\ & & 5 & 1 & & & \\ & & 0 & 5 & & & \\ & & & & -3 & 1 & 0 \\ & & & & 0 & -3 & 1 \\ & & & & 0 & 0 & -3 \end{bmatrix}$$

(b) Here $\Delta(t) = (t + 3)^3(t - 5)^4$. The exponent 3 comes from the fact that there are three -3s on the diagonal and the exponent 4 comes from the fact that there are four 5s on the diagonal. In particular, $\lambda_1 = -3$ and $\lambda_2 = 5$ are the eigenvalues.

(c) Here $m(t) = (t + 3)^3(t - 5)^2$. The exponent 3 comes from the fact that 3 is the order of the largest block belonging to $\lambda_1 = -3$ and the exponent 2 comes from the fact that 2 is the order of the largest block belonging to $\lambda_2 = 5$. [Alternatively, $m(t)$ is the least common multiple of the minimal polynomials of the blocks].

(d) Each block contributes one eigenvector to S. Three such eigenvectors are $v_1 = (1, 0, 0, 0, 0, 0, 0)$, $v_2 = (0, 0, 0, 1, 0, 0, 0)$, and $v_3 = (0, 0, 0, 0, 0, 1, 0)$, which correspond to the first, second, and third blocks, respectively. The entry 1 in each vector is the position of the first entry in the corresponding block.

11.39. Consider the following two Jordan matrices:

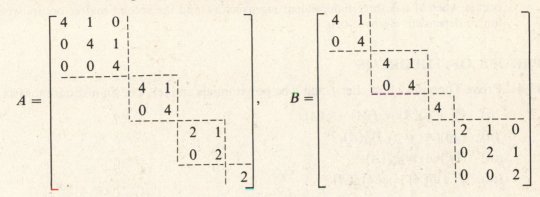

(a) Find the characteristic polynomial $\Delta(t)$ and eigenvalues of A and of B.

(b) Are A and B equivalent Jordan matrices?

(c) Find the minimal polynomial $m(t)$ of A and the dimension d_i of the eigenspace of each eigenvalue λ_i of A.

(d) Find the minimal polynomial $m(t)$ of B and the dimension d_i of the eigenspace of each eigenvalue λ_i of B.

(a) Both A and B have five 4s on the diagonal and three 2s on the diagonal. Hence $\Delta(t) = (t-4)^5(t-2)^3$ is the characteristic polynomial of both A and B, and $\lambda_1 = 4$ and $\lambda_2 = 2$ are their eigenvalues.

(b) No. Although A and B have the same characteristic polynomials and eigenvalues, A and B are not equivalent since the diagonal blocks are different. (In particular, A and B are not similar matrices.)

(c) Here $m(t) = (t-4)^3(t-2)^2$ since 3 is the order of the largest block in A, corresponding to $\lambda_1 = 4$, and 2 is the order of the largest block in A, corresponding to $\lambda_2 = 2$. Also, $d_1 = 2$ and $d_2 = 2$ since there are two blocks corresponding to both $\lambda_1 = 4$ and $\lambda_2 = 2$.

(d) Here $m(t) = (t-4)^2(t-2)^3$ since 2 is the order of the largest block in B, corresponding to $\lambda_1 = 4$, and 3 is the order of the largest block in B, corresponding to $\lambda_2 = 2$. Also, $d_1 = 3$ and $d_2 = 1$ since there are three blocks and one block, corresponding to $\lambda_1 = 4$ and $\lambda_2 = 2$, respectively.

11.40. Suppose A is a 5-square matrix with minimal polynomial $m(t) = (t-2)^2$. Determine all the possible Jordan canonical forms J for A.

 J must have one Jordan block of order 2 and the others must be of order 2 or 1. Thus there are only two possibilities,

$$
J = \begin{bmatrix} 2 & 1 & & & \\ 0 & 2 & & & \\ & & 2 & 1 & \\ & & 0 & 2 & \\ & & & & 2 \end{bmatrix} \quad \text{or} \quad J = \begin{bmatrix} 2 & 1 & & & \\ 0 & 2 & & & \\ & & 2 & & \\ & & & 2 & \\ & & & & 2 \end{bmatrix}
$$

Note that all the diagonal entries must be 2 since 2 is the only eigenvalue. The first matrix occurs when A has three independent eigenvectors, and the second matrix occurs when A has four independent eigenvectors.

PROOFS OF THEOREMS

11.41. Prove Theorem 11.1: Let f and g be polynomials and let A be an n-square matrix. Then

(i) $(f + g)(A) = f(A) + g(A)$.

(ii) $(fg)(A) = f(A)g(A)$.

(iii) $(kf)(A) = kf(A)$.

(iv) $f(A)g(A) = g(A)f(A)$.

Suppose $f = a_n t^n + \cdots + a_1 t + a_0$ and $g = b_m t^m + \cdots + b_1 t + b_0$. Then by definition,
$$f(A) = a_n A^n + \cdots + a_1 A + a_0 I \quad \text{and} \quad g(A) = b_m A^m + \cdots + b_1 A + b_0 I$$

(i) Suppose $m \leq n$ and let $b_i = 0$ if $i > m$. Then
$$f + g = (a_n + b_n)t^n + \cdots + (a_1 + b_1)t + (a_0 + b_0)$$
Hence
$$(f + g)(A) = (a_n + b_n)A^n + \cdots + (a_1 + b_1)A + (a_0 + b_0)I$$
$$= a_n A^n + b_n A^n + \cdots + a_1 A + b_1 A + a_0 I + b_0 I = f(A) + g(A)$$

(ii) By definition, $fg = c_{n+m}t^{n+m} + \cdots + c_1 t + c_0 = \sum_{k=0}^{n+m} c_k t^k$, where
$$c_k = a_0 b_k + a_1 b_{k-1} + \cdots + a_k b_0 = \sum_{i=0}^{k} a_i b_{k-i}$$
Hence $(fg)(A) = \sum_{k=0}^{n+m} c_k A^k$ and
$$f(A)g(A) = \left(\sum_{i=0}^{n} a_i A^i\right)\left(\sum_{j=0}^{m} b_j A^j\right) = \sum_{i=0}^{n} \sum_{j=0}^{m} a_i b_j A^{i+j} = \sum_{k=0}^{n+m} c_k A^k = (fg)(A)$$

(iii) By definition, $kf = ka_n t^n + \cdots + ka_1 t + ka_0$, and so
$$(kf)(A) = ka_n A^n + \cdots + ka_1 A + ka_0 I = k(a_n A^n + \cdots + a_1 A + a_0 I) = kf(A)$$

(iv) By (ii), $g(A)f(A) = (gf)(A) = (fg)(A) = f(A)g(A)$.

11.42. Prove the Cayley-Hamilton theorem, Theorem 11.2: Every matrix A is a zero of its characteristic polynomial $\Delta(t)$.

Let A be an arbitrary n-square matrix and let $\Delta(t)$ be its characteristic polynomial, say
$$\Delta(t) = |tI - A| = t^n + a_{n-1}t^{n-1} + \cdots + a_1 t + a_0$$
Now let $B(t)$ denote the classical adjoint of the matrix $tI - A$. The elements of $B(t)$ are cofactors of the matrix $tI - A$ and hence are polynomials in t of degree not exceeding $n - 1$. Thus
$$B(t) = B_{n-1}t^{n-1} + \cdots + B_1 t + B_0$$
where the B_i are n-square matrices over K which are independent of t. By the fundamental property of the classical adjoint (Theorem 10.9), $(tI - A)B(t) = |tI - A|I$, or
$$(tI - A)(B_{n-1}t^{n-1} + \cdots + B_1 t + B_0) = (t^n + a_{n-1}t^{n-1} + \cdots + a_1 t + a_0)I$$

Removing parentheses and equating the coefficients of corresponding powers of t,

$$B_{n-1} = I$$
$$B_{n-2} - AB_{n-1} = a_{n-1}I$$
$$B_{n-3} - AB_{n-2} = a_{n-2}I$$
$$\cdots\cdots\cdots\cdots\cdots$$
$$B_0 - AB_1 = a_1 I$$
$$-AB_0 = a_0 I$$

Multiplying the above matrix equations by $A^n, A^{n-1}, \ldots, A, I,$

$$A^n B_{n-1} = A^n$$
$$A^{n-1}B_{n-2} - A^n B_{n-1} = a_{n-1}A^{n-1}$$
$$A^{n-2}B_{n-3} - A^{n-1}B_{n-2} = a_{n-2}A^{n-2}$$
$$\cdots\cdots\cdots\cdots\cdots\cdots$$
$$AB_0 - A^2 B_1 = a_1 A$$
$$-AB_0 = a_0 I$$

Adding the above matrix equations,

$$0 = A^n + a_{n-1}A^{n-1} + \cdots + a_1 A + a_0 I$$

or $\Delta(A) = 0$, which is the Cayley-Hamilton Theorem.

11.43. Prove Theorem 11.6:   The following are equivalent:

(i)   The scalar λ is an eigenvalue of A.

(ii)   The matrix $\lambda I - A$ is singular.

(iii)   The scalar λ is a root of the characteristic polynomial $\Delta(t)$ of A.

The scalar λ is an eigenvalue of A if and only if there exists a nonzero vector v such that

$$Av = \lambda v \qquad \text{or} \qquad (\lambda I)v - Av = 0 \qquad \text{or} \qquad (\lambda I - A)v = 0$$

or $\lambda I - A$ is singular.   In such a case λ is a root of $\Delta(t) = |tI - A|$.   Also, v is in the eigenspace E_λ of λ if and only if the above relations hold.   Hence v is a solution of $(\lambda I - A)X = 0$.

11.44. Prove Theorem 11.8′:   Suppose $v_1, v_2, \ldots, v_n$ are nonzero eigenvectors of T belonging to distinct eigenvalues $\lambda_1, \lambda_2, \ldots, \lambda_n$.   Then $v_1, v_2, \ldots, v_n$ are linearly independent.

Suppose the theorem is not true.   Let $v_1, v_2, \ldots, v_s$ be a minimal set of vectors for which the theorem is not true.   We have $s > 1$ since $v_1 \neq 0$.   Also, by the minimality condition, $v_2, \ldots, v_s$ are linearly independent.   Thus v_1 is a linear combination of $v_2, \ldots, v_s$, say

$$v_1 = a_2 v_2 + a_3 v_3 + \cdots + a_s v_s \tag{1}$$

(where some $a_k \neq 0$).   Applying T to Eq. (1) and using the linearity of T yields

$$T(v_1) = T(a_2 v_2 + a_3 v_3 + \cdots + a_s v_s)$$
$$= a_2 T(v_2) + a_3 T(v_3) + \cdots + a_s T(v_s) \tag{2}$$

Since v_j is an eigenvector of T belonging to λ_j, we have $T(v_j) = \lambda_j v_j$.   Substituting in Eq. (2) yields

$$\lambda_1 v_1 = a_2 \lambda_2 v_2 + a_3 \lambda_3 v_3 + \cdots + a_s \lambda_s v_s \tag{3}$$

Multiplying Eq. (1) by λ_1 yields

$$\lambda_1 v_1 = a_2 \lambda_1 v_2 + a_3 \lambda_1 v_3 + \cdots + a_s \lambda_1 v_s \tag{4}$$

Setting the right sides of Eqs. (3) and (4) equal to each other, or subtracting Eq. (3) from Eq. (4), yields

$$a_2(\lambda_1 - \lambda_2)v_2 + a_3(\lambda_1 - \lambda_3)v_3 + \cdots + a_s(\lambda_1 - \lambda_s)v_s = 0 \tag{5}$$

Since $v_2, v_3, \ldots, v_s$ are linearly independent, the coefficients in Eq. (5) must all be zero. That is,

$$a_2(\lambda_1 - \lambda_2) = 0, \quad a_3(\lambda_1 - \lambda_3) = 0, \ldots, a_s(\lambda_1 - \lambda_s) = 0$$

However, the λ_i are distinct. Hence $\lambda_1 - \lambda_j \neq 0$ for $j > 1$. Hence $a_2 = 0, a_3 = 0, \ldots, a_s = 0$. This contradicts the fact that some $a_k \neq 0$. Thus the theorem is proved.

11.45. Prove Theorem 11.9: Suppose $\Delta(t) = (t - a_1)(t - a_2) \cdots (t - a_n)$ is the characteristic polynomial of an n-square matrix A, and suppose the n roots a_i are distinct. Then A is similar to the diagonal matrix $D = \text{diag}(a_1, a_2, \ldots, a_n)$.

Let $v_1, v_2, \ldots, v_n$ be (nonzero) eigenvectors corresponding to the eigenvalues a_i. Then the n eigenvectors v_i are linearly independent (Theorem 11.8), and hence form a basis for K^n. Accordingly, A is diagonalizable, that is, A is similar to a diagonal matrix D, and the diagonal elements of D are the eigenvalues a_i.

11.46. Prove Theorem 11.10′: The geometric multiplicity of an eigenvalue λ of T does not exceed its algebraic multiplicity.

Suppose the geometric multiplicity of λ is r. Then its eigenspace E_λ contains r linearly independent eigenvectors $v_1, \ldots, v_r$. Extend the set $\{v_i\}$ to a basis of V, say $\{v_i, \ldots, v_r, w_1, \ldots, w_s\}$. We have

$$\begin{aligned}
T(v_1) &= \lambda v_1 \\
T(v_2) &= \lambda v_2 \\
&\cdots \\
T(v_r) &= \lambda v_r \\
T(w_1) &= a_{11}v_1 + \cdots + a_{1r}v_r + b_{11}w_1 + \cdots + b_{1s}w_s \\
T(w_2) &= a_{21}v_1 + \cdots + a_{2r}v_r + b_{21}w_1 + \cdots + b_{2s}w_s \\
&\cdots \\
T(w_s) &= a_{s1}v_1 + \cdots + a_{sr}v_r + b_{s1}w_1 + \cdots + b_{ss}w_s
\end{aligned}$$

The matrix of T in the above basis is

$$M = \left[\begin{array}{cccc|cccc}
\lambda & 0 & \cdots & 0 & a_{11} & a_{21} & \cdots & a_{s1} \\
0 & \lambda & \cdots & 0 & a_{12} & a_{22} & \cdots & a_{s2} \\
\cdots \\
0 & 0 & \cdots & \lambda & a_{1r} & a_{2r} & \cdots & a_{sr} \\
\hline
0 & 0 & \cdots & 0 & b_{11} & b_{21} & \cdots & b_{s1} \\
0 & 0 & \cdots & 0 & b_{12} & b_{22} & \cdots & b_{s2} \\
\cdots \\
0 & 0 & \cdots & 0 & b_{1s} & b_{2s} & \cdots & b_{ss}
\end{array}\right] = \left[\begin{array}{c|c}
\lambda I_r & A \\
\hline
0 & B
\end{array}\right]$$

where $A = [a_{ij}]^T$ and $B = [b_{ij}]^T$.

Since M is a block triangular matrix, the characteristic polynomial of λI_r, which is $(t - \lambda)^r$, must divide the characteristic polynomial of M and hence that of T. Thus the algebraic multiplicity of λ for the operator T is at least r, as required.

11.47. Prove Theorem 11.15:   The minimum polynomial $m(t)$ of a matrix (linear operator) A divides every polynomial that has A as a zero.   Thus (by the Cayley-Hamilton theorem) $m(t)$ divides the characteristic polynomial $\Delta(t)$ of A.

Suppose $f(t)$ is a polynomial for which $f(A) = 0$. By the division algorithm there exist polynomials $q(t)$ and $r(t)$ for which $f(t) = m(t)q(t) + r(t)$ and $r(t) = 0$ or $\deg r(t) < \deg m(t)$. Substituting $t = A$ in this equation, and using that $f(A) = 0$ and $m(A) = 0$, we obtain $r(A) = 0$.   If $r(t) \neq 0$, then $r(t)$ is a polynomial of degree less than $m(t)$ which has A as a zero.   This contradicts the definition of the minimum polynomial.   Thus $r(t) = 0$, and so $f(t) = m(t)q(t)$, i.e., $m(t)$ divides $f(t)$.

11.48. Let $m(t)$ be the minimum polynomial of an n-square matrix A.

(a)   **Prove:**   The characteristic polynomial $\Delta(t)$ of A divides $(m(t))^n$.

(b)   **Prove Theorem 11.16:** The characteristic polynomial $\Delta(t)$ and the minimum polynomial $m(t)$ of a matrix A have the same irreducible factors.

(a)   Suppose $m(t) = t^r + c_1 t^{r-1} + \cdots + c_{r-1}t + c_r$.   Define matrices B_j as follows:

$$B_0 = I \qquad\qquad\qquad \text{so} \qquad I = B_0$$
$$B_1 = A + c_1 I \qquad\qquad \text{so} \qquad c_1 I = B_1 - A = B_1 - AB_0$$
$$B_2 = A^2 + c_1 A + c_2 I \qquad \text{so} \qquad c_2 I = B_2 - A(A + c_1 I) = B_2 - AB_1$$

$$\cdots\cdots\cdots\cdots\cdots\cdots\cdots\cdots\cdots\cdots\cdots\cdots\cdots\cdots\cdots$$

$$B_{r-1} = A^{r-1} + c_1 A^{r-2} + \cdots + c_{r-1}I \qquad \text{so} \qquad c_{r-1}I = B_{r-1} - AB_{r-2}$$

Then

$$-AB_{r-1} = c_r I - (A^r + c_1 A^{r-1} + \cdots + c_{r-1}A + c_r I) = c_r I - m(A) = c_r I$$

Set
$$B(t) = t^{r-1}B_0 + t^{r-2}B_1 + \cdots + tB_{r-2} + B_{r-1}$$

Then

$$(tI - A) \cdot B(t) = (t^r B_0 + t^{r-1}B_1 + \cdots + tB_{r-1}) - (t^{r-1}AB_0 + t^{r-2}AB_1 + \cdots + AB_{r-1})$$
$$= t^r B_0 + t^{r-1}(B_1 - AB_0) + t^{r-2}(B_2 - AB_1) + \cdots + t(B_{r-1} - AB_{r-2}) - AB_{r-1}$$
$$= t^r I + c_1 t^{r-1}I + c_2 t^{r-2}I + \cdots + c_{r-1}tI + c_r I$$
$$= m(t)I$$

Taking the determinant of both sides gives $|tI - A| |B(t)| = |m(t)I| = (m(t))^n$.   Since $|B(t)|$ is a polynomial, $|tI - A|$ divides $(m(t))^n$, that is, the characteristic polynomial of A divides $(m(t))^n$.

(b)   Suppose $f(t)$ is an irreducible polynomial.   If $f(t)$ divides $m(t)$, then since $m(t)$ divides $\Delta(t)$, $f(t)$ divides $\Delta(t)$.   On the other hand, if $f(t)$ divides $\Delta(t)$, then, by part (a), $f(t)$ divides $(m(t))^n$.   But $f(t)$ is irreducible; hence $f(t)$ also divides $m(t)$.   Thus $m(t)$ and $\Delta(t)$ have the same irreducible factors.

11.49. Prove Theorem 11.19: The minimum polynomial $m(t)$ of a block diagonal matrix M with diagonal blocks A_i is equal to the least common multiple (LCM) of the minimum polynomials of the diagonal blocks A_i.

We prove the theorem for the case $r = 2$. The general theorem follows easily by induction. Suppose $M = \begin{bmatrix} A & 0 \\ 0 & B \end{bmatrix}$, where A and B are square matrices. We need to show that the minimum polynomial $m(t)$ of M is the least common multiple of the minimum polynomials $g(t)$ and $h(t)$ of A and B, respectively.

Since $m(t)$ is the minimum polynomial of M, $m(M) = \begin{bmatrix} m(A) & 0 \\ 0 & m(B) \end{bmatrix} = 0$, and hence $m(A) = 0$ and $m(B) = 0$. Since $g(t)$ is the minimum polynomial of A, $g(t)$ divides $m(t)$. Similarly, $h(t)$ divides $m(t)$. Thus $m(t)$ is a multiple of $g(t)$ and $h(t)$.

Now let $f(t)$ be another multiple of $g(t)$ and $h(t)$. Then $f(M) = \begin{bmatrix} f(A) & 0 \\ 0 & f(B) \end{bmatrix} = \begin{bmatrix} 0 & 0 \\ 0 & 0 \end{bmatrix} = 0$. But $m(t)$ is the minimum polynomial of M; hence $m(t)$ divides $f(t)$. Thus $m(t)$ is the least common multiple of $g(t)$ and $h(t)$.

11.50. Here we use the following facts about the inner product in $\mathbf{C}^n$: (i) $\langle u, v \rangle = u^T \bar{v}$; (ii) $\langle ku, v \rangle = k \langle u, v \rangle$; and (iii) $\langle u, kv \rangle = \bar{k} \langle u, v \rangle$ (where $\bar{k}$, $\bar{v}$ and $\bar{A}$ denote the complex conjugates of k, v, and A). Suppose A is a real symmetric matrix viewed as a matrix over $\mathbf{C}$.

(a) Prove that $\langle Au, v \rangle = \langle u, Av \rangle$ for the inner product in $\mathbf{C}^n$.

(b) Prove Theorem 11.12: Any eigenvalue λ of A is real.

(c) Prove Theorem 11.13: Suppose u and v are eigenvectors of A belonging to distinct eigenvalues λ_1 and λ_2. Then $\langle u, v \rangle = 0$.

(a) Since A is real symmetric, $A = A^T = \bar{A}$. Thus

$$\langle Au, v \rangle = (Au)^T \bar{v} = u^T A^T \bar{v} = u^T \bar{A} \bar{v} = u^T \overline{Av} = \langle u, Av \rangle$$

(b) There exists $v \neq 0$ such that $Av = \lambda v$. Then

$$\lambda \langle v, v \rangle = \langle \lambda v, v \rangle = \langle Av, v \rangle = \langle v, Av \rangle = \langle v, \lambda v \rangle = \bar{\lambda} \langle v, v \rangle$$

But $\langle v, v \rangle \neq 0$ since $v \neq 0$. Thus $\lambda = \bar{\lambda}$, and so λ is real.

(c) Here $Au = \lambda_1 u$ and $Av = \lambda_2 v$ and, by (b), λ_2 is real. Then

$$\lambda_1 \langle u, v \rangle = \langle \lambda_1 u, v \rangle = \langle Au, v \rangle = \langle u, Av \rangle = \langle u, \lambda_2 v \rangle = \bar{\lambda}_2 \langle u, v \rangle = \lambda_2 \langle u, v \rangle$$

Since $\lambda_1 \neq \lambda_2$, we have $\langle u, v \rangle = 0$.

11.51. Let A be an n-square matrix. Without using the Cayley-Hamilton theorem, prove that A is a root of nonzero polynomial of degree $\leq n^2$.

Let $N = n^2$. Consider the $N + 1$ matrices $I, A, A^2, \ldots, A^N$. Recall that the vector space V of $n \times n$ matrices has dimension $N = n^2$. Thus the above $N + 1$ matrices are linearly dependent. Thus there exist scalars $a_0, a_1, a_2, \ldots, a_N$, not all zero, for which

$$a_N A^N + \cdots + a_1 A + a_0 I = 0$$

Thus A is a root of the polynomial $f(t) = a_N t^N + \cdots + a_1 t + a_0$.

11.52. Suppose A is an n-square matrix.   Prove the following:

(a) A is nonsingular if and only if the constant term of the minimum polynomial of A is not zero.

(b)   If A is nonsingular, then A^{-1} is equal to a polynomial in A of degree not exceeding n.

(a)   Suppose $f(t) = t^r + a_{r-1}t^{r-1} + \cdots + a_1 t + a_0$ is the minimum (characteristic) polynomial of A.   Then the following are equivalent: (i) A is nonsingular; (ii) 0 is not a root of $f(t)$; and (iii) the constant term a_0 is not zero.   Thus the statement is true.

(b)   Let $m(t)$ be the minimum polynomial of A.   Then $m(t) = t^r + a_{r-1}t^{r-1} + \cdots + a_1 t + a_0$, where $r \le n$.   Since A is nonsingular, $a_0 \ne 0$ by part (a).   We have

$$m(A) = A^r + a_{r-1}A^{r-1} + \cdots + a_1 A + a_0 I = 0$$

Thus

$$-\frac{1}{a_0}(A^{r-1} + a_{r-1}A^{r-2} + \cdots + a_1 I)A = I$$

Accordingly,

$$A^{-1} = -\frac{1}{a_0}(A^{r-1} + a_{r-1}A^{r-2} + \cdots + a_1 I)$$

Supplementary Problems

POLYNOMIALS IN MATRICES

11.53. Let $A = \begin{bmatrix} 2 & -3 \\ 5 & 1 \end{bmatrix}$ and $B = \begin{bmatrix} 1 & 2 \\ 0 & 3 \end{bmatrix}$.   Find $f(A)$, $g(A)$, $f(B)$, and $g(B)$, where $f(t) = 2t^2 - 5t + 6$ and $g(t) = t^3 - 2t^2 + t + 3$.

11.54. Let $B = \begin{bmatrix} 8 & 12 & 0 \\ 0 & 8 & 12 \\ 0 & 0 & 8 \end{bmatrix}$.   Find a real matrix A such that $B = A^3$.

11.55. For each matrix, find a polynomial having the matrix as a root:

(a) $A = \begin{bmatrix} 2 & 5 \\ 1 & -3 \end{bmatrix}$; (b) $B = \begin{bmatrix} 2 & -3 \\ 7 & -4 \end{bmatrix}$; (c) $C = \begin{bmatrix} 1 & 1 & 2 \\ 1 & 2 & 3 \\ 2 & 1 & 4 \end{bmatrix}$

11.56. Let A be any square matrix and let $f(t)$ be any polynomial.   Prove: (a) $(P^{-1}AP)^n = P^{-1}A^n P$; (b) $f(P^{-1}AP) = P^{-1}f(A)P$; (c) $f(A^T) = (f(A))^T$; (d) if A is symmetric, then $f(A)$ is symmetric.

EIGENVALUES AND EIGENVECTORS

11.57. For each matrix, find all eigenvalues and corresponding linearly independent eigenvectors:

(a) $A = \begin{bmatrix} 2 & -3 \\ 2 & -5 \end{bmatrix}$; (b) $B = \begin{bmatrix} 2 & 4 \\ -1 & 6 \end{bmatrix}$; (c) $C = \begin{bmatrix} 1 & -4 \\ 3 & -7 \end{bmatrix}$.

When possible, find the nonsingular matrix P which diagonalizes the matrix.

11.58. Let $A = \begin{bmatrix} 2 & -1 \\ -2 & 3 \end{bmatrix}$

    (a) Find all eigenvalues and corresponding linearly independent eigenvectors.

    (b) Find a nonsingular matrix P such that $D = P^{-1}AP$ is diagonal.

    (c) Find A^8 and $f(A)$, where $f(t) = t^4 - 5t^3 + 7t^2 - 2t + 5$.

    (d) Find a matrix B such that $B^2 = A$.

11.59. Repeat Problem 11.58 for $A = \begin{bmatrix} 5 & 6 \\ -2 & -2 \end{bmatrix}$.

11.60. For each matrix, find all eigenvalues and a maximum set S of linearly independent eigenvectors:

$$(a)\ A = \begin{bmatrix} 1 & -3 & 3 \\ 3 & -5 & 3 \\ 6 & -6 & 4 \end{bmatrix}; \ (b)\ B = \begin{bmatrix} 3 & -1 & 1 \\ 7 & -5 & 1 \\ 6 & -6 & 2 \end{bmatrix}; \ (c)\ C = \begin{bmatrix} 1 & 2 & 2 \\ 1 & 2 & -1 \\ -1 & 1 & 4 \end{bmatrix}.$$

Which matrices can be diagonalized and why?

11.61. For each linear operator $T: \mathbf{R}^2 \to \mathbf{R}^2$, find all eigenvalues and a basis for each eigenspace: (a) $T(x, y) = (3x + 3y, x + 5y)$; (b) $T(x, y) = (2x - 3y, 3x + 8y)$; (c) $T(x, y) = (3x - 13y, x - 3y)$.

11.62. Let $A = \begin{bmatrix} a & b \\ c & d \end{bmatrix}$ be a real matrix. Find necessary and sufficient conditions on a, b, c, d so that A is diagonalizable, that is, that A has two (real) linearly independent eigenvectors.

11.63. Show that matrices A and A^T have the same eigenvalues. Give an example of a 2×2 matrix A where A and A^T have different eigenvectors.

11.64. Suppose v is an eigenvector of linear operators F and G. Show that v is also an eigenvector of the linear operator $kF + k'G$, where k and k' are scalars.

11.65. Suppose v is an eigenvector of a linear operator T belonging to the eigenvalue λ. Prove:

    (a) For $n > 0$, v is an eigenvector of T^n belonging to λ^n.

    (b) $f(\lambda)$ is an eigenvalue of $f(T)$ for any polynomial $f(t)$.

11.66. Let $E: V \to V$ be a projection mapping, that is, $E^2 = E$. Show that E is diagonalizable and, in fact, can be represented by the diagonal matrix $M = \begin{bmatrix} I_r & 0 \\ 0 & 0 \end{bmatrix}$, where r is the rank of E.

DIAGONALIZING REAL SYMMETRIC MATRICES

11.67. For each symmetric matrix A, find an orthogonal matrix P such that $D = P^{-1}AP$ is diagonal:

$$(a)\ A = \begin{bmatrix} 5 & 4 \\ 4 & -1 \end{bmatrix}; \ (b)\ A = \begin{bmatrix} 4 & -1 \\ -1 & 4 \end{bmatrix}; \ (c)\ A = \begin{bmatrix} 7 & 3 \\ 3 & -1 \end{bmatrix}.$$

11.68. For each symmetric matrix B, find its eigenvalues, a maximal orthogonal set S of eigenvectors, and an orthogonal matrix P such that $D = P^{-1}BP$ is diagonal:

$$(a)\ B = \begin{bmatrix} 0 & 1 & 1 \\ 1 & 0 & 1 \\ 1 & 1 & 0 \end{bmatrix}; \ (b)\ B = \begin{bmatrix} 2 & 2 & 4 \\ 2 & 5 & 8 \\ 4 & 8 & 17 \end{bmatrix}.$$

11.69. Find a real 2×2 symmetric matrix A with eigenvalues $\lambda = 1$ and $\lambda = 4$ such that $u = (1, 1)$ is an eigenvector belonging to $\lambda = 1$.   Also find a matrix B for which $B^2 = A$.

11.70. Find a real 2×2 symmetric matrix A with eigenvalues $\lambda = 2$ and $\lambda = 3$ such that $u = (1, 2)$ is an eigenvector belonging to $\lambda = 2$.   Also find a matrix B for which $B^2 = A$.

CHARACTERISTIC AND MINIMUM POLYNOMIALS

11.71. Find the characteristic and minimum polynomials of each matrix:

$$(a)\ A = \begin{bmatrix} 3 & 1 & -1 \\ 2 & 4 & -2 \\ -1 & -1 & 3 \end{bmatrix}; \ (b)\ B = \begin{bmatrix} 3 & 2 & -1 \\ 3 & 8 & -3 \\ 3 & 6 & -1 \end{bmatrix}.$$

11.72. Find the characteristic and minimum polynomials of each matrix:

$$(a)\ A = \begin{bmatrix} 2 & 5 & 0 & 0 & 0 \\ 0 & 2 & 0 & 0 & 0 \\ 0 & 0 & 4 & 2 & 0 \\ 0 & 0 & 3 & 5 & 0 \\ 0 & 0 & 0 & 0 & 7 \end{bmatrix}; \ (b)\ B = \begin{bmatrix} 4 & -1 & 0 & 0 & 0 \\ 1 & 2 & 0 & 0 & 0 \\ 0 & 0 & 3 & 1 & 0 \\ 0 & 0 & 0 & 3 & 1 \\ 0 & 0 & 0 & 0 & 3 \end{bmatrix}; \ (c)\ C = \begin{bmatrix} 3 & 2 & 0 & 0 & 0 \\ 1 & 4 & 0 & 0 & 0 \\ 0 & 0 & 3 & 1 & 0 \\ 0 & 0 & 1 & 3 & 0 \\ 0 & 0 & 0 & 0 & 4 \end{bmatrix}.$$

11.73. Let $A = \begin{bmatrix} 1 & 1 & 0 \\ 0 & 2 & 0 \\ 0 & 0 & 1 \end{bmatrix}$ and $B = \begin{bmatrix} 2 & 0 & 0 \\ 0 & 2 & 2 \\ 0 & 0 & 1 \end{bmatrix}$.   Show that A and B have different characteristic polynomials (and so are not similar), but have the same minimum polynomial.   Thus nonsimilar matrices may have the same minimum polynomial.

11.74. Let A be an n-square matrix for which $A^k = 0$ for some $k > n$.   Show that $A^n = 0$.

11.75. Show that a matrix A and its transpose A^T have the same minimum polynomial.

11.76. Suppose $f(t)$ is an irreducible monic polynomial for which $f(A) = 0$ for a matrix A.   Show that $f(t)$ is the minimum polynomial of A.

11.77. Show that A is a scalar matrix kI if and only if the minimum polynomial of A is $m(t) = t - k$.

11.78. Find a matrix A whose minimum polynomial is: (a) $t^3 - 5t^2 + 6t + 8$; (b) $t^4 - 5t^3 - 2t + 7t + 4$.

JORDAN CANONICAL FORM

11.79. Consider the following matrices in Jordan canonical form:

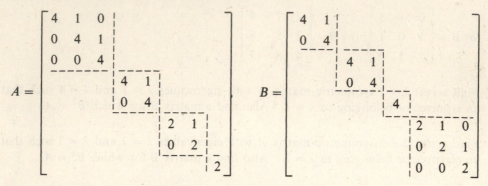

(a)   Find the characteristic polynomials of A and B.

(b)   Find the minimum polynomials of A and B.

(c)   Find a maximal set S of linearly independent eigenvectors of A.

(d)   Find a maximal set S of linearly independent eigenvectors of B.

11.80. Find all possible Jordan canonical forms whose characteristic polynomials $\Delta(t)$ and minimum polynomials $m(t)$ are as follows: (a) $\Delta(t) = (t-2)^4(t-3)^2$, $m(t) = (t-2)^2(t-3)^2$; (b) $\Delta(t) = (t-7)^5$, $m(t) = (t-7)^2$; (c) $\Delta(t) = (t-8)^4(t-1)^3$, $m(t) = (t-8)^3(t-1)^2$.

11.81. The six possible Jordan canonical forms with characteristic polynomial $\Delta(t) = (t-2)^3(t-5)^2$ follow:

$$B_1 = \begin{bmatrix} 2 & 1 & 0 & & \\ 0 & 2 & 1 & & \\ 0 & 0 & 2 & & \\ & & & 5 & 1 \\ & & & 0 & 5 \end{bmatrix}, \qquad B_2 = \begin{bmatrix} 2 & 1 & & & \\ 0 & 2 & & & \\ & & 2 & & \\ & & & 5 & 1 \\ & & & 0 & 5 \end{bmatrix},$$

$$B_3 = \begin{bmatrix} 2 & & & & \\ & 2 & & & \\ & & 2 & & \\ & & & 5 & 1 \\ & & & 0 & 5 \end{bmatrix}, \qquad B_4 = \begin{bmatrix} 2 & 1 & 0 & & \\ 0 & 2 & 1 & & \\ 0 & 0 & 2 & & \\ & & & 5 & \\ & & & & 5 \end{bmatrix},$$

$$B_5 = \begin{bmatrix} 2 & 1 & & & \\ 0 & 2 & & & \\ & & 2 & & \\ & & & 5 & \\ & & & & 5 \end{bmatrix}, \qquad B_6 = \begin{bmatrix} 2 & & & & \\ & 2 & & & \\ & & 2 & & \\ & & & 5 & \\ & & & & 5 \end{bmatrix},$$

In each case, find the minimum polynomial $m(t)$ and a maximal set S of linearly independent eigenvectors.

Answers to Supplementary Problems

11.53. $f(A) = \begin{bmatrix} -26 & -3 \\ 5 & -27 \end{bmatrix}$, $g(A) = \begin{bmatrix} -40 & 39 \\ -65 & -27 \end{bmatrix}$, $f(B) = \begin{bmatrix} 3 & 6 \\ 0 & 9 \end{bmatrix}$, $g(B) = \begin{bmatrix} 3 & 12 \\ 0 & 15 \end{bmatrix}$

11.54. *Hint*:   Let $A = \begin{bmatrix} 2 & a & b \\ 0 & 2 & c \\ 0 & 0 & 2 \end{bmatrix}$.   Set $B = A^3$ and then find a, b, and c.

11.55. Find $\Delta(t)$.   (a) $t^2 + t - 11$; (b) $t^2 + 2t + 13$; (c) $t^3 - 7t^2 + 6t - 1$.

11.57. (a) $\lambda = 1$, $u = (3, 1)$; $\lambda = -4$, $v = (1, 2)$; (b) $\lambda = 4$, $u = (2, 1)$; (c) $\lambda = -1$, $u = (2, 1)$; $\lambda = -5$, $v = (2, 3)$.   Only A and C can be diagonalized; use $P = [u, v]$.

11.58. (a) $\lambda = 1$, $u = (1, 1)$; $\lambda = 4$, $v = (1, -2)$; (b) $P = [u, v]$; (c) $A^8 = \begin{bmatrix} 21846 & -21845 \\ -43690 & 43691 \end{bmatrix}$,

$f(A) = \begin{bmatrix} 19 & -13 \\ -26 & 32 \end{bmatrix}$; (d) $B = \begin{bmatrix} \frac{4}{3} & -\frac{1}{3} \\ -\frac{2}{3} & \frac{5}{3} \end{bmatrix}$

11.59. (a) $\lambda = 1$, $u = (3, -2)$; $\lambda = 2$, $v = (2, -1)$; (b) $P = [u, v]$; (c) $A^8 = \begin{bmatrix} 1021 & 1530 \\ -510 & -764 \end{bmatrix}$;

$f(A) = \begin{bmatrix} 2 & -6 \\ 2 & 9 \end{bmatrix}$; (d) $B = \begin{bmatrix} -3 + 4\sqrt{2} & -6 + 6\sqrt{2} \\ 2 - 2\sqrt{2} & 4 - 3\sqrt{2} \end{bmatrix}$

11.60. (a) $\lambda = -2$, $u = (1, 1, 0)$, $v = (1, 0, -1)$; $\lambda = 4$, $w = (1, 1, 2)$.

(b) $\lambda = 2$, $u = (1, 1, 0)$; $\lambda = -4$, $v = (0, 1, 1)$.

(c) $\lambda = 3$, $u = (1, 1, 0)$, $v = (1, 0, 1)$; $\lambda = 1$, $w = (2, -1, 1)$.

Only A and C can be diagonalized; use $P = [u, v, w]$.

11.61. (a) $\lambda = 2$, $u = (3, -1)$; $\lambda = 6$, $v = (1, 1)$; (b) $\lambda = 5$, $u = (1, -1)$; (c) no real eigenvalues

11.62. Since $\Delta(t) = t^2 - tr(A)t + \det(A)$, we need $[-tr(A)]^2 - 4[\det(A)] > 0$ or $(a = d)^2 + 4bc > 0$.

11.63. $A = \begin{bmatrix} 1 & 1 \\ 0 & 1 \end{bmatrix}$

11.67. (a) $P = \frac{1}{\sqrt{5}} \begin{bmatrix} 2 & -1 \\ 1 & 2 \end{bmatrix}$;   (b) $P = \frac{1}{\sqrt{2}} \begin{bmatrix} 1 & 1 \\ 1 & -1 \end{bmatrix}$;   (c) $P = \frac{1}{\sqrt{10}} \begin{bmatrix} 3 & -1 \\ 1 & 3 \end{bmatrix}$

11.68. (a) $\lambda = -1$, $u = (1, -1, 0)$, $v = (1, 1, -2)$; $\lambda = 2$, $w = (1, 1, 1)$.

(b) $\lambda = 1$, $u = (2, 1, -1)$, $v = (2, -3, 1)$; $\lambda = 22$, $w = (1, 2, 4)$.

Normalize u, v, w, obtaining $\hat{u}$, $\hat{v}$, $\hat{w}$, and set $P = [\hat{u}, \hat{v}, \hat{w}]$.   (*Remark*: u and v are not unique.)

11.69. $A = \frac{1}{2} \begin{bmatrix} 5 & -3 \\ -3 & 5 \end{bmatrix}$, $B = \frac{1}{2} \begin{bmatrix} 3 & -1 \\ -1 & 3 \end{bmatrix}$

11.70. $A = \dfrac{1}{5}\begin{bmatrix} 14 & -2 \\ -2 & 11 \end{bmatrix}$, $B = \dfrac{1}{5}\begin{bmatrix} \sqrt{2}+4\sqrt{3} & 2\sqrt{2}-2\sqrt{3} \\ 2\sqrt{2}-2\sqrt{3} & 4\sqrt{2}+\sqrt{3} \end{bmatrix}$

11.71. (a) $\Delta(t) = m(t) = (t-2)^2(t-6)$; (b) $\Delta(t) = (t-2)^2(t-6)$, $m(t) = (t-2)(t-6)$

11.72. (a) $\Delta(t) = (t-2)^3(t-7)^2$, $m(t) = (t-2)^2(t-7)$; (b) $\Delta(t) = (t-3)^5$, $m(t) = (t-3)^3$;
(c) $\Delta(t) = (t-2)^2(t-4)^2(t-5)$, $m(t) = (t-2)(t-4)(t-5)$

11.78. (a) $A = \begin{bmatrix} 0 & 0 & -8 \\ 1 & 0 & -6 \\ 0 & 1 & 5 \end{bmatrix}$; (b) $A = \begin{bmatrix} 0 & 0 & 0 & -4 \\ 1 & 0 & 0 & -7 \\ 0 & 1 & 0 & 2 \\ 0 & 0 & 1 & 5 \end{bmatrix}$

11.79. (a) $\Delta_A(t) = \Delta_B(t) = (t-4)^5(t-2)^3$; (b) $m_A(t) = (t-4)^3(t-2)^2$, $m_B(t) = (t-4)^2(t-2)^3$;
(c) $\{10000000,\ 00010000,\ 00000100,\ 00000001\}$; (d) $\{10000000,\ 00100000,\ 00001000,\ 00000100\}$.

11.80. (a) $\begin{bmatrix} 2 & 1 & & & & \\ 0 & 2 & & & & \\ & & 2 & 1 & & \\ & & 0 & 2 & & \\ & & & & 3 & 1 \\ & & & & 0 & 3 \end{bmatrix}$, $\begin{bmatrix} 2 & 1 & & & & \\ 0 & 2 & & & & \\ & & 2 & & & \\ & & & 2 & & \\ & & & & 3 & 1 \\ & & & & 0 & 3 \end{bmatrix}$,

(b) $\begin{bmatrix} 7 & 1 & & & \\ 0 & 7 & & & \\ & & 7 & 1 & \\ & & 0 & 7 & \\ & & & & 7 \end{bmatrix}$, $\begin{bmatrix} 7 & 1 & & & \\ 0 & 7 & & & \\ & & 7 & & \\ & & & 7 & \\ & & & & 7 \end{bmatrix}$;

(c) $\begin{bmatrix} 8 & 1 & 0 & & & \\ 0 & 8 & 1 & & & \\ 0 & 0 & 8 & & & \\ & & & 8 & & \\ & & & & 1 & 1 \\ & & & & 0 & 1 \\ & & & & & & 1 \end{bmatrix}$

11.81. [Note: commas have been omitted for notational convenience.]
(1) $m(t) = (t-2)^3(t-5)^2$, $\{10000,\ 00010\}$,
(2) $m(t) = (t-2)^2(t-5)^2$, $\{10000,\ 00100,\ 00010\}$,
(3) $m(t) = (t-2)(t-5)^2$, $\{10000,\ 01000,\ 00100,\ 00010\}$,
(4) $m(t) = (t-2)^3(t-5)$, $\{10000,\ 00010,\ 00001\}$,
(5) $m(t) = (t-2)^2(t-5)$, $\{10000,\ 00100,\ 00010,\ 00001\}$,
(6) $m(t) = (t-2)(t-5)$, $\{10000,\ 01000,\ 00100,\ 00010,\ 00001\}$

Chapter 12

Quadratic Forms and Symmetric Matrices

12.1 INTRODUCTION

This chapter investigates the important notion of a quadratic form and its representation by means of a symmetric matrix. The main result in this chapter is that we can always choose a new coordinate system so that a given quadratic form is represented by a diagonal matrix. (This is not true for linear mappings.) We give two diagonalization algorithms. One uses elementary row and column operations, and the other uses eigenvalues and eigenvectors.

12.2 CONGRUENT SYMMETRIC MATRICES, LAW OF INERTIA

Let A be an arbitrary square matrix. A matrix B is said to be *congruent* to A if there exists a nonsingular (invertible) matrix P such that

$$B = P^T A P$$

Congruence is an equivalence relation (see Problem 12.37). Suppose A is a symmetric matrix, that is, suppose $A^T = A$. Then

$$B^T = (P^T A P)^T = P^T A^T P^{TT} = P^T A P = B$$

and so B is symmetric. Since diagonal matrices are special symmetric matrices, it follows that only symmetric matrices are congruent to diagonal matrices.

The next theorem plays an important role in linear algebra.

Theorem 12.1 (Law of Inertia): Let A be a real symmetric matrix. Then there exists a nonsingular matrix P such that $B = P^T A P$ is diagonal. Moreover, every such diagonal matrix B has the same number $\mathbf{p}$ of positive entries and the same number $\mathbf{n}$ of negative entries.

The *rank* and *signature* of the above symmetric matrix A are defined by

$$\text{rank}(A) = \mathbf{p} + \mathbf{n} \quad \text{and} \quad \text{sig}(A) = \mathbf{p} - \mathbf{n}$$

Thus these are uniquely defined by Theorem 12.1. (Section 5.5 defined the rank of a matrix to be the dimension of its row or column space; we note that the above definition agrees with the general definition.)

The following is an algorithm which diagonalizes (under congruence) a real symmetric matrix A, that is, the algorithm finds a matrix P such that $D = P^T A P$ is diagonal.

Algorithm 12.2 (Congruence Diagonalization of a Symmetric Matrix): Diagonalizes an inputted n-square real symmetric matrix $A = [a_{ij}]$.

443

Step 1. Form the $n \times 2n$ (block) matrix $M = [A, I]$, that is, A is the left half of M and the identity matrix I is the right half of M.

Step 2. Examine the entry a_{11}.

Case (i): $a_{11} \neq 0$. For $i = 2, \ldots, n$, apply the row operation "Add $-a_{i1}R_1$ to $a_{11}R_i$" and then apply the corresponding column operation "Add $-a_{i1}C_1$ to $a_{11}C_i$". These operations reduce the matrix M to the form

$$M \sim \begin{bmatrix} a_{11} & 0 & \star & \star \\ 0 & A_2 & \star & \star \end{bmatrix} \tag{$\star$}$$

Case (ii): $a_{11} = 0$ but $a_{kk} \neq 0$ for some $k > 1$. Apply the row operation "Interchange R_1 and R_k" and the corresponding column operation "Interchange C_1 and C_k". These operations bring a_{kk} into the first diagonal position. This reduces the matrix to case (i).

Case (iii): All diagonal entries $a_{ii} = 0$. Find i, j such that $a_{ij} \neq 0$. Apply the row operation "Add R_j to R_i" and the corresponding column operation "Add C_j to C_i". This brings $2a_{ij} \neq 0$ into the ith diagonal position. This reduces the matrix to case (ii).

Thus M is finally reduced to the form ($\star$), where A_2 is a symmetric matrix of order less than A.

Step 3. Repeat Step 2 with each new matrix A_k (by neglecting the first row and column of the preceding matrix) until A is diagonalized, that is, until M is transformed into the form $M' = [D, Q]$, where D is diagonal.

Step 4. Set $P = Q^T$. Then $D = P^T A P$.

Remark: We emphasize that in Step 2 the row operations will change both sides of M, but the column operations will only change the left half of M.

The justification of the above algorithm appears in Problem 12.27.

EXAMPLE 12.1 Consider the symmetric matrix $A = \begin{bmatrix} 1 & 2 & -3 \\ 2 & 5 & -4 \\ -3 & -4 & 8 \end{bmatrix}$. We apply the above algorithm to A to find a nonsingular matrix P such that $D = P^T A P$ is diagonal. First form the block matrix $M = [A, I]$, that is,

$$M = [A, I] = \begin{bmatrix} 1 & 2 & -3 & \vdots & 1 & 0 & 0 \\ 2 & 5 & -4 & \vdots & 0 & 1 & 0 \\ -3 & -4 & 8 & \vdots & 0 & 0 & 1 \end{bmatrix}$$

Apply the row operations "Add $-2R_1$ to R_2" and "Add $3R_1$ to R_3" to M, and then apply the corresponding column operations "Add $-2C_1$ to C_2" and "Add $3C_1$ to C_3" to obtain

$$\begin{bmatrix} 1 & 2 & -3 & \vdots & 1 & 0 & 0 \\ 0 & 1 & 2 & \vdots & -2 & 1 & 0 \\ 0 & 2 & -1 & \vdots & 3 & 0 & 1 \end{bmatrix} \quad \text{and then} \quad \begin{bmatrix} 1 & 0 & 0 & \vdots & 1 & 0 & 0 \\ 0 & 1 & 2 & \vdots & -2 & 1 & 0 \\ 0 & 2 & -1 & \vdots & 3 & 0 & 1 \end{bmatrix}$$

Next apply the row operation "Add $-2R_2$ to R_3" and then the corresponding column operation

"Add $-2C_2$ to C_3" to obtain

$$\begin{bmatrix} 1 & 0 & 0 & \vdots & 1 & 0 & 0 \\ 0 & 1 & 2 & \vdots & -2 & 1 & 0 \\ 0 & 0 & -5 & \vdots & 7 & -2 & 1 \end{bmatrix} \quad \text{and then} \quad \begin{bmatrix} 1 & 0 & 0 & \vdots & 1 & 0 & 0 \\ 0 & 1 & 0 & \vdots & -2 & 1 & 0 \\ 0 & 0 & -5 & \vdots & 7 & -2 & 1 \end{bmatrix}$$

Now A has been diagonalized. Set

$$P = \begin{bmatrix} 1 & -2 & 7 \\ 0 & 1 & -2 \\ 0 & 0 & 1 \end{bmatrix} \quad \text{and then} \quad D = P^T A P = \begin{bmatrix} 1 & 0 & 0 \\ 0 & 1 & 0 \\ 0 & 0 & -5 \end{bmatrix}$$

Note that D has **p** $= 2$ positive entries and **n** $= 1$ negative entry.

12.3   QUADRATIC FORMS

A quadratic form q in variables $x_1, x_2, \ldots, x_n$ is a polynomial

$$q(x_1, x_2, \ldots, x_n) = \sum_{i \leq j} c_{ij} x_i x_j \tag{1}$$

(where each term has degree 2).   The quadratic form q is said to be *diagonalized* if

$$q(x_1, x_2, \ldots, x_n) = c_{11} x_1^2 + c_{22} x_2^2 + \cdots + c_{nn} x_n^2$$

that is, if q has no *cross product* terms $x_i x_j$ (where $i \neq j$).

The quadratic form Eq. (*1*), may be expressed uniquely in the matrix form

$$q(X) = X^T A X \tag{2}$$

where $X = (x_1, x_2, \ldots, x_n)^T$ is the column vector of the variables and $A = [a_{ij}]$ is a symmetric matrix.   The entries of A can be obtained from Eq. (*1*) by setting

$$a_{ii} = c_{ii} \quad \text{and} \quad a_{ij} = a_{ji} = c_{ij}/2, \quad \text{for } i \neq j$$

that is, A has diagonal entry a_{ii} equal to the coefficient of x_i^2, and has entries a_{ij} and a_{ji} each equal to half the coefficient of $x_i x_j$.   Thus

$$q(X) = (x_1, \ldots, x_n) \begin{bmatrix} a_{11} & a_{12} & \cdots & a_{1n} \\ a_{21} & a_{22} & \cdots & a_{2n} \\ \cdots & \cdots & \cdots & \cdots \\ a_{n1} & a_{n2} & \cdots & a_{nn} \end{bmatrix} \begin{bmatrix} x_1 \\ x_2 \\ \vdots \\ x_n \end{bmatrix}$$

$$= \sum_{i,j} a_{ij} x_i x_j = a_{11} x_1^2 + a_{22} x_2^2 + \cdots + a_{nn} x_n^2 + 2 \sum_{i<j} a_{ij} x_i x_j$$

The above symmetric matrix A is called the *matrix representation* of the quadratic form q. Although many matrices A in Eq. (*2*) will yield the same quadratic form q, only one such matrix is symmetric.

Conversely, any symmetric matrix A defines a quadratic form q by Eq. (*2*).   Thus there is a one-to-one correspondence between quadratic forms q and symmetric matrices A.   Furthermore, a quadratic form q is diagonalized if and only if the corresponding symmetric matrix A is diagonal.

EXAMPLE 12.2

(a) The quadratic form

$$q(x, y, z) = x^2 - 6xy + 8y^2 - 4xz + 5yz + 7z^2$$

may be expressed in the matrix form

$$q(x, y, z) = (x, y, z) \begin{bmatrix} 1 & -3 & -2 \\ -3 & 8 & \frac{5}{2} \\ -2 & \frac{5}{2} & 7 \end{bmatrix} \begin{bmatrix} x \\ y \\ z \end{bmatrix}$$

where the defining matrix is symmetric. The quadratic form may also be expressed in the matrix form

$$q(x, y, z) = (x, y, z) \begin{bmatrix} 1 & -6 & -4 \\ 0 & 8 & 5 \\ 0 & 0 & 7 \end{bmatrix} \begin{bmatrix} x \\ y \\ z \end{bmatrix}$$

where the defining matrix is upper triangular.

(b) The symmetric matrix $\begin{bmatrix} 2 & 3 \\ 3 & 5 \end{bmatrix}$ determines the quadratic form

$$q(x, y) = (x, y) \begin{bmatrix} 2 & 3 \\ 3 & 5 \end{bmatrix} \begin{bmatrix} x \\ y \end{bmatrix} = 2x^2 + 6xy + 5y^2$$

Remark: For theoretical reasons we will always assume that a quadratic form q is represented by a symmetric matrix A. Since A is obtained from q by division by 2, we must also assume $1 + 1 \neq 0$ in our field K. This is always true when K is the real field $\mathbf{R}$ or the complex field $\mathbf{C}$.

12.4 CHANGE OF VARIABLES, CHANGE-OF-VARIABLE MATRIX

Suppose the list $x_1, x_2, \ldots, x_n$ of variables is to be changed to the list $y_1, y_2, \ldots, y_n$ by means of an invertible linear substitution of the form

$$x_i = p_{i1}y_1 + p_{i2}y_2 + \cdots + p_{in}y_n, \qquad i = 1, 2, \ldots, n$$

(Here *invertible* means that one can solve for each of the y uniquely in terms of the x.) Such a linear substitution can be expressed in the matrix form

$$X = PY$$

where

$$X = (x_1, x_2, \ldots, x_n)^T, \qquad Y = (y_1, y_2, \ldots, y_n)^T, \qquad P = [p_{ij}]$$

The matrix P is called the *change-of-variable matrix*. It is nonsingular since the linear substitution is invertible.

EXAMPLE 12.3 Consider a change of variables, say from variables x and y to variables s and t, by means of the linear substitution

$$\begin{aligned} x &= 2s - t \\ y &= s + t \end{aligned} \quad \text{or} \quad X = PY \quad \text{where} \quad X = \begin{bmatrix} x \\ y \end{bmatrix}, \quad Y = \begin{bmatrix} s \\ t \end{bmatrix}, \quad P = \begin{bmatrix} 2 & -1 \\ 1 & 1 \end{bmatrix}$$

Furthermore, consider the Cartesian plane $\mathbf{R}^2$ with the usual x and y axes. Then the above linear substitution determines a new coordinate system of the plane $\mathbf{R}^2$ with s and t axes as pictured in

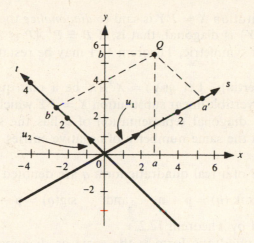

Fig. 12-1

Fig. 12-1.   That is, if we let u_1 and u_2 denote the columns of the change-of-variable matrix P, then

(a)   The s axis is in the direction of $u_1 = (2, 1)$, and its unit length is the length of u_1.

(b)   The t axis is in the direction of $u_2 = (-1, 1)$, and its unit length is the length of u_2.

Accordingly, if $[a, b]^T$ are the coordinates of a point Q relative to the x and y axes, then $[a', b']^T = P^{-1}[a, b]^T$ are the coordinates of Q relative to the s and t axes.   Furthermore suppose we are given an equation in the variables x and y, say

$$x^2 + 5xy = 25 \qquad (1)$$

Using the above substitution, we obtain the equation

$$(2s - t)^2 + 5(2s - t)(s + t) = 25 \qquad \text{or} \qquad 14s^2 + st - 4t^2 = 25 \qquad (2)$$

in the variables s and t.   The equations are related geometrically.   Specifically, plotting Eq. (1) in Fig. 12-1 using the x and y axes will yield the exact same set of points as plotting Eq. (2) in Fig. 12-1 using the s and t axes.

Remark: Any given nonsingular matrix P defines an invertible change of variables by the matrix equation $X = PY$.   [Here $X = (x_i)$ and $Y = (y_i)$ are lists of variables.]   Furthermore,

$$Y = P^{-1}X$$

yields the formula of the y in terms of the x.

12.5   CHANGE OF VARIABLES AND DIAGONALIZING QUADRATIC FORMS

Consider a quadratic form q in variables $x_1, x_2, \ldots, x_n$, say $q(X) = X^T A X$ (where A is a symmetric matrix).   Suppose a change of variables is made in q using the linear substitution $X = PY$.   Substituting $X = PY$ in q yields the quadratic form

$$q(Y) = (PY)^T A(PY) = Y^T (P^T A P) Y$$

Thus $B = P^T A P$ is the matrix representation of q in the new variables $y_1, y_2, \ldots, y_n$.   Observe that the new matrix B is congruent to the original matrix A representing q.

The above linear substitution $X = PY$ is said to *diagonalize* the quadratic form $q(X)$ if the derived quadratic form $q(Y)$ is diagonal, that is, if $B = P^T AP$ is a diagonal matrix. Since B is congruent to A and A is symmetric, Theorem 12.1 may be restated as follows.

Theorem 12.2   (Law of Inertia):   Let $q(X) = X^T AX$ be a real quadratic form. Then there exists an invertible linear substitution $X = PY$ which diagonalizes q. Moreover, every such diagonal representation of q has the same number **p** of positive entries and the same number **n** of negative entries.

The *rank* and *signature* of a real quadratic form q are denoted and defined by

$$\text{rank}\,(q) = \mathbf{p} + \mathbf{n} \qquad \text{and} \qquad \text{sig}(q) = \mathbf{p} - \mathbf{n}$$

These are uniquely defined by Theorem 12.2.

Since diagonalizing a quadratic form is the same as diagonalizing under congruence a symmetric matrix, Algorithm 12.2 may be used here.

EXAMPLE 12.4   Consider the quadratic form

$$q(x, y, z) = x^2 + 4xy + 5y^2 - 6xz - 8yz + 8z^2 \tag{1}$$

The (symmetric) matrix A which represents q is

$$A = \begin{bmatrix} 1 & 2 & -3 \\ 2 & 5 & -4 \\ -3 & -4 & 8 \end{bmatrix}$$

From Example 12.1 the following nonsingular matrix P diagonalizes the matrix A under congruence:

$$P = \begin{bmatrix} 1 & -2 & 7 \\ 0 & 1 & -2 \\ 0 & 0 & 1 \end{bmatrix} \qquad \text{and} \qquad D = P^T AP = \begin{bmatrix} 1 & 0 & 0 \\ 0 & 1 & 0 \\ 0 & 0 & -5 \end{bmatrix}$$

Accordingly q may be diagonalized by the following linear substitution:

$$x = r - 2s + 7t$$
$$y = s - 2t$$
$$z = t$$

Specifically, substituting for x, y, and z in Eq. (*1*) yields the quadratic form

$$q(r, s, t) = r^2 + s^2 - 5t^2 \tag{2}$$

Here $\mathbf{p} = 2$ and $\mathbf{n} = 1$. Hence

$$\text{rank}\,(q) = 3 \qquad \text{and} \qquad \text{sig}\,(q) = 1$$

Remark: There is a geometrical interpretation of the law of inertia (Theorem 12.2) which we give here using the quadratic form q in Example 12.4. Consider the following surface S in $\mathbf{R}^3$:

$$q(x, y, z) = x^2 + 4xy + 5y^2 - 6xz - 8yz + 8z^2 = 25$$

Under the change of variables,

$$x = r - 2s + 7t$$
$$y = s - 2t$$
$$z = t$$

or, equivalently, relative to a new coordinate system with r, s, and t axes, the equation of S becomes

$$q(r, s, t) = r^2 + s^2 - 5t^2 = 25$$

Accordingly, S is a hyperboloid of one sheet, since there are two positive and one negative entries on the diagonal. Furthermore, S will always be a hyperboloid of one sheet regardless of the coordinate system. Thus any diagonal representation of the quadratic form $q(x, y, z)$ will contain two positive and one negative entries on the diagonal.

12.6 ALTERNATE DIAGONALIZATION ALGORITHM

First we recall an important theorem from Chapter 11.

Theorem 11.14: Let A be a real symmetric matrix. Then there exists an orthogonal matrix P such that $D = P^{-1}AP$ is diagonal.

The matrix P is obtained by normalizing the (orthogonal) eigenvectors of A, and the diagonal entries of D are the corresponding eigenvalues.

Now if P is an orthogonal matrix, then $P^T = P^{-1}$. Accordingly,

$$D = P^{-1}AP = P^TAP$$

This means that the diagonal matrix D is also congruent to A. Consequently Algorithm 11.6 for the orthogonal diagonalization of a real symmetric matrix A can also be used to diagonalize a quadratic form q under an orthogonal change of coordinates. For completeness, we restate the algorithm in terms of quadratic forms.

Orthogonal Diagonalization Algorithm 12.6: Diagonalizes an inputted quadratic form $q(X)$.

Step 1. Find the symmetric matrix A representing q and its characteristic polynomial $\Delta(t)$.

Step 2. Find the eigenvalues of A, which are the roots of $\Delta(t)$.

Step 3. For each eigenvalue λ of A in Step 2, find an orthogonal basis of its eigenspace E_λ.

Step 4. Normalize all eigenvectors in Step 3, which then form an orthonormal basis for $\mathbf{R}^n$.

Step 5. Let P be the matrix whose columns are the normalized eigenvectors in Step 4.

Step 6. Set $X = PY$ to obtain the orthogonal change of variables.

Step 7. Set $q(Y) = \lambda_1 y_1^2 + \lambda_2 y_2^2 + \lambda_2 y_2^2 + \cdots + \lambda_n \lambda_n^2$, where the eigenvalues correspond to the eigenvector columns

EXAMPLE 12.5 Apply Algorithm 12.6 to the quadratic form $q(x, y) = 3x^2 - 4xy + 6y^2$.

Step 1. Its corresponding symmetric matrix A and characteristic polynomial $\Delta(t)$ are

$$A = \begin{bmatrix} 3 & -2 \\ -2 & 6 \end{bmatrix} \quad \text{and} \quad \Delta(t) = t^2 - 9t + 14 = (t - 2)(t - 7)$$

Step 2. Set $\Delta(t) = (t - 2)(t - 7) = 0$. The roots $\lambda_1 = 2$ and $\lambda_2 = 7$ are the eigenvalues of A.

Step 3.   (i)   We find an eigenvector of A belonging to the eigenvalue $\lambda_1 = 2$.   Subtract $\lambda_1 = 2$ down the diagonal of A to obtain the matrix

$$M = \begin{bmatrix} 1 & -2 \\ -2 & 4 \end{bmatrix} \quad \text{or the system} \quad \begin{matrix} x - 2y = 0 \\ -2x + 4y = 0 \end{matrix} \quad \text{or} \quad x - 2y = 0$$

A nonzero solution is $u_1 = (2, 1)$.

     (ii)   We find an eigenvector of A belonging to the eigenvalue $\lambda_2 = 7$.   Subtract $\lambda_2 = 7$ down the diagonal of A to obtain the matrix

$$M = \begin{bmatrix} -4 & -2 \\ -2 & -1 \end{bmatrix} \quad \text{or the system} \quad \begin{matrix} -4x - 2y = 0 \\ -2x - y = 0 \end{matrix} \quad \text{or} \quad 2x + y = 0$$

A nonzero solution is $u_1 = (1, -2)$.

(As expected from Theorem 11.13, u_1 and u_2 are orthogonal.)

Step 4.   Normalize u_1 and u_2 to obtain the orthonormal vectors

$$\hat{u}_1 = (2/\sqrt{5}, 1/\sqrt{5}) \quad \text{and} \quad \hat{u}_2 = (1/\sqrt{5}, -2/\sqrt{5})$$

Step 5.   Let P be the matrix whose columns are normalized vectors u_1 and u_2, that is

$$P = \begin{bmatrix} 2/\sqrt{5} & 1/\sqrt{5} \\ 1/\sqrt{5} & -2/\sqrt{5} \end{bmatrix} \quad \text{and thus} \quad D = P^T A P = \begin{bmatrix} 2 & 0 \\ 0 & 7 \end{bmatrix}$$

Step 6.   Let $X = PY$, where $X = (x, y)^T$ and $Y = (s, t)^T$:

$$x = \frac{2s}{\sqrt{5}} + \frac{t}{\sqrt{5}}, \quad y = \frac{s}{\sqrt{5}} - \frac{2t}{\sqrt{5}}$$

Step 7.   Then $q(s, t) = 2s^2 + 7t^2$.

12.7   POSITIVE DEFINITE SYMMETRIC MATRICES AND QUADRATIC FORMS

A real symmetric matrix A is said to be *positive definite* if

$$X^T A X > 0$$

for every nonzero (column) vector X in $\mathbf{R}^n$.   Analogously a real quadratic form q is said to be *positive definite* if

$$q(v) > 0$$

for every nonzero vector v in $\mathbf{R}^n$.

The following theorem gives alternate characterizations for a matrix to be positive definite.

Theorem 12.3:   Let A be a real n-square matrix.   Then the following are equivalent.

     (i) A is positive definite, i.e., A is symmetric and $X^T A X > 0$ for $X \neq 0$.

     (ii) $A = P^T P$ for a nonsingular matrix P.

     (iii) $A = B^2$ for a nonsingular symmetric matrix B.

Positive definiteness may also be characterized as follows.

Theorem 12.4: A real symmetric matrix A (or its quadratic form q) is positive definite if and only if any diagonal representation has only positive diagonal entries.

According to Theorem 12.4, a symmetric matrix A and its corresponding quadratic form q are positive definite if all eigenvalues are positive.

EXAMPLE 12.6 Consider the quadratic form $q(x, y) = 3x^2 - 4xy + 6y^2$ in Example 12.5. Its corresponding symmetric matrix is

$$A = \begin{bmatrix} 3 & -2 \\ -2 & 6 \end{bmatrix}$$

The eigenvalues are $\lambda_1 = 2$ and $\lambda_2 = 7$, and they are both positive. Thus q and A are positive definite. Using the diagonal factorization

$$A = PDP^T = \begin{bmatrix} 2/\sqrt{5} & 1/\sqrt{5} \\ 1/\sqrt{5} & -2/\sqrt{5} \end{bmatrix} \begin{bmatrix} 2 & 0 \\ 0 & 7 \end{bmatrix} \begin{bmatrix} 2/\sqrt{5} & 1/\sqrt{5} \\ 1/\sqrt{5} & -2\sqrt{5} \end{bmatrix}$$

we can find the symmetric matrix B such that $B^2 = A$. Specifically,

$$B = P\sqrt{D}P^T = \begin{bmatrix} 2/\sqrt{5} & 1/\sqrt{5} \\ 1/\sqrt{5} & -2/\sqrt{5} \end{bmatrix} \begin{bmatrix} \sqrt{2} & 0 \\ 0 & \sqrt{7} \end{bmatrix} \begin{bmatrix} 2/\sqrt{5} & 1/\sqrt{5} \\ 1/\sqrt{5} & -2\sqrt{5} \end{bmatrix}$$

$$= \frac{1}{5} \begin{bmatrix} 4\sqrt{2} + \sqrt{7} & 2\sqrt{2} - 2\sqrt{7} \\ 2\sqrt{2} - 2\sqrt{7} & \sqrt{2} + 4\sqrt{7} \end{bmatrix}$$

12.8 ORTHOGONAL MATRICES (REVISITED)

Suppose A is a (real) orthogonal matrix, that is, suppose

$$A^T = A^{-1} \quad \text{or} \quad AA^T = A^TA = I$$

Recall (see Theorem 3.3) that A is orthogonal if and only if its rows or columns form an orthonormal set of vectors.

Since A is a square matrix, it may also be viewed as a linear operator on $\mathbf{R}^n$. Note that for any (column) vectors u and v in $\mathbf{R}^n$, the usual inner product and norm (length) are defined by

$$\langle u, v \rangle = u^T v \quad \text{and} \quad \|u\| = \sqrt{\langle u, u \rangle} = \sqrt{u^T u}$$

The following theorem (proved in Problem 12.26) gives alternate characterizations for a matrix to be orthogonal.

Theorem 12.5: Let A be an n-square matrix. Then the following are equivalent:

  (i) A is orthogonal, i.e., $A^T = A^{-1}$.

  (ii) A preserves inner products, i.e., for any vectors u, v in $\mathbf{R}^n$, we have

$$\langle Au, Av \rangle = \langle u, v \rangle$$

  (iii) A preserves norms, i.e., for any vector u in $\mathbf{R}^n$, we have

$$\|Au\| = \|u\|$$

or, equivalently, $\langle Au, Au \rangle = \langle u, u \rangle$.

EXAMPLE 12.7   Let the matrix A be the linear operator on $\mathbf{R}^3$ which rotates each vector v about the z axis by a fixed angle θ, as shown in Fig. 12-2.   Then

$$A(x, y, z) = (x \cos \theta - y \sin \theta, \, x \sin \theta + y \cos \theta, \, z)$$

or, equivalently,

$$A = \begin{bmatrix} \cos \theta & -\sin \theta & \\ \sin \theta & \cos \theta & \\ & & 1 \end{bmatrix}$$

Note that lengths (distances from the origin) are preserved under A.   Thus A is an orthogonal matrix (operator).

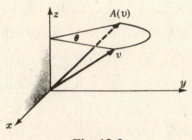

Fig. 12-2

An orthogonal matrix A need not be symmetric, and so it may not be similar to a diagonal matrix.   However, A does have a simple canonical representation, similar to the matrix in Example 12.7, which is described in the following theorem.

Theorem 12.6:   Let A be an orthogonal matrix.   Then A is orthogonally similar to a matrix B (that is, there is an orthogonal matrix P such that $B = P^{-1}AP$), where

$$B = \begin{bmatrix} I_r & & & & & \\ & -I_s & & & & \\ & & \cos \theta_1 & -\sin \theta_1 & & \\ & & \sin \theta_1 & \cos \theta_1 & & \\ & & & & \ddots & \\ & & & & & \cos \theta_m & -\sin \theta_m \\ & & & & & \sin \theta_m & \cos \theta_m \end{bmatrix}$$

The reader may recognize that each of the above 2×2 diagonal blocks represents a rotation in the corresponding two-dimensional subspace, and that each diagonal entry 1 in I_r, and each diagonal entry -1 in $-I_s$ represents, respectively, the identity mapping and a reflection in the corresponding one-dimensional subspace.

The proof of Theorem 12.6 lies beyond the scope of this text.

Solved Problems

CONGRUENT REAL SYMMETRIC MATRICES

12.1. Let $A = \begin{bmatrix} 1 & -3 & 2 \\ -3 & 7 & -5 \\ 2 & -5 & 8 \end{bmatrix}$. Find a nonsingular matrix P such that $D = P^T A P$ is

diagonal, and find sig (A), the signature of A.

First form the block matrix $M = [A, I]$:

$$M = [A, I] = \begin{bmatrix} 1 & -3 & 2 & \vdots & 1 & 0 & 0 \\ -3 & 7 & -5 & \vdots & 0 & 1 & 0 \\ 2 & -5 & 8 & \vdots & 0 & 0 & 1 \end{bmatrix}$$

Using $a_{11} = 1$ as a pivot, apply the row operations "Add $3R_1$ to R_2" and "Add $-2R_1$ to R_3" to M and then the corresponding column operations "Add $3C_1$ to C_2" and "Add $-2C_1$ to C_3" to A to obtain

$$\begin{bmatrix} 1 & -3 & 2 & \vdots & 1 & 0 & 0 \\ 0 & -2 & 1 & \vdots & 3 & 1 & 0 \\ 0 & 1 & 4 & \vdots & -2 & 0 & 1 \end{bmatrix} \quad \text{and then} \quad \begin{bmatrix} 1 & 0 & 0 & \vdots & 1 & 0 & 0 \\ 0 & -2 & 1 & \vdots & 3 & 1 & 0 \\ 0 & 1 & 4 & \vdots & -2 & 0 & 1 \end{bmatrix}$$

Next apply the row operation "Add R_2 to $2R_3$" and then the corresponding column operation "Add C_2 to $2C_3$" to obtain

$$\begin{bmatrix} 1 & 0 & 0 & \vdots & 1 & 0 & 0 \\ 0 & -2 & 1 & \vdots & 3 & 1 & 0 \\ 0 & 0 & 9 & \vdots & -1 & 1 & 2 \end{bmatrix} \quad \text{and then} \quad \begin{bmatrix} 1 & 0 & 0 & \vdots & 1 & 0 & 0 \\ 0 & -2 & 0 & \vdots & 3 & 1 & 0 \\ 0 & 0 & 18 & \vdots & -1 & 1 & 2 \end{bmatrix}$$

Now A has been diagonalized and the transpose of P is in the right half of M. Thus set

$$P = \begin{bmatrix} 1 & 3 & -1 \\ 0 & 1 & 1 \\ 0 & 0 & 2 \end{bmatrix} \quad \text{and then} \quad D = P^T A P = \begin{bmatrix} 1 & 0 & 0 \\ 0 & -2 & 0 \\ 0 & 0 & 18 \end{bmatrix}$$

Note that D has $\mathbf{p} = 2$ positive and $\mathbf{n} = 1$ negative diagonal elements. Thus the signature of A is sig $(A) = \mathbf{p} - \mathbf{n} = 2 - 1 = 1$.

12.2. Let $A = \begin{bmatrix} 0 & 1 & 1 \\ 1 & -2 & 2 \\ 1 & 2 & -1 \end{bmatrix}$. Find a nonsingular matrix P such that $D = P^T A P$ is diagonal,

and find the signature of A.

First form the block matrix $M = [A, I]$:

$$M = [A, I] = \begin{bmatrix} 0 & 1 & 1 & \vdots & 1 & 0 & 0 \\ 1 & -2 & 2 & \vdots & 0 & 1 & 0 \\ 1 & 2 & -1 & \vdots & 0 & 0 & 1 \end{bmatrix}$$

Here $a_{11} = 0$. [This is case (ii) in Algorithm 12.2.] Thus we first bring the nonzero diagonal entry -1 into the first diagonal position. Specifically, apply the row operation "Interchange

R_1 and R_3" and the corresponding column operation "Interchange C_1 and C_3" to obtain

$$\begin{bmatrix} 1 & 2 & -1 & | & 0 & 0 & 1 \\ 1 & -2 & 2 & | & 0 & 1 & 0 \\ 0 & 1 & 1 & | & 1 & 0 & 0 \end{bmatrix} \quad \text{and then} \quad \begin{bmatrix} -1 & 2 & 1 & | & 0 & 0 & 1 \\ 2 & -2 & 1 & | & 0 & 1 & 0 \\ 1 & 1 & 0 & | & 1 & 0 & 0 \end{bmatrix}$$

Now using $a_{11} = -1$ as a pivot, apply the row operations "Add $2R_1$ to R_2" and "Add R_1 to R_3" and then the corresponding column operations "Add $2C_1$ to C_2" and "Add C_1 to C_3" to obtain

$$\begin{bmatrix} -1 & 2 & 1 & | & 0 & 0 & 1 \\ 0 & 2 & 3 & | & 0 & 1 & 2 \\ 0 & 3 & 1 & | & 1 & 0 & 1 \end{bmatrix} \quad \text{and then} \quad \begin{bmatrix} -1 & 0 & 0 & | & 0 & 0 & 1 \\ 0 & 2 & 3 & | & 0 & 1 & 2 \\ 0 & 3 & 1 & | & 1 & 0 & 1 \end{bmatrix}$$

Next apply the row operation "Add $-3R_2$ to $2R_3$" and then the corresponding column operation "Add $-3C_2$ to $2C_3$" to obtain

$$\begin{bmatrix} -1 & 0 & 0 & | & 0 & 0 & 1 \\ 0 & 2 & 3 & | & 0 & 1 & 2 \\ 0 & 0 & -7 & | & 2 & -3 & -4 \end{bmatrix} \quad \text{and then} \quad \begin{bmatrix} -1 & 0 & 0 & | & 0 & 0 & 1 \\ 0 & 2 & 0 & | & 0 & 1 & 2 \\ 0 & 0 & -14 & | & 2 & -3 & -4 \end{bmatrix}$$

Now A has been diagonalized, and the transpose of P is in the right half of M. Thus set

$$P = \begin{bmatrix} 0 & 0 & 2 \\ 0 & 1 & -3 \\ 1 & 2 & -4 \end{bmatrix} \quad \text{and then} \quad D = P^T A P = \begin{bmatrix} -1 & 0 & 0 \\ 0 & 2 & 0 \\ 0 & 0 & -14 \end{bmatrix}$$

Note that D has $\mathbf{p} = 1$ positive and $\mathbf{n} = 2$ negative diagonal elements. Thus the signature of A is $\text{sig}(A) = \mathbf{p} - \mathbf{n} = 1 - 2 = -1$.

12.3. Let $A = \begin{bmatrix} 0 & 1 & 1 \\ 1 & 0 & 1 \\ 1 & 1 & 0 \end{bmatrix}$. Find a nonsingular matrix P such that $D = P^T A P$ is diagonal, and find the signature of A.

First form the block matrix $M = [A, I]$:

$$M = [A, I] = \begin{bmatrix} 0 & 1 & 1 & | & 1 & 0 & 0 \\ 1 & 0 & 1 & | & 0 & 1 & 0 \\ 1 & 1 & 0 & | & 0 & 0 & 1 \end{bmatrix}$$

Here all diagonal elements are zero. [This is case (iii) in Algorithm 12.2.] Since $a_{12} = a_{21} = 1$, bring $2a_{12} = 2$ into the first diagonal position. Specifically, apply the row operation "Add R_2 to R_1" and the corresponding column operation "Add C_2 to C_1" to obtain

$$\begin{bmatrix} 1 & 1 & 2 & | & 1 & 1 & 0 \\ 1 & 0 & 1 & | & 0 & 1 & 0 \\ 1 & 1 & 0 & | & 0 & 0 & 1 \end{bmatrix} \quad \text{and then} \quad \begin{bmatrix} 2 & 1 & 2 & | & 1 & 1 & 0 \\ 1 & 0 & 1 & | & 0 & 1 & 0 \\ 2 & 1 & 0 & | & 0 & 0 & 1 \end{bmatrix}$$

Now using $a_{11} = 2$ as a pivot, apply the row operations "Add R_1 to $-2R_2$" and "Add $-R_1$ to R_3" and then the corresponding column operations "Add C_1 to $-2C_2$" and "Add $-C_1$ to C_3"

to obtain

$$\begin{bmatrix} 2 & 1 & 2 & | & 1 & 1 & 0 \\ 0 & 1 & 0 & | & 1 & -1 & 0 \\ 0 & 0 & -2 & | & -1 & -1 & 1 \end{bmatrix} \quad \text{and then} \quad \begin{bmatrix} 2 & 0 & 0 & | & 1 & 1 & 0 \\ 0 & -2 & 0 & | & 1 & -1 & 0 \\ 0 & 0 & -2 & | & -1 & -1 & 1 \end{bmatrix}$$

Now A has been diagonalized and the transpose of P is in the right half of M. Thus set

$$P = \begin{bmatrix} 1 & 1 & -1 \\ 1 & -1 & -1 \\ 0 & 0 & 1 \end{bmatrix} \quad \text{and then} \quad D = P^T A P = \begin{bmatrix} 2 & 0 & 0 \\ 0 & -2 & 0 \\ 0 & 0 & -2 \end{bmatrix}$$

The signature of A is sig $(A) = \mathbf{p} - \mathbf{n} = 1 - 2 = -1$.

QUADRATIC FORMS

12.4. Find the quadratic form $q(X)$ which corresponds to each symmetric matrix:

$$(a)\ A = \begin{bmatrix} 5 & -3 \\ -3 & 8 \end{bmatrix}; \quad (b)\ B = \begin{bmatrix} 4 & -5 & 7 \\ -5 & -6 & 8 \\ 7 & 8 & -9 \end{bmatrix}; \quad (c)\ C = \begin{bmatrix} 2 & 4 & -1 & 5 \\ 4 & -7 & -6 & 8 \\ -1 & -6 & 3 & 9 \\ 5 & 8 & 9 & 1 \end{bmatrix}.$$

The quadratic form $q(X)$ which corresponds to a symmetric matrix M is defined by $q(X) = X^T M X$, where $X = (x_i)$ is the column vector of unknowns.

(a) Compute as follows:

$$q(x, y) = X^T A X = [x, y]\begin{bmatrix} 5 & -3 \\ -3 & 8 \end{bmatrix}\begin{bmatrix} x \\ y \end{bmatrix} = [5x - 3y, -3x + 8y]\begin{bmatrix} x \\ y \end{bmatrix}$$

$$= 5x^2 - 3xy - 3xy + 8y^2 = 5x^2 - 6xy + 8y^2$$

As expected, the coefficients 5 and 8 of the square terms x^2 and y^2 are the diagonal elements of A, and the coefficient -6 of the cross product term xy is the sum of the nondiagonal elements -3 and -3 of A (or, twice the nondiagonal element -3 since A is symmetric).

(b) Since B is a 3-square matrix, there are three unknowns, say x, y, z or x_1, x_2, x_3. Then

$$q(x, y, z) = 4x^2 - 10xy - 6y^2 + 14xz + 16yz - 9z^2$$

or $$q(x_1, x_2, x_3) = 4x_1^2 - 10x_1 x_2 - 6x_2^2 + 14x_1 x_3 + 16x_2 x_3 - 9x_3^2$$

Here we use the fact that the coefficients of the square terms x_1^2, x_2^2, x_3^2 (or x^2, y^2, z^2) are the respective diagonal elements $4, -6, -9$ of B, and the coefficient of the cross product term $x_i x_j$ is the sum of the nondiagonal elements b_{ij} and b_{ji} (or, twice b_{ij} since $b_{ij} = b_{ji}$).

(c) Since C is a 4-square matrix, there are four unknowns. Hence

$$q(x_1, x_2, x_3, x_4) = 2x_1^2 - 7x_2^2 + 3x_3^2 + x_4^2 + 8x_1 x_2 - 2x_1 x_3 + 10x_1 x_4 - 12x_2 x_3 + 16x_2 x_4 + 18x_3 x_4$$

12.5. Find the symmetric matrix A which corresponds to each quadratic form:

(a) $q(x, y, z) = 3x^2 + 4xy - y^2 + 8xz - 6yz + z^2$; (b) $q'(x, y, z) = 2x^2 - 5y^2 - 7z^2$

The symmetric matrix $A = [a_{ij}]$, which represents $q(x_1, \ldots, x_n)$, has the diagonal entry a_{ii} equal to the coefficient of the square term x_i^2 and the nondiagonal entries a_{ij} and a_{ji}, each equal to half of the coefficient of the cross product term $x_i x_j$.   Thus

$$\text{(a) } A = \begin{bmatrix} 3 & 2 & 4 \\ 2 & -1 & -3 \\ 4 & -3 & 1 \end{bmatrix}; \text{ (b) } A' = \begin{bmatrix} 2 & 0 & 0 \\ 0 & -5 & 0 \\ 0 & 0 & -7 \end{bmatrix}.$$

The second matrix A' is diagonal since the quadratic form q' is diagonal, that is, q' has no cross product terms.

12.6. Find the symmetric matrix B which corresponds to each quadratic form:

$$\text{(a) } q(x, y) = 4x^2 + 5xy - 7y^2; \text{ (b) } q(x, y, z) = 4xy + 5y^2$$

(a)   Here $B = \begin{bmatrix} 4 & \frac{5}{2} \\ \frac{5}{2} & -7 \end{bmatrix}$.   (Division by 2 may introduce fractions even though the coefficients in q are integers.)

(b)   Even though only x and y appear in the polynomial, the expression $q(x, y, z)$ indicates that there are three variables.   In other words,

$$q(x, y, z) = 0x^2 + 4xy + 5y^2 + 0xz + 0yz + 0z^2 \quad \text{and so} \quad B = \begin{bmatrix} 0 & 2 & 0 \\ 2 & 5 & 0 \\ 0 & 0 & 0 \end{bmatrix}$$

12.7. Consider the quadratic form $q(x, y) = 3x^2 + 2xy - y^2$ and the linear substitution

$$x = s - 3t, \qquad y = 2s + t$$

(a)   Rewrite $q(x, y)$ in matrix notation, and find the matrix A representing the quadratic form.

(b)   Rewrite the linear substitution using matrix notation, and find the matrix P corresponding to the substitution.

(c)   Find $q(s, t)$ using direct substitution.

(d)   Find $q(s, t)$ using matrix notation.

(a)   Here $q(x, y) = (x, y) \begin{bmatrix} 3 & 1 \\ 1 & -1 \end{bmatrix} \begin{bmatrix} x \\ y \end{bmatrix}$.   Hence $A = \begin{bmatrix} 3 & 1 \\ 1 & -1 \end{bmatrix}$ and $q(X) = X^T A X$ where $X = (x, y)^T$.

(b)   We have $\begin{bmatrix} x \\ y \end{bmatrix} = \begin{bmatrix} 1 & -3 \\ 2 & 1 \end{bmatrix} \begin{bmatrix} s \\ t \end{bmatrix}$.   Thus $P = \begin{bmatrix} 1 & -3 \\ 2 & 1 \end{bmatrix}$ and $X = PY$, where $X = (x, y)^T$ and $Y = (s, t)^T$.

(c)   Substitute for x and y in q to obtain

$$q(s, t) = 3(s - 3t)^2 + 2(s - 3t)(2s + t) - (2s + t)^2$$
$$= 3(s^2 - 6st + 9t^2) + 2(2s^2 - 5st - 3t^2) - (s^2 + 4st + t^2) = 3s^2 - 32st + 20t^2$$

(d)   Here $q(X) = X^T A X$ and $X = PY$.   Thus $X^T = Y^T P^T$.   Therefore

$$q(s, t) = q(Y) = Y^T P^T A P Y = (s, t) \begin{bmatrix} 1 & 2 \\ -3 & 1 \end{bmatrix} \begin{bmatrix} 3 & 1 \\ 1 & -1 \end{bmatrix} \begin{bmatrix} 1 & -3 \\ 2 & 1 \end{bmatrix} \begin{bmatrix} s \\ t \end{bmatrix}$$

$$= (s, t) \begin{bmatrix} 3 & -16 \\ -16 & 20 \end{bmatrix} \begin{bmatrix} s \\ t \end{bmatrix} = 3s^2 - 32st + 20t^2$$

[As expected, the results in parts (c) and (d) are equal.]

12.8. Let L be a linear substitution $X = PY$, where P is a square matrix and X and Y are columns of variables.

(a)   When is L nonsingular? orthogonal?

(b)   Describe advantages of an orthogonal substitution over a nonsingular substitution.

(c)   Is the linear substitution in Problem 12.7 nonsingular?   It is orthogonal?

(a) L is said to be nonsingular or orthogonal according to whether the matrix P representing the substitution is nonsingular or orthogonal.

(b)   Recall that the columns of the matrix P representing the linear substitution introduce a new coordinate system.   If P is orthogonal, then the new axes are perpendicular and have the same unit lengths as the original axes.

(c)   The matrix $P = \begin{bmatrix} 1 & -3 \\ 2 & 1 \end{bmatrix}$ is nonsingular, but not orthogonal.   Hence the linear substitution is nonsingular, but not orthogonal.

12.9. Consider the quadratic form

$$q(x, y, z) = x^2 + 4xy + 3y^2 - 8xz - 12yz + 9z^2$$

Find a nonsingular linear substitution expressing the variables x, y, z in terms of the variables r, s, t so that $q(r, s, t)$ is diagonal.   Also find the signature of q.

Form the block matrix $M = [A, I]$, where A is the symmetric matrix that corresponds to the quadratic form, that is,

$$M = [A, I] = \begin{bmatrix} 1 & 2 & -4 & 1 & 0 & 0 \\ 2 & 3 & -6 & 0 & 1 & 0 \\ -4 & -6 & 9 & 0 & 0 & 1 \end{bmatrix}$$

Apply the row operations "Add $-2R_1$ to R_2" and "Add $4R_1$ to R_3" and the corresponding column operations; and then apply the row operation "Add $2R_2$ to R_3" and the corresponding column operation to obtain

$$\begin{bmatrix} 1 & 0 & 0 & 1 & 0 & 0 \\ 0 & -1 & 2 & -2 & 1 & 0 \\ 0 & 2 & -7 & 4 & 0 & 1 \end{bmatrix} \quad \text{and then} \quad \begin{bmatrix} 1 & 0 & 0 & 1 & 0 & 0 \\ 0 & -1 & 0 & -2 & 1 & 0 \\ 0 & 0 & -3 & 0 & 2 & 1 \end{bmatrix}$$

Now A has been diagonalized (under congruence) by the nonsingular matrix P, which is the transpose of the final right half of M.   That is,

$$P = \begin{bmatrix} 1 & -2 & 0 \\ 0 & 1 & 2 \\ 0 & 0 & 1 \end{bmatrix}, \quad \text{corresponding to the substitution} \quad \begin{aligned} x &= r - 2s \\ y &= s + 2t \\ z &= t \end{aligned}$$

The linear substitution will yield the diagonalized quadratic form

$$q(r, s, t) = r^2 - s^2 - 3t^2$$

(which corresponds to the diagonal form of A in the final left half of M).   By inspection, $\text{sig}(q) = 1 - 2 = -1$.

12.10. Diagonalize the following quadratic form q by the method known as *completing the square*:

$$q(x, y) = 2x^2 - 12xy + 5y^2$$

First factor out the coefficient of x^2 from the x^2 term and the xy term to get

$$q(x, y) = 2(x^2 - 6xy) + 5y^2$$

Next complete the square inside the parentheses by adding an appropriate multiple of y^2 and then subtract the corresponding amount outside the parentheses to get

$$q(x, y) = 2(x^2 - 6xy + 9y^2) + 5y^2 - 18y^2 = 2(x - 3y)^2 - 13y^2$$

(The -18 comes from the fact that the $9y^2$ inside the parentheses is multiplied by 2.)   Let $s = x - 3y$, $t = y$.   Then $x = s + 3t$, $y = t$.   This linear substitution yields the quadratic form $q(s, t) = 2s^2 - 13t^2$.

ORTHOGONAL DIAGONALIZATION OF QUADRATIC FORMS

12.11. Let $q(x, y) = 3x^2 - 6xy + 11y^2$.   Find an orthogonal change of coordinates (linear substitution) which diagonalizes q.

Find the symmetric matrix A representing q and its characteristic polynomial $\Delta(t)$.   We have

$$A = \begin{bmatrix} 3 & -3 \\ -3 & 11 \end{bmatrix} \quad \text{and} \quad \Delta(t) = t^2 - \text{tr}(A)t + |A| = t^2 - 14t + 24 = (t - 2)(t - 12)$$

The eigenvalues are $\lambda = 2$ and $\lambda = 12$.   Hence a diagonal form of q is

$$q(s, t) = 2s^2 + 12t^2$$

(where we use s and t as new variables).   The corresponding orthogonal change of coordinates is obtained by finding an orthogonal set of eigenvectors of A.

Subtract $\lambda = 2$ down the diagonal of A to obtain the matrix

$$M = \begin{bmatrix} 1 & -3 \\ -3 & 9 \end{bmatrix} \quad \text{corresponding to} \quad \begin{matrix} x - 3y = 0 \\ -3x + 9y = 0 \end{matrix} \quad \text{or} \quad x - 3y = 0$$

A nonzero solution is $u_1 = (3, 1)$.   Next subtract $\lambda = 12$ down the diagonal of A to obtain the homogeneous system

$$-9x - 3y = 0, \qquad -3x - y = 0$$

A nonzero solution is $u_2 = (-1, 3)$.   Normalize u_1 and u_2 to obtain the orthonormal basis

$$\hat{u}_1 = (3/\sqrt{10}, 1/\sqrt{10}), \qquad \hat{u}_2 = (-1/\sqrt{10}, 3/\sqrt{10})$$

Let P be the matrix whose columns are $\hat{u}_1$ and $\hat{u}_2$.   Then

$$P = \begin{bmatrix} 3/\sqrt{10} & -1/\sqrt{10} \\ 1/\sqrt{10} & 3/\sqrt{10} \end{bmatrix} \quad \text{and} \quad D = P^{-1}AP = P^TAP = \begin{bmatrix} 2 & 0 \\ 0 & 12 \end{bmatrix}$$

Thus the required orthogonal change of coordinates is

$$\begin{bmatrix} x \\ y \end{bmatrix} = P \begin{bmatrix} s \\ t \end{bmatrix} \quad \text{or} \quad x = \frac{3s - t}{\sqrt{10}}, \qquad y = \frac{s + 3t}{\sqrt{10}}$$

One can also express s and t in terms of x and y by using $P^{-1} = P^T$, that is,

$$s = \frac{3x + y}{\sqrt{10}}, \qquad t = \frac{-x + 3y}{\sqrt{10}}$$

12.12. Let $q(x, y) = 4x^2 + 8xy - 11y^2$. Find an orthogonal change of coordinates (linear substitution) which diagonalizes q. Also, describe the graph of $4x^2 + 8xy - 11y^2 = 25$.

Find the symmetric matrix A representing q and its characteristic polynomial $\Delta(t)$. We have

$$A = \begin{bmatrix} 4 & 4 \\ 4 & -11 \end{bmatrix} \quad \text{and} \quad \Delta(t) = t^2 - \text{tr}(A)t + |A| = t^2 + 7t - 60 = (t - 5)(t + 12)$$

The eigenvalues are $\lambda = 5$ and $\lambda = -12$. Hence a diagonal form of q is

$$q(s, t) = 5s^2 - 12t^2$$

(where we use s and t as new variables). The corresponding orthogonal change of coordinates is obtained by finding an orthogonal set of eigenvectors of A.

Subtract $\lambda = 5$ down the diagonal of A to obtain the homogeneous system

$$-x + 4y = 0, \qquad 4x - 16y = 0$$

A nonzero solution is $u_1 = (4, 1)$. Next subtract $\lambda = -12$ (or, add 12) down the diagonal of A to obtain the homogeneous system

$$16x + 4y = 0, \qquad 4x + y = 0$$

A nonzero solution is $u_2 = (-1, 4)$. Normalize u_1 and u_2 to obtain the orthonormal basis

$$\hat{u}_1 = (4/\sqrt{17}, 1/\sqrt{17}), \qquad \hat{u}_2 = (-1/\sqrt{17}, 4/\sqrt{17})$$

Let P be the matrix whose columns are $\hat{u}_1$ and $\hat{u}_2$. Then

$$P = \begin{bmatrix} 4/\sqrt{17} & -1/\sqrt{17} \\ 1/\sqrt{17} & 4/\sqrt{17} \end{bmatrix} \quad \text{and} \quad D = P^T A P = \begin{bmatrix} 5 & 0 \\ 0 & -12 \end{bmatrix}$$

Thus the required orthogonal change of coordinates is

$$x = \frac{4s - t}{\sqrt{17}}, \qquad t = \frac{s + 4t}{\sqrt{17}}$$

One can also express s and t in terms of x and y by using $P^{-1} = P^T$, that is,

$$s = \frac{4x + y}{\sqrt{17}}, \qquad t = \frac{-x + 4y}{\sqrt{17}}$$

Since $5s^2 - 12t^2 = 25$ is a hyperbola, so is $4x^2 + 8xy - 11y^2 = 25$.

12.13. Let $q(x, y) = 5x^2 - 4xy + 8y^2$. Find an orthogonal change of coordinates (linear substitution) which diagonalizes q. Also describe the graph of $5x^2 - 4xy + 8y^2 = 25$.

Find the symmetric matrix A representing q and its characteristic polynomial $\Delta(t)$. We have

$$A = \begin{bmatrix} 5 & -2 \\ -2 & 8 \end{bmatrix} \quad \text{and} \quad \Delta(t) = t^2 - 13t + 36 = (t - 4)(t - 9)$$

The eigenvalues are $\lambda = 4$ and $\lambda = 9$. Hence a diagonal form of q is

$$q(s, t) = 4s^2 + 9t^2$$

(where we use s and t as new variables). The corresponding orthogonal change of coordinates is obtained by finding an orthogonal set of eigenvectors of A.

Subtract $\lambda = 4$ down the diagonal of A to obtain the homogeneous system

$$x - 2y = 0, \qquad -2x + 4y = 0$$

A nonzero solution is $u_1 = (2, 1)$. Next subtract $\lambda = 9$ down the diagonal of A to obtain the homogeneous system

$$-4x - 2y = 0, \qquad -2x - y = 0$$

A nonzero solution is $u_2 = (-1, 2)$. Normalize u_1 and u_2 to obtain the orthonormal basis

$$\hat{u}_1 = (2/\sqrt{5}, 1/\sqrt{5}), \qquad \hat{u}_2 = (-1/\sqrt{5}, 2/\sqrt{5})$$

The change-of-basis matrix P and the required change of coordinates follow:

$$P = \begin{bmatrix} 2/\sqrt{5} & -1\sqrt{5} \\ 1/\sqrt{5} & 2/\sqrt{5} \end{bmatrix} \quad \text{and} \quad x = \frac{2s - t}{\sqrt{5}}, \quad y = \frac{s + 2t}{\sqrt{5}}$$

One can also express s and t in terms of x and y by using $P^{-1} = P^T$, that is,

$$s = \frac{2x + y}{\sqrt{5}}, \qquad t = \frac{-x + 2y}{\sqrt{5}}$$

Since $4s^2 + 9t^2 = 25$ is an ellipse, so is $5x^2 - 4xy + 8y^2 = 25$.

12.14. Let $q(z, y, z) = 5x^2 + 2xy + 5y^2 + 2xz + 2yz + 5z^2$.

(a) Find the symmetric matrix A which represents q and its characteristic polynomial $\Delta(t)$.

(b) Find the eigenvalues of A or, in other words, the roots of $\Delta(t)$.

(c) Find a maximal set S of nonzero orthogonal eigenvectors of A.

(d) Find an orthogonal linear substitution which expresses the variables x, y, z in terms of the variables r, s, t so that $q(r, s, t)$ is diagonal.

(a) Recall that $A = [a_{ij}]$ is the symmetric matrix where the diagonal entry a_{ii} is the coefficient of the square term x_i^2 and $a_{ij} = a_{ji}$ is one-half the coefficient of the cross product term $x_i x_j$. Thus

$$A = \begin{bmatrix} 5 & 1 & 1 \\ 1 & 5 & 1 \\ 1 & 1 & 5 \end{bmatrix} \quad \text{and} \quad \Delta(t) = t^3 - 15t^2 + 72t - 112$$

(b) If $\Delta(t)$ has a rational root, it must be an integer which divides the constant term 112. Testing $t = 4$, we get

$$\begin{array}{r|rrrr} 4 & 1 - 15 + 72 - 112 \\ & \ \ 4 - 44 + 112 \\ \hline & 1 - 11 + 28 + \ 0 \end{array}$$

Thus $t - 4$ is a factor, and we find

$$\Delta(t) = (t - 4)(t^2 - 11t + 28) = (t - 4)^2(t - 7)$$

Hence the eigenvalues of A are $\lambda = 4$ (with multiplicity 2) and $\lambda = 7$ (with multiplicity 1).

(c) Find an orthogonal basis for each eigenspace. Subtract $\lambda = 4$ down the diagonal of A to obtain the homogeneous system

$$x + y + z = 0, \qquad x + y + z = 0, \qquad x + y + z = 0$$

That is, $x + y + z = 0$. The system has two linearly independent solutions. One such solution is $u_1 = (0, 1, -1)$. We seek a second solution $u_2 = (a, b, c)$, which is also orthogonal to u_1, that is, for which

$$a + b + c = 0 \qquad \text{and also} \qquad b - c = 0$$

For example, $u_2 = (2, -1, -1)$. Thus $u_1 = (0, 1, -1)$ and $u_2 = (2, -1, -1)$ form an orthogonal basis for the eigenspace of $\lambda = 4$.

Subtract $\lambda = 7$ down the diagonal of A to obtain the homogeneous system

$$-2x + y + z = 0, \qquad x - 2y + z = 0, \qquad x + y - 2z = 0$$

The system yields a nonzero solution $u_3 = (1, 1, 1)$. (As expected from Theorem 11.13, the eigenvector u_3 is orthogonal to u_1 and u_2.)

Thus u_1, u_2, u_3 form a maximal set S of nonzero orthogonal eigenvectors of A.

(d) Normalize u_1, u_2, u_3 to obtain the orthonormal basis

$$\hat{u}_1 = (0, 1/\sqrt{2}, -1/\sqrt{2}), \qquad \hat{u}_2 = (2/\sqrt{6}, -1\sqrt{6}, -1/\sqrt{6}), \qquad \hat{u}_3 = (1/\sqrt{3}, 1/\sqrt{3}, 1/\sqrt{3})$$

Let P be the matrix whose columns are $\hat{u}_1, \hat{u}_2, \hat{u}_3$. Then

$$P = \begin{bmatrix} 0 & 2/\sqrt{6} & 1/\sqrt{3} \\ 1/\sqrt{2} & -1/\sqrt{6} & 1/\sqrt{3} \\ -1/\sqrt{2} & -1/\sqrt{6} & 1/\sqrt{3} \end{bmatrix} \qquad \text{and} \qquad D = P^T A P = \begin{bmatrix} 4 & & \\ & 4 & \\ & & 7 \end{bmatrix}$$

Thus the required orthogonal change of coordinates is

$$x = \frac{2s}{\sqrt{6}} + \frac{t}{\sqrt{3}}, \qquad y = \frac{r}{\sqrt{2}} - \frac{s}{\sqrt{6}} + \frac{t}{\sqrt{3}}, \qquad z = -\frac{r}{\sqrt{2}} - \frac{s}{\sqrt{6}} + \frac{t}{\sqrt{3}}$$

Under this change of coordinates, q is transformed into the diagonal form

$$q(r, s, t) = 4r^2 + 4s^2 + 7t^2$$

12.15. Repeat Problem 12.14 for the quadratic form $q(x, y, z) = 8xz + 3y^2 + 6z^2$.

(a) Here

$$A = \begin{bmatrix} 0 & 0 & 4 \\ 0 & 3 & 0 \\ 4 & 0 & 6 \end{bmatrix} \qquad \text{and} \qquad \Delta(t) = t^3 - 9t^2 + 2t + 48$$

(b) If $\Delta(t)$ has a rational root, it must be an integer which divides the constant term 48. Testing $t = 3$, we get

$$\begin{array}{r|rrrr} 3 & 1 & -9 & +2 & +48 \\ & & 3 & -18 & -48 \\ \hline & 1 & -6 & -16 & +0 \end{array}$$

Thus $t - 3$ is a factor, and we find

$$\Delta(t) = (t - 3)(t^2 - 6t - 16) = (t - 3)(t - 8)(t + 2)$$

Hence the eigenvalues of A are $\lambda = 3$, $\lambda = 8$, and $\lambda = -2$.

(c) Find an eigenvector for each eigenvalue. Subtract $\lambda = 3$ down the diagonal of A to obtain the homogeneous system

$$-3x + 4z = 0, \quad 0x + 0y + 0z = 0, \quad 4x + 3z = 0$$

Here y is a free variable, and we get $z = 0$ and $x = 0$. Thus the system yields a nonzero solution $u_1 = (0, 1, 0)$.

Subtract $\lambda = 8$ down the diagonal of A to obtain the homogeneous system

$$-8x + 4z = 0, \quad -5y = 0, \quad 4x - 2z = 0$$

Here z is a free variable, and $y = 0$. Thus the system yields a nonzero solution $u_2 = (1, 0, 2)$.

Subtract $\lambda = -2$ (or, add 2) down the diagonal of A to obtain the homogeneous system

$$2x + 4z = 0, \quad 5y = 0, \quad 4x + 8z = 0$$

Again, z is a free variable, and $y = 0$. Thus the system yields a nonzero solution $u_3 = (-2, 0, 1)$.

(d) Normalize u_1, u_2, u_3 to obtain the orthonormal basis

$$\hat{u}_1 = (0, 1, 0), \quad \hat{u}_2 = (1/\sqrt{5}, 0, 2/\sqrt{5}), \quad \hat{u}_3 = (-2/\sqrt{5}, 0, 1/\sqrt{5})$$

Let P be the matrix whose columns are $\hat{u}_1$, $\hat{u}_2$, $\hat{u}_3$. Then

$$P = \begin{bmatrix} 0 & 1/\sqrt{5} & -2\sqrt{5} \\ 1 & 0 & 0 \\ 0 & 2/\sqrt{5} & 1/\sqrt{5} \end{bmatrix} \quad \text{and} \quad D = P^T A P = \begin{bmatrix} 3 & & \\ & 8 & \\ & & -2 \end{bmatrix}$$

Thus the required orthogonal change of coordinates is

$$x = \frac{s - 2t}{\sqrt{5}}, y = s, z = \frac{2s + t}{\sqrt{5}}$$

Under this change of coordinates, q is transformed into the diagonal form

$$q(r, s, t) = 3r^2 + 8s^2 - 2t^2$$

POSITIVE DEFINITE QUADRATIC FORMS

12.16. Let $q(x, y, z) = x^2 + 2y^2 - 4xz - 4yz + 7z^2$. Is q positive definite?

Diagonalize (under congruence) the symmetric matrix A corresponding to q (by applying the operations "Add $2R_1$ to R_3" and "Add $2C_1$ to C_3", and then "Add R_2 to R_3" and "Add C_2 to C_3"):

$$A = \begin{bmatrix} 1 & 0 & -2 \\ 0 & 2 & -2 \\ -2 & -2 & 7 \end{bmatrix} \sim \begin{bmatrix} 1 & 0 & 0 \\ 0 & 2 & -2 \\ 0 & -2 & 3 \end{bmatrix} \sim \begin{bmatrix} 1 & 0 & 0 \\ 0 & 2 & 0 \\ 0 & 0 & 1 \end{bmatrix}$$

The diagonal representation of q only contains positive entries, 1, 2, 1, on the diagonal. Hence q is positive definite.

12.17. Let $q(x, y, z) = x^2 + y^2 + 2xy + 4yz + 3z^2$. Is q positive definite?

Diagonalize (under congruence) the symmetric matrix A corresponding to q:

$$A = \begin{bmatrix} 1 & 0 & 1 \\ 0 & 1 & 2 \\ 1 & 2 & 3 \end{bmatrix} \sim \begin{bmatrix} 1 & 0 & 0 \\ 0 & 1 & 2 \\ 0 & 2 & 2 \end{bmatrix} \sim \begin{bmatrix} 1 & 0 & 0 \\ 0 & 1 & 0 \\ 0 & 0 & -2 \end{bmatrix}$$

There is a negative entry -2 on the diagonal representation of q. Hence q is not positive definite.

12.18. Show that $q(x, y) = ax^2 + bxy + cy^2$ is positive definite if and only if $a > 0$ and the discriminant $D = b^2 - 4ac < 0$.

Suppose $v = (x, y) \neq 0$.   Then either $x \neq 0$ or $y \neq 0$, say $y \neq 0$.   Let $t = x/y$.   Then

$$q(v) = y^2[a(x/y)^2 + b(x/y) + c] = y^2(at^2 + bt + c)$$

However, $s = at^2 + bt + c$ is positive for every value of t if and only if $s = at^2 + bt + c$ lies above the t axis and if and only if $a > 0$ and $D = b^2 - 4ac < 0$.   Thus q is positive definite if and only if $a > 0$ and $D < 0$.   [*Remark:* $D < 0$ is the same as det $(A) > 0$, where A is the symmetric matrix corresponding to q.]

12.19. Determine whether or not each quadratic form q is positive definite:

(a) $q(x, y) = x^2 - 4xy + 7y^2$; (b) $q(x, y) = x^2 + 8xy + 5y^2$; (c) $q(x, y) = 3x^2 + 2xy + y^2$

(a)   **Method 1:**   Diagonalize by completing the square:

$$q(x, y) = x^2 - 4xy + 4y^2 + 7y^2 - 4y^2 = (x - 2y)^2 + 3y^2 = s^2 + 3t^2$$

where $s = x - 2y$, $t = y$.   Thus q is positive definite.

Method 2:   Compute the discriminant $D = b^2 - 4ac = 16 - 28 = -12$.   Since $a = 1 > 0$ and $D < 0$, q is positive definite.

(b)   Compute $D = b^2 - 4ac = 64 - 20 = 44$.   Since $D > 0$, q is not positive definite.

(c)   Compute $D = b^2 - 4ac = 4 - 12 = -8$.   Since $a = 3 > 0$ and $D < 0$, q is positive definite.

12.20. Let B be any nonsingular matrix, and let $M = B^T B$.   (a) Show that M is symmetric; (b) show that M is positive definite.

(a) $M^T = (B^T B)^T = B^T B^{TT} = B^T B = M$.   Hence M is symmetric.

(b)   Since B is nonsingular, $BX \neq 0$ for any $X \neq 0$ in $\mathbf{R}^n$.   Hence $\langle BX, BX \rangle = (BX)^T(BX)$ is positive.   Thus

$$q(X) = X^T M X = X^T(B^T B)X = (X^T B^T)(BX) = (BX)^T(BX) > 0$$

Thus M is positive definite.

12.21. Show that $q(X) = \|X\|^2$, the square of the norm of a vector X, is a positive definite quadratic form.

For $X = (x_1, x_2, \ldots, x_n)$ we have $q(X) = x_1^2 + x_2^2 + \cdots + x_n^2$.   Now q is a polynomial with each term of degree 2, and q is in diagonal form where all diagonal entries are positive.   Thus q is a positive definite quadratic form.

12.22. Prove that the following two definitions of a positive definite quadratic form q are equivalent:

(a)   The diagonal entries are all positive in any diagonal representation of q.

(b) $q(Y) > 0$ for any nonzero vector Y in $\mathbf{R}^n$.

Suppose $q(Y) = a_1 y_1^2 + a_2 y_2^2 + \cdots + a_n y_n^2$.   If all the coefficients are positive, then clearly $q(Y) > 0$ whenever $Y \neq 0$.   Thus (a) implies (b).   Conversely, suppose (a) is not true, that is, suppose some diagonal entry $a_k \leq 0$.   Let $e_k = (0, \ldots, 1, \ldots, 0)$ be the vector whose entries are all 0 except one in the kth position.   Then $q(e_k) = a_k$ is not positive, and so (b) is not true.   That is, (b) implies (a).   Accordingly (a) and (b) are equivalent.

PROOFS OF THEOREMS

12.23. Recall that the usual inner product in $\mathbf{R}^n$ may be defined by $\langle u, v \rangle = u^T v$, where u and v are column vectors in $\mathbf{R}^n$. Let A be an n-square matrix. Prove:

(a) $\langle Au, v \rangle = \langle u, A^T v \rangle$ for every u, v in $\mathbf{R}^n$.

(b)   If $\langle Au, v \rangle = 0$ for every u, v in $\mathbf{R}^n$, then $A = 0$.

(c)   If A is symmetric and $\langle Au, u \rangle = 0$ for every u in $\mathbf{R}^n$, then $A = 0$.

(a)   Using $\langle u, v \rangle = u^T v$, we have $\langle Au, v \rangle = (Au)^T v = u^T A^T v = \langle u, A^T v \rangle$.

(b)   Set $v = Au$. Then $\langle Au, Au \rangle = 0$; and hence $Au = 0$. Since $Au = 0$ for every u in $\mathbf{R}^n$, we have $A = 0$.

(c)   For any u, v in $\mathbf{R}^n$, we have $\langle A(u + v), u + v \rangle = 0$. However,

$$\langle A(u + v), u + v \rangle = \langle Au + Av, u + v \rangle = \langle Au, u \rangle + \langle Au, v \rangle + \langle Av, u \rangle + \langle Av, v \rangle$$
$$= 0 + \langle Au, v \rangle + \langle Av, u \rangle + 0 = \langle Au, v \rangle + \langle Av, u \rangle$$

Accordingly, $\langle Au, v \rangle + \langle Av, u \rangle = 0$. Since A is symmetric, that is, $A^T = A$, we have

$$\langle Au, v \rangle = \langle u, A^T v \rangle = \langle u, Av \rangle = \langle Av, u \rangle$$

Hence

$$\langle Au, v \rangle + \langle Av, u \rangle = \langle Au, v \rangle + \langle Au, v \rangle = 2\langle Au, v \rangle = 0$$

Thus $\langle Au, v \rangle = 0$. Therefore, by (b), $A = 0$.

12.24. Suppose λ is an eigenvalue of a real n-square matrix A. Prove the following:

(a)   If A is orthogonal, i.e., $A^T = A^{-1}$, then $|\lambda| = 1$.

(b)   If A is positive definite, then $\lambda > 0$.

Since λ is an eigenvalue of A, there exists $u \neq 0$ such that $Au = \lambda u$.

(a)   Using properties of the inner product in $\mathbf{R}^n$,

$$\lambda^2 \langle u, u \rangle = \langle \lambda u, \lambda u \rangle = \langle Au, Au \rangle = \langle u, A^T Au \rangle = \langle u, Iu \rangle = \langle u, u \rangle$$

However, $\langle u, u \rangle \neq 0$ since $u \neq 0$. Dividing by $\langle u, u \rangle$ gives $\lambda^2 = 1$. Hence $|\lambda| = 1$.

(b)   By definition of a positive definite real matrix, A is symmetric and $\langle Au, u \rangle$ is positive for any $u \neq 0$. Hence $\langle Au, u \rangle = \langle \lambda u, u \rangle = \lambda \langle u, u \rangle$ is positive. However, $\langle u, u \rangle$ is positive since $u \neq 0$. Accordingly λ is positive. (By Theorem 11.12, λ is real.)

12.25. Prove Theorem 12.3:   The following are equivalent

(i) A is positive definite, i.e., A is symmetric and $\langle AX, X \rangle = X^T AX > 0$ for any $X \neq 0$.

(ii) $A = P^T P$ for a nonsingular matrix P.

(iii) $A = B^2$ for a nonsingular symmetric matrix B.

We show that (iii) implies (ii) implies (i) implies (iii).

(a)   Suppose (iii) holds. Then $A = BB = B^T B$ since B is symmetric. Thus (iii) implies (ii).

(b)   Suppose (ii) holds. Then $A^T = (P^T P)^T = P^T P^{TT} = P^T P = A$. Hence A is symmetric. Also, for $X \neq 0$,

$$\langle AX, X \rangle = \langle P^T PX, X \rangle = \langle PX, P^{TT} X \rangle = \langle PX, PX \rangle$$

Since P is nonsingular, $PX \neq 0$. Thus $\langle AX, X \rangle = \langle PX, PX \rangle$ is positive, as required. Thus (ii) implies (i).

(c) Suppose (i) holds. Then there exists an orthonormal basis of eigenvectors $u_1, u_2, \ldots, u_n$ belonging to eigenvalues $\lambda_1, \lambda_2, \ldots, \lambda_n$. Thus $A(u_i) = \lambda_i u_i$ for all i. By Problem 12.22, λ_i is positive. Hence $\sqrt{\lambda_i}$ is real. Let B be the matrix such that $B(u_i) = \sqrt{\lambda_i} u_i$. Then

$$B^2(u_i) = B(B(u_i)) = B(\sqrt{\lambda_i} u_i) = \sqrt{\lambda_i} B(u_i) = \sqrt{\lambda_i}\sqrt{\lambda_i} u_i = \lambda_i u_i$$

Thus A and B^2 agree on a basis of $\mathbf{R}^n$. Hence $A = B^2$. Also, B is symmetric since it is diagonalizable. Thus (i) implies (iii).

Accordingly (i), (ii), and (iii) are equivalent.

12.26. Prove Theorem 12.5:   The following are equivalent:

(i) A is orthogonal, i.e., $A^T = A^{-1}$.

(ii)   For any u, v in $\mathbf{R}^n$, $\langle Au, Av \rangle = \langle u, v \rangle$.

(iii)   For any u in $\mathbf{R}^n$, we have $\|Au\| = \|u\|$ or, equivalently, $\langle Au, Au \rangle = \langle u, u \rangle$.

We prove that (i) implies (ii) implies (iii) implies (i).

(a) Suppose (i) holds. Then $\langle Au, Av \rangle = \langle u, A^T Av \rangle = \langle u, Iv \rangle = \langle u, v \rangle$. Thus (i) implies (ii).

(b) Suppose (ii) holds. Then $\|Au\|^2 = \langle Au, Au \rangle = \langle u, u \rangle = \|u\|^2$.

(c) Suppose (iii) holds. Then, for every u in $\mathbf{R}^n$,

$$\langle A^T Au, u \rangle = \langle Au, Au \rangle = \langle u, u \rangle = \langle Iu, u \rangle$$

and so $$\langle (A^T A - I)u, u \rangle = 0$$

Since $A^T A$ and I are symmetric, $A^T A - I$ is also symmetric. Thus by Problem 12.23, $A^T A - I = 0$. Therefore, $A^T A = I$, and so $A^T = A^{-1}$. Hence (iii) implies (i).

Accordingly (i), (ii), and (iii) are equivalent.

12.27. Justify Algorithm 12.2, which diagonalizes (under congruence) a symmetric matrix A.

Consider the block matrix $M = [A, I]$. The algorithm applies a sequence of elementary row operations and the corresponding column operations to the left side of M, which is the matrix A. This is equivalent to premultiplying A by a sequence of elementary matrices, say $E_1, E_2, \ldots, E_r$, and postmultiplying A by the transposes of the E_i. Thus when the algorithm ends, the diagonal matrix D on the left side of M is equal to

$$D = E_r \cdots E_2 E_1 A E_1^T E_2^T \cdots E_r^T = QAQ^T \qquad \text{where} \qquad Q = E_r \cdots E_2 E_1$$

On the other hand, the algorithm only applies the elementary row operations to the identity matrix I on the right side of M. Thus when the algorithm ends, the matrix on the right side of M is equal to

$$E_r \cdots E_2 E_1 I = E_r \cdots E_2 E_1 = Q$$

Setting $P = Q^T$ we get $D = P^T AP$, which is a diagonalization of A under congruence.

Supplementary Problems

CONGRUENT REAL SYMMETRIC MATRICES AND QUADRATIC FORMS

12.28. For each matrix A, find a nonsingular matrix P and a diagonal matrix D such that $D = P^T A P$:

$$(a)\ A = \begin{bmatrix} 1 & 0 & 2 \\ 0 & 3 & 6 \\ 2 & 6 & 7 \end{bmatrix}; \quad (b)\ A = \begin{bmatrix} 1 & -2 & 1 \\ -2 & 5 & 3 \\ 1 & 3 & -2 \end{bmatrix}; \quad (c)\ A = \begin{bmatrix} 1 & -2 & 3 \\ -2 & 6 & -9 \\ 3 & -9 & 4 \end{bmatrix}$$

12.29. For each matrix B, find a nonsingular matrix P and a diagonal matrix D such that $D = P^T A P$:

$$(a)\ B = \begin{bmatrix} 1 & 1 & -2 & -3 \\ 1 & 2 & -5 & -1 \\ -2 & -5 & 10 & 9 \\ -3 & -1 & 9 & 11 \end{bmatrix}; \quad (b)\ B = \begin{bmatrix} 1 & -1 & 0 & 2 \\ -1 & 2 & 1 & 0 \\ 0 & 1 & 1 & 2 \\ 2 & 0 & 2 & -1 \end{bmatrix}.$$

In each case, find the rank and signature.

12.30. Find the symmetric matrix belonging to the following quadratic forms: (a) $q(x, y) = 3x^2 + 8xy - 7y^2$; (b) $q(x, y) = 2x^2 - xy + 5y^2$.

12.31. Find the symmetric matrix, belonging to the following quadratic forms:
   (a) $q(x, y, z) = 2x^2 - 8xy + y^2 - 16xz + 14yz + 5z^2$;   (c) $q(x, y, z) = xy + y^2 + 4xz + z^2$;
   (b) $q(x, y, z) = x^2 - xz + y^2$;   (d) $q(x, y, z) = xy + yz$.

12.32. Let $q(x, y) = 2x^2 - 6xy - 3y^2$ and $x = s + 2t$, $y = 3s - t$.

   (a) Rewrite $q(x, y)$ in matrix notation, and find the matrix A representing the quadratic form.

   (b) Rewrite the linear substitution using matrix notation, and find the matrix P corresponding to the substitution.

   (c) Find $q(s, t)$ using: (i) direct substitution; (ii) matrix notation.

12.33. Repeat Problem 12.32 for $q(x, y) = x^2 - 4xy$ and $x = 2s + 3t$, $y = s - 4t$.

12.34. For each quadratic form $q(x, y, z)$, find a nonsingular linear substitution expressing the variables x, y, and z in terms of variables r, s, and t such that $q(r, s, t)$ is diagonal:

   (a) $q(x, y, z) = x^2 + 6xy + 8y^2 - 4xz + 2yz - 9z^2$.

   (b) $q(x, y, z) = 2x^2 - 3y^2 + 8xz + 12yz + 25z^2$.

   (c) $q(x, y, z) = x^2 + 2xy + 3y^2 + 4xz + 8yz + 6z^2$.

In each case find the rank and signature.

12.35. Give an example of a quadratic form $q(x, y)$ such that $q(u) = 0$ and $q(v) = 0$ but $q(u + v) \neq 0$.

12.36. Show that any real symmetric matrix A is congruent to a diagonal matrix D with only 1s, -1s, and 0s on the diagonal.

12.37. Show that congruence of matrices is an equivalence relation.

ORTHOGONAL DIAGONALIZATION OF SYMMETRIC MATRICES AND QUADRATIC FORMS

12.38. Consider a real quadratic polynomial $q(x_1, \ldots, x_n) = \sum\limits_{i,j=1}^{n} a_{ij} x_i x_j$, where $a_{ij} = a_{ji}$.

(a)   If $a_{11} \neq 0$, show that the substitution

$$x_1 = y_1 - \frac{1}{a_{11}}(a_{12}y_2 + \cdots + a_{1n}y_n), \; x_2 = y_2, \ldots, x_n = y_n$$

yields the equation $q(x_1, \ldots, x_n) = a_{11}y_1^2 + q'(y_2, \ldots, y_n)$, where q' is also a quadratic polynomial.

(b)   If $a_{11} = 0$ but, say, $a_{12} \neq 0$, show that the substitution

$$x_1 = y_1 + y_2, \, x_2 = y_1 - y_2, \, x_3 = y_3, \ldots, x_n = y_n$$

yields the equation $q(x_1, \ldots, x_n) = \sum b_{ij}y_i y_j$, where $b_{11} \neq 0$, i.e., reduces this case to case (a).

This method of diagonalizing q is known as *completing the square*.

12.39. For each matrix A find an orthogonal matrix P and a diagonal matrix D such that $D = P^T A P$:

(a) $A = \begin{bmatrix} 6 & -1 \\ -1 & 6 \end{bmatrix}$; (b) $A = \begin{bmatrix} 9 & 4 \\ 4 & -6 \end{bmatrix}$; (c) $A = \begin{bmatrix} 7 & 3 \\ 3 & -1 \end{bmatrix}$.

12.40. Find an orthogonal transformation of coordinates which diagonalizes each quadratic form:
(a) $q(x, y) = 2x^2 - 6xy + 10y^2$; (b) $q(x, y) = x^2 + 8xy - 5y^2$.

12.41. For each quadratic form $q(x, y, z)$ find an orthogonal substitution expressing the variables x, y, and z in terms of variables $r, s,$ and t such that $q(r, s, t)$ is diagonal; and find $q(r, s, t)$:

(a) $q(x, y, z) = 5x^2 + 3y^2 + 12xz$;

(b) $q(x, y, z) = 2xy + 2xz + 2yz$;

(c) $q(x, y, z) = 11x^2 - 16xy - y^2 + 8xz - 4yz - 4z^2$.

POSITIVE DEFINITE QUADRATIC FORMS

12.42. Determine whether or not each quadratic form is positive definite:

(a) $q(x, y) = 4x^2 + 5xy + 7y^2$;

(b) $q(x, y) = 2x^2 - 3xy - y^2$; (c) $q(x, y) = x^2 - 6xy + 4y^2$.

12.43. Determine whether or not each quadratic form is positive definite:

(a) $q(x, y, z) = x^2 + 4xy + 5y^2 + 6xz + 2yz + 4z^2$;

(b) $q(x, y, z) = x^2 + 2xy + 2y^2 + 4xz + 6yz + 7z^2$.

12.44. Find the values of k so that the given quadratic form is positive definite:

(a) $q(x, y) = 2x^2 - 5xy + ky^2$;

(b) $q(x, y) = 3x^2 - kxy + 12y^2$;

(c) $q(x, y, z) = x^2 + 2xy + 2y^2 + 2xz + 6yz + kz^2$.

Answers to Supplementary Problems

12.28. $(a)\ P = \begin{bmatrix} 1 & 0 & -2 \\ 0 & 1 & -2 \\ 0 & 0 & 1 \end{bmatrix}$; $(b)\ P = \begin{bmatrix} 1 & 2 & -11 \\ 0 & 1 & -5 \\ 0 & 0 & 1 \end{bmatrix}$; $(c)\ P = \begin{bmatrix} 1 & 2 & 0 \\ 0 & 1 & 3 \\ 0 & 0 & 2 \end{bmatrix}$

$(a)\ D = \text{diag } (1, 3, -9)$; $(b)\ D = \text{diag } (1, 1, -28)$; $(c)\ D = \text{diag } (1, 2, -38)$

12.29. $(a)\ P = \begin{bmatrix} 1 & -1 & -1 & 2 \\ 0 & 1 & 3 & 7 \\ 0 & 0 & 1 & 3 \\ 0 & 0 & 0 & 1 \end{bmatrix}$; $(b)\ P = \begin{bmatrix} 1 & 1 & -1 & -4 \\ 0 & 1 & -1 & -2 \\ 0 & 0 & 1 & 0 \\ 0 & 0 & 0 & 1 \end{bmatrix}$

$(a)\ D = \text{diag } (1, 1, -3, 25)$, rank $(B) = 4$, sig $(B) = 2$; $(b)\ D = \text{diag } (1, 1, 0, -9)$, rank $(B) = 3$, sig $(B) = 1$

12.30. $(a)\ \begin{bmatrix} 3 & 4 \\ 4 & -7 \end{bmatrix}$; $(b)\ \begin{bmatrix} 2 & -\frac{1}{2} \\ -\frac{1}{2} & 5 \end{bmatrix}$

12.31. $(a)\ \begin{bmatrix} 2 & -4 & -8 \\ -4 & 1 & 7 \\ -8 & 7 & 5 \end{bmatrix}$; $(b)\ \begin{bmatrix} 1 & 0 & -\frac{1}{2} \\ 0 & 1 & 0 \\ -\frac{1}{2} & 0 & 0 \end{bmatrix}$; $(c)\ \begin{bmatrix} 0 & \frac{1}{2} & 2 \\ \frac{1}{2} & 1 & 0 \\ 2 & 0 & 1 \end{bmatrix}$; $(d)\ \begin{bmatrix} 0 & \frac{1}{2} & 0 \\ \frac{1}{2} & 0 & \frac{1}{2} \\ 0 & \frac{1}{2} & 0 \end{bmatrix}$

12.32. $(a)\ A = \begin{bmatrix} 2 & -3 \\ -3 & -3 \end{bmatrix}$; $(b)\ P = \begin{bmatrix} 1 & 2 \\ 3 & -1 \end{bmatrix}$; $(c)\ q(s, t) = -43s^2 - 4st + 17t^2$

12.33. $(a)\ A = \begin{bmatrix} 1 & -2 \\ -2 & 0 \end{bmatrix}$; $(b)\ P = \begin{bmatrix} 2 & 3 \\ 1 & -4 \end{bmatrix}$; $(c)\ q(s, t) = -4s^2 + 32st + 57t^2$

12.34. $(a)\ \ x = r - 3s - 19t,\ y = s + 7t,\ z = t;\ q(r, s, t) = r^2 - s^2 + 36t^2$; rank $(q) = 3$, sig $(q) = 1$

$(b)\ \ x = r - 2t, y = s + 2t, z = t; q(r, s, t) = 2r^2 - 3s^2 + 29t^2$; rank $(q) = 3$, sig $(q) = 1$

$(c)\ \ x = r - s - t,\ y = s - t,\ z = t;\ q(r, s, t) = r^2 + 2s^2$; rank $(q) = 2$, sig $(q) = 2$

12.35. $q(x, y) = x^2 - y^2$, $u = (1, 1)$, $v = (1, -1)$

12.39. $(a)\ P = \frac{1}{\sqrt{2}} \begin{bmatrix} 1 & 1 \\ 1 & -1 \end{bmatrix}$; $(b)\ P = \frac{1}{\sqrt{17}} \begin{bmatrix} 4 & 1 \\ 1 & -4 \end{bmatrix}$; $(c)\ P = \frac{1}{\sqrt{10}} \begin{bmatrix} 3 & 1 \\ 1 & -3 \end{bmatrix}$

$(a)\ D = \text{diag } (5, 7)$; $(b)\ D = \text{diag } (10, -7)$; $(c)\ D = \text{diag } (8, -2)$

12.40. $(a)\ x = \dfrac{3s - t}{\sqrt{10}}, y = \dfrac{s + 3t}{\sqrt{10}}$; $(b)\ x = \dfrac{2s - t}{\sqrt{5}}, y = \dfrac{s + 2t}{\sqrt{5}}$

12.41. $(a)\ \ x = \dfrac{3s + 2t}{\sqrt{13}}, y = r, z = \dfrac{2s - 3t}{\sqrt{13}}$; $q(r, s, t) = 3r^2 + 9s^2 - 4t^2$

(b) $x = \dfrac{r}{\sqrt{3}} + \dfrac{s}{\sqrt{2}} + \dfrac{t}{\sqrt{6}}, y = \dfrac{4}{\sqrt{3}} - \dfrac{s}{\sqrt{2}} + \dfrac{t}{\sqrt{6}}, z = \dfrac{r}{\sqrt{3}} - \dfrac{2t}{\sqrt{6}} ; q(r, s, t) = 2r^2 - s^2 - t^2$

(c) $x = \dfrac{-5s}{\sqrt{105}} + \dfrac{4t}{\sqrt{21}}, y = \dfrac{r}{\sqrt{5}} - \dfrac{8s}{\sqrt{105}} - \dfrac{2t}{\sqrt{21}}, z = \dfrac{2r}{\sqrt{5}} + \dfrac{4s}{\sqrt{105}} + \dfrac{t}{\sqrt{21}};$

$q(r, s, t) = -5r^2 - 5s^2 + 16t^2$

12.42. (a) Yes; (b) no; (c) no

12.43. (a) No; (b) yes

12.44. (a) $k > \frac{25}{8}$; (b) $-12 < k < 12$; (c) $k > 5$

Index